Fields, Fens and Felonies

Crime and Justice in Eighteenth-century East Anglia

Gregory J Durston

WATERSIDE PRESS

Fields, Fens and Felonies: Crime and Justice in Eighteenth-century East Anglia
Gregory J Durston

ISBN 978-1-909976-11-5 (Paperback)
ISBN 978-1-910979-18-1 (Epub ebook)
ISBN 978-1-910979-19-8 (Adobe ebook)

Main UK distributor Gardners Books, 1 Whittle Drive, Eastbourne, East Sussex, BN23 6QH. Tel: +44 (0)1323 521777; sales@gardners.com; www.gardners.com

North American distribution Ingram Book Company, One Ingram Blvd, La Vergne, TN 37086, USA. Tel: (+1) 615 793 5000; inquiry@ingramcontent.com

Cataloguing-In-Publication Data A catalogue record for this book can be obtained from the British Library.

Printed by Lightning Source.

e-book *Fields, Fens and Felonies* is available as an ebook and also to subscribers of Myilibrary, Dawsonera, ebrary, and Ebscohost.

Published 2016 by
Waterside Press
Sherfield Gables
Sherfield-on-Loddon
Hook, Hampshire
United Kingdom RG27 0JG

Telephone +44(0)1256 882250
E-mail enquiries@watersidepress.co.uk
Online catalogue WatersidePress.co.uk

Table of Contents

About the author

Gregory J Durston is a barrister-at-law who has taught in Law Schools in England and Japan. He was for many years Reader in Law at Kingston University, Surrey and is the author of the acclaimed *Whores and Highwaymen: Crime and Justice in the Eighteenth-century Metropolis* (Waterside Press, hardback 2012; paperback 2016).

Acknowledgements

I would like to acknowledge the invaluable assistance provided by the staff of the National Archives in Kew, the Norfolk Record Office in Norwich, the King's Lynn Borough Archives, and the Suffolk Record Office in Ipswich. Thanks are also due to the staff at Kingston University Library, Gray's Inn Library, Lincoln's Inn Library, and the British Library. Additionally, I am extremely grateful for assistance and advice from a wide variety of people on many different aspects of this book, and in particular to Philippa Russell, Paul Rock, Manuel Eisner, Peter King, Rhiannon Markless, Rhoda Koenig, and Nicholas Philpot. In a work with a significant element of synthesis, a huge debt is, inevitably, owed to the many scholars whose publications are cited in the text.

For each chapter to be comprehensible on its own, it has sometimes been necessary to restate points made elsewhere. These have been kept to a minimum by the use of cross-referencing; where such repetition is unavoidable, fresh illustrations have been used. Readers should note that abbreviated titles are often used in footnotes; the full versions of these sources can be found in the Bibliography. Until 1752 the year started on 25 March. Dates prior to this time have been modernised to accord with the Gregorian calendar.

Gregory Durston
London,
Whitsun, 2016

CHAPTER 1

Preliminary Matters

Introduction

This book examines crime and justice in eighteenth-century East Anglia. It is neither a micro-history of these phenomena in the context of a parish, hundred, or small town nor is it a national account. It is the criminal-justice history of a major English region, one that, unlike Cornwall and Northumberland, was not very far from the conurbation that had developed around London and Westminster, but not, like counties such as Kent, Essex, Hertfordshire, and Surrey, in its immediate hinterland. As such, it had much in common with large tracts of the rest of the country and can, to some extent, be considered as representative of the wider system under which most Englishmen of the era lived and died. This is important, as the large number and ready availability of records for London and Middlesex, many of which are now online, mean that the provinces have been slightly neglected in recent historiography, even though, to some extent, the Metropolis was *sui generis* in its crime problems and justice system.[1]

Of course, East Anglia had singularities of its own that set it apart from other regions, at least to a modest degree. These were most likely to be encountered at a local level, which lacked the unifying influence of the centrally based assizes judges. Nevertheless, by the 1700s these regional variations were relatively small compared to the situation 100

1. For more on this, see G. Durston, *Whores and Highwaymen: Crime and Justice in the Eighteenth-century Metropolis*, 2012, Hook: Waterside Press. To avoid unnecessary duplication between the two volumes there will be some cross-referencing to this work in footnotes.

years earlier, and they declined further as the century advanced. In this study comparison will be made with other parts of England and Wales, including the London area, to identify aspects of the system that were typical of the wider nation and to expose those that were unusual.

A recurrent problem for students of the era is the need to address the plethora of myths and misleading half-truths that are subscribed to by non-specialist observers. For example, contrary to popular belief, large numbers of people were not hanged for trifling and arcane offences established under the "Bloody Code," and children were almost never amongst those executed. Of course, myths normally have some connection to reality, even if it is rather tenuous. There were rare exceptions to these two generalisations, and on unusual occasions to both at once. As late as 1822, the capital conviction and execution of 16-year-old Benjamin Glover, the son of a career thief, for stealing goods worth more than 40 shillings from a dwelling-house (a Bloody Code offence) in Somerset, evinced acute shock and disquiet, as the crime was not "particularly atrocious."[2] Nevertheless, the quotidian reality, rather than the theoretical possibility, must be identified, and what was typical or "normal" separated from what was exceptional.

Time and Place

There is some debate as to the precise geographical boundaries of East Anglia. Many observers include Essex, Cambridgeshire, and Huntingdonshire in the region. However, whatever definition is employed it always includes Norfolk and Suffolk, the original components of the Anglo-Saxon kingdom of East Anglia. These two shires will be the focus of this book, and will be referred to when the term is used or "region" mentioned. Although the book primarily considers the 100 years after 1700, the years after 1688 and before 1815 –the "long" eighteenth century– will sometimes be touched on.

2. *Royal Cornwall Gazette, Falmouth Packet & Plymouth Journal*, 11 May 1822.

Sources of Information

Many of the rather sparse records from the assizes of the era have been preserved, but few match the thoroughness and completeness of some of those available for the Courts of Great Sessions in Wales (their equivalent in the principality). The majority (but not all) of the Norfolk Circuit's Gaol Books for the period from 1734 to 1800 are held at the National Archives in Kew (at ASSI 33) or, for the years from 1746 to 1750, in the library of Gray's Inn (under MS 45). Before 1734 the surviving records are often thin and spasmodic, but will be referred to occasionally. The gaol books or "calendars" usually (but not invariably) record in abbreviated form the names of defendants, the charges they faced, and the verdicts and sentences they received. They also record some (not many) recognisances to prosecute or give evidence and (much more reliably) provide details of any legal expenses and rewards paid out. In a minority of cases the occupations of those accused are recorded, but these are sometimes unreliable. The National Archives also hold a few volumes of the Crown Minute Books for the Norfolk Circuit. These were often drawn up as working documents by clerical staff on the Crown (criminal) side at assizes, and contain some information, albeit usually less than the gaol books.[3]

A complete decade of gaol books, from around the middle of the century, 1751 to 1760 (inclusive), is available, as are some shorter runs. These have been referred to extensively. Samples of one year for each decade after 1730 have also been employed. Unfortunately, no complete records prior to this time have been preserved, limiting coverage for the early part of the century. Gaps in the records after that date mean that the same year cannot be chosen for every decade. In this study, the fourth year in each decade has been the default choice, with the nearest year chosen where that has not been possible, this being taken at random where there are two that are equidistant. As a result, the longitudinal study will focus on the years 1735, 1747, 1754, 1764, 1774, 1784, and 1797.

3. J. S. Cockburn, *A History of English Assizes, 1558–1714*, 1972, p. 334.

It must be remembered that these records only cover the assizes courts of the region (three separate forums). They do not extend to the two towns with special jurisdiction to try the most serious cases in their own borough sessions: King's Lynn and Great Yarmouth. Furthermore, a few cases of smuggling (an offence against the Crown) and horse theft (viewed as a "continuing" crime when an animal was taken across a county border) that originated in Norfolk or Suffolk were tried in forums outside the area, such as the Old Bailey in London. Because there was no neat distinction in jurisdiction between the assizes and the lower jury courts of the region (quarter sessions and borough sessions), "counting" the less serious cases that were sometimes determined at the higher forum, such as misdemeanours, cases of petty theft, and even low-value grand larcenies, is of the most limited value.

Records for quarter and borough sessions are held at the relevant county record offices in Norwich and Ipswich or at satellite offices in towns such as Bury St Edmunds, King's Lynn (hereafter sometimes referred to simply as "Bury" and "Lynn"), and Great Yarmouth. Some records from almost all these forums have been lost or damaged, especially for the early years of the century. For example, the sessions "rolls" (working papers) for the Ipswich Borough Court were made up of documents generated by the court and its officers or submitted to them for further action or record. They survive for the whole of the eighteenth century after March 1722. Amongst them are, with varying degrees of completeness, calendars of prisoners in the local gaol and house of correction, lists of constables and jurors, coroners' inquisitions, the examinations of suspects, grand jury presentments, and certificates of summary convictions made out of sessions that were returned to the court. Some of these are better represented than others in the 78 years after 1722.

Unfortunately, few records for petty sessions have been preserved for the two counties prior to the 1840s, although they disposed of a great deal of legal work, both civil and criminal. Summary trials before a single justice pose similar problems.

Newspapers and Chapbooks

Contemporary newspapers provide a valuable source of information for the eighteenth century. They expanded greatly after 1695, when Parliament decided not to renew the Licensing Act that had permitted pre-publication censorship. Between 1690 and 1780, the total number of newspapers printed annually in England rose from under a million to about 14 million copies, an increase that greatly outstripped the growth in population.[4]

The newspaper industry was centred on the Metropolis. However, after this *de facto* monopoly ended in 1695, a significant provincial press quickly developed.[5] Francis Burges set up a printing-shop in Norwich, and in 1701 produced the *Norwich Post*, probably the first major provincial newspaper (Bristol followed shortly afterwards). It was a weekly, four-page publication, a common format for the era.[6] Several other local newspapers came out in the city over the next few years. Although the Stamp Act of 1712 affected them financially, and initially reduced their number, loopholes in the statute allowed a fairly swift recovery in circulation. An amalgamation of two of the city newspapers produced the popular *Norwich Mercury* in 1726. Three years later the long-lived *Ipswich Journal* joined it in the region. By 1746, there were 42 English provincial papers, several in East Anglia, although some were short lived.

At first many of these provincial papers contained little specifically local news, focusing instead on matters of national or metropolitan significance, although local issues sometimes achieved the former status. Indeed, many reports, taken directly from London publications or journalists, might be identical to those found elsewhere in the country, a practice that has sometimes led to their editors being called "scissors-and-paste men."[7] Their focus gradually changed during the course of the century, and the number of crime reports with an East Anglian focus

---

4. J. Black, "Newspapers and Politics in the 18th-century," 1986, pp. 36–42.
5. E. Snell, "Changing Discourses of Crime: Representations of Criminality in the Eighteenth-century Newspaper Press," 2007, pp. 13–47; E. Snell, "Representations of Criminality and Victimisation in Provincial Newspapers: The Kentish Post 1717 to 1768," 2005, pp. 48–75.
6. J. Wallis, "Representations of Justice Executed at Norwich Castle," 2013, p. 36.
7. J. Sharpe, "Reporting Crime in the North of England Eighteenth-century Newspaper: A Preliminary Investigation," 2012, p. 27.

slowly increased. They were especially common in peacetime, when a lack of war news left space to be filled.

Newspapers were not cheap, and their price rose faster than inflation during the era, in part because of the duty imposed by successive Stamp Acts. For example, the *Ipswich Gazette* sold for two pence in 1725, 2½d in 1757, three pence in 1776, three-and-a-half pence in 1789, four pence in 1792 and, with suddenly increased duty, six pence in 1797.[8] However, each edition was widely circulated. In 1711, Joseph Addison suggested that at least 20 people read every copy, as it was passed around in families, coffeehouses, and taverns. As a result, it was claimed that newspapers had "become the common conveyance of all information to the people."[9] This included news about crime. Indeed, they helped the phenomenon become a subject of popular interest in a way that it had not been in earlier centuries, when information about serious offences was often limited to chapbooks and sermons. Consequently, newspapers helped to create a climate of opinion that influenced policy decisions in the criminal justice system.

Nevertheless, the influence of newspapers, although important, can still be exaggerated. The space given to criminal news was often quite limited. Although some provincial newspapers dwelt at length on various crimes, many reported them briefly and in a matter-of-fact manner, sandwiched between mundane matters such as details of accidents, and often focusing on a summary of the cases tried at assizes or quarter sessions.[10] It would be a mistake to attribute to such reports the power of modern forms of mass media.

Newspapers were usually *reasonably* reliable when it came to reporting the basic facts of a case and its outcome, especially if it resulted in an execution. However, their habit of using common sources (or each other) meant that error could easily be multiplied, and they were often not strong on legal distinctions. For example, what is recorded in the gaol book as burglary is sometimes reported as housebreaking, a similar but legally distinct offence, or vice versa. The expression "robbery" is often

8. J. Black, "Newspapers and Politics in the 18th Century," 1986, pp. 36–42.
9. *Bingley's Journal*, 18–25 April 1772.
10. J. Sharpe, "Reporting Crime in the North of England Eighteenth-century Newspaper: A Preliminary Investigation," 2012, p. 31.

used quite indiscriminately for ordinary thefts and burglaries rather than those using or threatening violence (its legal definition).

Despite the rise of the newspaper, chapbooks and pamphlets on *causes célèbres* continued to be produced on a regular basis during the century, just as they had in the 1600s, although no longer holding centre stage amongst published accounts. Their accuracy was sometimes aided by the growth of effective systems of shorthand, which were increasingly used by court reporters. Typically, the accounts of two notorious murder trials from the region in the 1780s were offered at six pence each or bound together in marbled paper for a shilling.[11]

Justices' Notebooks

Magistrates' legal notebooks provide another important source of information, especially as they sometimes show how judges reached their decisions and how JPs often departed from the black letter of the law when "out of sessions." Edmund Bohun, like several other legal writers of the era, had stressed the importance of justices' keeping a personal record of their cases. He was himself an active JP in Suffolk from 1675 to 1694 (when he was excluded for political reasons), although his own notebook appears to have been lost. Nevertheless, such diaries were not official records and are not necessarily an exhaustive list of their authors' legal work; cases that were not noteworthy might be left out.

Nationally only a few such books survive from the eighteenth century. They include those of Richard Wyatt in Surrey, Edmund Tew in County Durham, Thomas Horner in Somerset, and William Hunt in Wiltshire (all of which have been published). Phillip Ward of Stoke Doyle in Northamptonshire, just under 50 miles west of the Norfolk border, served as a JP from (at least) May 1748 to September 1751, and kept fairly detailed notes of his cases and the rationales behind his legal decisions during this period, something that is of particular interest as he had qualified as a barrister.[12] Similarly, Samuel Whitbread (1758–1815), a Bedfordshire JP and owner of the famous brewery, kept notebooks recording in detail

11. *Ipswich Journal,* 12 April 1783.
12. D. Gray, "Making Law in Mid-Eighteenth-century England," 2013, pp. 211–215.

the cases he handled in his capacity as a county justice during the early years of the nineteenth century.[13]

Very few justicing notebooks appear to have survived in East Anglia itself. However, although written a little earlier than the period under consideration, that of Robert Doughty, a North Norfolk magistrate, provides some valuable insights from 1662 to 1665. He dealt with the normal range of administrative work for an active justice, as well as a few summary offences, and also issued arrest warrants, examined suspects, and questioned witnesses. Much more pertinently, Devereux Edgar (1651–1739), who owned extensive estates in Suffolk and was a JP for the county, kept a lengthy written record of his work over a period of several years early in the century. He was the son of a recorder of Ipswich and former reader of Gray's Inn. His own son became a member of Gray's Inn and was made the high sheriff of Suffolk in 1747. Edgar conducted a considerable amount of criminal work, most of it from his home, although, like other justices of the time, he dealt with significantly more civil matters. Nevertheless, in part because of his legal connections, his highly detailed record, kept after 1700 expressly to improve his understanding of the law, is exceptionally valuable (though still unpublished). For the years around the close of the eighteenth century, the "Entry Book" of the Reverend R. C. Barnard, another Suffolk magistrate, can be considered.[14]

General Diaries

Contemporary diaries of a more general type can also provide important insights into East Anglia during the era, although, of course, the diarists were often relatively wealthy people. The diaries are especially valuable if kept by those involved in the criminal-justice process. For example, although written slightly after the period, the notebook of the well-born Reverend John Longe (1765–1834), an affluent and active Suffolk JP during the early years of the nineteenth century, covers much legal business. James Oakes, an alumnus of Trinity College, Cambridge, who married a clergyman's daughter and became a prosperous businessman

13. A. Cirket (ed.), *Samuel Whitbread's Notebooks*, 1971.
14. SRO (Bury St Edmunds Branch) FL653/3/7.

of Bury St Edmunds,[15] kept a diary for almost 50 years which filled 14 volumes recording much of the minutiae of his daily life.[16] Oakes had an observant eye, and accumulated considerable wealth as, *inter alia*, a yarn manufacturer, coal merchant, and banker, while also serving as a deputy lieutenant, a grand juror, and a justice.[17] More famously, though he was not a magistrate, James Woodforde (1740–1803), a Norfolk cleric, was a prolific diarist. Oxford educated and conscientious about his duties, he began his career as a curate in Somerset but was granted the living of Weston Longville in Norfolk in 1773. For almost 45 years he kept a detailed account of his daily life and those of the people around him.

There were several female diarists in the region during this period, among them Elizabeth Freke (1671–1714). She portrays the late-seventeenth and early-eighteenth-century Norfolk gentry and their social world from the perspective of a somewhat bitter and litigious widow in an unhappy domestic situation who lived out her final years in increasingly poor health. Slightly more felicitously, Mary Hardy, born at Whissonsett in Norfolk in 1733 and the wife of a farmer-cum-maltster, brewer, and miller, wrote her diary daily from 1773 to her death in 1809.

A few foreigners also recorded their views of the area at this time. Thus, the 18-year-old Frenchman François de la Rochefoucauld visited Suffolk with his brother Alexandre in 1784, keeping a diary and noting what he saw of the county, including its criminal justice system. Although he was a well-educated and aristocratic young man, his observations were inevitably fairly superficial, and some were simply wrong, based on misheard conversations and incorrect information. They were also influenced by an awareness of the deteriorating domestic situation in his native country. Nevertheless, they provide a vivid picture of what was singular about many aspects of English provincial life at this time, including its justice system.

15. *World (1787)*, 22 October 1792.
16. J. Fiske (ed.), *The Oakes Diaries*, 1991.
17. *Morning Herald*, 1 September 1788.

Eighteenth-century East Anglia

Norfolk and Suffolk had much in common besides their Dark Age history. (The Kingdom of the East Angles was formed in the early sixth century by a merging of the North and the South Folk, who gave the two counties their names). Both were on the North Sea and had a flat or gently undulating topography partly composed of fenland and reclaimed marshland. Their climate was drier than that of most other parts of England. Legally, they were both situated on the Norfolk Circuit for their assizes hearings, unlike Essex, to the south (which was part of the Home Circuit), and Lincolnshire, to the north (part of the Midland Circuit).

According to one estimate, by the 1670s Norfolk had a population of about 181,000 and Suffolk approximately 125,000 people, both counties having grown slowly and unevenly over the previous century-and-a-half. Population continued to increase during the following 130 years, although not at a uniform rate. That of England as a whole was fairly stable between 1701 and 1731, before increasing sharply for the remainder of the century, and this pattern was broadly reflected in East Anglia.[18] The 1801 census (the first to be held) concluded that, by then, Suffolk had 207,148 inhabitants and Norfolk 273,629, making the latter county the fifth most populous shire in England, still slightly ahead of Surrey but behind Lancashire (swiftly industrialising and easily the largest), Devon, Kent, and, of course, partly metropolitan Middlesex.

Both Norfolk and Suffolk were heavily agricultural, more so than many other parts of provincial England. Well over three people in the region were engaged in farming for every two who were primarily employed in trade, handicrafts, mining, or manufacturing. In some respects, agriculture increased in importance during the period, as more land became available after fens and marshland were drained. However, land use also changed. At the start of the century much of it still provided pasture for wool-producing sheep. During the eighteenth century, a significant part of this land went under the plough, to produce rye, wheat, barley, and root vegetables, much of it for sale in London or provincial towns

---

18. M. J. Daunton, *Progress and Poverty: An Economic and Social History of Britain 1700–1850*, 1995, p. 391.

and cities. By 1796 it was estimated that two-thirds of land in Norfolk was used for arable farming.[19]

Both counties were to be in the forefront of agricultural developments during the era. Farming techniques improved throughout the century, especially after about 1740.[20] Better strains of livestock were bred and higher-yielding crops developed. Agricultural machinery also improved. Norfolk farmers played an especially important role in this process, and their county even gave its name to an improved "four course" regime of crop rotation, the "Norfolk husbandry" or "Norfolk method," phrases that were used in other parts of England.[21] Under this system, different root, legume, and cereal crops were grown on the same land over a four-year period so that none of it had to lie fallow to recover.

A fundamental change in land ownership also occurred in the region during the seventeenth and eighteenth centuries as both counties moved from open-field farming and a system of "commons" or "waste" to designated and delineated farms via the process known as "enclosure." In the early sixteenth century, complete dependence on wage labour had been rare outside towns. Even cottagers had small plots on which to grow crops and access to common pastures to graze animals. This changed over the ensuing 200 years. The poorest members of East Anglian communities became wage labourers on other people's farms and estates. As a result, the eighteenth century witnessed the emergence of what might properly be termed a rural proletariat.

Although a predominantly agricultural region, East Anglia boasted a major cloth-manufacturing industry at the start of the period. In 1722 weavers in Norwich had been unable to satisfy a huge national demand for the new style of calamancoes (a woollen textile), despite working incessantly to do so.[22] By the end of the century, Norwich's cloth production was in terminal decline, and small in comparison to that of the rapidly industrialising North. In 1810 it could be noted that combing

19. M. J. Armstrong, *History and Antiquities of the County of Norfolk*, vol. I, 1781, p. 95.
20. B. Campbell and M. Overton, "A New Perspective on Medieval and Early Modern Agriculture: Six Centuries of Norfolk Farming c.1250–c.1850," 1993, pp. 104–105.
21. *London Chronicle*, 7–9 September 1775.
22. *St. James's Journal*, 29 December 1722.

wool in the city: "used to employ a great number of hands; but since the invention of machines, their employ is in a great measure superseded."[23]

The region had a large number of small and medium-size towns. These varied greatly in size and wealth. For example, in the 1720s, Daniel Defoe thought that Sudbury was remarkable only for being "very populous and very poor." Its inhabitants, many engaged in cloth manufacture, were so numerous and impoverished that they were "almost ready to eat up the rich." By contrast, Bury St Edmunds, in the same county, was a vibrant, thriving, and prosperous commercial centre with many wealthy inhabitants and numerous fine houses.[24] Some relatively small towns were important administrative centres. Walsingham in Norfolk was the location for both quarter and petty sessions, these being held in the town's impressive shire hall after 1778. It acquired its own house of correction or "bridewell" in 1787. As would be expected of a coastal region, the two counties had numerous ports. Amongst them were the large boroughs of King's Lynn and Yarmouth and, on a smaller scale, Lowestoft, Wells, and Dunwich.

East Anglia's status within England changed markedly during the eighteenth century. In general terms, it was far more important to the nation at the start of the period than at its close, by which time it was becoming something of a backwater. For example, although the region had only one city, Norwich, it was the largest in provincial England during the early years of the era, albeit dwarfed by London. By 1730 Bristol had displaced it, and at the end of the century Norwich lagged behind six other provincial cities, most of them in the industrialising Midlands and North. Nevertheless, it bears special consideration, as it was by far the largest urban area in the region.

Norwich

On one estimate, Norwich had a population of 28,911 people in 1693. By 1752 this had increased to 36,396, and to 40,051 in 1786, before declining

23. C. Berry, *A Concise History and Directory of the City of Norwich: For 1811*, 1810, p. 1.
24. D. Defoe, *A Tour Through the Whole Island of Great Britain*, 1978, pp. 73–75.

to 36,854 inhabitants in 1801 (with a clear majority of women).[25] Whatever the precise total, Norwich was big enough to raise problems that were not encountered elsewhere in the region. A large number of poor people were concentrated in the city. In 1712 nearly all its parishes and liberties were united for Poor Law purposes by a statute aimed at the "meaner sort," who, it was claimed, multiplied rapidly and were increasingly lazy and debauched.[26] Two large workhouses were founded. In 1783 between 700 and 800 people were accommodated in these establishments, at a total cost of about £10,000 a year (almost £3,000 a year was also paid in outdoor relief to other poor people). Many inmates, especially children, were employed in spinning yarn.

Perhaps unsurprisingly the city faced some special crime problems. In 1781, after thieves broke into the cellar of the *Peacock Tavern* in the city, and stole four gallons of gin and some cheese, it was noted "[s]carce a night passes but robberies are committed."[27] This was reiterated the following year, when thieves broke into a laundry in the cathedral close and stole 15 tablecloths: "[S]everal other thefts of the like kind have been committed in the course of the week."[28] Norwich also had a major impact on crime rates in its immediate hinterland. For example, at about the same time, a gelding was stolen from a farmer in Crostwick, two miles outside the city gates, and it was thought that: "scarce a night passes but the like depredations are committed on the property of the different farmers near this city."[29] The following year, when the outhouse of a farmer in Bawburgh (about five miles from the city) was broken into, and 20 turkeys stolen, it was noted that the same man had lost several sacks of corn from his barn just a few weeks earlier. One observer suggested that farmers near Norwich would be well-advised to arm their servants and get them to "patrole nightly" in the area.[30]

The city authorities sometimes took radical steps to address their local crime problems. A series of burglaries over the summer of 1783 prompted

25. C. Berry, *Concise History and Directory of The City of Norwich For 1811*, 1810, p. v.
26. Anon, *A Bill for Erecting a Work-house in the City and County of the City of Norwich*, 1711, p. 1.
27. *Norfolk Chronicle*, 15 December 1781.
28. Ibid., 6 January 1782.
29. Ibid., 13 May 1780.
30. Ibid., 15 December 1781.

the Mayor's Court to ask that people give notice of anyone in their ward who had no visible means of support or who appeared to be of bad character. The city's constables were also ordered to be diligent about arresting the "lewd" women often found in its streets.[31]

Continuity and Change

It has long been appreciated that eighteenth-century English society was neither static nor always greatly cohesive in the years prior to the Industrial Revolution. Rank and hierarchy were powerful forces throughout the period, but they did not preclude social conflict. Society was undergoing significant and often rapid change throughout the 1700s, not just its final decades. Deference, though ever present and part of the currency of everyday life, was not as strong a social force as it had been in previous centuries. Class slowly started to replace the older terminology of "rank, order and degree" after the mid-century. Increasingly, there was a rejection of the "great chain of being," in which all living creatures were allocated their positions in the hierarchy at birth by God, with "[s]ome placed by Him in high stations, others in low estate."[32] Although clergymen continued to pay lip service to such an ideal, it was obviously untrue. New forms of wealth, whether commercial or industrial, eroded confidence in traditional identifications and encouraged social mobility. Critics of landed society emerged, and some trading and professional men began to term themselves "gentlemen" despite their commercial origins. New notions of politeness and sensibility also developed during the era, challenging previous norms of conduct.

There were other, more arcane, signs of social change. For example, members of the tiny (and fairly recently arrived) ethnic minority communities of East Anglia became both perpetrators and victims of crime. In March 1719, at the Bury Assizes, a "Blackmore was condemn'd for killing a carter on the road."[33] By contrast, in October 1784, the "negroe" servant of one Captain Peck, from Nacton near Ipswich, was stopped

31. Ibid., 16 August 1783.
32. T. Broughton, *Serious Advice and Warning to Servants, More Especially Those of the Nobility and Gentry*, 1800, p. 6.
33. *Post Boy (1695)*, 19–21 March 1719.

on Whitton Hill by two footpads and robbed of all his money.[34] By the final decades of the era a small number of Jews had settled in some of the region's towns beyond Norwich.[35] In 1783 David Aaron was committed to the Norwich Castle Gaol by the magistrate Roger Kerrison. Aaron was a Rabbi (a "Jew Priest"), who was accused of stealing a parcel from a common carrier's wagon containing stamps and a bill of exchange for £20.[36] In the same year Robert Fox was executed for robbing and "barbarously beating" 16-year-old Isaac Levi, a prosperous Jew from King's Lynn.[37] In a society that countenanced the slave trade abroad, it is perhaps surprising to find that black people were not greatly disadvantaged as victims, witnesses, or defendants at the Old Bailey.[38] This appears to have been replicated at provincial assizes. As Isaac Levi's case suggests, although Jews were subject to prejudice, they were also well-protected by the criminal law.

More generally, the advent of the Enlightenment or, as it is sometimes termed, the Age of Reason in late-seventeenth-century Europe, with its emphasis on rational analysis, its challenge to tradition and established practices, and its desire to reform society on clearly stated and evidentially supported principles, was also bound to have an impact on a criminal justice system inherited from a much earlier time. As belief in age-old and inscrutable custom weakened the question as to how modern society should be organized, including its systems of policing, prosecution, and punishment, moved onto the political agenda. Many, like the Yorkshire JP Christopher Tancred, felt that just as old-fashioned houses did not compare to "modern" (i.e. early-Georgian) architecture, traditional criminal justice systems were inferior to those specifically adapted for the eighteenth century.[39] Others feared such change and the manner in which the age was "running mad after innovation," to use Samuel Johnson's words on learning that public executions were being moved from Tyburn

34. *Ipswich Journal*, 30 October 1784.
35. See generally, R. Halliday and B. Susser, "The Ipswich Jewish Community in the Eighteenth and Nineteenth Centuries," 2002, pp. 151–163.
36. *Norfolk Chronicle*, 4 October 1783.
37. *London Chronicle*, 23–26 August 1783.
38. See generally, P. King and J. Carter Wood, "Black People and the Criminal Justice System," 2015, pp. 100–124.
39. C. Tancred, *Essay for a General Regulation of the Law*, 1727, p. 9.

to a space outside Newgate Prison.[40] This process was most visible in the Metropolis, but could not leave even the most rural areas untouched.

At the same time, innovation was qualified by the continuing survival of centuries of habits, beliefs, and practices, so that there was often a growing disjunction between elite and popular cultures. In many parts of East Anglia age-old superstition lingered throughout the era. This is unsurprising, as the provision of even basic education was limited. Although a few of the region's parishes, such as Mendlesham in Suffolk, had charity schools of long standing, many others had no form of education whatsoever for the children of the poor. As a result, numerous popular belief systems survived to the end of the century and beyond.

Illustrative of this survival, in 1776 a poor man who was suspected of being a wizard was "swum" in the River Deben at Farnham, Suffolk, in front of a crowd. He was thrown in with his feet and hands tied but sank immediately (traditionally deemed a sign of innocence), and would have drowned had one of the spectators not intervened. Those involved quickly: "dispersed, ashamed of themselves and angry at their own weakness and credulity."[41] In 1792 an elderly woman from Stanningfield in the same county, accused of witchcraft, allowed herself to be swum in front of her neighbours. She, too, sank, and so was cleared of being a witch, although she was almost drowned in the process.[42] As late as 1849 a farmer in Suffolk was fined £1 and costs for drawing blood from an old woman whom he called a witch by scratching her head with a nail.[43] (In ancient popular belief, drawing blood would break the witch's spell over her victim).

The Social Background

Many people in eighteenth-century East Anglia, as in other parts of England, lived close to the margins of existence. A selection of deaths from Norwich is indicative of this social background. In December 1724 Elizabeth Manclark, a 40-year-old widow who had been reduced to a

40. P. Corfield, "From Rank to Class: Innovation in Georgian England," 1987, pp. 36–42.
41. *Ipswich Journal*, 20 July 1776.
42. O. Davies, "Witchcraft: The Spell That Didn't Break," 1999, pp. 7–9.
43. *The Leicester Chronicle: Or, Commercial and Agricultural Advertiser*, 18 August 1849.

miserable condition by a combination of poverty and being "overrun with the itch and vermin," and who had no settled habitation in the city, lay down on a butcher's stall to rest, fell, bruised her head, and died.[44] In October 1749 the body of an unknown man was found in a small field in Norwich. He was believed to have died from "want of sustenance."[45] In January 1784, when Mary Howsden, a 45-year-old woman, was found dead in her lodging room in the parish of St Clement in the city, the coroner's jury noted that she had died from want and the inclemency of the weather.[46]

Although these are extreme cases, they represented the tip of a much larger pyramid of hardship. It has been estimated that in Staffordshire (not one of England's poorest counties) about ten per cent of households were unable to purchase enough bread for themselves over the course of a "normal" year, even if they devoted all their income to this end. During difficult times this proportion doubled, while in periods of dearth, such as 1766, it might reach 40 per cent or more.[47] Norfolk and Suffolk were broadly similar. Wages were often low, even for those in regular employment. Cloth workers in the towns were under constant economic pressure as a result of growing domestic and foreign competition, while labouring on East Anglian farms was poorly paid, hard, and often isolating work. Long hours were the norm. In theory, as a newspaper correspondent noted in 1765, conditions and terms of service were still regulated by the Statute of Artificers of 1562 and its 48 sections, most of which remained in force until the nineteenth century. These mandated penalties for leaving work before a contract was finished, so tying workers to a particular employer.[48] Theoretically, if not always in reality, the working hours of those employed by the day or week ran from 5:00 am until 6.30 pm for most of the period between the middle of March and the middle of September, though two-and–a-half hours were allowed for eating, drinking, and sleeping during the course of the day.[49]

44. NRO NCR Case 6a/5/6.
45. NRO NCR Case 6a/7/122.
46. NRO NCR Case 6a/11a/1.
47. J. Rule, "The Labouring Poor," 2004, p. 183.
48. D. Hay and P. Craven (eds), *Masters, Servants, and Magistrates in Britain and the Empire,* 2004, p. 6.
49. Letter to *Ipswich Journal,* 13 July 1765.

There was little or no improvement in agricultural wage levels for male farm workers during the eighteenth and early nineteenth centuries. In some places, there even appears to have been a fall in real earnings in the second half of the era.[50] In Norfolk the average weekly wage for agricultural workers between 1767 and 1770 was eight shillings. From 1794 to 1795 it was only a penny more.[51] In Suffolk, at the end of the century, Sir Frederic Eden could note that in the hundreds of Colneis and Carlford typical labouring wages had recently risen from one shilling and two pence, with beer, a day to one shilling and four pence, with beer. Additionally, those who grew corn would allow their workers to buy it at less than market price; if they did not produce it, they would pay as much as one shilling and six pence a day.[52] However, prices increased much more significantly during this period, partly as a result of regular shortages of grain. Furthermore, an increasing number of workers in the region were day labourers, with little security of service, and often idle outside harvest, the sowing season, and similar intense periods in the agricultural calendar.

By the early decades of the nineteenth century, rural conditions for many East Anglian workers were fairly desperate, and were aggravated by the advent of new, labour-saving, technology, such as threshing machines. This led to significant emigration, both internally within England to London and other parts and abroad to Australia and North America. Harsh rural conditions were to contribute to major disturbances in 1816 and the region's heavy involvement in the Swing Riots of 1830.

The Influence of London

Although London was at least 50 miles from even the closest parts of Suffolk, improved roads meant that the capital exerted a considerable and growing influence over the region. It was not always benign. In the

50. G. Clark, "Farm Wages and Living Standards in the Industrial Revolution: England, 1670–1869," 2001, p. 499.
51. M. J. Daunton, *Progress and Poverty: An Economic and Social History of Britain 1700–1850*, 1995, p. 427.
52. F. M. Eden, *The State of the Poor; Or, An History of the Labouring Classes in England*, vol. 1, 1797, p. 573.

1720s Daniel Defoe, noting that Ipswich had declined as a town, thought that this was largely due to the "neighbourhood of London, which sucks the vitals of trade in this island to itself, [and which] is the chief reason of any decay of business in this place."[53] Social trends, some of them negative, which began in the Metropolis, also spread to the provinces, though at times in a slightly muted form. Among them was the consumption of cheap spirits. In East Anglia largescale smuggling of gin and brandy from the Continent greatly exacerbated this problem. As Maurice Shelton warned the Suffolk Quarter Sessions grand jury in 1725, drunkenness was "so universal now (People of all ages, sexes, and conditions being infected with it) that it is become a national reproach."[54] As will be seen, London was also a place where East Anglian felons fled justice and marketed smuggled or stolen goods and animals and poached game from the region. Sometimes provincial authorities actively encouraged marginal members of their societies to move to the capital. By contrast, the Metropolis served as a source of offenders who might perpetrate local crimes while on excursion from the capital.

English Exceptionalism

England lacked an extensive national bureaucracy and large numbers of professional, state-funded, magistrates and policemen. In this regard, the country had taken a rather different route from that adopted in most of Continental Europe. Of course, English exceptionalism can be exaggerated. European jurisdictions often had common problems and, on examination, had recourse to similar solutions more frequently than is sometimes appreciated.[55] Nevertheless, England *was* different. Very significantly, there was no body specifically charged with preventing, investigating, or prosecuting crimes.

In the absence of professionally trained and paid magistrates or salaried law-enforcement officers there was widespread recourse to unpaid,

53. D. Defoe, *A Tour Through the Whole Island of Great Britain*, 1978, p. 68.
54. M. Shelton, *A Charge Given to the Grand-jury, at the General Quarter-sessions of the Peace, Holden at St. Edmunds-Bury For the Liberty Thereof*, 1726, p. 24.
55. B. P. Smith, "English Criminal Justice Administration, 1650–1850: A Historiographic Essay," 2007, p. 609.

amateur, participants in the criminal justice process, something that was not normally seen abroad. As late as 1819 Sir James MacIntosh noted that the entire English system proceeded on the assumption that the law would be aided by the public: "Wanting a spy in every house, and a crowd of police officers in every street, and a public prosecutor ever ready to undertake all labour and all expense, the presumption is that these deficiencies will be supplied by the active co-operation of the people."[56] Obviously this included the "political" nation's involvement as justices of the peace, but it went much further. As an observer noted in 1701, albeit with considerable exaggeration, it was hard to find any adult man in England who had not played some role in the justice system, whether by holding parish office as constable, churchwarden, or overseer of the poor, or by serving on a coroner's jury or on those summoned for the quarter sessions, assizes, and courts leet. As a result, he suggested that the "common people of England gain a greater experience in justice than the practice of law in foreign countries will allow to that sort of people."[57] This comment ignores a significant stratum of poor labourers who, in truth, had a fairly minimal role in the system. Nevertheless, a large proportion of Englishmen, probably more than half, played an active role in administering criminal justice in their society at some point in their lives. This had enormous ramifications.

An examination of a major French murder case highlights the contrast between the English and Continental criminal justice models during the early part of the century. In 1723, five English gentlemen embarked on a grand tour of Europe. Just outside Calais they were attacked by a gang of robbers, and all but one of them were killed.[58] A thorough search, under the immediate supervision of the local *lieutenant general de police*, was made for the murderers. The survivor, a Mr Mompessen, identified two suspects and made a deposition that would be legally admissible in his absence. The suspects were then interrogated at length, but denied any involvement. They were eventually subjected to "the torture, when they had still the resolution to deny that they knew any thing of the matter."

56. House of Commons Debate 2 March 1819, *Hansard*, vol. 39, cols. 777–845.
57. Anon, *The Claims of the People of England, Essayed, In a Letter from the Country*. London, 1701, p. 16.
58. *Daily Journal*, 16 September 1723.

The *lieutenant general de police* then sent the pair to Paris, where the authorities went more seriously to work on them. The evidence adduced was eventually found to be sufficient to declare them guilty of robbery and murder: "the Tryals in France being not by juries, as in England, but by the judgment of the court, or bench of judges." Both men were then executed. One of them was "[b]roke alive, in the extremest sense, not being allowed the coup de grace, and lived many hours on the wheel." The other was allowed the mercy of being put to death after suffering for a short time.[59]

Thus this serious but not untypical (for its gravity) case involved the work of several professional police officers, a large measure of central control from Paris, the use of deposition evidence for some prosecution witnesses, repeated interlocutory hearings, a bench of professional judges, investigative torture, and an aggravated form of death penalty. This apparatus survived largely unscathed until 1789 although the use of torture declined steadily during the course of the century, coming under fierce attack from philosophers such as Voltaire during the 1760s following the Jean Calas case, and was formally abolished in 1788, just before the French Revolution broke out.[60]

Many educated Englishmen, such as the Norfolk clergyman William Broom, were acutely aware of the differences between the two countries' systems, and proud of the fact that common law did not allow torture "like those of other countries, where men use engines to torment their fellow creatures." Nor did it normally aggravate death sentences by inflicting them on racks and wheels.[61]

The English attachment to amateurism and localism produced a system that was relatively cheap to run, less subject to pressure from central authority, provided reduced scope for state patronage, and was responsive to local needs. However, its dependence on the work of unpaid and untrained laymen, drawn from various ranks of the general public, placed considerable limits on its operation. The efforts of ordinary people were

59. Anon, *A Narrative of the Proceedings in France, for Discovering and Detecting the Murderers of the English Gentlemen, Sept. 21, 1723, Near Calais*, 1724, pp. 7–8, p. 102, and p. 108.
60. L. Silverman, *Tortured Subjects: Pain, Truth, and the Body in Early Modern France*, 2001, pp. 3–4, pp. 28–35, and p. 72.
61. W. Broome, *A Sermon Preach'd at the Assizes in Norwich, August 8th*, 1737, p. 12.

necessarily circumscribed by constraints of time, ability, training, and inclination, even as demands for better, more effective local government grew. In response, the era saw a steady erosion of its reliance on pure volunteerism at nearly all levels. This was partly achieved by a gradual infusion into the system of public money from national and local government, and private cash from a variety of individuals and organizations.

Philosophical Constraints

It was not just practical considerations that limited policing and judicial activism. There were strong philosophical constraints on the administration of criminal justice. The men behind the Glorious Revolution, several of whom were lawyers, had gone to considerable lengths to make their actions appear properly legal and in conformity with the English constitution. For example, they claimed that James had abdicated the throne by fleeing to France and they installed Mary as coequal monarch to keep up the appearance of a valid succession.[62] By the start of the eighteenth century, the "orthodox" interpretation of the events of 1688 had entered popular consciousness, with some help from establishment propaganda. They were viewed as a providential deliverance that had rendered traditional liberties secure from arbitrary power.[63] In the words of the Earl of Stamford to a grand jury, the country had been liberated from "tyranny and slavery *à la mode de France.*"[64]

Such attitudes had a considerable influence on the wider political culture. Englishmen were encouraged to esteem their legally regulated society as superior to that of most continental countries, let alone Turkey, where, it was thought, power was exercised *ex post facto* at the whim of those in authority.[65] More specifically, they believed that they were subject to publicly known laws, equal before the law, and equally subject to the law. In the words of a Norfolk justice, "No man is so great as to be

62. R. Kay, *The Glorious Revolution and the Continuity of Law*, 2014, pp. 1–12.
63. J. M. Neeson, "The Opponents of Enclosure in Eighteenth-century Northamptonshire," 1984, p. 115.
64. D. Lemmings, *Law and Government in England during the Long Eighteenth Century*, 2011, pp. 3–4.
65. M. Madan, *Thoughts On Executive Justice*, 1785, p. 117.

above its power, no man is so humble as to be below its protection."[66] Such beliefs had consequences. In the 1690s, the Suffolk JP Edmund Bohun warned that they meant that Englishmen had to be ruled with prudence and justice. Most important, they were conscious of anything that was done without proper legal authority. This attitude increased during the eighteenth century, which saw a steady growth in what might be termed legalism, an insistence that the agents of local and national government act according to law rather than the will of individuals. It reinforced slowly emerging notions of due process when dealing with suspects in the criminal justice system.

Paternalism was another key social concept throughout the period. It required social elites to have some regard to the wellbeing and interests of the poor. In exchange, the latter acknowledged the leadership of those elites and accepted that they should not have ideas above their station in life. This was a long-standing aspect of what might be termed the "organic" society. Of course, it was frequently honoured in the breach. All too often, the interests of the poor were disregarded in favour of those of landowners, such as the pursuit of profits. Nevertheless, as a widely promulgated ideal, it moderated the behaviour of those in authority, at least to some extent. More specifically, such political and social beliefs had numerous practical consequences for the criminal justice system.

A "Gentler" Society

There was a slow "gentling" in English society during the eighteenth century as attitudes towards violence, both criminal and legal, changed. The era witnessed a growing level of what might be termed squeamishness. This phenomenon was to have enormous social consequences in numerous different areas. For much of the period it led to a reduction in the incidence of potentially lethal violence and also to some previously tolerated forms of lesser violence becoming marginalised (see *Chapters 19* and *22*). It also produced growing concern at the excessive use of the death penalty for offences of dishonesty. Additionally, the latter decades

66. H. Jodrell, *A Charge Delivered to the Grand Jury of Norfolk, at the General Quarter Sessions Held on Wednesday, Jan. 16, 1793*, 1793, pp. 8–9.

of the era witnessed an increased reluctance to see people, especially women, being flogged or degraded, especially in public. Some brutal legacies of earlier times, such as the *peine forte et dure* (the pressing to death of those who refused to enter a plea), were abolished.[67] The first signs of sustained concern at the era's appalling prison conditions appeared, along with limited attempts to improve them.

Of course, this process should not be exaggerated. The vicious society that Hogarth graphically depicted in the middle of the century was still well-evidenced at its end. Nevertheless, the trend was apparent. The reasons for this general change in manners and social attitudes are complicated and contentious (some are considered in *Chapter 22*).

A More Mobile Society

At the start of the eighteenth century, travel in England was slow and expensive. This was partly because the country's roads were extremely poor. Traditionally, the parishes through which they ran had the responsibility for maintaining them. The wider county community had little involvement in the process. Every parish elected two unpaid Surveyors of Highways each year, and, under their supervision, its inhabitants provided labour, or compounded with monetary payments in lieu of work, to ensure that local roads were kept in a state of repair. This system worked reasonably well for small country roads linking farms and hamlets.

However, if a parish was unfortunate enough to have a major arterial route running through its bounds it would be required to carry out a great deal of work repairing the large ruts that were caused by heavy wagons, carts, and carriages, for little local benefit. Unsurprisingly, many were often reluctant to carry out more than the minimum amount of work necessary, although, if roads became decayed, a parish would risk being summoned to the county quarter sessions or assizes, and could be fined. For example, at the Norfolk Quarter Sessions held at Norwich on 11 July 1751, the inhabitants of Wymondham were presented for allowing "bad roads" in their parish.[68]

67. For more on the *peine forte et dure* see G. Durston, *Whores and Highwaymen*, 2012, pp. 495–497.
68. NRO MF 653 C/S 1/1.

Nevertheless, the most important East Anglian roads, like those elsewhere, improved greatly over the course of the eighteenth century. This was largely the result of their being removed from the traditional system and turned into commercial ventures. Although an informal toll system to pay for roads had operated in a few parts of England from the 1660s, this did not really expand until after 1695 and the advent of Turnpike Acts. These transferred authority over specific roads from their neighbouring parishes to a body of trustees that assumed responsibility for maintaining them in exchange for the power to levy tolls on travellers. In turn, improving the surfaces of these roads encouraged more people to use them, so boosting profits.[69]

The first private statute of this type in Suffolk was enacted in 1711. Numerous others followed, especially after the early-1730s, with the 1760s being particularly busy in this regard. Thus in 1782 an East Anglian newspaper could record a meeting of the Turnpike Trust that administered the road from Bury St Edmunds to Sudbury that was held in the *Swan Inn* in the latter town. It also noted that tolls paid at the Melford Gate on that road would be "lett by auction to the best bidder." (The trust would get a rental from this individual, who would pay it from his toll receipts.)[70] Evading toll payments was added to the list of summary offences that could be determined by a single magistrate. For example, in February 1781 William Taylor, a Norfolk JP, convicted two farmers from Halvergate for avoiding the toll at Filby Gate. They paid the statutory penalty of £5.[71] That August a farmer from Gimingham was convicted by Taylor of evading the same toll, and paid the same set fine.[72]

On some accounts, the process of privately funded improvement led to a fourfold increase in total road spending in England between 1730 and 1800. Road expenditure per mile may have increased by a factor of more than ten on roads that were taken over by turnpike trusts, although there was little change where parishes remained in control.[73] As a result

69. P. Langford, *Eighteenth-century Britain*, 2000, p. 65.
70. *Bury and Norwich Post*, 5 December 1782.
71. *Norfolk Chronicle*, 3 February 1781.
72. Ibid., 4 August 1781.
73. D. Bogart, "Did Turnpike Trusts Increase Transportation Investment in Eighteenth-century England?," 2005, pp. 439–468.

of these developments, journey times in the East Anglian region shrank. By December 1801, a new light coach (diligence) service could go from London to King's Lynn (almost as far from the capital as any place in Norfolk) in just 14 hours, passing through Cambridge and Ely on the way. It would leave the *Golden Cross* tavern in Charing Cross on Monday, Wednesday, and Friday mornings at 5:30 am, arrive in Cambridge at 1:00 pm, and be in Lynn at 8:00 pm. The same coach would return on Tuesday, Thursday, and Saturday mornings. It could carry four people in its cabin.[74] Such journeys also became cheaper. In 1750 the Sudbury-to-London stagecoach, which made the return journey to the capital three times a week, charged passengers just nine shillings each while allowing them 30 pounds of luggage.[75] Stagecoaches could carry at least six people inside their cabins, with more on top, and were usually drawn by four horses (unlike the two-horse diligences and even smaller post-chaises).[76] At the same time, transporting bulk goods in carts and wagons became quicker and less costly.

As will be seen, the improvement in lines of communication had considerable social, cultural and economic consequences. Even at the start of the century large numbers of small black cattle were driven down from Scotland to the meadows around Norwich, where they were fattened up on the rich pasturage. Local graziers then not only supplied the county, but also sent "great quantities of them weekly in all the winter season, to London."[77] Itinerant workers were also a regular feature of the period, with some "Scotchmen" walking to and from their native land to assist in the East Anglian harvest.

These changes had a major impact on crime and disorder, both directly and indirectly. For example, traditionally farmers had grown and harvested grain that was consumed in their own localities. This changed with the emergence of a national and international market, which drove up prices when harvests were poor and so encouraged grain riots in the region (see *Chapter 25*). More directly, improved roads made it easier to transport bulky smuggled and stolen goods. For instance, in 1783,

74. C. Mackie, *Norfolk Annals*, 1901, vol.1, p. 10.
75. *Ipswich Journal*, 28 April 1750.
76. N. Scarfe, *A Frenchman's Year in Suffolk*, 2011, p. 5.
77. D. Defoe, *A Tour Through the Whole Island of Great Britain*, 1978, p. 81.

several members of a gang were captured after they had committed a number of robberies on the river between Bungay and Yarmouth. One of them was a bricklayer who had frequently gone through the tollgate near Yarmouth during the night, unsuspected, with a cart loaded with sacks of stolen goods.[78]

Even more important, improved roads allowed felons to move about the country far more rapidly than before. After committing crimes in East Anglia they might flee the area, while those from other parts of the country could hide out or operate in the region. Many of those suspected of serious offences in Norfolk and Suffolk came from "out of area." Sometimes they were not even from the same region. For example, in September 1698 it was noted that three or four men who had come to Norwich from London a fortnight earlier were "now taken up for [foot] padding."[79] In 1722 a Quaker providing spiritual support to three men who were awaiting execution at Thetford observed that one of them came from Lincolnshire, while another was a "blackmore." Only one man was a native of Norfolk.[80] In 1783 the authorities in Norwich became concerned about a group of "itinerant cheats" that had arrived in the city.[81]

At the same time, the considerable mobility of certain types of victim posed problems for a legal system in which deposition and hearsay evidence was normally excluded. Those from out of area might be reluctant to wait months for an assizes or quarter sessions trial. In 1774 Tristram Harper of Aylsham in Norfolk was committed to Ipswich Gaol after a Scottish drover accused him of picking his pocket of four guineas and some silver coins. This was (in theory) a capital offence, but Harper was not subsequently executed, and may well not have stood trial.[82] Doubtless the drover had other business to attend to and a family in Scotland. This also helps explain the increased likelihood of being indicted for crimes committed not long before sessions compared to that for older offences.

78. *Norfolk Chronicle,* 9 August 1783.
79. *Flying Post Or The Post Master*, 22–24 September 1698.
80. R. Ashby, *A Relation of a Visit to Three Malefactors, Condemn'd at the Assizes at Thetford in Norfolk, Anno 1721–2,* 1724, p. 6.
81. *Norfolk Chronicle*, 16 August 1783.
82. *Ipswich Journal*, 26 November 1774.

In dealing with the problems occasioned by mobility, justices of the peace had to make greater efforts to liaise with their counterparts elsewhere in the country. For example, in 1790 a Welsh drover named John Jones murdered Robert Ellis, a colleague from the principality, while they were at Rayne in Essex (the county neighbouring Suffolk). When Ellis's body was discovered in a ditch, Jones was immediately suspected. It was known that he lived in Nant near Caernarvon. As a result, an urgent message was sent to the "magistrate in that neighbourhood, by whose vigilance he was apprehended, and is now lodged in Carnarvon Gaol, from when he will be removed to Essex."[83] The wife of the dead man was summoned from Wales, and gave evidence at Ellis's trial at the Essex Assizes, stating that on returning to the principality he had confessed to the crime and given her money not to prosecute him. There was considerable circumstantial evidence, and Ellis was convicted and executed.[84]

As this case suggests, in serious cases the authorities often went to considerable lengths to secure the return of suspects from other parts of the country. For example, in 1735 John Wilson took part in the murder of a dragoon who had been escorting customs officers near Hadleigh, in Suffolk. Wilson was later detained in London and then sent back to Suffolk for trial, where he was convicted.[85] In the same year John Davis, who was accused of bigamy and murder, was brought from Reading Gaol to Norwich by an order of *habeas corpus* directed to the Berkshire magistrates.[86]

Conversely, in 1759, when the philologist Eugene Aram was, belatedly, suspected of the murder of a man in Knaresborough, North Yorkshire, it was found that he had moved to King's Lynn in the years following the killing. William Thornton, a Yorkshire JP, issued a warrant for his arrest and sent two Knaresborough constables with it to Sir John Turner, a King's Lynn justice, who endorsed the document, making it valid within the county. Aram was then arrested at the grammar school

83. *Oracle*, 15 July 1790.
84. *Evening Mail*, 11–14 March 1791.
85. *London Evening Post*, 5–7 June 1735.
86. *General Evening Post*, 2–5 August 1735; TNA ASSI 33/1.

where he worked as an usher and escorted back to Yorkshire by the two constables.[87]

By the end of the period, the threshold for official involvement with "out of area" matters seem to have fallen as communications improved. For example, in 1809 the Mayor of Warwick sent a letter to the Bury Assizes noting that an army sergeant, who was due to stand trial in the Midlands county for shooting at a local farmer, had been found in possession of a pocketbook and a pair of half boots. On being questioned, he admitted that he had taken them from two shoemakers in Bury. A Bury alderman wrote back requesting that the sergeant be detained if he was acquitted at Warwick, with a view to being tried in East Anglia. (A later letter from the same mayor reported that the soldier had been capitally convicted).[88]

Transients and Crime

The large numbers of "transients" produced by improved communications occasioned other problems. In the middle of the century, one observer complained of an "amazing increase of beggars, vagabonds, and lawless people, who have no visible or honest way of getting their livelihood."[89] This explains why constables were urged to keep strangers under observation and to arrest those who appeared suspicious by their "garb or behavior."[90] For example, in December 1781, after two strangers burgled the home of Robert Purdey, an alehouse keeper at Weybourne in Norfolk, having loitered in the area for some time, it was noted that one was an elderly man in a "thread bare duffield coat," the other a youth dressed in a "long slop" (rough working dress).[91]

Membership of a community was an essential part of survival in eighteenth-century England. "Settlement" in a parish obliged its ratepayers

87. Anon, *The Genuine Account of the Life and Trial of Eugene Aram*, 1759, p. 13.
88. *Bury and Norwich Post*, 9 April 1809.
89. Philonomos, *The Right Method of Maintaining Security in Person and Property to All the Subjects of Great-Britain*, London, 1751, p. 2.
90. W. M. Godschall, *A General Plan of Parochial and Provincial Police*, 1787, p. 42.
91. *Norfolk Chronicle*, 8 December 1781.

to support those who became indigent.[92] Assistance was funded by a poor rate, paid by between a third and two thirds of householders. It was normally administered as financial outdoor relief (a cash dole), although food and clothes might sometimes be supplied as well. Up to 20 per cent of the population had recourse to poor relief, whether occasionally, to tide them over difficult times or an incapacitating illness, or on a long-term basis.

Annually elected overseers of the poor determined entitlement to Poor Law relief (it was a "right"). Their decisions could be appealed to a local JP, who might order relief as he saw fit, or refer the matter to quarter sessions for further consideration.[93] In practice, magistrates were often quite generous when it came to interpreting the law. In the economically difficult year of 1800, the Reverend William Holland even complained that the overseers of the poor in his Somerset parish were being "harassed to death" by insolent poor people appealing their decisions. Although poor rates had already increased fourfold over the previous two years, justices often acceded to such actions, as they were desperate to avoid public disorder, whereas overseers owed their primary allegiance to the parish ratepayers.[94]

Poor relief constituted a vital part of the country's policing system, as it discouraged "survival" crime.[95] However, although the Poor Law provided a public strategy for dealing with poverty that was unmatched in most of Continental Europe until the final years of the century, strangers, even those from neighbouring villages, did not enjoy this security when they fell on hard times, as parishes were obliged to assist only their own "settled" poor. They could be zealous about applying this restriction. For example, Frampton, in the Lincolnshire fens, appealed the decision in

92. B. Waddell, *God, Duty and Community in English Economic Life, 1660–1720,* 2012, p. 149; D. Bogart, "Did Turnpike Trusts Increase Transportation Investment in Eighteenth-century England?," *The Journal of Economic History*, 2005, vol. 65, no. 2, pp. 439–468.

93. P. Slack, *The English Poor Law, 1531–1782*, 1995, pp. 14–26.

94. J. Ayres (ed.), *Paupers and Pig Killers: The Diary of William Holland, A Somerset Parson, 1799–1818*, 1984, p. 48. Holland complained that it often had the opposite effect, as many poor people became insolent, so that all social "subordination" was lost.

95. J. Hanway, *The Defects of Police,* 1785, p. 142.

29 contested settlement actions between 1710 and 1770, and sometimes even actively searched its bounds for "louse fellers."[96]

Transients were also immune to some of the natural restraints and informal social controls that inhibited settled people. Local thieves had to be careful about what they stole if they were to avoid exposure. Frequently this limited them to petty crimes. Typically, in late seventeenth-century Myddle, in Shropshire, two brothers who were well-known for pilfering fruit, vegetables, and small things that were left lying about, never stole "any considerable goods." (One of their community's responses was to booby-trap stealable material). A local thief could not risk being seen in possession of distinctive items unless he was prepared to leave his parish after committing a crime. Occasionally this did happen. In 1781 John Todd, a labourer in his fifties from Mundham, in Norfolk, stole three pigs from a yard in the village and sold them at the market at Harleston the following day. He then disappeared. However, the published offer of a reward for his arrest noted that Todd had recently been living in Redenhall and was a veteran of the American war. Despite his comparatively advanced age, he was not, it appears, a "settled" man, and so was able to relocate elsewhere at short notice.[97]

If a local thief was caught stealing, or was even suspected of a crime, his life could easily be made uncomfortable, without having to invoke the law, with its formal evidential requirements. Ostracism was a powerful tool. Neighbours could refuse to help him in communal activities and exclude his wife from the gleaning field. More important, those who administered discretionary charity could withhold it from nefarious individuals; it was much harder to do this with Poor Law relief, which was a legal entitlement. This could be significant, as considerable amounts of money were available. For example, in 1780 a group of "worthy" gentlemen in Sudbury distributed 100 guineas among their local poor.[98] In early January 1783, on what would have been the old (pre-1752) Christmas Day, John Pike of Mendlesham, in Suffolk, gave a dinner of plum puddings and beef to all the poor people of his village and some ale and two

96. S. Hindle, "Power, Poor Relief, and Social Relations in Holland Fen, c.1600–1800," 1998, p. 87.
97. *Norfolk Chronicle*, 18 August 1781.
98. *Ipswich Journal*, 25 January 1780.

gallons of wheat to each of them for later consumption.[99] Local reprobates (those who were not "deserving") might not receive such charity.

A "carrot-and-stick" approach of rewards and informal sanctions was still probably highly effective in ensuring law-abiding behaviour among settled people, especially those in rural areas, as it had been for centuries. It did not work with strangers and transients.

Concern About Crime

During the eighteenth century there was a widespread and growing feeling amongst many interested observers, especially those in the London area, that crime was a major social problem. It was claimed, "[e]veryone is sensible, and loudly complains that there is some radical defect in our police and laws relating to ... the suppression of theft and roguery."[100] Whether this reflected reality, at least for most of the period, is doubtful. According to some modern estimates, the number of serious property crimes, as measured by indictments, declined steadily from the Restoration of 1660 until the latter decades of the 1700s, when they started to rise again.[101] Others have suggested that the expansion in offending started rather earlier, perhaps after the mid-century, although per capita indictment rates appear to have grown significantly only from the 1770s, and even this is not conclusive evidence of a real increase in law-breaking (rather than prosecution).[102] Many commentators probably attributed an increased sensitivity towards crime, and greater encouragement to prosecute offences, to a growth in the phenomenon. For example, in 1776, one thought that the then recent expansion in prosecution associations was "a sad proof, that the present times are worse than the former."[103]

There is no agreed explanation for this increase in concern about law and order. Some have attributed it to the rising influence of the "middling orders," a social group that was particularly vulnerable to crime.

99. Ibid., 11 January 1783.
100. Anon, *The Means of Effectually Preventing Theft and Robbery*, 1783, p. 3.
101. J. McMullan, "Crime, Law and Order in Early Modern England," 1987, p. 253.
102. D. Lemmings, *Law and Government in England During the Long Eighteenth Century*, 2011, p. 81.
103. T. Humphries, *A Preservative From Criminal Offences*, Shrewsbury, 1776, p. 6.

Others have linked it to the rapid growth in new forms of media, especially newspapers, which seemed to emphasise the problem. Even at the start of the century, an anonymous author, addressing the allegedly high national level of offending, thought that the existence of such a problem was self-evident, as otherwise the "Publick News [would not be] daily full of so many Relations of Robberies and Murthers."[104] Newspapers were not entirely unaware of their influence. A fear of encouraging copycat disturbances prevented the *Norwich Mercury* from reporting local food riots in 1766.[105]

Of course these two developments went together to a considerable degree; the growing middling orders provided much of the market for the expanding newspapers. The sociologist Jürgen Habermas has even suggested that late-seventeenth and early-eighteenth-century England was a pioneer in the process whereby a newly literate reading public of ordinary, if well-to-do, people influenced political affairs. They were no longer willing to uncritically accept authority. Governance was being debated, not simply projected.[106] This might affect the decision to prosecute or ignore perceived lawbreaking, whether by victims or committing magistrates, and influence other aspects of the administration of criminal justice.

Typically, the preamble to a statute from 1698 (11, W.3. c.23) took it as read that burglary, housebreaking, horse theft, and shoplifting "are of late Yeares much increased." Government also accepted that there was a need to be seen to "do" something about crime. In 1701 even a critic of the system of justice could accept that the Government had acted "vigorously" against crime and disorder, something that was evidenced in the divers laws that had been enacted to suppress offending.[107] As will be seen, there was often a hurried and ad hoc quality to the changes introduced to the criminal justice system after the end of the seventeenth century. Nevertheless, although the notion that crime was a growing problem was widespread, it was certainly not universal, even among

---

104. Anon, *Hanging, Not Punishment Enough*, London, 1701, p. 5.
105. P. King, "Newspaper Reporting, Prosecution Practice and Perceptions of Urban Crime: The Colchester Crime Wave of 1765," 1987, p. 424 and p. 464.
106. D. Lemmings et al., *Moral Panics, the Media and the Law in Early Modern England*, 2009, p. 246.
107. Anon, *Hanging, Not Punishment Enough*, 1701, p. 5.

magistrates. It was much more common amongst educated people and in the Metropolis than amongst common people and in the provinces. According to the Norfolk JP Sir Thomas Beevor (1726–1814), his was a "frivolous" age, not a "wicked" one.[108]

Arguments

At a superficial view, the eighteenth-century criminal justice system frequently appears brutal, incompetent, irrational, and grossly inefficient to modern eyes, and there was some support for such an analysis even at the time. In the words of Christopher Tancred, many of its features were "not so well adapted to the occasions of the Age we now live in, as that in which they were first form'd."[109] There are two possible responses to such a view, apart from accepting it unreservedly.

One is to find "method in the madness" by showing the system to be much more efficient and cost-effective than has often been suggested, albeit sometimes achieving its aims using different mechanisms and procedures to those of the modern era. For example, it may be that a preference for extreme but highly selective punishments, early in the century, reflected the greater cost of the obvious alternatives, especially that of lengthy imprisonment. Similarly, the use of private prosecution may have worked quite effectively because the possibility of compounding an offence, far from being a handicap, provided an incentive to prosecutors to pursue a matter and "punishment" for criminals even if they were not formally indicted.[110]

The other approach to such criticism is to note the system's strength in areas that were deemed important at the time but are less valued today. Most significantly, it accorded with the political ideal of the period. In 1700 a quasi-classical vision of government, including policing, had considerable resonance in English society. It was widely thought that criminal justice should be administered by locally resident men fulfilling

108. J. Innes, *Inferior Politics: Social Problems and Social Policies in Eighteenth-century Britain*, 2009, p. 217.
109. C. Tancred, *Essay for a General Regulation of the Law*, 1727, p. 9.
110. D. Friedman, "Making Sense of English Law Enforcement in the Eighteenth Century," 1995, p. 498.

their civic obligations to the wider society, according to their station and position in life, acting not for personal gain or pursuant to a career but out of a sense of duty. In this world, private action by members of the public appeared vastly superior to that of the state. The preference for professional, rather than popular, involvement in the justice systems found on the Continent was something to be deplored rather than emulated because of its political consequences. As these systems saw "little interference of the public, so there is little necessity for consulting their opinions."[111]

As will be seen, both approaches have some value. The criminal justice system was cheap and often more effective than it first appeared, if less so than desired. It also accorded with contemporary values to a much greater extent than the potential alternatives. However, something that will also become apparent is its lack of effective "quality control," which meant that there were regular and sometimes glaring failures throughout the system, even if they were not typical of its wider operation. At the start of the century, society took a fairly robust approach to these lapses, accepting them as the unavoidable collateral damage of its war on crime. As the era progressed, it became more alarmed by such failings, which were increasingly seen as unacceptable. Such a change in attitude helps to explain some of the developments of the 1700s.

111. House of Commons Debate 2 March 1819, *Hansard*, vol. 39, cols. 777–845.

CHAPTER 2

Justices of the Peace

Introduction

The eighteenth-century justice of the peace (or JP) was the mainspring of the country's criminal justice system as well as of much of its civil administration, despite being an unpaid, untrained, part-time, amateur magistrate, unlike most of his European counterparts. It was in the "English constitution alone that the security of the peace is committed by the Prince to men of ample fortunes in the respective neighbourhoods." Such men served at their own expense and were, in theory, familiar with their localities and neighbours, allowing them to make a proper assessment of any evidence presented before them. In this, they were (allegedly) unlike the "venal" professional magistrates of continental Europe, who were frequently strangers to the locations where they served and therefore unable to distinguish between the testimony of honest men and rogues.[1] Whatever the truth of such an analysis, the position warrants special consideration.

Appointment

In theory, the lord lieutenant of a county selected its new justices for approval and appointment by the Lord Chancellor. Indeed, the office of senior justice in a county, the *Custos Rotulorum* (Keeper of the Rolls), was usually held in tandem with that of lord lieutenant, a lifelong position

1. T. Barlow, *The Justice of Peace: A Treatise Containing the Power and Duty of That Magistrate*, 1745, p. vii.

normally granted to a major regional aristocrat that served as the main local vehicle for Crown patronage. In turn, his decisions on appointment were usually based on the advice of existing JPs and, to a much smaller extent, other local dignitaries. Periodically new commissions of the peace would be issued under the Great Seal, setting out the names of those who were allowed to act within the relevant county, adding some names and omitting others.

At the start of the era, a county magistrate was required to be literate and to possess an estate worth at least £20 a year, as had been the case since 1439. By then, it was claimed that inflation was allowing some poor men to "creep into the commission of the peace" to the detriment of the public.[2] An Act of 1732 for the "Better Qualification of Justices," which came into force in March 1733, provided that they should normally be resident in the county where they were appointed and have an estate worth not less than £100 a year. This was still a modest amount for a "gentleman"; an unsuccessful Parliamentary bill in 1701 had suggested that £400 a year was more appropriate.[3]

Prospective JPs had to swear that their assets met the £100 qualification. Typically, at the Suffolk Quarter Sessions held at Ipswich on 26 October 1751, the newly selected Reverend Thomas Tanner swore that he had two rectories and so possessed a sufficient estate "in law or in equity" to warrant the position.[4] Though this requirement prevented men of "mean estates" from being appointed, the 1732 legislation affected only county justices. Those selected for the benches of towns or cities, such as Norwich, Ipswich, Beccles, Yarmouth, and Lynn, were exempt from its provisions (see below).

Additionally, the 1732 statute provided that no magistrate was to be recruited from the inferior branches of the legal profession (solicitors, attorneys, proctors) "during such time as he shall continue in the business."[5] For this reason the active and extremely competent Yorkshire JP Samuel Lister, who came from a family of minor gentry, and had practised as an attorney between 1738 and 1751, gave up his legal work

2. Ibid., p. xiv.
3. N. Landau, *The Justices of the Peace 1679–1760,* 1984, p. 338.
4. SRO B105/2/24, p. 71.
5. Anon, *Abstract of Several Acts,* 1733, p. 2.

after being appointed as a magistrate for the West Riding.[6] All JPs were required to swear an oath of allegiance to the Monarch and the Protestant faith on assuming their position.

In the late seventeenth and early eighteenth centuries, political factors, particularly whether the individual put forward was a Whig or Tory, often influenced appointment and retention as a justice in East Anglia as elsewhere in the country. There could be considerable animosity between local magistrates over this issue, which reflected the acute tensions found in the wider nation. In 1715 toasting the success of the Old Pretender and putting up prayers for him in church led to prosecution at the Norwich Assizes.[7] Interestingly, the notorious Jacobite plotter Christopher Layer, who was executed in 1723, had been brought up in Norfolk and practised there as an attorney when a young man.[8]

JPs were sometimes added to, or left off, the county commissions of the peace purely because of their political allegiances, especially between 1689 and 1714. For instance, under Lord Chancellor William Cowper five Suffolk justices were put out of the county commission in March 1709. The following year, seven JPs were added to the Norfolk Commission.[9] When Devereaux Edgar and Orlando Bridgman were restored to the Suffolk bench in 1710, having been among the five excluded in 1709, it was noted that they had been removed as a result of misinformation from some "factious persons in Ipswich." Allegedly they were restored on Queen Anne's personal orders after she heard about the case. It was a popular move. When the two men went to Stowmarket, bells were rung, and they were met by the High Sheriff of Suffolk and up to 300 gentlemen, clergymen, and freeholders.[10]

However, political considerations were never entirely paramount in appointment. Although Norfolk saw Whig dominance of the commission after 1714, a minority of Tory JPs continued in office, including the crypto-Jacobite Sir John Wodehouse (1669–1754), who had been

6. J. Styles, "An Eighteenth-century Magistrate as Detective: Samuel Lister of Little Horton," 1982, p. 98.
7. *British Weekly Mercury*, 24–31 August 24 1715.
8. *Weekly Journal Or British Gazetteer*, June 15 1723; *Daily Post*, 29 January 1723.
9. L. Glassey, *Politics and the Appointment of Justices of The Peace 1675–1720*, 1979, p. 189 and p. 193.
10. *Post Boy (1695)*, 6–8 June 1710.

made Recorder of Thetford in 1701.[11] Their impact on appointment also declined rapidly after 1726, when George II instructed Lord Chancellor King to appoint "all gentlemen of rank and quality, unless they were in direct opposition to his government."[12] The role of political considerations largely disappeared after 1745, when it became apparent that most Tories were not incipient Jacobites. The general reluctance of gentlemen to sit as active JPs (see below) meant that those who were willing to do so could not normally be spared, whatever their political inclinations.[13]

There was no requirement that justices be formally trained in the law, although some had spent time at the Inns of Court. For example, the splendidly named Meux Rant, from Old Buckenham, had been called by Gray's Inn in 1716. He died at the age of 89 in 1780 and was remembered as a long-serving and active member of the Norfolk Commission of the Peace, with a good reputation "for his great skill in the profession of the law, and his integrity in the practice of it."[14] Almost 100 students who had a home address in Norfolk (63 men) and Suffolk (36 men) were admitted to the Inner Temple alone during the eighteenth century, and it was only one of the four Inns of Court.[15]

Nevertheless, by the 1700s such experience was much less common amongst magistrates than it had been in the previous century. Far fewer gentlemen sent sons who did not intend to become practising barristers to the Inns. In 1615 13 students joined Gray's Inn for each one who was called to the bar. In 1713 the ratio was 2.3 new students to each man called.[16] In Northamptonshire only about nine per cent of county JPs appointed between 1735 and 1795 were qualified as barristers.[17] By con-

11. L. Glassey, *Politics and the Appointment of Justices of the Peace 1675–1720*, 1979, p. 189, p. 193, and p. 260.
12. B. J. Davey, *Rural Crime in the Eighteenth Century: North Lincolnshire 1740–80*, 1995, p. 61.
13. N. Landau, *The Justices of the Peace 1679–1760*, 1984, p. 295.
14. *Norfolk Chronicle*, 5 August 1780.
15. The Inner Temple Admissions Database, www.innertemplearchives.org.uk, (Last accessed 1 March 2015).
16. R. Fletcher, *The Pension Book of Gray's Inn (Records of the Honourable Society) 1669–1800*, vol. II, 1910, p. x.
17. D. Gray "Making Law in Mid-Eighteenth-century England," 2013, p. 230.

trast, in Norfolk in 1636 more than a quarter (16 out of 62 JPs) had been barristers or serjeants-at-law.[18]

Of course, although there were fewer barristers than before in the commission, those who were legally qualified were likely to be highly active and (even more so) influential. Of the ten JPs who attended more than 50 Quarter Sessions in the West Riding of Yorkshire during the first 70 years of the eighteenth century, four belonged to Gray's Inn or the Inner Temple. Those who were practising barristers were particularly important.[19] Furthermore, despite the 1732 legislation, it was not uncommon for prosperous attorneys with a minor-gentry background to become justices of the peace, although, in theory, they could not continue to practise. It also seems that a few men who were intending to become JPs took active steps to familiarise themselves with their duties prior to appointment. The Reverend John Longe, for instance, seems to have attended petty sessions at Coddenham in Suffolk as an observer before becoming a magistrate, though this was far from universal.

Even so, many contemporary observers, like the visiting François de la Rochefoucauld, thought that it was unnecessary for English justices to have much general knowledge or education, let alone any form of legal training. One reason was that they used magistrates' well-indexed *vade mecums* ("very detailed" books) giving information on all the main offences and procedural matters, so that for a magistrate the "only requirement is to be able to read to dispense the law."[20] La Rochefoucauld was referring to handbooks by authors such as Jacob Giles, Samuel Blackerby, and Richard Burn. After 1755 *The Justice of the Peace and Parish Officer*, a compendious volume by Burn, appears to have become the most widely used and important of these, even being recognised as fairly authoritative by the Court of King's Bench, although would-be competitors, such as *The Magistrate's Assistant* (1784), by Samuel Glasse, continued to appear on a regular basis.[21]

18. W. Prest, *The Rise of the Barristers: A Social History of the English Bar 1590–1640*, 1986, p. 8 and p. 237.
19. M. E. W. Maddison, *The Justices of the Peace and the Administration of Local Government in the East and West Ridings of Yorkshire Between 1680 and 1750*, 1986, p. 42.
20. N. Scarfe, *A Frenchman's Year in Suffolk*, 2011 p. 87.
21. S. Devereaux, "The Promulgation of the Statutes in Late Hanoverian Britain," 2005, p. 85.

Whether such texts really were sufficient on their own is debatable. Some observers feared that legal ignorance meant that magistrates frequently degenerated into the "passive and mischievous" instruments of their clerks, who often did have a legal background, if only as a low-grade attorney, solicitor, or other "discarded underling of the law."[22] (Many others were simply literate local men or employees of the justice). It was feared that such clerks might try to maximise the fees from their unsalaried part-time position by resorting to corrupt practices. Others refuted these allegations, claiming that JPs normally employed the same attorney in the (occasional) position of clerk that they used for their own private legal business, so that most were notable for "legal skill and integrity."[23] Doubtless both types of clerk could readily be found, with most between these extremes. As in so many areas of the era's criminal justice system, there was a lack of effective quality control.

The number of JPs enrolled in the county Commissions of the Peace for both Norfolk and Suffolk increased considerably during the late seventeenth and early eighteenth centuries, as they did elsewhere in the country. In 1600 there were 1,200 justices in England; by 1714 there were well over 3,000.[24] More specifically, between the 1680s and the 1720s, the Commission for the West Riding of Yorkshire increased by approximately 160 per cent and that for the East Riding by 125 per cent. Expansion continued over the ensuing 30 years, albeit at a slower rate.[25] In Shropshire there were 45 magistrates in 1688, 102 in 1721, 145 in 1733, and 247 in 1761.[26] The situation was the same in East Anglia. In Norfolk there were, on average, 79 JPs between 1660 and 1675, but 133 from 1710 to 1718.[27]

However, as the number of JPs grew, those willing to devote a significant amount of time and energy to the administration of justice decreased, both proportionately and (more significantly) in absolute

22. T. Gisborne, *An Enquiry Into the Duties of Men in the Higher and Middle Classes of Society in Great Britain*, 1794, p. 288.
23. H. J. Pye, *Summary of the Duties of a Justice of the Peace Out of Sessions*, 1808, p. xiv.
24. M. J. Braddic, *State Formation in Early Modern England, c.1550–1700*, 2010, p. 134.
25. M. E. W. Maddison, *The Justices of the Peace and the Administration of Local Government in the East and West Ridings of Yorkshire between 1680 and 1750*, 1986, p. 44.
26. D. Cox, *Cinderellas and Packhorses: A History of the Shropshire Magistracy*, 2005, p. 27.
27. J. Rosenheim, "County Governance and Elite Withdrawal in Norfolk, 1660–1720," 1989, p. 108.

numbers, despite significant population increase after about 1730. This reluctance to serve actively was most marked amongst magistrates drawn from what might be termed the "social elite," the greater gentry and aristocratic families in a county.

There had always been "courtesy" JPs, appointed as a mark of esteem because of their prominent positions in national society (they were often Privy Councillors), without any expectation of their acting in the role. However, this profile gradually spread to many of the more substantial justices of the region. Such men were increasingly deterred by the many extra duties being placed on the office, and were more reluctant, as society became increasingly stratified, to mix intimately with the lower orders. They were also attracted by the new entertainments and diversions available in or near the capital or at spas such as Bath and Tonbridge Wells, which could be more easily reached on improved roads. The last consideration meant, "many persons of estate leave their antient country seats, and live in places that are better suited to the gaiety of luxurious inclinations."[28] Those with great wealth purchased town houses, and the "London Season" began to develop, while Parliament sat much more regularly than in the previous century, drawing justices who were also MPs (and so substantial men) to the capital for longer periods. For example, during the 1750s, the movements of Sir Cordell Firebrace, the chairman of the Suffolk Bench, between his seat at Melford Hall and his London home in North Audley Street were regularly reported in the newspapers.[29]

Major regional gentlemen continued to be appointed to the county commissions, almost as a matter of course, and would feel slighted if they had not been, but many of them did not serve actively. As Marc du Bombelles, a French diplomat who had toured the Midlands, noted in 1784, a typical lord lieutenant would select his neighbours and acquaintances as JPs purely out of politeness and as a personal mark of honour, even though they "do not exercise the functions for which they have sworn an oath."[30] Edmund Bohun, a Suffolk JP from 1675 to 1694, had identified this change as early as the 1690s. Indeed, the years around

28. T. Andrews, *An Enquiry Into the Causes of the Encrease and Miseries of the Poor of England*, 1738, p. 26.
29. *Public Advertiser*, 19 January 1753.
30. D. Cox, *Crime in England 1688–1815*, 2014, p. 19.

1690 appear to have been something of a watershed in this respect. For about three decades after the Restoration, the social elite had made considerable efforts to participate in county government and administration. This waned swiftly after the Glorious Revolution. In Norfolk old families such as the Gawdys, Calthorpes, and Spelmans were gradually replaced at sessions by newer names. This growth in "inactivism" was a nationwide phenomenon. The county commission for Gloucestershire that was issued in 1762 contained 262 names, but only 34 men attended any quarter sessions at all between 1750 and 1755.[31]

In 1718, in response to this development, William Nelson proposed that each English county should have eight magistrates who would sit on a regular basis, be properly rewarded financially for doing so, and punished if they failed to attend to their duties. These "workhorse" JPs would be balanced by eight men of the "best quality" who would sit as and when they chose.[32] His suggestion was not followed, and the problem of "non-practising" JPs became progressively more acute as the century advanced. In 1754 Lord Hardwicke urged assizes judges to remind gentlemen of their obligation to serve if appointed to the bench and lamented that many were "apt to be very pressing to get into the Commission of the Peace, and when they are appointed, to be very backward in acting."[33] A few years later, the Reverend William Jones deplored the "want of public spirit, and that aversion to business, which has prevailed of late years among our gentry."[34]

In some respects, this development was merely a facet of a much wider eighteenth-century process whereby members of the public, at whatever social level, became increasingly reluctant to discharge their "traditional" obligations to society purely out of a sense of civic duty, whether these entailed serving as a local constable or as a county magistrate. It was an

31. E. Moir, *Local Government in Gloucestershire 1775–1800*, 1969, p. 44.
32. W. Nelson, *The Office and Authority of a Justice of Peace: Collected Out of All the Books, Whether of Common or Statute Law*, 1718, p. 388.
33. J. M. Beattie, *Crime and the Courts In England 1660–1800*, 1986, p. 60.
34. P. Langford, *Public Life and the Propertied Englishman: 1689–1798*, 1991, pp. 390–391.

aspect of what gloomy contemporary observers called the "great decay of public virtue" in English life.[35]

Most members of the majority of English commissions of the peace did not attend quarter sessions during the eighteenth century. Many did not even take out their *dedimus potestatem*, the legal document that allowed them to work in any capacity, taking the title purely for its status. For example, in 1780 only 40 per cent of the JPs in Kent had ever taken out a *dedimus*.[36] From 1710 to 1718, an average 133 justices (apart from its borough magistrates) were on the Norfolk bench, but only 32 attended any sessions at all each year (24 per cent of the total). At the higher court, where their presence was more ornamental, and so less essential, the situation could be even worse. In 1724 only nine out of 115 county justices eight per cent of the total) attended assizes, although this number had increased to almost 30 pet cent a decade later.[37]

Suffolk had the same problem. Devereux Edgar (1659–1739), a JP of the late seventeenth and early eighteenth century, waited 15 years after becoming part of his county commission to be sworn into office as an active justice, finally succumbing to the blandishments of "persons of quality." When he became (highly) active in 1700, he noted that, before that year, "I entirely refused to act & would not be persuaded to be sworn."[38] He quickly became a vital member of the Suffolk county bench. During a heated struggle over its composition in March 1705, the then lord lieutenant threatened to remove Edgar from the Commission of the Peace. (His activism had made him unpopular in some quarters.) However, the Clerk of the Peace, a man named Kipling, immediately warned him that if Edgar were removed, "his grace must be sure to putt in such Justices as could doe the business and not fail attendance at sessions." Kipling noted that some other candidates who had been mooted for the Suffolk bench would not sit on a regular basis, making it impossible to hold

35. T. Andrews, *An Enquiry into the Causes of the Encrease and Miseries of the Poor of England*, 1738, p. 49. For the decline in communitarianism during the era, see G. Durston, *Whores and Highwaymen*, 2012, pp. 58–60.
36. N. Landau, *The Justices of the Peace 1679–1760*, 1984, p. 321.
37. J. Rosenheim, "County Governance and Elite Withdrawal in Norfolk, 1660–1720," 1989, pp. 108–109.
38. SRO QS 347.96, *The Devereux Edgar Notebook*, Transcribed by S. R. Schofield, 1956, vol. 1, p. 1.

sessions.[39] Although Edgar escaped removal on this occasion, he was one of four justices turned out of the County Commission in March 1708. Significantly, half the members of this small group were purely nominal magistrates, Edgar noting that "only Orlando Bridgeman and my selfe having been sworn and acting Justices."[40]

Furthermore, active JPs were unevenly distributed. There were "bald" spots in both East Anglian counties that forced some complainants to make long journeys to find a magistrate and which discouraged recourse to formal legal action. For example, the Norfolk port of Wells was prone to disturbances but, by the late 1600s, often had no resident JP. Efforts were sometimes made to cover these areas by appointing less prestigious local men to the position or by pressuring "active" JPs from other parts of the county to help cover them. At the Epiphany Sessions of the Norwich bench in 1698, a JP from "out of area" was named to join the single resident magistrate who was active in a particular hundred.[41]

Many magistrates were just as reluctant to participate in the justices' traditional and vital "out of sessions" legal work, such as examining suspects and issuing search and arrest warrants, as they were to attend sessions, although some were willing to perform the former duty but not the latter. In 1782, for instance, more than a third of Essex JPs did not commit a single person to quarter sessions.[42] In many counties the vast majority of work was done by as few as 30 magistrates, with a handful of these men sometimes being almost run ragged. In Staffordshire, during the years immediately after 1740, two or three JPs each committed more than eight per cent of those going for trial on indictment for the entire county. Similarly, a few magistrates returned dozens of summary convictions. Broadly the same pattern was found in East Anglia. Even in the 1660s Robert Doughty had been involved in some kind of legal

39. SRO QS 347.96, *The Devereux Edgar Notebook*, transcribed by S. R. Schofield, 1956, vol. 1, pp. 137–138.
40. Ibid., vol. 2, p. 211.
41. J. Rosenheim, "County Governance and Elite Withdrawal in Norfolk, 1660–1720," 1989, p. 101.
42. A. Brown, *Prosperity and Poverty: Rural Essex 1700–1815*, 1996, p. 86.

work every other day as a Norfolk JP. Usually this was as a single justice sitting "out of sessions."[43]

A shortage of appropriate men meant that alternatives to the shire's grandees (men of the "best reputation") necessarily had to be sought as magistrates.[44] As a result, eighteenth-century justice was increasingly administered by men drawn from what might be termed the lesser gentry, a few of whom might even have been called pseudo gentry, having acquired small estates with money made in commerce or the professions, despite the political dangers of empowering such men manifest during the Interregnum.[45] In the 1760s Blackstone could talk about the "present scarcity of magistrates" as something that encouraged the appointment of those who were not truly gentlemen to the office.[46] Lesser gentlemen were unlikely to have the resources to spend much time at spas or in London, or to become MPs. In several parts of the country, "winter justices," socially inferior men who did not participate in the London season or Parliament, and so were available in the colder months, were identified (many of them allegedly attorneys by training).[47]

Indicative of this process, in 1711 25 Norfolk justices, most of them newly appointed, took out their *dedimus*, allowing them to be active magistrates in the county and a strong indicator (though not a guarantee) that they would do at least some legal work (the fees charged for taking it out were about £4).[48] Twenty-one of these men, taken together, averaged a position of 109 in order of precedence in the (then) 130-member county Commission of the Peace. A similar pattern can be seen in immediately ensuing years. Active JPs tended to be disproportionately drawn from the more obscure members of the commission, although there were numerous exceptions to this general rule.[49]

---

43. J. Rosenheim, "Documenting Authority: Texts and Magistracy in Restoration Society," 1993, p. 593.
44. G. Jacob, *Every Man His Own Lawyer: Or, A Summary of the Laws of England in a New and Instructive Method*, 1736, p. 399.
45. N. Landau, *The Justices of the Peace 1679–1760*, 1984, p. 319.
46. W. Blackstone, *Commentaries on the Laws of England*, vol. 2, 1766, p. 279.
47. P. Langford, *Public Life and the Propertied Englishman: 1689–1798*, 1991, pp. 390–391.
48. L. Glassey, *Politics and the Appointment of Justices of the Peace 1675–1720*, 1979, p. 22.
49. J. Rosenheim, "County Governance and Elite Withdrawal in Norfolk, 1660–1720," 1989, p. 112.

Clerical JPs

The need for working magistrates meant that clerical JPs became vital to the county system after the mid-century. There had been a modest number of justices in holy orders in the early seventeenth century, but their appointment had quickly fallen out of fashion. In the 1620s members of the House of Commons had even complained about the Crown's appointment of clerics to the office. There were suggestions that only those clergymen who were bishops or deans should be appointed, or none at all. Even at their peak, in 1626, they made up less than eight per cent of all justices, and their numbers were allowed to decline significantly thereafter.[50] As a result, there were only about 50 justices in holy orders in the entire country in 1700. However, by 1761 there were more than 1,000, a particularly marked increase having occurred in the years after 1740.

Clerical livings counted towards the post-1732 financial qualification required of county magistrates, and were sometimes boosted by enclosure and the award of land in lieu of tithes. To the authorities, who were under pressure to find active justices, such magistrates became increasingly attractive especially as the fear that some men of the cloth were potential Jacobites waned swiftly after the early years of the century. Clergymen provided a ready source of university-educated, locally based, and settled recruits. They were also more resistant to the new diversions of the age, which discouraged other members of the "political nation" from investing their time in the administration of justice—a problem that continued well into the following century. As Francis Witts, a clerical magistrate from the West Country, noted as late as 1827, it was most desirable that younger squires should engage in such work and not "leave all to the clergy, as is too often the case, while their attention is absorbed in fox hunting, racing, London amusements, or the gay frivolities of Cheltenham, Brighton, etc."[51]

Clerical justices were also much less likely to behave poorly than some of the men who became JPs purely because of their social status,

50. C. Haigh, "Clergy JPs In England and Wales, 1590–1640," 2004, pp. 233–259.
51. D. Verey (ed.), *The Diary of a Cotswold Parson*, 2003, p. 65.

something that engendered increasing concern as the era progressed. In 1836 Witts noted that an active member of the Gloucestershire bench and frequent grand juror for that county had participated in a duel and also appeared in a London court charged with a serious assault. He had horsewhipped a man who had annoyed him and then "gloried in the shame."[52] By contrast, eighteenth-century clergymen in the diocese of Norwich were generally sober and well-behaved, the odd case of adultery and drunkenness apart. Whether they were clerics or minor gentlemen, it was particularly important that JPs who did not have the authority that came from being the "natural" leaders of their counties should, at least, behave correctly. A "patriarchal" rather than "bureaucratic" model of justicing came less naturally to them.

In their turn, clergymen were attracted by both the status of the office and the practical power that went with it.[53] This might be useful in disputes over tithes and dealings with potential religious rivals. For example, in 1785 Norfolk magistrates issued a general warrant for the arrest of "several disorderly persons who style themselves Methodist preachers [and] go about raising routs and riots to the great damage of his Majesty's liege people." (Unfortunately, this proclamation also helped legitimise outbreaks of mob violence against itinerant Methodist preachers in some parts of the county).[54] Many men of the cloth were worldly individuals, with little faith in a fear of damnation acting as an effective deterrent to potential felons, especially given the growing climate of scepticism towards religion: "The evils of another life, like objects of sight, the more remote they are, the less they appear."[55] Such men saw the value of concrete sanctions for misbehaviour.

As a result of these developments, clergymen became important "workhorses" in many local commissions of the peace, providing some of the most diligent, conscientious, and educated magistrates in rural parts.[56] In areas with few resident gentlemen they sometimes made up almost the

52. Ibid., p. 116.
53. P. Langford, *Public Life and the Propertied Englishman: 1689–1798*, 1991, pp. 411–420.
54. R. J. Lee, *Encountering and Managing The Poor: Rural Society and the Anglican Clergy in Norfolk 1815–1914*, 2003, p. 243.
55. F. Allen, *The Reasonableness and Necessity of Human Laws and Penalties*, 1739, p. 12.
56. G. Morgan and P. Rushton, "The Magistrate, the Community and the Maintenance of an Orderly Society in Eighteenth-century England," 2003, p. 59.

entire local bench. In late-eighteenth-century Lincolnshire, for example, 47 per cent of active JPs were clergymen, with almost all those in the Spalding district being men of the cloth.[57] In 1832, approximately a third of the working justices in England and Wales were still in holy orders. Their numbers declined thereafter, partly as a result of the influence of the Oxford Movement and public criticism from prominent bishops. Eventually openly middle-class magistrates replaced them. Ironically, clergymen achieved their power as justices even as their general influence on society as sources of information was becoming attenuated by the rise of newspapers and the de facto toleration after 1688 for much non-Anglican religious attendance.

Nevertheless, there was some opposition to clerical magistrates throughout the eighteenth century. Several lord lieutenants, in various parts of the country, were reluctant to appoint them if they could avoid it. At one point their number included the lord lieutenant of Norfolk, the Earl of Buckingham, who for several years refused to put any clergy into the county Commission other than the dean and chancellor for Norwich.[58] In 1761 Norfolk had only a handful of clerical JPs, but thereafter their numbers increased swiftly. In 1787 seven of 20 new Norfolk magistrates who were qualified to sit were clergymen. The following year there were nine out of 12. In 1789 eleven out of 15 were clergy, and in 1790 nine out of 18.[59] As late as 1837, 107 Norfolk Justices (31.5 per cent of the total) were clergymen.[60]

Suffolk was also well-provided with clerical JPs, a considerable number being appointed by the mid-century. In 1788, when the elderly Reverend Robert Butts, the rector of Melford in that county, died, he was remembered as a "magistrate, a Divine and a parent" in that order.[61] Between 1796 and 1833, men of the cloth made up between 34 per cent and 40 per cent of working justices in Suffolk.[62] Clerics also tended to be among

57. N. Yates, *Eighteenth Century Britain: Religion and Politics 1714–1815*, 2007, p. 134.
58. S. Taylor, *Church and State in England in the Mid-eighteenth Century: The Newcastle Years 1742–1762,* 1987, p. 16.
59. W. M. Jacob, *The Clerical Profession in the Long Eighteenth Century, 1680–1840*, 2007, p. 228.
60. R. Lee, *Rural Society and the Anglican Clergy in Norfolk 1815–1914: Encountering and Managing the Poor,* 2006, p. 105.
61. *Bury and Norwich Post,* 3 December 1788.
62. M. Stone (ed.), *The Diary of John Longe, Vicar of Coddenham, 1765–1834*, 2008, p. 247.

the most active of "active" magistrates in the region. For example, in the latter part of the era they were more likely than non-clerical justices to be regular attendees at quarter sessions in both the western and northern divisions of Norfolk, where there were fewer resident gentry.[63]

Inevitably there was a price to be paid for this development. It added to longstanding popular grievances about tithes and damaged any notion of the clergy as intermediaries between rich and poor. Their pastoral role was severely compromised by their responsibility for administering the criminal law. It was partly for this reason that the widespread disturbances in East Anglia in 1816 had a distinctly anti-clerical tinge. Several clergymen in the region, some of them JPs, received threatening and abusive letters or were targeted by rioters.[64] The existence of clerical JPs also appeared increasingly strange, given that, by the eighteenth century, it was generally recognised that clergymen should be exempt from service on a trial jury.[65]

Unfortunately for the county authorities, it was difficult to force magistrates to serve actively. Those who were conscientious usually did so through choice, whether they were prompted by a sense of duty, wished to enhance their local power and status, or found the work interesting. Some who were recruited from the less elevated sections of society would also know that their continued membership of the Commission was partly dependent upon "singing for their supper" by being effective justices. The desire for good governance in their immediate neighbourhoods was probably the single most important motivation for those members of the lesser gentry who sat actively. By the mid-eighteenth century an English "gentleman" could not hope to attain status that he otherwise lacked purely by being a working JP.[66] East Anglia did not have an equivalent of the metropolitan trading justices, attracted by the small fees that came with some of their work.[67]

---

63. W. M. Jacob, *The Clerical Profession in the Long Eighteenth Century, 1680–1840*, 2007, pp. 229–230.
64. E. J. Evans, "Some Reasons for the Growth of English Rural Anti-Clericalism c.1750–c.1830," 1975, pp. 102–105.
65. R. Pattenden, "The Exclusion of the Clergy from Criminal Trial Juries: An Historical Perspective," 1999, pp. 151–153.
66. N. Landau, *The Justices of the Peace 1679–1760*, 1984, p. 325 and p. 331.
67. For more on the trading justices see G. Durston, *Whores and Highwaymen*, 2012, at pp. 314–320.

The demand for active magistrates meant that those who were willing to serve, whether lay or clerical, might have long careers. In 1805, when John Blofield died at his seat at Hoveton in Norfolk, in his eightieth year, it was noted that he had been a deputy lieutenant and "upwards of 46 years an acting-magistrate, for that county."[68] When Robert Andrews died at his seat near Sudbury the following year, he was also in his eightieth year, and still an "active and impartial magistrate," one of the oldest in Suffolk.[69]

When considering the social background of working JPs it must be remembered that all things are relative. Drawing on his time in Suffolk, François de la Rochefoucauld thought that its magistrates were recruited from men of the "best reputation in the county." This was an exaggeration, at least when it came to active justices, and probably something that he had been told. Nevertheless, it was not entirely devoid of truth. It is apparent that a significant number of high-status men continued to serve as active JPs throughout the century. Members of aristocratic families might be among them, if they wished to secure a major role in county governance. For example, Sir Cordell Firebrace (1712–1759) was a conscientious member and eventually chairman of the Suffolk bench. He was also a Tory MP for the county and the Oxford-educated owner of an estate that, in 1750, was valued at £3,500 per annum, as well as having £30,000 in money and investments. More modestly, but perhaps more typically of rank-and-file justices, Davy Durrant (1704–1759) of Scottow, a Norfolk JP, had an average expenditure of £1,000 a year on his estate between 1738 and 1755. His household included three or four maids, a footman, coachman, gardener, and cook. He made regular trips to Norwich and Great Yarmouth but fewer to London. He could repair his home, but not rebuild it in a "fashionable" style, as more affluent gentlemen were doing.[70]

Even clerical magistrates tended to be recruited from the more prosperous elements in their profession, partly justifying the notion of "squarsons." Most of the 42 clergymen made JPs in Norfolk between

68. *The Gentleman's Magazine*, vol. 75, part 2, 1805, p. 884.
69. *Bury and Norwich Post,* 28 May 1806.
70. H. T. Dickinson, *A Companion to Eighteenth-century Britain*, 2002, pp. 183–195 and p. 165.

1787 and 1791 held rectories, making them entitled to both the greater and lesser tithes from their parishes. At least ten of them were members of longstanding gentry families, and almost as many again had some kind of connection to men of that status.[71] As late as 1834, 61.7 per cent of clerical magistrates in Norfolk still had what has been (very broadly) termed a "gentry" background.[72] The situation was similar in Suffolk. For example, the Reverend John Longe (1765–1834), the affluent vicar of Coddenham and an active JP for the county, had ten domestic servants. To a significant degree, the growth in clerical justices coincided with the growing number of aristocrats and men from major gentry families who were willing to consider the church as a profession by the middle of the eighteenth century, in a way that had been unusual 50 years earlier. As Bishop Warburton noted in 1752, the "grandees" had found their way back to the church.[73] The great majority of clergymen did not become JPs. Significantly, in counties such as Glamorgan in Wales, where there were few wealthy clergymen, the local gentry often appear to have been slow to accept them as justices.[74]

Although many high-status men were reluctant to serve as active magistrates, there were still normally enough of them to fill the most important positions, such as chairman of quarter sessions and of the various specialist sub-committees established by that court, even if more obscure men sometimes supplemented the ranks of ordinary justices. For this reason, in the light of his extensive personal experience, the metropolitan stipendiary justice Henry Pye (1745–1813) could still suggest, at the start of the nineteenth century, that country magistrates were normally a mixture of "gentlemen of the first consequence in the county, and clergymen of learning and respectability."[75]

71. W. M. Jacob, *The Clerical Profession in the Long Eighteenth Century, 1680–1840*, 2007, p. 229.
72. R. J. Lee, *Encountering and Managing the Poor: Rural Society and the Anglican Clergy in Norfolk 1815–1914*, 2003, p. 236.
73. J. H. Plumb, *England in the Eighteenth Century*, 1969, p. 43.
74. P. Jenkins, *The Making of a Ruling Class: The Glamorgan Gentry, 1640–1790*, 2002, p. 49.
75. H. Pye, *Summary of the Duties of a Justice of the Peace Out of Sessions*, 1808, p. xiv.

Reputation and Competence

In theory, as JPs were usually significant local gentlemen, and so the natural leaders of their communities, they should have commanded respect from those who appeared before them. In normative literature, the justice of the peace was often described as the "father of the country."[76] However, the reality was rather different. Whatever the ideal, justices were certainly not held in universal esteem. An apparently widespread lack of respect for the office troubled Maurice Shelton, a Suffolk JP who delivered a charge to the county's quarter-sessions grand jury at Bury in 1725. He urged them to punish those who made "unbecoming gestures" towards a justice or said, behind his back, that a particular magistrate was an: "ignorant fellow, and understands not the statutes."[77]

In 1748 another observer complained (with some justification) that magistrates were qualified by their wealth "not knowledge in the laws." Although there were some men of quality amongst their ranks, many others were "petty tyrants." He felt that they sapped rather than promoted English liberty.[78] Half a century later, Thomas Gisborne agreed with his analysis. He thought that justices were often a law unto themselves, and always at risk of becoming dictatorial, opinionated, dogmatic, aggressive, thick-skinned, and arbitrary when making decisions. They had a fairly free rein because the people they dealt with were usually drawn from the lowest ranks of society, often indigent and illiterate, and so unlikely to complain publicly or effectively.[79]

Reconciling the near contemporary but totally conflicting views of men like Pye and Gisborne is difficult. However, it appears that the provincial magistracy varied according to locality and practitioner, so that both opinions had merit. Problems were largely occasioned by the need to recruit enough men to carry out the office in any given place and, conversely, the difficulty of excluding unsuitable men of status from the

76. B. Waddell, *God, Duty and Community in English Economic Life, 1660–1720*, 2012, p. 125.
77. M. Shelton, *A Charge Given to the Grand-Jury, at the General Quarter-Sessions of the Peace, Holden at St. Edmunds-Bury For the Liberty Thereof*, 1726, p. 34.
78. Philalethes, *English Liberty in Some Cases Worse than French Slavery*, 1748, pp. 51–59.
79. T. Gisborne, *An Enquiry Into the Duties of men in the Higher and Middle Classes of Society in Great Britain*, 1794, p. 285.

position if they actively sought it out or of removing good magistrates who had lost some of their faculties due to age or illness. Some justices were outstanding, others were extremely poor; most were between these two extremes, doing a more or less competent job for most of the time.

Whether good or bad, JPs were not entirely free agents. Even magistrates had to take account of local feeling. Several were physically attacked. For example, at the Norfolk Assizes held at Norwich in July 1735, Thomas Benndish pleaded guilty to assaulting Thomas Betts in the execution of his office as a justice.[80] Others endured organized local hostility. In 1769, prior to his move to Norfolk, Parson Woodforde noted that an effigy of one of his friends, who was also a Somerset JP, had been paraded through the streets of Castle Cary and then burnt because he had summonsed the village churchwardens to sessions in Wells for failing to present a local man who had rioted in church.[81] Irrespective of such personal dangers, many JPs did not need much encouragement to exercise their powers in a restrained manner. Most were acutely aware of the need to preserve order and cohesion in their communities. This often precluded them from enforcing the criminal law too strictly, or acting purely in their own interests or those of their friends.

The Justices' Work

The bulk of a justice's legal work related to what were essentially civil matters. Typically, in early eighteenth-century Suffolk, Devereaux Edgar dealt with an enormous number of bastardy actions, such as that of Margaret Perryman, who claimed in 1707 that she had been impregnated by a fellow servant in Thorpe and asked Edgar for an affiliation order against the putative father of her child. On numerous other occasions, women who had already given birth to illegitimate babies asked him to arrange financial support. Yet more of Edgar's energy was spent on an endless succession of settlement actions in which parishes sought to avoid Poor Law responsibility for impoverished new arrivals, while a great deal more time was devoted to settling master-servant disputes over unpaid

80. NRO C/S1/12 mf 656 6, parts 1–4.
81. J. Beresford (ed.), *The Diary of a Country Parson, 1758–1802*, 1978, pp. 38–40.

wages or to endorsing changes to employment contracts, such as the mutually agreed discharge of a yearly hired man who, it transpired, was lame before he entered service.[82] On one estimate, about ten per cent of Edgar's time was spent on employment law alone.[83] Similarly, Phillip Ward, a magistrate in Oundle, Northamptonshire, around the middle of the century, appears to have spent more than a fifth of his judicial time on tax matters, and almost as much again on Poor Law and settlement disputes.[84] Half a century later, Samuel Whitbread (1758–1815), a Bedfordshire JP, was still heavily involved in resolving disputes between employers and employees.

Blurring boundaries, some master-servant disputes, particularly those involving recalcitrant apprentices, had a quasi-criminal aspect and ended with formal punishment being imposed. For example, Edgar committed at least 17 servants to the house of correction.[85] Thus, in March 1703 a master asked that his apprentice be released back to his service from Needham House of Correction because he had become "very orderly & penitent" since being committed there at his (the master's) behest.[86] Even "ordinary" servants could be punished in certain circumstances. In 1772 a magistrate committed John Meadows of Claydon Hall to Henley Bridewell in Suffolk for 14 days for absenting himself from his master on Sundays and being out for several nights without permission.[87] Numerous more arcane administrative matters also came within a justice's remit. For example, after the middle of the era, JPs became involved in militia recruitment. William Breese was excused service in the Norfolk Militia after Mary Hardy's husband went to a JP at Wroxham Bridge and spoke on his behalf.[88]

Less time was spent on more obviously (if broadly) "criminal" matters. Poaching and property crimes took up just ten per cent of Phillip Ward's time, with assaults and disturbances another five per cent, and

82. SRO QS 347.96, *The Devereux Edgar Notebook*, transcribed by S. R. Schofield, 1956, vol. 2, pp. 156–157.
83. D. Hay, "Master and Servant in England," 2000, p. 233.
84. D. Gray "Making Law in Mid-eighteenth-century England," 2013, p. 217.
85. D. Hay, "Master and Servant in England," 2000, p. 233.
86. SRO QS 347.96, *The Devereux Edgar Notebook*, transcribed by S. R. Schofield, 1956, vol.1, p. 53.
87. *Ipswich Journal*, 26 September 1772.
88. M. Bird (ed.), *The Diary of Mary Hardy 1773–1809*, 2013, p. 322.

public cursing between three per cent and four per cent. Together, these categories constituted less than a fifth of his work.[89] Even conscientious provincial JPs dealt with relatively few serious criminal offences that progressed to trial on indictment, especially at assizes. Samuel Lister, easily one of the most active magistrates in the West Riding of Yorkshire, committed only 19 suspected property offenders to the York Assizes between 1755 and 1768.[90]

Nevertheless, JPs played an absolutely vital role in the country's wider criminal justice system. They were its entry point, acting as filters for the higher courts. As was noted in 1706, in all criminal cases whatsoever they had "the first examination, and by them such offences are remitted to a further tryal."[91] The hearings that took place at quarter sessions or assizes were the culmination of a process that had started in a justice's parlour and were shaped by the decisions he had made. Some of these were reached in a decidedly off-the-cuff manner.

Equally important, many complaints that came before a justice went no further than his parlour, because they were dismissed out of hand, dealt with informally, or disposed of summarily. As the barrister Theodore Barlow noted in 1745, although justices could not formally deal with felons, "almost numberless are the sorts of people who may be defendants before them."[92]

The justices' policing and investigative work was primarily reactive. Sometimes it was only after a man had been taken into custody and produced before him that a magistrate became involved and "processed" the individual. However, on other occasions they had at least issued search and arrest warrants. For example, in 1782 the mayor of Norwich (an *ex officio* magistrate for the city) and two of its JPs issued a warrant whereby John Betts's house could be entered and searched for woollen yarn that, it was thought, had been embezzled and concealed there. Inside, dozens of different types of cloth were found. These were deposited for a month

89. D. Gray "Making Law in Mid-eighteenth-century England," 2013, p. 217.
90. J. Styles, "An Eighteenth-century Magistrate as Detective: Samuel Lister of Little Horton," 1982, p. 100.
91. T. Nourse, *Campania Folix. Or, A Discourse of the Benefits and Improvements of Husbandry*, 1706, p. 256.
92. T. Barlow, *The Justice of Peace: A Treatise Containing the Power and Duty of That Magistrate*, 1745, p. iii.

in the sword-bearer's office in the city's Guildhall so that: "Persons having lost such Materials may come and claim the same."[93]

If a petitioner did not get a search or arrest warrant from one magistrate, there was in theory nothing to prevent his going to another in the same commission area. In 1725, this practice prompted the Suffolk JP Maurice Shelton to complain about those who told a magistrate "if he will not do them Justice, they will go and seek it elsewhere."[94] Some JPs went beyond issuing warrants and became involved in basic detective work (see *Chapter 3*).

Unlike the metropolitan magistracy, that of East Anglia remained more or less viable throughout the century without radical reform. As with many other aspects of the criminal justice system in the region, and like most of provincial England, gradual and incremental change accompanied by administrative flexibility meant that the system of 1700 was still clearly recognisable a century later.

93. *Norfolk Chronicle*, 14 December 1782.
94. M. Shelton, *A Charge Given to the Grand-Jury, At the General Quarter-Sessions of the Peace, Holden at St. Edmunds-Bury For the Liberty Thereof*, 1726, p. 34.

CHAPTER 3

Policing

Introduction

Throughout the eighteenth century, England was, to a significant degree, a self-policing society. The notion of using paid, state-appointed officers to fulfil this function was anathema. As the visiting Frenchman François de la Rochefoucauld noted in 1784, the English constitution did not allow "even a small number of troops [specifically tasked] to deal with malefactors, like the Marshal's cavalry (*Maréchaussée*) with us." Like many others, he thought this stemmed from a popular fear that such a force might be used by the Crown to suppress its subjects.[1] Parliamentary bills that attempted to create what might loosely be considered a government police force quickly provoked anger and opposition. Instead, all parishes had at least one man who served as its part-time constable, and whose function it was to actively assist in law enforcement.

Constables

Constables held one of the four major parish offices, the others being overseer of the poor, surveyor of the highways, and churchwarden. Some men who served as constables also held one or more of these positions during the course of their adult lives. They were untrained, unsalaried, temporarily appointed officers drawn from locally resident ratepayers who

1. N. Scarfe, *A Frenchman's Year in Suffolk*, 2011, p. 80.

were under 60 (in practice, usually much younger) and not physically infirm, for a year of part-time service to their community. Ideally they were impartial, honest, and able individuals, physically healthy enough to carry out their duties and solvent enough to afford the time to do so.[2] Numerous categories of men, such as apothecaries, lawyers, JPs, physicians, clergymen, and even Oxford University barbers were exempt from serving, while publicans were supposed to be excluded from the office, for obvious reasons.[3]

Traditionally, constables were not volunteers. They were appointed to their positions, sometimes from a rota, by local courts leet, a situation that, in theory, persisted until 1842. Leets were manorial courts that had originally exercised a minor criminal as well as administrative jurisdiction. By 1700 this aspect of their work was moribund. Nevertheless, some leets continued to appoint parish officers. For example, the Castle Rising leet in Norfolk still elected local officials, including the two constables of the village, during the eighteenth century. By then, however, parish vestries often played a much more important role in selecting candidates, and it had often become customary for this body to choose who was to serve as a constable.[4] Indeed, the vestry formally took over this function in the provinces between 1842 and the arrival of the new police just over a decade later.

If a leet failed to meet or to select constables when it did, or if a constable proved unsuitable or died while in office, a justice could fill the vacancy on his own initiative, usually aided by a recommendation or advice from the relevant parish vestry. All constables, however selected, would be sworn into office in front of their local JP.[5] In November 1701 Devereaux Edgar of Suffolk recorded in his diary: "Jonathan Kempster sworn constable of Cobdock for yere following or till discharged."[6] As late as August 1831 the Reverend John Longe, a magistrate and the chairman of Crowfield (Suffolk) vestry, noted that while going through that

2. G. Jacob, *Every Man His Own Lawyer: Or, A Summary of the Laws of England in a New and Instructive Method*, 1736, p. 408.
3. J. Shaw, *Parish Law: Or, a Guide to Justices of the Peace*, 1733, p. 312; J. Ritson, *The Office of Constable*, 1791, pp. 4–5.
4. J. Bird, *The Laws Respecting Parish Matters*, 2nd edn., 1799, p. 60.
5. Ibid.
6. SRO QS 347.96, *The Devereux Edgar Notebook*, transcribed by S. R. Schofield, 1956, vol. 1, p. 15.

village he "saw & discharged James Brooke from his office of constable of Crowfield for continued drunkenness & misconduct." Longe then swore in another local man in his stead.[7]

As Brooke's case suggests, whatever the theory as to the qualities present in a good constable, the reality was sometimes rather different. The office could be onerous, discouraging men of "quality" from serving. Sometimes it was dangerous. For example, in January 1703 William Glandville, the constable of Shotley, in Suffolk, was informed that several men drinking at the *King's Head* in the village were committing "disorders." He went to the tavern and told them that it was time to go home. A local man immediately struck him on the head, while another tore off his neckerchief and ripped it into pieces. Glandville was then dragged about the premises and told that if he had been outside they would have beaten him to "within an inch of his life."[8] At the Suffolk Quarter Sessions held at Woodbridge on 12 July 1758, James Broadly was accused of wandering about the parish of Easton armed with a pitchfork and "resisting the constable." At the same sessions, James May pleaded guilty to assaulting the constable of Sudbury in the execution of his duty. May was fined just one shilling (presumably, he had arranged a private settlement with the officer).[9] The following year, John Bowle appeared at the same forum, held at Bury, for assaulting the constable of Monks Eleigh.[10] Other officers were sued in the civil courts for actions they had carried out as part of their work.

As a result, the position was often unpopular, so that the social profile of constables tended to be lower than that of men appointed to the other three major parish offices. As early as the 1660s, the Norfolk JP Robert Doughty complained that the position had been depressed by being given to the "most inconsiderable and unfit persons that could be picked."[11] This was just as marked during the eighteenth century. An analysis of 15 householders who served as constables in Ardleigh, a large rural parish in

7. M. Stone (ed.), *The Diary of John Longe, Vicar of Coddenham, 1765–1834*, 2008, p. 130.
8. SRO QS 347.96, *The Devereux Edgar Notebook*, transcribed by S. R. Schofield, 1956, vol. 1, p. 48.
9. SRO QS B105/2/32, p. 137.
10. *Ipswich Journal*, 13 October 1759.
11. R. Paley (ed.), *Justice in Eighteenth-century Hackney: The Justicing Notebook of Henry Norris and the Hackney Petty Sessions Book*, 1991, p. 117.

northeast Essex (just south of the Suffolk border) between 1767 and 1814 produces a fairly modest profile. Farmers and yeomen accounted for 43 per cent of the 58 years that these men served. Tradesmen and artisans, such as blacksmiths and wheelwrights, performed slightly more than a quarter. Even lower down the social scale, husbandmen and labourers conducted almost a third of the duty. Some of the men who served as constables even qualified for subsidised food in 1796. Their average status was also significantly lower than that of the men who served as overseers and churchwardens in the village.[12]

Those appointed could simply refuse to serve and pay a substantial fine in lieu. This was costly, and some men could not afford it. However, by the early eighteenth century many metropolitan constables were "substitutes," paid, by those originally selected to serve in their place, a sum lower than the fine. Substitution was much less common in the provinces, but it probably occurred in some urban areas, with their higher workloads. Other men who had been selected to serve accepted the office but made occasional use of paid deputies to assist them.[13] For example, the accounts of James Parkin, a constable in Barwick-in-Elmet (Yorkshire) between 1753 and 1754, mention a deputy constable who was paid 6s 8d for the year.[14]

More pertinently, by the eighteenth century, inducements were being offered by many provincial parishes to local men to serve (or continue serving) when they were not legally obliged to do so, saving others from the duty. Constables had always been paid a few shillings for each day they spent actively engaged in special duties, such as escorting prisoners and vagrants. They could also reclaim expenses they had incurred in office. Such payments appear to have become more common, and perhaps a little more generous, as the century advanced. In 1764 Richard Burn urged that they be extended, so that constables were reimbursed for almost all their work.[15]

Much more important, some vestries started to make small payments, often the equivalent of one or two months' income for a labourer, as a

12. P. King, *Crime, Justice, and Discretion in England 1740–1820*, 2003, pp. 66–69.
13. J. Ritson, *The Office of Constable*, 1791, pp. 4–5.
14. Anon, "The Parish Constable in Georgian Times," 2000, p. 50.
15. R. Burn, *The History of the Poor Laws: with Observations*, 1764, p. 249.

retainer to their constables, so that they stayed on beyond a year. For example, the Ardleigh vestry felt it necessary to pay some of its officers £2 a year.[16] As a result, by the end of the century there was a fairly widespread, but far from universal, tendency for men to be reappointed several times, or for several consecutive years, with their full agreement. This spared others from serving and ensured that the officer possessed a degree of experience.

Unsurprisingly, these developments often coincided with a further decline in the social status of those appointed to the position: well-to-do men would not serve for money. Although it would be wrong to call such regularly serving paid constables professional police officers, they were making something of a job, if not a career, of their service. This process seems to have started in towns such as Ipswich, where the demands of the office were greater. Even early in the eighteenth century, between a quarter and half of its petty constables served continuously for five years, while more than half served at least two consecutive terms throughout the era.[17] After the mid-century, this pattern slowly spread to some small towns and villages.

The Constables' Work

Constables had a huge range of duties and responsibilities, among them enforcing arrest and search warrants; apprehending offenders and taking them before area magistrates; imposing local punishments, such as putting minor offenders in the village stocks and keeping that apparatus in repair; billeting soldiers on taverns and alehouses; informing the coroner of suspicious deaths; assembling a coroner's jury and dealing with the corpse prior to an inquest; organising nightly watches in urban parishes; supervising vagrants and others in distress who were passing through their own parish; fighting local fires; raising the "hue and cry"; making recruitment arrangements for the militia, and collecting some local taxes.[18]

16. P. King, *Crime, Justice, and Discretion in England 1740–1820*, 2003, pp. 66–69.
17. J. D. Clemis, *Government in an English Provincial Town: The Corporation of Ipswich, 1720–95*, 1999, p. 143.
18. J. Bird, The Laws Respecting Parish Matters, edn 2, 1799, p. 74; Anon, "The Parish Constable in Georgian Times," 2000, p. 50.

Constables were primarily reactive when it came to dealing with crime. They did not normally carry out any form of deterrent patrolling, unlike the post-1829 police. However, they might act on their own initiative if they became aware of minor instances of local disorder or offending. For example, in June 1718, several youths amused themselves by throwing hay about in a riverside meadow in Norwich. When they saw a constable coming to "disperse" them, 17-year-old James Gardiner ran into the river to escape and drowned.[19] Much more commonly, constables would respond to requests for assistance or summons from members of the public, justices of the peace, high constables or, less commonly, their local sheriff or coroner. Men who ignored such requests and orders could be punished, although this was a regular problem during the era.

Occasionally constables from different parishes might work together to deal with larger-scale problems, under the control and legal authority of area high constables, especially, but not solely, in urban parts. Without his authorisation they had no powers outside their own parishes. For example, one night in 1784 the constables of Ipswich carried out a general search for "disorderly" women, who, apparently, had been parading the streets in unprecedented numbers: "[S]everal of these unhappy wretches were taken up in order to be passed to their respective parish."[20]

Where necessary, a constable could demand that other members of the public assist him in securing suspects. (In theory, anyone present when a felony was committed was legally obliged to apprehend the offender).[21] Very occasionally people were punished for breaching this duty. In 1772 David West was committed to gaol for refusing to assist the constable of St Mathews, Ipswich, in the execution of his office.[22] In November 1789 a bizarre incident occurred at Sudbury in this respect. A local whitesmith (a man who worked in "white" metals such as tin) was engaged in electioneering in the Suffolk town and got involved in a disturbance, during which he hit a woman. The mayor, who was (as normal) a de facto justice for Sudbury, issued an arrest warrant, "but the man being a bruiser the constable was afraid to execute it." The mayor

19. NRO NCR Case 6a/4/83.
20. *Ipswich Journal*, 18 September 1784.
21. Anon (An Attorney at Law), *The Law of Arrests in Both Civil and Criminal Cases*, 1742, p. 200.
22. *Ipswich Journal*, 31 October 1772.

told him he might charge some assistants to help him make the arrest. On hearing this, the constable selected the mayor himself, to considerable popular amusement, although he duly complied with the request and helped his officer detain the whitesmith.[23]

Constables also played an important part in the forensic process. One of their duties was to secure any property taken from or in connection with a suspect (this was also sometimes done by an examining JP). This included potential exhibits to be produced at trial, such as weapons and bloodied clothes. If constables were careless about letting these items out of their custody, before the hearing, they might find it legally difficult to swear to them as the originals at trial.[24]

Parish constables were often in an inherently awkward position. Knowing that they would return to ordinary life at the end of their term of office, they would frequently be reluctant to do anything that would cause controversy or risk making local enemies. In 1757 George Hyland, a labourer from Laughton, in Sussex, impregnated a young woman from a nearby village. Thomas Turner, her local overseer of the poor, obtained a magistrate's warrant for his arrest so that he could be produced before a JP on the issue of support. When he tried to enforce this with the assistance of the Laughton constable, that officer "refused to do [so] without more assistance, though there was two of us and the man we was a-going to take was a man with the use of one arm only." A complicated mixture of fear and local loyalty appears to have motivated his passivity.[25] For the same reason, constables were also advised to try to avoid serving arrest warrants on those with whom they had any personal dispute or "animosity" if it could be left to another officer (often difficult in rural areas).[26]

Conversely, constables might be pressured to act against unpopular local men, even when it was not warranted or wise. This may have occurred prior to the killing of the constable of Pattishall in Northamptonshire, who died while unnecessarily attempting to enforce an arrest

23. *Bury and Norwich Post*, 18 November 1789.
24. C. Halifax, *The Constable's Sure Guide: Or, Every Constable His Own Lawyer,* 1791, p. 21.
25. D. Vaisey (ed.), *The Diary of Thomas Turner, 1754–1765*, 1994, p. 87.
26. C. Halifax, *The Constable's Sure Guide: Or, Every Constable His Own Lawyer* 1791, p. 21.

warrant against a resented newcomer to the village, with a crowd of local people egging him on.[27]

Inevitably, abusive policing by such untrained officers was also a risk, although social pressure from neighbours probably restricted its extent. Even modestly prosperous men could succumb to the temptations of office. In 1753 John Mace, a farrier and blacksmith of "considerable business" as well as the constable of Hingham, in Norfolk, stole £44 from a house in his village while its owner was at church. When the crime was discovered, he went through the pretence of looking for suspects and even arrested three local men. One of them was produced before a JP and examined at length before having his case dismissed without further action. Mace eventually confessed to the crime and was sentenced to transportation, but escaped from prison before being sent to America, returning to the area some years later.[28]

As with other officeholders in the criminal justice system, some eighteenth-century constables were good, some bad, and most were in between, doing what they had to, but little more, within the numerous constraints (practical and legal) of their positions. As elsewhere in the system, eliminating bad men from the position was an intractable problem.

Watchmen

Major provincial towns and cities such as Norwich, Bury, and Ipswich had a force of parish-based night watchmen to patrol their streets, although these were usually a fairly pale imitation of their London counterparts when it came to numbers and organisation. Even so, they met with some success. For example, Henry Bexant and two other men, suspected of burglary at Ipswich in 1736, were "taken up by the Watch" and sent to gaol pending further investigation.[29] However, as in the Metropolis, there were perennial problems with the discipline and effectiveness of watchmen. In 1782 a Norwich coroner's inquest sat upon the body of Sarah Titter, who had been found dead in the street early the same morning.

---

27. D. Gray and P. King, "The Killing of Constable Linnell: The Impact of Xenophobia and of Elite Connections on Eighteenth-century Justice," 2013, p. 9.
28. *London Evening Post*, 21–14 July 1753.
29. *Daily Gazetteer* (London Edition), 15 June 1736.

It appeared that just before midnight she had been seen in the haymarket "very much intoxicated" by the watch for St Peter's parish. She asked them to lead her home. One of the watchmen took her in charge, but merely delivered her into the care of the neighbouring St Stephen's watch, who "at that time were drinking at the Nag's Head." Though requested to take care of Titter, they "very inhumanly" left her in the street, where she fell down and later expired.[30]

In smaller towns watch arrangements were often more ad hoc, being bolstered during apparent crime waves. In 1805, for instance, it was noted that "[i]n consequence of the many robberies committed in Woodbridge [Suffolk] and its neighbourhood, a patrole has been appointed from 6 o'clock in the evening to the same hour in the morning."[31] In practice many towns did not even manage this. In 1813, when John Hannah strangled his wife at Yarmouth during a prolonged domestic quarrel, the couple's female lodger went to the town watchhouse to secure assistance, but found that the watch had already gone off duty, although it was only just past 3 am. The lodger then returned to the room she rented in Hannah's house and went to bed. At 6 am a local constable attended, presumably having been alerted by neighbours, and arrested John, some three hours after the incident started, by which time his wife was dead.[32]

The Military

The army gave considerable aid to the civil power in dealing with crime, especially in East Anglia, where troops were often readily available. Sometimes their use in anti-smuggling operations and riot control was vital (see *Chapters 23* and *25*). There was limited use of troops in other areas of the criminal justice system, such as escorting prisoners or securing gallows. Some wished to see this go further. In 1738, during a parliamentary debate on the army, one observer claimed that the popular degeneracy of manners meant that only the military could "check the madness of a deluded rabble."[33]

30. *Norfolk Chronicle*, 12 January 1782.
31. *Ipswich Journal*, 2 March 1805.
32. *The Morning Post*, 13 September 1813.
33. *Gentleman's Magazine*, vol. 8, September 1738, p. 453.

Nevertheless, there was a widespread reluctance to use servicemen for policing when it was not absolutely necessary—unsurprisingly, since there was strong opposition to the very existence of a large standing army in peacetime, when it fell to as few as 17,000 soldiers based in Britain. Typically, during a parliamentary debate in 1752, William Thornton claimed that all armies maintained outside wartime were eventually "used against the liberties of the people, and at last enslaved them."[34] The acute concern occasioned in 1780 when the army became involved in pressing merchant sailors in Cromer is illustrative of such widely held attitudes. A naval press gang entered the small north Norfolk port shortly before dawn, supported by 20 dragoons who were posted around the town to prevent men fleeing while the press gang searched for suitable seamen. This greatly alarmed observers, who felt that it was illegal, unconstitutional, and "disgraceful to the liberty of Englishmen, and so great a stretch of arbitrary military usurpation, that it calls for immediate redress."[35]

The desire to have soldiers present when pressing sailors was understandable. Many merchant seamen would go to great lengths to avoid service in the harsh and dangerous conditions of a warship, and press gangs were correspondingly "robust." At the Suffolk Quarter Sessions held at Woodbridge in July 1762, John Ganagan, a midshipman, was committed to gaol to await trial at the following assizes accused of assaulting an ordinary labourer (not a mariner), threatening him with a pistol, and then impressing him.[36] At Beccles Quarter Sessions the same year, John Wayman, a lieutenant in the Royal Navy who was in command of a press gang, was indicted for assaulting and putting in irons Thomas Hawke from the same town, although he was a "person of property."[37]

As a result of such incidents, those in authority were usually cautious about authorising the military to support normal policing. It was widely recognised to be a blunt instrument. Many senior officers were reluctant to get involved in civil matters unnecessarily and without explicit orders. Practical objections to the use of troops in policing operations

34. J. Willis, "Transportation Versus Imprisonment in Eighteenth and Nineteenth-century Britain," 2005, p. 196.
35. *Norfolk Chronicle*, 12 August 1780.
36. *Ipswich Journal*, 17 July 1762.
37. Ibid., 17 July 1762.

also encouraged such attitudes. Until late in the century they would usually be forcibly billeted on reluctant (though remunerated) tavern and alehouse owners rather than housed in barracks. As the judge Thomas Rokeby noted in 1697, this process frequently occasioned "very great complaints" and allegations that the financial compensation offered was inadequate.[38] A military presence also posed considerable problems for local populations.

Crime and the Military

Off-duty soldiers attracted violent disturbances in East Anglia, as they did almost everywhere else in Europe. For example, in November 1757 three soldiers were "severely" whipped at the Castle Ditches in Norwich. One was punished for desertion, the other two for violent interaction with local civilians. One man had drawn his sword in a tavern and almost cut the hand off a master bricklayer who was drinking there. This soldier was whipped again the following week as part of his punishment. (Until the nineteenth century there was no formal limit on the number of lashes that could be imposed on a soldier by court martial).[39] The other man had threatened to shoot the landlady of the public house where he was billeted, and had even loaded his weapon for that purpose.[40] As these cases suggest, courts martial rather than domestic forums were often used to deal with soldiers who committed crimes against civilians.

There could be larger and fiercer disturbances and confrontations between soldiers and local people. In December 1795 a "most desperate" affray took place outside a tavern in Long Melford between men from the Dragoon Guards armed with swords and villagers carrying scythes. Many people, both soldiers and civilians, were injured (one soldier's hand was cut off), and two dragoons were committed to prison by the local magistrate, the Reverend John Lerco.[41] The following month, at the county

38. T. Rokeby, *The Diary of Mr Justice Rokeby,* 1887, p. 55.
39. J. R. Dinwiddy, "The Early Nineteenth-century Campaign Against Flogging in the Army," 1982, p. 311.
40. *Lloyd's Evening Post and British Chronicle*, 21–23 November 1757.
41. *The Times*, 2 January 1796, p. 4.

quarter sessions held at Bury, Sergeant David Doke and Private James McLauchlin were convicted of assaulting two men during the conflict.[42]

There could also be problems between rival groups of soldiers. In the early summer of 1796 the champion boxers of the Northumbrian and Warwickshire militia regiments, both of which were billeted in Norwich, challenged and fought each other. When the Warwickshire man was bested, his enraged comrades broke into the circle, and a pitched battle ensued between the two regiments, despite the efforts of their officers to restrain them. Bayonets were used, and 200 men were sent to the city hospital for treatment.[43]

Serving soldiers also committed conventional property crimes, usually (though by no means invariably) after stripping off their "regimentals" and putting on civilian clothes. At the Bury Assizes in April 1801, the presiding judge, when passing sentence on a long list of offenders, observed that among them he was sorry to see "so many soldiers, who had dared to lift their hands against the lives and properties of those whom they were paid to protect." He felt that there could be no excuse for such behaviour, as their pay had been greatly increased within the previous two years.[44] In 1741 Jonathan Mattox, a 22-year-old dragoon who originally came from Bury, together with Benjamin Smith, a gardener from Yarmouth, were executed on Castle Hill, in Norwich, for breaking open a house at Cantley, in the Norfolk Broads.[45] In the same year, Lawrence Spencer, a soldier in Colonel Druro's regiment, attacked William Ingold, a miller from Long Melford, in Suffolk, while he was on the road to Colchester. Spencer demanded his money and severely wounded him with a sword. Fortunately, other travellers came to Ingold's assistance.[46] Similarly, one night in 1783 two soldiers stopped a rider on his way from Bury to Stowmarket. When they found he had only eight pence on his person, they beat him in a "most cruel manner" and almost strangled him.[47]

42. *Norfolk Chronicle*, 20 January 1796.
43. *Oracle and Public Advertiser*, 9 June 1796.
44. *The Bury and Norwich Post: Or, Suffolk, Norfolk, Essex, and Cambridge Advertiser*, 1 April 1801.
45. *Daily Gazetteer* (London Edition), 15 April 1741.
46. *London Daily Post and General Advertiser*, 24 November 1741.
47. *Norfolk Chronicle*, 25 January 1783.

Even more problematic, there were many deserters from the military at large in East Anglia, as in other well-garrisoned English regions. These men were often far from their native counties or countries (in the case of Irishmen and Scotsmen), would frequently have recourse to crime to survive, were familiar with weapons, and being particularly fearful of the consequences of capture often quite desperate when confronted. In July 1760, when a robbery was committed by two footpads on the highway between Hintlesham and Hadleigh, in Suffolk, it was thought that one of the pair was Thomas King, a deserter from a locally based regiment of foot.[48] In 1787, when three very young men were executed at Rushmere after the Suffolk Assizes, it was noted that they had all been soldiers and that each of them had deserted several times.[49]

Even ordinary (i.e. non-criminal) recruits would often have recourse to crime when they deserted. On 9 May 1759, John Ludkin, a 23-year-old carpenter from near Holt in Norfolk, enlisted with a recruiting party from the 56th Regiment of Foot while in Norwich. He did not, however, make the journey to Musselburgh, in Scotland, to join his unit, deserting on 1 July that year. His regiment placed a large advertisement in a national newspaper offering a reward for his return.[50] By the time it came out, it seems that Ludkin was already in custody, as he appeared at the Norwich Assizes accused of theft and burglary in the same month. He was convicted of the former and sentenced to seven years' transportation.[51]

This problem was exacerbated because generous enlistment bounties encouraged a number of recruits to desert during wartime specifically in order to re-enlist elsewhere. In 1785, at a court martial held at Ipswich, George Smith, a private in the dragoons, was reported to have deserted 17 times from other regiments. Despite this, his sentence was ultimately commuted to service in the West Indies (a place with a high mortality rate for soldiers) for life.[52] Similarly, in 1801 John Day admitted at the gallows in Thetford that he had deserted 13 times from different regiments,

48. *Ipswich Journal*, 9 August 1760.
49. *World and Fashionable Advertiser*, 21 August 1787.
50. *Whitehall Evening Post Or London Intelligencer*, 28–31 July 1759.
51. TNA ASSI 33/3.
52. *Ipswich Journal*, 5 February 1785; *Ipswich Journal*, 12 February 1785.

having received the King's recruitment bounty from each one of them when he enlisted.[53]

Unsurprisingly, in these circumstances, political leaders who petitioned for a military presence in their areas during a crisis often quickly asked that the soldiers leave when it had been resolved.

53. *The Bury and Norwich Post: Or, Suffolk, Norfolk, Essex, and Cambridge Advertiser*, 8 April 1801.

CHAPTER 4

Crimes, Courts and Judicial Personnel

Crimes

There were three general degrees of crime: treason, felony, and misdemeanour. High treason included serious political crimes (outside the remit of this book) as well as, for arcane historical reasons, coining, that is the forging of the national currency. This was a statistically important form of serious crime in the Metropolis and in some parts of the North of England, such as Halifax. However, it was rather less significant in East Anglia, although cases occurred periodically. In 1719 a man was committed to gaol in Norwich after being found with counterfeit coins with Queen Anne's head on them.[1] The following year a man named Calthrope was sent to the same gaol for the same crime; on this occasion seven shillings "made in imitation of Queen's Ann's" were found on his person.[2] Not all currency offences constituted treason or were even felonies, and lesser forms of the crime were more common in the region. In March 1736, at the Suffolk Assizes in Bury, Henry Plumb was convicted of unlawfully getting some pieces of bare metal in the shape of silver sixpences and shillings with intent to cheat. He was merely sentenced to prison for three months and required to find sureties for his

1. *Weekly Journal Or Saturday's Post*, 20 June 1719.
2. *Applebee's Original Weekly Journal*, 13 August 1720.

good behaviour for 12 months.[3] In any event, no one was executed for coining in either East Anglian county between 1735 and 1799.[4]

All conventional criminal offences other than coining can be divided into felonies and misdemeanours. Despite its name, petty treason (the murder of a husband or master) was, for most purposes, treated as a felony.[5] Felonies could be tried only on indictment, in front of a jury, and encompassed the most serious crimes. Historically, and with one exception (petty theft), they all carried the theoretical possibility of a death sentence, even if it was almost always avoided for certain types of crime. Usually this was because the offence was "one which for the first offence is allowed clergy."[6] This crucial distinction requires examination.

Benefit of Clergy

Benefit of clergy had started life as a facet of the church-state struggles of the medieval period. Originally the privilege allowed offending clerics to escape temporal punishment after conviction in a secular forum. Literacy eventually became the sole test for clerical status, so that numerous laymen were able to claim the indulgence once the ability to read spread beyond the clergy. By the 1690s even this requirement was being abandoned in practice, and it was formally abolished in 1706 (6 Anne, c.9 s. 4). Women were allowed to claim an identical privilege to benefit of clergy, without any requirement of being able to read, by dint of two seventeenth-century statutes.

In theory laymen were limited to claiming clergy on only one occasion, and were branded to prevent subsequent claims. This was usually done on the brawn of the thumb, except for a few years at the start of the period (when it was on the face). They would then be released back into the community. However, the branding process was often being

3. TNA ASSI 33/1.
4. www.capitalpunishmentuk.org (last consulted 10 August 2015). The present author has confirmed nearly all of the executions listed for eighteenth-century East Anglia in this invaluable source using contemporary newspaper reports, and not firmly located any hangings that are missing from it.
5. S. Blackerby, *Cases in Law: Wherein Justices of Peace Have a Jurisdiction, As Well By Their Commission, As By Act of Parliament*, 1717, p. 85.
6. G. Jacob, *Everyman His Own Lawyer*, 4th edn., 1750, p. 434.

neglected by the early 1700s, and frequently did not leave a permanent mark. Indicative of this, in 1711 Elizabeth Freke belatedly discovered that one of her servants at West Bilney, in Norfolk, had been burnt in the hand for a clergyable felony committed before he was taken on.[7] Clearly the scar had not been apparent. This was not always the case. After the Norwich Assizes in 1753 a bigamist was "burnt in the hand severely."[8] It was not a superficial process on this occasion, and was perhaps done to warn future potential spouses. Nevertheless, this was unusual. As a result many felons successfully claimed clergy on more than one occasion during the 1700s. At the start of the period a City of London grand jury claimed that in the capital some offenders were being branded up to half-a-dozen times.[9]

Taken together, these developments meant that clergyable felonies were (effectively) no longer capital by the eighteenth century. As William Blackstone noted, the privilege had been converted by gradual mutations into a "merciful mitigation of the general law, with respect to capital punishment."[10] Although technically a felony, because petty larceny, the theft of goods worth less than twelve pence was (uniquely) not a capital offence, clergy was irrelevant. The sentence was usually a whipping. Ironically, this meant that punishment for the lesser form of theft could be more severe than that imposed for the greater, as, even at its worst, branding was not viewed as a severe penalty by the start of the century. As Timothy Nourse observed, "[F]rizzing them a little in the fist, is a punishment of no great pain, and of a short continuance."[11]

By the final years of the seventeenth century, attempts were being made to increase the punishment of clergyable offences. For seven years after 1699, this was done by moving the place of branding from the brawn of the thumb to the left cheek, near the nose. Many quarter sessions invested in new "engines" specifically to "burn" criminals in the

7. R. Anselment (ed.), *The Remembrances of Elizabeth Freke 1671–1714,* 2002, pp. 270–272.
8. *Public Advertiser*, 28 August 1753.
9. M. V. Muyden (ed.), *A Foreign View of England in the Reigns of George I and George II,* 1902, p. 125; T. Hitchcock and R. Shoemaker, *London Lives*, 2015, p. 64.
10. W. Blackstone, *Commentaries on the Laws of England,* vol. 4, 1769, p. 364.
11. T. Nourse, *Campania Folix. Or, a Discourse of the Benefits and Improvements of Husbandry,* 1706, p. 229.

appropriate place.[12] However, in 1706, this was abandoned because the public stigma that such brandings occasioned when carried out properly made it hard for clergied convicts to earn a living in "any lawful and honest way." As a result they were encouraged to return to crime. This danger often led to the authorities' not implementing it properly. Branding was restored to the hand.

Much more important, the 1706 act also included a provision allowing a custodial sentence of between six months and two years of hard labour in a house of correction or public workhouse for clergied offenders, at the trial judge's or magistrates' discretion (depending on jury forum), in *addition* to the customary branding. Eventually, in 1718, the advent of a power to impose seven years' transportation for clergied offenders who were guilty of property crimes, *instead* of branding, transformed the situation. (There had been unsuccessful parliamentary attempts in the same direction in 1663 and 1702).[13]

After it became possible to transport clergied offenders, branding followed by either immediate discharge or a short spell in a house of correction under the 1706 Act was still used periodically for cases of grand larceny. For example, the sentence passed on thieves can be identified in 20 cases at assizes sessions held for the region from the second half of 1734 to the end of 1736. Seventeen were sentenced to transportation, but at least three others were simply branded and discharged.[14] Amongst them was Elizabeth Dey, who was "burnt in the hand" and released at the City of Norwich Assizes after being convicted of stealing cambric (a dense, plain-weave cloth) from another woman.[15] This practice did not disappear until late in the century. In 1760 William Sturgeon was convicted at the Bury Assizes of stealing six pewter plates but merely burned in the hand and released.[16] At the same forum in 1767, Charles Rose and John Smith also received this disposal.[17] The incidence of branding and

12. J. Innes, "Parliament and the Shaping of Eighteenth-century English Social Policy," 1990, p. 71.
13. J. M. Beattie, *Crime and the Courts in England 1660–1800*, 1986, p. 471.
14. TNA ASSI 33/1.
15. *London Daily Post and General Advertiser*, 31 August 1736; *Universal Spectator and Weekly Journal*, 4 September 1736.
16. *Public Ledger Or The Daily Register of Commerce and Intelligence*, 5 August 1760.
17. *Ipswich Journal*, 8 August 1767.

discharge even increased slightly during the 1770s, when transportation to America became impossible.

Generally speaking, and unsurprisingly, those who were clergied and released after 1718 had been found guilty of lesser forms of grand larceny. Alluding to this, while on the Home Circuit in 1755, Sir Dudley Ryder noted that one Joseph Glover, who had been convicted of grand larceny after stealing seven deal boards was, "[b]urnt in hand and discharged."[18] The value of the stolen wood must have been quite modest. However, this was not always the case, especially where there was special mitigation. In 1746, when Thomas Stockdale was found guilty at the Bury Assizes of stealing goods worth more than 30 shillings, he was merely "[b]randed left hand."[19] In 1774, when a labourer named Thomas Cole was accused of burgling the house of Robert Cole and stealing a purse containing more than £50, he was not just convicted of the lesser offence of grand larceny, but also branded and discharged.[20] Presumably there was a family property dispute behind this crime, explaining the common surname for victim and complainant and justifying great leniency. More surprisingly, William Goodens received the same disposal after he was convicted at the Lent Assizes at Thetford, in Norfolk, in 1775, for stealing a silver watch from a farmer (possibly an early recognition of the impossibility of transporting prisoners to Revolutionary America).[21] It seems that such a sentence was also sometimes passed when the trial judge harboured doubts about the safety of a jury decision to convict for theft.

Branding for clergied cases of theft was finally brought to an end by section 3 of the Penitentiary Act of 1779 (19 Geo III, c 74). By then it was being applied in a most haphazard manner.[22] After this date clergied thieves could be whipped (usually just once and never more than thrice) or given a "moderate fine," which in practice was anything from 1s to more than £100, instead of being branded. For example, at the Norwich Assizes in August 1784 George Jurdan, a labourer, was convicted

18. Lincoln's Inn, Harrowby MSS 18–19, Document 19(f) *Legal Notebook of Sir Dudley Ryder*, 1754 and 1755, p. 18.
19. Gray's Inn MS 45.
20. TNA ASSI 33/5.
21. *Morning Chronicle and London Advertiser*, 30 June 1778.
22. Ibid., 11 May 1779.

and clergied for stealing gold rings and other items made of precious metal. He was whipped in Wymondham market on two occasions (in lieu of branding), and sentenced to six months' hard labour in a house of correction (under the 1706 act).[23] No such combined punishments are recorded in 1797, and their use appears to have petered out by then, given the new penal options available. Even so, the vestiges of benefit of clergy were not abolished until 1827.

The "Bloody Code"

The number of early-sixteenth-century felonies had been quite limited, largely being confined to long-standing common-law offences such as murder, arson, rape, sodomy, robbery, larceny, and burglary. Furthermore, many of these crimes were still clergyable in 1500.[24] During the early modern period, benefit of clergy was withdrawn by statute from many existing felonies. This meant that they became capital offences, even for those who could read. However, their number remained fairly limited.

This changed during the late-seventeenth and eighteenth centuries, as Parliament created numerous additional capital felonies by withdrawing clergy from existing offences or by establishing a new clergyless crime. Together, these constituted the so-called Bloody Code. Among the most important statutes in this regard was the Black Act of 1723 (9 Geo I, c 22). This was enacted as a response to the activities of a group of poachers in Windsor Forest (known as blacks because they darkened their faces at night). Depending on definition, the statute made between 21 and 50 offences capital, the lower figure probably being more realistic.

The Bloody Code was not a true legal code in any proper sense. The phrase was not used regularly until the 1820s, near the end of its supposed existence. Even employing it risks giving what was usually a fairly ad hoc and little-thought-out process far more unity and coherence than it properly deserves. The code emerged over many years and there was almost no detailed rationale for its creation — unsurprisingly, as it was almost

23. TNA ASSI 33/6–7; *Whitehall Evening Post (1770)*, May 15, 1784–May 18, 1784.
24. B. A. Hanawalt, "Fur-Collar Crime: The Pattern of Crime Amongst the Fourteenth-century English Nobility," 1975, p. 2.

entirely unplanned. Insofar as there was any thought behind the process, it was premised on a vague belief that the possibility (however remote) of draconian punishment might frighten some prospective offenders into remaining within the law, so that it was "not chiefly intended to punish the present criminal, but to hinder others from being so."[25] In practice, the extra power granted to the judiciary and Crown by Bloody Code statutes also allowed condign punishment to be imposed on those who had been convicted of relatively minor crimes but were thought to be of very bad character. As was noted in 1783, "[A]dvantage may sometimes be taken of a small crime to hang a great villain, who could not otherwise have been capitally convicted."[26] In this way, it increased judicial discretion.

Passing such legislation was, of course, also a quick way of being seen to do something about specific crime problems without being politically intrusive. It did not contribute to the power and patronage of the Crown and central government, which was a perennial post-1688 concern. Its apparent low cost suited another contemporary preoccupation. The expense of financing regular wars meant that England was one of the most heavily taxed European states for much of the eighteenth century, and there was little desire to add to the burden.

However, the Bloody Code was also a result of the greatly increased activism of Parliament. After 1688 this body was convened annually, and kept in being for four or more months in every year.[27] It had an unprecedented sense of its own importance and centrality to English society, and the will to put its legislative power to much more broadly conceived purposes than had previously been the case, without, perhaps, always appreciating the practical limits of such legislation.[28] Frequent meetings of Parliament provided interested parties and pressure groups with a novel opportunity to influence the law. As a result, in the period between 1689 and 1801, 13,600 statutes were enacted (fewer than 3,000 had been passed between 1485 and 1688). The final four decades of the

25. Anon, *Hanging, Not Punishment Enough*, 1701, p. 5.
26. J. Scott, *Observations On the Present State of the Parochial and Vagrant Poor*, 1773, p. 133.
27. J. Innes, *Inferior Politics: Social Problems and Social Policies in Eighteenth-century Britain*, 2009, p. 3 and p. 217.
28. S. Devereaux, "The Criminal Branch of the Home Office 1782–1830," 1998, p. 270.

eighteenth century saw a particularly high level of legislation.[29] In the middle of the era, Thomas Woodford blamed the huge growth in JPs' theoretical legal duties on the same process: Parliament sat every year and passed its time churning out statutes.[30]

Backbenchers, rather than the government, initiated many of the statutes establishing Bloody Code offences.[31] In 1772 Henry Dagge noted that the code's various pieces of enabling legislation were frequently drafted after a *cause célèbre* had incensed parliamentary feelings, so that laws were passed "*flagrante ira*, on some sudden occasion, when a combination of atrocious circumstances, attending some particular offence, inflamed the legislature."[32] The acts creating capital offences often went through Parliament swiftly, going before small committees and being voted on by thinly attended chambers. Frequently there was little debate as to the likely consequences of systematic and strict enforcement. In 1769 even William Blackstone complained about the lack of "care and attention" that went into passing them. Their introduction was often left to the "passions or interests of a few, who upon temporary motives may prefer or support such a bill." He believed that, had there been proper scrutiny by Parliament following legal advice, it would have been inconceivable that many of the more arcane Bloody Code offences would have become law.[33] He was not alone. In 1819 Sir James MacIntosh thought that the celerity with which men in the eighteenth century had been willing to gratify every petitioner to Parliament by enacting capital felonies was astonishing "[N]o man retired in disappointment, who only craved the indulgence of a 'felony without benefit of clergy.'" Such statutes were passed into law almost on a whim, being the fruit of a series of "perverse and malignant accidents, impelling the adoption of temporary and short-sighted expedients."[34]

---

29. S. Devereaux, "The Promulgation of the Statutes in Late Hanoverian Britain," 2005, p. 83.
30. T. Woodford, *A Discourse Concerning Some of the Most Important Branches and Parts, of the Office of the Justices of the Peace*, 1749, p. ii.
31. J. Innes, *Inferior Politics: Social Problems and Social Policies in Eighteenth-century Britain*, 2009, p. 3.
32. H. Dagge, *Considerations on Criminal Law*, 1772, pp. 224–225.
33. W. Blackstone, *Commentaries on the Laws of England*, vol. 4, 1769, p. 4.
34. House of Commons Debate 2 March 1819, *Hansard*, vol. 39, cols. 777–845.

Of course, this lack of care, though real, can be exaggerated. A considerable number of "criminal" bills were not passed after adverse scrutiny in Parliament. Government lawyers also sponsored a few of the more important statutes, such as the Forgery Act of 1727, while, towards the end of the century, it seems that the judiciary were often consulted about such legislation.[35] Nevertheless, these were exceptions to the general situation.

Because many of the new, unclergyable, offences were highly recondite, their precise number was a matter of some debate. It had grown quickly from about 50 at the time of the Glorious Revolution of 1688 (itself an increase from fewer than a dozen at the end of the medieval period). More than 30 were added during the reign of George II, and more than 60 in that of George III. By the 1760s Blackstone thought that there were at least 160 capital felonies. A Suffolk justice who examined the issue agreed. He thought that there were 249 felonies in 1779, of which only 89 were still within clergy. However, he also recognised that, during the six years following that date, there had been a "melancholy and almost continual addition" to the list.[36] By the end of the century, a figure of about 200 non-clergyable crimes was often cited, though some placed it even higher. In 1819 Sir James MacIntosh complained that there were people living who had been born into a country with fewer than 60 capital offences who had seen that number quadruple to about 233.[37] Crimes against property, the person, and the state were all found on the list, although expansion in the first category was the most important.[38]

A series of statutes then reduced capital offences to a tiny handful of very serious crimes, such as murder and piracy, by the middle of the nineteenth century. A century after the advent of the Black Act of 1723, it appeared the relic of a barbarous time and an almost ridiculous statute, one that had created capital felonies of the "most absurd description."[39] Its surviving provisions were finally repealed in 1823.

35. J. Innes, "Parliament and the Shaping of Eighteenth-century English Social Policy," 1990, p. 69 and p. 86.
36. J. Jebb, *Thoughts on the Construction and Polity of Prisons: With Hints for Their Improvement*, 1785, p. viii.
37. House of Commons Debate 2 March 1819, *Hansard*, vol. 39, cols. 777–845.
38. J. McCafferty, *Capital Punishment*, 2009, p. 8.
39. House of Commons Debate 2 March 1819, *Hansard*, vol. 39, cols. 777–845.

Many of the Bloody Code offences were rarely, if ever, prosecuted. Of those that were, few produced convictions, and few resulted in hangings. Although there may have been 200 capital felonies on the statute book, the returns from London and Middlesex indicated that only 25 of them had led to any executions between 1749 and 1819. At least 175 had never been used.[40] In East Anglia the situation was even more extreme. Between 1735 and 1799, people were executed for just 21 crimes, generously construed (treating infanticide as a different offence from murder, for instance). The vast majority of those hanged in the area died for one of four offences: murder, burglary, housebreaking, and horse theft. All of these offences had been unclergyable before 1700, some for centuries.

Several of the remaining 17 crimes that did produce executions led to only one or, at most, two hangings. Among them was the sole execution for capital assault under Lord Coventry's Act of 1670 (22 & 23 Car. II). More pertinent to the Bloody Code was the single hanging for stealing from a bleaching ground under an Act of 1745 (18 Geo II, c 27). This made it a capital felony to steal linen or cotton cloth worth more than 10s that had been laid out in the sun to be whitened. Spreading linen on a sheltered piece of ground was thought to be the best way of counteracting the yellowing caused by, *inter alia*, storage, urine, and the era's soap. It was hoped that the statute (which replaced a similar act) would reduce the need to keep such fabric under constant observation. Robert Mullinger was capitally convicted of the crime at the Thetford Assizes in 1791 and executed.[41] This was the only hanging for the crime in the region between 1735 and 1800, and on the entire circuit between 1768 and 1800.

Nevertheless, the offence was indicted slightly more regularly than this single execution might suggest. A few months after Mullinger's execution, another man was capitally convicted of the crime at the Norfolk Assizes at Norwich but subsequently reprieved.[42] In other cases the trial jury committed "pious perjury" and declared the cloth stolen to be worth less than ten shillings, making the crime simple larceny, as occurred with Robert Child at the Thetford Assizes in 1779, when an alleged 20

40. Ibid.
41. *Whitehall Evening Post (1770)*, 26–29 March 1791; *Evening Mail*, 13–15 April 1791.
42. Anon, *Report From the Select Committee on Criminal Laws*, 1819, pp. 196–211.

shillings worth of cloth was valued at only nine shillings.[43] Several other prosecutions, such as that of John Riches, accused at the Norfolk Assizes in 1753 of stealing 40 yards of linen worth £3, resulted in outright acquittals. (This was the only prosecution for the crime in the region during the decade after 1751).[44]

Interestingly, section 2 of the 1745 statute gave trial judges discretion to sentence those who had been found guilty to 14 years' transportation "instead of giving judgment of death."[45] This also avoided the need for hanging cabinet approval of a reprieve, and was indicative of reprieves being the normal disposal in such cases. Thus, at the Bury Assizes in 1807, John Turner was transported for 14 years after being convicted of stealing from a bleaching ground.[46]

Similarly, although forgery had been a misdemeanour for much of the seventeenth century, specific forms of the crime had become capital felonies by the early 1700s, with almost all types of forgery becoming an unclergyable felony by dint of a statute from 1729. The ensuing death sentences were only rarely reprieved.[47] There were dozens of capital convictions for the crime in the metropolitan area. However, only two men were hanged for forgery in the entire East Anglian region between 1735 and 1799. In 1754 William Scott was committed to Ipswich Gaol, accused of forging two letters and two handwritten notes purporting to be from a Daniel Richer, thereby defrauding George Almond of Ipswich of £20.[48] He was subsequently convicted and executed.[49] At the August Assizes for Bury in 1772, David Pigney was also convicted of forgery and "left for execution."[50]

This does not mean that the Bloody Code was entirely irrelevant to the region's criminal justice system in practice. Some of its offences did produce regular prosecutions and even hangings. The most important of

43. TNA ASSI 33/6.
44. TNA ASSI 33/2–3.
45. J. Raithby (ed.), *The Statutes at Large, of England and of Great-Britain*, vol. 10, 1811, pp. 179–180.
46. H. Barker, *History Of, and Guide to, Bury St. Edmund's*, 2006, p. 88.
47. R. McGowen, "From Pillory to Gallows: The Punishment of Forgery in the Age of the Financial Revolution," 1999, pp. 107–140.
48. *Read's Weekly Journal Or British Gazetteer*, 13 July 1754.
49. *Whitehall Evening Post Or London Intelligencer*, 17–20 August 1754.
50. *Bingley's Journal*, August 15–22 August 1772.

these were various forms of theft, committed in specific circumstances, which had been withdrawn from clergy after 1688. Clerks of assizes and JPs were reluctant to ignore these statutes in favour of prosecutions for simple grand larceny.[51] Among them were the theft of sheep and stealing from a dwelling-house (see *Chapters 15* and *16*). Nevertheless, the great majority of the code's more arcane felonies did not produce executions in eighteenth-century East Anglia, and many did not even result in prosecutions.

Misdemeanours

Misdemeanours were an ill-defined series of less serious crimes, whether common law or statutory, for which a death sentence could never be imposed and which were usually punished by fiscal, corporal, or short carceral sentences. They included most assaults and many offences of criminal damage as well as lesser cases of fraud, especially those in which the owner of goods voluntarily (albeit mistakenly) parted with them. For example, in 1781 William Dix, from Skeyton, in Norfolk, obtained the loan of a guinea from James Fulcher by leaving a box and its contents as security for the money. He claimed that it contained a large quantity of fine china, "but on opening the box, a quantity of stones packed up in straw only were found."[52] The following year, while a friendly society met at a public house in Debenham, in Suffolk, a "sharper" went to the house of the person who kept the club box, which he asked for and was given. He then fled with the £40 worth of goods that it contained.[53]

As they were defined as misdemeanours, and because the courts appear to have had little sympathy with foolish victims, such crimes were frequently punished quite modestly, whether tried at quarter sessions or assizes. For example, Morris Jones was convicted of obtaining money by false pretences at the Suffolk Quarter Sessions held at Beccles in 1724, after claiming that he was gathering alms for poor prisoners in the King's Bench Gaol. He was merely sentenced to a flogging in Beccles market.[54]

51. J. Innes, *Parliament and the Shaping of Eighteenth-century English Social Policy*, 1990, p. 71.
52. *Norfolk Chronicle*, 22 December 1781.
53. *Ipswich Journal*, 9 March 1782.
54. SRO QS B/105/20/14, p. 201.

At the Suffolk Quarter Sessions held at Ipswich in July 1784, James Wright was accused of obtaining four silk handkerchiefs, one pound of sugar, and two ounces of tea, "under false pretences." He pleaded guilty, and was publicly whipped and discharged.[55]

Most misdemeanours were tried on indictment before a jury. However, as the era advanced, an increasing number could be tried summarily, as a result of specific statutes (see below).

Courts with Criminal Jurisdiction

During the eighteenth century, there were four levels of criminal jurisdiction in East Anglia, and almost everywhere else in England outside the Metropolis. Going from the base of the criminal-justice pyramid to its apex, these were: summarily, in front of a single justice; summarily, in front of a bench of two or more JPs sitting at petty sessions; on indictment before a jury presided over by magistrates (often assisted by a legally qualified recorder) sitting at quarter sessions; and on indictment before a jury presided over by a professional judge from one of the three Westminster courts on circuit and sitting at assizes. These will be dealt with *seriatim*.

Summary Trial

Formal legal provisions allowing summary trial in criminal cases, whether before a single justice or in front of a bench of JPs sitting at petty sessions, had roots stretching back to the medieval period, but expanded significantly during the late-seventeenth and eighteenth centuries. Previously justices had a modest area of jurisdiction, but a plethora of enabling statutes extended their reach to a "vast variety" of new situations.[56] Magistrates could determine offences without any recourse to a jury and could impose small fines and corporal punishment on those they convicted.[57]

55. SRO QS B105/2/47, p. 77.
56. T. Gisborne, *An Enquiry Into the Duties of Men in the Higher and Middle Classes of Society in Great Britain*, 1794, p. 298; W. Paley, *The Law and Practice of Summary Convictions on Penal Statutes by Justices of the Peace*, 1814, p. 1, p. 7, p. xxvii, and p. xxix.
57. W. Blackstone, *Commentaries on the Laws of England*, vol. 4, 1769, p. 279.

In theory, such a jurisdiction had been expanded for the greater convenience of the subject, by "doing him speedy justice, and by not harassing the freeholders with frequent and troublesome attendances [as jurors] to try every minute offence."[58] It seems that the growth of summary jurisdiction during the 1700s replaced a previous willingness to have recourse to quarter sessions (which required a jury) to determine lesser criminal matters, and so reflects a major change in social attitudes towards the administration of justice.[59] In part, at least in the longer term, it was also a result of the disappearance or marginalisation of the manorial court leet and its minor jury-based criminal jurisdiction, as well as that of the penal jurisdiction of the lesser church courts, especially that of the archdeacon. By the early 1700s, even the most active of these, such as those in the diocese of Carlisle, tended to limit themselves to offences of sexual morality or crimes with a direct church connection, such as profaning the Sabbath by "leaping," playing football, or fighting cocks in the churchyard.[60]

Summary trial had a number of advantages. It was fast and cheap. Vitally, it was reliable, as there was "no intervention of a jury" that could nullify the law according to its own perception of right and wrong. Instead, the accused's fate was determined by: "such person only, as the statute has appointed for his judge."[61] This "person" was almost invariably a JP. Their jurisdiction was exercised in two situations: before a single justice sitting alone and in front of a bench of justices sitting at petty sessions.

Summary Trial Before a Single Justice

Frequently a single justice could try summary matters on his own. Throughout the eighteenth century, this was usually done in his home, at least in the provinces. As Thomas Gisborne noted in the 1790s, "The principal share of his business is transacted in his own house, before few

58. Ibid., p. 278.
59. D. Lemmings, *Law and Government in England during the Long Eighteenth Century*, 2011, pp. 19–25.
60. M. Kinnear, "The Correction Court in the Diocese of Carlisle, 1704–1756," 1990, p. 202.
61. W. Blackstone, *Commentaries on the Laws of England*, vol. 4, 1769, p. 278.

spectators."[62] Almost a century earlier, in 1700, the Suffolk JP Devereaux Edgar expressly decided to record in his legal notebook "[w]hat I transacted at my house as to warrants, mittimus to gaol, House of Correction, Examinations…"[63] Many of the country houses of the gentry contained a "justice room" or "parlour" for this purpose. It was only after the Summary Jurisdiction Act of 1848 that all such trials had to take place at formally constituted petty sessions, held before at least two magistrates.

Single justices could determine a range of matters, including cursing, stealing wood and vegetables, various alcohol-related offences, such as being drunk in a public place or tippling on the Sabbath, and minor cases of poaching under the Game Act of 1671.[64]

Summary Trial before Petty Sessions

Many summary matters were determined by groups of justices sitting together at "petty sessions" rather than by a single magistrate sitting alone. (Although dating back to the 1500s, the term was not widely used until the nineteenth century but is employed here for convenience). Indeed, some summary offences required the presence of more than one justice before they could be determined summarily.

JPs had first divided themselves into such groups to conduct lesser judicial and administrative business during the sixteenth century. The Book of Orders, issued in 1631, had required that they split their counties into divisions. The members of these divisions were directed to meet once a month. This explains why such hearings were often termed "monthly meetings" in the early 1700s.[65] However, during the eighteenth century, especially in its latter decades, some magistrates met more frequently. Fortnightly meetings of petty sessions became common in many areas.

From the late seventeenth century, petty sessions assumed greater responsibility for dealing with minor criminal offences. This was usually

---

62. T. Gisborne, *An Enquiry Into the Duties of Men in the Higher and Middle Classes of Society in Great Britain*, 1794, p. 285.
63. SRO QS 347.96, *The Devereux Edgar Notebook*, transcribed by S. R. Schofield, 1956, vol.1, p. 1.
64. P. B. Munsche, *Gentlemen and Poachers—The English Game Laws 1671–1831*, 1981, p. 212.
65. H. Langeluddecke, "'Patchy and Spasmodic'?: The Response of Justices of the Peace to Charles I's Book of Orders," 1998, p. 1231.

done with the active encouragement of the overburdened quarter sessions. However, petty sessions also dealt with a huge number of non-criminal administrative and local-government matters, such as settlement actions under the 1662 Act, bastardy, licensing, and poor relief. Such work was normally much more important than their criminal jurisdiction. Some petty sessions were held purely to register the employment of workers and servants.

Two or more JPs conducted petty sessions; one of them was usually a member of the quorum of supposedly experienced magistrates, albeit that this was a status that was almost universal by the eighteenth century. Although the bench acquired some extra powers over and above those of a solitary magistrate, they also conducted much work that could in theory have been done by a single justice, such as dealing with cases involving the theft of wood and vegetables, and sometimes even became involved in taking depositions or examining suspects in felony cases.

By the early nineteenth century, Norfolk had 25 petty sessional divisions, largely based on the county's old hundreds. However, divisional boundaries had changed several times during the 1700s, and were not put on a statutory basis until 1828. The arrangements for petty sessions were usually fairly informal, although, as the century advanced, JPs began to employ a small paid staff to assist in their administration. There was often a duly appointed clerk, who might have a copy of the statutes readily to hand.[66]

Typically petty sessions were held in a large room in a local tavern on a set day each month. For example, the *Crown Inn*, in Hartest, in Suffolk, was used for his purpose until at least 1766. As late as June 1833, John Longe recorded in his diary that he had attended petty-sessions sittings at the *Crown Inn* in Coddenham (also in Suffolk), "from where I did not return till 7 o'clock."[67] This was to be a regular entry in the clerical JP's diary. In the adjacent county, the *Black Lion Hotel*, a coaching inn at Walsingham, was regularly used as a venue during the 1700s. The arrangements for petty sessions were only fully regularised in the middle of the nineteenth century, by a combination of the Petty Sessions Act

66. D. M. M. Shorrocks, "Eighteenth Century Petty Sessions Records in Kent," 1954, pp. 10–13.
67. M. Stone (ed.), *The Diary of John Longe, Vicar of Coddenham, 1765–1834*, 2008, p. 155.

1849 and the Prosecution Expenses (Amendment Act) 1851. Together these provided for a regular procedure, a courthouse, and the use of salaried clerks.[68] Although they produced only a pale shadow of the pomp that attended quarter sessions, let alone assizes, even petty sessions attracted some custom and activity to the towns and villages where they were held. Indicative of this, in 1780 it was noted that a group of cardsharps were targeting individuals at those being held in Suffolk.[69]

As with quarter sessions (see below), the two counties' major boroughs, such as Great Yarmouth, King's Lynn, Norwich, Ipswich, and Thetford, had their own petty sessions, presided over by their own magistrates (usually the mayor and other local political figures). For example, the mayor's court in Norwich operated in this capacity. Most of the prisoners committed to the Norwich Bridewell in St. Andrew's parish for petty offences were sentenced at this forum.[70] As with most petty sessions, the majority of its work was made up of administrative matters, albeit that this included arrangements for the local criminal justice system. Thus, in August 1744 the mayor's court ordered that the city's chief constable pay Thomas Rawlins 7s 6d for attending a public whipping.[71] As its name states, the court was, ostensibly, presided over by the mayor, and would usually sit for a period on most weekdays in the imposing oak-panelled council chamber of the city hall. One or more senior aldermen would often join him, as might the legally qualified recorder, who "assists in the Mayor's court as Chief Judge." (The recorder was a qualified barrister and *ex officio* justice for the city.)[72]

As this suggests, borough petty sessions usually met much more frequently than those in their surrounding county, often twice a week or more in the larger urban areas. This, combined with geographical proximity, meant that residents of a town had much easier recourse to the criminal law than those in rural areas. In turn, this encouraged use of that law at the expense of alternative, informal methods of dispute resolution.

68. S. Flynn and M. Stevens, "Petty Criminals, Publicans and Sinners: Petty Sessions Records in the Berkshire Record Office," 1995, p. 43.
69. *Norfolk Chronicle*, 7 October 1780.
70. C. Mackie, *Norfolk Annals*, vol. 2, 1901, p. 286.
71. NRO Norwich City Quarter Sessions Minute Books MF 616.
72. C. Berry, *A Concise History and Directory of the City of Norwich; For 1811*, 1810 p. 43.

When it came to criminal matters, petty sessions would hear lesser cases of assault, occasional cases of poaching, minor property crimes (even the smallest felonies would be referred to quarter sessions or assizes), and many regulatory offences, such as those involving weights and measures, alehouses, and vagrancy. However, there was considerable variation over time, and between geographic locations, as to how much criminal business they would deal with, and how much it was felt could be left to a single justice sitting alone or should be sent to quarter sessions and a jury.

A selection of cases from the East Anglian region is illustrative of their typical criminal work. In October 1753 two JPs sitting at petty sessions convicted a Suffolk farmer "on his own confession" of driving infected cattle across the county during an outbreak of distemper; they fined him £100.[73] In 1762 Thomas Parminter, a servant from Brent Ely, in Suffolk, was convicted before two justices of the peace sitting at petty sessions for illegally shooting three pigeons in Milden. He was ordered to pay the statutory penalty of 20 shillings for each bird killed, this money going to the parish poor (as was common with summary fines).[74] In July 1781 Henry Hall, a miller from North Elmham, was accused of adulterating wheat meal with cheaper barley flour, contrary to statute (31 Geo II, s 22), before justices sitting at petty sessions at Dereham, in Norfolk. There was sworn testimony against him from several poor people (presumably purchasers) from nearby Mattishall. Hall agreed to pay the £5 statutory penalty, although he later claimed that a combination of his youth, ignorance of the law, and discomfiture at being in a room full of people made him desperate to get out at any cost, even if it meant admitting the allegation against him.[75] Similarly, in 1801, 18 people were convicted and fined for using deficient weights and balances at petty sessions held in the *White Lion* at Hadleigh, in Suffolk.[76]

73. *London Evening Post*, 11–13 October 1753.
74. *Ipswich Journal*, 22 May 1762.
75. *Norfolk Chronicle*, 25 August 1781.
76. *The Ipswich Journal*, 10 October 1801.

Appeal from Summary Conviction

In theory, it was usually possible to challenge a summary conviction, whether from an individual magistrate or petty sessions, at quarter sessions. (A few summary matters could not be appealed in this fashion.)[77] Henry Hall (see last section) claimed that he had not properly appreciated this in time. He thought that, for his offence, notice of appeal had to be lodged within 24 hours of the original hearing.[78] The certificates of most types of summary conviction, made by justices acting out of quarter sessions, were supposed to be returned to the higher forum (although this was frequently overlooked), and their decisions could often be challenged in a rehearing in front of the quarter-sessions justices, albeit sitting without a jury.[79] Such appeals were not uncommon after 1660. For example, at the Suffolk Quarter Sessions held at Woodbridge on 17 April 1751, the bench allowed James Wood's appeal of a summary conviction by Philip Carter Clerk, a county JP, for a regulatory offence relating to infected cattle. Perhaps significantly, Wood had been represented at the appeal hearing by counsel.[80]

Wood's success, however, was unusual. County magistrates would not lightly overturn a colleague's decision on the merits of a case. More typically, in 1816, when Joseph Dale brought an appeal against a summary conviction for poaching at Crowfield, in Suffolk, to the Ipswich Quarter Sessions, it was dismissed, and he was sentenced to six months in Botesdale Bridewell.[81] According to Thomas Gisborne, even if an appeal was successful, the justices involved in the original decision were unlikely to receive severe censure from their colleagues on the local bench, who would attribute any legal mistakes to an oversight or consider them to be of little importance, as they could easily be corrected.[82]

77. R. Burn, *The History of the Poor Laws: With Observations*, 1764, p. 274.
78. *Norfolk Chronicle*, 25 August 1781.
79. W. Paley, *The Law and Practice of Summary Convictions on Penal Statutes by Justices of the Peace*, 1814, p. xxx.
80. SRO QS B105/2/24, p. 58.
81. *Suffolk Chronicle*, 13 January 1816.
82. T. Gisborne, *An Enquiry Into the Duties of Men in the Higher and Middle Classes of Society in Great Britain*, 1794, p. 285.

A JP might also be called to account by the Court of King's Bench. This forum could consider the legality of a summary conviction by a writ of *certiorari,* which removed the record of the inferior court into the King's Bench for review.[83] Normally such challenges had to be based on a legal flaw "on the record" in the earlier proceedings, rather than the convicting magistrate's assessment of the evidence. For instance, in 1772 Daniel Bamford from Ipswich successfully appealed his summary conviction the previous year for allowing an early form of billiards to be played in his alehouse, for which he had been banned from selling beer and spirits for three years: "This conviction was removed by Certiorari into the King's Bench and on Saturday last it was squashed by this court."[84]

Appeal was an expensive process, and unsuccessful litigants could be subject to harsh costs. Several statutes effectively prohibited such actions, for certain common types of summary conviction, by establishing new, short, foolproof, model-form statutory convictions, deemed to be legally sufficient, in place of the elaborate, and so challengeable, common law form. For example, as a result of the Profane Oaths Act 1745 (which replaced a similar statute from 1694), convictions for swearing in public could not, effectively, be reviewed by *certiorari*, while the Alehouses Act 1753 had the same effect on some summary offences relating to the sale and consumption of alcohol.[85] Even in the absence of such statutes, the prospects of success during the 1700s were often fairly slim, much more so than in the previous century.[86] King's Bench appreciated that intervening too frequently in such cases would discourage men from sitting as active magistrates, so exacerbating what was a permanent problem during the era, and often did so only when a culpable intention on the JP's part had been clearly proved.[87]

83. W. Paley, *The Law and Practice of Summary Convictions on Penal Statutes by Justices of the Peace*, 1814, p. xxvii and p. xxix.
84. *Ipswich Journal*, 6 June 1772.
85. K. Costello, "The Writ of Certiorari and Review of Summary Criminal Convictions, 1660–1848," 2012, pp. 443–465.
86. D. Lemmings, *Law and Government in England during the Long Eighteenth Century*, 2011, pp. 34–35.
87. T. Gisborne, *An Enquiry Into the Duties of Men in the Higher and Middle Classes of Society in Great Britain*, 1794, p. 285.

Unsurprisingly in these circumstances, few cases were brought in this fashion, given the thousands of summary convictions that occurred nationally. Illustrative of this, no summary convictions were challenged by *certiorari* in the whole of Kent between 1743 and 1748.[88] Similarly, in Staffordshire there were just eleven cases between 1740 and 1800.[89] As a result, the procedure does not appear to have had a huge effect in controlling erring provincial magistrates, although its influence may have been slightly more significant in the Metropolis.[90]

More generally, those on the receiving end of summary justice were usually "too humble, ignorant, or timid" to think of seeking legal redress of any type in any but the most flagrant cases, in East Anglia as elsewhere. Even if they did, they were usually too poor to obtain it.[91]

Trial on Indictment before Quarter Sessions

Quarter sessions were the lower of the two types of provincial court that heard trials on indictment (before a jury). As their name suggests, they were usually held four times a year in each county, as the result of a medieval statute (2 Hen. V, c. 24). They were normally conducted at Epiphany (January), Easter (usually April), Midsummer (July), and Michaelmas (October). However, if pressure of business made it desirable, justices could hold additional sessions outside these times. For example, an extra sitting for Suffolk appears to have been held at Bury on 5 June 1751, with the usual hearing following at the same location on the 22 July.[92] This was not a common occurrence.

Some English counties, particularly the smaller ones, conducted all their quarter sessions in one location. Those in tiny Rutland were always held at Oakham. Some much larger but highly centralised counties, such as Gloucestershire, also conducted their quarter sessions in the same town. By contrast, Kent had two locations, Maidstone for its western

88. N. Landau, *The Justices of the Peace 1679–1760*, 1984, p. 354.
89. D. Lemmings, *The British and their Laws in the Eighteenth Century*, 2011, p. 65.
90. D. Hay, "Dread of the Crown Office: The English Magistracy and King's Bench 1740–1800," 2002, pp. 19–45.
91. T. Gisborne, *An Enquiry Into the Duties of Men in the Higher and Middle Classes of Society in Great Britain*, 1794, p. 285.
92. SRO QS B105/2/24, p. 61.

parts and Canterbury for those in the east. In other counties quarter sessions were held once yearly in each of four towns. Those that were large or had major natural barriers, such as Lincolnshire, Nottinghamshire, Derbyshire, Cheshire, and Wiltshire, held sessions four times a year in each of three or four locations in different parts of the county, producing a dozen or more sittings. This was also the pattern in Norfolk and Suffolk.

The quarter sessions for Norfolk usually sat four times a year in each of three places drawn from a list made up of Norwich, Walsingham, Holt, Swaffham, and King's Lynn, producing a dozen sittings in total. This was because the county had long been divided into three unequal divisions or limits: east, west and north. Norwich, where the sessions for the east division were held, was always one of the three venues selected and the first to hold its sessions. It was also by far the most important and largest of the divisions, with the longest-lasting quarter sessions, as it catered for 20 of the 33 hundreds in the county. Traditionally it was at Norwich that general orders relating to the whole of Norfolk were made. Technically the other two forums were "adjournments" of these sessions, although often treated as separate courts.[93] The north division was made up of seven hundreds, including King's Lynn, the west division of six hundreds, including Holt.

Although Norwich always hosted quarter sessions, the locations used for the other divisions varied slightly with the season, the summer sequence normally being different from those for the rest of the year. As a result, in 1740 the county quarter sessions for Easter opened at Norwich on 15 April, in Lynn on 22 April, and in Walsingham on 24 April 24. The next cycle started at Norwich on 15 July 1740 and in Swaffham on 22 July, and finished at Walsingham on 24 July. The Autumn Quarter Sessions began at Norwich on 7 October 1740, met at Lynn on 14 October, and opened at Holt two days later. The Winter Quarter Sessions started at Norwich on 13 January 1741, and were followed by those held at Lynn on 20 January, and then those at Holt two days later. The same pattern was adopted the following year.[94] This general distribution persisted for

93. D. E. Howell James (ed.), *Norfolk Quarter Sessions Order Book, 1650–1657*, 1955, p. 7.
94. NRO C/S 1/12.

decades. In 1788 those for Norfolk were held in Norwich on 10 October, in King's Lynn on 14 October, and the following day at Holt.[95]

Occasionally there was some variation to the pattern. For example, it appears that 1752 saw a reduced number of county quarter sessions.[96] Later in the century, Fakenham was occasionally added to the list, having a "spacious courthouse, in which the Justices of the county sometimes meet at adjournments of the Sessions."[97] A variety of other buildings were used. For example, the Beccles Town Hall, built in 1726, became the forum for both quarter and petty sessions.

The sittings of the Norfolk Quarter Sessions would last between one and four days, depending on the amount of business to be considered. In January 1712 the county JPs noted that the quarter sessions held in Norwich for the east division had traditionally started on a Tuesday and, because some of those with business did not arrive promptly, frequently lasted three or four days. (They urged all the county's JPs to return their recognisances by the Tuesday afternoon to speed up the process).[98] By contrast, hearings for the other divisions, such as those at Holt and Lynn, would often be completed within a day.

Suffolk was slightly different. For much of the century, the county quarter sessions met four times a year in each of four locations: Beccles, Woodbridge, Ipswich, and Bury St Edmunds. (Lowestoft occasionally substituted for Beccles.) In most years this produced 16 sittings in total. The Michaelmas Sessions in the final two decades of the century followed the pattern set for most of the era. In 1781 they were held at Beccles on 6 October, Woodbridge on 8 October, Ipswich on 10 October, and Bury three days later.[99] In October 1789 they followed the same pattern, almost to the day.[100] At Michaelmas 1797 they started at Beccles on Monday 2 October, Woodbridge on 4 October, Ipswich on 6 October, and Bury three days later.

---

95. *World (1787)*, 6 October 1788.
96. NRO C/S 1/12.
97. Anon, *The Norfolk Tour: Or, Traveller's Pocket Companion*, 1772, p. 20.
98. *Norwich Gazette Or The Loyal Packet*, 19 January 1712.
99. *World (1787)*, 6 October 1788.
100. Ibid., 3 October 1789.

In theory each quarter-sessions meeting was a general sessions for the whole county. All commission justices who had taken out their *dedimus* could sit at those held in any division. Indeed, they were supposed to attend each of these meetings. However, most active justices (and some court officers) attended only the quarter sessions for their own area.[101] In East Anglia few magistrates attended all the hearings in their county, and many attended none. On 3 October 1728, for instance, seven magistrates presided over the Norfolk County Quarter Sessions that met at Norwich. Four justices attended the adjournment at Lynn on 10 October, and the same number on 12 October at Holt. It seems that none of these 15 magistrates attended more than one session, so there was a complete change of judicial personnel with each move.[102]

This was not always the case. In Suffolk none of the magistrates who sat at the Epiphany Quarter Sessions held at Beccles on 14 January 1750 were among the three JPs who sat at Woodbridge two days later. However, both magistrates who sat at Ipswich on 18 January, John Woodbridge (an appropriate surname) and Edward Vernon, had sat at Woodbridge. Even so, all four magistrates who sat at the next hearing, held at Bury on 21 January, were appearing for the first time that month.[103] This change in personnel meant that there was significant de facto, unofficial, decentralisation in quarter sessions, although the legally qualified clerk of the peace (usually a solicitor or attorney) was nearly always present at such proceedings, wherever held. He administered the quarter sessions secretariat and also looked after the court records.[104]

As with the assizes, a grand jury would consider individual cases at quarter sessions before they were determined by a petty jury. The trials at such forums were held in front of a bench of magistrates rather than before the Westminster judge found at the higher forum. The bench had to have at least two JPs to be quorate.[105] Practice seems to have varied on this issue, some counties requiring more magistrates to be present as a

101. D. Lemmings. *Law and Government in England During the Long Eighteenth Century*, 2011, p. 27.
102. NRO C/S1/12 mf 656 6, parts 1–4.
103. SRO QS B105/2/24, p. 52.
104. D. Lemmings, *Law and Government in England During the Long Eighteenth Century*, 2011, p. 27.
105. W. Blackstone, *Commentaries on the Laws of England*, vol. 4, 1769, p. 268.

matter of custom, and a few powers needing more than two JPs on the bench before they could be exercised as a matter of law. For example, at the Norfolk County Quarter Sessions held at Little Walsingham on 3 May 1751, only two JPs attended. As a result, "This Sessions was dropt for want of two Justices to hold the same."[106] Fifty years earlier there had been a similar problem in the town, blamed on the poor weather and the "pretended illness" of several local JPs.[107]

In practice the number of magistrates present at East Anglian quarter sessions was usually greater than the minimum required, although far below that found in counties such as Kent, Surrey, Essex, Devon, Hertfordshire, Gloucestershire, and Shropshire.[108] For example, at the four Suffolk Quarter Sessions held in January 1750 (Epiphany was often unpopular because of poor weather), the number of JPs ranged from the bare minimum of two to a reported maximum of five. Typically, at the sessions held in Beccles that month, four JPs were present, including the baronet Sir Thomas Allen.[109] Sometimes significantly more JPs would be in attendance. In July 1708, the sessions for Norfolk held at Swaffham were conducted before eight JPs.[110] County quarter sessions held at Norwich were particularly well-attended.

The early eighteenth century saw a gradual increase in what might be termed professionalism when it came to the conduct of quarter sessions. This included a growth in recognised procedures and an increase in general decorum. For example, in 1707 the Norwich bench forbade those engaged in business at their court to stand on the tables. In 1710 the Little Walsingham Quarter Sessions insisted that counsel follow the Norwich precedent of always appearing in gowns.[111]

This period also saw the emergence of permanent chairmen at county quarter sessions, magistrates who would always preside over the hearings if in attendance, although a few counties did not go down this route,

106. NRO MF 653 C/S 1/1.
107. J. Rosenheim, "County Governance and Elite Withdrawal in Norfolk, 1660–1720," 1989, p. 110.
108. E. Moir, *Local Government in Gloucestershire 1775–1800*, 1969, p. 77.
109. SRO QS B105/2/24, p. 52.
110. R. Anselment (ed.), *The Remembrances of Elizabeth Freke 1671–1714*, 2002, p. 96.
111. J. Rosenheim, "County Governance and Elite Withdrawal in Norfolk, 1660–1720," 1989, p. 120.

and continued to rotate the position or appoint on an ad hoc basis (as had been common at the start of the century).[112] Regular procedures were established for electing these officers in most areas. They were usually chosen from the most experienced, active, and socially prominent JPs. The chairman played a vital role in setting general policy, and was backed up by an increasingly professional clerk and a hard core of active magistrates who often met at monthly adjournments of the quarter sessions for administrative purposes.[113]

It would be a mistake to think of quarter sessions as essentially criminal courts. By the eighteenth century they were overwhelmingly committed to county administration, unlike the relatively modest contribution made by the assizes in this regard; they conducted less criminal work proportionately than their predecessors in the seventeenth century. East Anglia JPs, like those elsewhere, made decisions relating to prisons, houses of correction, the maintenance of highways and bridges, licensing, the Poor Law, the law of settlement, rates, and many other areas.[114] This tendency became more marked as petty sessions assumed more responsibility for minor offences.

Criminal Jurisdiction

The staple diet of quarter sessions criminal jurisdiction consisted of regulatory offences, common-law misdemeanours, and cases of petty theft (which was in practice treated like a misdemeanour). For example, between 1740 and 1780, the quarter sessions for the Lindsey Division in Lincolnshire heard about 3,000 criminal cases. Approximately half were for regulatory matters, such as running unlicensed alehouses. There were nearly 700 assaults, of varying degrees of gravity. Theft (overwhelmingly petty larceny) was the second-largest category of crime, with 450 cases

112. P. King, *Crime and Law in England, 1750–1840: Remaking Justice from the Margins*, 2006, p. 50; E. Moir, *Local Government in Gloucestershire 1775–1800*, 1969, p. 91.
113. D. Eastwood, "Local Government and Local Society," 2002, p. 49.
114. D. Lemmings, *Law and Government in England During the Long Eighteenth Century*, 2011, p. 25.

being determined, to which can be added 16 cases of receiving and 45 of fraud.[115]

The same general pattern is found in East Anglia, where the quarter sessions also determined numerous regulatory offences. For example, at those for Suffolk held in October 1753, George Ruffles of Shimpling was convicted and fined £100 for buying and distributing cattle without a certificate.[116] At the same forum in May 1770, two men were indicted for committing a nuisance after erecting a public stage in Melford and performing "divers interludes of wire dancing etc."[117] At the Suffolk Quarter Sessions held at Bury in May 1775, Hannah Hunt was convicted of moving her three children into the parish of Lavenham while they were infected with smallpox. She was fined and committed to the local gaol until the money was paid.[118] At the same forum, held at Beccles in October 1797, several people from Lowestoft were fined five shillings each for allowing their pigs to wander around the streets.[119]

Throughout the era, conventional crimes, such as assault, that were legally defined as misdemeanours, also made up a significant part of East Anglian quarter sessions criminal jurisdiction. For example, at those held at Bury in 1782, John Nichols was fined £5 for assaulting a tailor from the same town.[120] Lesser crimes of disorder were also determined at this forum. At the quarter sessions held at Ipswich in 1785, Thomas Baker was sentenced to 14 days in the town bridewell and a whipping on discharge for keeping a house of ill fame. Margaret Dodd was sent to the bridewell for three months and whipped for the same crime.[121] As with Lincolnshire, various offences involving deceit, which were usually defined as misdemeanours, were dealt with at East Anglian quarter sessions. For example, at those held for Norfolk at Norwich on 11 July 1751, one Blake of Ashby was prosecuted as a "cheat."[122]

115. B. J. Davey, *Rural Crime in the Eighteenth Century: North Lincolnshire 1740–80*, 1995, p. 19.
116. *Ipswich Journal*, 27 October 1753.
117. Ibid., 5 May 1770.
118. Ibid., 13 May 1775.
119. *Oracle and Public Advertiser*, 9 October 1797.
120. *Norfolk Chronicle*, 16 November 1782.
121. *Ipswich Journal*, 19 March 1785.
122. NRO MF 653 C/S 1/1, MF 653.

However, when it came to crimes of dishonesty, petty theft was by far the most common offence tried at the lower jury court. As Maurice Shelton told the Suffolk Quarter Sessions grand jury, although it was only a "small offence, yet being frequently committed, [it] requires your care to suppress it."[123] This was the situation throughout England. In Oxfordshire during the second half of the eighteenth century, 597 people were tried at the county quarter sessions for larceny, the vast majority instances of petty theft, producing an average of about a dozen cases a year.[124]

A similar pattern can be seen in East Anglia. Typically, at the county quarter sessions held at Norwich on 11 July 1710, four men and one woman were convicted of petty larceny and whipped. At the same forum, on 15 July 1735, George Withy was convicted of stealing a shirt, whipped, and discharged. Ann Jones, a married woman, received a similar disposal after pleading guilty to stealing three aprons and as many shifts (very probably downvalued) from Mary Crisp. Stephen Briton was whipped after being convicted of stealing a knife. Another woman was acquitted of a similar crime.[125] Almost half a century later, in April 1782, two men and one woman were convicted of separate charges of petty theft at one sitting of the same forum. Two others accused of the same crime were acquitted.[126] Thus Suffolk presents a broadly similar picture to Oxfordshire, albeit that the number of prosecutions varied considerably from season to season and year to year. For example, only one case of petty theft was heard at all four sittings for the county in January 1751, while other quarters saw numerous trials for the same crime.

In theory quarter sessions could try any case other than treason until 1842, when statute (5 & 6 Vict. c.38) laid down what matters could be determined at the lower court and formally excluded a large number of serious offences, such as murder and capital felony, from its jurisdiction.[127] During the sixteenth century, such crimes had, sometimes, been tried at these forums. After 1590 this was expressly discouraged. As a result,

123. M. Shelton, *A Charge Given to the Grand-jury, at the General Quarter-sessions of the Peace, Holden at St. Edmunds-Bury For the Liberty Thereof*, 1726, p. 32.
124. A. Kilday, "'Criminally Poor?' Investigating the Link Between Crime and Poverty in Eighteenth Century England," 2014, p. 115.
125. NRO C/S1/12, mf 656 6, parts 1–4.
126. *Norfolk Chronicle*, 13 April 1782.
127. E. Melling, *Kentish Sources VI: Crime and Punishment*, 1969, p. 5.

quarter sessions abandoned hearing capital crimes in the seventeenth century, leaving such matters to the assizes. For example, at the Norfolk quarter sessions that opened at Norwich on 16 July 1717, Elizabeth Mountain(?) was "charged with breaking an house and & continued to the Assizes." Similarly, Benjamin Hipkin, accused of "breaking [into] a shop," was also referred to the higher forum.

Nevertheless, quarter sessions continued to determine some lesser examples of clergyable felonies, particularly grand larceny, for significantly longer. In this respect, practice varied greatly around the country, and over time. In some counties, such as Kent, quarter sessions were reluctant to hear the more serious form of larceny by the early 1700s, preferring to leave all such cases to the assizes, and confining themselves to petty theft. In others, such as Sussex, grand larceny was still heard on a fairly regular basis at the lower jury court during the early eighteenth century.

Of course stolen goods might be artificially downvalued to less than a shilling, so that offenders could be prosecuted for petty theft. This practice had occurred for centuries prior to 1700. At the Norfolk Quarter Sessions held at Fakenham in August 1662, three women were indicted for stealing five pewter plates with the owner's crest stamped on them, which were nominally (and wholly implausibly) valued at a total of ten pence.[128] This continued throughout the eighteenth century. For example, at the Suffolk quarter sessions held at Beccles on 10 July 1758, Mary Engle was indicted for petty theft after stealing three silver teaspoons, a shirt, and a pair of stockings, which together were undoubtedly worth more than a shilling; she pleaded guilty, was publicly whipped and then discharged.[129]

However, Norfolk Quarter Sessions were still hearing a significant number of grand larcenies that had been indicted as such in the late-seventeenth and early-eighteenth centuries. For example, at those held at King's Lynn in January 1685, Robert Amyab was "branded for felony" and discharged after he successfully claimed benefit of clergy having been convicted of the more serious form of theft. (Another person was whipped for petty larceny while yet more defendants were acquitted

128. J. Rosenheim (ed.), *The Notebook of Robert Doughty, 1662–1665*, 1991, p. 18.
129. SRO B105/2/32, p. 134.

after being accused of one or other of these crimes). A few years later, at the county quarter sessions held at the same forum on 1 January 1693, a man and a woman were clergied and branded for grand larceny, then released, while two others were whipped for petty theft and discharged. This pattern continued in the first two decades of the following century.

In some respects, benefit of clergy meant that those convicted of the lesser form of theft were often receiving greater punishment—a whipping rather than a cursory branding—than those found guilty of grand larceny. As a result, it is unsurprising that the Norfolk Quarter Sessions quickly made use of the enhanced (but discretionary) punishment available after 1706. In the ensuing decade, a majority of those clergied for grand larceny at the county quarter sessions received a sentence of penal hard labour on top of their branding. For example, at the Norfolk Quarter Sessions held at Norwich on 11 July 1710, Robert Warren, Matthew Nowell, and two other men were convicted of grand larceny, clergied, burnt in the hand, and sent to the house of correction at Wymondham for six months. At the same forum and location, on 9 January 1711, Augustin Kemp was burnt in the hand and sentenced to six months' hard labour in the house of correction at Acle. At the quarter sessions for the county held at Norwich in January 1718, William Wade, Robert Rix, and Richard Turner were convicted of grand larceny and received the same disposal. However, Benjamin Brooks and Gilbert Bacon were more fortunate. After being convicted at these sessions, they pleaded their clergy, were burnt in the hand, and immediately discharged.

By contrast, in the first eighteen years of the eighteenth century, the Suffolk County Quarter Sessions appear to have been slightly more nervous about hearing indictments for grand larceny. Petty larcenies were regularly prosecuted before them, as elsewhere in England, if only at an average rate of about two cases per session. For example, at the quarter sessions held at Beccles in April 1713, Samuel Bury was convicted of petty theft, flogged in the marketplace and discharged. At the same forum in January 1720, two men stood trial for the same crime, the only "mainstream" criminal offences heard on that occasion. Only one, Charles Singlar, was convicted. He was flogged the following day until his back was "bloody."[130] Many of these cases produced guilty pleas. A few defendants were described as being indicted "for felony" as well as petty larceny (technically also a felony), but nearly always merely punished by a whipping if convicted, suggesting a single count.

Nevertheless, there was clearly no local practice precluding clergyable grand larceny from being heard at the Suffolk Quarter Sessions, as in 1713 John Kerridge and two other men were indicted for the crime at those held at Ipswich, convicted, and "burnt in the hand for the same." They were then discharged.[131] This was not the only such case heard during the first two decades of the century. It seems that in Suffolk JPs were simply more reluctant to hear such cases than their Norfolk cousins. Instead, they normally preferred to refer them on to assizes for trial.

This situation changed throughout the country after 1718. Transportation for seven years, rather than custody, quickly became the favoured method of dealing with those convicted of the crime. It may be that in the ensuing decades this was felt to be rather too drastic a punishment to be imposed at the lower forum, while continuing to use the 1706 Act fell out of fashion at the inferior jury court, perhaps for reasons of cost. By the second quarter of the eighteenth century, the rule of thumb was that petty theft and misdemeanours went to the lower jury court, simple grand larceny and other felonies went to the higher forum. This pattern was normally found in both Norfolk and Suffolk, the special borough jurisdictions of Lynn and Yarmouth apart. It also accorded with the recommendations set out in most legal texts of the period. As Giles Jacob noted in 1736, "Justices, in their sessions, might originally hear and determine Felonies; but they at this time only try petty larcenies, other felonies being of course tried at the Assizes."[132]

In any event, for several decades after about 1720 the county quarter sessions appear to have heard very few cases of the more serious form of larceny, and this marked the nadir of their jurisdiction during the century. They continued to hear cases of petty theft on a regular basis, while the practice of undervaluing what were, in reality, cases of grand

130. SRO QS B/105/2014, p. 81 and p. 87.
131. SRO QS B/105/2014, p. 90.
132. G. Jacob, *Every Man His Own Lawyer*, 1736, p. 401.

larceny so that they could be dealt with as cases of petty theft may have received a boost after 1718, when transportation was, in theory, made available for the lesser form of larceny (albeit not commonly used in such cases in East Anglia).

In the third quarter of the eighteenth century, a further change became apparent in many parts of England, albeit with greatly varying degrees of completeness and speed. Quarter sessions in counties as diverse as Kent and Cheshire started to deal with cases of grand larceny again on a fairly regular basis. For example, there were no grand larceny cases at the Surrey quarter sessions in the five years prior to 1752. Within the next five years, over half of all such cases heard in the county were being determined at this forum.

Change was slower in some other parts of England. The Oxfordshire quarter sessions did not hear a case of grand larceny in the years after 1750 until 1768.[133] This broadly matches the situation in Suffolk. Until the mid-1760s, the county's quarter sessions were reluctant to hear any cases of grand larceny. Typically, at the sessions held on 14 January 1765, the theft of a watch was sent on to the assizes for determination.[134] However, the first case of grand larceny heard at this forum for many years appears to have followed just days later. On 16 January 1765, William Wilson was indicted and pleaded guilty to the crime, for which he was sentenced to seven years' transportation.[135] Other cases followed. At the quarter sessions held at Ipswich a year later, on 18 January 1766, William Brown pleaded guilty to stealing 33 ducks and was also sentenced to transportation.[136] Thereafter, grand-larceny prosecutions occurred quite regularly. Typically, at the Beccles Quarter Sessions held on 15 July 1782, James Aldredge was convicted of stealing a hempen shift from the guardians of the hundred of Wareford and sentenced to transportation.[137] At the same forum in April 1783, William Aldred was convicted of grand larceny after stealing wheat from Richard Knights. He was sentenced to transportation to the King's settlements in Africa for seven years (although only 200 men from the

133. Email from Anne-Marie Kilday on 21 October 2014.
134. SRO QS B105/2/39, p. 42.
135. SRO QS B105/2/39, p. 43.
136. SRO QS B105/2/39, p. 47.
137. SRO QS B105/2/47, p. 22.

entire country ever made this journey).[138] A similar process occurred in Norfolk, even quite significant thefts eventually ending up in the lower jury court. In July 1780 Elizabeth Adams was tried and acquitted at the Norfolk quarter sessions of stealing a silk cloak.[139]

Some counties took even longer to extend the de facto jurisdiction of their quarter sessions. In Sussex the first convictions for grand larceny appear to occur in 1780 (there being none during the previous five years).[140] In Cambridgeshire (the Isle of Ely was a separate jurisdiction), the county quarter sessions did not consider a case of grand larceny until January 1791, and it was not until Edward Gibson was tried in 1799 that a conviction for the full offence was secured.[141] Nevertheless, this was unusual. By the 1760s William Blackstone could note that quarter sessions were normally willing to try "small felonies within the benefit of clergy."[142] In the final decades of the eighteenth century, most English quarter sessions took a significant share of the less serious cases of grand larceny in the county.

This change does not seem to have occurred as a result of a central government directive. The post-1748 surge in prosecutions following demobilisation after the end of the War of the Austrian Succession may have contributed to the process. The gradual expansion of summary offences that involved an element of theft (although in very specific circumstances) could also have made it appear incongruous not to hear grand-larceny cases at quarter sessions.[143]

Employing quarter sessions had many advantages for theft complainants. They were often geographically closer, and so cheaper and easier to use, and they sat more frequently than did the assizes, making them more convenient. They also had ample powers to punish larceny, so that they were used by prosecutors who were aware that going to quarter sessions

138. SRO QS B105/2/47, p. 41.
139. *Norfolk Chronicle*, 15 July 1780.
140. S. Wilson, "The Court of Quarter Sessions and Larceny in Sussex, 1775–1820," 1986, p. 75.
141. CRO Q/SO 11, p. 76.
142. W. Blackstone, *Commentaries on the Laws of England*, vol. 4, 1769, p. 268.
143. J. M. Beattie, *Crime and the Courts In England 1660–1800*, 1986, pp. 284–287.

was: "attended with less expense and loss of time than the former, and wishing for nothing more than the transportation of the offender."[144]

Interestingly, Thomas Gisborne thought that indictable matters that might have gone to either jury forum were often punished more severely at quarter sessions than at assizes during the latter years of the century because presiding magistrates were more likely than the Westminster judges to be aware of a convict's antecedents and bad character.[145] The case of Benjamin Salmon is instructive in this regard. Salmon was convicted at the Suffolk Quarter Sessions in January 1774 for stealing a leg of mutton from one Brazillia Hare of Woolverstone. He was sentenced to seven years' transportation.[146] This was quite severe for a modest appropriation of food, even if it was meat. However, the previous month, Salmon had been arrested and committed to gaol "on suspicion" of involvement in a vicious robbery. John Talmarsh, a farmer, had been returning from market to his home in St Mary Stoke when he was "knocked down and terribly bruised" by a footpad. His pockets had been rifled and more than 3 guineas taken.[147] It is likely that this charge could not be made to stick, leading the authorities to seek an alternative that would stand up in court. The punishment reflected an offence for which he had not been indicted, let alone convicted (something that was beginning to occasion concern in the wider nation).

Despite these developments, quarter sessions continued to send serious or difficult cases of dishonesty that had been sent to them by examining justices to the higher jury court if they did not feel "comfortable" about dealing with them. For example, in 1781, at the Norwich Quarter Sessions, John and William Dunt, who were accused of stealing a linen bag, a book, razors, and tools from three people, and Mary Wilsea, accused of stealing a cask of butter, were all left for trial at the higher forum.[148] Similarly, in 1783 the Suffolk Quarter Sessions concluded that David Aaron's alleged offence of stealing from the wagon of a Diss carrier was

144. T. Gisborne, *An Enquiry Into the Duties of Men in the Higher and Middle Classes of Society in Great Britain*, 1794, pp. 301–302.
145. Ibid., p. 301.
146. *Ipswich Journal*, 22 January 1774.
147. *Public Advertiser*, 14 December 1773.
148. *Norfolk Chronicle*, 3 February 1781.

too grave for them to determine, and ordered that he remain in custody to take his trial at the following assizes at Thetford.[149]

Borough Sessions

Complicating matters, England had almost 200 incorporated boroughs of various sizes. During the medieval period, the municipal corporations for many of these towns, keen to increase their autonomy, had sought and been granted authorisation by charter to hold their own sessions of the peace before a jury. Thus, King's Lynn, in Norfolk, had first been allowed to do this by a charter granted in 1204, while Aldeburgh, in Suffolk, obtained the right to do so under a charter issued as late as 1529. At the same time, medieval corporations had often attempted to exclude the wider county authorities from excessive involvement in their own internal affairs. As a result, borough sessions were entirely separate from county quarter sessions, albeit that they were similar in appearance, and acted as their urban equivalents. As Blackstone noted, such borough sessions normally had "exactly the same authority as the general sessions of the county."[150]

Borough sessions were usually heard in front of magistrates drawn from the local corporation. In 1784 the visiting François de la Rochefoucauld was well aware that there were "two kinds of Justices of the Peace" in Suffolk (and England). Some had a jurisdiction confined to a specific town and an authority that could last only a year, as it was linked to temporary political office (though this was not always the case). Others had a jurisdiction that extended throughout the county, and were appointed for life by the Crown.[151] The former were the borough justices, the latter, of course, those for the county. It was possible to hold both positions simultaneously, but this was fairly rare.

In Norfolk borough sessions were held at Norwich, King's Lynn, Thetford, and Yarmouth. In Suffolk they were conducted at Bury, Ipswich, Southwold, Sudbury, Harwich, Eye, Orford, Aldborough, and tiny

149. Ibid., 11 October 1783.
150. W. Blackstone, *Commentaries on the Laws of England*, vol. 4, 1769, p. 269.
151. N. Scarfe, *A Frenchman's Year in Suffolk*, 2011, p. 86.

Dunwich. However, in many of these boroughs they were held much less frequently than four times a year during the eighteenth century. For example, in 1839 Robert Wake noted that "until lately" the borough sessions in Southwold had been held only once a year, though they were now convened on a quarterly basis (a statutory requirement after 1836).[152] The Dunwich sessions were also usually held just once a year (often in October), perhaps unsurprisingly given its size. Even in Ipswich the borough sessions were rarely held more than twice a year until the 1830s (the term "quarter sessions" first appears in the heading to the Sessions Roll there in April 1834). Even so, several of the large East Anglian boroughs, such as Bury, Lynn, and Yarmouth, held them just as regularly as their surrounding counties.

Slightly confusing for the modern observer, some of the county quarter sessions were held in towns that had their own borough sessions. Quarter sessions for Norfolk, for example, were regularly held at Great Yarmouth and King's Lynn. Similarly, three of the larger Suffolk boroughs, Ipswich, Bury, and Sudbury, had their own courts of borough sessions that were separate from the quarter sessions of the wider county that were also held within their limits.[153] Sometimes, in these situations, the venue for the two courts varied. In Norwich, for instance, quarter sessions for the city were usually held at the guildhall and those for the County of Norfolk were conducted at the nearby castle or shire hall. In some boroughs the same building was employed for both courts, albeit at different times. In King's Lynn the stone-and-flint guildhall was used for both forums, although St George's Hall in the town was also regularly used for county quarter sessions during the 1720s.

Prior to May 1836, when the Municipal Reform Act 1835 (5 & 6 Will. IV. c. 76) came into force, there was little consistency in the distribution of borough sessions and in their power to try crimes. Whether a town had its own sessions or not usually reflected its size or importance centuries earlier, rather than in the 1700s. Some boroughs had grown enormously in size and wealth since the medieval period, but without acquiring their own sessions. As a result, a few quite significant eighteenth-century towns

152. R. Wake, *Southwold and Its Vicinity, Ancient and Modern*, 2013, p. 128.
153. W. White, *History, Gazetteer, And Directory of Suffolk*, 1844, p. 27.

relied on county quarter sessions to determine middle and lesser-ranking matters that occurred within their bounds.

By contrast, some boroughs where sessions were held had shrunk over the centuries, so that several tiny municipalities still possessed such courts. Eye, in Suffolk, was among them. It had a population of just 1,000 people in 1700, and fewer than 2,000 in 1811.[154] Dunwich, on the Suffolk coast, was an even more extreme example. It may have been the smallest town in the entire country to hold borough sessions during the eighteenth century. Like its rotten-borough MPs, such sessions were a relic of the town's (literally) washed-away medieval glory days.[155] (In 1715 the Dunwich town gaol even fell into the sea, the result of the port's constant subjection to storm and coastal erosion).[156] In 1836 the town had only 232 residents.[157] Even so, a small number of lesser indictable crimes were heard at this forum over the years, although many sessions ended without any presentments being made.[158] Thus, in 1667 a local butcher named Thomas Spooner was given a fine of £5 for assaulting a town bailiff and was ordered to stay in prison until it was paid.[159] In October 1704 William Jessop, a Dunwich labourer, pleaded not guilty to stealing a beehive valued at ten pence (petty theft) but was convicted.[160] Almost a century later, in 1803, three more labourers were rather more fortunate when jointly accused of stealing a pipe stove (under) valued at ten pence, which was part of a locally wrecked ship. The Dunwich grand jury found that there was "no true bill" in this case, and the matter did not proceed to trial.[161] Of course, as with all such forums, many essentially administrative matters were also determined by the court. For example, in 1691 John Ead was tried and acquitted of exercising the trade of spicer in the town without qualification, contrary to the Elizabethan Statute of Apprentices.[162]

154. H. T. Dickinson, *A Companion to Eighteenth-century Britain,* 2006, p. 203.
155. SRO EE6/1144/120.
156. N. Gay, *Glorious Dunwich: Its Story Through the Ages*, 1947, p. 42.
157. Anon, *Penny Cyclopaedia of the Society For the Diffusion of Useful Knowledge*, 1836, p. 217.
158. SRO EE6/1144/122.
159. SRO EE6/1144/4.
160. SRO EE6/1144/5.
161. SRO EE6/1144/139/1.
162. SRO EE6/1144/6.

The wider county's degree of involvement in boroughs that had their own sessions varied considerably. Some boroughs had *non-intromittent* clauses in their commissions of the peace that excluded the county magistrates from any role in their proceedings, giving them an almost completely autonomous jurisdiction within their own bounds, something that they often guarded jealously. Others were, to some extent, under the supervision of the county quarter sessions.[163] In some English boroughs, the county even had a concurrent jurisdiction, allowing it to try matters from within the town boundaries that could also be heard at borough sessions (the doctrine of *autrefois acquit* prevented an adjudicated matter being tried again where this was the case). In others, the county could merely reconsider some (largely) administrative matters that had earlier been determined at borough sessions. Thus the Norwich justices had exclusive jurisdiction within their city, except in disputes as to settlement actions, where the Norfolk county JPs could overrule the city's magistrates. Similarly, in Ipswich, the borough general sessions were subject to little intervention by Suffolk JPs.[164]

Of course, borough magistrates could always leave difficult criminal cases to the assizes, and they were, if anything, more willing to do this than their county equivalents. For example, at the Bury Assizes, in 1782, Thomas Parker, and James Easy were tried for stealing lead off a church roof in Dunwich, although the latter had its own sessions. The verdict was eventually left for the legal opinions of the 12 judges in London, suggesting that their analysis of its complexity was correct.[165] As with the possession of borough sessions, there was little rhyme or reason as to those towns that had sessions that were almost entirely independent of the county quarter sessions and those which were not. Such variation was usually a matter of "accident or caprice" or reflected long-vanished historical factors and considerations.[166]

As La Rochefoucauld's comment suggests, borough justices were usually senior figures in their town government, men who were *ex officio* magistrates because they held, or had held, high municipal office. Most

163. B. Keith-Lucas, *The Unreformed Local Government System*, 1980, p. 28.
164. D. Allen et al, *Ipswich Borough Archives 1255–1835: A Catalogue*, 2000, p. 92.
165. *Norfolk Chronicle*, 27 July 1782.
166. Anon, *Penny Cyclopaedia of the Society For the Diffusion of Useful Knowledge*, 1836, p. 217.

commonly, they included the mayor (who often had a presiding role) and senior aldermen, burgesses, or jurats, depending on terminology (which varied around the country).

In Norfolk the mayor of Norwich, who was elected by its freemen on 1 May from amongst its 24 aldermen, was a "Justice of the quorum during his mayoralty, and afterwards Justice of the peace."[167] As this suggests, all Norwich aldermen who had previously been mayor were qualified to sit as magistrates, albeit that the serving mayor was the senior and most active justice for the city. Typically, in December 1781, when Philip Taylor was arrested on suspicion of stealing four silk handkerchiefs from a shop in Norwich, John Morse, the mayor, committed him to the city gaol.[168] Ostensibly, the mayor also presided over the city quarter sessions, although this was often under the *de facto* supervision of the city's legally qualified recorder or steward (the former's deputy), who were both barristers of at least seven years' standing.[169]

The Yarmouth borough sessions that opened on 17 July 1744 noted that the town had four "quorum" justices — the mayor, deputy mayor, recorder, and steward — and 13 non-quorum JPs.[170] A minimum of two magistrates had to be present at the towns powerful sessions, of whom at least one had to be from the quorum.[171] (Usually, far more men sat.) In King's Lynn the mayor normally sat with an alderman and other appointed magistrates. Similarly, the standard complement of justices for the Thetford Borough Sessions for much of the eighteenth century appears to have been the town mayor, recorder, and coroner, all of whom were *ex officio* JPs for the town. Thus, the proceedings that began there on 21 October 1751 were held before Mathew Smith, the mayor, Henry Cocksedge, the recorder, and John Walton, the coroner. The mayor would change regularly, if not annually, but the other two officeholders served for much longer. Cocksedge remained in place for many years until his death in 1762 (shortly before that, he helped Thomas Paine

167. C. Berry, *A Concise History and Directory of the City of Norwich; For 1811*, 1810, p. 43.
168. *Norfolk Chronicle*, 22 December 1781.
169. S. Renton, "The Moral Economy of the English Middling Sort in the Eighteenth-century: The Case of Norwich in 1766 and 1767," 1996, pp. 119–120.
170. SRO Y/S/ 2/1–4 MF 1031.
171. C. Parkin, *The History and Antiquities of Yarmouth, in the County of Norfolk*, 1776, p. 174.

get a position in the excise). Nevertheless, the borough sessions there were quorate with just two men. Thus on 7 May 1753, only the mayor and recorder were present, while on 18 April 1763 it was just the mayor and coroner.[172] Interestingly, although the town had the standard (for the era) division in its government between ten relatively elite aldermen and 20 slightly less prestigious common councilmen, the former do not normally appear to have sat at sessions.

In Suffolk the bailiffs and high steward (the equivalent of a mayor) of Southwold were *ex officio* justices of the peace for the town and presided over its fairly infrequent borough sessions, dealing with some of the assaults and minor thefts that took place within its boundaries. In these courts the town clerk, who was usually an attorney, would act as clerk of the peace (he would also be clerk to the magistrates when they sat in petty sessions).[173] Two bailiffs governed tiny Dunwich; during their year in office and in the succeeding year they were also JPs for the town. Many men served several times as bailiff, but not in successive years.[174] Being much bigger, Ipswich could field slightly larger benches; about five justices attended the general sessions at Ipswich in the years from 1721 to 1734, while only three or four normally sat in the 1750s and 1790s.[175]

The status of the men who were borough justices varied greatly. It should not be assumed that they were inferior in ability to those for the wider counties just because they usually held office by virtue of their political positions and were normally employed in trade rather than being landed men. In large or rich towns they were often affluent and well-educated individuals. In Norwich aldermen were required to have a property qualification of £10,000, and only those who had previously been mayor could serve as a magistrate. As a result, the city bench was almost entirely the preserve of wealthy merchants and manufacturers (though this was an extreme case.)[176]

172. NRO Quarter Sessions Minute Book for Thetford T/QS2.
173. B. Keith-Lucas, *The Unreformed Local Government System*, 1980, p. 23.
174. T. Gardner, *An Historical Account of Dunwich, Antiently a City, Now a Borough*, 1754, p. 87.
175. J. D. Clemis, *Government in an English Provincial Town: The Corporation of Ipswich, 1720–95*, 1999, p. 64.
176. S. Renton, "The Moral Economy of the English Middling Sort in the Eighteenth-century: The Case of Norwich in 1766 and 1767," 1996, p. 119.

The constraints on conduct imposed by conventions of gentlemanly behaviour were probably not so great amongst borough magistrates. Activity as a JP may also have been a more important ladder to local influence than it was for their county counterparts. This might explain why some of the provincial magistrates who were most active in criminal investigation during the second half of the eighteenth century were borough justices. John Hewitt, a Coventry alderman and magistrate, was one of them. He was so involved in detection that, when the celebrated metropolitan justice Sir John Fielding passed through Coventry in 1764, he met Hewitt and spent an evening with him discussing criminal law and investigations.[177]

However, it was also notorious that smaller, poorer, boroughs frequently found it difficult to produce men of sufficient quality and education to serve as magistrates for their quarter and petty sessions. Sometimes they depended on men engaged in relatively menial occupations to fill these positions.[178] Such men were often "shopkeepers or those engaged in mechanical trades," and their decisions could be influenced by a fear of losing custom or work.[179] A few borough justices, like those at Malmesbury, in Wiltshire, were reputed to be barely literate labourers.[180]

Fortunately, at borough sessions a legally qualified and formally appointed part-time recorder often assisted the mayor and magistrates on the bench, and in practice (if not always in theory) presided over hearings. Many of these men were successful lawyers in their own right, at least in the larger boroughs. For example, Sir William Thompson held the office of recorder of Ipswich between 1707 and 1739, during which time he was also an Ipswich MP, one of the Barons of the Exchequer, Solicitor General, and a notable recorder of London, the last of these giving him considerable (and unusual) expertise in criminal matters. In 1771 Humphrey Rant, a Cambridge graduate and barrister, became recorder of Harwich following the death of the Whig statesman and

177. J. Hewitt, *A Journal of the Proceedings of J. Hewitt*, 1790, p. 94 and p. 92.
178. Anon, *Penny Cyclopaedia of the Society For the Diffusion of Useful Knowledge*, 1836, p. 217.
179. T. Gisborne, *An Enquiry Into the Duties of Men in the Higher and Middle Classes of Society in Great Britain*, 1794, p. 303.
180. B. Keith-Lucas, *The Unreformed Local Government System*, 1980, p. 28.

barrister George Grenville.[181] Rant had been deputy recorder of the town since 1765.[182] He later became recorder of Ipswich. Similarly, in 1779 the mayor, aldermen, and capital burgesses of Sudbury appointed Arthur Murphy, a Lincoln's Inn barrister, as the town recorder after the death of George Weller Poley, his predecessor and an Inner Temple man.[183] More notably, in 1788 James Mingay was elected recorder of Aldeburgh after the death of William Mayhew.[184] Mingay (1752–1812), a one-armed alumnus of Thetford Grammar School, product of the Norfolk Circuit, and bencher of the Inner Temple, took silk at 34 and was thrice mayor of his home town. He was considered a "great and eminent lawyer."[185]

Many of the matters tried at borough sessions were of a regulatory nature, perhaps more so even than at county quarter sessions. For example, at those for King's Lynn there were dozens of instances of broken pavements, leaving a cart obstructing the King's highway, unlicensed hawking, selling ale without a licence, laying dirt or faggots in the streets, or keeping a disorderly house. Other cases were slightly more unusual. In 1733 John Bagge was indicted for common nuisance because his herd of 30 pigs were eating filth from drains, defecating in the streets, and producing "noisome and unwholesome smells." Traffic violations were particularly common in congested urban streets. Typically, in 1765 Edward Hayward was convicted at Sudbury and fined 20s for refusing to make way in his cart for the carriage of Edward Andrews.[186] Of the 32 matters that were put before the King's Lynn court on 10 August 1733, only two were what would be considered mainstream criminal offences in the modern era: one case of assault and one of petty larceny.[187]

Some boroughs even appear to have been reluctant to hold formal criminal hearings if these could be avoided, using other legal mechanisms or assizes to deal with local deviance. In the late 1720s the Ipswich Borough Sessions may have averaged just two contested trials a year. Thirty

181. *Public Advertiser*, 17 April 1771.
182. *Gazetteer and New Daily Advertiser*, 6 February 1765.
183. *St. James's Chronicle Or the British Evening Post*, 15–18 May 1779.
184. *St. James's Chronicle Or the British Evening Post*, 13–16 September 1788.
185. *Morning Chronicle*, 21 August 1794.
186. *Ipswich Journal*, 10 August 1765.
187. NRO, King's Lynn Sessions Book, KL/C 20/1.

years later, it was little more than one, although by the first half of the 1790s it had risen to an average of four a year.[188]

However, all borough sessions dealt with some mainstream criminal matters, whether misdemeanours, cases of petty theft, or even, towards the end of the period, minor clergyable felonies. Thus, at Thetford Borough Sessions on 18 April 1763 John Curry and two other men were prosecuted for assaulting Joseph Shepherd. They initially pleaded not guilty. However, at some point they reached a "cordial agreement" with Shepherd, presumably paying him compensation for his injuries. The three men then pleaded guilty and were fined just 3s 4d each as well as being required to give security to keep the peace for the following 12 months. At the Sudbury Borough Sessions held at the town Moot Hall in April 1782, Sarah Green was convicted of obtaining shoes by deception. She had asked for them in the name of respectable people (presumably cobblers). Green was whipped at the cart's tail as it was drawn around the local marketplace.[189] At the City of Norwich Quarter Sessions in May 1780, a man named Dublack was convicted of keeping a house of ill fame, and sentenced to stand in the pillory. His wife received a short sentence of imprisonment instead, because she was pregnant. Both were required to find two sureties of £50 for their good behaviour for the ensuing year.[190] Two months later, at the same forum, Hannah Blake was convicted of keeping a disorderly house in St Stephen's parish, and sentenced to stand in the pillory in the market, to serve a year in the city gaol, and to find two sureties of £50 for her future behaviour.[191]

As with county quarter sessions, the reluctance of borough sessions to hear mainstream criminal cases became slightly more muted in the latter stages of the century.[192] Prosecutions for petty theft (theft of goods with a real value of less than 1s) became more common. In January 1783 at the City of Norwich Quarter Sessions, a young man named Smart was convicted of stealing a greatcoat and sentenced to three months'

188. J D. Clemis, *Government in an English Provincial Town: The Corporation of Ipswich*, 1999, p. 64.
189. *Ipswich Journal*, 13 April 1782.
190. *Norfolk Chronicle*, 27 May 1780.
191. Ibid., 29 July 1780.
192. P. King, "Newspaper Reporting, Prosecution Practice and Perceptions of Urban Crime: the Colchester Crime Wave of 1765," 1987, p. 433.

imprisonment in the house of correction and to a public whipping.[193] More pertinently, a small number of cases of grand larceny were also heard at such forums. For example, at the Thetford Borough Sessions held in August 1781, Elizabeth Hubbard, was indicted for stealing a silver spoon valued at nine shillings belonging to a local surgeon, albeit merely convicted of petty theft.[194] In the same year, at the City of Norwich Quarter Sessions, Ann Crane was acquitted of stealing linen and a heater from a furnished lodging in St Laurence parish.[195] (This was a fairly common form of crime amongst women). A few people convicted of grand larceny were even transported from such forums. In 1789 John Symonds, the recorder of Bury, reported on the case of Elizabeth Edwards after her fitness for transportation to Australia was raised following her conviction for theft at the town's borough sessions.[196]

King's Lynn and Yarmouth

For a few eighteenth-century English towns and cities the historical legacy did not stop at a right to hold borough sessions. During the medieval period, various individuals and corporations, both lay and ecclesiastical, had at some time enjoyed (or at least claimed) judicial privileges that included "delivering" the local gaol, and so trying the most serious criminal offences that occurred within their bounds. Among them were Ipswich, Norwich, King's Lynn, Southwold, Thetford, and Yarmouth. In most cases these powers had gradually been ceded to the royal judges from the Westminster courts during the sixteenth century, as a result of economic and political pressure from the Crown.[197]

However, a few of these venues around the country had resisted, or at least not shared in, this process. As a result, nationally a handful of special borough sessions, such as those at Berwick, Bristol, Oxford, Tenterden, Lichfield, Canterbury, Rye, Sandwich, and Peterborough, had full power of gaol delivery, and continued to try small numbers of capital felonies

193. *Norfolk Chronicle*, 25 January 1783.
194. Ibid., 11 August 1781.
195. Ibid., 3 February 1781.
196. TNA HO 42/15/109, ff 353–355.
197. J. S. Cockburn, *A History of English Assizes, 1558–1714*, 1972, p. 27.

during the eighteenth century, even executing some of those found guilty. These trials were presided over by their recorders and magistrates, not the assizes judges, unlike cities such as Norwich that formed their own largely urban counties.

Suffolk had no towns with such special powers. However, in Norfolk the borough sessions at both King's Lynn and Yarmouth, two important ports, fell into this unusual category. As Daniel Defoe noted of Yarmouth in the 1720s, "They have particular privileges in this town, and a jurisdiction by which they can try, condemn, and execute in especial cases."[198] These powers were often exercised at special borough sessions with power of gaol delivery that were held just once or twice a year, rather than at all four of the quarter sessions conducted in the two towns. Their jurisdiction included a small rural hinterland, not merely the built-up area of the towns. Thus, in 1748 Lawrence Lee was sent to Yarmouth Gaol to await trial at its sessions after committing a highway robbery on a piece of road "within the jurisdiction of that corporation."[199]

The existence of such special powers did not necessarily preclude a matter's going to the assizes, instead of being tried locally, at least in some towns. For example, in 1743 John Breads became the only person to be executed after capital conviction for murder at the Rye Borough Sessions, in Kent, during the eighteenth century. He was also the first person to be hanged there for more than a century, and it was noted that had the mayor not been so jealous of, and keen to preserve, the town's "ancient privileges," Breads would have been sent to the county assizes for trial.[200]

During the eighteenth century, the borough courts at Yarmouth and Lynn periodically hanged those convicted of capital offences. Such cases would normally be presided over by a bench of at least three justices and, most important, their legally qualified recorder. For example, Henry Jodrell (1750–1814), the recorder of Yarmouth from 1792 to 1813, a Lincoln's Inn barrister, and MP for the town from 1796 to 1802, was present in November 1792 when special sessions were held to try several prisoners for capital offences arising out of riots in the town the previous

198. D. Defoe, *A Tour Through the Whole Island of Great Britain*, 1978, p. 92.
199. *Remembrancer (1747)*, 20 August 1748.
200. *Universal Spectator and Weekly Journal*, 18 June 1743.

month. The mayor, deputy mayor, local MP, and eight borough justices accompanied Jodrell on the bench. Although the mayor was, ostensibly, presiding over the trials, Jodrell gave the charge to the grand jury and dominated proceedings; this was probably fortunate, as senior counsel represented both the Crown and defendants.

In total, seven death sentences, resulting in five confirmed executions, were passed at borough sessions held at King's Lynn between 1735 and 1799. Several more occurred earlier in the century, including the double execution of a brother and sister in 1709. Thus, in January 1783 Joseph Beeton was capitally convicted at the Lynn borough sessions for robbing the mail, after a trial lasting six hours, and subsequently hanged in the town. Some observers thought the "sentence of death passed on him by the Recorder of Lynn, did great credit to him as an able Judge."[201] This was the last execution there during the eighteenth century.[202] The last man to be capitally convicted at the Lynn sessions and then hanged (the first for almost 30 years) was Peter Donahue, a sergeant in the 34th Regiment of Foot, who was convicted of knowingly circulating forged Bank of England £2 notes in 1801. He met his death in a "manly" fashion, acknowledging the legality of his sentence. He was married, with three children, including a newborn baby. Some local people viewed his sentence as slightly harsh, as it was felt that there was no need for such easily forged notes still to be in circulation. A group of women from the town raised money to support his widow and orphans.[203]

In Great Yarmouth, six people were executed (four for homicide offences, the other two for highway robbery) after ten capital convictions before the town borough sessions during the same period (1735–1799), and several others earlier in the century. One of them was Elizabeth Thompson, hanged in 1736 for murdering a Dutchman in a local tavern.[204] The last capital conviction at this forum that was not reprieved took place as late as 1813, when John Hannah was executed for strangling his wife.[205] He was hanged on the North Denes, an area of beach

201. *Norfolk Chronicle*, 25 January 1783.
202. *General Evening Post*, February 22–25 February 1783.
203. *The Bury and Norwich Post*, 18 November 1801.
204. *Daily Gazetteer*, 22 June 1736.
205. *The Ipswich Journal*, 24 April 1813.

outside what had been the town walls, and his body given to local surgeons for dissection.[206]

Great Yarmouth and King's Lynn sessions lost the power to impose death sentences only in May 1836, when the 1835 Municipal Reform Act (5 & 6 Wm. IV, c.76), came into force, limiting all borough sessions to trying the same crimes as county quarter sessions, although it had not been exercised in either town for many years prior to that date.

In seventeenth-century Yarmouth the power to execute had (apparently) sometimes been exercised without waiting for a death warrant from above.[207] However, throughout the eighteenth century the capital convictions of both ports were subject to close review from London, as were those from assizes, with the two town recorders being asked to comment on any local petitions for clemency to the Privy Council. For example, in 1813 Henry Jodrell gave his views on petitions made on behalf of Robert Gilbert, one of them by 56 people from Great Yarmouth, including its mayor and "principal inhabitants." Gilbert had been capitally convicted of burglary at the general sessions held in the town in September 1813. He was recommended for a reprieve on condition of transportation for life.[208]

Many more convictions for serious offences that did not result in executions were returned at both Yarmouth and Lynn during the eighteenth century, either because capital matters were reprieved (usually on condition of transportation) or, much more commonly, because the offences were clergyable. For example, at the Yarmouth Borough Sessions that opened on 12 July 1748, Sarah Jubs, a local spinster, was accused of stealing a silver teaspoon and other items. She pleaded not guilty but was convicted to the value of one shilling (only one penny over the limit for petty theft). She was sentenced to seven years' transportation to America. Thomas Webb was more fortunate. Accused of stealing two shirts valued by their owner at three shillings, along with other goods worth more than one shilling, he was convicted to the value of eleven pence (the limit of petty theft) and sentenced to the standard whipping.[209] In

206. *The Morning Post*, 13 September 1813.
207. D. Defoe, *A Tour Through the Whole Island of Great Britain*, 1978, p. 92.
208. TNA HO 47/47/24, ff 192–198.
209. NRO Y/S/ 2/1–4 MF 1031.

September of the same year, at the same forum, another woman was "cast for transportation" after conviction for grand larceny.[210]

As with death sentences, the recorders of Lynn and Yarmouth would be consulted by the Crown about applications for a reprieve from any sentence of transportation passed in their towns. Thus, in 1786 John Chamber, the recorder of Yarmouth, was asked for his views on a petition by Sir John Wodehouse on behalf of Roger Page, a bricklayer's labourer from Ludham, in Norfolk, who had been convicted of grand larceny at the town borough sessions in September 1785 after stealing a silver timepiece valued at 38s from a local watchmaker. Page had been sentenced to seven years' transportation. In light of his youth (he was 19), a previous good character that was vouched for by the minister and principal inhabitants of Ludham, and a recommendation from the trial jury for mercy, the recorder supported his application.[211]

Perhaps slightly worryingly, it appears that there was no legal requirement in either location that the town recorder be present for sessions to take place, and such sentences to be passed, even though this was normal practice. As late as 1785, it seems that the mayor of King's Lynn, William Bagge, presided over the town borough sessions unaided after the recorder for the town fell ill, and passed a sentence of transportation on John Bradley and another male convict.[212]

Whether the level of legal attainment of the recorders in either town (usually slightly lower than that of the assizes judges) made a significant difference to the quality of justice meted out at these forums is not clear. Nearly all of those executed in the two towns during the century were hanged for very serious offences. However, in 1750 25-year-old Charles Holditch was executed following conviction for burglary at King's Lynn after entering his father's house, and stealing money and goods worth just eight shillings and seven pence. This might, at first sight, appear rather draconian.[213] Nevertheless, Charles was of previous bad character and was believed to have carried a knife during the crime, possibly intending to

210. *Penny London Post Or The Morning Advertiser*, September 26–28 September 1748.
211. TNA HO 47/5/82.
212. W. Richards, *The History of Lynn: Civil, Ecclesiastical, Political, Commercial*, vol. 2, 1812, p. 1210.
213. *London Evening Post*, 13 March 1750; *Whitehall Evening Post Or London Intelligencer*, 1–3 March 1750.

kill his father had he not been prevented from doing so by the presence of a child in the same room.[214] He appears to have made admissions to this effect to the clergyman who ministered to him prior to execution.

There were also allegations of excessive leniency. In 1795 one of these prompted the recorder of Lynn to sue William Curtis for criminal libel at the Norwich Assizes. Curtis had published a pamphlet, *Lynn Law,* in which he claimed that the recorder who had presided over sessions when Curtis indicted a Captain Partridge for assault had shown malice, bad faith, and bias in office. Partridge had knocked Curtis's hat off in a local playhouse when he failed to remove it during the national anthem, and then issued a challenge. Although Partridge was convicted, the recorder merely fined him one shilling on one count and £10 on the other, a penalty that Curtis thought woefully inadequate. (The recorder succeeded in his *nisi prius* action at Norwich).[215]

Trial on Indictment before Assizes

Yarmouth and King's Lynn apart, all serious crimes in Norfolk and Suffolk were heard at the twice-yearly assizes. For the purposes of these courts, England was divided into six circuits (clusters of adjoining counties). Only the three palatinates of Lancaster, Durham, and Chester, along with Middlesex and the City of London, were outside this system. Thus Northumberland was part of the Northern Circuit, and Cornwall was situated in the Western Circuit. Gloucestershire could be found on the Oxford Circuit, Essex in the Home Circuit, and Lincolnshire was part of the Midland Circuit. Both the East Anglian counties under consideration were on the Norfolk Circuit, which, despite its name, included Bedfordshire, Buckinghamshire, Cambridgeshire, Huntingdonshire, and the City and County of Norwich. The last of these was an urban assizes county, covering the city and a tiny hinterland. Its small size meant that it usually tried significantly fewer cases than the surrounding Norfolk county jurisdiction. Indeed, at the City of Norwich Assizes in August

214. H. J. Hillen, *History of the Borough of King's Lynn*, vol. 2, 1907, p. 51.
215. *Oracle and Public Advertiser*, 7 August 1795.

1747, there was no need to empanel a petty jury at all, as there were "no prisoners to be tried."[216]

Twice a year, during Lent and in the summer, a pair of judges, usually drawn from the dozen members of the three Westminster courts (Common Pleas, King's Bench and Exchequer) would leave the capital and ride one of the six circuits over a period of several weeks. They would spend a few days in the assizes town in each county hearing local criminal and civil cases (empowered under temporary commissions of, *inter alia*, gaol delivery and *oyer and terminer*) before moving on to their next destination. At the same time, the judges passed on the concerns of central government to local elites and listened to their concerns. For example, in 1717 the Norfolk Circuit had one of the country's three highest judges (the Lord Chief Justice, Chief Justice, and the Lord Chief Baron) as part of its judicial pair. In this case it was Lord Chief Baron Bury, the senior judge for the Court of Exchequer.[217] One of the nine ordinary, or puisne, judges who sat at the Westminster courts partnered him.

If there were not enough judges available to cover all the circuits, due to their being engaged on other business, illness or infirmity, their numbers might be supplemented, on an ad hoc basis, by experienced serjeants-at-law drawn from what was technically the senior legal profession.[218] This was a fairly regular occurrence throughout the era. For example, at the Norfolk Assizes in 1775, Serjeant Whittaker accompanied Mr Justice Willes, "Lord Chief Justice de Grey being indisposed."[219] Similarly, Serjeant Simon Le Blanc accompanied Sir William Ashurst for the whole of the Norfolk Circuit during the Lent Assizes of 1788.[220]

Like the ordinary judges, serjeants could sit on both civil and criminal cases at assizes. Serjeant Raby, for example, who was also the Newgate deputy recorder, and therefore unusually experienced in criminal matters, went on the Norfolk Circuit in 1724.[221] Presumably he took many of the hearings determined on the Crown side. Similarly, at the Thetford

216. Gray's Inn MS 45.
217. *Post Boy (1695)*, July 6, 1717–July 9, 1717.
218. J. S. Cockburn, *A History of English Assizes, 1558–1714*, 1972, pp. 120–127.
219. *Morning Post and Daily Advertiser*, 22 August 1775.
220. *The Times*, 28 March 1788, p. 3.
221. *Daily Post*, 16 July 1724.

Assizes in 1803, "Serjeant Sellon tried most of the prisoners."[222] By contrast, at the Bury Assizes in 1813, Sir Nash Grose was aided by Serjeant Marshall "as assistant judge in the absence of Sir J. Mansfield." Marshall took the civil *nisi prius* hearings on this occasion.[223]

The judges' travelling itinerary on the Norfolk Circuit changed relatively little over the course of the eighteenth century. In the summer of 1701 they began at Buckingham, moved on to Bedford then went via Huntingdon, Cambridge, and Bury, to Norwich, before returning to London.[224] In 1713 the sequence was the same, except that the circuit started and finished two weeks earlier and used Aylesbury rather than Buckingham for the Buckinghamshire assizes.[225] During the Lent Assizes for 1736, Lord Chief Justice Reeves (Common Pleas) and Mr Baron Tempson (Exchequer) were scheduled to begin their circuit at Aylesbury on 8 March. They then went via Bedford, Huntingdon, and Cambridge to Thetford, where they were due to start their Norfolk cases on 18 March. They would finish off their tour by sitting at Bury four days later, returning to London a few days after this.[226] Exactly the same sequence of counties, towns, and cities, and almost the same timings (with the addition of an extra day at Thetford), was followed 50 years later, when Lord Chief Justice Loughborough and Mr Justice Nares (both from Common Pleas) covered the circuit at the same time of year.[227] Occasionally this order might be reversed, especially early in the century. For example, in March 1712 Bury was the first location and Thetford the second, followed by Cambridge, Huntingdon, and Bedford, and finishing at Aylesbury.[228] In 1723 the Lent Circuit started in Thetford, then moved on to Bury, Cambridge, Huntingdon, and Bedford, and finished at Buckingham.[229]

222. *The Bury and Norwich Post,* 30 March 1803.
223. *The Bury and Norwich Post: Or, Suffolk, Norfolk, Essex, Cambridge, and Ely Advertiser*, 31 March 1813.
224. *London Gazette*, 3–7 July 1701.
225. *British Mercury*, 9–16 June 1714.
226. *Weekly Miscellany (1732)*, 14 February 1736.
227. *London Gazette*, 14–18 February 1786.
228. *British Mercury*, 6–8 February 1712.
229. *Freeholder's Journal*, 20 February 1723.

The amount of time taken varied slightly, according to caseloads, and increased a little over the years. However, the first and last day of hearings on the circuit would normally be separated by less than three weeks. The judges would usually travel together, but in exceptional circumstances they might split up temporarily. For instance, in 1805 one judge left Bury for Thetford ahead of another who had been delayed there presiding over a complicated civil case on the *nisi prius* side, which required a few hours more.[230]

Even at the start of the period, not everyone approved of the assizes system. Timothy Nourse thought that having local judges who sat in county towns at least once a month would be superior to using twice-yearly itinerant judges. It would mean that large numbers of people were not kept in custody, at great expense, in a dangerous and corrupting environment, for long periods before trial. It would also mean that fewer men were held in prison at any one time, reducing the risk that they would band together in an escape attempt (a common occurrence). Nourse also thought that the regular execution of single felons would have a greater deterrent effect than twice-yearly hangings of several convicts at the same time, as sometimes occurred. Furthermore, inmates would have less time before trial to fabricate defences and arrange perjured witnesses.[231] This last concern was not an entirely idle fear. In 1788, after Henry Sell was sentenced to death for murdering his employer's wife, he admitted that the defence that he had run at trial, which was to blame his master for the killing, was unfounded. He claimed a fellow prison inmate, Joseph Saunders, who was awaiting trial for highway robbery, had suggested it to him.[232]

In a period when prosecutors often valued legal convenience, felonies that had been committed immediately before an assizes was held were much more likely to be indicted than those that occurred just after a sessions finished, the gravest cases apart. For example, the great majority of prosecuted shoplifting cases on the Northern Circuit during the century after 1726 occurred within three months of the biannual sessions' taking

230. *The Bury and Norwich Post: Or, Suffolk, Norfolk, Essex, and Cambridge Advertiser*, 7 August 1805.
231. T. Nourse, *Campania Folix. Or, a Discourse of the Benefits and Improvements of Husbandry*, 1706, p. 289.
232. *The Times*, 21 March 1788, p. 3.

place, many of them within the four weeks immediately preceding the assizes being held, so that complainants would not have to wait a long time for their hearings to come on. (During the latter part of the era some older cases may have been diverted to more convenient sittings of quarter sessions).[233]

Although travel on the Norfolk Circuit was usually less arduous than that on the Northern or even Western Circuits, it could still be difficult, especially in winter, and particularly at the start of the period, when roads were still largely unimproved. For example, at the Lent Assizes for the Norfolk Circuit in 1693 Mr Justice Rokeby noted that, after a heavy snowfall, he had hired a coach and six (rather than four) horses for transport "by reason of ye badness of ye ways."[234]

In Suffolk both of the year's assizes were usually heard at Bury St Edmunds, as they had been since 1584.[235] However, in an emergency a change of venue might be necessary. In March 1694 a specially improvised courtroom was used in Stowmarket (never previously employed for assizes), because there was an outbreak of smallpox at Bury and "ye Country was afraid of coming there."[236] A temporary booth was constructed at a cost of £14, with the judges' dinners being held at the Greyhound Inn in the town.[237] Ipswich, which had been used for assizes in the medieval period, was also occasionally pressed into service, as occurred in 1740; again, this was because of an outbreak of smallpox in Bury.[238] In 1796 it was claimed that between 1738 and 1743 the threat posed by this disease had been so severe that the assizes had been held at this venue on two or three occasions.[239]

In many respects it seemed to make sense to use Ipswich far more regularly, not least because it was the county town. In March 1690 it was noted that attempts had been made for some years, and "in all likelihood will be in the future," to persuade the Westminster judges

233. S. G. Tickell, *Shoplifting in Eighteenth-century England*, 2015, p. 54.
234. T. Rokeby, *The Diary of Mr Justice Rokeby*, 1887, p. 24.
235. F. Meeres, *A History of Bury St Edmunds*, 2010, p. 86.
236. T. Rokeby, *The Diary of Mr Justice Rokeby*, 1887, p. 39.
237. D. Allen, "Daniel Browninge of Crowfield; A Little-known High Sheriff of Suffolk and the Stowmarket Assizes of 1695," 1997, pp. 39–40.
238. F. Meeres, *A History of Bury St Edmunds*, 2010, p. 115.
239. S. Irvine, *Surgeons and Apothecaries in Suffolk: 1750–1830*, 2011, p. 197.

to hold at least one of the two Suffolk assizes there permanently. However, such proposals were always strongly resisted by the authorities in Bury St Edmunds. They were adamant that their shirehouse was a much more suitable trial venue than its equivalent in Ipswich. Even so, they appreciated that Bury could not take this state of affairs for granted. In March 1672 the corporation provided £15 for building new chambers at the shirehouse; it was feared that, if not built as "the judges expect, the assizes, as it is conceived, will be removed from the town." Eighteen years later, the corporation tried to encourage the continuance of its assizes by providing for the "generous entertainment of the judges and their associates." Local innkeepers, vintners, butchers, and bakers were urged to subscribe a reasonable sum of money to a fund set up for this purpose, something that, it was suggested, would "certainly return to their advantage."[240] This comment was a reflection of the trade that assizes hearings brought to local merchants.

Even so, the issue did not rest. In 1748 petitions from grand jurors, justices, gentlemen, and clergymen assembled at the county quarter sessions held at Beccles, Woodbridge, and Ipswich were presented to the House of Commons. They complained about the "extraordinary and unnecessary expense" occasioned by holding both Suffolk assizes in Bury, and asking that the Summer Sessions should always be held at Ipswich. Additionally, they argued that Ipswich was more convenient for trying people from the most populous (and so crime-prone) parts of the county, especially those located on the coast. They also claimed (less convincingly) that the town was easier for the Westminster judges to access when making their circuits. Perhaps most important, they pointed out that as the county gaol was located in Ipswich, prisoners often had to be taken from there to Bury for their trials. This was both costly and risky; in earlier decades, several had escaped on the way.[241] The last point was certainly true. The previous year one of the prisoners making the journey had been "rescued upon the road."[242] However, in practice many

240. Anon (Historical Manuscripts Commission), "The Corporation of Bury St. Edmunds: Minute-books (1652–1835)," 1895, pp. 144–155.

241. Anon, *Votes of the House of Commons, in the 2° Session of the 10th Parliament of Great Britain Appointed to Meet at Westminster the Tenth day of November 1747*, 1748, p. 131.

242. *Whitehall Evening Post Or London Intelligencer*, 15–18 August 1747.

prisoners were kept in the Bury gaol pending assizes, especially later in the period, reducing the extent of this problem. For example, of the 70 prisoners who went for trial at the Spring Assizes in 1801, 38 were held in Bury and just 32 in Ipswich.[243]

Despite such campaigns, opposition from Bury St Edmunds meant that it was not until well into the nineteenth century that one of the annual Suffolk assizes was regularly heard at Ipswich. In 1810 Robert Crockett failed in his petition to have assizes held at the county town. Similarly, in 1832 Rigby Watson MP unavailingly asked the House of Commons for permission to bring in a bill to remove the Summer Assizes from Bury to Ipswich.[244] However, from 1839 all Suffolk Summer Assizes were heard at Ipswich (the order was reversed 30 years later, when the county town took over the Lent sessions).

By contrast, Norfolk always had two assizes towns, Thetford and Norwich, both of which were normally used once each year. In the eighteenth century the Lent Assizes went to Thetford, while the Summer Assizes were heard at Norwich. In Thetford hearings were held in the town Guildhall, an impressive black flint building to which Sir Joseph Williamson, an MP for the town during the Restoration, had added a "fine court and Grand-Jury chamber" complete with a statue of Justice. (These were rebuilt in 1800). In the 1730s, the Westminster judges would normally lodge in a substantial mansion and former royal residence called the King's House, which was then owned by Sir John Woodhouse, the town recorder. In part this was because its large size made it "fit for the reception of much company." Largescale evening dinners for local dignitaries were an inherent part of every assizes.[245]

Norwich provided the location for the Summer Assizes in Norfolk. It also held assizes for the entirely separate City and County of Norwich. Both jurisdictions had their own carceral institutions. Norwich Castle had been the "publick gaol of the county of Norfolk" since at least the

243. F. Meeres, *A History of Bury St Edmunds*, 2010, p. 121.
244. House of Commons Sitting 3 July, 1832, *Hansard*, vol 14, cols. 49–50.
245. F. Blomefield, *The History of the Ancient City and Burgh of Thetford in the Counties, of Norfolk and Suffolk*, 1739, pp. 172–177.

fourteenth century.[246] It was used to house those awaiting trial (if they were not on bail) at both the county quarter sessions and its assizes, and would do so until 1887. However, the City of Norwich had its own "common gaol" for those destined for its assizes or quarter sessions. From 1597 to 1826 this prison was situated opposite the Guildhall, in what had been the Lamb Inn.

As with Suffolk, the use of an assizes' forum in Norfolk (Thetford) that was situated well away from the county gaol in Norwich Castle posed considerable logistical problems, albeit that Thetford was used only once a year. Prisoners awaiting assizes hearings in the market town were often detained in Norwich until just prior to trial, when they were taken to Thetford for their hearings, as occurred with the nine Norfolk men tried on assorted charges in March 1736.[247] The dungeon of the Thetford town gaol (its most secure area) was normally pressed into service during assizes week to accommodate them; the prison was sometimes almost empty outside this week.[248] As in Suffolk, the difference in location compromised security throughout the era.

Further complicating matters, those awaiting trial at the Norwich City and County Assizes were not sent to Thetford with the other prisoners during Lent, as their assizes could not, of course, be held outside the city, and the Westminster judges did not make an extra excursion to Norwich to accommodate them. This limited them to one occasion a year when their cases could be heard, so that, if detained at the wrong time in the cycle, the city "prisoners are often confined before their trials ten or eleven months." For example, Aaron Fakenham poisoned his wife in Norwich in September 1789 and was arrested almost immediately. He did not come for trial until the following July, being held in custody for almost a year before being convicted and hanged at Castle Ditches (the execution place for the jurisdiction).[249] It was partly for this reason that the prison reformer John Howard supported the mayor and

246. F. Blomefield, *An Essay Towards a Topographical History of the County Of Norfolk*, vol. iii, 1806, pp. 85–86.
247. *Daily Gazetteer* (London Edition), 23 March 1736.
248. J. Howard, *An Account of the Present State of the Prisons and Houses of Correction in the Norfolk Circuit*, 1789, p. 21.
249. *The Times*, 30 September 1789 and 3 August 1790.

citizens in their campaign to have the Lent Assizes for Norfolk moved from Thetford to Norwich (see below).[250]

The Norwich City and County Assizes hearings in the summer were conducted entirely separately, in a different court from those for the wider county and usually being held just before the latter. Typically, in August 1746 the judges started their trials at the City Assizes held in the medieval Norwich Guildhall (one of the largest city halls in the country), completed them on the same day, and then immediately moved to Norwich Castle, where they promptly began the Norfolk County Assizes.[251] (Later in the century the latter would be held in the nearby Shirehall).

Norwich was not unique in its status. Several other English provincial towns and cities were also counties in their own right, with assizes of varying degrees of activism, which usually opened just before or after those for the surrounding shire, and that were served by the same judges. Coventry, Lincoln, Leicester, Nottingham, Gloucester, Worcester, Poole, Southampton, York, Newcastle, Exeter, and Kingston-upon-Hull all fell into this category.[252] As with Norwich, several of them were also the seats of the assizes held for the surrounding county. Furthermore, the City of Norwich was not alone in having only one assizes a year. The four most remote counties of the Northern Circuit also held annual sessions, as did some of the towns listed above.

During the 1780s the mayor of Norwich petitioned Parliament to hold the County Assizes in his city twice a year and forgo those at Thetford.[253] He received considerable support from prominent people in both the city and wider county in his campaign. In 1796 the Norwich Corporation unanimously resolved to co-operate with the county magistracy in seeking this change.[254] However, when a bill was placed before Parliament in the same year, asking that the Lent sessions be moved to Norwich, the mayor and corporation of Thetford responded by sending a petition to the House of Commons, successfully arguing that they

250. J. Howard, *An Account of the Present State of the Prisons and Houses of Correction in the Norfolk Circuit*, 1789, pp. 18–19.
251. Gray's Inn MS 45.
252. B. Keith-Lucas, *The Unreformed Local Government System*, 1980, p. 38.
253. J. Howard, *An Account of the Present State of the Prisons and Houses of Correction in the Norfolk Circuit*, 1789, p. 18.
254. *Oracle and Public Advertiser*, 28 October 1796.

had been "held from time immemorial in the town of Thetford, and that removing them to Norwich would occasion great inconveniences to the North Western part of the county."[255] The bill failed.[256] It was not until 1832 that an Act of Parliament finally brought the move about and ended Thetford's glory days.[257]

The assizes were fairly major social occasions. They attracted a "vast concourse of people" from other parts of the county, including many members of the gentry.[258] They were so well-attended that four specialist hairdressers from Bath and London were present at Norwich during the Summer Assizes of 1771, 1773, and 1778, supplementing the work of local barbers.[259] In 1805 so many people attended the Thetford Assizes that there was "scarcely a bed being to be procured in the town."[260]

The sessions were marked by considerable ceremony, if only to uphold the majesty of the law. The assizes judges would be met after crossing the county borders and escorted into the relevant town or city by the high sheriff and his specially attired and armed "javelin men." In 1794, when Charles Purvis, the Suffolk High Sheriff, met the two county grand juries at Bury to discuss the heavy expense attendant on his position, it was unavailingly suggested that it was unnecessary that each new sheriff should personally be required to provide bailiffs and javelin men with liveries, javelins, hats, and stockings. Instead, it was proposed that these items should be replaced every five years, with serving sheriffs paying into a sinking fund to renew them.[261]

Before beginning their lists, the judges, robed in scarlet and ermine, would attend a service at the local parish church or cathedral, with the trumpeters, javelin men, court officers, sheriff, under-sheriff, and counsel in attendance. There they would listen to a special assizes sermon, usually delivered by a prominent clergyman from the area, on a religious and legal theme. For example, prior to the sessions at Bury in March

255. *Telegraph*, 6 December 1796.
256. Ibid., 2 January 1797.
257. W. White, *History, Gazetteer, and Directory of Norfolk,* 1845, p. 91.
258. M. Madan, *Thoughts On Executive Justice*, 1785, p. 24.
259. C. Rawcliffe and R. Wilson, *Norwich Since 1550*, 2004, p. 208.
260. *The Bury and Norwich Post: Or, Suffolk, Norfolk, Essex, and Cambridge Advertiser*, 20 March 1805.
261. Anon, *At a Meeting of the Grand Juries for the County of Suffolk ... For Taking Into Consideration the Present Very Heavy Expence That Attends Executing the Office of Sheriff*, 1795, pp. 1–2.

1708, the judges and other court personnel heard an edifying address from the Reverend George Raymond in which he finished by reminding them that all those concerned in the administration of justice "act before God, and for him; and are accountable unto him."[262] Almost a century later, at the same forum, the Reverend Samuel Kilderbee, the Suffolk sheriff's chaplain (and former Ipswich town clerk), delivered a sermon in which he "very appositely shewed, that our laws, when duly administered, were perfectly consonant with the divine religion of Jesus Christ." After hearing this, the judges immediately repaired to the shire-hall to begin the county assizes.[263]

The assizes had an important civil as well as criminal jurisdiction, that of *nisi prius*, which allowed trials to be conducted locally rather than at one of the three Westminster courts, although originally entered in the capital. For example, in *James v Bellinger*, heard at the Norfolk Assizes in 1794, a plaintiff successfully recovered £20 for libel.[264] Two years later, in *Rice v Tuby*, at the same forum, the plaintiff sought the return of 11 guineas he had paid for a colt that he had then rejected and returned without cause. His claim was dismissed by the trial jury, which decided that a "regular bargain in the usual way had been made."[265]

Criminal and civil matters would usually be heard simultaneously in adjacent courts, each one presided over by one of the two assizes judges. For example, at the Thetford Assizes in 1693, Mr Justice Rokeby presided over the civil cases during which he "entred 23 causes & tried 21."[266] The judges would often alternate between the *nisi prius* (civil) cases and the Crown side (criminal) matters, swapping with their coadjutors, from location to location, as they progressed around their circuit. Thus in 1746, at the Lent Assizes for Norfolk at Norwich, Sir Martin Wight presided over criminal matters, while a few days later at the Suffolk Assizes at Bury his colleague Sir James Reynolds was "on the Crown side."[267] At other times, personal preference, expertise, or seniority would influence allocation.

262. R. George, *Honour and conscience call'd upon: or, the duty of faithfulness and satisfying trust urg'd*, 1708, pp. 1–10.
263. *The Bury and Norwich Post: Or, Suffolk, Norfolk, Essex, and Cambridge Advertiser*, 7 August 1805.
264. *Morning Chronicle*, 12 September 1794.
265. *True Briton (1793)*, 3 August 1796.
266. T. Rokeby, *The Diary of Mr Justice Rokeby*, 1887, p. 25.
267. Gray's Inn MS 45.

Although civil cases were considered to be intellectually more demanding than criminal matters, if only because of the frequent presence of counsel, the case load was often slightly more modest than that found on the Crown side. This sometimes allowed the *nisi prius* judge to assist his colleague when he had finished his own list. Nevertheless, this was not always possible. At the Lent Assizes for Suffolk in 1788, it was noted that Serjeant Le Blanc (standing in for a Westminster judge) had "sat on the bench for the first time on this circuit on Saturday last, to assist the [other] judge in the trials of some of the prisoners." He had been too busy with civil causes prior to this point, even though Suffolk was the last stop on their circuit.[268]

One of the benefits of the circuit system was that the two paired judges might consult each other about difficult points of law or practice, if only over lunch or dinner. It also meant that, if one judge was suddenly indisposed, the other could deal with the most urgent matters, with the rest being adjourned to the following sessions. For instance, in August 1747, when Lord Chief Justice Willes arrived in Norwich, he was taken so ill that he could not sit, and half the scheduled criminal caseload had to be remitted to the following assizes at Thetford. His coadjutor sat on both sides at Norwich that month.[269] As a result, Daniel Mallows and his wife, Elizabeth, were eventually tried for poisoning Sarah Kimmin with arsenic at the Lent Assizes held at Thetford in 1748, rather than at Norwich six months earlier. This may have been for the best. In Norwich the populace was convinced of their guilt and physically attacked their carriage on its way to court.[270] However, both were acquitted when tried at Thetford.[271]

Although regulatory matters were much less important at assizes than at quarter sessions, they were not entirely absent from the higher forum. In 1764 George Hill appeared at the Norfolk Assizes at Thetford, accused of unlawfully exercising the trade of a baker. At the same forum, a decade later, John Ramsey was tried on indictment before a special jury for creating a public nuisance by building a coach house onto the back of New

268. *The Times*, 28 March 1788, p. 3.
269. *London Evening Post*, August 22, 1747–August 25, 1747.
270. *Old England*, 29 August 1747.
271. Gray's Inn MS 45.

Hall, in Yarmouth, a building he had leased from the town corporation. The jury—half of whom had had a view of the premises in question before reaching their decision—quickly found for the defendant, after concluding that the prosecution was unfounded and vexatious.[272] Rather more frequently, parishes were indicted and fined at assizes for failing to carry out repairs on their local highways.

Assizes courts could, of course, preside over lesser indictable crimes, whether misdemeanours or cases of petty theft. Sometimes these would be added to flesh out otherwise thin lists or because a minor offence had been committed conveniently close to the arrival of the Westminster judges. It was normal practice that such crimes should be tried in these forums only after the felony hearings had been completed, although there was no rule requiring this.[273] Thus four cases charged *ab initio* as petty theft were tried at sessions held at the three East Anglian assizes jurisdictions between the middle of 1734 and 1736, and this pattern continued during the remainder of the century. Some were extremely inconsequential, such as the alleged theft of a single rabbit listed for trial at the Bury Assizes in August 1794.[274] Most bizarrely of all, in July 1774, at the Bury Assizes, John Ellis and Abraham Merchant, a pair of labourers, were tried and acquitted of jointly stealing apples worth just 4d from Walter Waring.[275] Not only could this have been dealt with at quarter sessions, it might even have been triable summarily.

However, if the assizes were busy, judges would have no hesitation about remitting such cases to quarter sessions, as occurred with William Cook, who had been due to stand trial for petty theft at the Norfolk Assizes in March 1748.[276] Similarly, in 1801, when James Carter appeared at the Bury Assizes, accused of fraudulently obtaining money from John Branwhite of Lavenham (a misdemeanour), the matter was remanded to the lower court.[277]

272. *Public Advertiser*, 9 August 1774.
273. H. Twyford, *The Office of the Clerk of Assize*, 1676, p. 18.
274. Anon, *A Calendar of the Prisoners in the Custody of Margaret Baker, Keeper of his Majesty's Gaol of Bury St. Edmund's*, 1794, p. 1.
275. TNA ASSI 33/5.
276. Gray's Inn MS 45.
277. *The Bury and Norwich Post: Or, Suffolk, Norfolk, Essex, and Cambridge Advertiser*, 1 April 1801.

CHAPTER 5

Entering the Criminal Justice System

Introduction

Most felony (and some misdemeanour) defendants in East Anglia, as elsewhere in the country, entered the eighteenth-century criminal justice system by being arrested and then produced before a justice of the peace for examination. By contrast, lesser offenders were often summoned to appear before a magistrate, the document usually being served by a constable.

It has sometimes been suggested that a lack of investigative policing in the eighteenth century meant that a majority of serious criminals were caught red-handed.[1] Although this may have been true in the metropolitan area, far fewer suspects in the provinces were caught *in flagrante delicto* or even in the immediate aftermath of their crimes, owing to the relative absence of large numbers of people who were able to render swift assistance. For example, between 1748 and 1800, little more than a quarter of larceny defendants at the Essex Quarter Sessions had been "seen in the act."[2]

Nevertheless, many arrests were made within a short time of a crime being committed, whether by the victim, bystanders, or a parish constable who had been summoned to the incident. For example, in 1705, after William Gilbert butchered his wife and child in Norfolk, his brother-in-law and young nephew detained him almost immediately. Fortuitously, they had arrived on a visit just after the killing and seen large amounts

1. D. Lemmings, *The Journal of Legal History*, 2005, pp. 73–82.
2. P. King, *Crime, Justice, and Discretion in England 1740–1820*, 2003, p. 21.

of blood. They immediately doubted William's claim that his wife had killed their child and then herself while he was out. While the father held Gilbert, his son went for a local constable. This officer then "seized him for that night." Gilbert may have been secured in a cellar or village lockup. (Fifty years later, the highwayman Thomas Herring was held by his captors in a communal shared room at the *Red Lion* in Beccles.)[3] The next morning, the constable took Gilbert before a JP in King's Lynn, where he was examined and swiftly confessed to murder. He was then committed to Norwich gaol to await the forthcoming assizes, where he was convicted.[4]

Less gruesomely, in June 1715 John Frost, a Norwich sailor who was walking to Harwich to find a ship, went past a house in Bentley (Suffolk) where there were garments hanging on a hedge to dry. Frost helped himself to two shirts (a common form of theft), but was seen in the act. Although he dropped the clothes, his pursuers were not content merely with recovering them. They continued the chase until they caught him and then summoned a local constable. When apprehended, Frost quickly admitted the crime and repeated his confession to Devereaux Edgar after he was brought in for examination. Frost was then committed to the house of correction in Ipswich until the quarter sessions held the following month.[5] In 1740 Thomas Johnson from Beccles made a terrible mistake when burgling the home of a Norwich baker, as "contrary to his expectation, the family was not got to bed & he was taken." He had removed his coat and shoes and left them in the yard, making escape from the irritated occupants difficult.[6] Moving region, in 1768 the footpad James Earl robbed a man returning from market in Leicestershire. Just afterwards two fit young men happened to arrive on the scene. They immediately pursued Earl across the fields until he was captured.[7]

If felons were not captured red-handed they might be taken in the immediate aftermath of their crimes. For example, in 1748, Lawrence

3. *Read's Weekly Journal Or British Gazetteer*, 15 November 1755.
4. Anon, *The Wicked Husband, and Unnatural Father*, 1705, pp. 1–8.
5. SRO QS 347.96, *The Devereux Edgar Notebook*, transcribed by S. R. Schofield, 1956, vol. 2, p. 414.
6. *Norwich Gazette*, 7 March 1740.
7. *The Leicester Journal*, 24 December 1768.

Lee robbed a man named Alstron and another traveller on a highway near Yarmouth.[8] He then rode off towards nearby Gorleston. The next morning Alstron followed him there, describing his assailant and the (poor-quality) horse he had been riding. Local people quickly recognised the description, and said that such a man had entered their town at five am. Alstron swiftly located Lee's lodgings, found a constable, and together the two men arrested Lee while he was still in bed, after which they took him before a local justice, where Alstron swore positively to his identity as the robber.[9] (Lee was subsequently convicted and executed in Yarmouth.)[10] Similarly, the following year, when John Sullivan robbed Elizabeth Moon just outside Yarmouth and beat her unconscious, his capture was decidedly unsophisticated. As soon as Moon regained consciousness, she made her way to the town and reported the robbery. Several people then joined her search for Sullivan, and by chance met him in the street. Sullivan was seized and taken for examination before the town mayor, who committed him to gaol pending trial.[11] He, too, was convicted and executed.

A slightly more complicated case occurred in 1753, after William Mann separated 34 sheep from a flock that was on its way to market while they were still in Suffolk, and then offered them for sale at Ballingdon, just over the Essex border. He initially asked for eleven shillings an animal, but understandably was eager to get rid of them as quickly as possible, and swiftly reduced the price to the unusually low figure (for plump market-ready sheep) of five shillings and six pence each. This made the eventual purchaser suspicious, and he quickly came to believe that they had been stolen. He "charged a constable" with Mann, and, together they carried him before a local JP, who questioned him. Mann swiftly confessed to the theft. The owner of the animals and his shepherd (who had not yet missed the sheep) were sent for, and swore that 32 of them were the property of the former and two belonged to the latter.[12]

8. *Penny London Post or The Morning Advertiser*, 26–28 September 1748.
9. *Remembrancer (1747)*, 20 August 1748.
10. *General Advertiser (1744)*, 6 December 1748.
11. *General Advertiser (1744)*, August 29, 1749.
12. *Read's Weekly Journal Or British Gazetteer*, 4 August 1753.

Those without a personal connection to a crime might become involved in detaining suspects, especially if there was the possibility of a reward. In 1800 Sarah Lloyd was widely known to have been involved in a burglary-and-arson case at Hadleigh, in Suffolk. By chance Isaac Green saw her a few days later, some six miles from the crime scene. He knew she was a suspect, followed her through some fields, and made a citizen's arrest, despite her pleas that he let her go. He then forced her to accompany him to a nearby public house. From there he summoned both the local and the Hadleigh parish constable and saw her handed into the latter's custody. This officer, Thomas Simpson, questioned and searched Lloyd. She told him where the stolen goods were hidden, and these were recovered in her presence and later produced by Simpson as an exhibit. Lloyd was then taken before a magistrate, who examined her in the presence of his clerk, and committed her for trial at the assizes, where she was convicted.[13]

The "Hue and Cry"

A fleeing felon who was not arrested at the scene of a crime or in its immediate aftermath might be pursued by a "hue and cry" raised by his victim. In the eighteenth century, this communal call to action was still the primary mechanism for pursuit over longer distances. In theory it would travel from parish to parish until the offender was apprehended, even if many miles away. For example, one evening in March 1710, William Applewhite tied up his horse outside the house of Joseph Gall, a barber at Easton, in Suffolk. When he came out, the horse, with its saddle and bridle, was gone. Applewhite then made "great enquiry and search" for it, but without success. He was convinced that it had been stolen. A little belatedly he attended Devereaux Edgar, a county JP, provided him with a detailed description of the animal and its accoutrements, and "demanded of me this my hue and cry."[14] He wanted details of the stolen animal to be passed to neighbouring parishes until it was found.

13. W. Notcutt, *Trial of Joseph Clarke, the Younger, and Sarah Lloyd, at the Assizes, held at Bury St. Edmund's, March 20, 1800*, 1800, pp. 5–8.
14. SRO QS 347.96, *The Devereux Edgar Notebook*, transcribed by S. R. Schofield, 1956, vol. 2, p. 225.

The hue and cry was especially important in cases of highway robbery. The victim of such a crime would normally alert a constable in the first village that he reached, describing the physical appearance of the perpetrator and the direction in which he had escaped. The constable would then raise the inhabitants of his village or town to search for the offender. In theory members of the general public were obliged to participate on receipt of such a request. If the felon were not found quickly, the constable would send notice (ideally by horseman) to officers in adjacent parishes, especially those in the direction in which the criminal had fled. These constables would then raise a search in their parishes, while transmitting the notice of the hue and cry to their own neighbouring villages.[15] During the eighteenth century, some of these notices were sent on printed forms, on which information was filled in by hand, thus expediting the process. Constables and members of the public were given special protection from being liable for false imprisonment when arresting suspects while conducting a hue and cry.[16]

It was vital that the hue and cry be raised promptly after a crime was committed to lessen a criminal's chance of escape.[17] For example, in the middle of the eighteenth century, Benjamin Barker and his criminal associates purchased a consignment of bridles and, early one morning, stole horses from fields around Newmarket, in Suffolk. They then rode hard for London and "notwithstanding a Hue-and-Cry was soon after them, they fled with too much speed to be overtaken."[18] In 1809, after several male travellers were attacked by four footpads near Bradfield, in Suffolk, it was suggested that "had the parties raised the hue and cry when they reached Sicklesmere Turnpike Gate and returned to Bury with armed assistance these men could probably been apprehended."[19]

In theory any delay in reporting an incident might also have serious legal consequences. A surviving aspect of communal responsibility for local crime was that if the hue and cry failed to catch a robber who had

15. Anon (By an attorney at law), *The Law of Arrests in Both Civil and Criminal Cases*, 1742, pp. 200–202.
16. J. Morgan, *The Attorney's Vade Mecum, and Client's Instructor*, vol. 2, 1787, pp. 5–7.
17. M. Dalton, *The Country Justice*, 1661, p. 83.
18. Anon, *The Life of Benjamin Barker, A Notorious Highwayman, From His Youth to His Death*, 1750, p. 8.
19. *Bury and Norwich Post*, 4 January 1809.

operated in daylight, having been properly summoned by one of his victims, the hundred in which the offence occurred would have to make financial reparation for any loss. Although this obligation had long been in decline by 1700, a handful of victims successfully sued for their losses during the eighteenth century.

Nevertheless, the process of recovery was normally quite difficult, especially after the prerequisites for a successful claim were made more rigorous in 1735 (8 Geo II, c 16, s.11) and 1749 (22 Geo II, c 24). The authorities frequently evinced acute suspicion about such claims, which might be entirely fraudulent or at least grossly exaggerated. An example of the former occurred in 1750, when Thomas Chandler, a Clifford's Inn attorney, was convicted of falsely reporting a highway robbery, allegedly committed by three footpads, and then recovering the enormous sum of £975 from the Berkshire hundred, where, he claimed, the crime had occurred.[20] A considerable body of case law developed as to precisely when a hundred would be liable for failing to organise an effective hue and cry. (Chandler's legal knowledge had allowed him to satisfy the legal niceties for such an action). Much turned on the degree of notice that the victim had given when trying to raise it, and how detailed his description of his assailants had been.

The importance of these factors can be seen in a case that came to the summer assizes in Norfolk in 1759. One afternoon in February of that year two footpads, armed with large clubs, stopped a man named Whitworth while he was on the road from Bury St Edmunds to King's Lynn. Their victim, who resisted, was severely beaten and robbed of more than £82 and a silver watch. The two men turned his horse loose, but Whitworth managed to stagger a mile to Methwold Lodge and told people there about what had happened, asking them to pursue the robbers. Nobody was willing to do this, as it was almost dark. He then rode to Weeting, unknowingly passing the homes of two constables as he did so. Once there, he informed the occupants of several alehouses of the robbery before going on to the *Chequer Inn* in Brandon. By then considerably more than an hour had elapsed since the attack. At the inn,

20. E. Wise, *The Remarkable Tryal of Thomas Chandler, Late of Clifford's Inn, London, Gent. Who Was Tried and Convicted at the Lent Assizes at Reading, 1750,* 1751, pp. 1–69.

two men, one of them a serving soldier, agreed to pursue the robbers, and Whitworth hired a horse for the military man. This pair unavailingly searched Weeting, Wilton, Hockwold, and Feltwell for the robbers. It was only then that Whitworth formally informed Ambrose Whiteman, the Feltwell constable, of the robbery in the proper manner.

Subsequently, at the Norfolk Assizes, more than £85 in damages and £2 in costs were awarded to Whitworth against the Hundred of Grimshoe, where the robbery had occurred. However, the matter went to the Court of King's Bench for further consideration. The two constables at Weeting suggested that if notice of the robbery had been given promptly, so that they could have made an immediate pursuit, the footpads would have been captured. Additionally, the plaintiff's account of the robbery in the *London Gazette* and his description of his attackers was considered inaccurate. In reply Whitworth argued that his dazed and "miserable" condition at the time explained his delay in formally reporting the matter. Even so, King's Bench gave judgment for the hundred.[21]

The hue and cry could be a dramatic business. In 1776 a clerical observer expressed the hope that more godliness in the nation would mean that the entire country would not be alarmed periodically "with hue and cry, for the purpose of hunting down the miserably skulking offenders, like pernicious wild beasts."[22] Sometimes it worked efficiently, especially over short to medium distances, and where it was supported by armed and mounted men. For example, in May 1702 three prisoners who had escaped from the Ipswich county gaol by filing off their shackles and tunnelling out were recaptured a week later, "having been upon hue & cry taken."[23] In populous areas, scores of people could become involved. In 1745 a large posse pursued Jeremiah Pratt, a habitual thief and highwayman, through part of Suffolk. Although he made an "obstinate resistance" when cornered near Lakenham, brandishing a loaded pistol, two of his pursuers were also carrying firearms, and Pratt ultimately surrendered.[24] Similarly, in 1779, after a group of sailors robbed,

21. *Whitworth Qui Tam, &c. v The Hundred of Grimshoe in Norfolk* (1760), 2 Wilson, K. B. 109, 95 E. R. 713.
22. T. Humphries, *A Preservative From Criminal Offences*, 1776, p. 6.
23. SRO QS 347.96, *The Devereux Edgar Notebook*, transcribed by S. R. Schofield 1956, vol. 1, p. 25.
24. *St. James's Evening Post*, 12–15 October 1745.

shot, and wounded a fellow traveller on the Yarmouth road, a hue and cry was raised near Yoxford, in Suffolk. Two householders in the flight path of the robbers were asked to assist. Despite being warned that the sailors had firearms, they promised they would "venture their lives to take them." They did so, with the help of some neighbours, sealing the mariners in a room, securing their pistols, and sending for the local constable and sets of handcuffs.[25]

Most dramatically of all, in 1780 two highwaymen robbed several travellers outside Swaffham on a Saturday evening. The alarm was raised promptly in the town, and several local men immediately mounted their horses and pursued the robbers. One of the highwaymen was knocked off his horse, and then chased on foot until captured. The other got away. The following morning a local man made a fresh search with some of the victims, and caught up with this highwayman in Wisbech, 30 miles from Swaffham, where they pulled him off his horse, still in possession of some stolen items. Both highwaymen had robbed in other parts of England, and it was noted that "[t]oo much cannot be said in praise of the inhabitants of Swaffham, for their uncommon spirit and alacrity in pursuing and taking two such dangerous fellows."[26] However, as this comment suggests, such zeal was not typical.

Detection

Although many felons were caught in the act, in the immediate aftermath of their crimes, or by the hue and cry, a degree of detective work, even if rudimentary, was often necessary if a suspect was to be identified and brought to justice. Indicative of this, a significant number of people were arrested and prosecuted long after the commission of their crimes. At the Bury Assizes in 1751, Thomas Brook, John Cunningham and Francis Mayhew were convicted of breaking into the house of the Reverend Ward at Blakenham some three years earlier, and robbing him of a watch and other goods.[27] The following year Thomas Fidgett,

25. Anon, *The Trial at Large of Thomas Clarke, Thomas Carty, and John Deane*, 1779, p. 10.
26. *Norfolk Chronicle*, 26 August 1780.
27. *London Daily Advertiser and Literary Gazette*, 6 August 1751.

a notorious smuggler, was capitally convicted and executed for shooting an officer's servant on a customs sloop a decade before.[28]

The eighteenth century had not totally abandoned faith in supernatural methods of detection, at least for murder. For example, in 1707, an old soldier and two new recruits robbed a peddler near Oxford and cut his throat. They were pursued, captured, and according to "ancient custom, challenged to touch the Dead Body, which the old Soldier readily did; but one of the others was taken with a Trembling, and struck with such Terror, that he presently confess'd the horrid Fact."[29] The archaic custom referred to was cruentation; an alleged murderer was invited to touch the corpse, and was considered guilty if fresh blood flowed. Coroners' juries were still occasionally suggesting recourse to this technique in the 1730s.

Such beliefs were much less common by the end of the century, particularly among educated people. Nevertheless, popular faith in supernatural detection had not entirely disappeared. As late as 1828, a year after the suspicious disappearance of Maria Martin, in Suffolk, her stepmother allegedly dreamt on three successive nights that she had been murdered and buried in a local building known as the Red Barn. This reinforced her suspicion that Maria had been the victim of foul play. She eventually persuaded her husband to search the barn, where he found Maria's body in a makeshift grave.[30] Although this swiftly became part of the established mythology of the case, it was also quickly doubted. Neither prosecution nor defence counsel referred to it at trial.

More concrete means of detection were required. However, East Anglia did not acquire the quasi-professional bounty-hunting thieftakers who operated extensively in the capital for much of the era, while the metropolitan Bow Street Runners rarely operated in Norfolk or Suffolk towards the end of the century. Instead, crime victims conducted the bulk of eighteenth-century detective work.

28. *Read's Weekly Journal Or British Gazetteer*, 28 March 1752.
29. *The Post Boy*, 27 February –1 March 1707.
30. *The Morning Post*, 24 April 1828.

Detection by Victims

Sometimes a victim could readily identify a likely suspect. For example, in January 1714 Stephen Kerridge of Akenham went to a Suffolk JP to obtain an arrest warrant against Nathaniel Barney, a young man who had been his yearly hired servant but had "deserted his service" the previous night. At the same time, Kerridge's fine chestnut horse had disappeared from its stable. It did not take much to link the two events. Kerridge suspected that Barney had headed for Blowfield, seven miles from Norwich, and intended to follow him there with his arrest warrant.[31]

In a slightly more complicated case, in January 1715 Thomas Bloss of Belstead, in Suffolk, informed a JP that someone had broken into his study the previous night and stolen 20 guineas from his desk. The burglar had left behind a broken piece from a hammer that he had used to enter the premises. This was of a distinctive type, one that had also been used by a carpenter named Thomas Reeve who had done some work in the victim's house a few weeks earlier. Bloss's domestic servant backed up this identification. An arrest warrant was then issued against Reeve.[32]

Another typical example of such investigation occurred in Norfolk in early 1740, after George Riches broke into the shop of Richard Twist, in Coltishall, and stole three silver watches. He then sold one of them to an unnamed Norwich Jew, who, not knowing its source, tried to sell it back to Twist. Twist recognised the timepiece as his own, and detained the vendor until he gave a "satisfactory account how he came by it, which he did, when they both came to Norwich and had the prisoner secured."[33]

As this case suggests, the point at which stolen goods re-entered the legitimate market was always a dangerous one for the thief, especially if he did not use an experienced fence. Such men were much less common in the provinces than in London, and, in exchange for their services, would purchase items for only a small fraction of their worth. Handbills, flyers, and advertisements publicised recently stolen items. For example, in 1769, after two footpads robbed a man outside Sudbury, the victim

31. SRO QS 347.96, *The Devereux Edgar Notebook*, transcribed by S. R. Schofield, 1956, vol. 2, p. 390.
32. Ibid, pp. 440–441.
33. *Norwich Chronicle*, 9 February 1782.

advertised in a local newspaper, offering a reward and asking silversmiths, watchmakers, and others that, if a silver watch were offered for sale, they should "stop the person offering it and give information to G. Tabor of Waldingfield, Sudbury, Suffolk."[34] In 1762 the owner of a valuable greatcoat that had been taken from the Swan Inn in Sudbury and replaced with a greatly inferior garment went further. He published an advertisement in the *Ipswich Journal* warning the thief that if he did not return the coat to his residence, Borley Hall—in which case "no further notice" would be taken of the incident—he would have the thief's coat publicly displayed by the town crier on three market days and at all the inns in Sudbury so that the perpetrator could be identified.[35]

A more complicated case of victim investigation occurred in Suffolk in 1783. One winter evening a clergyman named Macro, from Barrow Hall, near Bury, was returning home from collecting tithes when he encountered a highwayman. The would-be robber shot at him but fled when his victim showed resistance. The following morning, Macro returned to the scene of the crime and found the tracks of a horse with the imprint of distinctive "bar" shoes. He followed these to a stable, where he apprehended the rider, a blacksmith named James Steggles, who was sitting in an adjacent kitchen. Macro had him committed to Bury gaol.[36] Steggles was subsequently capitally convicted at the assizes and executed locally.[37] (A stone set into the pavement near the modern village school allegedly marks the spot where he was hanged). As was later noted, "the extraordinary way in which Steggles was detected does great credit to Mr Macro."[38]

In 1786, after a carrier named John Raven was murdered in Norfolk, the same correspondence between the shoes of the suspect's horse and tracks in the snow at the crime scene was carefully noted.[39] A much less serious offence was proved in a broadly similar fashion when a farm labourer named Kettle was convicted at the Suffolk Quarter Sessions held in Ipswich at Easter 1800 of stealing 20 shillings' worth of stover (a

34. *Ipswich Journal*, 4 March 1769.
35. *Ipswich Journal*, 6 February 1762.
36. Ibid., 11 January 1783.
37. *London Chronicle*, 22–25 March 1783.
38. *Ipswich Journal*, 12 April 1783.
39. Anon, *The Trial of John Shilling, For the Wilful Murder of Mr. John Raven, of Burnham Westgate, Carrier*, 1786, p. 12.

mixture of clover and trefoil used as animal feed) from Ambrose Raynham, who farmed at Great Blakenham. Raynham had followed a trail of stover from his (depleted) stack to Kettle's yard.[40]

Traps were sometimes laid to identify suspected thieves. At a very elevated level, in 1782 Sir Gerard Vanneck, the wealthy MP for Dunwich, whose seat was at Heveningham Hall in Suffolk, became suspicious of a close friend and neighbour who had free access to his house after large amounts of cash went missing from a desk. He gave instructions to his steward to watch this man secretly, from a closet, when he next visited. The steward, together with another man who had been taken along for "security and better evidence," seized the man in the act of opening the bureau.[41]

More commonly, if people thought their cash was being stolen from them on a regular basis, by employees or other intimates they might secretly mark the coins. In 1777, after William Maplestone was committed to Beccles bridewell for stealing £1 2s 6d from the shop of a Mr Matchett in Ellingham, it was noted that many of the shillings taken had been marked with two letters from Matchett's name, establishing their provenance.[42] A few years later James Oakes, a Bury businessman, came to suspect that William Pulteney had been stealing small amounts of cash from him. He eventually caught him by leaving marked coins about; these were stolen by Pulteney, and then found on his person.[43]

Of course, the victim of a murder could not conduct detective work, but private individuals, such as close relatives, might become involved in the investigative process. For example, in 1740, after Charles Drew murdered his father in Long Melford, he was hunted down and eventually detained at a bagnio in Leicester Fields by Timothy Drew, an attorney and relative.[44] Nevertheless, the coroner would normally take the most important role in investigating homicides, and, as these were the most heinous offences committed, his office receives detailed consideration in the next chapter.

---

40. TNA HO 47/24/25, ff 188–199.
41. *General Advertiser and Morning Intelligencer*, 28 January 1782; *Public Advertiser*, 7 February 1782.
42. *Norwich Mercury*, 5 July 1777.
43. J. Fiske, *The Oakes Diaries*, 1991, p. 321.
44. *Ipswich Journal*, 12 April 1740.

Detection by JPs and Parish Officers

Although under their commissions justices had a vague duty to apprehend felons, it was unusual for them to take an active role in the detection of offenders on their own initiative, especially outside the Metropolis. As the Middlesex justice Sir John Fielding noted in the 1770s, most country magistrates, "however public spirited they may be, can only back our warrants, recommend peace officers to execute them, and examine offenders when taken."[45]

Nevertheless, even in the provinces, some English magistrates were much more than the passive recipients of others' investigations who limited themselves to issuing arrest and search warrants and examining suspects brought before them. This had always been the case. For example, when several skeletons were discovered in a Suffolk pond in 1620, an energetic JP had them laid out by a surgeon, and summoned local people to view the bones. This led to their identification and a subsequent murder prosecution.[46]

Only a few provincial magistrates matched the investigative zeal of Samuel Lister in Yorkshire or John Hewett in Coventry during the 1750s, and even they were fairly selective about the cases in which they became involved. Such activism was largely a matter of choice, attracting few personal benefits. After dealing with one Midlands criminal gang, Hewitt complained that he did not have the "least assurance of being paid my expenses, or rewarded for the unremitting pains that I took."[47]

Even so, there was more justice-initiated detective work in eighteenth-century Norfolk and Suffolk than is sometimes appreciated. Inevitably, it left relatively few formal records, making calculation difficult, although it is mentioned in some contemporary notebooks and diaries. The tradition survived into the following century. Thus, in June 1827 John Longe recorded that he had been at home in Suffolk, engaged in trying to "detect several persons concerned in the late burglaries in the neighbourhood."

---

45. J. Styles, "An Eighteenth-century Magistrate as Detective: Samuel Lister of Little Horton," 1982, p. 103.
46. T. Cooper, *The Cry and Revenge of Blood*, 1620, p. 42.
47. J. Hewitt, *A Journal of the Proceedings of J. Hewitt*, 1790, p. 94.

In August and September of the same year, he met other area justices in Ipswich to examine some members of the gang.[48]

Some lower-ranking local officials also became actively involved in criminal investigation, even if they were not required to do so. For example, while Jonathan Norman, from Ingham in North Norfolk, was being held in custody in Norwich Castle for taking oats from a barn, he was also accused of stealing a black gelding at Reydon, in Suffolk. This was the result of some investigative work by the Ingham parish officers. They had become suspicious after noticing Norman's wife riding such an animal to visit her husband while he was incarcerated, and scrutinised recent editions of the Norwich papers, where they found a reward advertised for the recovery of a horse answering to the same description. They told the owner, who came to identify the animal, and was bound over to prosecute the matter at the Norfolk Assizes (a prerequisite for recovering the horse).[49]

As some of these cases suggest, the availability of substantial rewards oiled the wheels of many eighteenth-century investigations and often motivated the pursuit and prosecution of criminals. In 1784 François de la Rochefoucauld thought that although English society would not tolerate a military type force to deal with crime it had "another, perhaps better, means. The government offers a good sum of money to the person or persons who bring in a wrongdoer together with proofs of his delinquency."[50] Leaving to one side his enthusiasm for the reward system (far from universal by the 1780s), he was correct in seeing it as fundamental to the eighteenth-century criminal-justice process.

The Reward System

Statutory rewards had been employed for hundreds of years prior to the late seventeenth century. Traditionally, they had been used to encourage the prosecution of minor, often regulatory, matters and involved the payment of small sums of money. Such rewards continued to be paid

48. M. Stone (ed.), *The Diary of John Longe, Vicar of Coddenham, 1765–1834*, 2008, p. 98 and p. 104.
49. *Ipswich Journal*, 29 April 1780.
50. N. Scarfe, *A Frenchman's Year in Suffolk*, 2011, p. 80.

out during the eighteenth century. For example, in 1786, after a servant named Charles Abbot was convicted and fined 20s for taking a loaded cart through a suburb of Bury on the Sabbath, "a third part [of the fine was] to be paid to the informer."[51]

Historically, statutory rewards had not normally been available in felony cases. However, during the half century after 1692, a series of acts offered major state-funded rewards to the successful prosecutors of a steadily growing number of serious crimes. These encouraged members of the public to risk their own security, and invest their own time and money, in catching, prosecuting, and convicting felons. Thus £40 was granted those who apprehended and gave evidence that convicted highway robbers, burglars, and housebreakers, while £20 was awarded those who prosecuted to conviction felons who returned prematurely from transportation. At a more modest level, those who convicted sheep and cattle thieves could receive £10.[52] Typically, the successful prosecutors of the East Anglian sheep thief Gibbon Houghton received such a sum (divided among themselves) in 1767.[53]

As a rough rule of thumb, sizable rewards were given for crimes that were viewed seriously, such as robbery, burglary, and housebreaking, but not for those that occasioned less concern, such as theft in a dwelling-house (despite its being, in theory, a capital felony). However, there was a lack of coherence to the system, in part because the enabling statutes were passed in a rather ad hoc fashion, like many other criminal-justice reforms of the time. Although the presence of the coroner might explain why no reward was felt necessary for successful murder prosecutions, they were not available in cases of horse theft (made a capital offence in the sixteenth century), despite eventually being provided for those stealing less valuable animals. (A "Tyburn Ticket" signed by the judge of the convicting court, exempting its holder from parish duties, might be given to those who successfully prosecuted horse thieves).[54]

51. *Bury and Norwich Post*, 10 May 1786.
52. Sir J. Fielding, *Extracts From Such of the Penal Laws, As Particularly Relate to the Peace and Good Order of this Metropolis*, 1762, p. 305.
53. *Gazetteer and New Daily Advertiser*, 28 October 1767.
54. Sir J. Fielding, *Extracts From Such of the Penal Laws, As Particularly Relate to the Peace and Good Order of this Metropolis*, 1762, p. 306.

Although placing prosecution on an entrepreneurial basis might appear strange to modern eyes, it was in keeping with many aspects of eighteenth-century society. In a world in which regimental commanding officers bought and sold their commissions, paid recruiting officers for their men, and profiteered from government payments for their units, it did not appear quite so peculiar.[55] This applied to many other public positions. Jerome Knapp (1722–1792) purchased his office as the clerk for the Home Circuit for £5,000 (the last man to do so).[56]

The sums paid out could be substantial, especially when more than one felon was prosecuted, as there would be a reward for each man convicted. Early in the eighteenth century there was litigation between Daniel Elsegood and the mayor and corporation of Norwich over the recovery of £120 for the conviction in the city of three highwaymen.[57] This was at a time when it was estimated that a typical poor man, in constant employment, might earn as little as 4s or 5s a week, and an entire family, with three or four children, might get by on between 1s and 1s 6d a day.[58]

To encourage popular activism, the authorities and the newspapers regularly publicised these rewards. When Roger Bicker and several other men were sought for a Suffolk burglary in 1736, an advertisement advised readers, "Whoever apprehends any of the last mentioned seven persons, upon their conviction, will be intituled to 40l. Reward for each person convicted."[59] In 1780 a Norfolk newspaper reminded its readers of the tangible rewards and other practical benefits that might accrue from prosecuting a highwayman to conviction, besides the "real satisfaction of doing so noble an act to serve their country."[60] Two years later, after a pair of footpads robbed a cart driver on a turnpike road near Hockering, in Norfolk, the local newspaper reporting the incident stated, "The

55. R. Porter, *English Society in the Eighteenth Century*, 1990, p. 135.
56. *Gentleman's Magazine and Historical Review*, vol. 62, part 1, 1792, p. 577. Knapp was also Clerk of the Haberdashers' Company and Treasurer of the Middle Temple; J. H. Langbein, "Shaping the Eighteenth-century Criminal Trial: A View from the Ryder Sources," 1983, p. 28.
57. NRO E 134/12–13 Wm3/Hil17.
58. J. Rule, "The Labouring Poor," 2002, p. 185.
59. *Daily Gazetteer* (London Edition), 15 June 1736.
60. *Norfolk Chronicle*, 18 November 1780.

reward for apprehending a highwayman, and prosecuting him to conviction, is 40 pounds."[61]

Such rewards were paid out after the assizes by the county sheriff, on receipt of a certificate signed by the trial judge. When there was more than one potential claimant, as was often the situation, the sums available were, in theory, divided according to the judge's discretion However, if Dudley Ryder's experience on the Home Circuit in 1754 and 1755 was typical, in many cases the judge would simply endorse a distribution that had been decided in advance by the claimants, making a decision only if they could not agree.

Thus, at the Summer Assizes held at Norwich in 1746, both Thomas and James Bird were rewarded with £20 (half each of the £40 allowed) as the "captors" of a woman who had burgled their house. Similarly, at the Norfolk Assizes that opened in Thetford on 18 March 1748, John Jarvis was convicted of burgling the home of Elizabeth Brooke so that (again) a £40 reward was payable. In this case, it was distributed among seven people. Elizabeth, the victim, who had prosecuted the matter and testified at Jarvis's trial, received £8. (Even if victims played no role in capturing suspects, this was usual, as, without their evidence, there could be no conviction.) Six men also received a share. Two of them got £10 each. Another received £5, with the remaining three being awarded £3, £2 10s, and £1 10s. It is likely that the two men who received £10 had been Jarvis's primary captors, while those with small awards had provided such assistance as, for example, helping to guard him on the way to a JP for examination.[62] In 1784 François de la Rochefoucauld saw £80 given to three men in Suffolk for securing two robbers, £40 to the complainant/prosecutor who called for help and gave evidence at trial, and £20 to each of the two men who actually secured the felons.[63]

In March 1777, when John Manning was convicted at the Norfolk Assizes for burglary, one of the victim's relatives received a single shilling, taken from another man's £5 reward.[64] Perhaps he was a juvenile who had carried a message. In an even more extreme case from the Bedfordshire

61. Ibid., 6 January 1782.
62. Gray's Inn MS 45.
63. N. Scarfe, *A Frenchman's Year in Suffolk*, 2011, p. 85.
64. TNA ASSI 33/6.

Assizes (also on the Norfolk Circuit) in March 1746, two £40 rewards for the capture and conviction of a pair of highwaymen, Thomas Harrison and John Tompkins, were divided 22 ways. For each conviction, one man received £12 10s, another £7 10s, and the remaining 20 men £1 each.[65] As this suggests, the possibility of a small share of a reward led numerous minor actors to lend assistance to those who apprehended felons.

Additionally, special rewards were frequently offered on top of the statutory scheme or in its absence, whether locally, nationally, or for a specific offence, and whether by the authorities, a private individual, prosecution association or other body. For example, the Crown offered a reward of £200 for the arrest and conviction of Edward Crispe's vicious (but non-lethal) assailants.[66] Although murder did not carry a statutory reward, if a killing was particularly heinous, substantial public or private rewards might be offered. Thus, after Charles Drew was murdered in 1740, John Gent, from Sudbury, in Suffolk, offered £100 to be paid on conviction of the killers, prudently excluding from those eligible "people who actually committed the murder."[67]

On a more quotidian basis, when the house of Widow Brook of Cretingham, in Suffolk, was broken into and 15 firkins of butter stolen, she offered 1 guinea to anyone who provided information that brought the thief to justice.[68] In like manner, after a large quantity of linen tablecloths, shirts, shifts, and capes was stolen from a rinsing tub in the yard of John Burkitt, in Sudbury, he offered three guineas to anyone giving information that would lead to the discovery of the offender.[69]

In Norfolk, the owner of 21 geese that had been killed and stolen from a farm went even further. Not only did he offer 5 guineas for the conviction of the perpetrator, he even promised that, if the person who gave such information was an accomplice to the crime, "he or she shall nevertheless have the Reward, and every legal Method taken to obtain his or her Free Pardon."[70] Similarly, when a dun stag was stolen from

65. Gray's Inn MS 45.
66. *Weekly Journal or British Gazetteer*, 13 January 1722.
67. *Ipswich Journal*, 16 February 1740.
68. Ibid., 15 November 1729.
69. Ibid., 17 November 1753.
70. *Norfolk Chronicle*, 14 October 1780.

a Widow Appleton at Cockfield, in Suffolk, she offered a £10 reward upon conviction of the thief, and promised, "If two or more were concerned the one who will turn evidence will receive the reward and [be] acquitted."[71] (Legally, this was more than she could guarantee.)

As some of these cases suggest, the growth of the provincial press provided an important medium for informing the public of non-statutory rewards. On one analysis, such advertisements were often successful in securing prosecutions in felony cases, those involving the theft of large animals possibly apart.[72] In 1725, when Josiah Math was suspected of robbing and brutally murdering Thomas Marsh at Culford, in Suffolk, an advertisement was placed in a newspaper offering 10 guineas for his capture and providing a detailed description of his appearance.[73] This appears to have been successful, as he was subsequently capitally convicted at the county assizes.[74] Even horse thieves were frequently caught by this means. For example, in 1722, Leonard Hendry, a Westminster man, travelled 110 miles to Beconthorp in Norfolk and stole a valuable colt before returning to the Metropolis. Its owner, John Lang "advertis'd it in the News Papers, by which means the Colt was found again, at Mr. Jones's Stable, in Petty France." When Hendry took the horse to Jones, offering to sell it at a fairly low price, this honest man, who had seen the newspaper, arrested him after "finding the Marks of the Colt exactly agree with those in the Advertisement."[75]

The reward system was certainly effective in encouraging members of the public to enforce the law. In 1733 the highwayman John Cullington was captured in Suffolk for a crime that he had committed in Middlesex a short while earlier. He had escaped from the metropolitan area and was riding on the road between Melford and Sudbury when, by chance, he fell from his horse and dislocated his neck. A passerby, John Felt, came to his aid, and, while he was helping Cullington, noticed some bullets fall out of his pocket. This, combined with the small arsenal of pistols he was carrying, made Felt "suspect him for a highwayman, and therefor

71. *Ipswich Journal*, 12 March 1763.
72. P. King, *Crime, Justice, and Discretion in England 1740–1820*, 2000, p. 61.
73. *Weekly Journal or Saturday's Post*, 28 November 1724.
74. *London Journal (1720)*, 7 August 1725.
75. OBSP, Trial of Leonard Hendry, 10 May 1722: t17220510–7.

I secur'd him."[76] Doubtless the prospect of a £40 reward greatly influenced him in this decision.

However, such success came at a price. The sums on offer were so substantial that they encouraged venal men to strain the truth or even to fabricate evidence to secure convictions. Many observers feared "[b]old and daring witnesses who in order to make sure of conviction, presume to make free with truth."[77] Indeed, the notorious John Waller, who made malicious capital allegations against innocent men, was exposed on the Norfolk Circuit. Daniel Bolton, the under clerk of assizes for the circuit, noted that Waller had come to him in Cambridge and given information against two men whom he accused of robbing him on the road from Newmarket, in Suffolk. They were both subsequently convicted and sentenced to death. Fortunately, suspicions developed about Waller, and Baron Cummins, one of the itinerant judges, ordered Bolton to investigate his character. After making enquiries of a man in Bury and another in Thetford, Bolton was told that Waller made a "[t]rade of swearing away Mens Lives for the Sake of the Reward, granted for convicting Robbers." Just in time, the execution of the two men was cancelled.[78]

The availability of rewards could also affect the evidence of ordinary people, not just those who were members of one of the era's entrapment gangs. As a result of several well-publicised scandals, there was, from the middle of the era, more judicial caution about receiving evidence for which a reward could be claimed. After George McCombe was acquitted of highway robbery at the Norfolk Assizes in 1764, his prosecutor, a travelling tinker named Breeze, was committed for trial at the ensuing sessions for wilful perjury.[79]

Accomplice Evidence

The use of accomplice evidence constituted another important eighteenth-century method for detecting and convicting serious criminals. In theory, some felons, especially those still at liberty, could come forward

76. OBSP, Trial of John Cullington, 5 December 1733: t17331205–19.
77. *Lloyd's Evening Post*, 6–8 September 1775.
78. OBSP, Trial of John Waller, 25 May 1732: t17320525–69.
79. *Public Advertiser*, 21 August 1764.

to admit their crimes, become an "approver" at common law or give evidence under various arcane statutes, impeach their criminal colleagues, then claim a pardon as of legal right. However, the former proceeding had fallen into disuse by the 1700s, while use of the latter was quite rare. Occasionally the Crown promised felons a pardon in exchange for evidence, with regard to specific offences, while they were still at large. For example, when Charles Drew was murdered at Long Melford, in Suffolk, in 1740, the King "promise[d] his most gracious pardon to anyone of them who shall discover his accomplice except the person who actually committed the murder, so that they be apprehended and convicted."[80] Again, such felons were, as Lord Mansfield noted in 1775, legally entitled to a pardon.[81]

Very much more commonly during the 1700s, an accomplice would make an informal deal, usually with an examining JP, after his own arrest, in which he offered to implicate, give evidence against, and convict other felons. These were usually his erstwhile colleagues. Such a pardon was not given as of legal right, but amounted to the promise of a recommendation for mercy if the accomplice fulfilled his part of the agreement and gave cogent evidence that produced convictions. This being done, the practice was to stop any prosecution and release the witness from custody.[82]

For example, in 1751 three men were taken from London's Newgate prison by *habeas corpus* to stand trial at the Ipswich Assizes (the town substituting for Bury that year), where they were capitally convicted of housebreaking. Shortly afterwards, it was noted that Jonathan Button, their former accomplice, who had been committed to Ipswich prison in April of the same year, "was the principal witness against Brook, Cunningham and Mayhew, [and] is discharged from the Goal [sic]."[83] The use of accomplice evidence continued to the end of the period. In 1802 William Bryant, John Cant, and William Bird were accused of several sheep thefts in Suffolk on such testimony, with: "William Murrills (an

80. *Ipswich Journal*, 16 February 1740.
81. *The King v Margaret Caroline Rudd* (1775) 1 Leach 115, 168 E.R. 160.
82. Sir W. Holdsworth, *A History of English Law*, vol. xii, 1938, p. 514.
83. *Ipswich Journal*, 6 April 1751, *General Advertiser (1744)*, 6 August 1751.

accomplice of the others) being admitted King's Evidence against the other prisoners."[84]

Such "evidences" would nearly always be detained in custody prior to trial but, for obvious reasons, were usually held safely away from those they were going to incriminate.[85] A failure to do this could have fatal consequences. Ideally, those who turned King's evidence would not be held in the same prison as those they intended to impeach. For example, in 1782, when the murderer Jeremiah Theobald was being carried to Bury gaol, he saw a former accomplice named Munsell and threatened him with death, having learnt that Munsell would be an evidence against him, "In consequence of which it was thought proper to lodge Munsell in a place of security, and he was committed to Mildenhall bridewell till the assizes."[86] If this were not practicable, an accomplice would have to be held in a secure part of the same establishment as the men against whom he would testify at trial. In 1793 the Suffolk Quarter Sessions stressed that the keeper of the new Ipswich Gaol should provide a separate place of confinement for any prisoners who intended to give evidence for the Crown.[87]

The accomplice-evidence system was certainly effective. In 1788 Parson Woodforde noted in his diary that, on a visit to the family of a Norfolk JP the magistrate had been called away to examine a man named Joseph Wakefield, who was suspected of murdering an elderly gamekeeper, bludgeoned to death by a gang of poachers some three years earlier. Wakefield had been arrested after being impeached by an accomplice named Beales, who was held in the castle gaol at Norwich as one of the gang. It was "also reported that he [Beales] has impeached about ten more of the said gang."[88] Wakefield was subsequently convicted and hanged.[89]

Under the threat of the noose, even close family loyalties could break down, as there was usually little honour among thieves. John Bicker, a shoemaker and suspected burglar, was capitally convicted at the Lent

84. *Bury and Norwich Post*, 13 January 1802.
85. Anon, *General Regulations for the Government of the New Goal* [sic], *At Ipswich*, 1791, p. 1.
86. *Norfolk Chronicle*, 16 November 1782.
87. Anon, *General Regulations for the Government of the New Goal* [sic], *At Ipswich*, 1791, p. 4.
88. J. Beresford (ed.), *The Diary of a Country Parson, 1758–1802*, 1978, p. 314.
89. *General Evening Post*, 20–22 March 1788.

Assizes for Suffolk in 1737 and hanged as a result of his own sibling (and fellow shoemaker) Roger Bicker's testimony.[90] At the Suffolk Assizes held in the summer of 1795, Charles Blyth was convicted and executed for horse theft, largely on the testimony of his brother, who had been his accomplice in the crime, and who had become a Crown evidence to save himself.[91]

Ideally, those chosen as Crown witnesses would have had peripheral roles in the crimes about which they gave evidence; they would be the "least guilty of the gang."[92] For example, although Munsell had been involved in Jeremiah Theobald's earlier crimes, he had refused to take part in the brutal murder perpetrated by the latter. However, this was not invariably the case. Sometimes the authorities would be forced to accept the most culpable individuals as evidences, even in the most heinous cases. For example, James Fleming and Samuel Windham, two dragoons convicted at the Thetford Assizes for the rape of eleven-year-old Rebecca Brighton, who had subsequently died (in part because of her injuries), were found guilty and executed only because an equally guilty colleague "was admitted an evidence for the crown, without which (the child being dead) it was thought the prisoner could not have been convicted."[93]

There was usually little merit in those who were reprieved, who normally acted out of self-interest and were devoid of any real remorse; many reoffended swiftly after release. Despite his narrow escape from death, Roger Bicker was not deterred from crime. Only months later he went to the gallows after being convicted of another capital offence at the same forum, despite attempting to avoid the noose once more by impeaching his new criminal associates. (Immunity was usually only granted once in such cases.)[94] In 1783 Samuel Oxer, held in Bury Gaol as prospective Crown evidence against two men accused of robbing the mayor of Sudbury, attempted to escape. After he was caught with another

90. *London Evening Post*, 13–16 August 1737; *Daily Gazetteer* (London Edition), March 29, 1737.
91. *Lloyd's Evening Post*, 19–21 August 1795.
92. M. Madan, *Thoughts On Executive Justice*, 1785, p. 162.
93. *London Chronicle*, 26–28 March 1799; *Courier and Evening Gazette*, July 26, 1799. The child's pre-mortem statement was also admitted.
94. *London Evening Post*, 13–16 August 1737; *Daily Gazetteer* (London Edition), 29 March 1737.

prisoner, Oxer confessed that they had considered murdering a turnkey and the gaoler as part of their bid for freedom.[95] Oxer appears to have lost his status as a result of this incident, and was executed the same year.

The accomplice system was fraught with other dangers. As Lord Mansfield observed in 1775, it would not be used if it were not "absolutely necessary for the execution of the law against notorious offenders that accomplices should be received as witnesses, [as] the practice is liable to many objections."[96] Desperate men sought to save themselves at the expense of others, even if they had to embroider the truth or completely fabricate accusations to gain the authorities' interest. Robert Lambert, who was executed at Bury in 1735 for burglary, announced at the gallows that, after his arrest, he had implicated two other men in the crime with a view to hanging them, "hoping at the same time to save himself by being an evidence, and now he declared them both innocent."[97]

A growing awareness of this danger and an increased sensitivity to ensuing miscarriages of justice, fanned by a series of well-publicised scandals, eventually prompted much greater judicial care in the reception of accomplice evidence, which, depending on the decade, either had to be corroborated by other testimony or subject to a firm jury warning of its inherent dangers.[98] For example, in 1807, when Martha Alden was tried for petty treason (murder of her husband) at the Norfolk Assizes, Mary Orvice, who had helped to dispose of the corpse, gave important evidence for the Crown. The trial judge, however, instructed the jury that her evidence "was to be received with extreme caution."[99]

The Justice's Examination

After a felony suspect reached a JP, the magistrate would conduct a formal examination pursuant to statutes dating from the reign of Mary I. Usually he did this sitting alone with a clerk, in his own home. Occasionally it would be done with colleagues present. Sometimes this was

95. *Morning Chronicle and London Advertiser*, 24 February 1783.
96. *The King v Margaret Caroline Rudd* (1775), 1 Leach 115, 168 E.R. 160.
97. *London Evening Post*, 12–15 April 1735.
98. J. H. Langbein, *The Origins of Adversary Trial*, 2005, pp. 205–214.
99. *Hampshire Telegraph and Sussex Chronicle etc.*, 17 August 1807.

in a tavern or other public building, or even at petty sessions (although this was rare for a first examination). Such examinations were much less common when misdemeanours were alleged.

The justice or his clerk would write down any statement the suspect made, which he might then be invited to sign or mark (if illiterate). It was not normally a verbatim record, but a mediated summary of the questions and answers. Any admissions made by the suspect might later be adduced at trial as a confession. Borough justices would perform the same function within the confines of their towns. For example, in 1726 Grace Baldwin stole a substantial sum of money from her employer's shop in the Metropolis. She then fled from the capital to East Anglia. Her master advertised the crime in the *Publick News* and eventually received information about her whereabouts. He then "took her at Thetford in Suffolk, I had her before the Mayor, and she confessed the Fact." The confession she made during her examination by this *ex officio* magistrate in Thetford was later adduced against her at the Old Bailey, and she was convicted.[100]

The duration and thoroughness of the examination varied greatly according to the JP involved and the crime alleged. After being arrested in London for murdering his father at Long Melford, in Suffolk, Charles Drew was subjected to a six-hour examination by the legendary quasi-professional magistrate Colonel Thomas de Veil before being committed to Newgate prison and then sent back to Suffolk for trial.[101] This was certainly not typical, especially in provincial England. Many examinations in East Anglia were much more cursory. Nevertheless, in 1750, after John Barchard was arrested for murder in Yarmouth he did not come clean to a JP immediately, but a "few hours after confinement confessed the fact."[102] Clearly the process had not been rushed. Similarly, in 1796, when John Osborn was tried at the Bury Assizes for stealing 27 turkeys and some wheat from barns and outhouses, "his confession made before a magistrate was read, including a history of his life for more than seven

100. OBSP, Trial of Grace Baldwin, 7 December 1726: t17261207–37.
101. *London Daily Post and General Advertiser*, 14 March 1740.
102. NRO Y/S/ 2t1–4 MF 1031.

years." It was apparently a litany of crimes, and obviously the fruit of a lengthy questioning process.[103]

Some suspects firmly denied all allegations made against them. For example, in 1737 John Hewes, from Burnham Market, in Norfolk, broke into a miller's house and stole clothing while the family was at work. Although captured in possession of the garments, he "would not make any confession."[104] However, many examinations did produce admissions. Thus, when ten-year-old William York was accused of murdering another child in Suffolk, his confession, taken and attested by a justice of the peace, was "in part, proved on his trial."[105] In like manner, in 1752 Thomas Hill was committed to the county gaol, charged with stealing 25 sheep from Thomas Hammond of Aldham, in Suffolk, to which he "confessed on his examination."[106] In a more complicated case from 1737, William Tink and Geoffrey Leaks robbed a man on a Suffolk highway of a gold watch, chain, and seal. While being questioned by a JP, Leake said nothing, but Tink admitted the offence and also stated that he and Leake had committed several other similar robberies in the wider East Anglian region.[107] In legal theory, the confession could only be used against Tink, but both men were ultimately convicted and executed.

Those being questioned, usually without legal advice, could easily make admissions that they subsequently regretted. Many did not appreciate how legally weak the prosecution case against them often was in the absence of a confession. Most important, the *corpus delicti* of a crime normally had to be established before a conviction could be secured. In an increasingly mobile world, this was often a problem for the authorities. It could be difficult to prove that goods found in extremely suspicious circumstances were actually stolen, however likely this might appear. For example, in April 1702 Devereaux Edgar committed Thomas Arnold to gaol in Ipswich after he was arrested at a market while in possession of a silver mug and a pair of silver buckles. In 1730 William Pope from Castle Rising, in Norfolk, was committed to prison in Bury after three valuable

103. *Sun*, 31 March 1796.
104. *Daily Gazetteer* (London Edition), 17 November 1737.
105. *London Evening Post*, 21–24 May 1748.
106. *London Daily Advertiser*, 26 September 1752.
107. *Daily Gazetteer* (London Edition), 6 December 1737.

cased silver watches and eight horses had been found in his possession or under his control. This was highly suspicious in a man who admitted to having no place of legal settlement.[108] In both cases considerable efforts would have to be made to identify the provenance of apparently stolen goods while the suspect was held in custody, if a conviction was to be secured. Sometimes advertisements might be placed to find victims. In 1752 an elderly Scottish woman was committed to the house of correction at Colchester, in Essex, for vagrancy. She had over £100 on her person, and an advertisement was published, "to acquaint the publick that it is suspected she did not come by this fairly."[109]

In exceptional cases it might be legally possible to circumvent the requirement that such goods be provably stolen. For example, at the Suffolk Quarter Sessions held at Woodbridge on 16 April 1760, John Row was convicted of stealing a quantity of wheat, "the property of persons unknown."[110] However, this was unusual. Much more typically, in 1783 William Webb and George Watling, privates in the East Suffolk militia quartered in Bury, were committed to prison after four geese and two turkeys were found in their quarters, which were "supposed stolen." A few days later they were discharged from custody without any action being taken against them.[111] Presumably it had been impossible to find the original owners of the birds and so identify them as stolen, while the soldiers had made no admissions.

If a suspect admitted that goods had been stolen this problem did not arise. In 1780 James Buncle was examined and committed to the Norwich city gaol by the mayor on suspicion of stealing six chickens from someone at Heigham. Although this person had yet to be identified, a confession had been extracted from Buncle. In its absence, he may have been released.[112] More than 30 years later, Robert Gilbert was convicted of a serious burglary at the Yarmouth Borough Sessions purely on his own

108. *Read's Weekly Journal Or British Gazetteer*, 21 November 1730.
109. *Ipswich Journal*, 6 June 1752.
110. SRO B105/2/32, p. 273.
111. *Ipswich Journal*, 11 and 18 January 1783.
112. *Norfolk Chronicle*, 11 October 1783.

confession, there being no other evidence against him. (This was unusual, and subsequently advanced as a ground for reprieve from execution).[113]

Aggravating this problem, numerous suspects had to make a difficult decision when questioned: continue to deny the allegations made against them in the hope of walking free at trial, or co-operate with the authorities in the hope that they would be made a Crown evidence against accomplices or, at the least, be reprieved from any ensuing capital conviction. Early admissions to a JP could be an important factor in granting clemency. Before he was executed for armed robbery at the Suffolk Assizes in 1733, the fairly youthful but uneducated Samuel Partridge claimed that he was innocent and had made admissions only because a fellow inmate in Halsted bridewell, where he had initially been held after arrest, had advised him that "if he confessed the fact he would come off very well, and advised him to say that he had made use of a bolt [i.e., a fake gun] instead of a pistol." (Interestingly, it seems that a bolt was subsequently found hidden where Partridge suggested it would be.)[114] Similarly, Nathan Nicholls made a belated confession to a JP while in prison, largely blaming his father for the murder of his sister. After conviction he sought to retract it, claiming that he had "only done it by advice of a prisoner in Ipswich Gaol, with a hope of saving his own life."[115]

The courts became more careful about admitting confessions as the century advanced, especially after the 1740s.[116] As Lord Mansfield noted in 1775, all too often people made confessions under threats or promises. As a consequence, frequently "such examinations and confessions have not been made use of against them on their trial."[117] For example, in December 1754 it was reported that David Dent had "sacrilegiously" stolen brass plate and bell metal from the church of South Creek, in Norfolk (his native parish), a crime to "which he has confess'd."[118] Despite this, he was acquitted at trial. Increasingly, as Lord Mansfield's comment suggests, the courts investigated confessions and excluded or disregarded

113. TNA HO 47/47/24, ff 192–198.
114. *London Journal (1720)*, 14 April 1733.
115. Anon, *The Trial of John and Nathan Nichols*, 1794, p. 8.
116. J. H. Langbein, *The Origins of Adversary Trial*, 2005, p. 220.
117. *The King v Margaret Caroline Rudd* (1775) 1 Leach 115, 168 E.R. 160.
118. *Whitehall Evening Post Or London Intelligencer*, 28–31 December 1754.

those obtained by duress or inducements. JPs appreciated this. In 1800, after Sarah Lloyd was arrested for burglary and arson, she was taken before a local Suffolk magistrate, Thomas Gooch, who examined her in the presence of his clerk, George Parsons. Parsons ultimately produced Lloyd's marked (she was illiterate) confession at the assizes, after assuring the court that it had been "made voluntarily, without promises or threatenings."[119]

However, the rough and tumble of provincial trials, which were less subject to public scrutiny than those at the Old Bailey, meant that there was much variation and latitude in this regard. As late as 1835 a clerical magistrate attending a murder trial at the Gloucestershire Assizes, in which the most important evidence was the young defendant's confession, witnessed a remarkably robust approach to this issue from the trial judge. During cross-examination, it was put to the keeper of the bridewell where the defendant had initially been incarcerated that he had offered him inducements to make admissions. The keeper "hesitated a good deal" when replying. The magistrate who took the confession admitted that he had not cautioned the defendant before receiving it. Nevertheless, and despite a vigorous submission from defence counsel that the confession should be excluded, it was admitted, the judge feeling that there should not be an "over scrupulous adherence to a punctilious rule."[120] Many aspects of the pre-trial examination remained unregulated until 1848.[121]

Committal for Trial

Having conducted his examination, and taken sworn depositions from the prosecutor and potential prosecution witnesses, a justice would decide whether to commit a matter for trial and, if so, to what forum and for what crime. In the absence of a confession, he would have to be satisfied that an offence had been committed and that there was at least one credible witness willing to swear to the suspect's being guilty of it. Thus, in December 1781 John Fenn committed Benjamin Jessop of Weasenham to

119. W. Notcutt, *Trial of Joseph Clarke, the Younger, and Sarah Lloyd, at the Assizes, held at Bury St. Edmund's*, 1800, pp. 6–8.
120. D. Verey (ed.), *The Diary of a Cotswold Parson*, 2003, pp. 95–96.
121. W. Pue, "The Criminal Twilight Zone: Pre-trial Procedures in the 1840s," 1983, pp. 335–364.

the Norfolk gaol, in Norwich, "charged on the oath of Thomas Gunton, of Tittleshall, wheelwright, on a violent suspicion of stealing a quantity of ash wood, from out of a wheelwright's yard."[122] At about the same time, John Cook was committed to the same prison, "charged on the oaths of several persons with stealing three guineas."[123] The following year Mary Baldwin was committed to the Norwich city gaol "charged on the oath of Mary Stannard with stealing from her dwelling-house some wearing apparel, her property."[124] Of course, such allegations could be mistaken. In 1764 Mary Taylor spent almost two weeks in Ipswich gaol on suspicion of stealing over £25 from James Massers before being discharged, the money having been found in Massers' house.[125]

In practice, even at the start of the period, magistrates could use their personal authority to dissuade complainants from swearing to weak cases. For example, in 1707 an apparently mistaken allegation of highway robbery was made against two respectable travellers in Kent. After they were arrested, three JPs sat in on their examinations and those of their accusers. The magistrates unanimously concluded that the accusation was "frivolous and vexatious." As a result, they warned the complainant of the possible consequences of swearing a "rash oath" in support of his allegation. The complainant initially decided not to press charges. The justices then cleared and discharged the two suspects.[126] As the century advanced, JPs became slightly more robust and open about throwing out cases that appeared inherently weak, even if a witness was prepared to swear to them, whatever legal theory dictated.[127]

As in other parts of eighteenth-century England, during the latter decades of the period, a practice developed in East Anglia of holding additional examinations for suspects in serious or debatable cases after the initial questioning was over, with the suspect being remanded in custody in the meantime. This allowed time for further investigations to be conducted into both the crime and the detained man or woman.

122. *Norfolk Chronicle*, 22 December 1781.
123. Ibid., 15 December 1781.
124. Ibid., 26 October 1782.
125. Ibid., 18 February 1764.
126. Anon, *An Impartial Account of the Malicious Prosecution of John Comyn, and Chadwick Chambers*, 1709, p. 9.
127. J. H. Langbein, *The Origins of Adversary Trial*, 2005, p. 47.

For example, one Friday in 1784 George Jordan, a former soldier in the Scots Fusiliers who had been discharged from the army a year earlier and lived at Cranworth, was apprehended near Norwich after trying to sell gold rings and silver spoons to local people. When examined by Sir Thomas Beevor on suspicion of theft, he claimed to have found the goods abandoned in a paper parcel on a road near Swaffham. Perhaps unsurprisingly, he was remanded in custody to Wymondham bridewell for further examination on the following Monday.[128] Jordan was ultimately convicted of theft at the Norfolk Assizes in August 1784.[129] By contrast, in 1782 the victim of a burglary at Carrowe Abbey Farm, near Norwich, announced that a suspect who had been taken into custody was no longer in the frame: "I do declare that, upon the strictest Enquiry being made, he appeared perfectly Innocent."[130] If there was a regularly sitting petty sessions nearby, this second examination might be conducted by two or more justices when it next convened. Nevertheless, the legality of multiple examinations was often questioned.

Recognisances to Prosecute

Having decided to indict a matter, justices would usually bind over in recognisances the person who would prosecute the suspect and sometimes those who might be required to give evidence for the Crown. Thus, in 1740, when Charles Drew was sent to trial for murder, it was noted that "four persons are bound over to prosecute him at the next Assizes to be held at Bury."[131] In theory such individuals would forfeit their recognisances if they failed to appear to testify. These were usually for at least £20 and often £40 or more. In practice, the courts were sometimes merciful if a satisfactory excuse for non-attendance was advanced.

Although most commonly used for felonies, a few individuals were also entered into recognisances to prosecute misdemeanours. For example, in 1733 Thomas Cowley and Robert Ashley were bound over in the sum of £10 each to appear at the King's Lynn sessions to prosecute Stephen

128. *Whitehall Evening Post (1770)*, 15–18 May 1784.
129. TNA ASSI 33/6–7.
130. *Norfolk Chronicle*, 2 March 1782.
131. *Ipswich Journal*, 15 March 1740.

Harris and Thomas Carr for "cheating at play." This seems to have been a fairly standard sum for those prosecuting the lesser form of indictable crime at the lower forum, as the same year John Sykes was bound over in the sum of £10 to prosecute Thomas Cross for assault and battery.[132]

As these cases suggest, the magistrate-issued recognisance played a crucial role in processing suspects through the eighteenth-century criminal justice system. However, it had other vital functions. JPs could bind over those involved in disturbances to be of good behaviour, and misdemeanour suspects to appear at quarter sessions even if there had, as yet, been no decision to indict them for an offence. An important measure was that defendants could enter recognisances to appear at trial if bailed.

Bail

If an examining justice committed a suspect for trial, he or she would have to decide whether to bail him or her for the intervening period, or remand him or her to the county gaol to await the hearing. All misdemeanours were bailable, provided that fairly modest recognisances were available to guarantee the suspect's appearance. These were usually only a problem for the very poor, especially those who were far from home, friends, and family, although a somewhat higher proportion of suspects were held in prison for a few specific misdemeanours, such as attempted sodomy. Typically, when Judith Vincent was accused of buying stolen goods from Peter Jarrard in 1733 (a misdemeanour in this case), she was allowed to attend the Lynn sessions under her own steam, having personally entered into a recognisance of £20 to do so, with William Vincent (presumably husband, father or brother) guaranteeing the same amount of money for her appearance. (She was acquitted at trial.)[133] Frequently the sums pledged were much smaller.

Those suspected of felony would find it much harder to obtain release pending trial, and the great majority of them were remanded in custody. Nevertheless, the law governing bail was notoriously complicated and sometimes quietly ignored. Exceptionally, even murder suspects might

132. NRO Lynn Sessions Book 1726–1752, KL/C 20/1.
133. NRO Lynn Sessions Book 1726–1752, KL/C 20/1.

be bailed, although there was some legal debate as to whether this was entirely proper. In 1753 two wealthy gentlemen, John Sheppard and John Jenkinson, were indicted for the murder of an ash gatherer at Sweffling, in Suffolk. Nevertheless, they did not appear to take their trials, indicating that they were on bail at the time. The pair appeared at the following assizes, where they were acquitted. Their high social status may help to explain why they were not held in custody.[134] In 1736 there were rumours that Christopher Hewett, accused of murder after a knifing in Suffolk, was to be bailed, although this does not appear to have transpired.[135]

Cases of burglary, housebreaking, and robbery were also bailed on rare occasions. Relevant factors included the gravity of the offence, the strength of the evidence against the suspect, his reputation and any previous criminal record, his state of health (prison was gruelling), and, vitally, his ability to arrange recognisances.[136] The latter required men of some means. These were not always easily found. In May 1702, after it was alleged that Captain Samuel Spicer had fraudulently obtained money from wool producers, Devereaux Edgar warned him that "unless he had very good sureties" he would commit him to gaol. The captain then went into Ipswich with a constable and two other men (to prevent him escaping), in an unsuccessful attempt to find acquaintances willing to stand surety for his appearance at the ensuing assizes.[137]

Many felt that, even for a potentially clergyable felony like grand larceny, the sum for those bailed should never be set at less than £40, in many situations much more.[138] If suspects were accused of a serious non-clergyable crime or were wealthy, amounts could be considerable. In 1800 William and Jemima Woltin, a brother and sister, who committed perjury when prosecuting a former maid at Suffolk Assizes, were detained in the county gaol "but on the same evening were admitted to bail, on finding sureties for 500l each."[139] If suspects failed to appear for trial, recognisances would be forfeited. In 1763 a man named Ray from

134. *Ipswich Journal*, 18 August 1753.
135. *Daily Gazetteer*, 31 March 1736; *London Daily Post and General Advertiser*, 30 December 1735.
136. A. Highmore, *A Digest of the Doctrine of Bail in Civil and Criminal Cases*, 1783, pp. 152–155.
137. SRO QS 347.96, *The Devereux Edgar Notebook*, transcribed by S. R. Schofield, 1956, vol. 1, p. 27.
138. Anon (By an attorney at law), *The Law of Arrests in Both Civil and Criminal Cases*, 1742, p. 237.
139. *The Times*, 8 August 1800, p. 3.

Saxmundham, committed to prison for sodomitical practices and, "afterwards admitted to Bail, not appearing, his Recognizance was estreated."[140]

Individuals (other than the accused) who vouched money for bail had to be acceptable to the magistrates, as well as personally solvent. In 1796 Richard Stroud, an excise officer, was arrested for stealing 6 pounds of candles, worth four shillings, from the workshop of a Yarmouth tallow chandler. His superior, William Goodrick, the supervisor of the excise at Yarmouth, later noted that he had offered to put up money to bail the prisoner, but this was refused because both of them were strangers to the area, having come from Greenwich, in Kent.[141]

The vagaries of the bail system attracted regular criticism. In the Culling case, a newspaper correspondent noted that both men accused of sodomy had been granted bail by the same magistrate. However, Culling had been unable to make the enormous sum required of him as security, unlike his wealthier partner, of whom less had been demanded. It was not obvious "[w]hy two hundred Pounds Security was taken from the accused, a man not worth a Shilling, and one hundred Pounds only from a Gentleman of five hundred Pounds a Year."[142]

The absence of bail could have unfortunate consequences. Some people were incarcerated in atrocious circumstances for crimes of which they were innocent. In 1741, just before he was executed for burglary at the Suffolk Assizes, Henry Crack noted that, after he had broken into a house in Parham, some three years earlier, three "entirely innocent" men had initially been committed to Ipswich gaol for the crime, although later discharged at Woodbridge sessions.[143] When examined in 1755, the highwayman Thomas Herring admitted robbing a clergyman just outside Norwich the previous month, and declared that a man who was then in the city's gaol for the same crime was "entirely innocent."[144]

140. *The Ipswich Journal*, 26 March and 6 August 1763.
141. TNA HO 47/22/16, ff 73–75.
142. *St. James's Chronicle*, 7–9 April 1763.
143. *London Evening Post*, 8–11 August 1741.
144. *Read's Weekly Journal Or British Gazetteer*, 15 November 1755.

CHAPTER 6

The Coroner and His Inquest

Introduction

Coroners performed a vital function in the investigation and prosecution of all forms of homicide. There were three types in eighteenth-century England, depending on the jurisdiction. By far the most important were those appointed for the counties, each of which normally had between two and (more commonly) four designated officers. Occasionally they had more: Norfolk had five coroners in 1616, as did Kent in 1797.[1] A few large counties had six men. However, franchise jurisdictions in certain liberties and a tiny number of individual manors had their own officers, independent of those for the surrounding county. Nationally there were about 80 of these in 1726, including three in Suffolk and five in Norfolk.[2] For example, the Liberty of St Etheldreda, in Suffolk, had a dedicated coroner, as did the Liberty of the Duchy of Lancaster, in Norfolk, albeit that this position was usually combined with another office, such as that of bailiff. The latter jurisdiction was based around East Dereham and included some 250 parishes, mainly in the north of the county, but with some, like Castle Acre, much further away. It included towns such as Aylsham, Cromer, Fakenham, Holt, Hunstanton, Reepham, North Walsham and Wells-next-the-Sea. East Dereham itself was outside the jurisdiction for which it was the centre.

1. E. Hasted, *The History and Topographical Survey of the County of Kent*, Volume 1, 1797, pp. 214–215.
2. P. J. Fisher, *The Politics of Sudden Death: The Office and Role of the Coroner in England and Wales, 1726–1888*, 2013, p. 66.

Many of the individual towns and cities also had their own officers responsible for investigating deaths within their limits, having successfully excluded the county coroner in the medieval period. Thus Norwich had been authorised to elect two coroners during the reign of Henry II. Typically, in May 1758 Jehosaphat Postle and Christopher Newman were elected to the office at the city assembly.[3] Postle was a prosperous brewer who was active in local politics. Newman would continue to serve as a coroner for many years to come. Sometimes the two officers of a city worked together on difficult cases. For example, in 1789 both Thomas Marks and Edward Crane were present at the ten-hour inquest that concluded that Aaron Fakenham had murdered his wife by putting arsenic in her breakfast tea.[4] Great Yarmouth also had two coroners (elected annually), as did Ipswich.[5] Many other East Anglian towns had at least one.

Quite frequently borough coroners were *ex officio* positions for those holding political office in the smaller towns. Such coroners were dependent on another trade to secure a livelihood, as they did not earn enough from their fees to make a living. Most did not conduct enough inquests to develop much expertise in the role, and this could be a weakness in the system.

Coroners represented the interests of the state, but, unlike the Crown-appointed justices, were normally elected by freeholders (*ex officio* officers apart) if there was more than one nomination for the position, whether at county quarter sessions or borough session. If a vacancy arose unexpectedly, an ad hoc election might be called. For example, when Francis Munhall resigned his position as a Norfolk coroner in 1795, an election was held at the shirehall in Norwich. Some 1,500 Norfolk freeholders, including gentlemen, husbandmen, gardeners, weavers, ironmongers, thatchers, farmers, millers, and even labourers, voted in a contest between two men for the position.[6] There was often little competition from suitably qualified individuals for the less remunerative borough positions. In Ipswich during the eighteenth century, no polls appear to have been

3. Anon, *The History of the City and County of Norwich*, 1768, Volume 1, p. 352.
4. *Whitehall Evening Post (1770)*, 1–3 October 1789.
5. SRO Y/S/ 2/1–4 MF 1031.
6. Anon, *The Poll for Electing A Coroner for Norfolk, Occasioned by the Resignation of Mr. Francis Munhall*, 1795, pp. 1–36.

held to elect the two nominated officers.[7] Some coroners in liberties appear to have been appointed without election.

Many coroners served until death or physical incapacity prevented their continuing in office. It was difficult to dismiss them against their wishes, especially for incompetence. In general, they could be removed only for wilful neglect of duty, after conviction for extortion, or for committing a misdemeanour in office (25 Geo II, c 29). The last of these was a rare occurrence. An examination of the circumstances leading to the election of more than 500 county coroners between 1730 and 1888 produces just one vacancy created by a prosecution on this ground—in Shropshire in 1823—although the magistrates of Kent came close to bringing another in 1806.[8]

In earlier centuries, when the county office had been held in considerable regard, it had attracted some high-ranking men. For example, Sir Nathaniel Bacon, a Cambridge-educated member of Gray's Inn, became a Norfolk coroner in 1599, was knighted in 1604, and served as deputy lieutenant for the county from 1605.[9] By the eighteenth century, the office did not carry great prestige or high levels of remuneration. The only prerequisite for appointment was that the candidate owned freehold land in the relevant county. Nevertheless, some education and native ability was required. Until 1733 a basic knowledge of Latin was helpful when preparing documents for the assizes. As a result, the position often appealed to minor gentlemen. Typically for the eighteenth century, John Hubbard, a Suffolk coroner of the 1760s, was simply given the suffix "Gent" in contemporary newspaper reports, as were most county coroners of the era.[10]

The county positions could be fairly demanding, involving a considerable amount of travelling, often at short notice. At petty sessions held in February 1709, the newly appointed James Woods from Bramford, in Suffolk, who had been chief (high) constable of the Bosmere and Claydon Hundred, asked to be discharged from his former office specifically

7. J. D. Clemis, *Government in an English Provincial Town: The Corporation of Ipswich, 1720–95*, 1999, p. 102.
8. P. J. Fisher, "Edmund Whitcombe and the Detection of Homicide in Georgian Shropshire," 2011, p. 4.
9. D. J. Murray, *Crown and Community: The Coroner in Early Modern England, 1580–1630*, 2013, pp. 23–24.
10. *Lloyd's Evening Post*, 16–19 September 1763.

because it was "highly inconvenient with his Coronorship." Another man from the same town was immediately sworn in as a replacement.[11]

Although it was not an essential requirement, most eighteenth-century county coroners were lawyers (usually attorneys) or doctors by training, the former being significantly more common than the latter.[12] In the late eighteenth and early nineteenth centuries, only about a quarter appear to have had a medical background. However, there was no formal requirement for any form of professional status (legal or medical) until 1926. Inevitably, and not unreasonably, most of those who served in a county position were motivated by the "perquisites and fees which they are by statute allowed to take."[13] An archaic, medieval scale governed these until 1752, when it was substantially revised by Parliament (25 Geo II, c 29). Salaries were not introduced until 1860.

While county coroners could not hold inquests within boroughs or in most liberties that had their own officers, they could act anywhere else in their shires. Even so, for reasons of convenience and expense, parishes would normally send for the coroner who lived closest to them, creating customary areas of responsibility for these officers. Some counties even stipulated that full travelling expenses and allowances would be paid only if the coroner nearest to a death had been summoned. Ideally, therefore, the coroners would reside in different parts of the county. At the Suffolk Quarter Sessions held at Beccles on 14 April 1760, a coroner named Hubbard was awarded £7 12s for holding four inquests at the standard (non-homicide) rate of 20 shillings each, combined with a nine pence per mile travelling allowance of £3 12s. The last figure suggests an average journey of 12 miles each way for the hearings.[14]

Adjournments were permitted during inquests, unlike assizes trials (until the 1790s), although they were often impractical, given the travelling distances involved and the lack of additional fees for any further appearances by the coroner. Nevertheless, if there was a strong possibility

11. SRO QS 347.96, *The Devereux Edgar Notebook*, transcribed by S. R. Schofield, 1956, vol. 2, p. 202.
12. P. J. Fisher, *The Politics of Sudden Death: The Office and Role of the Coroner in England and Wales, 1726–1888*, 2013, p. 91.
13. E. Hasted, *The History and Topographical Survey of the County of Kent*, vol. 1, 1797, pp. 214–215.
14. SRO B105/2/32, p. 269.

that an important witness or suspect would become available for examination within a reasonably short time, a hearing might be delayed slightly. For example, when Thomas and Elizabeth Carter were found butchered at Cratfield, in Suffolk, one Thursday morning in October 1793, the coroner did not sit on their bodies until the Monday, and then adjourned the hearing to the following Friday "on account of various suspicions."[15] When it met again, it adjourned once more for a week, "not being able to discover the perpetrators thereof."[16] Unfortunately, when it met for the third time it was still unable to identify the killer, and so returned a verdict of "wilful murder against some person or persons unknown."[17]

The Coroner's Work

The coroner's most important duty was to enquire into suspicious, sudden, or violent deaths, whether occasioned by homicide, suicide, accident, or unexplained medical problems. Coroners also investigated all deaths, however caused, that occurred in prisons. This could be important in towns with several custodial establishments. For example, of the 119 preserved inquests from Norwich for the first two decades of the century, 44 (about 37 per cent) were investigations into the deaths of prison inmates. A majority were incarcerated debtors rather than felons, which was probably a reflection of their numbers and greater average age and vulnerability to sickness. As this suggests, disease was by far the most common cause of death in these cases. However, prisoners could also be vulnerable to abusive treatment by those in charge, and this was one reason for holding such inquests. The Norwich figures include an investigation into the death of a female prisoner in the city gaol after alleged mistreatment by its keeper.[18] Similarly, in 1763 it was claimed that Jane Tolworthy, a young inmate of the Mildenhall Workhouse, had died of the bruises she received from Thomas Eagle, the keeper. An inquest presided over by John Hubbard, a Suffolk county coroner, committed Eagle to

15. *Morning Chronicle*, 1 November 1793.
16. *Lloyd's Evening Post*, 4–6 November 1793.
17. *Morning Post*, 22 November 1793.
18. NRO NCR Case 6a/4/68/1 and 2.

Bury Gaol to await trial at the forthcoming assizes.[19] Although indicted for murder in March 1764, he was acquitted of any offence; such cases were often hard to prove to a satisfactory standard at trial.[20]

More generally, and ignoring prisons, a verdict of accidental death was one of the most common outcomes for an inquest. In eighteenth-century Cheshire it was given five times as often as all forms of deliberate killing taken together.[21] In many places the proportion was much higher. In Norwich it seems that cases of homicide, whether murder, manslaughter, or infanticide, made up less than a tenth of all surviving inquests during the first 20 years of the eighteenth century. The proportion then rapidly fell even further. In Suffolk, complete bundles of inquests for the Liberty of St Etheldreda have survived for each year from 1767 to 1858 (1856 apart). The great majority were for accidents (44.7 per cent of the total) or cases in which death was due to natural causes (34.9 per cent), with a significant number of suicides (12 per cent) and those washed up on the coast, having drowned at sea (6.1 per cent), also being considered. Only 21 cases (about 3 per cent) were identified as instances of murder or manslaughter, and this figure includes the killing of seven unwanted babies.[22]

A typical example of a coroner's practice can be seen in December 1753, when one of the Norfolk county officers dealt with the case of a poor nine-year-old boy who had drowned in a small river in Forncett St Peter's on a Friday, and the following Monday investigated the death of a man who had been killed by a kick from a bullock near Wroxham.[23] Nevertheless, although investigating potential homicides was only a small part of the coroner's work, it was vital for the prosecution of murder, and he would receive an enhanced fee in such cases after 1752.

The inquest had to "sit" on a body that was physically set in front of it for inspection (by both the coroner and his jury), although the corpse did not have to be present during the hearing. This was a limitation to the process when individuals had disappeared in suspicious circumstances,

19. *Lloyd's Evening Post*, 16–19 September 1763.
20. TNA ASSI 33/4; *London Chronicle*, 17–20 September 1763.
21. J. Dickinson and J. Sharpe, "Coroners' Inquests in an English County, 1600–1800: a Preliminary Survey," 2011, p. 257.
22. D. Smith and L. Smith, *Sudden Deaths in Suffolk 1767–1858: A Survey of Coroners' Records in the Liberty of St Etheldreda*, 1995, pp. 1–6.
23. *Public Advertiser*, 25 December 1753.

and it was feared they had been murdered. However, coroners had the power to order exhumation where necessary, to allow an inquest to be held if suspicions arose after burial. For example, in August 1771 Christopher Newman, a Norwich coroner, issued a warrant for the exhumation of a five-year-old named Henry Pearson who had been buried the previous week. At the inquest, it transpired that almost two months earlier the boy had refused to come in from playing to have his dinner. This had infuriated his mother, who, in her annoyance, had thrown a small piece of iron at him. Unfortunately, this hit him and pierced his skull. Although he was taken to a surgeon and trepanned, the boy died from his wounds a few weeks later. The coroner's jury returned a verdict of manslaughter.[24] Four years later, Richard Wood, a Suffolk coroner, ordered that the body of Sarah Smith be dug up three days after she had been buried. There were suspicions that her husband had poisoned her. An autopsy by two surgeons "confirmed" this, and, along with other evidence, it led to a finding of murder by the inquest.[25]

Of course, decay placed an effective time limit on exhuming bodies, after which it would become a pointless exercise. There were also fears that rotten corpses could "infect the people by being dug up." In many cases, two weeks underground appears to have been a practical limit, although there were some cases in which bodies that had been interred for a longer time were exhumed.[26]

The coroner's jury was recruited from householders drawn from the parish in which a corpse had been found or those that adjoined it; frequently they were a mixture of the two. There was no other property requirement for membership. The local constable automatically became the coroner's officer for the purpose of raising this body, acting by strength of a warrant issued by the official. The social status of coroner's jurors varied considerably but was often quite modest. A significant number of the men selected for inquests in the City of Norwich early in the eighteenth century were unable to sign their names, but made a personal mark

24. *The Gentleman's Magazine and Historical Chronicle*, vol. 41, p. 375.
25. *Public Advertiser*, 31 January 1775.
26. T. Barlow, *The Justice of Peace: A Treatise Containing the Power and Duty of that Magistrate*, 1745, p. 148.

instead, something that by then was usually indicative of relatively low status amongst urban males.

However, because inquest jurors were local to a killing (unlike most assizes jurors), they would often have some background knowledge as to what had occurred, in the same way that *viceinage* had ensured that medieval trial juries knew something of a case before it came to court. This knowledge is likely to have had an affect on their verdicts. For example, in 1739, when Francis Trumble was tried for highway robbery at the Old Bailey, he called Thomas Steed, a former neighbour from his hometown of Ipswich, as a character witness. Steed noted that Trumble's parents had lived next door to him, and, when the defendant's mother had killed herself, after many unsuccessful attempts to do so, and a long history of mental disturbance, he (Steed) had sat "upon the Coroner's Inquest, and she was brought in Lunatick, for she had been reputed as such."[27] Clearly he was steeped in knowledge about the dead woman before becoming a juror in her case.

Nevertheless, in homicide inquests men summoned to serve on a coroner's jury who had a history of personal animosity towards an already identified suspect might be discharged, to prevent bias in adjudication.[28] Unfortunately, this did not preclude wider, more general, local prejudices affecting inquest jurors. For example, in March 1755, at the Bury Assizes, George Tufnell was swiftly acquitted of any offence when accused of murdering William Roberts during a disturbance arising from the election of bailiffs in Ipswich the previous September. There were strong doubts about identification and whether it was, in any event, a case of justified self-defence. The dead man had led a mob that tried to break into Tufnell's house around midnight while shouting, "[M]urder them all, pull the house down." They had already broken open the front door when Roberts was stabbed.[29] Despite this being a weak case, the coroner's jury, which finished its deliberations five days after the killing, swiftly signed and returned an inquisition implicating the well-to-do Tufnell in the full crime of murder. The coroner then issued an arrest warrant

27. OBSP, Trial of Francis Trumble, 18 July 1739: t17390718–10.
28. P. J. Fisher, "Edmund Whitcombe and the Detection of Homicide in Georgian Shropshire," 2011, p. 10.
29. *Read's Weekly Journal Or British Gazetteer*, 5 April 1755; TNA ASSI 33/2.

against him, as he had been absent from the hearing (it was mistakenly reported that he had "gone out of the kingdom").[30]

An inquest was usually assembled hurriedly after a suspicious or sudden death came to light, not least to prevent putrefaction setting in. As soon as a parish officer or magistrate made a coroner aware of the death, he was supposed to "go to the place forthwith."[31] He might be roused at the crack of dawn to do this. Sometimes an inquest sat on the very day that a body was discovered, especially if it was found in an urban area that had its own coroner or close to where a county coroner resided. (Inquests could not be conducted on a Sunday.) For example, on the same day in 1766 that Mary Stacy's illegitimate baby was found in Norwich with its throat cut, an inquest was held into the death and returned a verdict of wilful murder.[32] In more remote areas it might take a day or two for a county officer to arrive. Thus James Smyth, the coroner who sat on the deaths of William Webb and William Green, a dragoon and customs officer shot by smugglers at Old Hunstanton in 1785, arrived from Dereham a day after Green succumbed to his injuries.[33]

Inquests were frequently held in taverns. Alternatively, a church or workhouse might be used, as a large building was required to house all those involved in the process, as well as spectators. (Hearings were open to the public, something that helped preserve their independence.) For example, the inquest into William Webb and William Green was held in the *Cutter* alehouse. Occasionally even the house of a well-to-do murder victim might be pressed into service if it was sufficiently large, as occurred in Suffolk after the killing of Charles Drew in 1740 and Frances Phillips in 1782. Alternatively, the house of one of the dead person's neighbours might be used for this purpose.

30. *Public Advertiser*, 24 September 1754.
31. Anon, *The Coroner's Guide*, 1756, p. 10.
32. *St. James's Chronicle Or the British Evening Post*, 19–22 July 1766.
33. N. Holmes, *The Lawless Coast: Murder, Smuggling and Anarchy in the 1780s on the North Norfolk Coast*, 2008, p. 55.

The Quality of the Coroner's Work

According to some of the early historians of English forensic medicine, the coroner's inquest was woefully inadequate prior to the nineteenth century, being characterised by unqualified or even corrupt officials, uninterested and uneducated jurors, and the virtual absence of expert evidence. There was some contemporary support for such an analysis, and several scholars have reiterated it in the recent past.[34]

Certainly a few coroners were not competent or energetic, and some inquests were conducted in an inept or lackadaisical manner.[35] For example, in 1655 it was claimed that Newcastle coroners were not even looking at the bodies of those found drowned in the River Tyne, near the city, despite a legal duty to do so, and even though some of the dead were "respectable" people.[36] More than a century later, the Middlesex coroner Edward Umfreville claimed that many of his colleagues did not exercise a "becoming care and diligence" in their work.[37] One modern study suggests that, even in the early years of the nineteenth century, coroners in London were often fairly sanguine about what might be viewed as suspicious deaths, at least where the deceased had been poor and there were no obviously criminal wounds or suspects.[38] The limited forensic abilities of the era and coroners' lack of resources greatly compounded these problems, and meant that they were not nearly as effective at identifying subtle killings as the police are today.

The inquest conducted into the notorious domestic murder of John Beddingfield, for instance, the day after it occurred in Suffolk, in 1762, appears to have been lamentably incompetent. Although the coroner had been summoned because the death was clearly suspicious, the servants in the house were not questioned properly, and the physician who

34. M. Jackson, "Suspicious Infant Deaths: The Statute of 1624 and Medical Evidence at Coroners' Inquests," 1994, p. 64.
35. P. J. Fisher, "Edmund Whitcombe and the Detection of Homicide in Georgian Shropshire," 2011, pp. 3–23.
36. R. Gardiner, *England's Grievance Discovered, in Relation to the Coal-trade with the Map of the River of Tine,* 1655, p. 70.
37. E. Umfreville, *Lex Coronatoria*, 1761, p. iv.
38. M. Emmerichs, "Getting Away With Murder?: Homicide and the Coroners in Nineteenth-century London," 2001, pp. 93–100.

examined the body failed to spot obvious signs of manual strangulation. The inquest appears to have concluded that Beddingfield accidentally throttled himself while tossing in his sleep! The whole process was conducted in a rushed manner; the surgeon who testified arrived a little late, examined the body for just five minutes, and noted that the inquest members were "in a great hurry, the jury had been there a long time, particularly the coroner had been there so long he wanted to go home."[39]

Nevertheless, despite these reservations and examples, more recent work, examining a broader range of sources than the thin official records or the jaundiced views of individuals such as Umfreville, has qualified the traditional picture to a significant degree. Most of the inquests of the time were not as perfunctory as has sometimes been suggested. Many were fairly thorough in examining the bodies set before them, carefully searching for a wound that would explain the death and an explanation as to how the person came by it. Theories were often advanced and then tested by both coroner and jurors. For example, in a late seventeenth-century murder case from Gough, in Shropshire, the entire jury travelled several miles to determine whether an alleged killer had been visible from a particular window.[40] Inquest juries might also physically examine the place where a corpse was found and request that other evidence be adduced if available. When the inquest into the murder of Charles Drew (senior) was held in the dead man's house at Long Melford in 1740, his son and (as it eventually transpired) killer was in the same building "[S]everal of the jury requested of him, that he would attend the enquiry; but he absolutely refused to appear." (Unsurprisingly, this aroused suspicion).[41] The coroner would usually conduct a lengthy personal examination of a murder suspect during his inquest. The jurors and any representatives of the dead man might also ask questions.

Furthermore, by the start of the eighteenth century, inquests had recourse to expert testimony and to forensic autopsies much more frequently than was once thought, in provincial England as well as in the

39. Anon (an eminent short-hand writer), *The Genuine Trial of Margery Beddingfield and Richard Ringe*, 1763, p. 26.
40. C. Loar, "Medical Knowledge and the Early Modern English Coroner's Inquest," 2010, p. 489.
41. Anon, *The Suffolk Parricide; Being, the Trial Life, Transactions, and Last Dying Words of Charles Drew*, 1740, p. 8.

capital, even if there was no legal requirement that they take place. Their use, which dated back to at least the sixteenth century, increased steadily as the 1700s advanced. A selection of cases from East Anglia is indicative.

In November 1753, after an apparently newborn male baby was found in a "cockey" near Privy Lane, Norwich, the inquest into his death received the opinion of two local surgeons, who suggested that the baby had been deliberately thrown in and then drowned in the mud.[42] The use of two medical men in these situations appears to have been almost standard practice in the city at this time (it had a large number of doctors and surgeons), even for infanticide cases.

Doctors often demonstrated a considerable awareness of suspicious pathologies. In October 1782 the Mildenhall (Suffolk) surgeon John Syer told an inquest that he knew immediately he saw the elderly Frances Phillips's body that she had been strangled, due to the "very great prominence and fullness of the eyes and the lips."[43] In March 1798, when two surgeons, John Kinnell from Framlingham and William Goodwin from Earl Soham, attended a coroner's inquest into the death of Samuel Lanceter, they were expressly requested to open the deceased's head and examine his brain. On doing so, they found a considerable effusion of blood beneath the part of the skull where the dead man had been bruised, which, they concluded, "arose from external violence and to have been the Cause of the death of the S'd Samuel Lanceter."[44] By then these developments were causing novel problems, as doctors and physicians were often reluctant to provide a professional opinion without being paid for it, and parishes did not wish to burden ratepayers with the extra cost involved.

Even without expert evidence, an inquest could be quite thorough. For example, in November 1764 Thomas Turner, a shopkeeper from East Hoathly, in Sussex, who was also the local overseer of the poor, sat as the foreman of a 13-man jury at an inquest into the sudden death of Matthew Lewer, a poor lath cleaner who had been found dead in a

42. NRO NCR Case 6a/8/29.
43. T. Notcutt, *The Trial at Large of Jeremiah Theobald*, 1783, p. 7.
44. *William Goodwin of Street Farm, Earl Soham, Diaries dated from 1785–1810*, Vol. 3, HD 365/3, transcribed by Mrs. J. Rothery of Earl Soham, August 2001. www.earlsoham.org (Last accessed 15 December 2015).

nearby wood the previous evening. The coroner for the eastern part of the county was immediately sent for, and sat on the body the day after its discovery. Lewer was a fairly old man who had complained of feeling unwell, left work early, and died on his way home. Although medical evidence does not appear to have been received, the two men who found his corpse testified that there was no evidence of other people's footprints near the body or of a scuffle. Additionally, the coroner's jury carefully examined the corpse and could not find "any cut, bruise, stab or any other appearance of hurt." They quickly returned a verdict of natural death by the visitation of God.[45]

A case from Somerset occasioned rather more problems in 1774, but indicates a real attempt at getting to the truth. The body of a haymaker was found in the River Frome, missing some clothes, but without apparent marks of violence. However, it was discovered a short distance from a tavern with a notoriously bad reputation. Some jurors thought there had been foul play; others disagreed. They argued through the night and into the following day before compromising on a fairly non-committal narrative verdict, which allowed them to be discharged and the body to be buried.[46]

Coming to Notice

Coroners could act only if they were alerted to a sudden or suspicious death, whether by JPs, constables, members of the public, or parish searchers (women employed to lay out bodies and, *inter alia*, examine them for signs of foul play). The process of informing the coroner of a suspicious death could be a weakness in the system. In an increasingly transient society, yet one that still had limited means of communication, a significant number of deaths occasioned by homicide probably went entirely undetected rather than merely unsuspected.

For example, Richard Nobbs, a Norfolk brickmaker, hanged himself at Hempnall in 1785, after the skeletal remains of his son were found buried

45. D. Vaisey (ed.), *The Diary of Thomas Turner, 1754–1765*, 1994, pp. 307–308.
46. M. McGarvie (ed.), *The King's Peace, The Justice's Notebooks of Thomas Horner of Mells, 1770–1777*, 1997, p. 124.

in a local ditch. For several years he had explained the lad's absence by saying that he had enlisted as a soldier. The coroner's jury returned a verdict of "self-murder" on Richard and, as was normal with eighteenth-century suicides, he was buried at a nearby crossroads (still named for him).[47] In 1808 labourers clearing a ditch in Glemsford, in Suffolk discovered the skeletons of a woman and child. On investigation it was thought that they had been murdered eight or nine years earlier.[48]

Even when there was a body available, there might be an element of chance as to whether a death was identified as suspicious, or reported to a coroner when it was, at least where violence was not blatant. Although many people seem to have been keen to alert the authorities in such situations, others were reluctant to become involved. Similarly, some searchers were observant, others less so. Some might be bribed or susceptible to local pressure to turn a blind eye to suspicious deaths. Looking back over half a century, one observer described them as "gin drinking old women" and claimed that they performed their duties in a very inefficient manner.[49] However, some were clearly quite diligent and incorruptible. For example, after Benjamin Brett mortally wounded his adopted infant son in Suffolk during an outburst of temper, the child's mother (Brett's third wife) did not expose the crime. Instead, a local woman, summoned to assist in preparing the boy's body for burial, became suspicious after viewing his injuries. She informed a parish officer about the death and her concerns, which were fanned because Brett was "known to be naturally cruel." He had also disappeared. A thorough search followed, and he was detained a day or so later and committed to prison.[50] An inquest was duly held.

A case from 1799 is indicative of the slightly haphazard identification of suspicious deaths throughout the era. An inquest was hurriedly and belatedly arranged at Hundon, in West Suffolk, for John Hale, who had died some time after a fracas in a public house at Saffron Walden. At first nothing untoward had been suspected. When his corpse was being

47. *St. James's Chronicle Or the British Evening Post*, 16–18 June, 1785.
48. *Bury and Norwich Post*, 9 May 1808.
49. A. Andrews, *The Eighteenth Century Or Illustrations of the Manners and Customs or Our Grandfathers*, 1856, p. 50.
50. Anon, *Last Dying Speech and Full Confession of Benjamin Brett*, 1794, pp. 1–2.

conveyed into church for the burial service, one of the attendants discovered bruising and other marks on the body and informed the presiding minister, who immediately asked for an inquest to be held. This led to medical evidence and the testimony of 20 witnesses. It was discovered that the dead man had violent contusions to his loins and that, shortly before he died, had mentioned that a few days earlier he had fallen heavily in a public house after drinking and "receiving an unlucky blow from a person he had been in dispute with." (Even so, and indicative of a continuing robustness about lower-level violence, the coroner's jury returned a verdict of accidental death.)[51]

Coroners could also be discouraged from excessive activism by area magistrates. This became more common after the medieval system of remuneration was replaced in 1752 by providing a fee of £1 from the county purse for every inquest "duly taken" in a place that contributed to the county rates, as well as a supplement in homicide cases and a small allowance for travelling.[52] Payments for batches of completed inquests were usually authorised by JPs sitting at quarter sessions. Thus, at those for Suffolk held at Ipswich in July 1784, John Turner, a coroner for the county, was paid £8 14s 9d for holding six non-homicide inquests, his fees ranging from £1 2 3d to £1 18s 6d (including travelling allowances).[53]

Although fairly modest, such payments became a minor political issue in some parts of England during the latter years of the eighteenth century, being deemed "highly burdensome to the county."[54] Magistrates could refuse payment if they thought an inquest had been unnecessary—for example, if it was based on a vague suspicion of foul play that proved to be entirely unfounded. The higher courts were resistant to attempts to challenge such decisions. In 1808 Lord Chief Justice Ellenborough, sitting in the Court of King's Bench, even claimed that there had been many instances of coroners exercising their office in a highly vexatious and oppressive manner by "obtruding themselves into private families

51. *Bury and Norwich Post*, 6 February 1799.
52. P. J. Fisher, *The Politics of Sudden Death: The Office and Role of the Coroner in England and Wales, 1726–1888*, 2007, p. 6.
53. SRO B105/2/47, p. 77.
54. E. Hasted, *The History and Topographical Survey of the County of Kent*, vol. 1, 1797, pp. 214–215.

to their great annoyance and discomfort, without any pretence of the deceased having died otherwise than a natural death."[55]

Inevitably this must have encouraged a degree of official caution about investigating deaths where there was only a modest level of suspicion. This could have unfortunate consequences, as was to be seen in the following century. In 1843 the Norfolk Quarter Sessions resolved that a parish constable should not inform the local coroner of a death until he had obtained an official certificate stating that an inquest was necessary. Three years later a county coroner declined to hold inquests into the deaths of eight-month-old Elizabeth Pestle and her grandfather Jonathan Balls, despite local rumours that this was a murder and suicide, as he had no certificate and feared he would not be paid. Finally, after several requests, inquests were held and poison was found in both exhumed bodies. A further eight exhumations of other family members followed, with clear evidence of poison found in five of them.[56]

The Inquest Hearing

The coroner's jury was usually made up of about 15 men, who were normally sworn into office three or four at a time. There was no formal upper limit but it was almost never more than 24 jurors. Conversely, many Norwich city inquests in the early eighteenth century, like that which sat on the discovery of a baby girl's body on 21 March 1712, had the bare minimum of a dozen men.[57] Although it was supposed to show a degree of deference to the directions of the coroner, the jury was free to return whatever verdict appeared appropriate to the evidence, even if he disagreed with it. The jury did not have to be unanimous, but at least a dozen of its members had to agree on its decision. Possible verdicts ranged from accident to murder as well as, *inter alia*, Act of God (lightning, etc.), Visitation of God (natural causes), suicide, and manslaughter. Thus the coroner's inquest that sat on the body of William Brokenham, a 74-year-old man who was thrown from a cart and run

55. P. J. Fisher, "Getting Away with Murder? The Suppression of Coroners' Inquests in Early Victorian England and Wales," 2007, pp. 47–62.
56. Ibid., p. 50.
57. NRO NCR Case 6a/4/12.

over in Norwich marketplace, dying from his injuries the following day, found nothing of general concern: "The Jury after some consideration on the nature of the evidence, and the view of the body... brought in their verdict accidental death."[58]

If the jury was unsure how a death was occasioned, they might deliver a narrative verdict. Thus in June 1752, after the corpse of ten-year-old John Pickerell was pulled out of the river between Blackfriars Bridge and Fye Bridge in Norwich, the inquest could not determine how he came to fall in: "[W]hether he threw himself or was thrown is unknown."[59] Similarly, in 1823 a Shropshire coroner's jury decided that a woman had died from loss of blood "but how occasioned we could not find." When the coroner asked them if they meant that she had died by the Visitation of God, they expressly denied agreeing to such an interpretation. (After the inquest, new evidence eventually led to a murder prosecution.)[60]

By contrast, other inquests ended up setting the ground for homicide trials. Coroners were required to attend assizes to produce accounts of any findings of murder or manslaughter to the clerk of that forum.[61] At the Lent Assizes for Norfolk in 1777, two coroners, one for the county and the other for the Duchy of Lancaster (in Norfolk), were each fined 40s for non-attendance at the higher jury court (one fine was later remitted).[62] Their decisions would be used to found prosecutions, and were kept with the files of the relevant circuit (rather than being sent to King's Bench like other inquests). Because a suspect could be tried on their "inquisitions," coroners effectively had the power to indict directly to an assizes trial without the intervention of that body's grand jury.

How far inquest verdicts influenced the counts later brought at assizes is a matter of some debate. Those accused of a homicide offence would normally stand trial on both the coroner's inquisition and an indictment approved by the court's own grand jury, with verdicts being returned on both at the same time. The offence alleged was frequently, but not

58. *Norfolk Chronicle*, 28 December 1782.
59. NRO NCR Case 6a/8/12.
60. P. J. Fisher, "Edmund Whitcombe and the Detection of Homicide in Georgian Shropshire," 2011, p. 11.
61. Anon, *The Coroner's Guide*, 1756, p. 22.
62. TNA ASSI 33/6.

invariably, the same. During the eighteenth century, it was normal practice for an assizes grand jury to indict for murder if it decided there was any type of case to answer for homicide, even where a manslaughter verdict had been returned at an inquest and this was clearly the more pertinent charge. This might mean a trial proceeding simultaneously on a grand-jury indictment for murder and a coroner's "inquisition" for manslaughter. The verdicts on the two types of indictment were, of course, always the same. Thus, when Robert Cary was accused at the Lent Assizes for Suffolk in 1747 of killing John Lock, that court's grand jury committed him for trial on the full charge of murder. Rather more realistically on the facts, the coroner's inquisition had committed him only for trial for manslaughter. Cary was acquitted of both forms of homicide, the jury concluding that Lock "came to death by misfortune and chance medley."[63]

It was possible for a defendant to be tried solely on a grand-jury indictment or purely on a coroner's inquisition. The former was unusual, but not unheard of, especially when suspicions of murder arose after a coroner's inquest had been held but before a suspect (or even a homicide) had been identified. In 1754 two gentlemen who had been indicted for the murder of Robert Martin, a Suffolk ash gatherer, were acquitted, although it was reported that the coroner's inquest that considered the case the previous year had brought in a verdict of chance medley (by then, normally used for non-culpable homicide). As a result, they may have stood trial purely on the grand-jury indictment.[64] Conversely, a defendant might be tried solely on a coroner's inquest, the grand jury having thrown the case out. This appears to have been the situation at the Bury Assizes in March 1752, when John Wright was tried for "slaying John Rich" (an allegation of manslaughter). Two other men, James Hunt and Ellis Goddard, were prosecuted for aiding and abetting the crime. All were acquitted of any offence. There does not appear to have been a grand-jury indictment in this case, suggesting that they did not feel that there was any homicide case to answer, a view with which the

63. Gray's Inn MS 45.

64. TNA ASSI 33/2; *Ipswich Journal*, 21 April 1753; T. S. *A Dissertation Concerning the Evil Nature and Fatal Consequence of Immoderate Anger and Revenge*, 1725, p. 59.

trial jury appears to have agreed.[65] Similarly, Abraham Northern seems to have stood trial purely on a coroner's inquisition of manslaughter, after accidentally shooting a man in Norwich.[66] He, too, was acquitted of "slaying" John Wright, at the City of Norwich Assizes in July 1755.[67]

Parish officials or even private individuals could be bound over to prosecute homicide suspects by the coroner (an example of quasi-public prosecution), who could also bind over witnesses to appear at the assizes to give evidence (just as he could summon them to appear at his own hearing). Furthermore, the coroner could commit a suspect to prison pending such a trial. Thus Daniel Mallows and his wife, Elizabeth, were tried for murdering Sarah Kimmin as the result of a coroner's inquest held in 1747. Although Daniel had carried the dying Sarah to Thorpe, in Norfolk, the coroner and his jury became suspicious after viewing her body, and concluded that she had been poisoned with arsenic ingested in a glass of wine the couple had served her. The coroner had Daniel committed to the county gaol to await trial. His wife followed shortly afterwards.[68] (Both were acquitted at the Thetford Assizes).[69]

In like manner, in 1742, after two babies were found dead in Ipswich, sealed in a locked box with bunches of lavender to mask the smell of decay, the "Coroner's opinion was that Mary Howe was the mother and brought in a verdict of wilful murder[;] she was committed to gaol and to be try'd at the next Assizes."[70] In a similar crime in January 1782, it was noted that Elizabeth Usher, who had been "charged with the wilful murder of her newborn bastard child, was conveyed to Ipswich gaol, by virtue of the coroner's warrant."[71]

There would often be close liaison between coroner and assizes, just as there was between the assizes and the examining justice, and between the latter official and a coroner. The coroner might also arrange for exhibits to be sent to trial. For example, in 1794, at Samuel Hammond's hearing for murder at the Lent Assizes in Bury, the coroner who had investigated

65. TNA ASSI 33/2.
66. *Read's Weekly Journal Or British Gazetteer*, 19 July 1755.
67. TNA ASSI 33/2.
68. *Whitehall Evening Post Or London Intelligencer*, 15–18 August 1747.
69. Gray's Inn MS 45.
70. *Ipswich Journal*, 20 February 1742.
71. *Norfolk Chronicle*, 12 January 1782.

the death sent a parcel of bloodstained clothes for examination by the tribunal.[72]

Any admissions made during an inquest, like those made before an examining JP, would be summarised in writing and admissible at an ensuing assizes trial, provided they had been obtained without duress or inducements. The coroner might be called to prove this at the hearing, just like an examining JP or his clerk. Thus Samuel Ward, a Suffolk coroner, conducted an inquest into the death of Thomas Briggs in 1792. The suspected killer, the youthful Thomas Harper, had been held overnight in Lakenheath after arrest, and was then taken before a magistrate for questioning. Shortly afterwards he was produced at, and gave evidence to, the inquest into Briggs's death. He made a full confession to the murder at this forum, which the coroner recorded and which was then marked by the illiterate youth. Ward later gave evidence at Harper's trial at the Bury Assizes. (Before the confession was admitted into evidence, the presiding judge was careful to ensure that it had not been obtained by inducements).[73] Similarly, Aaron Fakenham made admissions to poisoning his wife when questioned at the coroner's inquest into her death. These, too, were adduced against him at his trial at the City of Norwich Assizes in July 1790, where "the prisoner's own voluntary confession for the coroner was proved."[74]

The sequence of involvement between examining JP and coroner was reversed in 1748, when ten-year-old William York was suspected of murdering a young girl. He was first questioned at the inquest into her death. After initially denying the allegation, he was "closely interrogated," started crying, and made admissions. The next morning he was taken before a neighbouring JP for examination and repeated his confession.[75] As this case suggests, admissions might be made to both the investigating magistrate and the coroner, as also occurred in July 1750,

72. *Public Advertiser or Political and Literary Diary*, 28 January 1794.
73. Anon, *The Trial of Thomas Harper, for Shooting Thomas Briggs, of Lakenheath in the County of Suffolk*, 1788, pp. 16–17.
74. *The Times*, 30 September 1789 and 3 August 1790.
75. *The Case of William York*, 1 January 1748, Foster 70 168 E.R. 35.

when John Barchard confessed to committing a murder in Yarmouth to a local justice and then admitted his crime at the ensuing inquest.[76]

Conclusion

As a mechanism for detecting homicides and murderers, the eighteenth-century inquest had some major weaknesses. These were manifest in all phases of the process, from reporting and investigating suspicious deaths to the hearing itself. However, there were numerous examples of the system working very well, with good-quality expert evidence being received where necessary (if available) and cases being carefully considered by the tribunal. The swift and highly localised nature of the forum allowed vital knowledge of the background to a death to be accessed while matters were still fresh in people's memory, unlike most assizes trials.

As with so many aspects of the justice system of the period, occasional instances of gross incompetence were probably not typical, but seemed almost unavoidable because of a general lack of institutional safeguards, particularly the acute difficulty of dismissing poorly performing officers. Too much turned on the ability, energy, and inclinations of individual coroners. Additionally, too much was dependent on other situational variables, such as the presence of diligent searchers and medical men in remote areas who could or would examine bodies; when these were lacking or absent, problems arose and mistakes were made.

76. NRO QS Y/S/ 2/1–4 MF 1031.

CHAPTER 7

Prosecution

Introduction

Although the Crown provided the state's courts and judges, the responsibility for prosecuting a crime was largely placed on ordinary people. Indictments were brought "in the name of the king, but at the suit of any private prosecutor."[1] Normally, though not invariably, these were the victims of the relevant crime (see below). The new form of nineteenth-century police took over primary responsibility for this role only in the 1840s and 1850s, and the Director of Public Prosecution's (very limited) office was not set up until 1879. However, there were numerous reasons not to indict suspects in eighteenth-century England, even if they could readily be identified and detained, and these need to be considered to understand the system.

Reasons not to Prosecute

As in all eras, some victims did not prosecute for highly personal reasons. For example, in 1782 a genteel but financially pressed young man stole up to £1,400 from a wealthy neighbour, Sir Gerard Vanneck of Heveningham Hall, in Suffolk. Even so, Sir Gerard "positively refused to institute judicial process against him, but commanded him to be turned out of his house without a word of invective or reproach."[2] Nevertheless, there

1. Anon (By a Friend to the Constitution), *Observations On the Duty and Power of Juries, As Established by the Laws of England,* 2nd edn., 1796, p. 16.
2. *General Advertiser and Morning Intelligencer*, 28 January 1782; *Public Advertiser*, 7 February 1782.

were also sound practical reasons for not pursuing a matter through the courts. The most important of them was the sheer "expense and trouble of prosecuting offenders."[3]

The cost of indicting a crime could be considerable. Court and recognisance fees would usually have to be paid by the prosecutor, as would a lawyer, if one was employed to conduct the case. Out-of-pocket expenses such as lodgings and travel would also have to be covered, for the prosecutor and (frequently) his witnesses. The cost entailed in keeping the latter fed and accommodated at assizes until a hearing came on might be considerable, something that was not aided by poor listing. Some indication of this is given in Elizabeth Freke's diary, though it may have been describing a civil *nisi prius* action. Freke noted that in July 1708 she had travelled to the Norwich Assizes with eight of her tenants as witnesses and "kept them there a week drinking." Ultimately the court would not even permit them to be called.[4] There was little encouragement for a victim to indict someone who had broken into his house and stolen 30 or 40s worth of goods if it would require him "to throw 5 or 10 pounds after it, to have him Try'd, and perhaps Acquitted."[5]

Inconvenience was another major factor behind popular reluctance to prosecute. In a society where the criminal justice system had to be actively sought out, ease of access was prized.[6] Unlike their metropolitan counterparts, those in awkwardly situated rural parishes might have to walk many miles to find a JP ready to receive their initial complaint and issue an arrest warrant. As was noted in 1765, in a large county like Norfolk "there now are, and always will be, many towns above eight miles from a Justice of the Peace."[7] In 1794 Thomas Gisborne, in a vague echo of metropolitan practice, urged provincial JPs to keep regular hours for discharging their legal duties so that parish officers and the general public would at least know when and where to find them, so avoiding wasted

3. J. Fitzsimmonds, *Free and Candid Disquisitions, on the Nature and Execution of the Laws of England, Both in Civil and Criminal Affairs,* 1751, p. 52.
4. R. Anselment (ed.), *The Remembrances of Elizabeth Freke 1671–1714,* 2002, p. 258.
5. C. Jones, *Some Methods Proposed Towards Putting a Stop to the Flagrant Crimes of Murder, Robbery, and Perjury,* 1752, pp. 14–15.
6. J. Ritson, *The Jurisdiction of the Court Leet,* 2nd edn., 1809, p. xix.
7. Anon, *A Proposal For the Relief and More Comfortable Maintenance of the Poor of the County of Norfolk,* 1765, p. 6.

journeys. However, many failed to do this. Subsequent trips to testify at trials held at assizes or quarter sessions could be even greater than those made to a magistrate. For example, Emneth, near the Norfolk border with Cambridgeshire, was almost 58 miles from Norwich by road, making attending hearings in the county capital a time-consuming business.

Even at the time, it was widely recognised that victims were much more likely to resort to law if they lived near active JPs, quarter sessions, or assizes, and more likely to settle matters privately if they lived in remote spots that would require long journeys to and from legal hearings. As a result, apparently similar parishes in different parts of a county might produce different per capita indictment rates: "[T]he greater frequency of commitment is caused by the greater facility to commit."[8] Partly for this reason, indictment rates also tended to be higher in towns than in rural areas.

However, it was not solely the cost in time and money that discouraged prosecution; there were other practical considerations. If a local man was indicted, enemies might be made. There were cases in which prosecutors were attacked, their animals were killed, or their property damaged. In other situations, if a breadwinner was convicted it might force his family onto the parish, and so increase the poor rates which were paid by the "respectable," ultimately costing them more than they lost from his theft.

There was another important factor behind popular reluctance to prosecute capital felonies, one that seems to have become steadily stronger as the century advanced and social attitudes changed. Prosecutors, like judges and jurors, appear to have become increasingly reluctant to have a suspect's death on their consciences for all but the most serious crimes (such as murder and highway robbery). This was part of a wider "gentling" in eighteenth-century society. Interestingly, it was a banker who carried on business in Norfolk, Daniel Gurney, who warned the 1819 Select Committee about the effects of severity on implementation of the harsh law against forgery. He claimed that many felons had avoided prosecution for the crime because his colleagues had a "dread of being

8. G. O. Paul, *Address to his Majesty's Justices of the Peace for the County of Gloucester*, 1789, p. 47.

instrumental in inflicting death."[9] As Sir James MacIntosh noted in the same year, although centuries earlier people may have been quite bloodthirsty, they had become fearful of "burdening their consciences with the blood of a fellow-creature." Even if they did give evidence, prosecutors and other witnesses might suppress or downplay incriminating facts to avoid such an outcome.[10]

Indicative of such increased prosecutorial compassion, in 1748, when Thomas Chestney was found guilty at the Old Bailey of stealing a horse from Henry Coxhead in Thetford (Norfolk), he was also able to produce a letter from his victim asking that, if capitally convicted, Chestney be "recommended for mercy."[11] Although Coxhead lived 100 miles from the thief, and so would have been subject to no local opprobrium if he had allowed him to hang, he was still reluctant to have a man's death on his conscience for a £3 nag.

Most important of all, when it comes to explaining legal inaction by crime victims, there were often practical alternatives to pursuing a formal prosecution.

Alternatives to Prosecution

For all but the most serious crimes, such as murder and highway robbery, an informal resolution between perpetrator and victim was always a possibility, especially if local people were involved. Strangers were a different matter; frequently they could not offer reliable restitution, or be subject to many types of informal sanction, and there was less disruption to social harmony in prosecuting them. They also appeared more frightening than local miscreants. However, the latter could usually be dealt with in other ways than by indictment, at least for low-to middle-ranking offences.

For example, if suspects stole from an employer, they could simply be dismissed from their position without a reference. This might explain why it was rare for servants to be prosecuted for petty larceny; only major

9. Anon, *Report From the Select Committee on Criminal Laws*, 1819, p. 15.
10. House of Commons Debate, 2 March 1819, *Hansard*, vol. 39, cols. 777–845.
11. OBSP, Trial of Thomas Chestney, 7 September 1748: t17480907–1.

thefts by employees normally warranted the trouble of court action. Typically, in February 1780 Mary Hardy noted that she had replaced one of her farmhands in Norfolk for workplace theft and "[s]ett a new thresher in the barn, Old Master Davy having carried home straw &c. feloniously."[12] Apart from dismissal, no further action appears to have been taken against Davy for stealing the straw.

Informal sanctions could also include low-level physical violence, such as a beating or ducking. In 1767 a group of women in Leicestershire caught a horse thief. After recovering the animal, they severely whipped him and then "filled his eyes with dust and salt, and his mouth with excrement; and having as they thought sufficiently punished him, they let him go inform his companions."[13] He escaped prosecution for a capital felony.

In many cases, ostracism, the withdrawal of co-operation and mutual support, might be deemed sufficient to punish a minor criminal and deter him from re-offending. On other occasions, a suspect might be forced to enlist in lieu of prosecution, without the authorities ever becoming involved. When James Oakes caught William Pulteney stealing from him in Bury, he was reluctant to indict the lad, noting that he had sent for the youth's mother and "instead of presenting him mean, if possible, sending him to sea."[14]

Alternatively, a private arrangement might be reached involving "compromises or underhand dealings between the criminal and the person injured."[15] Sometimes the victim might secure a public apology in lieu of prosecution, perhaps one that was published in a newspaper, which would add to his local status as a magnanimous man and humiliate the perpetrator. In 1783 Michael Piper from Stoke, in Suffolk, threatened John Bare with a large hedge stake after mistakenly accusing him of child murder. Piper later publicly noted that Bare had "consented to drop further prosecution against me on making this public acknowledgement of my

12. M. Bird (ed.), *The Diary of Mary Hardy 1773–1809*, 2013, p. 364.
13. *The Leicestershire Journal*, 4 July 1767.
14. J. Fiske (ed.), *The Oakes Diaries*, 1991, p. 321.
15. J. Fitzsimmonds, *Free and Candid Disquisitions, on the Nature and Execution of the Laws of England, Both in Civil and Criminal Affairs*, 1751, p. 52.

fault and making a payment to the poor of Nayland of 20s."[16] Similarly, in 1808 John Perry launched a drunken, vicious and unprovoked assault on John Fenn while he was on the road from Melford to Sudbury, in Suffolk. Perry was subsequently forced to publish an advertisement in a local paper explaining what he had done and apologising to his victim as part of a deal to avoid being indicted for the crime: "I humbly beg his pardon and am grateful that he will not prosecute me in consideration of my family of children and I will pay 5s to be given in bread to the poor of Melford."[17] In a case from 1782 involving a highly arcane statutory offence, Edward Symonds, a carrier from Garvestone, in Norfolk, received a quantity of satins from two Norwich merchants with orders that it be given to John Tilney for weaving, but delivered it to another man. He avoided court action by publishing an apology, in which he noted that the two named merchants had determined to prosecute him "but in Compassion to my Family, upon my asking their Pardon in the Public Newspaper, and paying the Expense of this Advertisement, they have humanely agreed to drop their intended Prosecution against me; for which Lenity I think myself much obliged to them." The apology was witnessed and marked by two other carriers.[18]

Most important of all, a crime victim might "compound" the offence and accept payment from its perpetrator for not prosecuting it as part of such a settlement. This was technically illegal but widespread for felonies, and entirely lawful and commonplace for misdemeanours. Cases of the former rarely led to successful prosecutions, and, although ostensibly a serious offence, were usually dealt with by modest punishments on the rare occasions when a conviction was secured. As Timothy Nourse noted at the start of the century, most crime victims preferred to "compound in private with such felons, than be at farther costs to prosecute such offences."[19]

Indeed, the practice was so common that members of the Harleston Association for Prosecuting Felons in Suffolk were expressly warned that

16. *Ipswich Journal*, 13 December 1783.
17. *Bury and Norwich Post*, 4 July 1808.
18. *Norfolk Chronicle*, 6 April 1782.
19. T. Nourse, *Campania Fœlix, Or, A discourse of the Benefits and Improvements of Husbandry*, 1700, p. 290.

they would themselves be prosecuted by the society if, having become the victim of crime, they compounded a felony (something that would reduce the deterrent effect of membership).[20] In many criminal cases that were indicted, prosecutors reported unavailing attempts by defendants to compound matters.

In some respects, compounding can be viewed as a privately administered fine. As such, it may be seen as an exceptionally cheap, swift and efficient way to deal with offences. It also merged seamlessly with the broadly legal payment of compensation for the losses sustained by a crime victim, another regular phenomenon of the period. For example, in 1764 some fishermen seeking mussels went ashore at Bradwell on the Essex coast and killed and stole poultry belonging to a local farmer. They farmer saw and pursued them and, on catching up with the thieves, "offered to forgive them on payment of a fair market price." Unfortunately, they refused to pay up and, when he took one of them by the collar, the men beat and mortally wounded him.[21]

Numerous other cases did result in mutually acceptable settlements, without the authorities' becoming involved. Typically, in late-seventeenth-century Myddle, Richard Challoner was bound over to appear at the Shropshire Assizes for stealing a cow from one of his relatives, who also entered into a recognisance to prosecute the matter. However, an uncle told the prosecutor that it would be a disgrace to have Challoner hanged if found guilty, as he was illiterate and so unable to claim benefit of clergy (this being prior to 1706); his friends would therefore raise £5 to pay for the cow in lieu of indictment, "To this the prosecutor agreed; received the £5, preferred noe bill and Challoner was quitt by proclamation."[22]

As the result of a combination of these factors, the great majority of lesser crimes seem to have been resolved without any type of formal prosecution, and so do not show up in official records. This helps to explain why so few matters went for trial relative to the size of the population, and why the state's formal sanctions were administered so sparingly,

20. Anon, *Rules and Regulations, Entered Into by the Members of the Harleston Association for Prosecuting Felons,* 1799, pp. 1–14.
21. *Ipswich Journal,* 27 August 1762.
22. G. Gough, *The History of Myddle,* 1981, p. 55. Even the £5 was eventually returned after the perpetrator threatened to report the prosecutor for compounding.

especially in the provinces. For example, in Oxfordshire, during the 1780s, the county quarter sessions averaged only ten committals a year for theft.[23] (Obviously, some cases also went to assizes). In 1751 just 16 people were sentenced to death within the entire East Anglian region. Most of them were reprieved on condition of transportation for 14 years. Only six were actually executed. The same year 18 people were sentenced to seven years' transportation at the assizes. Some of these would have been reprieved from this penalty after petitioning the Crown. Two other men were branded and released after being clergied for manslaughter and bigamy.[24] Thus, in a region with a combined population of about 400,000 people, there were at most six hangings, two brandings, and a score of transportations. The remaining criminal cases that resulted in a conviction were dealt with by fiscal penalties, floggings, the pillory, and short carceral sentences. There were not huge numbers of these.

However, the availability of alternative methods of dealing with offenders does not mean that formal prosecution in the criminal justice system was irrelevant where it was not used, as is sometimes suggested. It was a constant presence, lurking in the background. It was fear of formal prosecution that forced offenders to apologise in public, made them compound crimes, or prevented them from reporting punishment beatings to the authorities. Even where a crime victim took no action over a detected crime, the knowledge that he might have done could enhance his local reputation for neighbourliness and compassion and the perpetrator's sense of future indebtedness.

Even so, despite the many reasons for not prosecuting offences, some victims were willing to do whatever was necessary to pursue crimes to trial, even if they were not "atrocious." For example, in 1781 James Youngs advertised a reward of two guineas for the arrest and prosecution to conviction of whoever had broken into his alehouse in St Martin's parish, in Norwich. He had lost two pounds in weight of candles, a tin of tea, a large quantity of eggs, and a till containing between 40s and 50s.[25] The reward he offered was worth at least half the total loss he had sustained,

23. D. Eastwood, "Local Government and Local Society," 2002, p. 46.
24. TNA ASSI 33/2.
25. *Norfolk Chronicle*, 29 December 1781.

and he would also have to pay for the advertisement and court charges. He was highly unlikely to recover his cash and goods, even if a conviction were secured. In an even more extreme case, from 1806, after four ewes were taken from a drove of sheep between Cowlinge and Hartest, in Suffolk, two local clergymen advertised a reward of £30 for bringing the offender to justice. This was many times what the animals were worth.[26]

By some national comparisons, indictment rates were fairly "average" in East Anglia. One examination of indictments and populations suggests that in 1801 there were 59 "criminals" prosecuted per 100,000 people in Norfolk, and 51 in Suffolk. Inevitably these figures were dwarfed by the figure of 148 found in heavily urban Middlesex and significantly smaller than the 73 people found in partly urban Surrey. They were also smaller than the numbers found in Essex, Kent, and Wiltshire, but about the same as those for Gloucestershire, Berkshire, and Nottinghamshire. Nevertheless, the two counties' indictment rates were much higher than those found in many of England's extremities, such as Northumberland (24), Cumberland (15), Cornwall (23), and Devon (27).[27] To some extent these variations probably reflect the incidence of crime in these areas. However, they also reflect differences in local willingness to prosecute offences. (The metropolitan area had more "strangers" and was much better served by readily available courts). Distinguishing between the two is difficult if not impossible.

Prosecutors who did bring formal actions were motivated by anger, a sense of civic responsibility, a desire to send out a warning to others who might target them in future, the possibility of a reward, or a combination of all these factors. Interestingly, it was not just wealthy victims who indicted those crimes that did come to trial. A significant number of prosecutors were labourers and husbandmen. A study of the Essex Quarter Sessions from 1760 to 1800 suggests that this group made up 21.5 per cent of felony prosecutors (they made up about 40 per cent of the population), although, perhaps unsurprisingly, the most active

26. *Bury and Norwich Post*, 1 October 1806.
27. T. Plint, *Crime in England: Its Relation, Character, and Extent, as Developed from 1801 to 1848*, 1851, p. 10.

prosecutors appeared to be farmers, tradesmen, and artisans.[28] Norfolk and Suffolk were broadly similar.

Private Prosecution

In its reliance on private prosecution, as with its lack of professional police officers, eighteenth-century England was different from most Continental countries, where the entire process of prosecution largely rested on the state: "One set of officers paid by the Crown, arrest the offenders; another set of officers search out the evidence; a third conduct the prosecution; and a fourth pronounce their verdict."[29] Only the last was always provided by the state in England. As late as the early 1830s, the lack of a public official in England who was tasked with enquiring into and prosecuting crimes appeared astonishing to many foreign visitors.[30]

Such a system had not developed entirely unchallenged. For example, as early as 1534 Henry VIII had unavailingly attempted to introduce a limited form of public prosecution via "sergeants of the common weal." It was intended that these county-based law-enforcement officers would take over responsibility for instituting many prosecutions in their localities. (The proposal was rejected by Parliament).[31] Similar suggestions were periodically made during the eighteenth century. In 1751 the barrister Joshua Fitzsimmonds urged that officers be appointed to conduct all criminal prosecutions in the name of the attorney general and at public expense.[32]

Despite such proposals, in England ordinary members of the public not only arrested offenders (albeit often with the assistance of local constables) and arranged for them to be examined by a magistrate but also found witnesses who could testify against them and then marshalled the evidence that would appear for the prosecution at trial. In theory this could be done by anyone. As a senior judge noted in 1767, it was

28. P. King, *Crime, Justice, and Discretion in England 1740–1820*, 2003, p. 37.
29. House of Commons Debate, 2 March 1819, *Hansard*, vol. 39, cols. 777–845.
30. A. de Tocqueville, *Journeys to England and Ireland*, 1835, p. 63.
31. Y. Ma, "Exploring the Origins of Public Prosecution," 2008, p. 195.
32. J. Fitzsimmonds, *Free and Candid Disquisitions, On the Nature and Execution of the Laws of England, Both in Civil and Criminal Affairs*, 1751, p. 52.

not only lawful "but the duty of every subject to apprehend a felon, and take him to a justice of the peace, who is to examine, bail, or to commit him."[33] In practice, and for obvious reasons, it was usually the victim of a crime who indicted it, although male relatives sometimes prosecuted on behalf of female victims.

Such procedures meant that prosecution could be a very personal affair. In 1761 John Long was capitally convicted at the Thetford Assizes for stealing a mare from his brother, who then indicted him for the crime.[34] William Goodrick, the supervisor of excise at Yarmouth in the mid-1790s, thought that a key reason that one of his juniors, Richard Stroud, had been convicted of stealing four shillings' worth of candles from a tallow chandler whose premises he was inspecting was that Stroud had been led to believe that the prosecutor would not appear against him at the Yarmouth Borough Sessions, and so was "lulled into a fatal and unprepared security."[35] He had offered the chandler £10 to keep quiet.[36]

Conversely, private individuals who had initiated the criminal process prematurely might be forced into public retractions to avoid the risk of civil actions for slander or malicious prosecution. In 1766 Josiah Sharsfield of Melford, in Suffolk, publicly accused Mordecai Reynolds and Thomas Gibling of committing highway robbery but was later forced into a recantation in a local newspaper: "I now hereby acknowledge what is false and without foundation and do heartily ask pardon from the said."[37] Similarly, in 1780 William Oliver, a commercial traveller from Staffordshire, alleged that the wife of a tavern landlord in Briston, Norfolk, had stolen from his pack. He was later forced to withdraw this claim as entirely untrue by placing similar advertisements in local papers.[38]

That the prosecutor, or someone acting on his behalf, would normally help marshal the evidence could also encourage interference with witnesses. In 1707 it was noted that a man of high status had been very active on behalf of a prosecutor in an alleged highway robbery case in

33. *Anonymous* (1767), Parker 247, 145 E. R. 771.
34. *London Chronicle*, 21–24 March 1761. He was subsequently reprieved.
35. TNA HO 47/22/16, ff 73–75.
36. TNA HO 47/22/18, ff 93–96.
37. *Ipswich Journal*, 25 January 1766.
38. *Norfolk Chronicle*, 13 May 1780.

Kent. He had even approached likely defence witnesses. By pointing out inconsistencies in their version of events, he tried to "stagger them in their evidence." One witness later claimed at trial that this man had been "tampering with him also to give in a wrong evidence."[39]

However, it would be a mistake to view all decisions to prosecute as being entirely within a victim's unfettered discretion. Pressure could be brought both for and against indicting a matter, depending on circumstances. For example, William Aldred from Halesworth, in Suffolk, was an unpopular man in his village and suspected by his neighbours of several petty crimes. In 1783 he was convicted of stealing three pecks of wheat at the Suffolk Quarter Sessions, where he was sentenced to seven years' transportation. The loss of America meant that five years later he was still in custody in Ipswich Gaol. When he sought early release, it was noted in his favour that the victim of his crime claimed to have been "pushed into prosecution by Halesworth people and without their doing so he would not have pursued the case."[40] In other instances, pressure might have been brought not to indict a popular local man.

In exceptionally serious cases, potential prosecutors might not be given *carte blanche* by local JPs as to whether to indict a matter. After the murder of Charles Drew (senior), suspicion initially fell on a man named Humphreys. The examining justice, Sir Cordell Firebrace, sent for Drew's son (and real killer), who was understandably reluctant to become involved, but still "bound him over in a Bond of 500l. to prosecute."[41] However, this was unusual.

Not only did a crime victim normally have the option of not prosecuting, they often had the discretion to indict for a lesser felony than that committed if they did decide to go to court. This was especially important when it made the difference between a capital and non-capital matter. For example, theft in a dwelling-house or shoplifting could be indicted as simple larceny. More generally, there were "comparatively few capital offences in the catalogue, in which the prosecutor has not

39. Anon, *An Impartial Account of the Malicious Prosecution of John Comyn, and Chadwick Chambers*, 1709, p. 27.
40. TNA HO 47/7/120, ff 499–504.
41. Anon, *The Suffolk Parricide; Being, The Trial Life, Transactions, and Last Dying Words of Charles Drew*, 1740, p. 17.

his election of indicting on a minor charge."[42] This was frequently done in practice. However, as with the decision to prosecute, this was not entirely unfettered. Some magistrates might pressure complainants not to "down charge" crimes.

Public Prosecution

There *were* some important exceptions to the general pattern of private prosecution. Continental tourists (like some modern historians) tended to underestimate the variety of public or publicly funded mechanisms that could lead to a matter's coming to court, and which probably explain, in part, why reform was so slow in arriving in England.

In homicide cases, with the victim dead, the coroner and his inquisition took a significant role in the prosecution process. They had the power to send matters directly for trial at assizes and to bind over parish officers to prosecute them (see *Chapter 6*). Additionally, from the end of the seventeenth century several new or emerging government organisations, such as the mint, the Bank of England, the Post Office, and the Treasury took an active role in investigations and prosecutions within their own fields, appointing officers for this purpose. They were also willing to pay for competent prosecution counsel where necessary.

Furthermore, during the reigns of Queen Anne, George I, and George II, the Crown became increasingly willing to become directly involved in prosecuting very serious but "ordinary" crimes rather than confining itself to treason. These often involved *causes célèbres*. For example, in 1722 Arundel Coke was prosecuted at the Bury Assizes at the Crown's expense for a heinous and carefully planned assault (an attempted murder).[43] Indeed, the deputy solicitor to the Treasury in criminal matters came from London to assist in the prosecution. He ran up a bill of £85.[44] It may be that the defendant's status as a barrister meant that they did not want the Crown to be legally outgunned. Although unusual, this was not an isolated case.

42. Anon (By a Juryman), *Notes and Observations On Criminal Trials*, 1819, p. 23.
43. *Applebee's Original Weekly Journal*, 17 February 1722.
44. *Daily Journal*, 10 March 1722; J. H. Langbein, *The Origins of Adversary Trial*, 2005, p. 120.

Individual parishes were also increasingly willing to fund the prosecution of felonies that occurred within their borders, or that involved their own officers, such as an assault on a village constable, or an attack on someone for whom they had a modicum of responsibility, such as one of their parish apprentices. The money to do this was often supplied by local rates. For example, in March 1734 the vicar and 22 prominent residents of Pattingham, in Staffordshire, met and agreed that henceforth their parish would fund the cost of prosecuting any felonies committed within the village, its churchwardens paying out the relevant money. In the following decade several people were indicted there at parish expense. In some cases a churchwarden was also charged to personally prosecute a matter at quarter sessions.[45] Similarly, in 1801, after two boys died following abusive treatment by the Essex farmer who employed them, it was noted, "[t]he officers of the 2 parishes, to which the boys severally belonged, have laudably come forward as prosecutors."[46] This sort of activism was sometimes matched in Norfolk and Suffolk.

It was not only felonies that were publicly prosecuted: the growth of summary crimes that could be prosecuted by constables or other minor officials, without the involvement of a victim, and sometimes with a legal burden placed on the accused to establish his innocence, was of some significance. In October 1701 a search warrant was issued against Daniel Estoe, a labourer from Coddenham, in Suffolk, for pilfering and being a "common wood stealer." It was granted at the behest of a local "complainant constable" rather than a victim. The constable then searched Estoe's home, and found bits of sawn wood under his bed. Perhaps foolishly, Estoe confessed to stealing them when examined by a JP. (The *corpus delicti* might otherwise have been hard to establish.) He was committed to Ipswich gaol.[47] However, many offences of this type, such as the theft of metal, were much less important in the provinces than in London, and only rarely prosecuted in East Anglia.

Nevertheless, these remain exceptions to a general rule of private prosecution, one that applied throughout the period, even for serious crimes,

45. J. R. Kent, "The Centre and the Localities: State Formation and Parish Government in England, circa 1640–1740," 1995, pp. 363–364.
46. *Bury and Norwich Post*, 22 April 1801; *Ipswich Journal*, 18 April 1801.
47. SRO QS 347.96, *The Devereux Edgar Notebook*, transcribed by S. R. Schofield, 1956, vol.1, p. 14.

and which would not see drastic change until the nineteenth century. Indicative of this, at the Norwich Assizes in 1801, Robert Hardy was discharged, "no prosecutor appearing." He had been accused of rape.[48] To encourage more people to bring prosecutions, increased provision was gradually made by statute after the mid-century to reimburse the costs of those who indicted serious criminals. This indirectly increased the Crown's role in prosecution. There was also a growth in private initiatives to bring about the same aim, the most important of which were the prosecution associations.

Prosecution Costs

By the middle of the eighteenth century there were regular suggestions that the cost of felony prosecutions be reimbursed by the state (as had been tried during the Interregnum).[49] Under an act of 1752, successful but poor felony prosecutors were able to recover at least some of their expenses. It was not necessary that a conviction for the charge initially indicted be secured, as long as there was a finding of guilty for *some* offence. For example, at the Bury Assizes in August 1764, John Gore indicted John Gathercote for grand larceny (stealing goods worth 3s). The jury returned a conviction for stealing goods worth ten pence (petty theft). Even so, Gore was awarded £1 2s.

An award of costs also helped sweeten slightly the disappointment of a prosecutor who had seen an allegation of burglary or housebreaking artificially down-valued to simple larceny by a jury's "pious perjury," so depriving him of a £40 reward.[50] (Costs were rarely given when a substantial reward was paid out). Thus in 1764, after James Rampley was convicted of simple theft on a burglary indictment at the Thetford Assizes, the prosecutor was allowed £2 2s.

At first the 1752 act was interpreted quite strictly. In 1754 Sir Dudley Ryder granted costs to several poor prosecutors on the Home Circuit who had secured convictions but refused it to another "because he appeared to

48. *The Bury and Norwich Post: Or, Suffolk, Norfolk, Essex, and Cambridge Advertiser*, 5 August 1801.
49. C. Jones, *Some Methods Proposed Towards Putting a Stop to the Flagrant Crimes of Murder, Robbery, and Perjury*, 1752, pp. 14–15.
50. TNA ASSI 33/6.

be an innkeeper of external [prosperous] appearance."[51] Judicial practice seems to have become rather more liberal in ensuing years. Increasing numbers of middling members of society received their costs, as did a few prosecutors who had failed to secure any form of conviction, even though this was not, in theory, covered by the 1752 act.

In 1754, another statute (27 Geo II, c 3) allowed poor prosecution witnesses (other than the prosecutor) who had been bound over by recognisance to give evidence, to recover some of their expenses. At the Norfolk Assizes held in August 1754, two witnesses were allowed 15s each after Francis Wessells was convicted of stealing a mare.[52] The power to reimburse prosecution witnesses under this statute (unlike the prosecutor under the 1752 act) does not appear to have been contingent on a conviction being secured, even in theory. Although Thomas Dowsing was acquitted of any crime when accused of murdering John Mays at the Bury Assizes in 1764, two of the witnesses involved in his prosecution, Nathaniel Mills and Timothy Gorman, were each allowed expenses of £1 4s. In a more mundane case, at the Thetford Assizes the same year, Robert Gold was allowed 10s 6d after giving evidence at Thomas Hull's trial for stealing 3s worth of goods from John Mitchell (presumably also the prosecutor), even though Hull was acquitted outright.[53] In 1778 Parliament formally allowed deserving but unsuccessful prosecutors to claim their costs (18 Geo III, c 19, ss 7–8). By the close of the century, some assizes judges were even granting costs to prosecutors whose bills of indictment had been rejected by the grand jury, and so not come to trial.[54]

Although these provisions were being employed in East Anglia almost immediately after their introduction, total expenditure in the region was initially fairly small, and remained quite modest to the end of the century. Just one award of prosecution costs was made in the three assizes jurisdictions in 1752: Elizabeth Whiskard received £5 after she secured a theft conviction on a burglary indictment at the Norfolk Assizes in Norwich. No awards were made in 1753. There were three awards of

51. Lincoln's Inn, Harrowby MSS 18–19, Document 19(f) *Legal Notebook of Sir Dudley Ryder*, 1754 and 1755, p. 7.
52. TNA ASSI 33/2.
53. TNA ASSI 33/4.
54. J. M. Beattie, *Crime and the Courts in England 1660–1800*, 1986, p. 45.

prosecution costs the following year. At the Lent Assizes in Thetford, £3 5s was awarded after Henry Chapman was capitally convicted of stealing a brown mare belonging to David Maycroft. At about the same time, £4 was allowed after James Beckham was convicted at the Bury Assizes for stealing a gelding. At the same sessions, James Damant was convicted of simple grand larceny after being indicted with a capital form of house-breaking, but 50s prosecution costs was still allowed. There was also one award of witness expenses to two men under the (then) new 1754 act. In 1755 three people received their prosecution costs, and the witnesses in two other cases were given their expenses.

The courts of East Anglia became slightly more willing to grant costs during the second half of the 1750s. In 1756 15 cases are recorded as leading to awards of prosecution costs and/or witness expenses in the region. The highest was for £5, but most were between £2 and £4. In 1757 there were only seven awards of prosecution costs or expenses. In ensuing years the number and size of awards made at assizes fluctuated. In 1759 13 people received prosecution costs or witness expenses, at a total expense of just under £11. In 1764 there were just four awards to prosecutors, averaging a little more than £1 17s. One prosecution witness also received expenses of 10s 6d.[55] In 1774 there were awards of prosecution costs in six cases to seven people.

Nevertheless, costs were not granted lightly, even late in the period. In 1788 the reluctant prosecutor of William Aldred, a Suffolk grain thief, complained that he had been promised his expenses when indicting the matter but that these had not subsequently been forthcoming.[56] As a result, cost remained an important consideration for many prosecutors. It was not until the advent of the Criminal Law Act of 1826 (7 Geo IV, c 64) that the payment of expenses to prosecutors could be described as the normal state of affairs.[57] However, the state was not the only body at this time seeking to make prosecution easier and less costly for private individuals. There were also private initiatives. The most important of these were the prosecution associations.

55. TNA ASSI 33/4.
56. TNA HO 47/7/120, ff 499–504.
57. D. Cox, *Crime in England 1688–1815*, 2014, p. 83.

Prosecution Associations

Early in the eighteenth century, Robert Nelson asked (rhetorically) how respectable people could expect magistrates to punish wickedness without taking active steps themselves, "either by giving information against offenders, or by contributing money, or otherwise, for the detecting of them."[58] Prosecution Associations were one answer to this question. They also appeared to square the circle identified in 1721 by J. J. Lockhart, the MP for Oxford. He claimed that crime had reached a level at which it not only endangered property, but also menaced personal security. Unfortunately, as he also noted, one obvious response to this problem, a military type of police, would itself be an evil because it would be "dangerous to the public liberty." Lockhart felt that the best course of action would be for citizens to come forward and enforce the existing law on a more effective basis by forming societies to prosecute felons.[59] This was not an entirely novel idea even then. Prosecution associations dated back to the late seventeenth century; one was formed in Stoke-on-Trent in 1693, and it was probably not the first. Despite this, the great majority were set up after 1760. It is just possible that a decline in the quality of parish constables made a small contribution to this process.

Hundreds of associations were established in the late eighteenth and early nineteenth centuries. Indicative of this, in 1776 an observer noted that an improvement in public morality would mean that "[h]onest men will no longer have occasion to form themselves into societies, for their safety against the wicked, as they have found it necessary to do of late."[60] Similarly, in 1793, a humorous pamphlet could complain about the "associations, which by the contagion of example, are spreading fast over England; supported by the subscriptions of opulent men, for the avowed object of suppressing and prosecuting felons."[61] Their precise number is impossible to establish, as many of the smaller societies left

58. R. Nelson, *An Address to Persons of Quality and Estate ... To Which is Added, An Appendix of Some Original and Valuable Papers*, 1715, p. 156.
59. M. Koyama, "Prosecution Associations in Industrial Revolution England: Private Providers of Public Goods?," 2012, pp. 95–130.
60. T. Humphries, *A Preservative From Criminal Offences*, 1776, p. 6.
61. Anon, *An Address to the Public, From the Friends of Freedom*, 1793, p. 5.

few records, and some were quite short-lived. Even so, there were at least 1,000 of them, and there could have been up to four times that number.[62]

Such associations were created to share some of the costs and inconveniences, especially the legal expenses and attendant administrative tasks, associated with being the victim of a serious property crime and going to law. A few dealt with lesser offences as well, especially after the 1780s. Their existence was premised on a belief that the leniency that was often shown to criminals encouraged further offending, rather than the reform of those who were (undeservedly) released.[63] Most important, as Lockhart had anticipated, prosecution associations provided a practical response to public concern about crime without requiring increased governmental involvement.

Associations normally consisted of up to 100 members, living in roughly the same locality, whether borough or hundred, or engaged in the same trade. For example, in June 1782 it was noted that the "Diss Association for apprehending and prosecuting Horse-Stealers" had just over 100 members, including several women. At least nine of them were clergymen; a similar number were described as "gentlemen."[64] Members adopted articles of association and made a payment, usually between 5s and 1 guinea a year, into a common fund. When the Suffolk JP and clergyman John Longe joined the "Coddenham Association for Prosecuting Felonies" in June 1796 he paid 10s 6d.[65] Occasionally the scale of these payments was dependent on individual incomes. For example, the members of the "Harleston Association for Prosecuting Felons" instead of a fixed sum, paid according to their contribution to the local poor rate.[66]

If members of such an association were the victims of a crime covered in their agreement, the society would usually pay the expenses of criminal investigation, including the gathering of evidence, and prosecution (court fees, a solicitor, and even counsel where necessary). Frequently they would also offer and advertise rewards for the return of goods and

62. J. H. Langbein, *The Origins of Adversary Trial*, 2005, pp. 131–136.
63. *World and Fashionable Advertiser*, 11 January 1787.
64. *Norfolk Chronicle*, 22 June 1782.
65. M. Stone (ed.), *The Diary of John Longe, Vicar of Coddenham, 1765–1834*, 2008, pp. 12–13.
66. Anon, *Rules and Regulations, Entered Into by the Members of the Harleston Association for Prosecuting Felons*, 1799, pp. 1–14.

the apprehension of culprits. For example, in 1790 a large bay mare was stolen out of a yard in Sproughton, in Suffolk; the "Association for apprehending and prosecuting horse-stealers within the Hundred of Sandford" put a detailed description of the missing animal in the national press, and offered a £10 reward for information that led to the conviction of the thief.[67] (Such rewards were usually contingent on a conviction being secured). In 1795 the Cavendish Association in Suffolk offered 50 shillings for anyone who revealed the identity of a person who had stolen a Norfolk breed cow.[68] This sometimes produced results. In 1780, after William Broughton was arrested for stealing a horse in Griplesham, in Norfolk, it was noted, "This mare was advertised last Saturday in the Ipswich paper, by the association held at Downham, offering a reward of five guineas for apprehending the person who stole her."[69] In the same year Jeremiah Harvey (an "old offender") was committed to Ipswich gaol for stealing a horse in Ashwelthorpe (Norfolk) after "[t]en Guineas reward was advertised for the taking him, by the Brooke Association."[70] He was capitally convicted at the ensuing Norfolk Assizes, albeit reprieved from execution by the trial judge.[71]

A few prosecution associations even insured their members against some of the financial losses occasioned when stolen goods were not recovered. Thus members of the Harleston Association who lost a horse that was not retrieved within six months could be reimbursed half its value, up to a maximum of £20.[72] Potential criminals would often be made aware of who was in the association, as lists of members were frequently published in local newspapers or periodicals. This might, in turn, discourage them from stealing from such individuals and gave members an immediate return on their subscription. (The great majority of societies did not fund prosecutions by non-members).[73] For example, the "Diss Association for apprehending and prosecuting Horse-Stealers," which

67. *St. James's Chronicle Or the British Evening Post*, 8–11 May 1790.
68. *Ipswich Journal*, 29 April 1795.
69. *Norfolk Chronicle*, 22 January 1780.
70. Ibid., 29 July 1780.
71. Ibid., 15–17 August 1780.
72. Anon, *Rules and Regulations, Entered Into by the Members of the Harleston Association for Prosecuting Felons*, 1799, pp. 1–14.
73. L. James, *The Middle Class: A History*, 2006, p. 201.

met at the *King's Head* in the town, advertised a reward of 10 guineas, together with incidental expenses, to anyone who arrested and prosecuted to conviction those who stole a horse from their members. Their names were then publicly listed.[74]

During the second half of the eighteenth century it became increasingly common for solicitors or attorneys to manage associations. Although some still left it to their members to institute prosecutions and then seek reimbursement for the expenses that they had incurred, in others the association's lawyer actively conducted the initial investigation and subsequent prosecution.[75] To that extent, they qualified the highly personal form of English prosecution, so that criminals indicted in this fashion were "impeached, not by the people heated with a sense of individual danger [the crime victims], and personally mixing themselves with the charge and the evidence."[76] (The prosecution was still normally brought in the victim's name).

Prosecution associations were particularly common in East Anglia. Some of them were specialist, confined to dealing with the theft of a certain type of item or animal. Many, especially the early societies, were primarily established to deal with horse thieves, such animals being valuable and relatively easy to transport long distances. For example, "The Association for the apprehending and convicting of Horse Stealers, etc. in the Hundred of Weyland, and adjoining Hundreds" offered a set reward of 10 guineas plus expenses for the conviction of anyone who stole a horse belonging to its members. However, its treasurer also had a discretion to offer such a reward as should seem proper for apprehending and convicting anyone who committed any other type of serious property crime against its members, "to be paid, with the Expences of such Prosecution, upon Conviction of such Offenders."[77] In 1780 members of the "Association for Norwich, Yarmouth, South Town, and the several Branches of the North River," who were merchants and shippers trading to and from Yarmouth and Norwich, resolved to offer 10 guineas as

74. *Norfolk Chronicle*, 22 June 1782.
75. J. H. Langbein, "The Prosecutorial Origins of Defense Counsel in the Eighteenth-century: The Appearance of Solicitors," 1999, pp. 314–365.
76. Anon, *An Address to the Public, From the Friends of Freedom*, 1793, p. 8.
77. *Norfolk Chronicle*, 1 December 1781.

a reward to anyone who gave information that led to the conviction of those who stole or embezzled their goods and merchandise.[78] A more specialised group, though one that covered the region, was an association set up in April 1783 by the principal owners of rabbit warrens within Norfolk and Suffolk to defray the expense of prosecuting those who stole their conies. It was felt that, as this sort of property was "more likely to be infringed or trespassed upon than any other, it is necessary to form a separate and distinct Association from those already undertaken for the Prosecution of other Felonies." [79]

By contrast, the Harleston Association for Prosecuting Felons was catholic in the goods it protected. It was established at a meeting held at the Crown Inn in the village in October 1786 and, as with all such societies, a set of rules was drawn up (it was amended some 12 years later). The association funded prosecutions for all crimes committed against its members, whether misdemeanours or felonies, including wood theft. Rewards of up to £10 (in the most serious cases) would be offered for the arrest of offenders. It also, unusually, rewarded people involved in unsuccessful prosecutions, albeit at a lower rate than those securing convictions. Furthermore, "all reasonable expenses" incurred during prosecutions by members of the society, such as living expenses while waiting for a trial to come on, up to a maximum of seven shillings and six pence a day, would be reimbursed. However, its members could not claim the cost of hiring an attorney to manage their prosecutions without first getting permission from the society. The association met four times a year, shortly before quarter sessions sat.[80] It should be noted that there was a tendency for prosecution associations to become more generalist in the offences they were prepared to indict during the 1780s.

Malicious Prosecution

A system of private prosecution meant that accusations were sometimes made for malign reasons, whether spite or as part of a blackmail attempt.

---

78. Ibid., 18 November 1780.
79. Ibid., 12 April 1783.
80. Anon, *Rules and Regulations, Entered Into by the Members of the Harleston Association for Prosecuting Felons,* 1799, pp. 1–14.

The main deterrent to an unfounded criminal action was the risk of a civil suit for malicious prosecution or slander, or a criminal prosecution for perjury. However, both posed considerable evidential problems, making them only a fitful discouragement. (The fear of being sued for slander could also prompt complainants not to back down from indicting obviously weak cases once they had made an allegation).[81]

Despite these problems, in an action for malicious prosecution William Hurry, a Yarmouth merchant, secured £3,000 in damages against John Watson from a special jury sitting at *nisi prius* at the Thetford Assizes after the latter had brought an indictment against him (ironically) for perjury, allegedly committed at the same forum the previous year. The trial judge had quickly dismissed this charge as being without foundation. Aggravating his conduct, Watson had later placed an advertisement in several provincial papers untruthfully claiming that the case had been thrown out purely on a legal technicality. Both parties had recourse to expensive legal representation to argue their cases.[82]

An example of a criminal prosecution for perjury occurred at the Suffolk Assizes in 1800, when siblings William and Jemima Woltin were indicted for lying on oath after prosecuting a former maid for the same crime. They were detained when their case against the maid was thrown out, and committed for trial at the following sessions. Their maid had stated publicly that they had had incestuous sexual relations with each other, something that, it transpired, was probably true.[83]

Proving cases of perjury was difficult, if only because a verbatim record of evidence given in court was not normally made. Many prosecutions related to untruthful affidavits in civil matters, rather than testimony at criminal trials, where this problem did not arise, as with Robert Sturridge's false chancery documentation considered at the Norfolk Assizes in August 1749 (and even this case produced an acquittal).[84]

Furthermore, during the early years of the century, the punishment for perjury, even if it could be proved, was relatively modest. The Perjury

81. See for example, Anon, *An Impartial Account of the Malicious Prosecution of John Comyn, and Chadwick Chambers*, 1709, p. 6.
82. *The Times*, 31 March 1787, p. 3.
83. Ibid., 8 August 1800, p. 3.
84. Gray's Inn MS 45.

Act of 1728 (2 Geo II, c 25) allowed those convicted of the crime in certain specific circumstances to be transported for up to seven years or to be sentenced to the same amount of time at hard labour in a local house of correction. Nevertheless, such convictions and sentences were unusual. More typically, in 1729 Thomas Walker, the serjeant of the mace for King's Lynn, was found guilty at the Norfolk Assizes in Norwich of perjury, fined 10 marks, pilloried in Lynn, and sentenced to three months' imprisonment.[85] (A mark was a unit of account, not currency, amounting to about 16s.) Similarly, in August 1801 two men stood in the pillory in Bury marketplace with a board affixed above them on which was written "for wilful and corrupt perjury in open court."[86] Many contemporary observers thought that this level of punishment was woefully inadequate as a deterrent.[87]

85. *Daily Journal*, 6 August 1729.
86. *Bury and Norwich Post*, 5 August 1801.
87. C. Jones, *Some Methods Proposed Towards Putting a Stop to the Flagrant Crimes of Murder, Robbery, and Perjury*, 1752, p. 15.

CHAPTER 8

Jury Trial

Introduction

English criminal trials stressed "day in court" justice: the trial took place as a single uninterrupted meeting of the tribunal during which the judge and jury heard all the evidence in a case, along with any legal submissions, and then made a decision on guilt. It was not practical to have numerous hearings in a system that used a lay jury, as individual jurors might not attend later sittings if adjournments were allowed.[1] As a result, they were not permitted, even overnight, until 1794. English trials were also held in public, and emphasised the primacy of oral over written testimony. This made them quite different from most continental systems based on Roman Law with their professional fact-finders, heavy reliance on deposition evidence, and frequent preliminary and interlocutory hearings.

Apart from the indictment, the English process was largely verbal, and most forms of documentary evidence were excluded.[2] The only major qualification to this general rule was that a defendant's confession, which had been put into writing when made to an examining JP or coroner, could normally be produced at trial, unlike most other out-of-court statements.[3] There were a few more, arcane, exceptions, the prerequisites for which became ever more stringent as the century advanced.[4] Nevertheless,

1. J. H. Langbein, "The Disappearance of Civil Trial in the United States," 2012, p. 529.
2. P. J. Grosley, *A Tour to London: Or, New Observations On England, and Its Inhabitants*, vol. 3, 1772, p. 34.
3. T. W., *The Clerk of Assize*, p. 14.
4. For more on this, see G. Durston, *Whores and Highwaymen*, 2012, pp. 349–351.

they seem to have been met in 1799, when the statement of a young Norfolk rape complainant to Roger Kerrison, an examining magistrate, was admitted at the trial of her assailants at the Thetford Assizes, as the girl had since died. Defence counsel vigorously opposed this course, arguing that the statement was not evidence. However, the 12 judges upheld the decision as (unusually) several complicated requirements had been met. Not only was the maker of the statement dead, but it had been made on oath by a competent witness, written down immediately, read back to her, signed by the examining magistrate, and, most important, all this had been done in the presence of the two defendants.[5]

The emphasis on live testimony (and private prosecution) meant that, if nobody appeared at trial to give evidence against a defendant, he or she would be discharged by proclamation (as would those whose cases were thrown out by a grand jury) unless the court had received a satisfactory explanation for the prosecutor's absence and was prepared to adjourn the case to the following sessions.[6] A failure by the prosecutor to appear was a fairly regular occurrence during the period, even though he risked having his recognisances estreated. This might be because circumstances made it too difficult for him to attend, he had forgotten the date, or he had privately compromised the matter.

The last possibility was fairly common. However, such pre-trial arrangements were not always honoured. In February 1766 John Brock and John Francis burgled William Doe's house in Thornton (Suffolk) and took two bags of money containing the enormous sum of £180.[7] It appears that during the break-in they threatened Doe into giving them the key to the chest containing the bags.[8] Despite this, the two men were bitterly aggrieved as, after their arrest, Doe had promised that if they returned the money taken they "should not be hurted. We returned the money, except what we had spent, now instead of keeping his promise he appeared against us, and we must die."[9]

5. *The King v Flemming and Windham* (1799), 2 Leach 854.
6. M. Grosley, *A Tour to London: Or, New Observations On England, and Its Inhabitants*, vol. 3, 1772, p. 33.
7. *London Evening Post*, 27–29 March 1766.
8. *Public Advertiser*, 25 February 1766.
9. D. Edwards, *Sermons For the Use of Condemned Kalefactors*, 1774, p. 233.

Even so, few sessions passed without at least one defendant walking free for want of prosecution. Thus, after the Norfolk Assizes in August 1726, two men were discharged for this reason (as many as were acquitted after trial).[10] Edward Mayhew, who had been charged with stealing from his master in Pulham, in Suffolk, was discharged for want of prosecution at the Bury Assizes in August 1751.[11] At the same forum in 1813, it was noted that a woman was released because "no prosecutor appeared against Mary Dye for privately stealing a 1l. note."[12] Sometimes the numbers involved were much greater. For example, at the Summer Assizes for Norfolk in 1734 eight men were discharged for want of prosecution.[13] (The following year, one of them was made the subject of a £100 reward, having returned to crime.)[14] A failure to prosecute also occurred fairly frequently at quarter sessions, although fewer people were formally bound over to give evidence at this forum.

Exigencies of time, the inability to adjourn a trial overnight, and heavy caseloads meant that the sitting hours of eighteenth-century assizes and (to a smaller extent) quarter sessions were often much greater than those of a modern court. This could produce long working days for both judge and jury. Frequently they started in the early morning. For example, anticipating a lengthy hearing, the trial of Charles Drew at the Bury Assizes in 1740 began at 7 am. Sessions could also last late into the night if necessary. Tempers might become frayed as a result. In 1749 John Hall was committed to gaol for insulting both the trial judge and the high sheriff of Norfolk at about 2 am while testifying as a witness at the higher forum.[15]

Assizes judges spent most of their working lives in London dealing with civil, not criminal, matters. This meant that they were usually not experts in the latter field when first appointed. All judges, especially neophytes, leant on their coadjutors and, even more so, the clerks of assizes for advice. The latter were qualified barristers who were responsible for

10. *London Journal (1720)*, 20 August 1726.
11. *London Daily Advertiser and Literary Gazette*, 6 August 1751.
12. *The Bury and Norwich Post: Or, Suffolk, Norfolk, Essex, Cambridge, and Ely Advertiser*, 31 March 1813.
13. TNA ASSI 33/1.
14. *London Gazette*, 10–13 May 1735.
15. Gray's Inn MS 45.

most of the administration of the circuit, albeit assisted by a secretariat of associates.[16] In the 1750s, for example, Jerome Knapp, the clerk for the Home Circuit, regularly gave tips on practical matters to the newly appointed Sir Dudley Ryder.[17] It is clear from Ryder's diary that Knapp expressed his opinion on the merits of some issues, such as the granting of administrative reprieves, quite forcibly, although Ryder ignored it when he felt it appropriate to do so. An examination of Ryder's assizes diary for 1754 and 1755 also reveals how much judicial uncertainty there was about a number of criminal-justice issues, including the legality of certain sentences, with practices and views differing greatly between judges.

Commencement of Proceedings

The King's Lynn Sessions Book for the years between 1726 and 1752 contains a handwritten formula for trying felons, as the town (like Great Yarmouth) had power of gaol delivery, unlike most other borough sessions (there was another formula for holding ordinary quarter sessions of the peace to try lesser crimes).[18] With local variations, these set out the basic structure for most English felony trials on indictment, including those at assizes.

Typically, the court crier would open the sessions and then call on those who had entered into recognisances to prosecute to identify themselves, or risk forfeiting their money via estreatment. He would then swear them to bills of indictment. In the eighteenth century these were usually drafted on behalf of the prosecutor with the assistance of a JP's clerk, the clerk of assizes, a solicitor, or an attorney. The cryer would then send both the bills and witnesses to the room containing the grand jury (sometimes known as the grand inquest) for consideration.

16. J. S. Cockburn, "Seventeenth-century Clerks of Assize—Some Anonymous Members of the Legal Profession," 1969, p. 317.
17. J. H. Langbein, "Shaping the Eighteenth-century Criminal Trial: A View from the Ryder Sources," 1983, p. 28.
18. NRO Lynn Sessions Book 1726–1752, KL/C 20/1.

The Grand Jury

Grand juries were found at assizes, quarter sessions, and borough sessions, wherever criminal matters were tried on indictment. Although Suffolk had only one assizes venue, it had two grand juries. One sat for the Liberty of Saint Edmund, the other for the "body" of the county (sometimes referred to as the franchise and guildable grand juries respectively).

In 1793, while addressing the grand jury at the Suffolk Quarter Sessions, the magistrate John Chedworth noted that its members were called upon to exercise one of the highest privileges that could be enjoyed by the citizens of a free state, that of assisting in the administration of its criminal justice system. In theory grand jurors did this in two ways. It was their duty to "decide on the Truth of all such Bills of Indictment as shall be laid before You, likewise to present all Offences against the Public Peace, Convenience, and good Order which You know of from your own Knowledge."[19] Grand juries had been introduced in the twelfth century specifically to perform the latter function. However, in the ensuing centuries, the first task, scrutinising bills of indictment proffered by members of the public (rather than by the grand jury itself) to ensure that there was a prima facie case against the accused, had been added to their duties. As will be seen, over time this function had become paramount.

In 1746 and 1747 the number of men found on East Anglian assizes grand juries ranged from 15 (the legal minimum was 13) to 23 (the maximum allowed). They decided by a simple majority, albeit that at least 12 men had to be in favour of a matters going for trial, while only a majority was needed to dismiss a bill.[20] In practice, it seems that they usually came to the same decision, working in reasonable harmony. However, at the Thetford Assizes in 1736, John Woolston's bill of indictment for felony was returned to the court by the grand jury, "they not being in agreement."[21] Although there was a mild preference for an uneven number of jurors, there were regular exceptions. Thus the guildable and

19. J. Howe, *A Charge Delivered to the Grand Jury at the General Quarter Sessions of the Peace for the County of Suffolk,* 1793, pp. 1–10.
20. Anon, *The Complete Juryman: Or, A Compendium of the Laws Relating to Jurors*, 1752, p. 12.
21. TNA ASSI 33/1.

franchise grand juries for the Lent Assizes at Bury in 1747 had eighteen and 16 men respectively.[22]

A similar situation was found at the lower jury forum, whether borough or county. For example, on 25 July 1787, when Thomas Bailey was accused at the Thetford Quarter Sessions of stealing a peahen, his case was considered by a grand jury of 14 men before going for trial in front of the crown jury (as the petty jury was termed there), where he was acquitted.[23] Perhaps unsurprisingly, in tiny Dunwich, the legal minimum of 13 men was normally employed for the borough sessions, as occurred with those held on 24 October 1720. There were too few suitably qualified men for any to be used unnecessarily.[24]

Although the property qualification for membership varied, it was usually much greater for the grand than for the petty (trial) jury at assizes. Thus, in the early 1700s, it was £80 a year freehold for the former and only £10 a year freehold or copyhold for the latter.[25] After the Restoration, in the provinces at least (London was rather different), the membership of the assizes grand jury included increasingly large numbers of gentlemen and some clergymen, with fewer members of the "middling orders" being summoned. Even more significantly, growing numbers of JPs and local aristocrats were recruited to the body, further raising its prestige.[26] By 1677 the Norfolk Assizes grand jury included several baronets and justices.[27] Over a century later, in August 1781, when Baron Skynner and Mr Justice Ashurst opened the Norwich City Assizes, its 22-man grand jury contained five baronets. Their foreman was the Honourable Henry Hobart. Several of them, such as Sir Harbord Harbord, were also active JPs for the county.[28] Indeed, of 399 identifiable grand jurors in Norfolk between 1661 and 1707, more than a third (36 per cent) were JPs, more than half of whom had served as grand jurors prior to appointment to the

22. Gray's Inn MS 45.
23. NRO Quarter Sessions Minute Book for Thetford, T/QS2.
24. SRO EE6/1144/120.
25. G. Jacob, *The Compleat Parish Officer*, 7th edn., 1734, p. 24.
26. J. M. Beattie, *Crime and the Courts in England 1660–1800*, 1986, p. 321.
27. N. Landau, *The Justices of the Peace 1679–1760*, 1984, p. 56.
28. *Norfolk Chronicle*, 11 August 1781.

bench. This may suggest that grand-jury service was being used, to some extent, to make an assessment as to their suitability to be magistrates.[29]

The mid-eighteenth-century guildable grand jury for Suffolk that assembled at the Summer Assizes in August 1746 had two baronets, including Sir Thomas Allen, nine "esquires," and just four men ranked as ordinary "gents" amongst its 15 members. The socially more modest franchise grand jury for the county lacked aristocrats, but was made up of 12 esquires and three gentlemen.[30] Unsurprisingly, in these circumstances, when François de la Rochefoucauld visited the Bury Assizes in 1784, he noted that the grand jury there was made up of the most prosperous and "best thought of" gentry in Suffolk.[31] The government recognised that such men represented an important concentration of the political elite of a county and consulted them on a wide range of matters. For example, in 1794, when it was considering various plans to raise volunteer corps to resist a French invasion, the proposals for Suffolk were put to the assizes grand jury at Bury, on the basis that they represented the natural leaders of the area.[32]

Membership of the county quarter sessions grand jury was much less prestigious than that gathered for assizes, and its composition correspondingly less exclusive. Indeed, there was no clearly defined qualification for serving on it. Nevertheless, its jurors were still expected to be reasonably substantial men, and tended to be considerably more prosperous than those selected to adjudicate over trials. The list for the quarter sessions held at Caistor, in Lincolnshire, at Epiphany 1775 describes (albeit a little formulaically) nine as being gentlemen, along with one yeoman, one tanner, one joiner, one carpenter, and a gardener.[33] In Surrey and Sussex, grand juries commonly included high constables drawn from the counties' various hundreds amongst their members. The men empanelled to serve on grand juries at the Devon Quarter Sessions were also markedly superior to those who sat to hear trials at the same forum. For

29. J. Rosenheim, "County Governance and Elite Withdrawal in Norfolk, 1660–1720," 1989, p. 125.
30. Gray's Inn MS 45.
31. N. Scarfe, *A Frenchman's Year in Suffolk,* 2011, p. 82.
32. M. Thomas and N. Sign, *The Loyal Suffolk Hussars,* 2012, pp. 1–5.
33. B. J. Davey, *Rural Crime in the Eighteenth Century: North Lincolnshire 1740–80,* 1995, p. 92.

example, at Michaelmas 1741, 37 of the 40 men on the grand-jury panel (a maximum of 23 would have been selected) were described as gentlemen, the others being a merchant, an ironmonger, and a mercer. The petty-jury panel, by contrast, summoned 36 yeomen, a clothier, a tailor, a serge-maker, and a maltster. At the subsequent Christmas sessions, all 39 of those summoned to the grand jury were termed 'gentlemen', compared with the 37 yeomen, a serge-maker and a shopkeeper who were called for the petty jury panel.[34]

On a more statistical basis, two-thirds of quarter sessions petty jurors for late-eighteenth-century Essex had an estate worth between just £10 and £19 a year, while only 15 per cent of those selected for the court's grand jury fell into this category.[35] Very similar profiles were found in East Anglia. In 1793 Henry Jodrell addressed the grand jury for the Norfolk Quarter Sessions as "respectable farmers and gentlemen, under whom laborers and the lower classes of society are employed."[36]

The social standing of grand jurors selected for borough quarter sessions was usually less elevated than that of the men who performed the same role for their county. However, the townsmen chosen for this body were still, on average, more prosperous than those selected to be trial jurors. In Ipswich during the 1750s, 75 per cent of grand jurors were in the highest quarter of all ratepayers, whereas the same proportion of petty jurors were merely in the top half. When it came to paying rates, the profile of grand jurors in the town was broadly comparable with that of the men who became churchwardens.[37]

More specifically, at the Ipswich Borough Sessions that commenced on 28 June 1755, the grand-jury panel of 24 men (of whom 17 were eventually sworn) had several individuals drawn from the same trades as the court's trial jurors, but a significant number who were obviously in more well-to-do lines of business. Among them were a draper, bookbinder, miller, brazier, plumber, glazier, shoemaker, grocer, ironmonger, brewer,

34. Devon Heritage Centre, Quarter Session Bundles, QS6/1–5.
35. P. King, "Illiterate Plebeians, Easily Misled: Jury Composition, Experience and Behaviour in Essex 1735–1815," 1988, p. 274.
36. H. Jodrell, *A Charge Delivered to the Grand Jury of Norfolk, At the General Quarter Sessions Held on Wednesday, Jan. 16, 1793,* 1793, p. 9.
37. J. D. Clemis, *Government in an English Provincial Town: The Corporation of Ipswich, 1720–95,* 1999, p. 122.

tallow chandler, carpenter, baker, and linen draper.[38] As late as 1839 Robert Wake noted that in Southwold the grand jury for the town borough sessions were taken from its "chief inhabitants" while trial jurors were drawn from the "tradesmen of the town." (The town bailiffs empanelled both groups.)[39]

Frequently borough grand jurors were members of the common council, the body below that of the aldermen of a town. On a specific basis, amongst the 14 grand jurors for the borough sessions held at Thetford on the 25 October 1781 was one John Theodorick, who also served on several other grand juries for the town during the period.[40] He may have been the same person as a baby of that unusual name christened in Market Downham in 1740. He was almost certainly the same man who sat on Thetford's 20-man common council in 1781. Theodorick later donated a handsome portrait of the figure of Justice with sword in hand to the town in 1792. It is safe to assume from this that he was a prosperous man.

For some borough grand jurors, service could be quite demanding. For example, the grand jury for King's Lynn assembled numerous times (far more than four) each year during the 1730s, even if many of their meetings were not effective or were for administrative purposes. The same names recur regularly on the lists of 20 or so men summoned. Thus, in the year from 1733 to 1734, Joshua Edwards, like two other men, attended three in succession, and several others went to two of the three sessions.[41]

The Work of the Grand Jury

As previously noted, the grand jury had started its life as a jury of presentment. This was the "notice taken by a grand jury of any offence from their own knowledge or observation, without any bill of indictment laid before them at the suit of the king."[42] Indicative of this historic role, its members were supposed to come from different parishes and hundreds,

38. SRO Sessions Roll 42, 2 July 1755, c/2/9/1/1/1/77–2 and 10.
39. R. Wake, *Southwold and Its Vicinity, Ancient and Modern*, 2013, p. 128.
40. NRO Quarter Sessions Minute Book for Thetford, T/QS2.
41. NRO Lynn Sessions Book 1726–1752, KL/C 20/1.
42. W. Blackstone, *Commentaries on the Laws of England*, vol. 4, 1769, p. 298.

so bringing "the whole county into one spot."[43] However, by the beginning of the seventeenth century only a tiny number of felonies were being presented by the assizes grand jury on its own initiative, and they were exceptionally rare in the eighteenth century.

Presentment was slightly more common at quarter sessions. In some parts of England presenting juries, usually for the old hundreds, still lingered at the lower forum, bringing to court offences that affected public welfare, such as disorderly conduct. More important, constables were still, in theory, required to present local cases, pursuant to 14 designated articles of enquiry, for endorsement by the quarter sessions grand jury. Nevertheless, regular admonitions to this body by JPs and the judiciary make it clear that relatively few cases were being initiated in this manner, especially after the early decades of the eighteenth century, even though some members of the grand jury, being high constables, could have encouraged their subordinate officers to be more active in this regard. Henry Jodrell, the recorder of Yarmouth in the 1790s, complained that the reluctance of petty constables to bring matters of which they were personally aware to the quarter sessions grand jury, and a lack of concern amongst that body about this reticence, helped explain the low-level disorder found in many parishes. All too often, constables simply stated as a matter of course that there was "nothing to present" in their parishes, under the articles of enquiry. This would then be accepted by the grand jury without further investigation, which would formally note, "We present the presentments of the petty constables hereunto annexed and we have nothing else to present." The attachment would normally be a nil return.[44]

There were occasional exceptions to the general situation. For example, though all but one of the constables attending the Ipswich Borough Sessions in March 1797 had "nothing to present," Jeremiah Burch from St Nicholas's parish presented Eleanor Askew, a local widow, for keeping a disorderly house, to the "disturbance of the neighbourhood and in breach of the peace." The grand jury found this to be a "true bill," although a

43. H. Jodrell, *A Charge Delivered to the Grand Jury of Norfolk, at the General Quarter Sessions Held on Wednesday, Jan. 16, 1793*, 1793, p. 6.
44. Ibid, pp. 6–8.

not-guilty verdict was returned at trial, even though several local women gave evidence against Askew.[45] Very rarely, a cluster of minor cases might be presented at the same time. This occurred at the borough sessions held for Ipswich in August 1735. All these offences were alcohol-related. Most involved selling spirits, whether "Geneva" or cheap brandy, without a licence, contrary to then recent legislation. Of the 14 constables making declarations for the town parishes, half (as usual) had nothing to present. However, Ashburne Hardy, the constable of St Peter's parish, presented Joseph Miller for "selling Geneva by retail" without a licence. The remaining six constables brought similar cases. Interestingly, at the same sessions, the grand jury presented the repair of a bridge in the town on its own initiative.[46] Nevertheless, at quarter sessions, as at assizes, the scrutinising role of the grand jury had become absolutely paramount.

Scrutiny of Bills of Indictment

After its members were sworn in, the grand jury would consider any bills of indictment tendered by complainants and the evidence to support them. Such scrutiny was done in private, normally in a chamber near the main courtroom. Ostensibly this was to prevent external pressure being brought to bring in a certain decision, although such privacy also allowed irrelevant considerations to be discussed. Additionally, in theory, it avoided unfavourable publicity for those whose cases were thrown out, although negative decisions were sometimes reported in the newspapers, especially later in the period, undermining this rationale.

Normally grand jurors considered only prosecution evidence, whether oral testimony or (much less commonly) depositions, when making a decision. They merely looked for a *prima facie* case. In January 1797, when Henry Jodrell, chairman of the Norfolk Quarter Sessions, delivered a charge to its grand jury at the shirehall in Norwich, he noted that its members were tasked with deciding whether there was a "reasonable ground to call upon the person accused for a denial and defence."[47] A

45. SRO Sessions Roll C/2/9/1/1/1/145, 3 and 1.
46. SRO Sessions Roll C/2/9/1/1/1/56, 2.
47. H. Jodrell, *A Charge Delivered to the Grand Jury of Norfolk, at the General Quarter Sessions Held on Wednesday, Jan. 16, 1793,* 1793, p. 4. All the cases before them involved larceny.

positive decision indicated only that the matter was "fit for enquiry."[48] If a grand jury decided that a bill of indictment was well-founded they would write "*billa verra*" on its back (or "true bill" after 1733). If they did not find a case to answer, they would write "*ignoramus*" ("no true bill" or "not found" after 1733), and the suspect would be discharged by proclamation, as occurred with John Ward at the Norfolk Assizes in March 1749.[49] This did not constitute an acquittal, and so did not preclude a further prosecution if more evidence came to light, although this was quite exceptionally rare.

The grand jury might take several hours to complete its business. For example, at the Bury Assizes that opened on Saturday, 22 March 1800, it met at 10:30 am and finished its work at 4:30 pm the same day. The bills of indictment of 42 prisoners were marked "true" during this time and sent for trial.[50] Procedures varied slightly between forums. The grand jury at King's Lynn would consider a batch of several bills at a time, and then return to court to be asked whether they had agreed upon any of them. At this point they would hand over the "true bills" and also indicate that they were content for any mistakes in English, or on technical matters that did not affect their "substance," to be corrected by the court on its own initiative. The grand jury would then go back to their room to consider a fresh batch. In other locations, individual true bills were sent to the court for trial as soon that they were found. If a suspect was on bail and failed to appear at his hearing, the grand jury could still consider the prosecution case against him in his absence, and indict if they thought fit, though he could not then be tried.

It has sometimes been suggested that, by the eighteenth century, the English grand jury was largely an anachronism, being more ceremonial than functional. Certainly its scrutinising role led to only a minority of cases being thrown out. For example, the Surrey Assizes grand juries rejected between 10 per cent and 20 per cent of the bills brought before them during this period. In like manner, indictments were dismissed for about a seventh of those indicted for property crimes in the major

48. J. Parker, *Conductor Generalis, Or, The Office, Duty and Authority of Justices of the Peace*, 1749, p. 392.
49. Gray's Inn MS 45.
50. J. Fiske, *The Oakes Diaries*, 1991, pp. 386–387.

criminal courts in Essex between 1740 and 1805.[51] Perhaps unsurprisingly, the pattern in East Anglia was broadly similar. For example, of the 44 people who were indicted at the Suffolk Assizes at Bury in August 1736, only three (about 7 per cent) were marked in the gaol calendar as having received *ignoramus* decisions from the grand jury. Thus the case of Philip Caton, who was accused of highway robbery after assaulting John Wythescomb and stealing his goods and money, was dismissed, as were those of an alleged housebreaker and a cattle thief.[52] Between 1734 and 1737, just seven of the 251 felony cases (about 3 per cent) sent to assizes in Norfolk and Suffolk were thrown out by the grand jury.[53] Moving to the end of the era, at the Lent Assizes in Bury in 1803, only four out of 23 prosecutions (about 15 per cent) were rejected (six more resulted in acquittal after trial).[54] At the same forum in March 1813, just four men had their cases thrown out, a little over 10 per cent of the cases put before this body on that occasion.[55]

However, such low levels of intervention were not invariably characteristic of eighteenth-century assizes grand juries. In Norfolk and Suffolk there were occasional exceptions to the general pattern, when a significant number of cases were "not found," especially early in the century. At the Norfolk Assizes in July 1725, it was noted that, "six other persons in prison were discharged, the Bills being returned ignoramus."[56] As late as 1784, at the City of Norwich Assizes, the grand jury rejected the bills of indictment of five people (four men and a woman), while eleven people went for trial.[57] (Eleven men and three women were recorded as having had findings of "no true bill" from the grand jury in the gaol calendars for all the assize jurisdictions in the region that year).[58] Even the most serious cases might be dismissed in this fashion. Among them was the allegation of murder made against John Clowes, which was thrown out

51. P. King, "Illiterate Plebeians, Easily Misled: Jury Composition, Experience and Behaviour in Essex 1735–1815," 1988, p. 255.
52. TNA ASSI 33/1.
53. J. Sharpe, *Crime in Early Modern England 1550–1750*, 1998, p. 94.
54. *The Ipswich Journal*, 2 April 1803.
55. *The Bury and Norwich Post: Or, Suffolk, Norfolk, Essex, Cambridge, and Ely Advertiser*, 31 March 1813.
56. *Evening Post*, 31 July–3 August 1725.
57. TNA ASSI 33/6.
58. TNA ASSI 33/6–7.

by the grand jury at the Lent Assizes for Norfolk in 1735 (although this would not preclude trial on a coroner's inquisition).[59]

Even so, by the end of the period it seems that only weak or unsupported cases normally failed to survive this stage of the process, something that may have reflected a more efficient pre-trial investigation. For example, in 1782 the Suffolk Assizes grand jury sitting at Bury did not find a true bill against William Day for attempting to murder his wife, Margaret, by throwing her into a well, for "want of evidence."[60] In like manner, in 1800 William Wells and his two sons were committed to gaol in Bury for breaking into the house of John Daking at Cavendish. However, when the matter came for trial at the Suffolk Assizes, "no true bill" was found against the three men.[61]

The county and borough quarter sessions grand juries in East Anglia also periodically threw out cases during the century. At the Suffolk Quarter Sessions held at Bury in July 1784 Ann Walker was indicted for stealing a 2d loaf, but the case was found "no true bill" and she was discharged.[62] At the same forum in July 1789, a bill of indictment was proffered by the landlord of a Sudbury tavern against a man suspected of stealing a turkey off a spit in his establishment. Again, the grand jury decided that there was no case to answer.[63]

The figures for Yorkshire suggest that in some parts of England the grand juries for the lower jury court were still quite active in this respect, perhaps more so than they were at assizes. Just over a fifth of all bills of indictment brought against men at Yorkshire Quarter Sessions between 1735 and 1775 were rejected in this fashion.[64] This was not necessarily the case in East Anglia, even though some of the allegations were fairly trivial. For example, of 40 bills of indictment presented at the grand inquest for the King's Lynn sessions in September 1726 (the great majority were for regulatory matters), only one was returned *ignoramus*. However, there were occasional exceptions, even at this forum. In April 1738, of ten bills

59. *Weekly Miscellany (1732)*, 17 May 1735.
60. *Norfolk Chronicle,* 27 July 1782.
61. *Bury and Norwich Post,* 6 August 1800.
62. SRO B105/2/47, p. 78.
63. *Bury and Norwich Post*, 22 July 1789.
64. R. Markless, *Gender, Crime and Discretion in Yorkshire, 1735–1775*, 2013, p. 88.

of indictment (including two pairs of defendants), only six were found true while four were dismissed.[65]

Quarter sessions and, to a greater extent, borough sessions were normally much more localised than those for assizes (the City and County of Norwich apart). Perhaps as a result, it seems that their grand juries, with greater access to local knowledge, were more willing to make an assessment of the credibility of complainants when making their decisions. For example, in July 1708, Thomas Garrett, a Norfolk tenant farmer, laid charges of assault and battery against his landlord, Elizabeth Freke. He appears to have made the allegations directly to the sessions, rather than to a JP, as Freke does not seem to have been aware of them until they were dismissed. Freke thought that he acted maliciously because she had threatened him for cutting down 16 large elms and 27 ash trees on the property for timber. Although Garrett personally swore to his account before the county quarter sessions grand jury at Swaffham, the bill was thrown out. It appears that Garrett's reputation counted against him, especially when combined with Freke's high social status. She later noted that the "grand jury were so civil to me as to send me word that they had brought it in ignoramus and that they were glad they could serve me against such a rogue as Garrett was."[66] Nevertheless, such extraneous considerations were not entirely absent in the higher forum, information sometimes being supplied to the assizes grand jury about the credibility of those submitting bills, as occurred with a rape complainant at the end of the period, even if this was not supposed to happen.[67]

It has sometimes been suggested that what kept the grand jury from being abolished altogether (it survived in a residual form until the twentieth century) was the prestige that it brought to its members. Even at the end of the period, grand-jury meetings at assizes towns were opportunities for local social elites to meet and participate in the pageantry of the courts.[68] However, given that petty jurors were drawn from people of relatively modest social status, and grand jurors were drawn from

65. NRO Lynn Sessions Book, KL/C 20/1.
66. R. Anselment (ed.), *The Remembrances of Elizabeth Freke 1671–1714*, 2002, p. 96.
67. *The Bury and Norwich Post: Or, Suffolk, Norfolk, Essex, and Cambridge Advertiser*, 24 March 1802.
68. J. H. Langbein, "The English Criminal Trial Jury on the Eve of the French Revolution," 1987, pp. 22–24.

elements of the "political nation," at least at assizes, and met in private, the grand jury seems to have provided an important filter before a matter was subjected to the uncertainty of a public trial. That only a relatively small number of cases were rejected does not alter the importance of this function. Its presence probably deterred some hopeless cases from being brought.

The assizes grand jury also played an important role behind the scenes on many criminal-justice matters, even if much of this was unrecorded (or has since been lost). They regularly made recommendations on convicts to circuit judges and even directly to the Crown in London. For example, a petition from a prisoner who had been sentenced to seven years' transportation at the Norfolk Assizes in 1785 for stealing pigs, and then spent two years in prison, was supported by a covering letter from the county grand jury signed by its foreman, Henry Hobart.[69] They also played a broader role in regional crime control, law enforcement, and penal policy. Typically, during the summer of 1781, the Norfolk Assizes grand jury granted money for food to prisoners held in the two main Norwich prisons.[70] In August 1797 all members of the Suffolk grand jury who were present at assizes signed a letter expressing concern at the lack of security on the mail coach to Newmarket and suggesting that either a safer route be adopted or that the vehicle be guarded. The jury foreman arranged for this to be delivered to the Postmaster General.[71]

It might be tempting to suggest that the enhancement of the social complexion of the assizes grand jury helped to preserve the oversight and role of the social elite in the criminal justice system at a time when many were abandoning active service as JPs. Nevertheless, it would appear that political factionalism in the late seventeenth century played a greater role in this development.

69. TNA HO 47/6/38, ff 138–142.
70. *Norfolk Chronicle*, 11 August 1781.
71. J. Fiske, *The Oakes Diaries*, 1991, p. 354.

Arraignment and Plea

On receipt of a positive decision from the grand jury, the clerk of the court would arraign those prisoners for whom a true bill had been found, reading their indictment to them (in English, even before 1733) and asking them to plead guilty or not guilty. Very occasionally a defendant might not be sufficiently *compos mentis* to enter such a plea. For example, at the Bury Assizes in August 1753 the case against Robert Studd, accused of stealing a gelding in Grundisburgh, was adjourned until the following sessions, with Studd being kept in gaol in the meantime.[72] His counsel claimed that he was "disordered in his senses."[73] (Interestingly, he appears to have been acquitted at the same forum on another charge some two years earlier.)[74] In March 1754 the matter was put over again. The trial finally took place at the August sessions that year, when Studd was found not guilty.[75]

Similarly, in 1789 the judge Sir Nash Grose reported on a petition from the high sheriff of Norfolk and Henry Hobart, the foreman of that county's assizes grand jury at Thetford, on behalf of John Kerrison. Kerrison had been indicted for several burglaries the previous year, but did not enter a plea or stand trial as he was thought to be mad. He was held in gaol chained to the floor until the following assizes. When this came on, he was certified as insane and unlikely to recover. The officers of his home parish, North Elmham, in Norfolk, said they were willing to provide for him, and Kerrison was recommended to mercy.[76]

Guilty pleas were fairly common for both misdemeanours and petty theft (the only non-capital felony). For example, at the county quarter sessions that opened at King's Lynn on 9 October 1739 there were ten criminal defendants. None of them went to trial (this was unusual). Nine of them pleaded guilty. The one exception, Thomas Barber, had his case quashed without going for a hearing.[77] Even at assizes, a very

72. *Public Advertiser*, 21 August 1753.
73. TNA ASSI 33/2.
74. *General Advertiser (1744)*, 6 August 1751.
75. TNA ASSI 33/2.
76. TNA HO 47/8/5.
77. NRO, C/S 1/12.

high proportion of misdemeanour indictments produced guilty pleas. Thus, at the start of the Summer Assizes held at Bury in 1746, two large groups of men (several dozen in total) accused, *inter alia*, of "riotously assembling themselves" or "riotously assaulting" each other, all pleaded guilty and were fined 3s 4d each.[78]

However, guilty pleas were discouraged in cases of felony, throughout the eighteenth century, especially at the assizes, and particularly where an offence was unclergyable. As a member of the judiciary noted to John Hewett in April 1764, an assizes judge would, as a matter of course, seek to dissuade a defendant from following such a course.[79] Guilty pleas in felony cases were, therefore, rare. Whole assizes might, and frequently did, pass without any being entered. In the entire decade after 1751, only two people "confessed" to felony indictments at the regional assizes. At those held for Norfolk in July 1755, John Longden pleaded guilty to two indictments for horse-theft in Caister, one involving a valuable black gelding and the other a less expensive animal. He was sentenced to death but subsequently reprieved on condition of transportation for 14 years. This was, apparently, done at the behest of the Secretary of State, who sent a letter on his behalf that was produced at the same forum. Longden, a professional horse thief, had disclosed a "great variety of facts committed by him and others in Norfolk and Suffolk, and to whom and in what manner they disposed of the horses they stole."[80] It seems that his co-operation with the authorities saved his neck, probably explaining the guilty plea. Less obviously, the following year, Margaret Howard, a married woman, pleaded guilty to a minor case of grand larceny at the City of Norwich Assizes in August 1756.[81]

Guilty pleas in felony cases were frowned on because they deprived the trial judge of important information for sentencing, and might also be entered in ignorance of a potential defence, especially by those who were not legally represented (a common situation). The case of John May, who pleaded guilty to horse theft at the Bury Assizes in 1789, is indicative of the problems that this could occasion. He had been sentenced to

78. Gray's Inn MS 45.
79. J. Hewitt, *A Journal of the Proceedings of J. Hewitt*, 1790, p. 90.
80. *Whitehall Evening Post Or London Intelligencer*, 28 June – 1 July 1755.
81. Ibid., 24–27 April 1756; TNA ASSI 33/3.

seven years' transportation in lieu of execution and was initially sent to the *Lion* hulk at Portsmouth. Charles Cropley, a fellow of King's College, Cambridge, petitioned for clemency on his behalf. The trial judge, William Ashurst, was asked to comment on the merits of the petition. There was some delay, as he could not find any notes on the case, because there had been no trial, so that he needed to look at the records kept by the clerk of assize.[82]

A plea of guilty also precluded the trial jury from having recourse to "pious perjury" to make an offence less serious. In the case of Margaret Howard, the small sum alleged against her (goods worth just 2s) and the fact that she was a married woman could well have led them to convict her of petty theft. This possibility may have influenced the trial judge's comparatively lenient sentence. Rather than receiving the usual seven years' transportation, she was clergied, branded, and sentenced to 18 months' hard labour in a house of correction under an act of 1706.[83]

Nevertheless, guilty pleas were sometimes entered in even the most heinous cases. For example, at the King's Lynn Borough Sessions in January 1766, John Rudderham pleaded guilty to murdering Leonard Wilson, a local bricklayer.[84] He was duly hanged. In 1785 Robert Randall, when arraigned at the Thetford Assizes, accused of a highway robbery which had involved shooting at and cruelly treating his victims, would "not put himself on his trial, but persisted in pleading guilty to the indictment."[85] He, too, was executed, on Castle Hill in Norwich.[86]

Judicial opposition to such pleas continued to the end of the century and beyond. In 1805, when Henry Green insisted on pleading guilty to stealing a pig worth 20s at the Suffolk Assizes, it was noted, "it was in vain that the Judge (Macdonald) recommended him to stand the event of his trial." (However, the judge did take the plea into account when sentencing the defendant.)[87] In 1819 this was still considered the normal state of affairs in felony cases.[88] As late as 1835 a clerical JP visiting the

82. TNA HO 47/8/63.
83. *Whitehall Evening Post Or London Intelligencer*, 24–27 April 1756.
84. *Gazetteer and New Daily Advertiser*, 28 January 1766.
85. *Public Advertiser*, 26 March 1785.
86. *Whitehall Evening Post* (1770), 7–9 April 1785.
87. *The Bury and Norwich Post: Or, Suffolk, Norfolk, Essex, and Cambridge Advertiser*, 7 August 1805.
88. Anon (By a juryman), *Notes and Observations On Criminal Trials*, 1819, p. 11.

Gloucestershire Assizes disapprovingly watched the trial judge successfully persuade a murder defendant to change his plea from guilty to not guilty. (On doing so, he was swiftly convicted and executed).[89]

After the arraignment, a trial jury would be sworn in. Its members would not normally hear the defendant's plea. However, the clerk would identify the accused man to them, inform them as to the counts against him, and charge them with delivering a just verdict on the matter.[90]

Adjournments

Pressure of work, and a need to clear out local gaols, meant that courts normally took a fairly robust approach to applications to postpone hearings with a view to securing further evidence. Charles Drew's counsel asked for an adjournment at the start of his murder trial at the Suffolk Assizes in 1740, on the grounds that the defendant's "most material witness" was too ill to attend court to testify. This was opposed by prosecution counsel, who felt that the defendant had had adequate time to prepare for trial and had not furnished the court with the name and address of this witness, or properly prepared affidavits setting out his condition. The presiding judge accepted this argument, and the trial proceeded.[91] Judges were often equally firm about prosecution applications to put trials back without good reason.

Of course, if the accused were very ill, legal hearings would have to be adjourned. In 1764 James Knights, a suspected burglar who had been held for less than three months was not able to take his trial at the Thetford Assizes, "being sick in gaol."[92] (The journey from Norwich would have been punishing.) The condition proved fatal; he died a week later of a "mortification of his leg."[93] A decade further on, William Bennett was unable to take his trial at the same forum for a similar reason.[94]

89. D. Verey (ed.), *The Diary of a Cotswold Parson*, 2003, p. 92.
90. NRO Lynn Sessions Book 1726–1752, KL/C 20/1.
91. Anon (By a gentleman of Bury), *The Genuine Trial of Charles Drew*, 1740, p. 6.
92. TNA ASSI 33/4.
93. *Lloyd's Evening Post*, 30 March –2 April 1764.
94. TNA ASSI 33/5.

The Trial Jury

Assizes petty (trial) jurors were reasonably healthy men between the ages of 21 and 70, recruited from the same county as the tribunal. In practice, many—sometimes about three quarters of them—were over the age of 40, due to patterns of property inheritance, something that was significant in an age when average life spans were shorter than they are today.[95] Certain men were always exempt or disqualified from service by reason of their profession, occupation, or possession of a serious criminal record.

Throughout the eighteenth century, assizes jurors had to own property that produced an annual income of £10, as a result of a statute dating from 1692. According to some modern research, this limited jurors to the top third of the income scale. Nevertheless, given the distribution of earnings in the period, it meant that most were small farmers, artisans (such as carpenters or blacksmiths), and tradesmen or shopkeepers. To a significant extent, membership of the assizes trial jury overlapped with that of the 400,000 people nationally who could attend vestry meetings at the end of the eighteenth century, and from whom parish officers were elected.[96]

Many contemporary observers thought that people of any real education and property did their best to avoid service on petty juries.[97] Opulent men usually found it to be an "irksome occupation."[98] As a result, even a strong believer in the system like William Blackstone was concerned at the "general incapacity" of the best jurors to determine complicated questions.[99] In 1785 the Reverend Martin Madan was blunter. He complained that assizes jurors were usually "low and ignorant country people" given to excessive drinking over their lunchtime breaks.[100] At about the same time, a visiting Frenchman, François de la Rochefoucauld, described the trial jury at the Bury Assizes as being made up of farmers and the

95. P. King, "Illiterate Plebeians, Easily Misled: Jury Composition, Experience and Behaviour in Essex 1735–1815," 1988, p. 261.
96. D. Eastwood, "Local Government and Local Society," 2002, p. 47.
97. *The Times*, 13 October 1788, p. 3.
98. Anon (By a juryman), *Notes and Observations On Criminal Trials*, 1819, p. 2.
99. W. Blackstone, *Commentaries on the Laws of England*, vol. 1, 1765, p. 8.
100. J. Langbein, "The English Criminal Trial Jury on the Eve of the French Revolution," 1988, pp. 24–26.

"peasants of the county." Like Madan, he thought they were largely uneducated men, albeit equipped with an innate "very rough good sense."[101]

Even so, there would usually be one or two men of fairly considerable means on a typical assizes trial jury. For example, about a tenth of jurors in late-eighteenth-century Essex had an estate worth more than £100 a year. It is possible—indeed, likely—that these individuals had more influence than their poorer colleagues and were more commonly elected as foremen. In 1737 one observer complained (with some exaggeration) that, although typical defendants might see some men of their own rank on assizes trial juries, they would also see "one or more of them in all matters of moment, as far removed above them in wealth and power as many barons are."[102] Nevertheless, such men were clearly the exception.

Those chosen for service at the lower jury court were of even more modest backgrounds than their assizes counterparts. At the Ipswich Borough Sessions held in June 1755, the petty jury panel of 24 men included four shoemakers (the most common trade) and three carpenters. The remainder included at least one blacksmith, tailor, breeches-maker, tallow chandler, bricklayer, upholsterer, baker, saddler, innkeeper, and locksmith.[103]

As a result of their social provenance, most assizes and quarter sessions jurors were not divorced from the reality of everyday life for ordinary Englishmen. They were not marginal members of society, but nor were they members of the social elite in any way. They may not, quite, have represented the many, but their lives were not secure. The uncertainties of the marketplace could bankrupt the most carefully run small business, while mortality and illness, accident or injury, too few or too many offspring might also bring about its ruin.[104] This helps explain the frequent sympathy shown by juries to those defendants who committed modest non-violent property crimes when in desperate straits.

The names of those who met the property requirement for jury service were compiled annually under the supervision of the relevant county's

---

101. N. Scarfe, *A Frenchman's Year in Suffolk*, 2011, pp. 82–84.
102. Anon, *A Dissertation on the Constitution and Effects of a Petty Jury*, 1737, p. 21.
103. SRO, Sessions Roll 42, 2 July 1755, c/2/9/1/1/1/77, 2 and 10.
104. S. D'Cruze, *A Pleasing Prospect: Social Change and Urban Culture in Eighteenth-century Colchester*, 2009, p. 176.

justices. This list was then sent to the sheriff, who, with the support of his full-time and permanent under-sheriffs, selected and summoned a group of between 48 and 72 potential jurors for the Crown side of each assize sessions; a separate panel was summoned for *nisi prius* hearings. (The sometimes ill-informed François de la Rochefoucauld thought they were drawn by random selection from a panel of 110 names, perhaps conflating the two). When a special assizes was held at Norwich to try rioters in 1766, it was noted that the petty-jury panel summoned from the city consisted of 60 of the "principal manufacturers and tradesmen," 59 of whom appeared in court.[105] It appears that special care had been taken to ensure a somewhat more elevated social composition than usual for this jury, if only to reduce the risk of excessive sympathy for the rioters.

In some parts of England, it seems that assizes jurors were disproportionately taken from men who lived within relatively easy reach of the towns and cities where they would serve, if only to avoid excessive journeys to court and their attendant financial expense. However, this was not necessarily the case. In 1765 a newspaper correspondent complained that tradesmen who owned a small piece of land and a couple of cottages (so just fulfilling the assizes property requirement), and who were required to serve as jurors, might be "called 20 or 30 miles from home, on that duty at much expense and loss of time."[106] This certainly was true in East Anglia.

Of course, those who sat for the City and County of Norwich Assizes must, by definition, have lived close by, because of the city's tiny hinterland, but such proximity was not necessarily found in county juries for Norfolk and Suffolk. The trial of Roger Benstead for murder, held at the Bury Assizes in 1792, provides an obvious example. None of his petty jurors came from Lakenheath, where the defendant lived and had arranged the killing. This is unsurprising, as any requirement of *viceinage* had disappeared centuries earlier. Jurors merely had to be from the same county, with two taken from the same hundred.[107] They would normally be "utter strangers" to the defendants.[108] More significantly,

105. *Public Advertiser*, 9 December 1766.
106. *St. James's Chronicle Or the British Evening Post*, 5–7 September 1765.
107. Anon, *The Complete Juryman: Or, A Compendium of the Laws Relating to Jurors*, 1752, pp. 21–22.
108. Anon, *A Charitable Visit to the Prisons*, 1709, p. 10.

none of the jurors in the Benstead case came from near Bury, where the trial was held. One man came from Norton, about eight miles away. Seven were from Melford, on the Suffolk/Essex border, about 15 miles from the assizes town. The remaining four came from Ashfield, approximately 25 miles away.[109]

Two years later the trial of John and Nathan Nichols at the same forum, for murdering their daughter/sister, produced a similar pattern. Five jurors came from Hitcham, some eleven miles from Bury; three came from Newmarket, 12 miles to the West; two came from Brettenham, ten miles away; and one each came from Hawkedon and Shimpling, five and seven miles distant, respectively.[110] At a murder trial held at the Thetford Assizes in March 1785, two jurors came from Attleborough, about 15 miles away, and two from Great Ellingham, which was a similar distance. One man each came from: Upwell (about 20 miles away); Shouldham (slightly further); Foulden (almost as far); Hilborough (more than ten miles away); Carbrooke (about the same); Bridgham (about seven miles); Wimbotsham (20 miles); and Great Hockham (more than ten miles).[111] In this distribution of jurors, the two counties were broadly similar to Essex, where men were chosen from the various hundreds, and those distant from Chelmsford were just as likely to be selected as men resident near the Assizes.[112]

Unsurprisingly, quarter sessions jurors tended to be somewhat more local to their forums, which sat at more locations than did assizes, and had a sub-county area of responsibility as a result. Those sitting at borough sessions, including those at the powerful sessions held at King's Lynn and Yarmouth, necessarily came from the relevant town.

Inevitably, some summoned jurors failed to keep their appointments, whether at assizes or quarter sessions, and accepted the penalties for doing so. By the early nineteenth century, one man with personal experience of the metropolitan area thought that as many as half those summoned did

109. Anon, *The Trial of Roger Benstead the Elder, and Roger Benstead the Younger*, 1792, p. 1.
110. Anon, *The Trial of John and Nathan Nichols*, 1794, p. 2.
111. N. Holmes, *The Lawless Coast: Murder, Smuggling and Anarchy in the 1780s on the North Norfolk Coast*, 2008, pp. 69–70.
112. P. King, "Illiterate Plebeians, Easily Misled: Jury Composition, Experience and Behaviour in Essex 1735–1815," 1988, p. 284.

not appear, or advanced a "trifling excuse" for evading the office if they did, although the figure was probably lower in the provinces.[113] Nevertheless, at one sitting of the Beccles Quarter Sessions in 1766, five local men were fined for non-appearance after being selected.

Statute required that the 48 or more names on the jury panel be written on as many slips of paper, which were put into a box. Twelve slips were then drawn. If any of the men selected failed to appear, was successfully challenged by the accused, had an acceptable excuse, or proved not to be financially qualified for jury service (a not uncommon occurrence), additional names were drawn until there were a dozen jurors ready to sit. Those who were not selected were then normally allowed to go home. An Act of 1730 imposed a two-year interval for repeat service on county juries, though this did not affect cities that, like Norwich, had separate assize sittings. This legislation remained in force to the end of the era. At most eighteenth-century assizes, only a single criminal trial jury was needed; occasionally, there might be two, so that the court was not delayed while the first jury considered its verdicts.

A felony defendant could peremptorily challenge up to 20 potential jurors as of right, and more for cause (such as bias). In practice, this rarely happened, because defendants were unaware of this power, were too slow to exercise it, or were afraid of antagonizing the men who replaced those originally called. In theory the prosecution could also ask jurors to stand by for the Crown, and so not serve, but this power also was only rarely exercised, the occasional smuggling case in East Anglia apart.[114]

The Hearing

Most trials conducted at assizes were brief by modern standards, as there were numerous cases to be determined within the few days allotted to each location. At the middle of the eighteenth century they may have averaged 30 minutes each (itself a small increase from the 1600s).[115] The average was certainly much less than an hour. The defendant would

113. Anon (By a juryman), *Notes and Observations On Criminal Trials*, 1819, pp. 1–2.
114. J. H. Langbein, "The English Criminal Trial Jury on the Eve of the French Revolution," 1987, pp. 24–26.
115. J. H. Langbein, *The Origins of Adversary Trial*, 2005, p. 17.

stand throughout the proceedings, unless infirm. However, although felony cases could not normally be adjourned overnight until the end of the period (1794), grave cases that might produce a death sentence that was unlikely to be reprieved, and in which there was a serious dispute of fact, received much more thorough attention than this figure might suggest, and possibly slightly more than the equivalent cases tried at the Old Bailey. Defendants who pleaded not guilty but then made little effort to deny the allegations against them (as often occurred) significantly reduced the average length of trials. For grave and contested matters hearings of several hours were unusual but not uncommon, and jury deliberations could take up further time.

For example, the trial of Charles Drew for murder at the Bury Assizes in 1740 lasted more than five hours and involved at least 16 witnesses (only two of them called for the defendant).[116] That of Thomas Otley, a Sudbury barber accused of murdering his wife, lasted four hours at the same forum in 1752, even though he had little to say in his own defence.[117] In 1788 Henry Sell, an apprentice of 17, was convicted at the Lent Assizes at Thetford, after a trial of almost five hours, for poisoning his master's wife. (Poisoning was always difficult to establish, usually requiring medical evidence.) The jury went out for another 20 minutes to consider their verdict.[118]

More unusually, in 1754 the trial of John Sheppard and John Jenkinson for the murder of an ash gatherer from Sweffling lasted more than eleven hours at the Bury Assizes. (They were both acquitted.)[119] In one of the most extreme cases, the trial of Henry Steward and Elizabeth Burroughs for murdering the former's live-in servant lasted almost 13 hours at the Bury Assizes in 1766. Steward was eventually acquitted, but Burroughs was convicted and executed.[120] Such lengthy trials were not confined to cases of murder, although homicides provided the majority of examples.

116. *Ipswich Journal*, 29 March 1740.
117. *Ipswich Journal*, 1 August 1752.
118. Anon, *The Trial of Henry Sell, for the Wilful Murder of Mrs. Elizabeth Clark*, 1788, pp. 18–22.
119. *Read's Weekly Journal Or British Gazetteer*, 13 April 1754.
120. *London Chronicle*, 22–25 March 1766.

At the Norfolk Assizes in 1790, Thomas Jackson was capitally convicted, after a trial of seven hours, of robbing the mail.[121]

Throughout the era there were some observers who thought that the pressures of time placed on circuit judges at assizes, with criminal hearings sometimes confined to just one day at a location (although this was rare, jurisdictions such as the City and County of Norwich apart) was unhelpful. They suggested that the matters of life and death over which the judges presided "ought to be examin'd with leisure and caution."[122]

The eighteenth-century trial on indictment has been the subject of intense study over the past 30 years, and can be dealt with here in outline.[123] At the start of the era, felony hearings were still fairly unmediated, relatively informal, usually unlawyered, confrontations between prosecutors and defendants. It was primarily for the accused, the presiding judge or chairman of quarter sessions, and even the jury, to elicit and probe evidence.[124] Illustrative of this, in 1709, after a prosecution witness in a case of highway robbery tried at the Kent Assizes had finished his evidence, the "court gave the prisoners leave to ask him what questions they thought fit." The court (i.e., the judge) necessarily had to be highly interventionist to stop the proceedings' drifting into irrelevant matters. In the same Kentish case it was noted that the next witness said a great deal but to "so little purpose, that the court was frequently oblig'd to ask him if he had done, what he talk'd of, and the like."[125]

By contrast, in the 1790s the criminal trial on indictment was much closer to its modern counterpart. Lawyers were present in nearly all murder trials and many of those for other serious crimes. Such representation may even have become more common at assizes than it was at the Old Bailey.[126] Major rules of evidence had emerged or become

121. *World (1787)*, 18 March 1790.
122. T. Nourse, *Campania Folix. Or, a Discourse of the Benefits and Improvements of Husbandry*, 1700, pp. 288–299.
123. See generally, J. H. Langbein, *The Origins of Adversary Criminal Trial*, 2005, and G. Durston, *Whores and Highwaymen*, 2012, pp. 445–532.
124. S. Landsman, "The Rise of the Contentious Spirit: Adversary Procedure in Eighteenth-century England," 1990, pp. 505–506; J. Hawles, *The Englishman's Right*, 1680, p. 4.
125. Anon, *An Impartial Account of the Malicious Prosecution of John Comyn, and Chadwick Chambers*, 1709, p. 17 and p. 24.
126. J. H. Langbein, *The Origins of Adversary Trial*, 2005, pp. 256–257.

much more rigid than they were in 1700.[127] Trial procedure was more structured and less informal than it had been at the start of the century, and judges and juries had become increasingly passive, often leaving it to counsel to adduce and test the evidence. By the early nineteenth century, an experienced observer could note that witnesses were "not often questioned by the jury." He urged judges to allow unrepresented defendants to make comments on the evidence as it emerged, even if these were ill timed, in order to reduce the risk that they would later forget what they intended to say. Such extempore comments had been normal at the start of the period.[128]

Eighteenth-century criminal hearings were not for the fainthearted. Those being tried were often in a physically poor condition, so that it was suggested that an observer in a crowded court should "begin by first resolving most courageously, not to be affected with the least dread of whatever he may smell or feel."[129] To modern eyes, there was often a lack of forensic decorum, although this became less marked as the century advanced. In 1709 one observer felt it necessary to warn defendants that if their carriage was rude and insolent in court or "vain and careless, as I have sometimes seen that of some prisoners to be, you may well expect this would redound to your temporal disadvantage."[130] It was not just those on trial who were ill mannered. At the August Assizes for Suffolk in 1736, Ambrose Keddington, the county under sheriff, accused a witness of "misbehaving." The man was bailed on two sureties of £100 to appear on a future occasion, when the matter would be determined.[131] In the 1780s Martin Madan deplored the drunkenness often found amongst both jurors and witnesses at assizes after alcohol-fuelled luncheon adjournments.[132]

There was also a slightly disorganised quality to many hearings. When a neighbour of Parson Woodforde's (then resident in Somerset) was tried

127. For more on eighteenth-century rules of evidence see G. Durston, *Whores and Highwaymen*, 2012, pp. 465–470.
128. Anon (By a Juryman), *Notes and Observations On Criminal Trials*, 1819, p. 2, p. 8 and p. 16.
129. D. Layard, *Directions to Prevent the Contagion of the Jail-distemper: Commonly Called the Jail-fever*, 1772, p. 39.
130. Anon, *A Charitable Visit to the Prisons,* 1709, p. 12.
131. TNA ASSI 33/1.
132. M. Madan, *Thoughts On Executive Justice*, 1785, at pp. 141–142.

at the Wells Assizes in 1775 for murdering his wife, the trial lasted fully ten hours, and the judge did not leave the court once during this time. Woodforde had been summonsed as a good character witness for the accused man, but had less stamina, and was out of court having a meal when he was called, and so failed to testify on the defendant's behalf. The man was convicted and executed.[133] A few hours after Sarah Stave was found guilty at the Bury Assizes in 1746, and sentenced to seven years' transportation, she gave birth to a baby boy.[134] Whether she was in an ideal position to testify in her own defence is debatable.

The criminal courts of the period had a preference for direct testimony. Circumstantial evidence on its own had to be strong to found a conviction, as eighteenth-century judges and juries were often nervous about inferring guilt in this fashion, especially early in the period. It was feared that such evidence could lead to mistaken inferences, "tho' ever so probable."[135] However, it could still be important when combined with a confession or eyewitness testimony. For example, in 1786 a man lurking in a hedgerow shot John Raven, a carrier on his way from Burnham Market to Norwich. The gunman then fled the scene.[136] Two balls entered Raven's thigh, but he did not die for 17 hours and positively identified his assailant as John Shilling from South Creake before he expired. Shilling was arrested and questioned by a local magistrate, although he does not appear to have made any admissions. Nevertheless, the carrier's last statement satisfied the requirements of a "dying declaration" exception to the hearsay rule, despite objection from defence counsel, who: "several times held a conversation with the Judge, relative to the propriety of admitting the verbal declarations of the deceased." As a result, it was adduced at trial.[137] Bolstering the victim's identification, the suspect's powder horn was found near the crime scene, and when searched he had in his pocket balls of the same calibre and type as those used in the killing. Additionally, there was snow on the ground at the relevant time, and Raven left behind a fairly distinctive pattern from the nails on the

133. J. Beresford (ed.), *The Diary of a Country Parson, 1758–1802*, 1978, p. 80.
134. *London Evening Post*, 22–25 March 1746.
135. *Lloyd's Evening Post*, 6–8 September 1775.
136. *Whitehall Evening Post (1770)*, 4–7 March 1786.
137. Anon, *The Trial of John Shilling, For the Wilful Murder of Mr. John Raven*, 1785, p. 14.

soles of his shoes. There were also "several other strong circumstances against him."[138] He was convicted and executed.

Identification was often a key issue at trial. Defendants, if not arrested *in flagrante*, would simply deny that they were the same people as those involved in a crime. The courts were sensitive to such claims, and well aware that miscarriages of justice had been occasioned by mistakes in this regard. Some guilty defendants would take steps to make it harder for the Crown's witnesses to pick them out. When a new county gaol for Suffolk was opened at Ipswich in 1791, its rules included a requirement that prisoners should not be allowed to "disguise themselves during their being in prison, by cutting off their hair, or by letting it grow so as to deceive the prosecutor." They were also supposed go to their trials in the same condition as they arrived at the prison.[139] Martin Madan thought the practice that had developed at some quarter sessions of clothing defendants produced from prison in clean carters' smocks rather than their own garments, in the interests of hygiene, was mistaken for this reason.[140] Defendants would often bolster a denial by advancing an alibi. For example, at the Bury Assizes in 1788, John Hills was acquitted of burgling a house at Assington in Suffolk after a blind man swore that he had heard Hills' voice at his father's house at the time of the crime.[141] Inevitably, these alibis were sometimes fabricated.

Judicial Directions

At the close of a hearing, the trial judge would direct the jury on the law and sum up the evidence. This was done with varying degrees of thoroughness, but was often fairly brief. If he wished, a judge could give his opinion on the "proper" verdict quite firmly. The celebrated *Bushel's Case* of 1670 merely decided that jurors who ignored strong judicial advice could not be punished for their recalcitrance; it did not prevent such guidance being given. At the end of the period, in 1800, the jury at Bury Assizes swiftly convicted Sarah Lloyd after the trial judge advised them

138. *Whitehall Evening Post (1770)*, 4–7 March 1786.
139. Anon, *General Regulations for the Government of the New Goal* [sic], *At Ipswich*, 1791, p. 11.
140. M. Madan, *Thoughts On Executive Justice*, 1785, p. 149.
141. *Bury and Norwich Post*, 26 March 1788.

that, although it was theoretically open to them to find her not guilty of stealing from a dwelling-house, "I have been looking into this case, and can find no loop hole whereby you might be induced to acquit her."[142] As late as 1815, Lord Chief Justice Gibbs, presiding over the murder trial of Elizabeth Woolterton at the same forum, warned jurors that they "should not create doubts for the purpose of acquitting her."[143] However, by the end of the eighteenth century a reminder that it was ultimately for the jury to decide the matter would often accompany such a direction. The judge in Lloyd's case advised the jurors that they should not be "led away by me." (He also directed them to acquit on a separate burglary count that was not made out on the evidence).[144]

In practice, conflicts between judge and jury were fairly rare. Contemporary newspapers often recorded that a verdict in the region, particularly an acquittal, had been "returned to the satisfaction of the court."[145] In other situations, when a jury acquitted against the evidence because of mitigating factors pertaining to the defendant—youth, inebriation, previous good character—the judge would merely congratulate the accused on his narrow escape and tell him that he had had a "very merciful jury."[146]

Jurors normally took their lead from the judge if he expressed a strong view, if only because many held the judiciary in awe, thinking it "presumptuous" to reject their suggestions.[147] For example, at the trial of Frances Cheek on the Home Circuit in 1754, the primary issue was whether the defendant was insane when she killed her six-month baby with a hook. (She had recovered by the time her trial took place). The jury initially returned to say that, although fully satisfied that she had killed the baby, they "doubted her sanity." This was not acceptable to Sir Dudley Ryder, the assizes judge, who "explained again the nature of the case rather against the prisoner." They went out once more and

142. W. Notcutt, *Trial of Joseph Clarke, the Younger, and Sarah Lloyd, at the Assizes, Held at Bury St. Edmund's*, 1800, pp. 6–8.
143. T. Middleditch, *The Trial at Large of Eliz. Woolterton, for the Wilful Murder of Robert Sparkes, a Child Six Years Old*, 1815, p. 20.
144. W. Notcutt, *Trial of Joseph Clarke, the Younger, and Sarah Lloyd, At the Assizes, held at Bury St. Edmund's*, 1800, pp. 6–8.
145. *General Evening Post*, 20–23 April 1751.
146. M. Madan, *Thoughts On Executive Justice*, 1785, p. 38.
147. Anon (By a Juryman), *Notes and Observations On Criminal Trials*, 1819, pp. 4–5.

an hour-and-a-half later returned with a verdict of "guilty of murder," which led to Ryder's sentencing her to death.[148] She was duly hanged.

Similarly, at the Thetford Assizes in 1802, John Wilson, who had recently been discharged from a warship, was accused of stealing a horse from a stable. He had quickly been pursued and caught. At trial the jury initially returned a verdict of "guilty of taking but not of stealing." They may have thought the prisoner intended using the animal for his journey and then abandoning it. The trial judge would not accept this, and directed them that if they thought he intended to return the horse to the stable from which it came they should find Wilson "not guilty." The jury reconsidered their decision and then convicted him.[149]

Nevertheless, juries did, occasionally, resist strong judicial or magisterial pressure to convict. At the Norfolk Quarter Sessions in 1810, Edward Stubbing from Wymondham was accused of uttering seditious words in a tavern, in the presence of men from the West Norfolk Regiment. He had allegedly said that Napoleon Bonaparte was a better man than King George, and expressed the hope that he (Napoleon) would soon come to England. There was no serious challenge to the prosecution evidence, although the defendant called character witnesses to his general good conduct and loyalty to the Crown. The jury, "to the surprise of the whole Court, returned a verdict of *Not Guilty.*"[150]

One reason for the lack of judicial concern about jury verdicts was that, in many situations, judges had the power to render them nugatory, especially after the Transportation Act of 1718 came into force. For example, if they felt that a jury's under-valuing of stolen goods in a grand larceny case to below 1s was manifestly unreasonable, they could still sentence the convict to transportation for petty theft. Thus, at the Summer Assizes held at Norwich in 1746, Thomas Blofield and Nicholas Hooke were accused of stealing naval stores. They had a benign jury who were prepared to value the items taken at an unrealistic ten pence. Hooke was publicly whipped (the usual penalty for petty larceny). However, Blofield was sentenced to transportation for seven years. An explanation for

148. Lincoln's Inn, Harrowby MSS 18–19, Document 19(f) *Legal Notebook of Sir Dudley Ryder, 1754 and 1755*, p. 4.
149. *The Bury and Norwich Post: Or, Suffolk, Norfolk, Essex, and Cambridge Advertiser*, 24 March 1802.
150. *The Times*, 7 May 1810, p. 3.

their radically different treatment can be gleaned from the gaol calendar for the sessions, which notes, "It appearing to the court that Blofield is a dangerous man." Similarly, at the Norfolk Assizes in August 1747, Moses Howard was accused of grand larceny, after stealing goods valued at 20s. He was merely convicted to the value of 6d. The trial judge was not impressed with this degree of downvaluing, and sentenced him to transportation.[151]

In 1752 Thomas Hines was accused of stealing goods worth 5s from Abraham Church at the Lent Assizes for Suffolk. Although only convicted to the value of ten pence, he was sentenced to transportation. The fact that he had been separately accused and acquitted outright of theft from a dwelling-house under a statute from 1713 may have influenced the judge's decision.[152] In an even more extreme case, at the Norfolk Assizes held in March 1749, Stephen Goodwin was accused of stealing a wether sheep valued at 6s. Technically, this was a capital crime after 1741. However, the jury merely found him guilty of petty theft to the value of ten pence. Instead of ordering him to be whipped, the judge sentenced Goodwin to seven years' transportation, evidently feeling that the verdict was far too lenient.[153] Even so, Goodwin still received significant benefit from the jury's compassion. He avoided any possibility of execution (albeit that this was always highly improbable for taking a single sheep) or, much more realistically, the imposition of 14 years' transportation as a condition of reprieve. As this suggests, the major limits on judicial discretion occurred when the jury returned a non-capital verdict but the trial judge felt that the death penalty was appropriate or when they returned an outright acquittal but he felt that there should have been some form of conviction. This did not happen often.

Conversely, if a defendant was capitally convicted when the judge had doubts about the safety of the jury's verdict (as was sometimes the case), he could advise the Crown that clemency be granted, unconditionally if necessary. Similarly, there are occasional suggestions that a trial judge thought that a jury might have been too harsh in failing to

151. Gray's Inn MS 45.
152. TNA ASSI 33/2.
153. Gray's Inn MS 45.

reduce a charge via pious perjury. At the Norfolk Assizes in July 1748, Henry Rush was found guilty of grand larceny after being accused of stealing goods worth 9s, as was Simon Catchpole, who had been accused of taking items worth just 4s. The trial judge allowed both of them to be clergied, branded, and discharged, rather than imposing the usual sentence of transportation.[154] Perhaps he thought that these particular cases, like some others at a similar value, should have been returned as petty-theft convictions.

Jury Decision-Making

At the start of the eighteenth century, some assizes petty juries were still returning verdicts on several trials at the same time, having sat through a series of hearings before withdrawing to reach their decisions on the entire batch. Thus one contemporary observer noted that a jury at the Kent Assizes in 1707, faced by an apparently weak case, could not acquit without retiring as they were still "oblig'd to withdraw upon other causes which lay before them."[155] After the early years of the century, felony juries returned their verdicts on each prisoner at the end of his trial, rather than in batches, in East Anglia as elsewhere.[156]

If a case appeared straightforward, jurors would often simply put their heads together and whisper among themselves, without leaving court, before reaching a decision, which was then delivered by their foreman. For example, at the Bury Assizes in 1754, John Sheppard and another man named Jenkinson, accused of murder, were swiftly acquitted, the "jury giving favour without going out of the court."[157] At the trial of Thomas Harper for murder at the same forum in 1792, "The Jury, without quitting the court, found him guilty."[158]

If a case were more complicated, the jury would retire to a room under the supervision of a court bailiff and debate the matter for a few minutes.

154. Gray's Inn MS 45.
155. Anon, *An Impartial Account of the Malicious Prosecution of John Comyn, and Chadwick Chambers*, 1709, p. 31.
156. NRO Lynn Sessions Book 1726–1752, KL/C 20/1.
157. *Ipswich Journal*, 6 April 1754.
158. Anon, *The Trial of Thomas Harper, for Shooting Thomas Briggs, of Lakenheath in the County of Suffolk*, 1788, p. 20.

Longer deliberations were rare, but not unheard of. Exceptionally, they might last more than an hour. Some observers were cynical about the speed with which jurors normally reached their decisions, feeling that they sometimes deferred to the views of their foreman because of his "supposed gravity and experience" and to avoid having their dinners spoilt by any delay in adjudication.[159]

While discussing their verdict, jurors were supposed to be kept without fire, food, and drink until they reached a unanimous decision, however long it might take. It was thought that this rule discouraged delay and disagreement, so that unanimity was often reached suspiciously quickly.[160] In theory this practice lasted until 1858. However, it was not followed at the Sudbury Quarter Sessions of October 1791. A woman had brought an indictment for assault against a local man. The trial started at 11 am and went on for about hour. At its close, the jury retired to consider their verdict. Very unusually, there was a "great want of unanimity" among its members, who were too committed to their views to settle the matter in a legally improper manner, such as by flipping a coin, as sometimes apparently occurred in these situations. The case was repeatedly put back, but the jurors still could not agree. At 10 pm the court noted that it would meet again at 10 am the next day, leaving the jury to continue its deliberations overnight. At midnight the jurors, feeling hungry, decided to go home, broke down the door of the jury room, and left. They returned the next morning to complete their office, but the mayor, presiding over the case as senior magistrate for the town, noted that, because of their absence, legally they were no longer the same jury as the one that had sat the previous day. He decided to write to the Attorney General to determine what sort of penalty should be imposed on them.[161] The jurors were probably punished for their deviation from the "established laws of the land for securing a uniformity of verdict."[162]

---

159. Anon (By a Friend to the Constitution), *Observations On the Duty and Power of Juries, As Established by the Laws of England* (2nd edn.), 1796, p. 6.
160. Anon, *A Dissertation on The Constitution and Effects of a Petty Jury*, 1737, p. 9.
161. *The Times*, 17 October 1791, p. 3.
162. *Bury and Norwich Post*, 19 October 1791.

Verdicts

Prospects for acquittal at a jury hearing were much higher during the eighteenth century than in the Victorian period, despite the considerable level of attrition between the commission of an offence and it going for trial. In the major criminal courts in Essex, between 1740 and 1805, petty jurors acquitted almost a third of those who came before them, and brought in partial verdicts in a further 10 per cent of cases. Just over half of those tried were convicted of the full offence indicted, and this seems to have been about the same for the other counties in the Home Circuit.[163]

Perhaps unsurprisingly, given its geographic proximity, the distribution of verdicts in Norfolk and Suffolk was broadly in accordance with those in Essex. Even cases that survived the grand-jury procedure produced large numbers—often at least a third—of not-guilty decisions. According to one estimate, of the 251 felony cases tried at assizes in Norfolk and Suffolk between 1734 and 1737, 98 (37 per cent) produced outright acquittals, while another seven cases (three per cent) were thrown out by the grand jury before trial.[164] Thus 40 per cent of defendants escaped any form of conviction. Similarly, of the 33 people tried for property crimes at the regional assizes in 1751 (some cases involved multiple defendants), where the outcome of their trials can be firmly determined, ten were acquitted outright (slightly less than a third). Another five (about 15 per cent) were convicted of lesser offences, while 18 (somewhat over half) were convicted of the full offence indicted.[165] The following year, 45 people were accused of property crimes at the regional assizes. Of these, 19 (just over 42 per cent) were convicted of the offences charged, 13 of lesser offences, and the same number acquitted outright (about 29 per cent for both categories).

More specifically, and taking an individual sessions, at the Lent Assizes for Norfolk held at Thetford in 1741 eight men were capitally convicted, four convicted of a clergyable offence for which they received seven years'

163. P. King, "Illiterate Plebeians, Easily Misled: Jury Composition, Experience and Behaviour in Essex 1735–1815," 1988, p. 255.
164. J. Sharpe, *Crime in Early Modern England 1550–1750*, 1998, p. 94.
165. TNA ASSI 33/2.

transportation, and ten acquitted. Thus 12 men were found guilty of some type of felony and another ten found not guilty of any offence.[166] At the Suffolk Assizes held at Bury in August 1774, seven defendants were acquitted, and five were convicted of offences ranging from petty larceny, in the course of housebreaking, to stealing more than 40s in a residence or burglary.[167] Eight years later, at the same forum, John Sones was capitally convicted for stealing a horse, and John Prime was found guilty of stealing flour, and sentenced to three years' hard labour on the Thames. Three other men were convicted and imprisoned for six months for offences of theft and fraudulently obtaining cloth, shoes, and stockings from shopkeepers. However, five defendants (half the total) were acquitted outright.[168]

Trial on indictment at the lower forum also frequently resulted in acquittals, even for misdemeanours and cases of petty theft, but this is less surprising. A much higher proportion of these accusations produced guilty pleas, unlike felonies heard at assizes. This probably meant that proportionately more cases that went for trial were intrinsically weaker than their equivalents at assizes.

A significant increase in conviction rates for felony occurred in the nineteenth century. Perhaps an early indication of this change is that at the Bury Assizes in 1813, and ignoring cases where the grand jury returned a finding of "no true bill," six defendants were acquitted outright but about 28 (more than 80 per cent) were convicted of some form of offence.[169]

Despite (as he believed) the low social provenance and poor education of most trial jurors, François de la Rochefoucauld thought that 95 per cent of Suffolk Assizes jury verdicts were legally correct, i.e., justified by the evidence, something that, he felt, was partly explained by the firm advice and guidance they received from the trial judge.[170] The precision of this figure suggests that it was taken from English observers he had

166. *London Evening Post*, 21–24 March 1741.
167. *Public Advertiser*, 9 August 1774.
168. *Norfolk Chronicle*, 27 July 1782.
169. *The Bury and Norwich Post: Or, Suffolk, Norfolk, Essex, Cambridge, and Ely Advertiser*, 31 March 1813.
170. N. Scarfe, *A Frenchman's Year in Suffolk*, 2011, pp. 82–84.

spoken to. Juries may have made their decisions quickly, but they were often highly discriminating in their verdicts when there was more than one count against the same defendant or several co-accused.

The risk of mistaken convictions in capital cases was well-known. Even at the start of the period, a few observers expressed concern that not enough was being done to prevent them.[171] The situation was aggravated by the use of rewards and accomplice evidence (see *Chapter 5*). Several major miscarriages of justice occurred, or were narrowly avoided, in eighteenth-century East Anglia as elsewhere. In 1783 Jeremiah Theobald, having been found guilty of the murder and robbery of a Suffolk woman, confessed at the gallows to having burgled the house of Thomas Newman of Burnham. John Bunch and Elizabeth Holmstead had been executed at Chelmsford (Essex) the previous summer for this crime.[172] The deaths of two innocent people had apparently weighed heavily on his conscience.[173] Elizabeth had been a servant in the house that was burgled, and it was assumed that the crime must have been the work of an insider. Although her execution was delayed because of pregnancy, she was eventually hanged.[174]

More fortunately, when Thomas Herring was awaiting death at Ipswich in 1756 for stealing a horse, he cleared a man named Whimer who was being held in Norwich Gaol for the robbery of a vicar near Hartford Bridge. Herring felt compelled, "in justice to the said Whimer, to confess that he was the only person who robbed Mr Fox."[175] In a neat bit of courtroom drama, after Stephen Rolfe was acquitted of murdering a customs officer near Yarmouth, at the Bury Assizes in 1771, it was noted that the Crown witness who had testified against him was himself "committed on strong suspicion of his having perpetrated the fact."[176]

It was partly the general awareness of such miscarriages of justice that explains why gallows confessions by those about to die were so keenly

171. R. Smith, *Mistaken Justice: Or, Innocence Condemn'd, in the Person of Francis Newland*, 1695, p. 36.
172. T. Notcutt, *The Trial at Large of Jeremiah Theobald, Otherwise Hasell, and James May, otherwise Folkes*, 1783, pp. 1–4.
173. *London Chronicle*, 3–5 April 1783.
174. *Parker's General Advertiser and Morning Intelligencer*, 30 November 1782. For more on pregnant women and execution see G. Durston, *Whores and Highwaymen*, 2012, pp. 514–516.
175. *Gazetteer and London Daily Advertiser*, 20 April 1756.
176. *Craftsman or Say's Weekly Journal*, 10 August 1771.

sought by the authorities: they reassured the public. Their absence could occasion concern. In 1748 a spectator at the execution of William Salter for robbery and murder in Norfolk noted that he vehemently maintained his innocence until the end, despite considerable pressure from the attending clergyman to make a confession. The apparently worried observer concluded that Salter was "either very obstinate and fool-hardy; or entirely innocent."[177]

However, the authorities and many educated and well-to-do people could be extremely sanguine about the risks of mistaken conviction, especially early in the century. In 1709 one observer suggested that those who were about to be executed for crimes that they had not committed might console themselves by reflecting on the fact that they had probably offended against God on many other occasions![178] Similarly, the generally mild-mannered Parson Woodforde was untroubled about the prospects of a miscarriage of justice if a Norfolk defendant who had called him as a character witness, and been capitally convicted, was innocent. He left such matters to God, he said, on the basis that if the man, though innocent, was executed: "I doubt not he will be amply rewarded."[179]

In part this lack of concern could be attributed to the slight chance that "respectable" people would be on the receiving end of such verdicts. This was not just because they were tried less frequently. Unsafe convictions often involved slightly nefarious individuals who were not given the benefit of any doubt as a result. In 1738, musing on the dangers posed by perjured, reward-driven evidence, an observer accepted that a "good character, is, indeed, some protection to the innocent."[180] Having well-to-do connections willing to vouch for a suspect might even prevent a matter's coming for trial. In January 1774 Mary Hardy noted that Thomas Holesworth, an innkeeper, had gone to St Faiths, in Norfolk, where he was "taken for goose stealing." Five days later her husband secured his release on bail at the Norwich sessions. Two days after that Mr Hardy got

177. *Westminster Journal or New Weekly Miscellany*, 23 April 1748.

178. Anon, *A Charitable Visit to the Prisons*, 1709, p. 16.

179. J. Beresford (ed.), *The Diary of a Country Parson, 1758–1802*, 1978, p. 80.

180. T. Andrews, *An Enquiry into the Causes of the Encrease and Miseries of the Poor of England*, 1738, p. 49.

him "cleared."[181] Conversely, poor travellers accused of crimes of which they were entirely innocent, many miles from anyone who could readily establish their bona fides, were frequently disadvantaged.

Nevertheless, society seems to have become more concerned about miscarriages of justice as the century advanced, and notions of due process strengthened. This was probably accelerated when fraud, which was not normally a plebeian crime, was made a capital felony in almost all circumstances in 1729, threatening more well-to-do people with the noose.

Pious Perjury and Partial Verdicts

As some of the verdicts considered above suggest, eighteenth-century juries were often keen to convict for less serious felonies than those initially indicted by the prosecutor. This was most commonly done to mitigate the consequences for the defendant of being found guilty, rather than a true reflection of the evidence adduced. As a result, the practice was termed "pious perjury" by the jurist William Blackstone. It was medieval in origin, but reached its apogee during the eighteenth century.[182] Pious perjury was used to reduce clergyable grand larceny to petty theft and capital felonies to non-capital crimes. Juries appear to have been much more willing to let compassion influence what they would convict for than to allow it to produce an outright acquittal.[183]

An understanding of partial verdicts is vital, as they were of crucial importance to the wider system. For example, taking those cases where a verdict can be identified from entries in the appropriate gaol calendar, it seems that 15 people were convicted of some form of property crime at the assizes held in the East Anglian region during the summer of 1734. Of these, seven (almost half) were convicted of a legally less serious offence than that initially indicted, and three of the full convictions involved indictments for robbery, which was inherently unlikely to produce a lesser verdict compared to other property offences.[184]

181. M. Bird (ed.), *The Diary of Mary Hardy 1773–1809*, 2013, pp. 9–10.
182. T. A. Green, *Verdict According to Conscience*, 1985, p. 276.
183. P. King, "Illiterate Plebeians, Easily Misled: Jury Composition, Experience and Behaviour in Essex 1735–1815," 1988, p. 255.
184. TNA ASSI 33/1.

Pious Perjury and Grand Larceny

Sympathetic juries regularly reduced grand larceny counts to convictions for petty theft. As one observer noted in 1775, "The mercy of juries will oftentimes make them strain a point, and bring in larceny to be under the value of twelve-pence, when it is in reality of so much greater value."[185] A valuation of ten pence was frequently used in these situations. For most of the century, this was likely to make the difference between flogging and seven years' transportation.

The incidence with which this occurred varied greatly. In the summer of 1734, ten individuals are identifiable from the Norfolk Circuit gaol calendar as having been tried in the three East Anglian assizes jurisdictions for simple grand larceny (two were co-defendants). Four were acquitted outright. However, just as many were convicted of the lesser offence of petty theft, the goods taken being valued at ten pence, as were convicted of the full offence (three in each case). In all cases, this had important ramifications. The three convicted of the full offence were transported for seven years, while those convicted of the lesser form of the crime were merely whipped, the trial judge accepting the jury's apportionment of culpability.[186] By contrast, only one such case occurred at the regional assizes in 1751, while there were nine cases in which at least one conviction was secured for the full offence and five that resulted in acquittals.[187] Moving on to the three years from 1777, there were three cases, making up about 20 per cent of those heard.[188]

When stolen goods were worth only slightly more than 1s but indicted as grand larcenies, defendants were usually convicted for petty theft, unless there were severely aggravating features. Thus, at the Bury Assizes in March 1755, George Harvey was accused of stealing goods valued at just 18d from William Alp but convicted to the value of six pence.[189] At the same forum in August 1764, John Gathercote was accused of stealing three shillings' worth of goods from John Gore, but convicted to the

185. *Lloyd's Evening Post*, 6–8 September 1775.
186. TNA ASSI 33/1.
187. TNA ASSI 33/2.
188. TNA ASSI 33/6.
189. TNA ASSI 33/2.

value of just ten pence.[190] A decade later at the Bury Assizes, Elizabeth Herrington was accused of stealing clothing valued at two shillings and one penny, but also convicted to the value of ten pence.[191] In 1767 Wadwell Rose, a gardener, was accused of stealing 112 pounds of hay worth just 18 pence at the Thetford Assizes. This was valued at nine pence by the trial jury.[192] This sort of down valuing is unsurprising. Jurors would have been well aware that many identical cases were prosecuted *ab initio* as the lesser form of larceny.

Slightly higher-value grand larcenies, worth between (roughly) 3s and 10s were also regularly down valued to below 12 pence. For example, at the Norfolk Assizes of August 1747, Ruben Pritchard was prosecuted for stealing goods worth four shillings from Thomas Crispe in Norwich. At trial they were valued at the standard sum of ten pence by the jury, and the judge sentenced Pritchard to the normal whipping. At the Suffolk Assizes in July 1748, John Skelton was accused of stealing goods worth six shillings, but received the same verdict.[193] In March 1774 William West, who had stolen two coats allegedly worth eight shillings, was convicted to the value of ten pence at the Thetford Assizes and publicly whipped on Castle Hill in Norwich.[194]

Defendants convicted of such relatively low-value grand larcenies were usually shown leniency if there were no aggravating circumstances, such as a breach of trust (theft from an employer), a generally suspicious defendant (perhaps an "old offender"), a wealthy perpetrator, or a prevalent local problem requiring a deterrent example. If any of these factors were present, even the theft of fairly small sums could be returned as grand larceny. For example, at the Bury Assizes in March 1797, John Gill was convicted of the full offence charged after stealing halters valued at just three shillings.[195] Even so, cases of down valuing could be much more extreme. For example, John Lilley had allegedly stolen goods valued at more than £2 from Daniel Devereaux, but was convicted to the value

190. TNA ASSI 33/4.
191. TNA ASSI 33/5.
192. TNA ASSI 33/6.
193. Gray's Inn MS 45.
194. TNA ASSI 33/5.
195. TNA ASSI 33/6.

of ten pence at the Bury Assizes in 1774. However, these nearly always involved extremely unusual or specially mitigating factors.

Inevitably, pious perjury could produce marked discrepancies in verdict in essentially similar cases. At the Bury Assizes in March 1751, Sarah Lanham, a spinster, was accused of stealing goods worth 18 shillings from William Garnham. She was convicted to the value of just ten pence and whipped in Ipswich market. At the same sessions, Samuel Sparke was accused of stealing two packages of goods worth a total of nine shillings and two pence. He was convicted of the full offence and sentenced to transportation. However, few cases matched the disparity that occurred at the Bury Assizes in 1753, when John Alcock and John King were jointly accused of stealing two cheeses worth (together) seven shillings. King was convicted of the full offence charged and sentenced to transportation. For Alcock the value of the cheese miraculously fell to just ten pence, allowing a conviction for petty theft, for which he was whipped. It is likely that the jury thought King was the leader in the venture.[196]

Pious Perjury and Capital Offences

Pious perjury was regularly used to reduce capital property crimes, such as pickpocketing, shoplifting, burglary, housebreaking, and stealing in a dwelling-house, to cases of grand larceny or even petty theft. This was done by valuing the goods taken at less than the amount required in the definition of the offence or not finding other essential elements of the felony to have been made out on the evidence.

Using the former mechanism, cases involving the pickpocketing of goods worth a shilling or more, shoplifting those valued at over 5s, housebreaking of empty premises during which goods worth more than 5s had been taken, or stealing goods worth more than 40 shillings from a domestic residence, produced convictions for simple theft or petty theft (in the case of pickpocketing) by going just below these values. For example, jurors might find that someone who had taken large amounts of silver plate, watches, jewels, and money from a dwelling-house was

196. TNA ASSI 33/2.

guilty "of stealing to the value of thirty-nine shillings only, in order to prevent his being hanged."[197]

On other occasions, juries might commit pious perjury by finding that a legal prerequisite for a capital offence, *other* than value, had not been made out. For example, when, at the Bury Assizes in 1746, John Corbold was accused of the capital offence of stealing goods worth more than 40s from a dwelling-house, the gaol book was endorsed, "Jury say guilty but not guilty of stealing in house." This would then become an ordinary case of (clergyable) grand larceny, irrespective of the value of the goods taken, for which he could only be (and duly was) transported for seven years.[198]

When it came to burglary this approach was essential, as down-valuing stolen items would have no effect on the verdict if the other situational prerequisites for the crime were present. Thus, at the Lent Assizes for Norfolk in 1747, Samuel More was accused of committing a burglary during which items worth a total of £1 15s 4d were stolen. The jury suggested that there had been no nocturnal break-in, and so returned a verdict "[g]uilty felony not guilty of burglary."[199] Similarly, at the Bury Assizes in March 1764, James Rampley was accused of burglary during which goods worth six shillings had been stolen but convicted of simple grand larceny.[200] In a more extreme case, Lydia Coats, a married woman, was tried for burglary at the Bury Assizes in 1751. It was alleged that she had broken into the house of Joseph Rolph during the night, and stolen goods worth 30s. She, too, was merely convicted of grand larceny.[201] Perhaps the jury suspected that she was driven by need, possibly even put up to it by her husband (in his absence the doctrine of *feme covert* did not apply). Most important, she was not a physical threat.

Exceptionally, both circumstances and value might be ignored. In one of the more extreme examples of pious perjury, from the Bury Assizes held in March 1774, Virtue Clarke, a labourer's wife, was accused of a burglary during which she allegedly stole food worth more than four

197. *Lloyd's Evening Post*, 6–8 September 1775.
198. Gray's Inn MS 45.
199. Gray's Inn MS 45.
200. TNA ASSI 33/4.
201. TNA ASSI 33/2.

shillings. Not only did the jury decide that this was a case of theft, rather than burglary, they also valued the items stolen at ten pence, so that it was just petty theft, for which Clarke was sentenced to be privately whipped in prison and then discharged. Stealing moderate amounts of food was often treated leniently because it was seen as indicative of pressing need rather than greed.[202]

Of course, in some cases there was a genuine valuing of property that had initially been overvalued by the prosecutor (perhaps in the hope of a reward); in some, the evidence for one of the other essential elements of a capital crime was truly absent. However, it is clear that a majority of the cases in which findings benefited the prisoner were examples of pious perjury. For example, in 1802 Elizabeth Hutchinson, a 16-year-old girl, was indicted at the Thetford Assizes on three counts of burglary from as many houses in Swaffham. She was acquitted on all of them but found guilty of three offences of grand larceny and sentenced to seven years' transportation.[203] It is almost inconceivable that the criminal allegations contained in all three of the indictments were truly mistaken.

On a more statistical basis, in the decade from 1751 to 1760 there were 48 prosecutions for burglary in the regional assizes (counting as a single prosecution those cases with multiple defendants). Of these, 15 cases produced at least one conviction for the full offence indicted (just over 31 per cent), leading to four executions. A further 20 cases (just under 42 per cent) produced at least one conviction for a lesser offence (normally larceny), usually via pious perjury. Finally, thirteen cases (about 27 per cent) produced outright acquittals, the accused being found not guilty of any offence.[204]

Of course, such verdicts required that jurors be aware of the financial values or the other legal prerequisites that made property offences capital. Members of the judiciary often instructed them on key aspects of this subject as part of their directions. Indeed, this would have been vital when it came to down valuing for arcane offences, such as stealing from a bleaching ground, as occurred with Robert Child in 1799.[205] As this

202. TNA ASSI 33/5.
203. *The Bury and Norwich Post: Or, Suffolk, Norfolk, Essex, and Cambridge Advertiser*, 24 March 1802.
204. TNA ASSI 33/2.
205. TNA ASSI 33/6.

case also suggests, such practices were usually not only tolerated without demur by judges but were even actively encouraged, in appropriate cases, so that they were committed "under the direction of the Court."[206] This was a longstanding phenomenon. In late-seventeenth-century Myddle (Shropshire), when a mentally backward local man was indicted for stealing 24 chickens, the assizes judge told the jury that they must find the prisoner guilty but that they would be well-advised to value the birds at less than a shilling (an absurd under-estimate).[207] The same approach often prevailed in eighteenth-century East Anglia.

However, such information cannot have come purely from the trial judge, as juries sometimes down valued goods to strategic totals, such as 39 shillings or four shillings and six pence, that were irrelevant to the offence charged. Although some jurors usually had previous experience of jury service, and could pass on the knowledge they had gleaned on earlier occasions, this might have become confused or garbled over time. For example, in 1754 John Damant was accused at the Bury Assizes of stealing in a dwelling-house, contrary to the 1713 Act, the allegation being that he had taken goods and cash worth £2 8s (just over the 40 shillings limit). He was convicted to the value of four shillings and ten pence, when reducing the value to 39 shillings would have been sufficient. However, the figure selected might have been vital if Damant had been indicted for housebreaking.[208] There were several other cases in which a petty jury opted for what was clearly a "technical" sum without apparently realising that it would have no effect on their verdict.

Sentencing

During the first half of the century, murderers were often sentenced immediately after conviction, and in 1752 this became mandatory. However, for much of the period those who had been found guilty of other crimes were usually dealt with together, at the end of the sessions. It was fairly common in these situations to start with the lowest penalties,

206. *Lloyd's Evening Post*, 6–8 September 1775.
207. R. Gough, *The History of Myddle*, 1981 (originally written 1701), p. 146.
208. TNA ASSI 33/4.

imposed on those convicted of misdemeanours and petty theft, and then work up to those sentenced to death for capital felonies other than murder.[209] This changed in the latter decades of the century. By 1785 Martin Madan was deploring the new "fashion" whereby assizes judges sentenced prisoners individually, immediately after they had been convicted, for all offences, suggesting that, by then, this practice had been extended well beyond murder.[210]

Appeal

It was almost impossible to challenge a jury's decision on the merits of a case. However, after the sixteenth century it was customary for doubtful legal questions that arose at assizes to be reserved for further consideration by the 12 Westminster judges. (They also sometimes discussed civil matters from *nisi prius*). This was usually done on the initiative of the trial judge, but might be suggested to him by defence counsel or even by other lawyers who were present in court. Most commonly, this would occur when jurors could not apply the substantive law to the facts of a case, or a trial judge was personally unsure about the correct legal position. Such referrals became more common during the second half of the century, as the presence of defence counsel increased, and more matters of statutory interpretation were debated.

At the start of the century, referral was normally done by the trial jury returning a "special" verdict. In this situation, the jury made a finding of the relevant facts, which were then recorded, and the matter reserved for the consideration of the Westminster judges. This was quite a cumbrous procedure, and later in the century the practice developed of returning a general verdict (normally guilty) and then referring the matter to the judges. If the 12 judges thought a conviction was wrong, they would recommend to the Crown that the convict receive a pardon.

The judges would normally meet informally at Serjeants' Inn, consulting collegially and, if they disagreed, deciding by a simple majority.

209. Lincoln's Inn, Harrowby MSS 18–19, Document 19(f) *Legal Notebook of Sir Dudley Ryder*, 1754 and 1755, p. 10.
210. M. Madan, *Thoughts On Executive Justice*, 1785, p. 3.

Although in theory advisory, when it came to recommendation, decisions were recorded and regarded as setting binding legal precedents.[211] Thus in 1785 William Newland was executed after his conviction for forgery against the Bank of England at the Norfolk Assizes was "referred to the opinion of the 12 judges, and confirmed."[212] Similarly, after William Gowan was capitally convicted of arson at the Suffolk Assizes in 1787, his case was referred to London. He had burnt down a dwelling-house that had been provided by the parish of Laxford for his own use and that of his family. Unfortunately, the case was remitted back to the assizes with an unhelpful decision, and he, too, was hanged.[213] Others experienced more success. Some contemporary observers were critical of special verdicts, feeling that, by definition, they were indicative of a doubt and so should have produced acquittals from the trial jury.[214]

Occasionally judicial meetings appear to have petered out without a decision being reached. In 1779, 17 members of a press gang were committed to the Bury Assizes by a coroner's inquest for the wilful murder of Thomas Nicholas, one as principal and 16 as accessories to the killing.[215] Led by a midshipman, and armed with staves, they had been sent to Ipswich to find seafaring men. They located some in a local tavern, but when they tried to press them the merchant seamen resisted violently. Nicholas was mortally wounded, but the man who inflicted the injury could not be positively identified.[216] At trial the jury found the facts "special, and left [them] for the opinion of the Court of King's Bench."[217] The case may have resulted in manslaughter verdicts for the Royal Navy men, although the gaol calendar lists them as acquittals.[218] Certainly none was convicted of murder.

If, after a normal guilty verdict, information arose that cast a serious doubt on the merits of a conviction, and the relevant convict was still

211. J. Oldham, "Informal Law-Making in England by the Twelve Judges in the Late 18th and Early 19th Centuries," 2011, pp. 181–183.
212. *Public Advertiser*, 26 March 1785.
213. *Whitehall Evening Post (1770)*, 28 April – 1 May 1787.
214. Anon (By a Friend to the Constitution), *Observations On the Duty and Power of Juries, As Established by the Laws of England* (2nd edn.), 1796, p. 6.
215. TNA ASSI 33/6.
216. *Lloyd's Evening Post*, 9–11 June 1779.
217. *Public Advertiser*, 23 March 1779.
218. *Lloyd's Evening Post*, 9–11 June 1779.

alive, the Crown might grant a free pardon. For example, after Ambrose and Alexander Goodbody were found guilty of sheep theft at the Norfolk Assizes in 1800, doubts quickly set in about the safety of their verdicts. Eventually the two men received a free pardon, "[s]trong circumstances since their trials having appeared to confirm the declaration they made of innocence."[219]

In 1784 a seaman, Nicholas Goddard, was capitally convicted at the Bury Assizes for an "atrocious" burglary in a woman's house at Coombes, near Stowmarket (Suffolk). Fortunately his defence counsel obtained a temporary respite from execution because of a technical error in the indictment, and the matter was left for the consideration of the 12 judges.[220] Doubts appear to have arisen almost immediately about Goddard's conviction, even ignoring the technical objection to the indictment (which was not substantial). In his report on the case, Lord Loughborough noted that, after further investigation, he was not inclined to believe the evidence that had led to the guilty finding and noting that it had not been in the prisoner's power to produce at the hearing evidence of his innocence. However, at the same time, the judge was concerned about the "great danger in reviewing cases out of court upon evidence not produced at the trial." He considered the use of a free pardon, although noting that opinion would always be divided as to Goddard's guilt or innocence of what was a very serious crime. Because of this, and the prisoner's being a sailor (i.e. a flight risk) Loughborough thought it might be more expedient to pardon him on condition of transportation.[221] This was an interesting halfway house that would necessarily be either too lenient or too harsh. Goddard was ultimately kept in Ipswich gaol for almost four years, under sentence of death, being respited from time to time, until the "return of his captain, and other circumstances, should prove his innocence." This being done, he was granted a free pardon by the King in 1787, along with an order for his immediate release.[222]

219. *The Bury and Norwich Post: Or, Suffolk, Norfolk, Essex, and Cambridge Advertiser*, 18 November 1801.

220. *London Chronicle*, 3–6 April 1784; *St. James's Chronicle Or the British Evening Post*, 3–6 April 61784.

221. TNA HO 47/4/71.

222. *London Chronicle*, 3–6 February 1787.

In the lower jury forum, King's Bench exercised a supervisory function when it came to procedural errors, although it was expensive and complicated to refer cases to the court. At the Norfolk Quarter Sessions held at Holt in 1810, John Prentice was found guilty of embezzling £300 in the course of his employment as a farm bailiff. After conviction, his counsel moved for an arrest of judgment, but the court refused the request, after pointing out that the prisoner might "take advantage of any errors in the record or proceedings of that Court [Quarter Sessions] by an Appeal to the Court of King's Bench."[223]

Nevertheless, as with the assizes, if doubts arose about the safety of a conviction at quarter sessions, a pardon might follow, although this was fairly uncommon, as less usually turned on it. In 1807 Robert Alderson, the recorder of Ipswich, was asked to comment on a petition on behalf of two soldiers who had been convicted at the town borough sessions, one for stealing meat from a slaughterhouse, the other for receiving it. He supported the application for a pardon for John Foster, the thief, on the basis (*inter alia*) that he thought that Foster should have been acquitted. He was duly pardoned from his sentence of transportation.[224]

---

223. *The Bury and Norwich Post: Or, Suffolk, Norfolk, Essex, Cambridgeshire, and Ely Advertiser*, 31 January 1810.
224. TNA HO 47/39/43, ff 404–407.

CHAPTER 9

Summary Disposal

Introduction

Most allegations of criminal activity went no further than a magistrate, being dealt with summarily. According to one estimate, in eighteenth-century Staffordshire the assizes dealt with just eleven per cent of criminal matters, quarter sessions another five per cent, while magistrates sitting "out of sessions," whether alone or with colleagues, disposed of 83 per cent.[1] Of course these forums considered offences of different degrees of gravity, and the dividing line between criminal and administrative matters varied considerably, according to definition used. Nevertheless, these figures do at least suggest the importance of the summary process to the wider system.

Justices dealt with criminal matters using a variety of mechanisms. Obviously these included formal summary trial. However, they disposed of far more cases using informal mediation, the vagrancy legislation, and prosecution by recognisance.

Summary Trial

Some aspects of formal summary trial have already been discussed (in *Chapter 4*) but require further consideration, as do the crimes that were most commonly dealt with in this fashion. Such trials, especially when conducted by a single justice, were swift and informal: the magistrate

1. D. Lemmings, *The British and Their Laws in the Eighteenth Century*, 2005, p. 63.

would have a suspect brought before him (usually by a summons delivered by a constable) and then swiftly proceed to a hearing and verdict.[2] The statutes creating many summary offences expressly stipulated the evidence on which a conviction could be secured. Typically this might include a confession by the suspect, the testimony of one or two witnesses, or a personal view of the offence itself by the relevant JP.

In the 1733 edition of his guide for JPs, Joseph Shaw provided specimen documentation for cursing, drunkenness, selling by false weights or measures, and refusing to produce a hawker's licence, so providing some indication as to where a magistrate's power of summary trial was most often exercised.[3] However, other alcohol-related offences, as well as the theft of wood and (to a lesser extent) vegetables, also regularly featured in their lists.

Profane Oaths

Cursing in public was often the most common summary crime dealt with by JPs when sitting alone, particularly during the first part of the century, even though it normally had to be charged promptly after being committed. (It was also most likely to be notified to quarter sessions, exaggerating its apparent significance for modern scholars). Unusually, under enabling statutes from 1694 (6 & 7 Will. & Mar., c.11) and 1745 (19 Geo. II, c.21), the fine imposed on those found guilty was linked to their social status and any similar convictions that they had accrued on earlier occasions. It started at 1s (the most common sum) per incident for workingmen and women, such as servants and labourers, but was twice that for most others. The amount would, in theory, double for a second offence and treble for a third.[4]

Typically, in July 1701 Elizabeth Stanton obtained a warrant against Sarah Harthing and had her arrested for "swearing three oaths within ten days against the statute." At the hearing, Harthing was convicted

2. Anon (A Middlesex Freeholder), *A Dialogue Between a Lawyer and a Country Gentleman, Upon the Subject of the Game Laws*, 1771, pp. 6–7.
3. J. Shaw, *Parish Law: Or, a Guide to Justices of the Peace*, 1733, pp. 2–7.
4. J. Shaw, *The Practical Justice of Peace, and Parish and Ward-officer: Or, A Treatise Shewing the Present Power and Authority of these Officers*, vol. 1, 1756, p. 258.

by Devereaux Edgar, who dealt with numerous cases of this type, and fined one shilling for each offence, this money going to the local poor in Needham (Suffolk), as was normal with summary fines. If the money was not paid, her husband's goods were to be seized to that value. If that was not successful in raising the full amount, the local constable was to "sett her in the stocks for 2 hours."[5] A year later, after hearing sworn evidence from Cecilia Bulbrook, Edgar convicted William Plumb, a labourer from Sproughton, having decided that he "did openly in a prophane manner swear 6 oaths." Imposing the standard fine for each offence, Plumb was ordered to pay six shillings, in default of which he, too, would be set in the stocks. However, in September 1701 William Parker from Washbrook was fined at double this rate, four shillings for swearing two oaths, after Edgar received a complaint and sworn evidence from a local woman.[6] A selection of summary convictions for cursing made by a variety of Suffolk magistrates in Ipswich between December 1753 and December 1754, then notified to quarter sessions, record between one and seven convictions occurring on each occasion, with about three being the average number for each hearing.[7]

As in other parts of the country, the crime was also sometimes used as a way of obtaining summary jurisdiction over minor instances of assault, which in theory were only determinable by a jury sitting at quarter sessions or assizes. Such offences were usually accompanied by cursing, which a magistrate *could* punish summarily. As each profanity warranted a fine—it was rare for a single curse to be uttered during a disturbance—the punishment could also be graduated to match the defendant's means and culpability.[8]

For example, in December 1708 Devereaux Edgar received a sworn complaint from Philip Nevill, a Norwich worsted weaver, that Thomas Dallby had attacked him at the *Falcon Inn* in Claydon the previous night. While doing so, Dallby had "prophanely muttered" five curses. He was duly summoned and convicted on Nevill's evidence and then

5. SRO QS 347.96, *The Devereux Edgar Notebook*, transcribed by S. R. Schofield, 1956, vol. 1, p. 7.
6. SRO QS 347.96, *The Devereux Edgar Notebook*, transcribed by S. R. Schofield, 1956, vol. 1, p. 37 and p. 8.
7. SRO Sessions Roll 41, 9 July 1754, c/2/9/1/1/1/76, 46–53.
8. B. J. Davey, *Rural Crime in the Eighteenth Century: North Lincolnshire 1740–80*, 1995, p. 73.

fined 10s for the five oaths, the money to be paid to the overseer of the poor at Claydon.[9] Similarly, in February 1711 Elizabeth Chapman, John Piggot and his very pregnant wife Mary, were on the highway near Woodbridge when two mounted men, Joseph Farry and Philip Sarjent, came up, swearing and threatening to ride over them. They forced the group to climb into a field and tried to jump in after them, until Piggot hit one of their horses on its nose with a hedge stake. Chapman and the Piggots later complained to Devereaux Edgar, who issued an arrest warrant against the two men. They had been heard to utter at least six curses each, and, when they attended the magistrate, these were proved against them, so that they were each fined six shillings as well as having to produce sureties for future good behaviour. Interestingly, the complainant, John Piggot (who may have been known to the magistrate), was also fined 1s for cursing during the incident.[10]

Other Summary Offences

Alcohol related offences provided another important field for summary justice. They included the sale of ale without a licence and "tippling" in an alehouse on the Sabbath or permitting it to occur (on the part of the landlord). Such summary crimes were long established by 1700. For example, in December 1663 the Norfolk justice Robert Doughty convicted an alehouse keeper from Felmingham for allowing a customer to drink for five hours outside designated times, and the drinker himself for tippling during this period. In February 1665 he convicted two widows for selling beer without a licence at Runton on the North Norfolk coast. The women were fined 20 shillings each.[11]

Simple drunkenness had been made an offence by an act of 1606, and those convicted were liable to a fine of five shillings or six hours in the stocks. It could be determined by a single justice or at petty sessions, and a conviction could be based on the word of just one witness (many other summary offences required two). However, unlike some other

9. SRO QS 347.96, *The Devereux Edgar Notebook*, transcribed by S. R. Schofield, 1956, vol. 2, p. 190.
10. Ibid., p. 259.
11. J. Rosenheim (ed.), *The Notebook of Robert Doughty, 1662–1665*, 1991, p. 30 and p. 48.

alcohol-related crimes, it was not prosecuted frequently, although it must have been extremely common. Apparently, a blind eye was often turned to such behaviour if it did not cause other problems.[12]

The alleged use of defective weights and measures was also an important area for summary jurisdiction, though usually tried at petty sessions rather than by a single JP. For example, at sessions held in August 1800 at the *Half Moon* tavern at Clare, in Suffolk, three magistrates for the Risbridge Hundred convicted and fined 39 people for using or having in their possession false weights and balances.[13] Very significantly for East Anglia, in the years after 1671, lesser cases of poaching were largely taken out of the remit of quarter sessions, where they would have been heard by a jury, and became a crime that could be dealt with by a single justice sitting alone or at petty sessions. It took several years for such summary prosecutions to occur on a regular basis, but they were relatively common by 1700.[14]

Unsurprisingly, and less controversially, many administrative offences were determined summarily. Traffic regulations were prominent among them. Typically, in October 1783, after John Matthews from Topcroft in Norfolk violated safety regulations, he was convicted before a county JP for "riding upon his cart in the common highway, and paid the penalty accordingly."[15] This issue was a perennial concern. Five years later, after a youth at Fornham St Martin, in Suffolk fell from his master's wagon and was run over and badly injured, local justices resolved to enforce the statutory penalty against riding on carts or wagons without holding reins to the horse or having someone on foot to guide it.[16] Prosecutions for avoiding the fees at the new turnpikes were another important area for summary jurisdiction. Typically, in January 1781 the driver of a farmer's cart was fined by Roger Kerrison, a Norfolk justice, for avoiding payment of the toll at the Postwick gate.[17]

12. P. Jennings, "Policing Drunkenness in England and Wales from the late Eighteenth Century to the First World War," 2012, pp. 70–71.
13. *Morning Post and Gazetteer*, 14 August 1800.
14. D. Lemmings, *Law and Government in England During the Long Eighteenth Century*, 2011, p. 32.
15. *Norfolk Chronicle*, 18 October 1783.
16. *Bury and Norwich Post*, 13 August 1788.
17. *Norfolk Chronicle*, 20 January 1781.

However, by the eighteenth century summary jurisdiction also extended to some very specific forms of minor theft and embezzlement. These included the theft of wood, as a result of a variety of statutes dating back to the Elizabethan period. This may have been the most common rural crime of "dishonesty." These statutes reflected a general move to proscribe what may previously have been viewed as customary rights to fallen timber and "snapwood" (wood that could easily be broken off trees).[18] The Destruction of Trees Act of 1663 authorised the summary conviction of those found in possession of wood, underwood, poles, or young trees who could not give a "good account" of how they came by such materials. (This reversal of the burden of proof was to become much more common for new summary offences during the eighteenth century.)[19] By the 1660s, it seems, encouraging summary trial for this offence was also a realistic acknowledgement that the forums that would previously have dealt with such crimes, particularly the manorial courts leet, were moribund. It seems that many, if not most, of those convicted of this offence were caught red-handed.[20] Devereaux Edgar dealt with numerous cases of wood theft during the early 1700s. Typically, in March 1701 he received a complaint from one John Brownrigg accusing Thomas Page of stealing "Thatching stuff" from his grounds. Two men gave evidence on Brownrigg's behalf, and the matter was "proved." Page was ordered to pay 10s in compensation to the complainant within as many days, or to be whipped by the local constable in Elmsett (Suffolk).[21]

Three more statutes supplemented or supplanted the 1663 act in 1715, 1719, and 1766.[22] Illustrative of their operation, in January 1783 Thomas Beales of Tivetshall, in Norfolk, was convicted by John Kerrich, a local JP, on the sworn evidence of one William Arnold, for unlawfully cutting down a large bough from an ash tree in a wood owned by Lord Walpole

18. R. Bushaway, "'Groveley, Groveley and All Groveley': Crime and Conflict in the English Woodland," 1981, pp. 37–45.
19. See generally, B. Smith, "The Emergence of Public Prosecution in London, 1790–1850," 2006, pp. 29–62.
20. N. Landau, "Summary Conviction and the Development of the Penal Law," 2005, p. 176 and p. 186.
21. SRO QS 347.96, *The Devereux Edgar Notebook*, transcribed by S. R. Schofield, 1956, vol. 1, p. 4.
22. D. Lemmings, *The British and Their Laws in The Eighteenth Century*, 2005, p. 64. R. Bushaway "'Groveley, Groveley and All Groveley': Crime and Conflict in the English Woodland," 1981, pp. 37–45.

and let to a tenant farmer. He was fined £5, and, when he refused to pay, committed to prison for six months or until the money was forthcoming.[23] That this case occurred in midwinter was not a coincidence. As a valuable source of fuel, the theft of wood occurred most commonly in the colder months.

At the start of the eighteenth century, some cases of vegetable and fruit theft were also dealt with summarily under an Elizabethan statute from 1601 (43 Eliz. I, c 7). Under this provision, if the thief was unable or unwilling to pay a fine or damages to the victim, he or she could be whipped.[24] Robert Doughty dealt with such cases in Norfolk during the 1660s, as did Henry Norris, a Middlesex JP in the 1730s and 1740s.[25] For example, in July 1741 Norris convicted two men and a woman who had been caught stealing beans in Mile End. They were each told to pay 20 shillings to their victim as "satisfaction." When they were unable to do so, Norris issued a warrant to a local constable to whip them. In the same month, another bean thief received a similar disposal after being unable or unwilling to pay ten shillings to the owner of the field where they had been growing.[26]

Summary provisions for punishing vegetable theft were updated in the latter part of the eighteenth century, partly, it seems, because magistrates were becoming slightly more nervous about the use of general vagrancy provisions to deal with pilfering. Under a statute from 1772 (13 Geo III, c 32), stealing or maliciously uprooting cabbages, peas, carrots, turnips, or parsnips was made an offence that could be prosecuted in front of a single justice sitting alone or two or more at petty sessions. A conviction could be secured on the confession of the suspect or the sworn evidence of one witness. If he were found guilty, the defendant would forfeit the value of the vegetables along with a maximum of ten shillings. This fine was divided between the victim and the local poor. A sentence of up to a month's hard labour in a house of correction could be

23. *Norfolk Chronicle*, 25 January 1783.
24. R. Shoemaker, *Prosecution and Punishment: Petty Crime and the Law in London and Rural Middlesex, c 1660–1725*, 1991, p. 83.
25. J. Rosenheim (ed.), *The Notebook of Robert Doughty, 1662–1665*, 1991, p. 61.
26. R. Paley, *Justice in Eighteenth-century Hackney: The Justicing Notebook of Henry Norris and the Hackney Petty Sessions Book*, 1991, pp. 56–62.

imposed in default of payment. As a safeguard against malicious allegations, the whole fine would be given to the local poor where a conviction was secured solely on the sworn evidence of the owner of the vegetables, rather than a neutral source.[27] Thus in December 1772, when James and Hester Biggs were convicted by Thomas Horner, a Somerset JP, of stealing turnips from a field some 12 days earlier, they were each ordered to pay 15d to the owner of the land and to the local overseer of the poor.[28] Single justices were trying such cases well into the nineteenth century.[29]

It seems that this general pattern of summary prosecution was almost universal within England (outside the Metropolis). For example, in Gloucestershire conviction certificates returned from petty sessions and single magistrates to quarter sessions during the 1780s were dominated by four offences: wood theft; minor cases of poaching, particularly of hares; public swearing; and selling ale without a licence. Stealing potatoes, turnips, and cabbages from the fields occasionally appeared in the lists, as did embezzling wool and a few other minor crimes.[30]

Concern About Summary Justice

The expansion of summary justice was not universally welcomed. It had a bad reputation among many legal commentators, including William Blackstone and Henry Zouch, who thought that use of the jury was fundamental to English freedoms.[31] There was also a degree of popular concern at the novel powers that magistrates acquired during the eighteenth century. In 1748 a lay observer urged that any matter that could not be compromised by mediation by a justice (see below) should go for a jury trial, even if it meant that a few "knaves" would ultimately go unpunished.[32] Towards the end of the period, Thomas Gisborne thought that many Englishmen feared the "suspicious" summary jurisdiction that

27. W. Marriot, *The Country-Gentleman's Lawyer; and the Farmer's Complete Library*, 1795, pp. 25–26.
28. M. McGarvie (ed.), *The King's Peace, The Justice's Notebooks of Thomas Horner of Mells, 1770–1777*, 1997, p. 81.
29. T. Shakesheff, *Rural Conflict, Crime and Protest: Herefordshire 1800–1860*, 2003, p. 115.
30. I. Wyatt, *Calendar of Summary Convictions at Petty Sessions 1781–1837*, 2008, pp. 1–59.
31. W. Blackstone, *Commentaries on the Laws of England*, vol. iv, 1769, p. 277; H. Zouch, *Hints Respecting the Public Police*, 1786, p. 1.
32. Philalethes, *English Liberty in Some Cases Worse than French Slavery*, 1748, pp. 51–59.

had been granted to JPs over previous decades. He urged that it be exercised in a suitably cautious manner.[33] More than two decades into the nineteenth century, a clergyman from Little Massingham in Norfolk, who based most of his views on his experiences in that county and neighbouring Suffolk, was still appalled at the growth of magistrates' powers and, in particular, the quality of justice meted out in the "upstart court" of petty sessions. He felt that this forum modified the general law at whim. Summary convictions were returned without proper foundation and after "hearing only one side, without a precedent, without oath of witnesses or the intervention of a jury, without a record or even a reporter, and on parole authority, by 'winks, frowning, and countenance.'"[34]

Although this was an exaggeration, there was a kernel of truth to the cleric's analysis. It seems that, during the eighteenth century, summary justice was often administered according to customary practice rather than by express statutory authority.[35] In 1764 Richard Burn felt it necessary to urge that JPs mirror the basic trial structure and procedures of the higher courts when exercising such a jurisdiction, even if this was not mentioned by the enabling statute, with prosecution witnesses being put on oath before testifying and the accused having time to prepare his defence.[36] Much would depend on the inherent fairness of the magistrate concerned.

Inevitably, many of the actors in those parts of the criminal process that took place before JPs would be familiar with one another, especially in rural parts. Such areas produced tiny, close-knit groups of men drawn from what might loosely be termed the "political nation" out of whose ranks most magistrates came. When John Beckett was held for a brutal murder in 1790, he was taken before his local Norfolk JP, Daniel Collier, "for whom Becket had worked as labourer." Beckett quickly made admissions to his erstwhile employer and was committed to gaol to await the assizes.[37] In Somerset, the curate and future Norfolk parson

33. T. Gisborne, *An Enquiry Into the Duties of Men in the Higher and Middle Classes of Society in Great Britain*, 1794, p. 298.
34. C. D. Brereton, *The Subordinate Magistracy and Parish System Considered*, 1827, pp. 5–7.
35. P. King, *Crime and Law in England, 1750–1840: Remaking Justice from the Margins*, 2006, p. 15.
36. R. Burn, *The History of the Poor Laws: With Observations*, 1764, p. 253.
37. *General Evening Post*, 16–18 February 1790.

the Reverend James Woodforde regularly socialised with his local JP, Justice Creed. They dined at each other's houses, played cards, and drank coffee together. When, in January 1770, Woodforde suspected two local brothers of stealing wood from his sister's ash tree, he obtained a summons against them from Creed, for which he paid the standard fee of 6d. It required the two brothers to appear before the justice at his (Creed's) house at 2 pm the following Friday. Woodforde sent the summons with a servant to a local tithingman (a type of constable), who then served it on the men. Woodforde duly attended the justice along with the suspects at the designated time. The two men were examined in his presence by the magistrate, and one was convicted, while the other was found not guilty. The guilty brother was ordered to pay Woodforde six shillings within two weeks, with an order that he be whipped if he failed to do so.[38] Presumably he was convicted on the sworn evidence of the parson or another witness. That one of the men was acquitted suggests that the hearing was not a mere formality, and Woodforde comes across in his diary as a man of integrity. Nevertheless, his intimate relationship with the magistrate determining his case would not be considered remotely proper today, and where less honest men were complainants the process must sometimes have been abused.

Occasionally, if not commonly, a magistrate became a judge in his own cause; for example, by presiding over a poaching case committed on his land. This attracted much popular criticism and features heavily in some contemporary literature, although it was unusual at the start of the period, and viewed as clearly improper by its end, quite exceptional cases apart. This principle led to a *cause célèbre* in 1811, after General Batterbee, a strangely named young Norfolk labourer, contracted to work on Thomas Hoseason's farm during the harvest. After several earlier problems, Batterbee refused to curtail his hour-long lunch break to labour in the fields. Hoseason's bailiff then assaulted him. However, when Batterbee complained to Hoseason, who was also a local magistrate, Hoseason struck him as well, and had Batterbee committed to the Swaffham house of correction for a month, with an order that he be "corrected" (beaten)

38. J. Beresford (ed.), *The Diary of a Country Parson, 1758–1802*, 1978, p. 46.

under a rarely used statute from 1747 (20 Geo II, c 19). Despite a letter from a King's Lynn attorney asking that the flogging be remitted and pointing out that the law did not permit a man to be a judge in his own cause, Batterbee was duly beaten. This resulted in Hoseason being prosecuted in the Court of King's Bench for committing a misdemeanour while in office as a magistrate. At trial Lord Ellenborough accepted that a magistrate acting in his own cause constituted a "gross abuse of position." However, he also concluded, somewhat improbably but diplomatically, that an independent magistrate would have reached the same decision on the facts of the case.[39]

Mediation and Arbitration

Eighteenth-century justices, faced by minor criminal allegations, would often avoid formal action altogether by supervising mutually acceptable settlements between complainants and suspects, just as they did in many lesser civil disputes.[40] It was widely thought that one of a JP's most important functions was the "healing of differences and preventing vexatious prosecutions."[41] Such settlements required that JPs act as mediators rather than by dint of any legal authority, although the parties involved may not always have appreciated this.[42] When the Northamptonshire justice Phillip Ward reconciled an apprentice watchmaker with the master he had assaulted, he was careful to conceal his "want of power" in such situations.[43]

Critics sometimes claimed that such informal settlements were prompted by magistrates' indolence and legal ignorance. However, they usually reflected more laudable motives. Among them was a realistic appreciation that many criminal allegations made in the heat of the moment would not ultimately go to trial; in 1725, the Suffolk JP Maurice Shelton deplored the behaviour of time-wasters who went to justices and

39. D. Hay, "Patronage, Paternalism, and Welfare," 1998, pp. 42–43.
40. T. Andrews, *An Enquiry into the Causes of the Encrease and Miseries of the Poor of England*, 1738, p. 26.
41. W. Blackstone, *Commentaries on the Laws of England,* vol.1, 1765, p. 8.
42. *The Gentleman's Magazine*, 1732, vol. 2, p. 910.
43. D. Gray, "Making Law in Mid-eighteenth-century England," 2013, p. 223.

made "complaints without prosecution."[44] A desire to avoid the already overburdened justice system being overwhelmed with minor or meritless cases was another significant factor. Most important of all, such arrangements usually reflected the magistrate's views of the justice of any given situation and the need to preserve community cohesion, something that could easily be damaged by litigation.

Somewhat unhelpfully, but capturing the acute tension between conflicting demands within the criminal justice system in this regard, Thomas Gisborne advised magistrates not to substitute their own ideas of equity for the law, yet also urged them to refrain from proceeding to a formal legal hearing while "reasonable hopes remain that the aggressor might be induced, by the reiterated application of the person injured, to make satisfaction."[45] Satisfaction could be given in several ways, the most common being the payment of a small amount of money. However, sometimes a private or public apology to the victim might suffice. In September 1811 John Cooper was arrested and brought before the Bedfordshire JP Samuel Whitbread at the behest of his employer. Whitbread "[o]rdered him to beg his master's pardon; he did and was forgiven."[46]

Such justice-initiated settlements appear to have occurred less frequently in the years prior to the Restoration. This may have reflected a greater seventeenth-century willingness to refer minor matters to quarter sessions for formal determination by a jury. Mediation became especially common in the late 1600s and early 1700s. It lasted into the early nineteenth century. Nevertheless, the frequency with which rural JPs were willing to act in this capacity seems to have fallen in the late 1700s, and gradually petered out during the first half of the following century, even though some observers still preferred negotiated compromises to formal summary trials.[47]

As Thomas Gisborne's use of the word "aggressor" suggests, informal resolution was most commonly used to deal with lesser assaults.

---

44. M. Shelton, *A Charge Given to the Grand-Jury, at the General Quarter-Sessions of the Peace, Holden at St. Edmunds-Bury For the Liberty Thereof*, 1726, p. 34.
45. T. Gisborne, *An Enquiry Into the Duties of Men in the Higher and Middle Classes of Society in Great Britain*, 1794, p. 281.
46. A. Cirket (ed.), *Samuel Whitbread's Notebooks*, 1971, p. 46.
47. N. Landau, *The Justices of the Peace 1679–1760*, 1984, p. 191; P. King, "Summary Justice and Social Relations in Eighteenth-century England," 2004, p. 166.

For much of the period, most such crimes were dealt with in this fashion, without the alleged perpetrator being formally tried in any forum, although magistrates acting summarily did not even have the power to fine those who had committed an assault until 1828. In 1780 Sir John Hawkins, chairman of the Middlesex bench, advised his colleagues that, where there was only a small injury, the magistrate to whom the initial complaint had been made "cannot better exercise his humanity, and I may add, his wisdom, than by persuading the parties to peace and reconciliation." Nevertheless, he also felt that if a magistrate thought it proper, and there was "probable evidence" to found such an allegation, the JP should bind the offender over to the quarter sessions.[48] The latter procedure was most commonly employed in more serious cases, but was only rarely used for most of the era. For example, only 3 per cent of assault accusations made at the Lexden and Winstree Petty Sessions in Essex between 1788 and 1792 resulted in a suspect's being bound by a recognisance to appear at a higher forum.[49]

The process of arbitration can be seen most clearly in the City of London, where detailed minute books were kept because of the sheer volume of legal business dealt with in the Square Mile and the variation in legal personnel involved. Numerous allegations went no further than an alderman sitting as an *ex officio* magistrate for the city. Frequently he presided over an agreed settlement. In other situations, he might decide that it was too "trifling" to warrant going further and discharge it. In 1762 an allegation of assault was dismissed and the female suspect released, because the prosecutor had already "taken her own revenge."[50]

The same process occurred in rural areas and provincial towns, even if they were not so well-documented, usually only showing up in surviving justices' notebooks. For example, at times, the Reverend Edmund Tew, a County Durham magistrate, personally dealt with almost as many cases of assault as were determined at that county's quarter sessions.[51] In

48. J. Hawkins, *A Charge to the Grand Jury of the County of Middlesex*, 1780, pp. 26–27.
49. P. King, "Summary Justice and Social Relations in Eighteenth-century England," 2004, p. 148 and p. 149.
50. G. T. Smith (ed.), *Summary Justice in the City: A Selection of Cases Heard at the Guildhall Justice Room, 1752–1781*, 2013, p. 56.
51. G. Morgan and P. Rushton, "The Magistrate, the Community and the Maintenance of an Orderly Society in Eighteenth-century England," 2003, p. 68.

the 1770s Thomas Horner, a Somerset JP, also settled many complaints in this manner, albeit not as many as Tew had 20 years earlier. Thus he used a letter to urge a well-born man who had assaulted a tavern waiter to make his victim "ample satisfaction" so that the matter would not have to proceed further. In other cases he directly oversaw the payment of money, having made an assessment of the veracity of a claim. For example, in November 1771 he was present when ten shillings and six pence was paid to a marine sergeant by a local man "as recompense" for an assault. Another soldier got nothing from a second suspect, as he "failed in proving anything" against him.[52] In the early years of the following century, the Bedfordshire JP Samuel Whitbread was still dealing with some assaults in this fashion, if fewer than Horner, let alone Tew. For example, in 1811, when William Biggs of Potton complained about being assaulted by a local clergyman while seeking repayment of a debt, Whitbread initially wrote to the cleric "advising him to compromise the matter." The same year, when Dennis Beaumont was brought before him for assaulting his wife, the justice merely "[r]ecommended them to part." In September of that year, Whitbread dismissed a complaint against a man who had been arrested for assaulting a woman, but required that the man pay the cost of the constable who had enforced the arrest warrant (an informal and minor punishment).[53]

The use of informal resolutions was not confined to minor crimes of violence. Sometimes they were employed to deal with allegations of criminal damage and even lesser offences of dishonesty. In eighteenth-century Wiltshire, William Hunt, a county justice, regularly dealt with petty theft by "reconciling" the parties.[54] This could come perilously close to the judicially supervised compounding of a felony, although Thomas Gisborne stressed that magistrates should not allow this to happen. (Misdemeanours such as assault could be compounded quite legally.)[55] However, by the latter years of the eighteenth century, many JPs were

52. M. McGarvie (ed.), *The King's Peace, The Justice's Notebooks of Thomas Horner of Mells, 1770–1777*, 1997, p. 35 and p. 58.
53. A. Cirket (ed.), *Samuel Whitbread's Notebooks*, 1971, p. 30, p. 65 and p. 46.
54. E. Crittall (ed.), *The Justicing Notebook of William Hunt, 1744–1749*, 1982, p. 13 and p. 62.
55. T. Gisborne, *An Enquiry Into the Duties of Men in the Higher and Middle Classes of Society in Great Britain*, 1794, p. 283.

becoming nervous about compromising property crimes in this fashion. In the 1770s Thomas Horner sent even minor thefts for trial at quarter sessions, rather than dealing with them informally.

Of course, some suspects were not in a financial position to make any form of acceptable satisfaction, forcing recourse to formal punishment, even early in the period. In October 1701 Devereaux Edgar signed a *mittimus* to send Samuel Boar to the house of correction at Needham, in Suffolk, for a month, after it transpired that he could not pay compensation for cutting down young trees and pulling up hedges. He was to be "well whipt & kept to hard labour his damage committed being soe great & his inability such as not able to recompence."[56] If Boar had been possessed of means, an informal settlement might well have been reached.

As this case suggests, East Anglian JPs were certainly involved in supervised reconciliation. It seems that Robert Doughty was arranging settlements in Norfolk during the 1660s, if not as frequently as many justices did fifty years later. For example, in August 1665 three women were brought before him for stealing peas near Cromer, on the Norfolk coast. One, Elizabeth Swan, admitted stealing a handful of the vegetables and the other two half a peck each. Swan "offered for satisfaction a day's work in harvest." Another offered to pay for her peas, and the third "being a poor silly lame wench he [the complainant] forgave"[57] The Reverend John Longe, also a Suffolk JP, makes less mention of informal settlements in his diary for the early decades of the nineteenth century, by which time it seems that they were less common than they had been in Devereaux Edgar's time. Nevertheless, in May 1831 Longe noted that he had endeavoured to "settle a charge of assault" committed by two youths on another young man, even though it involved a "shameful" attack. He visited the father of one of the perpetrators, a tailor, but without success and "therefore issued the summons that the charge may be heard next sittings."[58] By then magistrates had acquired the power to fine for assault after a summary hearing. In the many decades between Doughty and Longe, numerous cases must have been settled informally, although a

56. SRO QS 347.96, *The Devereux Edgar Notebook*, transcribed by S. R. Schofield, 1956, vol. 1, p. 13. Boar was also notorious as an idler, being "very slothful in worke."
57. J. Rosenheim (ed.), *The Notebook of Robert Doughty, 1662–1665*, 1991, p. 61.
58. M. Stone (ed.), *The Diary of John Longe, vicar of Coddenham, 1765–1834*, 2008, p. 123.

shortage of justices' notebooks for the era and area means that this must often be an assumption.

Prosecution by Recognisance

In a significant number of eighteenth-century misdemeanour cases, suspects were merely bound over to appear at forthcoming quarter sessions. Anyone who refused to be bound over in this manner, or who was not able to provide sureties guaranteeing their attendance, might be committed to gaol in the meantime, but this was fairly uncommon, at least for local people (if not for transients).[59] Sometimes the recognisance would include a requirement that the suspect keep the peace in the meantime.[60] Many of these cases did not result in a trial, as prosecutors had not entered into a recognisance to pursue the matter and ultimately decided not to do so. Instead, the suspect would attend court, pay a small fee, and then, in the absence of the prosecutor, be discharged.[61]

For example, at the start of the eighteenth century the Suffolk JP Devereaux Edgar issued an arrest warrant at the behest of Elizabeth Bond against one Joan Bretton for being a "lewd & disorderly person a common mover of discord in the neighbourhood." (Preserving community cohesion from scolds and barraters was part of a justice's work). When she came before him, Bretton was merely required to provide a surety for her good behaviour and her appearance at the next sessions. Similarly, in February 1707 a married woman complained that Thomas Alderton, a wheelwright in Needham Market, had been banging on her house door, shouting abuse ("whore"), and threatening her. Alderton was personally bound over in the sum of £40, with another man also entering into a recognisance for £40 pounds for his good behaviour and appearance at the next county quarter sessions.[62] Sometimes such a course of action was only pursued after a magistrate-supervised agreement could not be

59. W. Sheppard, *A Sure Guide for his Majesties Justices of Peace*, 2nd edn., 1669, p. 197.
60. R. Burn, *The Justice of the Peace and Parish Officer*, 1755, vol. 1, p. 538 and vol. 2, pp. 317–318.
61. R. Shoemaker, *Prosecution and Punishment: Petty Crime and the Law in London and Rural Middlesex, c 1660–1725*, 1991, p. 25.
62. SRO QS 347.96, *The Devereux Edgar Notebook*, transcribed by S. R. Schofield, 1956, vol. 2, p. 177.

reached. Although this type of recognisance became much less common as the eighteenth century advanced, the Bedfordshire JP Samuel Whitbread was still using them as late as 1811.

Punishment for Vagrancy

Eighteenth-century JPs had a statutory power to punish "idle and disorderly" individuals by committing them to bridewells and houses of correction as "vagrants," whether until the following quarter sessions or for shorter periods, such as a month. Alternatively, they might order that vagrants be whipped (usually by a parish constable) and released immediately using the same authority. Frequently magistrates would combine the two punishments.[63] This power dated back to the early seventeenth century and was reiterated using slightly different wording in successive eighteenth-century Vagrancy Acts, such as those of 1714 and 1744. Under the former, people who were apprehended as rogues or vagabonds could, "if the Justice think fit, be order'd to be openly whippd, or sent to the House of Correction, for hard Labour." A single JP, sitting alone, could exercise the power, after examining a suspect.[64]

The power to commit for vagrancy was used frequently by metropolitan magistrates. However, it was also employed on a fairly regular basis in the provinces. For example, Robert Burton and Henry Smith appeared at the Suffolk Quarter Sessions held at Beccles in January 1720, having been committed as vagrants to a local house of correction by a JP. The bench ordered that they be "whipt & sent away."[65] At many quarter sessions the attendant justices would consider a tranche of cases of this type from their local house of correction; the outcomes would be recorded together in the sessions order book. Thus, at Beccles, on 14 January 1751 seven people were produced from custody, three women and four men. The Bench ordered that three of them be discharged. Another three were

63. Anon, *Statement and Propositions from the Society for Giving Effect to His Majesty's Proclamation Against Vice and Immorality*, 1790, p. 5.

64. O. Ruffhead, *The Statutes at Large*, vol. 3, 1763, p. 76. Clause four of this statute had envisaged that many such commitments would be made at quarter sessions rather than out of sessions, as often proved to be the case in practice; *The Times*, 14 October 1789, p. 3.

65. SRO QS B/105/2/14, p. 87.

to be kept in the house of correction for between three and six months and ordered to "receive the correction of the house" while they were incarcerated (i.e., be flogged). The remaining man, Edward Ives, who was from "out of area," was to remain in custody for one month and then to be passed to his place of last legal settlement.[66]

A few vagrants were described as "incorrigible rogues," having accrued previous convictions for the same crime. They might receive several floggings and longer sentences before being discharged with a pass to carry them back to their home parish. For example, at the Suffolk Quarter Sessions held at Bury on 8 October 1764, James Silver was found to be a rogue and vagabond with a previous conviction for the same offence in Norfolk. He was sentenced to two years' hard labour and several floggings.[67]

The power to punish for vagrancy was frequently used to deal with beggars, unruly drunks, and itinerants who were living rough. Typically, at the Norfolk Quarter Sessions held at Norwich in July 1751, Charles Macdonald, an Irishman who had been wandering and begging, was sentenced to three months in Aylsham bridewell followed by a whipping in North Walsham market.[68] However, the meaning of phrases like "idle and disorderly" were often manipulated by magistrates to deal with a much broader range of apparently nefarious individuals and situations, even if these had not been anticipated by Parliament or the enabling legislation. By 1700 many justices used them as a catchall to deal with minor substantive offences, such as petty larceny or assault. This was particularly attractive if it was feared that the available evidence would not support trial on indictment before a jury at quarter sessions or assizes, or if the victim of the crime was unwilling to go to the trouble of prosecuting the matter (a common situation).[69]

A typical example can be seen in a case from Northamptonshire in 1748. A county JP there, Phillip Ward, received a complaint that Anne Monk, a wandering vagrant, had stolen a butter-straining cloth worth about 1s, which she had then attempted to sell for eight pence. A local

66. SRO QS B105/2/24, pp. 52–53.
67. SRO QS B105/2/39, p. 38.
68. *General Advertiser* (1744), 23 July 1751.
69. A. Eccles, *Vagrancy in Law and Practice Under the Old Poor Law*, 2012, pp. 145–147.

woman was identified as the likely owner of the cloth, but "could not be positive" it was hers. There were also reports that Monk had taken another unidentified object from an outhouse. Both cases were weak and might not even survive a quarter sessions grand jury scrutiny if indicted as petty theft or (much less likely) grand larceny, although, strictly speaking, this is what should have happened if there was a case to answer. Instead Ward resolved this problem by dealing with Monk as a vagrant (something that she had more or less admitted), and committing her to the local house of correction. This was felt to be punishment enough. Ward was open about his reasons for such a disposal, noting that the "proof being not precise and value trivial [it was] not worth prosecution."[70] Similarly, in Middlesex, when Susan Newcome was brought before the magistrate Henry Norris in August 1736, accused of stealing fruit from a garden, she was sent to bridewell for a month "as a vagrant."[71]

The Suffolk Justice Devereaux Edgar used the power in this fashion on an occasional basis during the early 1700s. For example, in October 1701 he committed Thomas Clark, described as a "boy," to the house of correction in Needham after conducting an examination that found him to be a "pilfering & lyeing Raschall guilty of great misdemeanours in diverse places."[72] "Pilfering" would suggest the commission of small thefts. Much later in the century, on 18 July 1783, Mary Soer was produced at the Suffolk Quarter Sessions held in Ipswich. A county magistrate had committed her to a local bridewell on 5 June, "charged on the oath of Elizabeth Shallow on a suspicion of stealing a certain quantity of Bohea tea." The quarter sessions ordered that she be committed for a further 14 days and then discharged. Mary does not appear to have been indicted for, let alone convicted of, larceny.[73]

Nevertheless, there were jurisprudential and practical objections to committing for vagrancy, limiting the frequency with which it was employed, especially in the provinces.[74] As the century advanced, these

70. D. Gray "Making Law in Mid-eighteenth-century England," 2013, pp. 225–226.
71. R. Paley (ed.), *Justice in Eighteenth-century Hackney: The Justicing Notebook of Henry Norris and the Hackney Petty Sessions Book*, 1991, pp. 32–46.
72. SRO QS 347.96, *The Devereux Edgar Notebook*, transcribed by S. R. Schofield, 1956, vol. 1, p. 12.
73. SRO QS B105/2/47, p. 52.
74. F. Dabhoiwala, "Summary Justice in Early Modern London," 2006, p. 797.

increased, legal scrutiny of such decisions grew, and the number of people committed to short-term custody in this manner declined. Magistrates became particularly nervous about using such powers to deal with mainstream offenders, rather than genuinely disorderly individuals. Instead, there was greater recourse to the growing array of summary offences that expressly authorised JPs to deal with specific crimes.

CHAPTER 10

Capital Punishment

Introduction

At the start of the eighteenth century, England had a relatively ungraduated penal regime for serious and middle-ranking crimes. Clergyable felonies had (effectively) ceased to be capital, and normally led to the immediate discharge of a convict (after branding), while the only sentence for unclergyable crimes was death, even if it was eventually reprieved. If clemency was granted, it frequently resulted in the convict's immediate discharge and return to the community without any further punishment. As a result, most convicted felons faced either death or immediate liberty.

This regime could produce inconsistencies. As Charles Jones noted in 1752, there was, in theory (whatever the practice), no legal difference between a sheep thief (whose offence was by then unclergyable), who had tried to feed his impoverished family, and a murderer. Like several others, he pointed out that the lack of penal graduation in England was unusual among other nations, almost all of which "adapt their punishments to the nature of the offence."[1] Thirty-five years further on, Hewling Luson was still making the same comparison between murder and stealing sheep.[2]

Nevertheless, by the time Jones was writing, the situation was not nearly as serious as it had been 50 years earlier. Despite its historic roots, the traditional penal system was occasioning concern by the end of the

1. C. Jones, *Some Methods Proposed Towards Putting a Stop to the Flagrant Crimes of Murder, Robbery, and Perjury*, 1752, p. 7.
2. H. Luson, *Inferior Politics*, 1787, p. 114.

seventeenth century, and ensuing years witnessed a sustained attempt at introducing a more finely calibrated system of punishment. As part of this process, the penalty for clergyable offences was enhanced after 1699. Initially, this was by branding the convict's face rather than their hand. In 1706 this change was reversed, but a new power to append a short sentence of imprisonment to a successful claim of clergy was introduced (see *Chapter 4*). Most important of all, after 1718 the majority of convicts who were entitled to benefit of clergy were transported to America instead of being branded (see *Chapter 12*).

By contrast, the punishment of less serious but unclergyable felonies was modified by the greater use of conditional (rather than unconditional) reprieves (see *Chapter 11*). Finally, after 1752 there was a modest attempt at enhancing the death penalty when it was imposed for murder (the most heinous felony), not by aggravating it in the fashion found in some continental countries of the era (breaking on the wheel, etc.), but by making post-mortem medical anatomisation or public gibbeting—effectively, desecration of the body—a designated part of the sentence (see below). As a result of these developments, by the 1750s the English penal system was already far removed from the death or liberty approach that had, in part, characterised it at the start of the century, with further major change occurring following the American Revolution.

It should also be noted that, in theory, being found guilty of a felony would lead to forfeiture of the convict's estate (if he had one of any value) to the Crown, although, in practice, this power was sometimes tacitly ignored or expressly waived. For example, after being convicted of murder in 1740, Charles Drew was anxious about his mother and sisters being deprived of the £600 value of his property in Long Melford, as the Suffolk High Sheriff had already "seized on all his Estate and Effects." However, the King was subsequently "graciously pleas'd to send down a remittance of the estate in behalf of the family."[3]

3. Anon, *The Suffolk Parricide; Being, The Trial Life, Transactions, and Last Dying Words of Charles Drew*, 1740, p. 42.

Centrality to Criminal Justice

The English penal system revolved around capital punishment. It was cheap to administer and required no continuing supervision, so allowing for "light" government. Although it prevented reoffending, it was freely admitted that its primary purpose was to act "in terrorem" on the basis that a draconian public punishment might deter potential felons from committing crimes.[4] There were always some doubts about whether it was effective at doing this.

Arguably, many offenders were too young or impulsive for considered reflection about the consequences of their actions, making it a "vain supposition that the light of such punishment will deter others from the commission of that crime."[5] Some were too desperate. As Henry Dagge noted, although well-to-do men naturally thought that what frightened them most (death) would have a similar effect on potential criminals, this was not necessarily true for those *in extremis*.[6] Throughout the period, many observers, such as John Scott, thought the punishment ineffective, believing it possible that "no nation on earth, is so prodigal of life as the English, and [yet] perhaps no nation on earth is so much infested with thieves."[7]

As Scott's comment suggests, England made much greater use of the death penalty than most continental countries, and this was widely known. Some even thought that there were "more persons executed in the British Dominions, than in all Europe besides."[8] As Scott also hints, many of those executed were hanged for non-violent property offences, something that occasioned particular concern.[9] To many observers this seemed manifestly disproportionate and excessive, or, in the words of the Reverend Dr. Patrick Delaney, "unrighteous and unequitable."[10] Even as

4. F. Allen, *The Reasonableness and Necessity of Human Laws and Penalties*, 1739, p. 13.
5. Anon, *The Means of Effectually Preventing Theft and Robbery*, 1783, p. 3.
6. H. Dagge, *Considerations on Criminal Law*, 1772, pp. 224–225.
7. J. Scott, *Observations On the Present State of the Parochial and Vagrant Poor*, 1773, pp. 133–134.
8. C. Jones, *Some Methods Proposed Towards Putting a Stop to the Flagrant Crimes of Murder, Robbery, and Perjury*, 1752, p. 8.
9. Anon, *A Compassionate Address to the High and Mighty in Behalf of the Poor Distressed Prisoners*, 1753, p. 3.
10. *The British Magazine, or, Monthly Repository for Gentlemen & Ladies*, July 1766 p. 346.

they prepared condemned prisoners for death, and advised them on the justice of their sentences, numerous clergymen could not help noting that Biblical law did not condone execution for theft in any circumstances. Crimes of great violence might require a hanging, but for offences against property unaggravated by "acts of cruelty, the laws of God, of nature, and of equity, certainly require a different penalty."[11] Those clerics who supported the regime — and there were many — felt obliged to justify their positions.[12] By the 1760s criticism of the extent of the capital code had become a well-established feature of public debate, and had prompted a considerable amount of published and widely disseminated literature.[13]

Nevertheless, to the end of the era and beyond, the value of draconian deterrent example also had strong supporters, some of them in government and the judiciary. As late as the economically difficult years at the start of the following century, it made a sudden, albeit extremely short-lived, return in the execution of those who stole sheep and other animals in circumstances that would certainly have received clemency just a few years earlier.

According to one assessment, between 1735 and 1799 there were 6,233 confirmed executions and another 241 possible or probable hangings in England and Wales.[14] London and Middlesex saw high per capita execution rates, while close proximity to the metropolitan area appears to have driven up those for men (most of those hanged) in counties such as Kent, Essex, and Surrey. Conversely, the country's extremities, such as Cumberland, Westmorland, Northumberland, Cornwall, and much of Wales usually experienced much more modest execution levels. At times between 1750 and 1775 their per capita rates fell to as little as two per cent of those found in London.[15] The bulk of the country outside the Metropolis, both in area and population, fell between the extremes set by the London collar counties and those at its fringes.

---

11. J. Scott, *Observations On the Present State of the Parochial and Vagrant Poor,* 1773, pp. 133–134.
12. F. Allen, *The Reasonableness and Necessity of Human Laws and Penalties,* 1739, p. 18.
13. S. Devereaux, "The Making of the Penitentiary Act, 1775–1779," 1999, p. 405 and p. 409.
14. www.capitalpunishmentuk.org (Last consulted 10 August 2015).
15. P. King et al, "Rethinking the Bloody Code in Eighteenth-century Britain: Capital Punishment at the Centre and on the Periphery," 2015, pp. 166–167.

Norfolk witnessed 138 executions between 1735 and 1799, taking together those for the county, the City of Norwich, Yarmouth, and Kings Lynn. This is a little over two per cent of the national total. Suffolk saw 116, possibly 117 executions (just less than two per cent). Given that Suffolk had a significantly smaller population than Norfolk throughout the period, the per capita execution rate for the two counties appears to have been broadly similar over the century, albeit somewhat higher in Suffolk, which was closer to London and bordered Essex, a county adjacent to the Metropolis and with a correspondingly high execution rate.

Combining these figures, there were 254 executions in the region during a 65-year period, or just under four a year (roughly two per county) on average. It was not a "blood fest" and was significantly lower than the per capita incidence of execution seen in Singapore in 1994 and 1995 (then one of the highest in the world).[16] By contrast, during the same period London and Middlesex saw 2,034 executions at Tyburn and (after 1783) outside Newgate Prison, an average of more than 31 a year. The Metropolis had (very approximately) almost twice the population of East Anglia for much of the period. This suggests a per capita execution rate that was up to four times as high in the London area as in Norfolk and Suffolk. Going to the other extreme, Cornwall appears to have witnessed just over 40 executions in the final two-thirds of the century, despite having a population that was (again, very approximately) about 30 per cent of the East Anglian total, producing a per capita rate of about half that found in the region.

More particularly, on one assessment England (excluding Wales) had a population of 6,310,338 people in 1761. Of these 251,435 lived in Norfolk and 176,499 in Suffolk.[17] Thus the former county made up almost exactly four per cent of the national population, and the latter about 2.8 per cent. (The East Anglian share of the national population declined in the latter decades of the century). Arguably, this would place their execution rate below the national average, as they performed roughly about four per cent of the country's executions but 6.8 per cent of its

16. UN Commission on Crime Prevention and Criminal Justice, Tenth Session, Vienna, 8–17 May 2001.
17. E. A. Wrigley, "English County Populations in the later Eighteenth-century," 2007, pp. 35–69.

population. However, the national figures are greatly distorted by the high incidence of hanging found in and around the metropolitan area.

In comparison to other provincial areas, the East Anglian execution rate was neither particularly low nor especially high. For instance, in 1761 Sussex had 103,237, Wiltshire 190,751, Staffordshire 157,680, Durham 128,875, and Oxfordshire 103,237 inhabitants.[18] In the period from 1760 to 1769 inclusive, there were 12 executions in Norfolk (including one each at King's Lynn and Great Yarmouth). There were also 12 executions in Suffolk. Both Sussex and Durham saw just three executions each during this period. Oxfordshire had eight executions, Staffordshire ten. Wiltshire witnessed 15, the most hangings in the group. When executions are divided into population for this decade, Suffolk saw one hanging per 14,708 inhabitants, while Norfolk experienced one per 20,952. The other counties varied considerably. Staffordshire saw one execution per 15,768; Oxfordshire, one per 12,904; Wiltshire, one per 12,716; Sussex, one per 34,412; and in Durham one for every 42,958 people.

Obviously, the figures and ten-year time period are too small to produce firm conclusions. Nevertheless, it seems that the East Anglian execution rate was unexceptional for what might be termed "Middle England." As in much of the country, it declined significantly in the early years of the century, but was relatively stable for most of the period after the 1730s, which, allowing for an increase in population, points to a mild (albeit extremely uneven) underlying decline after about 1740. In Norfolk 26 people were hanged during the decade after 1735, while 42 were executed in the ten years following 1785, with the 1750s and 1760s having seen somewhat lower rates (as they did elsewhere in the country). In Suffolk the figures were 29 (possibly 30) and 27, respectively. As this suggests, the number of hangings fluctuated considerably from year to year. Thus in 1782 no one was executed in the entire region; by contrast, in 1785, 17 people went to the gallows in the two counties.

The decline in the per capita incidence of execution after 1700 was a modest continuation of a trend that was already longstanding, and which had been much more dramatic in the previous century. The English

18. E. A. Wrigley, "English County Populations in the later Eighteenth-century," 2007, pp. 35–69.

execution rate between 1580 and 1630 may have been up to ten times higher than that found in the early eighteenth century, having risen substantially after the medieval era in what may have been an aspect of early modern state formation.[19] It had then declined swiftly, with a particularly sharp fall in the decades leading up to the middle of the seventeenth century.[20]

Preparing for Death

While awaiting execution, convicts would be ministered to by prison chaplains and other (outside) clerics, who would also accompany them to their deaths. For example, in 1736, the murderer Elizabeth Thompson went to the gallows in Great Yarmouth with four clergymen in attendance.[21] Some of the condemned needed considerable spiritual instruction in the basics of religion. Before he was hanged for robbery, after conviction at the Suffolk Assizes in 1733, it was noted that 22-year-old Samuel Partridge, a native of Debden, was "entirely ignorant of the first principles of Christianity."[22]

Of course, not all convicts were Anglicans. Some were non-conformists or Catholics, and a tiny number (in the provinces) were Jews. When John Sullivan, an Irish sailor, was executed at Yarmouth in 1749 he was penitent but declared his intention of "dying in the Romish persuasion, crossing himself several times before he was turned off."[23] For most of the century it appears that such men could receive religious support from within their own denomination, if it was available (not always the case). At the Thetford Assizes in 1722, Richard Ashby, a local Quaker, apparently driven by the Spirit, volunteered himself as spiritual counsellor to three men (not Quakers) awaiting execution in the town. He visited

19. J. Sharpe, "Crime, Order and Historical Change," 2001, p. 129.
20. P. King et al, "Rethinking the Bloody Code in Eighteenth-century Britain: Capital Punishment at the Centre and on the Periphery," 2015, p. 164.
21. *Daily Gazetteer* (London Edition), 15 June 1736.
22. *London Journal (1720)*, 14 April 1733.
23. *Whitehall Evening Post Or London Intelligencer*, 21–24 October 1749.

them several times with the agreement of the gaol authorities. They even provided him with a room in which to minister to the condemned.[24]

As this case suggests, many convicts availed themselves of the chance of spiritual redemption. When giving an assizes sermon at Thetford, the Reverend Thomas Pyle claimed that the prospect of execution concentrated their minds in a way that simple reasoning could not.[25] The Reverend Fifield Allen agreed. He thought that it was only in the condemned cell that fears of another world began to display themselves "in their full force."[26] This appears to have worked with Benjamin Brett, who spent an hour preparing himself for execution at Bury St. Edmunds in 1794, requesting and reading a Bible at the gallows. When questioned as to whether he was ready to be "turned off," he asked for, and was granted, another half hour, as he found himself "not sufficiently strengthened in faith" to meet his maker.[27] However, several prisoners firmly rejected all tendered spiritual assistance prior to their deaths.

Throughout the era, some of the condemned went to execution in their grave clothes. For example, in 1736, Elizabeth Thompson went to the gallows wearing a shroud.[28] The following year, three men who were executed in Norwich also went to their deaths "drest in their shrouds, with the burial-caps stitched under their chins, and without shoes and stockings."[29] This had the additional benefit of preventing the hangman from claiming their clothes, one of the traditional perquisites of his office. For most of the period, prisoners were hanged with their faces covered. Thus Robert Carlton was hooded in 1742. Similarly, while awaiting execution, Jonathan Sawyer, who was hanged near Ipswich for burglary in 1780, pulled up the handkerchief that had been put over his face several times to warn the attendant crowd against following his wicked course in life.[30]

---

24. R. Ashby, *A Relation of a Visit to Three Malefactors, Condemn'd at the Assizes at Thetford in Norfolk*, 1724, p. 3.
25. T. Pyle, *The Wisdom of a Government in Distributing Punishment or Mercy to State-criminals*, 1716, p. 17.
26. F. Allen, *The Reasonableness and Necessity of Human Laws and Penalties*, 1739, p. 16.
27. Anon, *Last Dying Speech and Full Confession of Benjamin Brett*, 1794, pp. 1–2.
28. *Daily Gazetteer* (London Edition), 15 June 1736.
29. *Daily Gazetteer*, 29 March 1737.
30. *Gazetteer and New Daily Advertiser*, 18 April 1780.

The Place of Execution

Execution was carried out in public, as it would be until 1868. This was usually at the designated county gallows, which were normally in or near the assizes town where the condemned person had been convicted. Thus, felons from Norfolk who were executed in Norwich were hanged on Castle Hill until April 1800. Those from the city itself, who were convicted at the City and County of Norwich Assizes, were hanged on the meadow at nearby Castle Ditches until 1822. People who were capitally convicted at the assizes held at Thetford, in the same county, were sometimes hanged in or near the town, like the three men put to death there in 1722. There had been a gap of some years during which Thetford was not used for executions before William Bennington and Stephen Watson were hanged in the town for separate murders after the Lent Assizes in 1795. This was, it seems, motivated by a fear that the maximum two day delay allowed under the Murder Act would require unseemly haste if the men were sent back to Norwich.[31] Alternatively, like Thomas Boddy and three other men convicted of burglary at Thetford in 1779, they were returned to Norwich for execution.[32]

Felons convicted at the Bury Assizes were normally executed at the designated county gallows at Rushmere, a village just outside Ipswich (the county town of Suffolk), although a few were hanged near the town's North Gate. The short distance from the county gaol to the gallows allowed a formal procession to be held. In April 1784, when William Simpson and Joseph Lambert were executed at Rushmere, the bells were tolled in each parish as their cart passed through it on their way from the prison.[33] Typically, in March 1766 John Brock and John Francis sat next to the coffins that would receive their bodies while making the same journey.[34]

---

31. Poole, S. (2015), "'For the Benefit of Example': Crime Scene Executions in England, 1720–1830," p. 82.
32. R. Ashby, *A Relation of a Visit, to Three Malefactors, Condemn'd at the Assizes at Thetford in Norfolk*, 1724, p. 5; *Public Advertiser*, 23 March 1779.
33. *Ipswich Journal*, 17 April 1784.
34. D. Edwards, *Sermons For the Use of Condemned Malefactors*, 1774, p. 251. A clergyman joined the prisoners during the journey.

This use of places of execution some distance from the gaol was common in England until late in the century, when, following the example set by the Metropolis in 1783, locations adjacent to the county gaol started to be used, so that there was no need for convicts to make a short journey to be hanged. In Ipswich the change occurred in 1795, although some counties, such as Kent, delayed such a move until well into the following century.

If an exemplary role for an execution was seen to be desirable, convicts might be sent to a gallows specially erected near the location of their crime, even if one had to be hurriedly improvised. On one account there were at least five such cases in Norfolk during the years between 1720 and 1830, but none in Suffolk.[35] However, Toby Gill *may* have been hanged near Blythburgh (the scene of his crime) in the latter county, although this is not certain (he was certainly gibbeted there). As this might suggest, murderers were more likely than other felons to be executed at the scene of their killings. For example, in January 1700 Robert Watts, a weaver who had cut his wife's throat in a "barbarous" fashion, was hanged in front of his own house in St Augustine's parish, Norwich.[36] Similarly, the notorious poisoner Robert Carlton was returned to Diss, in Norfolk, for execution in 1742. Such localised executions became less frequent in the final years of the eighteenth century, and petered out during the early 1800s, three arsonists who were hanged in Somerset in 1830 being the last.[37] Of course, those felons who were capitally convicted at the special Lynn or Yarmouth Borough Sessions were necessarily hanged in or near the relevant town.

Executions were popular forms of entertainment and moral instruction, although, inevitably, the crowds were normally much smaller in East Anglia than at Tyburn. This was due to the lower population density in the region and the reduced dissemination of information about forthcoming hangings. Nevertheless, executions in *causes célèbres* still attracted

35. Poole, S. (2015), "'For the Benefit of Example': Crime Scene Executions in England, 1720–1830," p. 80.
36. Anon, *The History of the City and County of Norwich: From the Earliest Accounts to the Present Time*, 1768, p. 288.
37. S. Poole, "'A Lasting and Salutary Warning': Incendiarism, Rural Order and England's Last Scene of Crime Execution," 2008, p. 165.

large attendances. In 1742, when Robert Carlton was hanged on Diss Common, it was claimed that a crowd of more than 10,000 people was present. His body was then exhibited for two pence a view in the nearby house where he had poisoned his victim.[38] By contrast, when William Hawke and Thomas Mayhew were executed for murder at Norwich in 1787, they asked to be hanged at 11 am, "which being before the usual time, but few spectators attended."[39]

Although it has been suggested that executions were becoming more unruly during the course of the eighteenth century, so undermining their role as "moral theatre," and that "respectable" people were increasingly nervous about attending them, it seems that this was more of a metropolitan than provincial phenomenon until relatively late in the period. Certainly the respectable Mary Hardy and her husband appear to have viewed attending executions in Norwich as a valuable part of the moral training of their children and younger servants. In April 1775 Mary, along with her offspring and maid, saw 22-year-old Thomas Green, a burglar from Diss, being hanged on Castle Hill. After watching him die in a suitably penitent manner they "drank tea." The following year Mr Hardy took two of their children to watch Henry Jex and James Jacques hanged there for housebreaking.[40]

Despite its use as a form of moral instruction, there seems to have been a considerable element of straightforward entertainment involved in watching executions, even among educated people. The mild-mannered Parson Woodforde recorded several visits to Norwich from his home in Weston Longueville, eight miles away, to see hangings. If he was ill or otherwise engaged when a hanging took place, he would sometimes send a servant with instructions to bring him back a description of what had occurred. As late as 1828 a large number of females were amongst the 7,000 spectators who watched the execution of the murderer William Corder at Bury. Of these, a significant proportion were women of a "much superior grade."[41]

38. *Norwich Gazette*, 3–19 April 1742.
39. *The Times*, 6 April 1787, p. 3.
40. M. Bird (ed.), *The Diary of Mary Hardy 1773–1809*, 2013, p. 109 and p. 31.
41. *The Hull Packet and Humber Mercury*, 19 August 1828.

At Corder's execution those in attendance behaved in a "decent and orderly" manner. Unfortunately, this was no longer always the case by the last quarter of the era, even in the provinces. In 1777 the crowd at the execution of the murderer John Rye in Norwich gave vent to their feelings by "pulling and tossing" his dead body as it hung from the gallows.[42] By the end of the century, the lack of public decorum was beginning to occasion concern, as it was thought to undermine the deterrent value of execution. In 1799 it was noted that some hangings in Ipswich had been accompanied by the "most indecent actions and expressions."[43]

There was a generally approved form of gallows conduct for those about to be executed, and this was often followed, albeit usually with active encouragement from attending clergymen and the high sheriff, the latter being in charge of the county gallows as part of his office. Thus it was noted that the habitual criminal Jeremiah Pratt, awaiting execution at Norwich in 1746, behaved in the "extraordinary decent manner, that all persons under his unhappy circumstances ought to do."[44] Some indication as to what this entailed can be seen in the case of the domestic murderer William Gilbert, who made a contrite speech at the gallows and carefully prayed with the attending minister before being "turned off" on Castle Hill in 1705.[45]

Similarly, Jonathan Mattox and Benjamin Smith, executed at Norwich in 1741, both admitted that they were guilty of the crime for which they were to be hanged, were heartily sorry for their previous lives, behaved "very decently at the gallows, and prayed very devoutly before they were turn'd off the ladder, desiring the spectators to pray for them."[46] In like manner, the teenage arsonist John Sherwood, executed there in 1768, showed no anxiety at his forthcoming death, took an affectionate leave of his fellow prisoners, but at the same time behaved in a "very decent manner." He prayed fervently and acknowledged the gravity of his crime.[47]

42. *Norfolk Chronicle*, 22 March 1777.
43. J. Bransby, *The Ipswich Magazine, For the Year 1799*, 1799, p. 108.
44. *Westminster Journal or New Weekly Miscellany*, 19 April 1746.
45. Anon, *The Wicked Husband, and Unnatural Father*, 1705, p. 8.
46. *Daily Gazetteer* (London Edition), 15 April 1741.
47. *Public Advertiser*, 23 August 1768.

Those who failed to express suitable contrition and admissions of guilt could come under considerable pressure to conform. Nevertheless, not a few ignored conventional demands. When John and Elizabeth Wilkinson were executed at Rushmere for the murder of their daughter Martha, they denied their guilt at the gallows and appeared unconcerned at their fate. Elizabeth even called on several people who were present to shake hands with her, and "when the executioner was going to put the rope about her neck, she put him aside, and said she would talk a little longer."[48] Some were openly defiant. George Chandler, a horse thief facing execution in 1736, admitted the crime for which he was to hang, but behaved boldly, having resolved to "die intrepid." He refused to consider his spiritual condition and merely requested (unavailingly) that he be buried at Saxtead, where he was born, after being cut down.[49] Similarly, in 1785 Parson Woodforde noted that James Cliffen, hanged on Castle Hill in Norwich for murder, had "behaved most daringly audacious" at the scaffold.[50]

It is apparent that at East Anglian gallows, as at Tyburn, dying "game" attracted popular admiration. Indeed, an inadvertently revealing line in a newspaper report of the execution of a pair of experienced housebreakers after the Bury Assizes in April 1737 noted that when John Wallage died he seemed penitent, while John Bicker "died with more courage."[51] Of course, not everyone could display such *sangfroid.* Elizabeth Burroughs appeared "like a person insane" after she was condemned to death in 1766.[52] In 1816 Thomas Thody was so terrified that he had to be physically supported to the Norwich gallows.[53] Other convicts may have been in a state of shock or denial. In 1787 it was observed that, of three men awaiting execution for a Suffolk burglary, one, George Chamberlain, "seemed depressed," while another, John Mayes, "appeared in a kind of stupidity."[54] By contrast, when Jonathan Vincent went to the gallows for murdering his illegitimate child he talked to his son about farming and

48. *Public Advertiser*, 2 April 1785.
49. *Daily Gazetteer* (London Edition), 20 April 1736.
50. J. Beresford (ed.), *The Diary of a Country Parson, 1758–1802*, 1978, p. 167.
51. *Daily Gazetteer* (London Edition), 14 April 1737.
52. *London Chronicle*, 22–25 March 1766.
53. C. Mackie, *Norfolk Annals*, 1901, p. 137. *The Morning Chronicle*, 12 September 1816.
54. *World and Fashionable Advertiser*, 21 August 1787.

appeared "totally regardless of his future state." Something of a miser, the day before his execution he sent for a carpenter to make his coffin and bargained ferociously over its price; he also attempted to avoid paying for his attorney and the bed he had rented while incarcerated at Bury Gaol.[55]

The Manner of Execution

Most of those hanged in the eighteenth century met their deaths by strangulation (rather than a broken neck). This was initiated in two ways: by a convict being placed on a ladder that was suddenly twisted away from him so that he or she was no longer supported except by the noose, and by "roped-up" convicts being turned off the back of a horse-drawn cart after the vehicle moved off. The former was common when there was only one person to be hanged. For example, in 1705 it was noted that William Gilbert, who had murdered his family in Norfolk, was "turned beside the ladder."[56] However, more than 30 years later, it was recorded that when Elizabeth Thompson was executed she "gave a shriek and clapped her hands, just as the cart drew away."[57]

Proceedings did not always run smoothly. In 1785 three men were taken to Rushmere to be executed for robbing a sailor. Unfortunately, the hangman did not realise until they had finished singing psalms at the gallows that he had forgotten their halters, and had to return to nearby Ipswich for them. This caused an unexpected delay of 20 minutes.[58] In the same year, the hangman at Castle Hill in Norwich was very drunk when conducting an execution, leading to the "awful business" being carried out ineptly and unnecessarily prolonged. Compounding the misery of the two men being hanged, just as they were about to be "turned off," someone mistakenly or maliciously called out that a late reprieve had arrived, further delaying their deaths. It was apparently "impossible to express the agitation of their countenances, during the moment of suspense."[59]

55. *Ipswich Journal,* 22 July 1769.
56. Anon, *The Wicked Husband, and Unnatural Father,* 1705, pp. 1–8.
57. *Daily Gazetteer* (London Edition), 15 June 1736.
58. *Ipswich Journal,* 1 August 1785.
59. *Public Advertiser,* 13 August 1785.

How long the process of strangulation took to kill the convicts, or at least render them unconscious, depended on their weight, the muscularity of their necks, the quality of the rope used, the position of the ligature, and the skill of the executioner. When the robber Thomas Clarke was hanged at Norwich he "died very hard owing to the rope being improperly fixed from the trepidity of the hangman who shook like an aspen leaf." His partner in crime, John Deane, tried to avoid such a risk. When the cart moved off, he threw himself backwards, either hoping to break his neck or at least to produce a tight noose. Unfortunately, this did not accelerate his death by very much. However, the third man to be executed, Thomas Carty, died quite easily and was not seen to struggle.[60]

As was common practice in the Metropolis—but not found on the Northern Circuit—informal steps were sometimes taken to expedite the process of strangulation, by both executioner and observers. For example, when Andrew Lister and Robert Bezett were awaiting execution at Norwich in 1740 they begged those who stood nearby to "put them out of their misery as fast as they could, by pulling them by the legs as soon as turn'd off." They were hanged separately, Bezett going first. As he was suspended, Lister again urged the crowd to quicken his companion's death.[61]

Towards the end of the eighteenth century, a short drop was introduced in many parts of England, following the example set by the new gallows set up outside Newgate in December 1783. The fall was normally a maximum of 18 inches and sometimes less than a foot, so it was not usually enough to guarantee a broken neck, but at least it produced a tighter ligature, speeding up strangulation. After its introduction at Ipswich, convicts were no longer escorted to Rushmere but hanged outside the county gaol. As late as April 1800, when Thomas Shop was executed, the apparatus was still referred to as "the new drop at the top of the gateway of the new gaol at Ipswich."[62] However, it was first used five years earlier, when Charles Blyth, a horse thief, and James Dosser, a burglar were hanged in the town.[63] The former was "dead in an instant"

60. *Ipswich Journal*, 1 August 1785.
61. *Universal Spectator and Weekly Journal*, 6 September 1740.
62. *Bury and Norwich Post*, 23 April 1800.
63. *St. James's Chronicle Or the British Evening Post*, 4–6 August 1795.

while the latter took more than seven minutes to die.[64] A "long drop" that almost always broke the prisoner's neck to produce a swift death would not become universal in England until the 1880s.

Those put to death for petty treason — the murder of a husband or superior — were subject to a special execution regime. Both men and women found guilty of this offence would be taken to the gallows sitting backwards on a sledge rather than in the normal cart or carriage. Once there, their disposals differed. Men would be hanged in conventional fashion, as occurred in 1795 with Henry Bennington, a servant, who had been convicted of killing his employer, a farmer from West Dereham in Suffolk. Bennington died in exactly the same way as a man who had murdered his wife who was executed with him.[65]

By contrast, until 1790 women would be burned, not hanged, albeit nearly always strangled first by the hangman, using a pulley system. Occasionally, early in the century, this either failed or was omitted so that the woman died from asphyxiation. For example, Mary Taylor, convicted at the Thetford Assizes in 1731 for murdering Ann Wright, the publican who employed her, and executed at King's Lynn, "gave a few shrieks when the fire began to burn about her, and lifted up her hands amidst the flame, but was soon suffocated." She was then burned to ashes. Her male accomplice, a man named George Smith, who had apparently performed the killing, as well as committing robbery, was hanged alongside her, on a gallows set up 17 yards from the stake.[66] Both forms of petty treason (male and female) were present in a notorious case in 1762, when Margaret Beddingfield and her husband's young farmhand, Richard Ringe, murdered her spouse/his master. The pair were subsequently convicted at the Lent Assizes at Bury in 1763. Both were drawn on sledges to the gallows at Rushmere, just to the north of Ipswich, where Richard was hanged and Margaret strangled and burned.[67]

64. P. Wright, *Death Recorded: Capital Punishment In Suffolk 1732–1900*, 2006, p. 51.
65. *St. James's Chronicle Or the British Evening Post*, 26–28 March 1795.
66. *Fog's Weekly Journal*, 27 March 1731 and 3 April 1731. B. Mackerell, *The History and Antiquities of the Flourishing Corporation of King's-Lynn in the County of Norfolk*, 1738, p. 242.
67. Anon (an eminent short-hand writer), *The Genuine Trial of Margery Beddingfield and Richard Ringe*, 1763, pp. 3–43; *Ipswich Journal*, 9 April 1763.

After 1790 women convicted of petty treason were treated in the same way as men. As a result, in 1807, when Martha Alden was convicted of killing her husband at the Norfolk Assizes, she was drawn on a hurdle along an extended route to the place of execution and hanged, her body then being given to the surgeons to be dissected (see below).[68]

Burial, Dissection, and Display

After a body had hung for about an hour it would be cut down, and the issue of disposal would arise. Some, especially (but not solely) those convicted of murder during the first half of the century were buried near the gallows in unconsecrated ground, as was the case with the horse thief George Chandler, who was interred near the scaffold at Ipswich in 1736.[69] Others might be laid to rest in a churchyard following a normal funeral service, if sometimes in a paupers' grave. Thus, in the same year, after Elizabeth Thompson was cut down, her body put into a hearse and taken to Gorlstone to be buried.[70] The following year, the horse-thief John Painter was buried in a local Norfolk churchyard.[71] Similarly, in 1768 the body of the arsonist and horse thief John Sherwood was recovered from the Norwich gallows by his "sorrowful" mother and taken home to Snetterton for burial.[72] In 1785 Thomas Carty and the two men hanged with him at Rushmere were interred in a communal grave in nearby St Mathew's churchyard the morning after their execution.[73]

By contrast, the corpses of executed murderers (cases of infanticide apart) and highway robbers were sometimes hung in chains, near the scene of their crimes, for exemplary effect. The use of such "gibbeting" peaked in the 1740s, when an average of between six and seven cases a year received such a disposal in England and Wales, but remained fairly constant after the 1750s (when there were four to five cases annually), until declining rapidly at the start of the nineteenth century prior to

68. *The Bury and Norwich Post: Or, Suffolk, Norfolk, Essex, and Cambridge Advertiser*, 5 August 1807.
69. *Daily Gazetteer* (London Edition), 20 April 1736.
70. *Daily Gazetteer* (London Edition), 15 June 1736.
71. *Daily Gazetteer* (London Edition), 29 March 1737.
72. *Public Advertiser*, 23 August 1768.
73. *Ipswich Journal*, 1 August 1785.

abolition.[74] This practice was found to varying degrees throughout much of England. It was fairly common in the southeast and around London but rare in the northeast (as it was in Scotland).[75] In this regard, Norfolk and Suffolk had more in common with the Home Counties than with Northumberland.

The bodies of gibbeted men were usually kept together by a chain cage and sometimes lightly tarred to help preserve them from decay. They were hung from a tall wooden post, often 30 feet high, with a cross beam at the top from which a short chain attached to the apparatus containing the felon's corpse was suspended. Frequently, this was designed to allow the body to twist in the wind. Although a majority of gibbets were designed for just one man (women were not normally dealt with in this manner) the Reverend Thomas Kerrich provided an illustration of a double gibbet that was situated on Brandon Sands in Suffolk during the period. It shows the main support as being bound with several iron bands, to prevent attempts at cutting it down.[76] A selection of cases is indicative of use of this disposal in East Anglia.

In 1705 William Gilbert was hung in chains before his own door at Toddington in Norfolk "as a terror to all such wicked murtherers."[77] In 1734 John Norton received the same disposal on Rymerton Heath, in Suffolk, near where he had poisoned his wife.[78] In 1742 the sodomist and murderer Robert Carlton was displayed on a gibbet on the common in his native Diss.[79] Eight years later, the rapist and murderer Toby Gill was gibbeted at Blythburgh in Suffolk. More than 30 years further on again, two men who had robbed and murdered an elderly woman in an isolated Suffolk village were hanged and "afterwards (at the request of the prosecutor) hung in chains at Eriswell."[80] Roger Benstead was due to have been anatomised for murder in 1792, but was, instead, hung in

74. S. Tarlow and Z. Dyndor, "The Landscape of the Gibbet," 2015, p. 73.
75. R. A. Houston, *Punishing the Dead?: Suicide, Lordship, and Community in Britain, 1500–1830*, 2010, p. 257.
76. A. Hartshorne, *Hanging in Chains*, 1891, p. 75.
77. Anon, *The Wicked Husband, and Unnatural Father*, 1705, pp. 1–8.
78. *Universal Spectator and Weekly Journal*, 20 April 1734.
79. *Norwich Gazette*, 3–10 April 1742.
80. T. Notcutt, *The Trial at Large of Jeremiah Theobald, Otherwise Hasell, and James May, Otherwise Folkes*, 1783, pp. 1–4.

chains a quarter of a mile from his home at Lakenheath in Suffolk. He dreaded this even more than being dissected.[81]

However, as the case of Benstead suggests, medical anatomisation was the typical (statutory) disposal for murderers' corpses after 1752, when the Murder Act of that year included a provision for better deterring such crimes by requiring that "some further terror and peculiar mark of infamy be added to the punishment." Even before this date, it had occasionally been used as an alternative to gibbeting in heinous cases, and not just those involving murder. For example, Robert Bird, a habitual criminal, horse thief, and housebreaker, was anatomised after the Bury Assizes in 1735.[82] Two years later it was noted that, after being cut down, the bodies of John Johnson ("Black Jack") and William Wright, a highwayman and a horse thief respectively, were delivered to surgeons in Norfolk, who began "picking their bones, in order to their being anatomiz'd."[83]

After 1752 medical dissection became the set punishment for all murderers, unless they were hung in chains. For example, after execution following the King's Lynn Borough Sessions in January 1766, John Rudderham's body was handed over to surgeons.[84] Similarly, in 1790, after John Beckett was convicted at the Thetford Assizes of murdering a lime burner from Wroxham, he, too, was executed and dissected.[85] There were two unavailing attempts in Parliament in the decades after 1752 to extend automatic anatomisation to the corpses of other executed felons, such as those hanged for highway robbery and burglary, if only to supply medical schools with specimens.[86]

It seems that it was normally the business of the presiding judge at assizes to ensure that a surgeon was available to take the convict's body.[87] Some of these medical men can be identified by name. The prominent Ipswich surgeon John Clubb (1741–1811) received the corpses of at least three murderers for dissection and teaching purposes. Among them was

81. Anon, *The Trial of Roger Benstead the Elder, and Roger Benstead the Younger,* 1792, p. 14.
82. *Daily Courant*, 22 April 1735.
83. *Daily Gazetteer* (London Edition), 29 March 1737.
84. *Gazetteer and New Daily Advertiser*, 28 January 1766.
85. *Whitehall Evening Post (1770)*, 20–23 March 1790.
86. R. Ward (ed.), *A Global History of Execution and the Criminal Corpse*, 2015, p. 9.
87. Lincoln's Inn, Harrowby MSS 18–19, document 19(f), *Legal Notebook of Sir Dudley Ryder*, 1754 and 1755, p. 7.

that of the child-killer Jonathan Vincent, who was executed following the Bury Assizes in 1769.[88] When John Wilkinson and his wife, Ellen, were hanged at Rushmere in 1785 for the murder of their youngest daughter, Wilkinson's body was delivered to John Bucke (1756–1839), a well-connected surgeon then resident in Ipswich, while that of his wife was given to Robert Abbott (1750–1830), a surgeon from Needham Market.[89]

One reason that hanging in chains rather than anatomisation continued periodically in East Anglia after 1752 was that, unlike the Metropolis and Cambridge University, the two counties lacked major medical schools that needed a constant supply of fresh cadavers for instruction. They had no equivalent of the Surgeons' Hall, in London. This also meant that even where "dissection" was carried out it could sometimes be quite cursory; occasionally it was just a few token cuts. As was noted by a Suffolk journal in 1799, albeit with some exaggeration, in the (frequent) absence of medical students, corpses were often indecently mangled and the "mutilated remains of a human body are commonly carelessly thrown away, to be dragged about the streets by dogs."[90]

Not every anatomised corpse ended this way. At her request, the dissected remains of Rebecca Howard were buried next to the body of her illegitimate five-week-old baby, for whose murder she had been capitally convicted.[91] Furthermore, a number of experienced surgeons in East Anglia performed thorough dissections on the corpses of executed convicts to enhance their own medical knowledge or that of students or the junior doctors who were apprenticed to them. When Robert Abbott of Suffolk advertised for an apprentice in February 1784, he noted that "[m]orbid and comparative anatomy [would be] taught."[92]

Such dissections were often done publicly. In 1787 the murderer William Hawke was anatomised in the Shire House in Norwich. An "incredible number" of people came to see his body being taken apart. A distinguished surgeon from the city later delivered an anatomical lecture based on the examination. At about the same time, the corpse of

88. *Middlesex Journal or Chronicle of Liberty*, 22–25 July 1769.
89. *Ipswich Journal*, 2 April 1785.
90. J. Bransby, *The Ipswich Magazine, For the Year 1799*, 1799, p. 109.
91. *Observer*, 20 August 1797.
92. S. Irvine, *Surgeons and Apothecaries in Suffolk: 1750–1830*, 2011, pp. 70–71.

Hawke's co-defendant, Thomas Mayhew, was taken to Thetford and dissected there by a surgeon from the town.[93] Additionally, the Norfolk and Norwich Hospital conducted a number of thorough dissections after it was founded in 1771. That of John Rye, in 1777, served as the basis for several public lectures, as various parts of his body (brain, lungs etc.) were anatomised individually.[94] (Many other counties also used their hospitals for this task).[95]

By the end of the century, a change in social attitudes meant that both dissection and gibbeting were increasingly felt to be counter-productive, failing to deter criminals, shocking "tender" travellers, and even being "disgraceful to a civilized nation."[96] In 1813, when Ann Arnold was anatomised at the shirehall in Ipswich, a newspaper lamented the crowds of women and children going there to view "so disgusting a sight."[97] However, as late as 1828, when William Corder was executed in Suffolk, he was partially dissected in the *nisi prius* court at the shirehall in Bury, in front of members of the public, and then moved to the town hospital, where, before an audience of doctors and students from Cambridge University, the process was completed. His sternum was opened, and the internal organs closely examined. A galvanic battery was even attached to his limbs to demonstrate the contraction of muscles.[98] Corder's skeleton was eventually put on display. Dissection was only formally abolished in 1832, hanging in chains following in 1834. By contrast, The Netherlands abolished the latter as early as 1795 and Prussia in 1811.

93. *The Times*, 6 April 1787, p. 3.
94. M. J. Armstrong, *The History and Antiquities of the County of Norfolk*, 1781, p. 213.
95. D. Bentley, *Capital Punishment in Northern England, 1750–1900*, 2008, p. 43.
96. J. Bransby, *The Ipswich Magazine, For the Year 1799*, 1799, p. 109.
97. *Ipswich Journal*, 3 April 1813.
98. *The Hull Packet and Humber Mercury*, 19 August 1828.

CHAPTER 11

Reprieves from Execution

Introduction

Executions were merely the tip of an iceberg of capitally convicted felons, most of whom avoided the gallows. This process of reprieve was vital to the entire eighteenth-century criminal justice system, is of paramount importance in understanding it, and warrants special consideration as a result.

Even as capital offences and death sentences started to burgeon under the "Bloody Code," the per capita execution rate was falling, while the proportion of capitally convicted felons who were hanged plummeted. By the middle of the era, the number of executions, although high by continental standards, was much lower than it had been a century earlier (see *Chapter 10*), and the proportion of death sentences actually carried out much smaller than it had been even in the late 1600s. This had largely been brought about by the increased use of reprieves.

Looking back from the vantage point of 1819, Sir James MacIntosh was well aware of a gradual change in this regard, a ripening in "humane feelings" when it came to execution, during the century after the Glorious Revolution of 1688.[1] Although huge numbers of felons could have been hanged, this would have exceeded most people's idea of vengeance or example. As Edmund Burke observed in 1780, the execution of one man might excite awe; that of multitudes would occasion disgust. As a result, and as the Reverend William Broom noted in an assizes sermon

1. House of Commons Debate 2 March 1819, *Hansard*, vol. 39, cols. 777–845.

delivered at Norwich in 1737, English law manifested a "happy mixture of severity and mercy."[2] Selective examples were made of some of those sentenced to death but the majority escaped hanging.

The eighteenth-century decline in the per capita execution rate was especially pronounced between 1700 (when a marked post-1690 fall in hangings was already a decade old) and the early 1740s. Even by the first decade of the eighteenth century, only 12 per cent of all convicted felons in Norfolk and Suffolk were being hanged, although this figure includes those who were clergied.[3] The fall was particularly marked during the 1720s, when it became possible to reprieve those condemned to death on condition of a reliable sentence of transportation. For example, in Somerset, during the decade prior to 1720, 72.5 per cent of those who had been capitally convicted were executed. In the following decade, this declined to half. Hampshire, Devon and Cornwall also saw major falls (Wiltshire and Dorset saw little or no change).[4]

This decline in the execution rate did not necessarily continue in a uniform manner for the rest of the era. It has been suggested that in much of provincial England it was fairly stable for some years after 1740, and may not have shown a further marked and sustained decrease until the late 1700s or even the early years of the following century.[5] Indeed, nationally there was an upward surge in executions during the mid-1780s (after a period of decline) and again, briefly, at the start of the nineteenth century, when judges experimented with a policy of severity.[6]

Against this, the reprieve rate (the proportion of capitally convicted felons who received clemency) does seem to have increased in Norfolk and Suffolk during the last three decades of the eighteenth century, albeit that this must be seen against the background of an increased number of capital convictions. In the five years from the start of 1768 to the end of 1772, 31 people were capitally convicted at the regional assizes, of whom 15 (just under half) were "left for execution" and hanged. By

2. W. Broome, *A Sermon Preach'd at the Assizes in Norwich, August 8th, 1737,* 1737, p. 11.
3. J. Briggs et al, *Crime and Punishment in England: An Introductory History*, 1996, p. 64.
4. M. Eder, *"At the Instigation of the Devil": Capital Punishment and the Assize in the Early Modern England, 1670–1730*, 2014, pp. 137–138.
5. P. King, *Crime, Justice, and Discretion in England, 1740–1820*, 2000, pp. 277–278.
6. P. King and R. Ward, "Rethinking the Bloody Code in Eighteenth-century Britain," 2015, p. 172.

contrast, during the five years from 1795 to 1799 (inclusive) 63 people were capitally convicted at the same forums, of whom 18 (well under a third) were hanged.[7] There were also two executions in King's Lynn and Great Yarmouth during the former period, but none in the latter. After 1805 only two per cent of those capitally convicted of property crimes at the Norfolk Assizes (rather than offences against the person) were hanged; 98 per cent were granted clemency.[8] As elsewhere in England, this change brought about the "final separation between the letter and the practice of the law."[9]

According to one estimate, between the start of 1735 and the end of 1799, 446 death sentences led to just 114 confirmed executions at the Norfolk Assizes, while 55 death sentences passed at the City of Norwich Assizes produced only 13 hangings. Thus, about 75 per cent of capital convicts in the county were ultimately reprieved, although one or two individuals may have died of natural causes between sentence and execution. (This figure also ignores the small number of capital convictions, reprieves, and executions at the sessions in Yarmouth and Lynn). At the Suffolk Assizes, the figures were broadly similar: 377 death sentences led to 116 executions, producing a reprieve rate of about 70 per cent.[10]

The reprieve rate was lower in the Metropolis, where it varied between 42 per cent and 67 per cent of capital cases in the years from 1700 to 1790, after which it *may* not have shown a further marked and sustained decline until the early years of the following century.[11] During the decade from 1765, it stood at 57 per cent. This partly explains the differences in execution rates between East Anglia and the metropolitan area. (Another explanation is the much higher per capita indictment rate in and near the city).[12]

On a more specific level, at one session of the Bury Assizes in 1742, five people received the death sentence but all were reprieved. Three of

7. Anon, *Report From the Select Committee on Criminal Laws*, 1819, pp. 188–201. www.capitalpunishmentuk.org/circuits.html (Last accessed 9 July 2015).
8. J. Wallis, "Representations of Justice Executed At Norwich Castle," 2013, p. 34.
9. House of Commons Debate 2 March 1819, *Hansard*, vol. 39, cols. 777–845.
10. www.capitalpunishmentuk.org (Last accessed 12 August 2015).
11. V. Gatrell, *The Hanging Tree: Execution and the English People 1770–1868*, 1996, p. 616.
12. T. Plint, *Crime in England: Its Relation, Character, and Extent, As Developed from 1801 to 1848*, 1851, p. 10.

them had been convicted of sheep stealing (only recently made a capital offence), one of forgery, and one of horse theft.[13] Three years later, at the same forum, four felons were capitally convicted and sentenced to death but "all were reprieved." Amongst them were Thomas Hart, for breaking into a house in Westhall and stealing a watch and three silver spoons; John King, for stealing a horse in Milden; and William Fuller, for stealing several pieces of silver from the house of a clergyman in Monks Ely.[14]

Not all parts of England and Wales were treated with the same strictness when it came to clemency. For example, those who were capitally convicted in the principality appear to have received more favourable treatment than many of their counterparts across Offa's Dyke, including those in East Anglia. This leniency might be explained by the small numbers being processed through Welsh courts for serious felonies and the reduced need for deterrence, the large amount of information available to the judiciary in such cases, greater personal ties between gentry and ordinary people in Welsh communities (encouraging intercession), and the distance from London (and scrutiny), allowing more freedom of action. Interestingly, on one occasion a judge expressly pointed out that a particular Welsh offender's crime did not warrant the kind of alarm that it would have attracted if committed in the great farmlands of Suffolk.[15]

There were two means by which capitally convicted prisoners could be reprieved: by the trial judge, shortly after he had passed sentence of death, or, if he failed to do this, by subsequent petition to the Crown. Thus, at the Bury Assizes in 1790, 14 prisoners were convicted and sentenced to death for offences ranging from sodomy to highway robbery. Before the presiding judge left the town to continue his circuit he personally reprieved four of the men: a housebreaker, a burglar, and two horse thieves.[16] This left ten people awaiting death. However, only six men were ultimately executed, after successful interventions on behalf of the other four.

13. *Ipswich Journal*, 14 August 1742.
14. *Ipswich Journal*, 10 August 1745.
15. D. Jones, "Life and Death in Eighteenth-century Wales," 1981, p. 538.
16. *General Evening Post*, 27–30 March 1790.

Administrative Reprieves

At the conclusion of each circuit those initially sentenced to death normally had a report on their cases forwarded by the trial judge in a certificate/memorial/circuit letter (the terminology varied over time) to the Secretary of State. This contained his recommendation as to whether they should be "left for execution" or reprieved, and the terms on which a reprieve should be granted. Although, in theory, the final decision was for the Crown, the judge's advice was almost invariably followed if he recommended clemency. As a result, and unlike the situation at the Old Bailey, judges would openly announce their decisions on this issue before leaving an assizes town. They would also usually publicly state the conditions that they would recommend should be imposed in exchange for clemency. It would have been highly embarrassing, and undermined the reputation of the law, for the Crown to go back on such a public decision, although this *may* have occurred in a tiny number of quite exceptional cases during the late seventeenth century.[17] A formal letter would then be sent to the judge presiding over the next assizes ordering that the convict receive mercy on the stipulated terms, which he would accede to.[18]

A selection of cases is indicative of the award of immediate reprieves in the region. For example, William Holding was convicted of stealing sheep (a newly capital offence) at the Norfolk Assizes in 1743, but promptly granted clemency by his trial judge.[19] At the Bury Assizes in 1787, ten prisoners were capitally convicted and sentenced to death. However, the presiding judge, Henry Ashurst, reprieved seven of them before leaving the town. He left only three people, two highwaymen and an arsonist, for execution.[20] At the Bury Assizes in 1796, nine people were capitally convicted of various property offences: burglary; shoplifting; sheep theft; stealing from a dwelling-house; and housebreaking. Nevertheless, "[b] efore the judge left the town, they were all reprieved."[21]

---

17. M. Eder, *"At the Instigation of the Devil": Capital Punishment and the Assize in the Early Modern England, 1670–1730*, 2014, p. 96.
18. M. Madan, *Thoughts On Executive Justice*, 1785, p. 101.
19. *Westminster Journal or New Weekly Miscellany*, 26 March 1743.
20. *St. James's Chronicle Or the British Evening Post*, 10 12 April 1787.
21. *Sun*, 31 March 1796.

These immediate acts of judicial clemency have sometimes been termed administrative reprieves or pardons because they did not require a convict to petition for them. Exceptionally, a judge could change his mind while still on circuit, and order such a reprieve where he had initially failed to do so. He would then send word back to the relevant assizes town, announcing his change in decision.[22] Administrative reprieves were normally used for less serious capital crimes, such as lesser forms of animal theft, housebreaking, and stealing in a dwelling-house. They were not usually thought appropriate for very serious offences, such as rape, sodomy, and murder.

It seems that trial judges would often let those receiving administrative pardons stew for a short period between passing sentence of death on them in open court and revealing their decision to reprieve and on what terms. For example, on the last day of the Lent Assizes at Bury in 1801, a large number of men were sentenced to hang. A few hours later, on the same afternoon, "when the gaoler carried in the reprieves for ten of the unhappy men, it was a very effecting scene." A Russian convict was apparently quite overcome by the realisation that he would not be executed, as he had assumed would automatically be the case.[23]

If an administrative reprieve spared a convict from death, he might still petition against the condition imposed by the judge, who would then usually be asked to comment on its merits, just as he would with petitions against a death sentence (see below). An example of such a report can be seen in the response of Judge William Ashurst to a petition signed by 21 people from Great and Little Fransham in Norfolk, on behalf of 18-year-old James Askoe, along with an individual petitioning letter from the prisoner himself. Askoe had been capitally convicted at the Norfolk Assizes held at Norwich in August 1787 for stealing a gelding. He had immediately been reprieved from death on the fairly standard condition of transportation for 14 years. Reviewing the case, the judge felt that there were grounds for further clemency based on his youth, his suffering from "imbecility" following a violent fever, and his

22. Lincoln's Inn, Harrowby MSS 18–19, Document 19(f) *Legal Notebook of Sir Dudley Ryder*, 1754 and 1755, p. 18.
23. *The Bury and Norwich Post: Or, Suffolk, Norfolk, Essex, and Cambridge Advertiser*, 1 April 1801.

previous good character. In the light of this, a much milder condition of one year's imprisonment with hard labour in the Wymondham house of correction was imposed.[24]

Reprieve by Petition

Those capitally convicted felons who were not included in the first tranche of immediate reprieves did not automatically hang. The second method of securing a pardon, if an administrative reprieve had not been granted, was to petition the Crown for mercy. (Petitions were also regularly made against sentences of transportation and, later in the century, imprisonment). Sometimes, such petitions raised doubts about the safety of a conviction, but far more commonly they argued that the convict's merits and crime warranted clemency.

The normal delay between conviction and execution, usually several weeks (post-1752 murder cases apart), gave the condemned man the opportunity to ask for mercy. In 1728 the Crown urged the Lord Chief Justice to advise his fellow judges, when on circuit, not to appoint an "unusual distant time" for the execution of capitally convicted criminals, in cases where there was not a reasonable possibility that such petitions would be acceded to.[25] However, if necessary, extra time could be granted to allow further consideration of the issue. For example, in 1789 the Right Honourable William Grenville arrived with a temporary respite of seven days for William Mayhew, who was under sentence of death in Norwich Gaol for breaking into the house of a Colonel Goate. This would give time for the "[j]udge's reply on the case to be known." A week later, the King granted a pardon to Mayhew on condition of being transported to the coast of Africa for life.[26]

In these situations, a petition or letter supported by members of the public (preferably men of some standing, such as JPs, clergymen, and former employers) would be sent to the Secretary of State asking for clemency. Revealingly, when two burglars awaiting execution after the

24. TNA HO 47/6/6, ff 138–142.
25. TNA SP 36/9.
26. *Bury and Norwich Post*, 10 and 17 June 1789.

Suffolk Assizes in March 1766 were asked by an attendant clergyman whether they had any prospect of a reprieve, they replied, "No, Sir, we are Friendless."[27] The major public campaign for clemency for Matthew Barker, who had been convicted of burglary at the Norfolk Assizes in 1784, was typical of a high-powered intercession. Two collective petitions, one from 33 Norfolk magistrates assembled at quarter sessions, the other from 15 prominent people in his home village of Nacton, the local rector and his last employer among them, urged mercy, as did two individual petitions, one of them from Sir Thomas Beaver.[28] This approach paid off; he eventually received a free pardon.[29]

Sometimes even the victim of the relevant crime would endorse such a petition. This was always helpful, although no guarantee of mercy. For this reason, after his conviction at the Bury Assizes in 1722, Arundel Crispe begged his brother-in-law and erstwhile victim, in the "most submissive terms," to support his application, although he had attempted to murder him in a particularly brutal fashion. (Perhaps unsurprisingly, his brother-in-law "appeared inflexible" in the matter).[30] Twenty-three-year-old James Clark was more fortunate. After he was capitally convicted of burglary at the Bury Assizes in 1800, the prosecutor and victim, George Suggate, interceded on his behalf with "great liberality and humanity."[31] Two years later, 19-year-old Christopher Smith, capitally convicted at the Norwich Assizes for stealing five ewes and six lambs belonging to Ann Young, was equally lucky. Young wrote in support of his petition for mercy and Smith was reprieved from death on condition of transportation for life.[32]

Of course, many petitions were not successful, even when they had the best support available. For example, in 1797 Robert Scott, a 58-year-old man, was executed at Norwich for cattle theft, committed in what were thought to be severely aggravated circumstances, despite attempts by Prince William of Gloucester to secure a reprieve "from motives of

27. D. Edwards, *Sermons For the Use of Condemned Malefactors,* 1774, p. 233.
28. TNA HO 47/1/65.
29. *St. James's Chronicle Or the British Evening Post*, 9–11 November 1784.
30. *Daily Journal*, 20 March 1722.
31. *True Briton (1793)*, 8 August 1800.
32. TNA HO 47/29/19, ff 145–150.

humanity."[33] Similarly, in 1799 Sarah Lloyd, a young maid who had let her lover into her employer's home, where they took some jewellery and set the building on fire, was convicted at Bury Assizes and condemned to death for stealing in a dwelling-house. By then this was a capital offence that was nearly always reprieved. However, because of the fire, her trial judge warned her: "I cannot advise his majesty to shew you any grace or pardon whatsoever."[34] Even so, a prominent local magistrate subsequently organized a petition and engaged in "much fruitless endeavour" to get her reprieved.[35] The Home Secretary rejected his efforts because of the aggravating features in the case, (it was suspected that the fire had been intended to kill Lloyd's mistress), and she was executed.[36] In Northamptonshire in 1788, a petition against the execution of an unpopular man from Pattishall, convicted of murder in legally rather dubious circumstances, was not acceded to, although it included four dukes and duchesses.[37]

The so-called hanging cabinet of privy counsellors, which had emerged under Queen Mary when her co-regent, King William III, was away, and it was felt that a woman might need support for such an emotionally onerous task, would consider the petitions. This situation changed little during the eighteenth century, even after March 1782, when the Home Office was formed by renaming the existing Southern Department, transferring the latter's small staff to it, and moving all domestic responsibilities to the new ministry. It continued dealing with petitions to the king in much the same manner as its predecessor.

Throughout the era trial judges would be consulted about such petitions, and their opinion was of vital importance. As was noted in a communication to the Lord Chief Justice in 1728, petitions to the King asking for pardons for people convicted of capital crimes before the assizes judges: "are of course referred to them [the relevant judge] as best able to inform his Majesty how far such criminals may be proper objects

33. *Evening Mail*, 24–26 April 1797.
34. *The Times*, 11 April 1800, p. 3. Anon, *Trial of Joseph Clark, the Younger, and Sarah Lloyd*, 1800, pp. 7–10.
35. J. Fiske, *The Oakes Diaries*, 1991, p. 389.
36. *The Times*, 11 April 1800, p. 3.
37. D. Gray and P. King, "The Killing of Constable Linnell: The Impact of Xenophobia and of Elite Connections on Eighteenth-century justice," 2013, pp. 15–21.

of mercy."[38] This continued to the end of the century and beyond. The judges' opinions would usually be based on their own notebooks and records of the case. For example, in 1784 James Riches was convicted of burglary at the Suffolk Assizes at Bury after stealing a "great quantity" of property from the Reverend John Spurgeon in Melton.[39] The trial judge, Sir George Nares, was asked about clemency and initially recommended that no mercy be shown. At the same time, he apologised for the lateness of his report, as he had been ill "at Bath, and had not my Circuit Books with me."[40] (Ultimately, Riches appears to have been reprieved on condition of transportation for 14 years). Similarly, in March 1795 James Churchyard was capitally convicted at the Thetford Assizes for stealing 17 wether sheep belonging to a farmer from Billingford at the start of the year.[41] His trial judge, James Mingay, was initially unable to produce a report on the case for the Duke of Portland, who was the Home Secretary, as his notebook was in Thetford, while Mingay was in Derby. However, he noted that he had written to the Norfolk authorities asking that the execution be suspended and promising to provide a full report as soon as he returned to Thetford.[42]

Judicial responses varied greatly. Sometimes justices supported such an application. This might occur if: the judge had initially been close to ordering an administrative reprieve and had been impressed by the evidence adduced in a petition; the crime was of a type that could not normally be dealt with by an immediate reprieve, because of its ostensible gravity (such as rape), but warranted clemency for special reasons; or there were lingering doubts about the safety of the guilty verdict. Thus, when James Mingay eventually prepared his report on James Churchyard he supported clemency because the convict had behaved well in gaol, was of good previous good character, had shown contrition, and had received petitions in support of mercy from people of high social status.[43]

38. TNA SP 36/9.
39. *St. James's Chronicle Or the British Evening Post*, 3–6 April 1784.
40. TNA HO 47/1/71.
41. *St. James's Chronicle Or the British Evening Post*, 26–28 March 1795.
42. TNA HO 47/18/9, ff 35–36.
43. TNA HO 47/18/11, ff 41–48.

In other cases, judges would be fairly neutral, merely identifying the factors that supported, and those that militated against, clemency. Occasionally in these situations they withheld a recommendation, and left it entirely to the cabinet to make a decision. However, judges would often be opposed to such applications, sometimes strongly so, giving their reasons in explicit terms. Strong judicial opposition was always taken seriously, although it was not conclusive of the issue. George III was particularly reluctant to go against such advice.

For example, at the Bury Assizes in 1801 William Baldwin, a private in the Third Dragoon Guards, was convicted of highway robbery after assaulting a farmer near Ipswich and taking from him a watch, two guineas, and seven shillings. He was sentenced to death. The trial judge, Lord Chief Baron Archibald Macdonald, made it clear that he should not expect mercy because his crime had been accompanied by "violence and cruelty." The judge was also determined to make an example of the soldier, without which he feared that no one who resided near a garrison town would be safe.[44] Even so, there was a major attempt to obtain a reprieve for Baldwin. A petition signed by 55 Suffolk residents, including the prosecutor (and victim) was produced on his behalf, arguing that he was a suitable case for clemency. Nevertheless, when asked to comment, Macdonald was unimpressed. He opposed mercy, noting that the need to secure farmers from billeted soldiers required that the law be "left to take its course."[45] Baldwin was duly executed at Ipswich a few days later.

The Privy Council would normally consider petitions for mercy and the judicial responses to them together. The King might take an active role in these proceedings. Indeed, George I (whose English was not perfect) had some petitions translated into French (in which he was fluent) to allow detailed personal consideration, and even dealt with a few while in his hunting lodge in Hanover.[46] George III also became very involved in

44. *The Bury and Norwich Post: Or, Suffolk, Norfolk, Essex, and Cambridge Advertiser*, 29 July 1801.
45. TNA HO 47/28/33, ff 252–259.
46. Paper delivered by Dr Thomas Krause at the British Legal History Conference, Glasgow, 10–13 July 2013.

decisions, sometimes even meeting petitioners and granting temporary respites to allow further consideration of any issues raised.[47]

Conditions for Reprieve

Only a few reprieves were granted as free pardons; most were conditional. In exchange for clemency, the Crown could impose any requirement it desired, but usually settled on transportation. This was so common that, until shortly before his execution, Robert Bird, a Suffolk horse thief and housebreaker who had been capitally convicted in 1735, hoped for what a contemporary newspaper expressly termed a "[t]ransportation pardon."[48] For most of the eighteenth century after 1718, the recommendation would be for 14 years' transportation, although seven years was often set down following the American Revolution. For very serious crimes, transportation might be for life. Thus, at the assizes held for Norfolk and Suffolk in 1774, the last full year before events in America affected the system, seven people were capitally convicted and reprieved, six on condition of transportation for 14 years, and one for life.[49]

During wartime, reprieves were also frequently granted to younger and healthier men on condition that they join the army, navy, or marines, especially if the crime for which they had been convicted was considered a lesser capital offence. For example, in 1780 Thomas Hudson was accused of stealing 19 lambs from two farmers at Elden, in Suffolk.[50] He was capitally convicted at the ensuing assizes but "reprieved on condition of enlisting."[51] Two years later, James Thompson, who had been capitally convicted at the Norfolk Assizes for housebreaking in Rainham, and John Ewston, a highwayman whose erstwhile colleague in crime had already been hanged, were pardoned on condition that they entered the military service of the East India Company (a particularly hazardous occupation). They were escorted to London, under heavy guard, to

47. D. Gray and P. King, "The Killing of Constable Linnell: The Impact of Xenophobia and of Elite Connections on Eighteenth-century Justice," 2013, p. 18.
48. *Daily Courant*, 22 April 1735.
49. TNA ASSI 33/5.
50. *Gazetteer and New Daily Advertiser*, 11 October 1780.
51. *Whitehall Evening Post (1770)*, 22–24 March 1781.

be put on board an *Indiaman* bound for the subcontinent.[52] Mistakes were occasionally made in these situations as to suitability for military service. In 1777 Robert Cracknell was reprieved at the Bury Assizes on condition of enlisting in the army but granted a free pardon after he was found to have a bad leg.[53]

Other conditions were sometimes imposed in exchange for clemency. For some years after transportation became impossible following the American Revolution, it was commonplace to make reprieves for less serious capital cases conditional on a relatively short custodial sentence (often as little as two years) being served in a local bridewell or house of correction rather than have convicts lingering in prisons waiting for a voyage that could not take place or being sentenced to the hulks. Thus, at the Bury Assizes in 1785, Robert Gooding was convicted of stealing a cow from a farmer in Weybread, and Robert Woods was found guilty of a housebreaking during which a purse and some money were taken. The trial judge reprieved both men before he left the town.[54] Instead of putting further pressure on the town gaol, the judge recommended them to two years' hard labour in their local house of correction.[55] Similarly, in 1787 Robert High, William Wilson, William Moore, and Edmund Sinclair were capitally convicted at the Lent Assizes in Thetford.[56] Rather than sending them to the overcrowded hulks in the Thames, the Secretary of State sent a reprieve to the four men on condition of their being kept to hard labour for two years in Wymondham bridewell.[57]

An unusual condition of reprieve was imposed after Roger Benstead persuaded a youthful employee named Thomas Harper to shoot Thomas Briggs, a man with whom he (Benstead) was engaged in a bitter legal dispute over the ownership of a cow. He then tried to aid the lad's escape. Harper was convicted of murder but given a full pardon in exchange for a promise to give evidence against his erstwhile master. When Lord Kenyon, the trial judge, requested that such a course of action be taken,

52. *Norfolk Chronicle*, 5 January 1782.
53. TNA ASSI 33/6.
54. *Morning Herald and Daily Advertiser*, 25 July 1785.
55. TNA HO 47/5/11.
56. *Whitehall Evening Post (1770)*, 29–31 March 1787.
57. *The Times*, 20 August 1787, p. 4.

he suggested that it might be "right to pardon Harper, in order to make Him a competent Witness against the other Prisoners." (Harper's youth and his having acted under the influence of Benstead also influenced this decision).[58] The pardon was read out in court at the following gaol delivery for Suffolk. It meant that Harper ceased to be an accomplice, and so did not require corroboration or a corroboration warning.[59]

Conditions might vary considerably between convicts who had been found guilty at the same sessions, even for the same type of offence. For example, at the Lent Assizes held at Bury in 1788, six people were capitally convicted and reprieved before Sir William Ashhurst left the town. The most heinous offender, Nathaniel Lillie, who had been convicted of burglary, had a recommendation of transportation for life. John Wiseman, who had been found guilty of housebreaking, during which he had stolen clothes, was recommended to just seven years' transportation. John May, who had stolen a gelding, received the same disposal, as did John Lovell, who had taken a mare. However, Stephen Pike and William Argent were treated quite leniently after being capitally convicted of either larceny in a dwelling-house or shoplifting under the 1699 act (it is not clear which), even though they had stolen purses containing 15 guineas in gold and 80s in silver from a till in the shop of a grocer in Sudbury.[60] They were both recommended to just two years hard labour in the Bury St Edmunds house of correction.[61]

Although those reprieved from execution would feel great relief at their escape from death, the conditions imposed had terrors of their own. In 1778, after James Kilborne was reprieved at the Bury Assizes, he was very frightened and "chopped his hand in a most terrible manner, in order, as it is supposed, to incapacitate himself from serving in the army, or working on the Thames."[62]

58. TNA HO 47/14/4, ff 22–23.
59. Anon, *The Trial of Roger Benstead the Elder, and Roger Benstead the Younger*, 1792, p. 1.
60. *The Times*, 28 March 1788, p. 3.
61. *Whitehall Evening Post*, 27–29 March 1788; TNA HO 47/7/66.
62. *Public Advertiser*, 21 April 1778.

Communicating a Reprieve

Reprieves could be granted right up until execution, even after the death warrant came down, although such a delay was unusual. Normally, local authorities would ensure that the Crown was kept aware of time constraints and so avoided last-minute decisions. In 1800, when a petition was submitted for Edmund Roberts after he had been capitally convicted of horse theft at the Bury Assizes, it was accompanied by a covering letter from Charles Stisted, the committing magistrate, carefully pointing out that 12 April, just eight days later, was "the day upon which the unhappy convict expects to suffer."[63] This would encourage a speedy decision or the granting of a temporary reprieve to allow more time for consideration.

Nevertheless, this process did not always work smoothly. In August 1734, a King's messenger arrived with a reprieve for a highwayman named John Broughton the day before he was due to be executed at Norwich.[64] (The King's messengers, of whom there were 16 in 1772, helped with liaison within the national criminal justice system and were sometimes employed to report on, and even help prosecute, notorious cases).[65] In April 1737 John Crisp was reprieved the night before he was due to be hanged in Ipswich after conviction at the Suffolk Assizes.[66] In August 1784 Matthew Barker, an agricultural labourer, escaped hanging by an even narrower margin after he was capitally convicted at the Norfolk Assizes of burgling a widow's house in Beetley.[67] He was "left for execution" at the end of the sessions.[68] At the appointed time he was "coming out of the gaol door, with his shroud on, to be executed, when he was respited for a few days."[69] This temporary reprieve appears to have been granted by the under sheriff, something that the trial judge, Lord Loughborough, was later to complain about as "unconstitutional" in his report on the case. Barker then benefited from what appears to have been a major

63. TNA HO 47/24/9, ff 75–80.
64. *London Journal (1720)*, 31 August 1734.
65. D. Cox, *Crime in England 1688–1815*, 2014, p. 83.
66. *Daily Gazetteer* (London Edition), 14 April 1737; *London Evening Post*, 12–14 April 1737.
67. *General Evening Post*, 12–14 August 1784.
68. *Felix Farley's Bristol Journal*, 21 August 1784.
69. *St. James's Chronicle Or the British Evening Post*, 9=11 November 1784.

campaign to save his life.[70] He escaped execution. By contrast, in 1767 two men were hanged for horse theft following the Chelmsford Assizes in Essex just hours *before* a reprieve for both of them arrived.[71]

The remote possibility of a late reprieve sometimes encouraged irrational optimism. Jonathan Sawyer, who was executed for burglary near Ipswich in March 1780, still had "hopes of life on the day he suffered." He had convinced himself that the prison governor had a reprieve in his pocket and was merely leaving it late in the process to reveal this to him because he wanted to see how Sawyer would react under pressure. It was only when his arms were pinioned that the reality sank in. Despite his disappointment he died bravely.[72]

Reprieves and Meta-Narratives

The discretion provided by reprieves was so important that their use has contributed to various meta-narratives and explanations for the operation of the era's criminal justice system. As far back as the early 1970s, it led Douglas Hay to conclude that the system of criminal law between the Glorious Revolution of 1688 and the early years of the nineteenth century, which was much less severe than it appeared, was not the result of legal inefficiency; in fact, it had an important role in promoting a political ideology that sustained the dominance of the propertied class. According to this analysis, the pardon system allowed the judiciary to evaluate the respectability of those seeking clemency and encouraged the latter to seek the influence of members of the upper classes when seeking a reprieve. This reinforced "vertical" loyalties in the wider society.[73]

Although containing valuable insights, Hay's interpretation was quickly challenged. Legal historians stressed that in most cases the decision to reprieve, whether by trial judge or after petition to the Crown, was based on clearly identifiable and rational criteria.[74] Certainly those identified as significant have a repetitive, almost mechanical, quality. This has even

70. TNA HO 47/1/65, ff 275–280.
71. *Ipswich Journal,* 22 August 1767.
72. *Gazetteer and New Daily Advertiser*, 18 April 1780.
73. D. Hay, "Property, Authority, and the Criminal Law," 1975, pp. 44–48.
74. J. H. Langbein, "Albion's Fatal Flaws," 1983, p. 120.

allowed attempts to be made at estimating their relative importance, by counting the frequency with which they were employed in successful petitions. For example, during the years from 1784 to 1787, the most significant were previous good character, youth, the circumstances of the crime, the poverty of the convict, and, finally, his "respectability."[75] These factors, along with several others, warrant detailed consideration.

Factors Influencing Reprieve

Unsurprisingly, the gravity of the crime and the convict's degree of culpability were crucial. Not all eighteenth-century capital offences were viewed in the same way. Their inherent seriousness, the number of offences for which the defendant had been convicted, his level of involvement and motivation, were all vitally important. In 1819, Sir James Macintosh divided capital crimes into three classes. In the first category was murder, a crime on which he felt the law was "invariably executed," though this was a slight exaggeration; in the second he placed arson, highway robbery, and seven or eight other offences in which the law was carried into effect in a "great many" but not all cases. In the third category were up to 150 ostensibly capital offences, some of the most "frivolous and fantastic description." In these the law was almost never put into effect by 1819, and, on the exceptionally few occasions that it had been implemented in the recent past, usually excited horror and disgust. MacIntosh felt that it was the theoretical existence of these rarely enforced capital offences that led people to believe that English law was much more sanguinary than it really was.

Although social attitudes had changed by the early 1800s, MacIntosh's division was a sound one for the eighteenth century, albeit with appropriate modifications. For example, the second category of offences was a little larger for much of the previous 100 years than it was in 1819 and, although extremely uncommon, slightly more "frivolous" offences from the third category led to execution in the years before 1800.[76]

75. P. King, *Crime, Justice and Discretion in England 1740–1820*, 2003, p. 299.
76. House of Commons Debate 2 March 1819, *Hansard*, vol. 39, cols. 777–845.

Some ostensibly capital eighteenth-century crimes, such as stealing goods worth more than 40 shillings from a domestic residence and shoplifting, were highly likely to result in a reprieve, especially in the provinces. In others, for example burglary or robbery, such a result was a strong possibility, something to be hoped for until the death warrant came down, even if they did not produce an administrative reprieve at trial. For murder, rape, and sodomy there was much less prospect of clemency.

Within a single offence description there could also be major differences in gravity that would have an enormous effect on the prospects of reprieve, especially for felonies in the second category. As MacIntosh noted, the imposition of capital punishment in cases of burglary and robbery largely depended on their "particular circumstances."[77] For example, in 1753 John Watling and John Kent were both capitally convicted of housebreaking at the Bury Assizes. The trial judge reprieved Kent, while Watling was left for execution and hanged.[78] This was probably because Watling had broken into an attorney's house at Carleton on three occasions, stealing a large silver spoon, a damask tablecloth and some clothes.[79] By contrast, Kent had broken into a house, at Kessingland, just once. Judges were particularly sympathetic if a crime had been committed to secure the necessities of life.

As has long been appreciated, the previous character of individual felons played a vital role in the decision to reprieve. Were reputable people willing to vouch for the accused? Typically, when the clerk of assizes on the Home Circuit tried to pressure Sir Dudley Ryder into reprieving a felon on condition of transportation, the judge declined because "nobody spoke to his character." Although some judges became case hardened about low-status character witnesses, a clergyman, local squire, or former employer (ideally, several of them) were always useful in this regard.

Conversely, an ascertainably bad previous character would make a reprieve much less likely. In one of the most controversial examples, William Potter was hanged at the Essex Assizes in 1814 for maliciously

77. House of Commons Debate 2 March 1819, *Hansard*, vol. 39, cols. 777–845.
78. *London Evening Post*, 16–18 August 1753.
79. *London Daily Advertiser*, 24 April 1753.

cutting down 70 trees in an orchard. This was an exceptionally rare, and extraordinarily late, example of an arcane Bloody Code offence (one created by the 1723 Black Act) actually being pursued to execution. It had almost never happened before. The sentence was also carried out despite appeals for clemency from the prosecutor, the defendant's neighbours, and the committing magistrate. However, there was a simple explanation for this apparently bizarre disposal. Potter was hanged "because he was believed to be habitually engaged in other offences." Foolishly, he apparently admitted many of them to a ministering prison chaplain.[80]

The Potter case was merely an extreme (and late) example of a practice that was widespread during the eighteenth century. For example, in 1784 two cousins, both named Simon Tuffs, and both allegedly "old offenders," were capitally convicted of stealing a mare worth eight guineas from a miller and a cheaper horse from another man. They were rumoured (but not proven) to have been involved in several other crimes and to be part of a gang.[81] The older man was left for execution and hanged.[82] By the 1780s men who were considered neophytes to crime would have been extremely unlikely to die for stealing two fairly standard horses. The executed man's fate was probably the result of his rumoured associations and activities. These may have been mentioned during his examination, or have been purely the result of hearsay.

However, by the end of the period the use of such information was beginning to offend against increasingly strong notions of due process. There was growing concern about the role that previous character, real or suspected, had on sentence (and verdict). According to Thomas Gisborne, writing in the 1790s, a good judge would not inflict "chastisement disproportioned to the transgression immediately before him, by way of wreaking vengeance on the prisoner for some former act of misconduct."[83] The 1819 Select Committee was very critical of William Potter's treatment,

80. Anon, *Report From the Select Committee on Criminal Laws*, 1819, p. 6.
81. *Whitehall Evening Post (1770)*, 1–4 May 1784; *General Evening Post*, 12–14 August 1784.
82. *Felix Farley's Bristol Journal*, 21 August 1784.
83. T. Gisborne, *An Enquiry Into the Duties of Men in the Higher and Middle Classes of Society in Great Britain*, 1794, p. 387.

not least because he had not been tried, let alone convicted, for any of the other crimes that influenced the decision to execute him.[84]

An appeal from a trial jury might also influence clemency. Even where jurors convicted on a capital matter, it was "common experience" for them to recommend the defendant to the King's mercy, in an attempt to save his life, although some observers thought that it would be better to acquit outright or convict of a lesser charge, to avoid uncertainty.[85] This seems to have occurred with female felons in eighteenth-century Wales, where juries often pre-empted the need for state clemency by ensuring that they were convicted of non-capital crimes whatever the offence originally indicted (pious perjury).[86] Jury recommendations were frequently—but not invariably—followed or supported by the trial judge.

The need to set a deterrent example in a particular locality, at a certain time, or with regard to a specific type of offence, could also be vital to the reprieve process. This was the one factor that was usually entirely independent of the merits and actions of a defendant and which often could not be anticipated by the accused, especially if his trial took place some length of time after the crime. Thus in 1754 Ryder refused a reprieve to a capitally convicted felon at the Surrey Assizes largely because a royal directive had recently been issued to judges discouraging excessive leniency.[87] Similarly, in his report on John Edward, a yeoman from Brecon (Wales) who was convicted on a number of charges of sheep stealing in 1784, the trial judge, John Wilson, argued that not only was Edward a bad character but that, as there had been no executions over the previous 20 to 30 years, his death would help deter future crimes.[88]

Such considerations were also taken into account in East Anglia. Sometimes this was for national, sometimes for local, reasons. For example, at the Bury Assizes in August 1784 four men were convicted of burglary and left for execution.[89] Two of them, John Lenny and Joseph Hartley, appeared promising candidates for a reprieve following petition. Lenny

84. Anon, *Report From the Select Committee on Criminal Laws,* 1819, p. 6.
85. *Lloyd's Evening Post*, 6–8 September 1775.
86. K. Watson, "Women, Violent Crime and Criminal Justice in Georgian Wales," 2013, p. 246.
87. Lincoln's Inn, Harrowby MSS 18–19, Document 19(f), *Legal Notebook of Sir Dudley Ryder,* 1754 and 1755, p. 17 and p. 13.
88. N. Woodward, "Seasonality and Sheep-stealing: Wales, 1730–1830," 2008, p. 31.
89. *Felix Farley's Bristol Journal*, 14 August 1784.

had stolen low-value items, had not used or threatened violence, was unemployed and hungry (he "devoured" a loaf that he had taken) when he offended, and had previous worthy service as a soldier. Hartley was just 16, an orphan, had also taken low-value goods, and his victim was an uncle who was uneasy about prosecuting him. Despite this mitigation, Lord Loughborough was fairly lukewarm about recommending reprieves because he felt that burglary was then prevalent in Suffolk.[90] Neither man was ultimately executed, but others were not so fortunate. In 1824 Robert Gibson, the last man to be hanged for sheep theft in East Anglia, was executed, in part, because the crime had become so prevalent in the region that it was felt necessary to set an "absolute example."[91]

Lingering doubt about the evidence that had secured a conviction could also encourage clemency (and shows that jurors were sometimes more conviction minded than the judiciary). Ryder reprieved three capital property cases from a single Home Circuit assizes sitting in 1754 because the evidence appeared "doubtful" or was "not clear." This appears to have been widespread judicial practice, and was expressly referred to and approved by Martin Madan. It was especially likely to occur when a judge's encouragement to acquit in his summing up, following ambiguous evidence, had been disregarded by the jury.[92] Illustrative of this, in 1729 John Gooch was capitally convicted of horse theft at the Suffolk Assizes. He appears to have been reprieved on condition of transportation by the trial judge, Lord Chief Justice Raymond, at the end of the sessions. He subsequently petitioned for further clemency, requesting not to be sent to America, and Raymond was asked to comment on his application. The judge noted that he would not have censured the jury had they returned a not-guilty verdict at trial. In light of the good character given to Gooch in the petition, Raymond had no objection to his being granted a pardon. It is likely that he had entertained doubts about the safety of the conviction from the start, initially manifest in

90. TNA HO 47/1/52, ff 209–216.
91. *The Bury and Norwich Post: Or, Suffolk and Norfolk Telegraph, Essex, Cambridge, & Ely Intelligencer*, 31 March 1824.
92. M. Madan, *Thoughts On Executive Justice*, 1785, p. 49.

the decision to grant an administrative reprieve and later in his lack of opposition to a full pardon.[93]

Age was a particularly important factor. As Askoe's case suggests, extreme youth or old age could encourage clemency. One example of the latter is a case from the Suffolk Assizes in March 1790. Robert Heron was one of a pair of gypsies who were capitally convicted for the highway robbery of Edward Surridge on the road between Haverhill and Withersfield and left for execution by the trial judge. However, in the light of a petition for clemency, he was recommended for transportation instead of hanging. One reason given for mercy was that Heron was 70 years old.[94]

More commonly, it was the young who received special consideration. By the eighteenth century, a lower age limit of seven years for criminal responsibility had long been accepted at common law. Those below that age could not commit a crime. Between seven and 14 years there was a presumption of *doli incapax*, so that it had to be proved that the child knew right from wrong before a conviction could be secured. In practice, this could be quite difficult to establish; juvenile defendants had significantly higher acquittal rates than those who were over 14 years of age. Most important, even where convictions were secured, children were more likely to benefit from leniency.

There was a particular reluctance to hang those who were below the age of 16, even if they had been found guilty of fairly heinous offences. It was suggested in 1812 that Michael and Ann Hammond or Hammont (a brother and sister), whose ages were given as seven and eleven respectively, had been hanged outside the South Gate in King's Lynn in 1709. If true, this would easily make them the youngest children executed in the whole country during the entire century.[95] However, modern research strongly suggests that the executions referred to, which occurred on 29 September 1709, involved two young, albeit physically immature, adults. The baptismal records of St Margaret's Church indicate that they were aged 20 and 17 years, respectively, and from a poor family, perhaps explaining their slight physiques.[96] (Benjamin Mackerell makes no mention of

93. TNA SP 36/10.
94. *General Evening Post*, 27–30 March 1790.
95. W. Richards, *The History of Lynn: Civil, Ecclesiastical, Political, Commercial*, vol.2, 1812, p. 888.
96. I am grateful to Susan Maddock, Norfolk Record Office, for this information.

them at all in his history of the town published in 1738). Nationally, a few 15-year-olds were executed during the course of the century, with largely unconfirmed reports of one or two who were even younger being hanged, such as the supposedly 12-year-old housebreaker William Jennings at Tyburn in 1716. Even so, most children escaped death, in East Anglia as elsewhere.

In 1748 William York tested the system in this regard. York was a ten-year-old parish pauper who had been lodged with a couple at Eye, in Suffolk. He was convicted of murdering his bedfellow, five-year-old Susan Mayhew (also "on the parish"), after a minor quarrel; she was "sulky" and may have soiled their shared bed, although it appeared clean when examined. It was a particularly gruesome, indeed psychopathic, killing, the infant's wrists having been cut with a knife and other bodily parts slashed with a hook before she was buried in a dunghill. York then cleaned himself up and calmly went to breakfast.[97] He was found guilty of murder at the Bury Assizes in August that year, and sentenced to death, but Lord Chief Justice Willes, the presiding judge, "put over" his execution to November to allow high-level consideration with his colleagues in London.[98] At this meeting in Serjeants Inn, Willes and most of the judges present suggested that the aggravating features in the case warranted death and clearly showed that York was possessed of a "mischievous discretion," despite his youth. However, a couple of the judges present suggested further investigation, in case the boy had been acting at the behest of another person. York's execution was (again) temporarily respited.[99] Although a death warrant was later issued, it was not implemented.[100] The respite was eventually made permanent by the Secretary of State, on account of York's age, despite his apparent lack of remorse at the crime.[101] Instead, he was kept in custody until 1757, when he was pardoned at the Bury Assizes on condition that he enlist in the Royal Navy. By then he was a young man of 19.[102]

---

97. *London Evening Post*, 2124 May 1748.
98. *General Evening Post*, 11–13 August 1748.
99. *The Case of William York* (1748) *Foster* 70, 168 E.R. 35.
100. *Whitehall Evening Post Or London Intelligencer*, 30 May – 1 June 1749.
101. *Penny London Post Or The Morning Advertiser*, 8–10 August 1748; *Old England*, 19 November 1748.
102. *Lloyd's Evening Post and British Chronicle*, 2–5 September 1757.

This was an extreme and unusual case. A much more typical one relating to a child involved a trial from the Bury Assizes in 1743, in which James Cheese and William Hunt received a death sentence, but the latter "being only 13 years old was reprieved."[103] However, age could be a vital factor in the award of clemency for much older youths, in both administrative and petition-based reprieves. In August 1774 Edward Abbott, an attorney's clerk in Ipswich, was capitally convicted of breaking open his master's study and taking 40 guineas. At first he was not recommended for an administrative reprieve by the trial judge. However, Abbott, in a "most pathetic speech addressed his Lordship, entreating him to consider his youth, and earnestly begged for Transportation." His request was granted forthwith, and he was sent to the Americas for 14 years.[104] In 1783, Abraham Carman, Henry Cabell, and 17-year-old Henry Cabell (junior) were capitally convicted at the Norfolk Assizes for burgling the house of Abigail Hambling.[105] The first two were executed, the last reprieved on account of his youth and because he was thought to have been led into crime by his father.[106] The following year, Joseph Hartley and John Murrills were capitally convicted at the Suffolk Assizes in separate trials for burglary and cattle theft, respectively. However, they were temporarily respited from execution for two weeks and subsequently received clemency. The explanation for such mercy was that both were "only 17 years old."[107]

Indeed, youth was regularly cited as a factor (among others) justifying mercy for young adults up to about 23 years of age. Of course, this was not necessarily enough. When Joseph Loads, a man of less than 20 years of age, was executed for a routine burglary after the Norfolk Assizes of 1785, it was noted as significant that such a young man suffered for his "first offence." Nevertheless, by then, this was thought to be unusual.[108]

Some (but by no means all) evidence suggests that women tended to receive more favourable outcomes when it came to reprieves. For

---

103. *Ipswich Journal*, 6 August 1743; *London Evening Post*, 9 August 1743.
104. *Public Advertiser*, 9 August 1774.
105. *Whitehall Evening Post (1770)*, 20–22 March 1783.
106. *Public Advertiser*, 26 March 1783.
107. *Bury and Norwich Post*, 19 August 1784; *Bury and Norwich Post*, 8 August 1784.
108. *Public Advertiser*, 13 August 1785.

example, capitally convicted female property offenders on the Western Circuit may have obtained significantly more conditional pardons than their male counterparts during the early part of the century.[109] By contrast, evidence from Yorkshire, slightly later in the era, indicates that, although they received better outcomes earlier in the criminal-justice process (verdict, etc.), for post-conviction reprieves their success rate was broadly the same as that for men.[110] Similarly, in Norfolk, during the first half of the nineteenth century at least, it seems that, once capitally convicted, women had about the same prospect of clemency as their male counterparts.[111]

In so far as women did benefit from greater leniency with regard to reprieves, it was most clearly manifested when they offended with men. Thus, in 1769 Cornelius Green was capitally convicted at the Norwich City Assizes, along with his wife, for housebreaking (the doctrine of *feme covert* not being applicable in the particular circumstances of the case). She was reprieved on condition of transportation, but he was hanged.[112] However, Cornelius was not obviously more culpable than his spouse. He was a "very ignorant" man who had stood at the door of the residence that they targeted, receiving stolen goods from his wife as she "stripped" the house.[113] Similarly, when Samuel Place and his wife, Ann, were capitally convicted of burglary and robbery at the Bury Assizes in 1771, Ann was immediately reprieved; Samuel was executed.[114] In like manner, in 1803 Richard Brown was hanged for burgling the house of two men at Wickhambrook, in Suffolk, and stealing linen and other valuables worth up to £100. His female accomplice, Hannah Jones, who was capitally convicted with him, ultimately received clemency.[115]

The recovery of stolen items and the convict's record of co-operation with the authorities were also relevant to any decision to grant clemency. Thus, in 1753 William Mann avoided the death penalty he had received

109. M. Eder, *"At the Instigation of the Devil": Capital Punishment and the Assize in the Early Modern England, 1670–1730*, 2014, pp. 160–161.
110. R. Markless, *Gender, Crime and Discretion in Yorkshire, 1735–1775*, 2013, p. 16
111. J. Wallis, "Representations of Justice Executed at Norwich Castle," 2013, p. 3.
112. *Gazetteer and New Daily Advertiser*, 26 July 1769.
113. *Public Advertiser*, 16 August 1769.
114. *London Evening Post*, 3–6 August 1771.
115. *The Ipswich Journal*, 2 April 1803.

at the Bury Assizes for stealing 34 sheep that were part of a large flock being driven from Suffolk to London. The animals were ready for market and so quite valuable. However, all of them were safely recovered (almost immediately), and the crime was, apparently, impulsive and opportunistic. Most important, Mann made swift admissions when arrested and assisted the authorities in finding the animals.[116] At the Thetford Assizes in March 1759, John Cross was convicted of a fairly serious highway robbery, during which he had taken £4 9s. He was sentenced to death and his execution appointed for early the following month. Even so, he was subsequently reprieved in favour of 14 years' transportation. This was probably because he was co-operative after conviction: "Cross, since his condemnation, has impeached several of his accomplices of committing divers robberies in Berkshire, Huntingdonshire and Northamptonshire."[117] This was too late for him to become an evidence for the Crown, but enough to escape the gallows.

For former military men (though not deserters), previous exemplary service to the Crown in time of war could be significant. At the Summer Assizes held at Bury in 1800, 23-year-old James Clark was capitally convicted of burglary. He had stolen 31 watches and other items to a total value of £200 from a house in Halesworth. This was about as heinous an example of the offence as could be found without threatening or using violence. His trial judge, the Lord Chief Baron, left him for execution, despite Clark's mitigation, which was that as a naval midshipman he had shown great gallantry at the Battle of Camperdown in 1797 and during other incidents and engagements.[118] He was given "no hopes" of a reprieve.[119] Even so, a temporary respite was obtained, to allow time for further consideration, and this was subsequently renewed.[120] Nineteen men from Ipswich supported Clarke's petition, which noted that he was well-regarded by his superior officers, particularly for his conduct during a mutiny, and had been injured in the line of duty. (He had also, allegedly, fallen into bad company, was suitably penitent, and the prosecutor

116. *Public Advertiser*, 21 August 1753.
117. *Universal Chronicle Or Weekly Gazette*, 24–21 March 1759.
118. *The Ipswich Journal*, 9 August 1800.
119. *True Briton (1793)*, 8 August 1800.
120. *The Ipswich Journal*, 30 August 1800.

had requested mercy.)[121] Clark was not subsequently executed. For more mundane crimes and older defendants, even a record of "solid service" to the Crown earlier in life might be influential.

As several of the cases already cited suggest, most successful petitioners relied on a multiplicity of grounds. For example, in 1784 those sent on behalf of Matthew Barker argued that he deserved mercy because: the crime was his first offence; he was of previous good character; lies had been told in court suggesting that he was cohabiting with his accessory, a "woman of bad fame," blackening his character; no violence had been used; most of the money taken had been recovered; and some of the goods he was accused of stealing had been legitimately given to him after the crime was committed. Furthermore, Barker had behaved well while in prison and, it was claimed, had been led into the crime by need, or the "great and unusual scarcity and Dearness of all the necessaries of life."[122] Finally, he received a late, temporary reprieve while on the way to execution. When consulted, the trial judge felt that although Barker was not necessarily a fit subject for mercy (his victim had been a widow), in the light of his narrow and stressful escape from hanging and general mitigation, his life should be spared.[123]

121. TNA HO 47/24/39.
122. TNA HO 47/1/65.
123. TNA HO 47/1/65.

CHAPTER 12

Transportation

Introduction

In some respects, given the frequency of its imposition and the gravity of its consequences, transportation was the most important form of punishment in England between 1718 and 1775, and highly significant during those parts of the century that fell outside these dates. Although less draconian than execution, its consequences, including long-term banishment, forced labour, and the risk of death on the voyage out, were much more serious than those entailed in short custodial sentences and feared accordingly.[1]

Transportation was not a new punishment in 1718. As Mr Justice Heath noted in 1793, it was "usual, long before, for the Crown to grant pardons on condition of transportation."[2] Its roots dated back to 1617, and it had been used as a prerequisite for granting a reprieve from execution from the middle of the seventeenth century, especially during the reign of William III, albeit that those transported would often have to make their own travel arrangements. By 1700, it seems, some 4,500 people nationally had been granted clemency on these terms. This process continued during the first 18 years of the century, with hundreds more being sent (or at least ordered) across the Atlantic in lieu of execution. Inevitably, this affected East Anglia, though to a modest degree. As early as 1663 ten people who had been capitally convicted on the Norfolk Circuit

1. J. Willis, "Transportation Versus Imprisonment in Eighteenth-and Nineteenth-century Britain," 2005, p. 174.
2. *Fleetwood v Finch* (1793), 2 Blackstone (H.) 220.

were reprieved on condition of transportation. Between 1700 and 1717, it appears that a total of 41 people who had been convicted on the same circuit were granted clemency in this fashion.[3]

However, the Transportation Act of 1718 (4 Geo I, c 11), passed due to a fear of rising crime (especially in the London area) and the desire to improve secondary punishments, transformed the situation. For the first time it provided that those convicted of clergyable offences of dishonesty, most particularly grand larceny, could be sentenced to transportation for seven years instead of being branded, if they claimed benefit of clergy.[4] (It was an alternative, not a supplement, to the latter). As the 1718 act noted, it would be imposed if the judges "think fit, instead of ordering any such offenders to be burnt in the hand or [in the case of petty theft] whipped." Although this power was couched in permissive, not mandatory, terms, such a sentence quickly became by far the most common disposal for even quite modest cases of grand larceny, largely (though not entirely) replacing both branding and immediate discharge, and branding and imprisonment in a house of correction. Typically, in 1754, when Richard Mays was convicted at the Bury Assizes of stealing just two shirts, he was sentenced to seven years' transportation.[5]

The Transportation Act also allowed those convicted of petty larceny to be sentenced to seven years' transportation rather than the customary whipping. However, this disposal was relatively uncommon in most parts of provincial England, including East Anglia, where flogging followed by immediate discharge remained by far the most common punishment for the lesser form of theft. (Transportation was used fairly frequently for those convicted of petty theft in parts of the West Country and, at times, the Old Bailey).

The 1718 act, supplemented by another statute passed in the following year (Geo I, c 23), also placed the process by which those sentenced to transportation for larceny, or reprieved from execution on condition of transportation, would be sent to America on a properly organised and financed basis. This allowed for the effective removal of convicts

3. P. W. Coldham, *The Complete Book of Emigrants in Bondage, 1614–1775*, 1988, p. 916.
4. G. Ollyffe, *An Essay Humbly Offer'd, for An Act of Parliament to Prevent Capital Crimes*, 1731, p. 2.
5. *Ipswich Journal*, 17 August 1754.

from the country after they had received their sentences, encouraging both its use as a condition of clemency in capital cases and as a sentence for lesser felonies. This was effected by arranging for the appointment of merchants who were then contracted to transport the convicts for a fee that covered much of the expense of the journey (initially £3, it was quickly raised to £5), while also granting them the right to sell for their own benefit the convicts' (forced) labour for seven years on their arrival in the New World. Panels of three senior justices of the peace were expressly authorized to contract with such merchants. Thus, at the Suffolk Assizes held in August 1746, Sir Jasper Cullum and two other Justices were appointed, "any two of them to contract for the transportation of felons now ordered to be transported for the liberty of Bury St Edmunds." At the same time, John Sparrow and two other magistrates were appointed to perform the same role for the rest of Suffolk.[6]

At least 50,000 convicts from the British Isles (including those sent from Ireland), 36,000 of them from England, were transported between the advent of the 1718 act and the American Revolution of 1776. (Some estimates are considerably higher). By then almost 1,000 were being sent across the Atlantic every year, although this was a lower figure than a decade earlier, something that may have been aided by withdrawal of the government subsidy in 1772. During this period, between two and six convict ships made the journey each year, with about three or four sailings being the norm, and some making the voyage in other vessels.[7] Half of all transports were sent from the metropolitan area and its environs. Nevertheless, penal transportation was also used regularly, if less frequently, in the provinces.

Criticism

Throughout the era, some observers were dismissive of transportation, not viewing it as an effective punishment. Several proposed that felons suffer a "miserable and painful life" in England instead, suggesting, *inter alia*, that they be kept underground and forced to work as coal miners

6. Gray's Inn MS 45.
7. P. W. Coldham, *The Complete Book of Emigrants in Bondage, 1614–1775*, 1988, p. 914.

or at a similarly unpleasant task while being fed on bread and water.[8] Others favoured greater use of imprisonment.

Many of these commentators feared (probably mistakenly) that "great numbers" of those transported returned illegally, before their time in exile was even half finished.[9] Nevertheless, such concerns were not entirely without foundation. For example, John Gulliford, a Londoner who had been transported to America for seven years, escaped from his "owner" (the person who had purchased his service for that period) in Maryland and took passage as a sailor for England; he had been to sea before turning to crime. Gulliford disembarked at Great Yarmouth, in Norfolk, where, needing money for his journey to London, he swiftly "robb'd a House of a Watch and a Silver 3 Pint Mug."[10]

In the early 1750s these fears resurfaced in an acute form, amid concern that returnees were contributing to an apparent crime wave in the wider country. It was suggested that clergied convicts should, instead, be set to forced work in the royal docks. However, not everyone was comfortable with this idea, fearing that using convicts for such vital work, instead of transporting them, could threaten national security. The proposal was not followed.[11]

Despite its critics, transportation still had had considerable attractions to contemporary observers, even after 1775. Some felt that forced labour for long periods within England smacked of slavery and executive tyranny. Perhaps strangely to modern eyes, it was more acceptable for government to distance itself from the supervision of convicts. This helps to explain why transportation was reintroduced once Australia was identified as a potential destination.[12]

The island continent was not selected for some years after 1775. Jamaica, Nova Scotia, New Zealand, the Falkland Islands, and British Honduras were all considered as potential destinations. A brief and extremely unsuccessful attempt was made to use West Africa. Eventually,

---

8. R. Hodshon, *The Honest Man's Companion: Or, The Family's Safeguard*, 1736, p. 49.
9. *British Journal (1722)*, 3 April 1725.
10. Ordinary's Account, 13 January 1742: OA17420113.
11. C. Jones, *Some Methods Proposed Towards Putting a Stop to the Flagrant Crimes of Murder, Robbery, and Perjury*, 1752, p. 11.
12. J. Willis, "Punishment and the Cultural Limits to State Power in Late 18th-century Britain," 2008, p. 416.

in August 1786, as the pressure of mounting numbers of convicts sentenced to transportation but held in custody became intolerable, the cabinet settled on Botany Bay. The "first fleet" of six transport vessels, two warships, and three store ships carrying 717 convicts (48 of whom died on the journey) left England in May 1787, arriving at Sydney Cove in January 1788. Others quickly followed.

Nevertheless, transportation did not regain the penal dominance it had held prior to 1775. Australia could take only a share of English convicts, selected by their offence, age, health, skills, gender, etc. Many (more than half) of those sentenced to transportation had to remain in England, forcing the continued use of prisons, as well as hulks moored in ports and on the River Thames, to accommodate them (see *Chapter 13*).

Transportation in East Anglia

Although the 1718 legislation had been introduced because of concerns in London, transportation for theft was quickly used in East Anglia, while the number of those reprieved from execution on condition of transportation also increased swiftly. For example, at the Lent Assizes held at Thetford in 1721, two men were sentenced to seven years' transportation for grand larceny. Another capitally convicted housebreaker was reprieved, presumably on condition of transportation [13] The region's speed in employing the punishment is unsurprising. The use of the Westminster judges at assizes courts ensured a rapid degree of uniformity in national practice.

In 1751, at the various East Anglian assizes courts, 18 people were sentenced to transportation for seven years for grand larceny, and another seven received 14 years' transportation as a condition of reprieve from a capital sentence. One or two more may have received a reprieve on the same condition, without its being recorded, after petitioning for clemency from execution, while a few of the seven-year sentences were probably not imposed after petitions against sentence were received by the Crown. Nevertheless, it is probably safe to assume that about 20 people were

13. *London Journal (1720)*, 25 March 1721.

sent to the Americas from the region in 1751. Similarly, in 1752 the figures were 20 sentences of seven years' transportation and eight reprieves on condition of 14 years in America. Thus it also seems that about 30 per cent went across the Atlantic as a condition of reprieve from capital punishment and 70 per cent as a sentence for clergyable felony. This split between the two mechanisms is broadly in accordance with most other studies. Even so, the proportion of English convicts sentenced to transportation from the Norfolk Circuit (5.6 per cent) was smaller than that in other circuits, such as the Northern (8.5 per cent), the Midland (6.5 per cent), the Oxford (10.9 per cent), or the Western (12.8 per cent).[14]

During the 1750s very few convicts were transported pursuant to sentences passed by East Anglian quarter or borough sessions, other than the special sessions held for Great Yarmouth and King's Lynn, which did add several men or women to the total. For example, in 1753, at Yarmouth, two people convicted of grand larceny, one of them a man who stole from fish houses in the town and the other a girl who stole from a tavern where she had been employed, were both sentenced to seven years' transportation to the Americas.[15] However, county quarter sessions and ordinary borough sessions were not *always* so reticent about having recourse to the disposal during the era.

Use of Transportation at Quarter Sessions

Throughout the country the willingness of quarter and borough sessions, other than those with special powers (such as Lynn and Yarmouth), to impose seven years' transportation for grand larceny or, much less commonly, petty theft under the 1718 act varied greatly. In part, it was contingent on the number of clergyable felonies that the lower jury courts were willing to hear (usually very few between 1718 and the middle of the century). However, it was also dependent on the willingness of the magistrates who presided over them to have recourse to the punishment. In some parts of the North of England they were reluctant to

14. W. Meyer, *Beyond the Seas: Eighteenth-century Convict Transportation and the Widening Net of Penal Sanctions*, 2011, p. 48.
15. *London Daily Advertiser*, 24 April 1753.

use transportation in the decades after its introduction. In Cumberland they did not apply the 1718 act until the 1740s, and Westmorland applied it only twice before the American Revolution (both cases occurring in 1737).[16] This may have been influenced by the logistical problems involved in removing convicts from such parts. In Surrey the disposal was not used by quarter sessions between 1718 and 1750. By contrast, the Devon Quarter Sessions acquired a reputation for imposing the punishment fairly readily quite soon after its introduction. The infamous "King of the Beggars," Bampfylde Moore Carew, claimed that he had been sentenced to transportation by that forum in 1739 merely for being an "idle rogue," an exceptionally unusual disposal. He had the presence of mind to ask by what legal authority this was done as he was "not accus'd of any crime."[17] Similarly, during the three decades after 1718 the West Riding justices in Yorkshire transported an average of six people a year.[18]

In Norfolk there was an initial reluctance to use the punishment at county quarter sessions after 1718. The court largely abandoned hearing cases of grand larceny for several decades, so avoiding any pressing need for it. Nevertheless, it was being imposed quite regularly at this forum in the final decades of the century. For example, John Cooper and John Fuller were convicted at the Norfolk Quarter Sessions held on 21 January 1788 and sentenced to seven years' transportation. They sailed with the second fleet to Australia in December 1789.[19] Similarly, at the Norfolk Quarter Sessions held at Holt in 1810, John Prentice was found guilty of embezzling £300 and received the same disposal.[20]

Perhaps surprisingly, given its conservatism over jurisdiction earlier in the century, Suffolk appears to have been a little different. Several sentences of transportation were passed at the county quarter sessions in the years after 1720. For example, in January 1721 Mary Fiske faced

16. P. Rushton and G. Morgan, *Eighteenth-century Criminal Transportation: The Formation of the Criminal Atlantic*, 2004, p. 19.
17. Anon, *An Apology for the Life of Bampfylde Moore Carew*, 1749, pp. 8–9. It was claimed that he was one of 32 people transported at about the same time from this location.
18. M. E. W. Maddison, *The Justices of the Peace and the Administration of Local Government in the East and West Ridings of Yorkshire Between 1680 and 1750*, 1986, p. 153.
19. Australian Joint Copying Project; microfilm roll 87, no. HO11/1.
20. *The Bury and Norwich Post: Or, Suffolk, Norfolk, Essex, Cambridgeshire, and Ely Advertiser*, 31 January 1810.

indictments for felony and petty larceny at the Suffolk County Sessions sitting at Bury, and "confessed the same." She was not flogged but, instead, was sentenced to seven years' transportation to the Americas under the 1718 act.[21] This occasioned some practical problems that had to be resolved by a subsequent meeting of the court. Similarly, at the Suffolk Quarter Sessions held at Bury in January 1725, Richard Bush and Samuel Finch were sentenced to transportation after being convicted of felony and/or petty larceny.[22]

As with Norfolk, by the final decades of the century sentences of transportation were being imposed quite regularly at the Suffolk Quarter Sessions. Thus, at those held at Beccles in January 1771, Martha Marsh was convicted of stealing thirteen turkeys and sentenced to seven years' transportation.[23] Joseph Everitt received the same disposal for stealing chickens when the county sessions were held at Bury in October 1782 (he may have been reprieved after spending 18 months in custody).[24] Robert Churchfield was also sentenced to transportation after being convicted of stealing six pecks (12 gallons) of barley at the Suffolk Quarter Sessions at Ipswich in 1785. By then, even some borough sessions in the region had occasional recourse to the disposal.

Australia

After the American Revolution broke out in 1775, sentences of transportation could not be carried out. Such sentences were still passed, but convicts were held in prison while the government tried to find somewhere else to send them. For example, in 1783 John Roberts was convicted at the Suffolk Assizes of highway robbery but reprieved from death on condition of seven years' transportation. In 1789 he petitioned for a free pardon after spending six years in prison in England.[25] Others in this situation were sent to the hulks (see *Chapter 13*). Unsurprisingly, in these circumstances East Anglia contributed to the early convict transportations

21. SRO QS B/105/2014, p. 180.
22. SRO QS B/105/2014, p. 220.
23. *Ipswich Journal*, 19 January 1771.
24. TNA HO 47/3/53.
25. TNA HO 47/8/24.

to Australia after the continent was eventually chosen as an alternative destination in 1787.

It seems that only a handful of people from the region, perhaps just four adults and a child, were on the first fleet, albeit that three of them made up a remarkable family unit. The youthful Henry Cable (1763–1846) had been convicted of burglary at the Thetford Assizes in February 1783 and sentenced to death. This was commuted to 14 years' transportation, but there was, at first, nowhere to send him. He was held in Norwich Castle for several years until he embarked for Australia. While in custody, he formed a relationship with Susannah Holmes, who was also under sentence of 14 years' transportation. A son, Henry, was born to them in the prison, and they went to the Antipodes together, where they married shortly after their arrival. The couple went on to have nine more children, and Henry became a prominent figure in the new colony.

Far more men and women from East Anglia were on subsequent convict sailings. It appears that the ill-starred second fleet had at least 36 men and women from the region out of more than 1,200 who embarked. The majority came from Norfolk, with just eight coming from Suffolk. Most had been sentenced at the assizes for the two counties, but three came from the special borough courts at Lynn and Yarmouth and, on one assessment, five more came from ordinary quarter sessions. Among them was Henry Cone, who had been convicted of stealing money at the Lent Assizes in Norwich in 1787.[26] John Levell, who stole a horse and was capitally convicted but reprieved at the Suffolk Assizes in March of the following year, also sailed with this fleet.[27] They arrived in Australia in 1790, to face seven and 14-year banishments, respectively.

The third fleet of eleven ships sailed in early 1791 and arrived in the colony later the same year with more than 2,000 convicts. Of those who embarked from England, it seems that about 51 originated in Norfolk and Suffolk. Amongst them were James Cam and "Royal" James King, who had been capitally convicted at the Norfolk Assizes of highway robbery at Chisworth and expected to hang, but were reprieved on condition of

26. *St. James's Chronicle Or the British Evening Post*, 10–12 April 1787.
27. *General Evening Post*, 27–29 March 1788.

transportation for life.[28] James Waterson received a similar disposal after being capitally convicted of stealing goods from a shop. Even so, most convicts on these voyages were sent for just seven years.[29]

The numbers of those sent to Australia from England fell to more sustainable levels after the third fleet, with a total of 419 men and women making the journey in the latter part of 1791, 418 the following year, and the lowest total, 84, sailing in 1794. However, numbers were back up to 403 in 1797.[30] Many convicts from East Anglia were among these prisoners or sailed in subsequent years.

The journey to Australia was long and arduous, far more so than that to America. Infirm convicts could not embark on it. In 1789 Elizabeth Edwards, a 60-year-old woman, was sentenced to transportation at the borough sessions for Bury. However, the apothecary of the gaol where she was held was of the opinion that she was physically incapable of travelling to Botany Bay, forcing the town's recorder to reconsider her case.[31] It swiftly became relatively uncommon, though not unheard of, for those over 50 to be sent to the Antipodes.

Embarkation

Some assizes courts used provincial ports, such as Barnstaple, Bideford, and Liverpool to ship their convicts to the New World. The Northern Circuit frequently employed Newcastle. However, the vast majority of transports went through either London or Bristol. Of those who went to Maryland (one of the most common destinations) between 1746 and 1775, more than 56 per cent sailed from the former and about 36 per cent from the latter. Only about 8 per cent went through other ports.[32] Thus the Oxford Circuit usually employed Bristol for its convicts. By contrast, London served as the dispatching point for many counties on the East Coast, as well as its own and Home Circuit convicts. Typically,

28. *Whitehall Evening Post* (1770), 20–23 March 1790.
29. *Oracle Bell's New World*, 12 August 1789.
30. P. Colquhoun, *A Treatise on the Police of the Metropolis*, 1800, p. 472.
31. TNA HO 42/15/109, ff 353–355.
32. W. Meyer, *Beyond the Seas: Eighteenth-century Convict Transportation and the Widening Net of Penal Sanctions*, 2011, p. 48.

in 1725 a small vessel moored in the Humber picked up those going from Lincoln and then sailed to the Metropolis. Once there, they were put on board a larger vessel for the Atlantic crossing.[33]

Similarly, East Anglia was close enough to London for most of its prisoners to be marshalled there for transportation to the Americas. Some made the journey to the capital overland from the region, others by sea. For example, in June 1748 several convicts "loaded with irons" were brought from the Norfolk County Gaol in Norwich Castle to the Green Dragon Inn in Bishopsgate Street, London "in order to be transported to some of his Majesty's colonies in America."[34] Two years later Jonathan Paul, James Edwards, and Ann Gillet, who had been capitally convicted but reprieved at the Bury Assizes, were put aboard a vessel in London in order to cross the Atlantic.[35] Conveying convicts to London could be an expensive business. In 1763 the Cambridgeshire Quarter Sessions paid the gaoler Thomas Williamson £6 6d for taking a single felon to the Metropolis for transportation.[36]

Sometimes the process of transportation happened quite expeditiously. In late September 1751 nine men who had been sentenced at the assizes for Norfolk and the City of Norwich were sent to London for transportation less than two months after being convicted.[37] At other times, there would be longer delays, with inmates held in prison for significant periods pending the journey. In 1768 a statute (8 Geo III, c 15) required that those who were to be transported as a condition of reprieve from execution (rather than as a sentence for clergyable theft) should go immediately. Even so, four years later it was suggested that a separate holding prison be established for those waiting to go to the Americas, with improved inmate hygiene.[38]

Because of the distance involved, and the nature of the shipping making the voyage, transports were not normally carried to Australia from

33. P. W. Coldham, *Emigrants in Chains*, 2011, p. 74.
34. *Jacobite's Journal*, 18 June 1748.
35. *Whitehall Evening Post Or London Intelligencer*, 12–15 August 1749; *Ipswich Journal*, 7 April 1750.
36. CRO Q/SO 6, p. 145.
37. *Whitehall Evening Post Or London Intelligencer*, 28 September – 1 October 1751.
38. D. Layard, *Directions to Prevent the Contagion of the Jail-distemper: Commonly Called the Jail-fever*, 1772, p. 17.

London, as they had been when sent to America. Instead, they were usually marshalled at Portsmouth. Thus, in 1788 it was noted that those sentenced to transportation and held in Norwich Gaol had been sent to Ipswich, where they joined inmates from that town prison who were also being sent to Botany Bay. There were 17 of them in total. The combined group, together with two gaolers, was then put on a wherry (a type of coastal sailing barge) in which they sailed to Portsmouth.[39] From there they embarked on a much larger vessel for the island continent. Similarly, in 1791 John Boreham and John Lilley were conveyed from the gaol at Bury to Portsmouth to be put aboard vessels destined for Botany Bay.[40] In 1801 the notorious horse thief Margaret Catchpole and two other female convicts, Elizabeth Barker and Elizabeth Killet, made the same journey from Ipswich gaol.[41]

Reprieves from Transportation

Throughout the era, and especially after 1718, many of those sentenced to transportation petitioned against its implementation, in a process that mirrored that of convicts who tried to avoid execution; a considerable number succeeded. As was noted in 1772, it was a "frequent occurrence that persons sentenced for transportation are set at liberty, by his Majesty's most gracious pardon, on account of some favourable circumstances appearing in their behalf, and the small amount of value of the theft committed."[42] Between 1761 and 1770 alone almost 300 petitions from around the nation for reprieve from transportation were successful.[43] Such appeals became particularly common after the relatively swift voyage to America ended in 1775, and those under such a sentence might spend their entire sentence in custody in England, giving plenty of time for requests for clemency. For example, in 1786 Thomas Black was convicted at the Norfolk Assizes of stealing three iron bars from a cargo ship that

39. *Bury and Norwich Post*, 13 July 1788.
40. Ibid., 2 February 1791.
41. Ibid., 3 June 1801.
42. D. Layard, *Directions to Prevent the Contagion of the Jail-distemper: Commonly Called the Jail-fever*, 1772, p. 18.
43. A. R. Ekirch, *Bound for America: The Transportation of British Convicts to the Colonies, 1718–1775*, 1987, p. 40.

had been wrecked off the coast. He petitioned against his sentence of seven years' transportation with the support of the mayor of Yarmouth and the foreman of the assizes grand jury. William Ashhurst, the trial judge, recommended that Black be granted a free pardon.[44]

A tiny number of inmates went through both reprieve procedures successively, petitioning to avoid transportation after being successful in escaping execution in the same manner, although this took a degree of "chutzpah." Many more petitioned against transportation, having received an administrative reprieve from a trial judge or been sentenced to seven years abroad after conviction for grand larceny.

Of course, many petitions were not successful. In 1808 three poachers were capitally convicted at the Thetford Assizes for shooting at William Bussey, the assistant gamekeeper to Lord Cholmondley. Before Sir Nash Grose departed from the town, he granted clemency to one of them, Robert Chapman, on condition of transportation for life.[45] Chapman was just 22 years old, of previous good character, and had, allegedly, been encouraged to commit the crime by his older brother. He subsequently petitioned for a free pardon. The judge, when consulted, was opposed to this, but did suggest that he could eventually be allowed to return from transportation if he behaved well in Australia.[46]

Many of the factors considered in a decision to reprieve from execution were also relevant to petitions against transportation.[47] For example, in 1786 Thomas Black was reprieved from transportation (see above) because he was old and infirm, and stole only to procure common necessities; he was also of previous good character, and had spent his youth in the King's service.[48] The petition of Frances Cranmer, convicted at the Thetford Assizes on 23 March 1793 for a minor burglary, stressed her youth; she was just 21 years old.[49]

---

44. TNA HO 47/4/60, ff 350–354.
45. *The Bury and Norwich Post: Or, Suffolk, Norfolk, Essex, and Cambridge Advertiser*, 30 March 1808. The conviction was under the Black Act of 1723 or Lord Ellenborough's Act of 1803 (reports differed).
46. TNA HO 47/40/19.
47. K. Morgan, "Petitions Against Convict Transportation, 1725–1735," 1989, pp. 110–113.
48. TNA HO 47/4/60, ff 350–354.
49. TNA HO 47/16/76, ff 319–324.

Exactly the same process might apply to sentences of transportation imposed at quarter sessions, although in such cases it would be the chairman of the bench who was asked to comment on petitions. For example, in October 1782, 18-year-old Joseph Everitt was convicted of stealing chickens at the Suffolk County Quarter Sessions held at Bury St. Edmunds.[50] He was initially sentenced to seven years' transportation, along with his co-defendant James Cream, but appears to have successfully petitioned for a reprieve some 18 months later (the American War meant that he was still in custody in England). One of his grounds for clemency was that he had been unable to provide a character reference at trial, as he lived in a remote part of Suffolk. A testimonial to his previous good behaviour, dated February 1784, accompanied the petition. It was signed by four of Everitt's former masters, who described him as being a generally well-behaved and honest man and emphasised his youth and good behaviour while in custody.[51] Similarly, at the Ipswich Quarter Sessions in 1801, James Mudd, a carpenter, was convicted of stealing wheat and sacks worth 36s from a barn and sentenced to transportation.[52] He requested mercy with the support of his victim, a parish constable, and a local clergyman. Lord Chedworth (1754–1804), a Suffolk JP and chairman of the county bench, was asked to comment on the matter. Although he was initially unenthusiastic, it seems that a free pardon was eventually secured.[53]

Prosecution for Premature Return

Very few people who had been successfully transported abroad were executed in the East Anglian region for returning "prematurely"—that is, before the expiry of their term, whether it was for seven years, 14 years, or life, although doing so was a capital offence. To a significant extent, this probably reflected the incidence of early return for those who had made the forced voyage abroad. Escape was not easy, and the attractions of life in America, if not initially Australia, considerable for those who

50. *Norfolk Chronicle*, 26 October 1782.
51. TNA HO 47/3/53, ff 166–169.
52. *The Bury and Norwich Post: Or, Suffolk, Norfolk, Essex, and Cambridge Advertiser*, 28 January 1801.
53. TNA HO 47/31/11, ff 105–125.

did manage to get away from their masters, although it is also likely that most who returned early to England from abroad were not detected.

However, escape after sentence of transportation had been passed, but before it had been carried out, was more common, especially after 1775. Legally it was the same crime as returning from America itself, often being referred to simply as "being at large." In both situations, the prospects of being detected and convicted were greatly increased by two factors: returning to the area where the transport had originally been convicted or in which he had lived, and resuming a criminal career, arrest for which then brought him to notice. Quite commonly, both factors were combined.

Even if detected, a returned convict often avoided conviction because of the considerable evidential difficulties involved in proving (in a pre-fingerprint age) that he was the same man as the one originally sent to America, especially if he had been transported from a court far from the place where he was arrested. For example, in 1739 John Pixley was convicted at the Thetford Assizes and sentenced to seven years' transportation. He escaped from the keeper of the Norfolk prison and some escorting dragoons while on his way to a port for shipment to America (this still constituted "returning").[54] About a year later he was caught in London and indicted for being at large and for further offences under the Black Act of 1723. However, when his case was called for trial at the Old Bailey, he successfully argued that he had not had sufficient time to prepare his defence, and it was put over to the following sessions.[55] Subsequently he was taken to Norwich by order of *habeas corpus* to face trial, but not executed for the crime.[56]

There might be other legal problems in prosecuting such cases. John Mace was convicted of grand larceny at the Norfolk Assizes in 1753, and sentenced to seven years' transportation.[57] Before this could be carried out he escaped from prison, and was not heard of for 15 years, when he was arrested in London, and brought back by order of *habeas corpus* to his native county. He stood trial for "being at large" while under a sentence

54. *Daily Gazetteer* (London Edition), 25 April 1739.
55. OBSP, supplementary material for John Pixley, 3 September 1740: s17400903-1.
56. *London and Country Journal*, 24 February 1741.
57. TNA ASSI 33/2, *Public Advertiser*, 28 August 1753.

of transportation (the seven-year period after his escape) at the Norfolk Assizes in 1768. Even so, the case was thrown out by the grand jury, as it could not be proved that he was "resident in the kingdom during his time of banishment."[58]

Some returnees were not even prosecuted, if there appeared to be serious evidential problems, but simply sent back to America. Thus in July 1751 William Ellsden was acquitted of stealing goods worth 15s from Viscount Townshend at the Norwich Assizes.[59] However, he was not released: "[I]t appearing to the Court, that Ellsden had been transported, and returned before his time is expired, he is to be transported again for the remainder of that time."[60]

Most important, and contrary to much popular belief (then and now), many of those returnees who were prosecuted successfully in the provinces were not hanged, especially if they had returned early from a seven-year sentence for clergyable larceny or (much less commonly) petty theft. Instead, they were reprieved from execution and sent back across the Atlantic, with their seven-year terms increased to 14 years or life, as occurred with William Stratton, who was convicted at the Norwich Assizes in 1775.[61]

Similarly, at the Thetford Assizes in March 1788, Thomas Fisk was indicted for being "feloniously at large" before his seven years had expired. Fisk had originally escaped while awaiting transportation or in the process of being moved to a hulk after sentence. Unusually, he pleaded guilty to "returning."[62] He was reprieved from execution with a recommendation that he be transported for life.[63] Fisk sailed to Australia with the second fleet. The following year John Allington was also convicted at the Suffolk Assizes for being at large before the expiration of his seven-year sentence of transportation. Again, he was not executed, but recommended to transportation for life.[64] Samuel Codham was even luckier. He had been

58. *Gazetteer and New Daily Advertiser*, 3 August 1768.
59. TNA ASSI 33/2.
60. *London Daily Advertiser and Literary Gazette*, 6 August 1751.
61. G. Morgan and P. Rushton, *Eighteenth-century Criminal Transportation*, 2004, p. 122; *Morning Post and Daily Advertiser*, 22 August 1775; *Public Advertiser*, 22 August 1775.
62. *Whitehall Evening Post (1770)*, 20–22 March 1788.
63. TNA HO 47/7/66.
64. TNA HO 47/8/123.

convicted at the Norfolk Quarter Sessions held at Norwich in January 1787, and sentenced to seven years' transportation, but escaped from prison before his time had expired or he was sent abroad. At the Norfolk Assizes in late July 1792, he was capitally convicted, but reprieved by the trial judge, Beaumont Hotham, before he left the city.[65] Hotham's circuit certificate subsequently cited "favourable circumstances" when recommending a free pardon.[66]

Returning prematurely from a 14-year or life term that had been imposed after reprieve from a capital offence was viewed rather more seriously, although it did not invariably end in execution. In October 1736 Samuel Sawyer, who was awaiting transportation for burglary, escaped from Ipswich Gaol. He was recaptured the following April in Norfolk, and returned there, but not hanged.[67] At the Lent Assizes at Thetford in 1776, William Goodens was capitally convicted of burglary but reprieved on condition of seven years' transportation (this term sometimes replacing 14 years by then). He was put on board a transport ship but subsequently took part in a convict revolt with 40 others, and escaped. He then made the mistake of returning to his native Norfolk, with a view (somewhat strangely) to enlisting in the East India Company's army at their military recruiting office in Norwich. When he went to the mayor's parlour, to be sworn into its service, someone who had read of Goodens' escape in Sir John Fielding's *Hue and Cry* policing journal recognized his name, and he was immediately arrested.[68] Nevertheless, after spending two more years in Norwich Gaol, he was reprieved on condition of enlisting in the navy and was put on board a warship off Yarmouth.[69]

Even so, between 1735 and 1799, five men were executed in Norfolk and Suffolk for returning to England. At least three had not actually left the country, but escaped before being shipped abroad. Some of the five, such as Robert Reeve, had been convicted of other capital crimes at the same time as being found guilty of being at large, which helps to explain their draconian disposal. Reeve was convicted at the Bury Assizes of horse

65. *General Evening Post*, 4–7 August 1792.
66. TNA HO 47/14/70, ff 292–293.
67. *Common Sense Or The Englishman's Journal*, 2 April 1737; TNA ASSI 33/1.
68. *London Packet or New Lloyd's Evening Post*, 9–111776.
69. *Morning Chronicle and London Advertiser*, 30 June 1778.

stealing and robbing on the highway as well as returning.[70] Presumably, it was arrest for the first two offences that led the authorities to investigate his status. Perhaps unsurprisingly, he was hanged.

In 1764 John Holloway was found in Essex, despite having been sentenced to transportation at the Norwich Assizes the previous year.[71] It appears that he had escaped while awaiting disposal. He was sent back to his original convicting court (something that made prosecution much easier), found guilty of being at large, and, despite both a temporary reprieve and another escape attempt, executed.[72] At trial, he disputed identity, as was common in such cases, and unsuccessfully claimed to be one William Brentnall rather than Holloway.[73] The £20 statutory reward for prosecuting returnees to conviction was duly distributed among his three captors.[74]

In the same year, John Carman was executed for being at large in Norfolk. Carman had been sentenced to 14 years' transportation at Thetford Assizes in 1759 after reprieve from a capital offence, and presumably had made the journey across the Atlantic before escaping from his master there and returning to England. Five years later, he was one of two men seen lurking around Honningham in Norfolk at about the same time as a series of burglaries occurred in the area. A posse organized by a local farmer arrested them while they were drinking from a five-pint bottle of rum in a local wood, with housebreaking implements found nearby.[75] Carman was subsequently convicted and executed at Norwich (some weeks after Holloway).[76]

In 1769, Isaac Skinner, a carpenter from Bures, in Suffolk, was also capitally convicted and executed for returning from transportation.[77] He appears to have been unfortunate. He was found guilty of stealing an elm plank (not a capital offence) at the same time. It was being apprehended for the theft that initially brought him to the authorities' attention, and

70. *London Evening Post*, 27–30 March 1742.
71. London Evening Post, 21–23 August 1764; London Chronicle, 20–23 August 1764.
72. *London Evening Post*, 21–23 August 1764.
73. *Westminster Journal and London Political Miscellany*, 25 August 1764.
74. TNA ASSI 33/4.
75. *Public Advertiser*, 5 June 1764.
76. *Public Advertiser*, 11 September 1764.
77. *Ipswich Journal*, 18 March 1769.

led them to appreciate that he had returned early.[78] Almost two decades later, John Clarke was hanged at Norwich for horse theft and being at large.[79] He had apparently gone under the name of John Haynes, and presumably his trial revolved around whether Haynes and Clarke were the same man. The latter had escaped from Norwich Castle the previous March, having been sentenced to transportation. Had he merely been found guilty of stealing a horse, it is likely that he would have been reprieved from execution.[80]

Returning prematurely from Australia was much harder than it was from America, because of the distance involved and the much smaller number of ships making the journey. Only a few cases occurred before the end of the century. In 1788 Nathaniel Lilley was capitally convicted at the Bury Assizes for burgling the house of Nathaniel Summerset, a Sudbury baker.[81] He was not executed, and it seems that his sentence was eventually commuted to transportation. In 1791 a man by the same name, and presumably the same individual, escaped in an open boat from Botany Bay with a group of other convicts, citing a near-starvation level of rations in the Australian colony. Despite this, when they set sail from Sydney Cove late one night in March, they had amassed 100 pounds of flour, some pork, rice, and seven gallons of water. They were eventually picked up by a Dutch vessel and taken to Timor. There, they were joined by the survivors of a British warship that had foundered who arranged to have the convicts shipped back to England, via the Cape of Good Hope, for trial. The Bow Street magistrate who initially examined them seems to have been fairly sympathetic to their plight.[82]

78. *Ipswich Journal*, 18 February 1769.
79. *London Chronicle*, 25–28 August 1787.
80. *The Times*, 20 August 1787, p. 4.
81. *Bury and Norwich Post*, 26 March 1788.
82. *Evening Mail*, 29 June – 2 July 1792.

CHAPTER 13

Imprisonment, Penal Enlistment, and Corporal Punishment

Imprisonment

Historically, custody had been used to hold suspects awaiting trial or convicts pending execution or transportation, rather than as punishment, at least for serious crimes. As the visiting Frenchman François de la Rochefoucauld noted in 1784, it was thought that English prisons "should serve only to secure the persons detained, and not provide their first stage of punishment."[1] Even so, by the time La Rochefoucauld was writing, his analysis was certainly not correct, and it had never been entirely accurate.

Penal imprisonment for felonies, an expensive and highly intrusive punishment, was of marginal significance at the start of the era and of relatively limited importance until well into the 1770s, as John Howard discovered on his first tour of English prisons.[2] Indeed, there were no penitentiaries in the modern sense at any time in eighteenth-century England. The proposed construction of two highly regulated national prisons pursuant to the Penitentiary Act of 1779 (19 Geo III, c 74), in which the Norfolk Circuit would have been allocated 20 places a year, failed to occur. Fear of the potential expense and local opposition to central-government initiatives prevented such a development until 1816.[3]

1. N. Scarfe, *A Frenchman's Year in Suffolk*, 2011, p. 81.
2. J. Sinclair, "Why Has Imprisonment Emerged as the Predominant Form of Punishment for Serious Crimes in England?," 2007, pp. 37–52.
3. D. Lemmings, *Law and Government in England During the Long Eighteenth Century*, 2011, p. 102.

However, imprisonment had become a significant part of the penal repertoire long before then. By 1700 it had been imposed on a regular basis for petty offences and vagrancy for well over a century, with short sentences being served in bridewells or houses of correction. Felonies were a different matter. At the start of the period, those who successfully pleaded their clergy were usually branded and discharged without further ado, although a little-known and rarely used act of 1576 had authorised judges to imprison clergied offenders for up to a year, and there had been a similar experiment during the Interregnum. Additionally, in the late seventeenth century, a few reprieves were granted to those who had been sentenced to death on condition of being committed to a house of correction rather than the more normal requirement of transportation or enlistment in the military. Nevertheless, these were exceptions to the general situation.

The 1706 Act

By the start of the eighteenth century, attitudes were beginning to change. Timothy Nourse, regretting the lack of continental-style penal galleys in England, suggested that convicted felons who did not warrant execution should be forced to work in a house of correction.[4] He was not alone, especially in the Metropolis, where the City actively petitioned for change. Shortly afterwards, in 1706, statute (5 Anne, c 6) gave the courts a discretion to sentence those who were clergied for a felony to between six months' and two years' imprisonment in addition to their branding.

Use of the new power varied across the country. In some places it was employed only intermittently in the 12 years after 1706. In others it was used much more frequently. For example, in Devonshire a quarter of clergied felons received a custodial sentence between 1707 and 1716.[5] It was also adopted enthusiastically at both county quarter sessions and assizes in East Anglia. It was employed in well over half of all clergyable cases that produced convictions at the Norfolk Quarter Sessions during

4. T. Nourse, *Campania Folix. Or, A Discourse of the Benefits and Improvements of Husbandry*, 1706, p. 229.
5. J. M. Beattie, *Crime and the Courts In England 1660–1800*, 1986, p. 499.

the 12-year period after 1706, though all were for the bare minimum of six months. Comparatively few clergied convicts anywhere in England, at either jury forum, received the full two years that the judges could have imposed. In part, this was because no provision was made to increase prison capacity, so that the space was simply not there to accommodate them. Typically, at the Norfolk Quarter Sessions held at Norwich on 11 July 1710, Robert Warren and three other men were convicted of grand larceny, clergied, burnt in the hand, and sent to hard labour at the house of correction at Wymondham for six months.

After the advent of the 1718 Transportation Act, which appeared to provide an effective secondary punishment for those accused of clergyable larceny, was cheaper to impose than imprisonment, and did not permit reoffending in England (because the convicts were banished), use of the 1706 act quickly became relatively rare. Nevertheless, it did not cease altogether, at least at the higher jury court. For example, in the decade after 1751, 19 people (including four women) were convicted of theft and clergied at the regional assizes rather than being transported for seven years under the 1718 act. Most were simply branded and discharged. However, three received short custodial sentences as well, including a woman who was sentenced to 18 months in a house of correction pursuant to the 1706 act. More typically, in 1755, after Thomas Steward was convicted of stealing goods worth 5s, he was branded and sentenced to six months in a house of correction.[6]

Such sentences continued to be passed occasionally in ensuing years and even increased during the 1770s, especially after political difficulties in America affected use of the 1718 act. At the Bury Assizes in 1774, three men received seven years' transportation for various offences of grand larceny, but another, William Smith, who had stolen five silver teaspoons and a pair of silver tongs at Stratford, was simply "branded, and is to be imprisoned six months."[7] He was one of three people at East Anglian assizes that year who were clergied after being convicted of grand larceny and also sentenced to six months' hard labour in a local

6. *St. James's Chronicle Or the British Evening Post*, 28–30 July 1768.
7. *Public Advertiser*, 9 August 1774.

house of correction under the 1706 act.[8] Some received longer sentences. In August 1778, Sarah Alden was convicted of grand larceny at the City and County of Norwich Assizes, after being convicted of stealing a shirt worth 2s, branded on the left hand, and sentenced to 12 months in a house of correction.[9]

Sections three and four of the Penitentiary Act of 1779 (19 Geo III, c 74), which abolished branding for clergied thieves in favour of whipping or a fine, expressly preserved the power to append a sentence of six months'-to-two-years' hard labour established under the 1706 statute. Thus, at the Norwich Assizes in July 1779, Samuel Redgrave, a labourer who had stolen £4 worth of clover seeds, was sentenced to a whipping in the city marketplace (in lieu of branding) and nine months in custody.[10] Similarly, at the Thetford Assizes in March 1784, George Barham was convicted of stealing stockings and sentenced to be whipped in gaol (in lieu of branding) and to serve six months' hard labour in a house of correction. At the same time, in the same forum, Robert Newsham was convicted of stealing 39s worth of goods from a dwelling-house (simple grand larceny) and received an identical disposal.[11]

Attractions of Penal Imprisonment

Despite the post-1718 decline in the use of penal imprisonment, several observers over ensuing decades, such as Bishop George Berkeley, proposed that it be employed more frequently, especially if it was to be combined with hard labour. It appeared to offer the possibility of a more graduated and proportionate system of punishment, yet one that, because it was highly visible, might be more effective than transportation at deterring potential felons from criminal activity. Others feared that sending felons to America was not sufficiently unattractive to deter offenders, especially after the mid-century, when shipping conditions improved and mortality rates on the voyage out fell sharply. Furthermore, the punishment was increasingly unpopular with the colonial authorities and most

8. TNA ASSI 33/5.
9. TNA ASSI 33/6.
10. TNA ASSI 33/6.
11. TNA ASSI 33/6.

Americans (if not the plantation owners) in Maryland, Virginia, and Pennsylvania, the most common convict destinations after 1718. (Prior to this time, many had been sent to the Caribbean). In 1770, noting that it had been suggested that convicts be sent to Africa or Asia instead, the *Ipswich Journal* recognized that America had originally been selected as a destination when it was much more sparsely populated, and that the "people of Maryland in America have complained for many years of being over-stocked by transported felons."[12]

The Rise of Penal Imprisonment

The use of imprisonment increased significantly during the 1770s. Although the statutory framework by which this occurred can be identified, the underlying motivation behind such a change is still a matter of considerable debate. Was it prompted by an increase in humanitarian idealism which itself had been influenced by Enlightenment thought and writers such as Beccaria (the traditional Whig interpretation)? Was it a desire to discipline and regulate a rapidly growing industrial working class in a more efficient and effective manner, as suggested, *inter alia*, by Michel Foucault? Or was it a simple response to the loss of transportation to America and other situational imperatives? A combination of some or all of these factors is possible, indeed likely.

Whatever the motivation, by the start of the 1770s a slow shift towards the use of imprisonment in place of transportation, especially for those accused of non-capital crimes against property, can be discerned. Initially, this was largely based on use of the 1706 act (see above). This development focussed attention on the country's various prisons and houses of correction. These institutions still lacked uniform standards of accommodation, security, and, more important to most contemporary observers, the space for extra inmates. There were various government initiatives aimed at improving this situation during the 1770s. A statute from 1773 required magistrates to ensure that clergymen were available to conduct divine service in county gaols (14 Geo III, c 59). Two more

12. *Ipswich Journal*, 12 May 1770.

acts the following year (14 Geo III, c 20 and 14 Geo III, c 59) relieved acquitted prisoners from having to pay gaolers' fees before their release (which freed a small amount of space), required local officials to see that prisons were clean and ventilated, and ordered that provision be made to promote personal hygiene among inmates.[13] This last requirement was not prompted purely by humanitarian motives. There were considerable fears that such institutions might be the source of typhus epidemics in the wider community—a danger throughout the era. Chief Baron Pengelly and several other lawyers, court officers, and local people had died at the Taunton Assizes in 1730 after catching the disease from defendants.[14] In the latter decades of the century, these concerns were sometimes as persuasive as Enlightenment penal theory in encouraging local reform.[15]

The use of domestic custody in some form necessarily received a huge fillip with the outbreak of the American Revolutionary War in 1775. Transportation became impossible, initially encouraging recourse to unusually lenient disposals. In 1777 Jeremiah Harvey was clergied and immediately released after being convicted at the Bury Assizes for stealing four valuable pigs.[16] This was still sometimes happening eight years later. In 1785 Judge William Ashurst recommended that John Jacob be given a free pardon after he was sentenced to seven years' transportation, following conviction at the Suffolk Assizes for a modest case of grand larceny. Ashurst cited the considerable logistical problems involved in transporting prisoners. Indeed, it had become impossible, with those so sentenced spending their time in prison or on the hulks (see below) awaiting a voyage that could not take place.[17] This situation would change only when Australia was selected as an alternative venue. Even then, the island continent could not take the majority of convicts sentenced to transportation during a time of rising population and convict numbers. This encouraged several observers and officials, such as William Eden, to

13. S. Devereaux, "The Making of the Penitentiary Act, 1775–1779," 1999, pp. 407–9.
14. *Weekly Journal Or British Gazetteer*, 18 April 1730.
15. See generally, P. Hardman, "Fear of Fever and the Limits of the Enlightenment: Selling Prison Reform in Late Eighteenth-century Gloucestershire," 2013, pp. 511–531.
16. TNA ASSI 33/6.
17. TNA HO 47/2/43. ff 153–157. Jacob's good previous character, repentance, and the fact that his neighbours were "not afraid" of his returning to the area were also influential in the decision.

promote incarceration as an alternative form of punishment for middle-ranking offences.

In 1775, faced by overflowing gaols, especially in London, where many of those to be transported from the provinces were marshalled, and initially as a short-term expedient, convicts were housed in the *Censor* and *Justitia* hulks on the Thames at Woolwich "as if in due course for transportation."[18] These vessels, and the many others that followed them, were dismasted and heavily modified former warships.[19] Their inmates were put to work in guarded groups dredging docks and building a new embankment during the day, returning to the vessels each night.[20]

In 1776 William Eden introduced a bill before Parliament to formally authorize what was already taking place and produce a long-term solution to the "inconveniences" occasioned by the American war. It provided that any convict who was liable to be transported could be sent to a hulk instead. The bill attracted some criticism. Several observers thought that such punishment smacked of slavery and was not suitable for "freeborn" Englishmen. Against this, its supporters argued that the new system had some advantages over transportation. Those so sentenced could not buy their freedom on arrival in America (as occurred with wealthy transports) or, if skilled or well-educated, be "cosseted" by their new masters in easy positions.[21] It was approved by Parliament in May of the same year.

Under section one of the 1776 "Hulks Act" (16 Geo III, c 43), also known as the "Hard Labour Act," males who could have been sentenced to transportation for grand larceny might, instead, be sentenced, at the court's discretion, to hard labour in a hulk for between three and seven years. This would be spent dredging sand and gravel on the Thames. Under the same statute, those who were capitally convicted could be reprieved from execution on condition of hard labour in a hulk for a maximum of ten years (it was usually seven in practice) in lieu of transportation. Inmates were to be fed on bread or "coarse or inferior foods." More positively, their sentences could be shortened if they showed signs

---

18. S. Devereaux, "The Making of the Penitentiary Act, 1775–1779," 1999, p. 414.
19. *London Evening Post*, 16–18 July 1776.
20. *Daily Advertiser*, 11 June 1777.
21. *Gazetteer and New Daily Advertiser*, 28 May 1776.

of reformation, and they were to be given between 40s and £5 on discharge, depending on their conduct when incarcerated.[22]

The new provisions were quickly employed in East Anglia. In July 1776 John Cheny was convicted at the Ipswich Quarter Sessions of stealing hens in Wetheringsett. He was sentenced to "get sand and gravel and cleanse the river Thames for 7 years."[23] In March 1778, Robert Lowe was slightly more fortunate, after he was convicted of attempting to rob James Horslee of Melford on the highway, and sentenced to five years' labouring on the Thames.[24] (Both were clergyable offences.) More seriously, in 1777 George Rudrum, a 23-year-old labourer, was capitally convicted of theft in a dwelling-house at the Norfolk Assizes in 1777 but reprieved on condition of seven years on the river.[25]

Such disposals necessitated that formal arrangements be made to transfer provincial prisoners from their convicting counties, in East Anglia as much as anywhere else. Thus, in November 1781, those sentenced to hard labour on the Thames at the Norfolk Assizes a few months earlier were conveyed from Norwich Castle gaol and the city gaol to Woolwich.[26] This process sometimes occasioned administrative difficulties. In 1778 six convicts were brought from Norwich to the "new gaol" (King's Bench Prison) in Southwark, prior to going aboard hulks to work on the Thames. Unfortunately, a problem with their paperwork meant that they were turned away.[27]

Life and work on the hulks was gruelling, requiring considerable physical robustness. In 1780 it was noted that Thomas Galloway, who had been convicted of stealing a gelding at the Thetford Assizes in March 1779, and ordered to hard labour on the Thames, could not be "removed without danger of his life, being in a deep consumption, [so] was ordered to remain in custody."[28] Furthermore, such a disposal was open only to men. As a result, the 1776 statute also allowed both convicted females and those males who were not physically capable of the heavy work required

22. Ibid., 17 May 1776.
23. *Ipswich Journal*, 20 July 1776.
24. Ibid., 28 March 1778.
25. TNA ASSI 33/6.
26. *Norfolk Chronicle*, 1 December 1781.
27. *Gazetteer and New Daily Advertiser*, 18 May 1778.
28. *Norfolk Chronicle*, 12 August 1780.

on the river to be sentenced to up to three years' imprisonment and (in theory) hard labour in a local house of correction. In practice, it seems that this disposal was also used for those men who were not thought so "bad" as to warrant working on the Thames while living in a hulk.

For example, at the Thetford Assizes in 1782, Edward Bennet was sentenced to three years' hard labour in a house of correction for stealing six pigs in Scoulton. On the same occasion, John Mitchell received a similar sentence for stealing 36 rabbits from a warren in Beachamwell, as did George Riches, for taking three silver watches from a shop in Coltishall.[29] However, and perhaps in light of the carceral capacity in the area, not all such convicts received the full sentence potentially available, especially if their crimes were not particularly serious. In 1788 William Ford was sentenced to two years in a house of correction for stealing 3s from a woman in Cavendish.[30] Almost 20 years later, John Woodgate received just a year for stealing a bushel of his master's barley in Sudbury.[31] By then such disposals meant that the penal distinction between petty theft and grand larceny was becoming attenuated.

As a result of these developments, three kinds of custodial sentences were given to those convicted of grand larceny at the regional assizes during 1777. Six were clergied, branded, and sent to a house of correction for six or 12 months pursuant to the 1706 act. Two were sentenced to up to three years' hard labour in a house of correction under the 1776 act. Six more were sent to hard labour on the Thames for periods of three or four years under the same statute.[32]

The second bill that Eden proposed to Parliament in this area was not passed until three years after the Hulks Act. The 1779 Penitentiary Act extended the use of prison hulks and established new terms of confinement. Offenders liable to seven years' transportation could be sentenced to not less than one or more than five years on a hulk, and offenders sentenced to transportation for 14 years could have their terms commuted to seven years on board such a vessel. By 1784 the impact of these new types of custodial sentence had produced a crude, de facto

29. Ibid., 23 March 1782.
30. *Bury and Norwich Post*, 26 March 1788.
31. Ibid., 22 January 1806.
32. TNA ASSI 33/6.

division in punishment for people convicted of simple grand larceny. Those who were male, healthy, and accused of relatively serious forms of theft, a total of five men (two of them jointly charged) according to the gaol calendar, were "sent to River Thames and 2 yrs hard labour on a vessel." Thus, a 40-year-old labourer named William Smith received this disposal for stealing a box and cash valued at more than £20 from John Earthy. Perhaps more surprisingly, 50-year-old Thomas Hearne was sentenced to the same punishment for stealing 60 pounds of honey and beehives worth just over £1. Anthony Heedham, a 23-year-old labourer, who had initially been charged with a capital form of housebreaking, but was merely convicted of stealing goods worth 4s 6d, also went to the Thames for two years, probably because the trial judge concluded that the verdict was a case of pious perjury rather than a true reflection of the gravity of his crime.[33]

By contrast, women, the frail, and those who had committed less serious forms of grand larceny were sentenced to shorter periods of labour in a local house of correction. Typically, Maria Gay, who had been convicted at the Norfolk Assizes in Norwich, received six months in such an establishment for stealing wood, blankets, and sheets. Mary Haslup received the same disposal from the City of Norwich Assizes, for the theft of ribbons.

Significantly, over the whole of 1784 only one man in the entire region was formally sentenced to seven years' transportation for larceny. Robert Livsey was convicted of stealing £5 worth of yarn at the City of Norwich Assizes. Why he should have been sentenced to this punishment is not obvious; his offence was serious, but not the worst imaginable, and he would in any event be kept in prison (or a hulk) as he could not be transported anywhere at that time (something that explains the paucity of such disposals).[34] An act passed in 1784 expressly allowed convicts under sentence of transportation to pass their entire terms on board hulks.

Taken together, these developments meant that in the final decades of the century there was a decisive national shift towards the use of imprisonment as a primary punishment, whether de jure or de facto.

33. TNA ASSI 33/6 and ASSI 33/7.
34. Ibid.

The number of those who were incarcerated in England increased substantially, doubling between 1770 and 1800 (a much greater increase than can be explained by the rising population), and this was reflected in East Anglia.

Carceral Conditions

Imprisonment was a dangerous, squalid, and corrupting experience throughout the era, though conditions improved significantly towards the end of the century. For much of the period JPs and high sheriffs, although theoretically responsible for their local gaols, rarely put into effect the many laws giving them power to repair, regulate, and inspect them. Reluctant to assume the onerous and unpleasant tasks of managing carceral institutions, they appointed prison masters or "keepers" who ran their establishments on a quasi-commercial basis, selling alcohol and other commodities to the inmates.[35] As a result, for much of the era prisons were largely unsegregated, with civil debtors, those on remand prior to trial, convicts awaiting punishment, males and females often mixing together. Those with friends or money could sustain a life of relative comfort while the poor suffered badly.

This state of affairs was widely known, throughout the century, not discovered at its end. At the start of the period, one observer referred to the "Scandalous Wickedness and Corruption of Prisons." He felt that their keepers were usually infamous men and the establishments they presided over sanctuaries for villains.[36] A few years later, another complained that inmates were exposed to drunkenness, debauchery, and "uncleanness, even such as are not to be named among Christians."[37] During the 1730s William Hay introduced several parliamentary bills for the construction of local prisons. However, it was only late in the period that such knowledge started to occasion serious concern in the wider country.

35. J. Willis, "Transportation Versus Imprisonment in Eighteenth- and Nineteenth-century Britain," 2005, p. 186.
36. Anon, *Hanging, Not Punishment Enough*, 1701, p. 1.
37. Anon, *A Charitable Visit to the Prisons*, 1709, p. 3 and p. 6.

Prisoners had high mortality rates. Coroners investigated all deaths, however caused, that occurred within their walls. This was primarily done to ensure that the death was not the result of the "duress and ill usage of the gaoler."[38] Such brutality was a real risk. For example, in October 1715 an inquest into the death of Henry Munford, a prisoner in the common gaol in Norwich, concluded that Peter Harrold, the late keeper of the gaol, had struck, abused, and mortally wounded him. A Latin copy of the inquest was prepared to allow a prosecution at assizes.[39]

Nevertheless, far more commonly, inquests concluded that inmate deaths were the result of disease. It was regularly claimed that many more English prisoners died from sickness than were executed, even though doctors and surgeons would attend the ailing and injured and also had some role in supervising standards of cleanliness and general health amongst the inmates. They were normally local medical practitioners working on a part-time basis, appointed and paid for by the county justices sitting at quarter sessions.[40]

In Norwich, which had both county and city gaols, along with a bridewell and other custodial establishments, numerous prisoners died from a multiplicity of medical conditions. For example, in the 12 months from January 1689 to December 1689, thirteen inquests were heard on prisoners who had expired in the common gaol alone. Of these, eleven were civil debtors, and not even suspected of crimes. Fatal illnesses cited in the inquests included scurvy, dropsy, and consumption.[41] Typhus was particularly common in prisons, where it was known as "gaol fever," as a result of poorly nourished inmates being huddled together in dirty and unventilated cells in which lice (the primary carrier of the pathogen) easily spread. In June 1769, when Simon Hewitt, a 40-year-old vagrant, died in the St Andrew bridewell in Norwich, it was noted that the vermin he had acquired there had brought on a wasting disease.[42]

38. G. Jacob, *Every Man His Own Lawyer: Or, A Summary of the Laws of England in a New and Instructive Method*, 1739, p. 396.
39. NRO NCR Case 6a/4/48/1 and 2.
40. S. Irvine, *Surgeons and Apothecaries in Suffolk: 1750–1830,* 2011, p. 197.
41. NRO NCR Case 6a/1/24–25, 28, 30, 32, 34, 36–37, 39–42, 44.
42. NRO NCR Case 6a/9 /119.

The deaths of inmates often clustered together when a severe outbreak of disease took hold. In March 1731 John Dover, a 23-year-old prisoner in the Norwich common gaol, died after being afflicted with a fever for about a fortnight. Less than a week later Robert Bear, a 40-year-old man in the same establishment, died in identical circumstances. Other inmates died from longer-lasting conditions. In the same month and prison, Thomas Tewke, aged 51, expired after being in a "consumptive condition" for a considerable time. At Bury in 1763 it was noted that John Culling, who had been capitally convicted of sodomy, had fallen sick and "lies dangerously ill with small pox."[43] (He recovered to be reprieved from execution). Inmates released from prisons, whether through acquittal or discharge for some other reason, might carry disease home with them into the civil population, sometimes creating localised epidemics.[44]

For much of the century, criminal inmates were heavily dependent on a basic allowance of a penny or twopenny loaf a day. This was the only food supplied to those accused of crimes as of right, at public expense. Fortunately, this meagre allowance was supplemented by charitable donations from private individuals, public bodies, and officials. Thus, in 1763 the poor prisoners in Bury gaol returned their "most hearty thanks" to Sir William Bunbury after he sent them 2 guineas.[45] Such gifts were made fairly frequently, especially during the festive season. A selection of cases for Norwich alone, over a two-year period, is suggestive of their importance.

In January 1781 the prisoners in the Castle gaol thanked an unknown benefactor who had given them 64 pounds of beef and a small amount of bread and money, another unknown philanthropist who had donated 1 guinea's worth of bread, and yet another who had given them 38 threepenny loaves and a pint of beer each. These charitable donations were, apparently, a great comfort to a "number of distressed objects of pity and compassion."[46] During the summer of 1781, the Norfolk Assizes grand jury granted the prisoners held in the Norwich city gaol £2 2s. This was spent by the prison governor on bread, beef, and beer for each inmate,

43. *Ipswich Journal*, 2 April 1763.
44. G. O. Paul, *A Second Address on the Subject of a Reform of Prisons*, 1783, pp. 6–9
45. *Ipswich Journal*, 12 November 1763.
46. *Norfolk Chronicle*, 20 January 1781.

and "proved a great relief to many individuals." At the same time, the prisoners for the county who were being held in the nearby Castle gaol were given £1 15s, which was divided equally among them.[47] A few months later, those in the Norwich city gaol returned their thanks to John Morse, the mayor, for providing each of them with a Christmas dinner of beef and plum pudding, a threepenny loaf, and a quart of beer. They also thanked two unknown benefactors, one of whom left them half a guinea, and the other 7s 6d.[48] In January the following year, the poor prisoners in the Castle gaol also expressed their heartfelt thanks for 58 twopenny loaves that had been sent from St Stephen's parish "being the first gift this winter."[49] At the end of 1782 the inmates in the same establishment thanked an unknown benefactor for £1 1s that had been given to them on Christmas Day, and "for the hot dinner and a quart of strong beer each, being 47 in number."[50]

Conditions on the hulks were even worse than in terrestrial prisons, with mouldy food and an absence of bedding being commonplace. They produced particularly high mortality rates, especially in their early years. A quarter of inmates died within the first 20 months of the hulks' existence. All too typically, it was noted in 1781 that Thomas Rumney, the noted horse thief, sent from the Norwich city gaol to the *Justitia* hulk at Woolwich, had died within a few months of arrival.[51] Incarceration in the vessels certainly did not reform inmates. By 1783 the first prisoners sentenced to transportation who had spent their entire seven years in a hulk (if they received no reduction) were being released. In June of that year the *Ipswich Journal* suggested, albeit not entirely convincingly, that newly discharged men had perpetrated many recent murders and robberies in the region. Nevertheless, the hulks ultimately lasted for 80 years as Parliament regularly renewed the 1776 act and even extended its scope. Conditions improved slightly after the first decade.

47. Ibid., 11 August 1781.
48. *Norfolk Chronicle*, 29 December 1781.
49. Ibid., 5 January 1782.
50. Ibid., 28 December 1782.
51. Ibid., 8 December 1781.

Prison Security

For most of the eighteenth century, prisons were only casually and indirectly supervised by their keepers and were usually situated in buildings that were not originally built as carceral institutions. As a result, they were often very insecure. Escape attempts were frequent, and a considerable number were successful, in East Anglia as elsewhere in the country.

To counter this risk, most prisons had dungeons that were separate from their main wards, and which might be used to secure high-risk inmates, such as those awaiting execution. A large number of inmates were also fettered with heavy ankle irons, often attached to large weights, to enhance security. Some high-risk prisoners were even "double ironed," with weights on both ankles. These were difficult to remove. In 1796 two convicts managed to escape from Norwich gaol by using blankets to lower themselves from the prison wall onto the roof of the neighbouring shirehall. One was captured a few days later, as "he had not been able to get [rid of] his irons."[52] However, they were certainly not foolproof. In 1751 some inmates in Ipswich gaol successfully sawed through their chains; they were discovered by a keeper, then "doubly ironed and closely confined" to prevent any recurrence.[53] A few years later, several prisoners in Norwich gaol attempted to escape with the help of a fellow inmate who was a whitesmith (tin worker) by trade, and who successfully removed their fetters while they were still incarcerated.[54]

Various techniques were employed to get beyond prison walls. Several men used physical violence to break out. In the early 1730s, James Macdowal, a young Irish highwayman, was committed to Norwich gaol. As he and two companions were walking about the gaol, a "Turnkey going to open the Door, they knock'd him down, and took the Keys from him, and let themselves out (before any-body could come to the Turnkey's Assistance) so that they got entirely off."[55] Less successfully, in 1736, a group of six felons in Norwich Castle attacked the governor and one of the turnkeys. They attempted to wrestle the keys from the former while

52. *True Briton (1793)*, 12 September 1796.
53. *Ipswich Journal*, 21 December 1751.
54. *Lloyd's Evening Post and British Chronicle*, 11–14 August 1758.
55. See Ordinary's Account, 11 February 1734: OA17340211.

threatening to murder him. However, on this occasion, the governor kept hold of the internal door to the prison, despite receiving several wounds. Assistance eventually arrived, and the convicts were recaptured and heavily ironed.[56]

Other felons tried to climb out of their prisons. In October 1736 Samuel Sawyer, awaiting transportation, escaped from Ipswich gaol with the "help of a rope thrown over the wall." He was recaptured the following year at Filby, in Norfolk, and returned to the same establishment.[57] When Gibbon Houghton attempted to break out a few days before his execution at Norwich in 1768, he made a breach in his cell wall and got onto the roof of a building adjacent to the prison yard, but was unable to fix a rope to the battlements that would allow him to climb into a neighbouring road. He then came back down, covered himself in muck, and hid in the prison vaults, hoping to avoid detection, but some incarcerated debtors saw him and alerted the keeper. A man with a pitchfork was sent down to prod the muck, forcing Houghton to reveal himself. Bizarrely, his cell was "reckoned the strongest in England."[58]

Other inmates tried to tunnel their way to freedom. Amongst them was Thomas Rumney, incarcerated at the Norwich city gaol in 1780. He was held in solitary confinement, chained to a post. Even so, he managed to cut off his irons, make a hole through a plank in the cell, and then burrowed underground for 16 feet, planning to come out next to a grocer's shop. However, he was missed before he emerged, and labourers were set to work to dig him out. After they had been excavating for five hours, Rumney called out, by which time he was "almost suffocated for want of air."[59] Only a month later, at the same institution, a group of men who were awaiting trial combined with four convicted highwaymen to dig under the castle foundations. Parson Woodforde later noted that they "very near completed an escape."[60] Even so, they were captured and "double ironed and yoked."[61]

---

56. *Daily Gazetteer* (London Edition), 4 January 1737.
57. *Common Sense Or The Englishman's Journal*, 2 April 1737.
58. *Public Advertiser*, 26 April 1768.
59. *Norfolk Chronicle*, 18 November 1780.
60. J. Beresford (ed.), *The Diary of a Country Parson, 1758–1802*, 1978, p. 117.
61. *Norfolk Chronicle*, 23 December 1780.

Some escape tools were improvised. Robert Bird was caught in Ipswich Gaol in 1735 with a "knife notched like a saw."[62] Others were brought in from outside. In 1737 Katherine Woods was arrested for smuggling in the implements used by a group of felons in Norwich Castle to remove their fetters.[63] In 1779, after two convicts awaiting execution broke through the wall of their cell in Ipswich gaol and escaped, Luke and James Spooner were arrested for furnishing them with various chisels, saws, hammers, and files. (They were both acquitted at trial.)[64] By contrast, at the Thetford Assizes in 1756, William Culham was convicted of assisting his brother escape by conveying him to Norwich after he broke out of the local gaol. He was sentenced to seven years' transportation, but this was later respited by order of the Secretary of State.[65] (The following year he was pardoned on condition of enlisting in the army).[66]

It was unusual for a woman to escape, but a tiny number managed to do so. At the Bury Assizes in August 1800, Margaret Catchpole was convicted of breaking out of Ipswich gaol the previous March. She had been confined there for three years while awaiting transportation for horse theft. Catchpole had used a clothesline to climb the 22-foot wall of the prison. She was sentenced to death once more but, again, reprieved before the judge left town.[67]

The frequent willingness of fellow inmates to alert the authorities to escapes might appear surprising. However, this was expressly encouraged by the provision of tangible rewards, and so provided an extra layer of security. Most important, exposing such breakouts was regularly cited as a ground for clemency in inmate petitions for reprieve from execution, transportation, or imprisonment, as prisoners well knew. Inevitably, currying favour in this manner had its risks. In 1783 several felons led by a footpad from King's Lynn attempted to escape from Norwich Castle by breaking through their cell wall. They were discovered and chained to the floor. Subsequently, another prisoner, whom they suspected had

62. *Daily Courant*, 22 April 1735.
63. *Daily Gazetteer*, 4 January 1737.
64. *Public Advertiser*, April 13, 1779. TNA ASSI 33/6.
65. TNA ASSI 33/3.
66. *London Evening Post*, 10–13 September 1757.
67. *Bury and Norwich Post*, 6 August 1800.

revealed their escape attempt, was badly wounded in the head with a stick; he had then to "be kept by himself, to prevent their murdering him."[68]

As these cases suggest, escaping was not without considerable physical danger. In 1783 two men, one of them awaiting transportation and the other trial, broke out of their cells in the Norwich city gaol and scaled the prison walls using ropes. Although they got away, it was thought that they had been severely wounded by the "hooks upon the top of the wall, as a great quantity of blood was apparent both on the ground and wall."[69]

As with many aspects of the eighteenth-century criminal justice system, financial incentives were used both to prevent escapes and to recover escapees. The keeper or governor of a prison that "lost" a prisoner might be fined heavily. This encouraged diligence in securing them and attempts at recapturing those who did get away. For example, in February 1741 John Ablett and Francis Knights broke out of Ipswich gaol. The keeper, Jonas Edrington, immediately published descriptions of the two men and their clothes and offered £5 a head to anyone who recaptured them.[70] Similarly, in February 1772 5 guineas were offered for the recapture of Harvey Harrison, a bargeman who had been incarcerated for stealing a sheep, after he broke out of Bury gaol.[71] More dramatically, in April 1779 a publican challenged Ronald Hoy and William Lay after they escaped from the same institution. They overpowered him and fled, but he quickly informed the prison of the breakout. The governor of the gaol immediately commandeered a horse and set off after the two men, capturing both with local assistance.[72]

Reform

Although, by the middle of the eighteenth century, many thought it necessary that a "thorough Reformation be made in our gaols," major reform would wait until the final decades of the era.[73] Conditions slowly

68. *Norfolk Chronicle*, 9 August 1783.
69. Ibid., 11 October 1783.
70. *London Evening Post*, 7–10 February 1741.
71. *Ipswich Journal*, 29 February 1772; *Ipswich Journal*, 28 March 1772.
72. *Public Advertiser*, 13 April 1779.
73. C. Jones, *Some Methods Proposed Towards Putting a Stop to the Flagrant Crimes of Murder, Robbery, and Perjury*, 1752, p. 11.

improved after the early 1770s. Under the permissive regime that was established by the 1779 act, more than 60 new penal institutions were either built or converted throughout the country in the last 20 years of the eighteenth century alone.[74] During the 35 years after 1780, most English county gaols were rebuilt or remodelled, in East Anglia as elsewhere.[75] After visiting Suffolk in 1784, François de la Rochefoucauld even thought, albeit with considerable exaggeration, that prisons "are very healthy in England."[76]

Much would depend on the character of the keeper and the ethos that he or she instilled in their establishment. (The keeper of the Bury gaol in 1794 was female).[77] Thus, in the 1780s Howard thought that the Norwich city prison was still in a poor condition: "The gaol very dirty: the rules not enforced. No proper separation of the sexes." By contrast, at about the same time, he noted that its counterpart at Ipswich "as usual was very clean."[78]

The regime at the Wymondham bridewell in Norfolk during the 1780s is indicative of a "reformed" prison. Its improvement was largely the work of Sir Thomas Beevor, an important county JP. The establishment had two wings, each containing 13 cells. When John Howard visited, there were 12 male and four female inmates. Each prisoner had a space with a bed and work materials to beat or spin hemp. The prison was provided with an infirmary and a chapel. It was clean, and no prisoners were fettered or ironed. Breakfast consisted of a penny loaf of 13 ounces in weight. Dinner varied, but was largely made up of staples. For example, it might be another loaf of bread, potatoes, or boiled peas. However, on Sunday the prisoners had ox cheek. Only water (rather than ale) was permitted to inmates. Howard thought that the diet was inadequate for men engaged in hard labour. Even so, he felt the prison was likely to reform the idle and dissolute and provided one of the "best examples of the proper

74. P. Hardman, *The Origins of Late Eighteenth-century Prison Reform in England,* 2007, p. 41.
75. D. Eastwood, *Government and Community in the English Provinces, 1700–1870,* 1997, p. 50.
76. N. Scarfe, *A Frenchman's Year in Suffolk,* 2011, p. 81.
77. Anon, *Last Dying Speech and Full Confession of Benjamin Brett,* 1794, pp. 1–2.
78. J. Howard, *An Account of the Present State of the Prisons and Houses of Correction in the Norfolk Circuit,* 1789, p. 18 and p. 23.

management of a house of correction." Howard also felt that the other bridewells in Norfolk were improving, if still behind Wymondham.[79]

The new approach and attitudes towards incarceration, and an indication of the "old regime" they replaced, were reflected in the *General Regulations for the Government of the New Goal* [sic], *At Ipswich* that were drawn up at the Suffolk Quarter Sessions in February 1791, even if these rules were not always strictly implemented. They stated that every "denomination" of prisoner was to be kept "entirely separate" from the others, as required by a then recent statute (24 Geo III, c 54). Thus civil debtors, those accused of misdemeanours or suspected of felonies, convicts, and individuals preparing to turn Crown evidence, would be held apart from each other, as would men and women. The gaoler was not to take "garnish" or fees from new inmates or allow other prisoners to do so. He was also to make sure that the county allowance of bread was correct and that well-behaved inmates received half a pound of beef and broth on Sundays. Anything brought in for prisoners from outside was to be inspected by the turnkeys. Fresh water was to be provided in jugs and washing tubs, and slopping-out buckets emptied, on a daily basis. The wives and children of prisoners would not be allowed to sleep overnight in the establishment. The gaoler was not to sell liquor to the prisoners, while wine and spirits were only to be brought in for medicinal purposes. The gaoler was also required to inspect the cells every day and to be particularly careful that those awaiting execution were limited to milk and water, rather than alcoholic beverages. Visitors motivated by "curiosity" would no longer be allowed to see prisoners for a money payment. There was also to be better documentation and more exercise for each inmate. Those awaiting trial would also be allowed to wear their own clothes until conviction and then dressed in a prison uniform of yellow and blue. Convicts would face work of the "hardest and most servile kind, in which drudgery is chiefly required." Local JPs and the high sheriff would inspect the prison on a regular basis.[80]

---

79. Ibid., pp. 15–17.
80. Anon, *General Regulations For the Government of the New Goal* [sic], *At Ipswich*, 1791, p. 1 and pp. 16–30.

Penal Enlistment

Finding sufficient volunteers for military and naval forces was a constant problem during times of conflict. In the eighteenth century England (and, after the 1707 Act of Union, Britain) was involved in regular warfare, and so forced to expand (and then demobilise) its army and navy very rapidly. In these circumstances, recruiting convicts had obvious attractions. In wartime, enlistment in the army or navy could be made a condition of reprieve from capital punishment; it could also be allowed as an alternative to seven years' transportation for a clergyable felony, or even in lieu of the punishment normally imposed for a summary offence. In other situations enlistment could be offered instead of formal prosecution.

Penal recruitment was common in East Anglia, throughout the era. For example, in January 1706 Devereaux Edgar and two other Suffolk magistrates sat at the White Horse Inn in Ipswich, pursuant to statute, to recruit soldiers. They had sent out requests to local high constables and, via them, parish constables, to bring in suitable men. Amongst them were some volunteers. However, there were also men taken from prison, whether undergoing punishment or awaiting trial. In the latter situation, where a man was diverted from the justice system altogether, it seems that regard was often had to the view of the complainant before allowing them to enlist in lieu of prosecution.[81] Such recruits included 35-year-old Daniel Lamb from Barton, who had been "laid into gaol for stealing hoggs." Another was Robert Carr, a man of almost 50, who was in custody for fathering a bastard that he could not support, "the parish consenting & remitting the charge against him."[82]

Three-quarters of a century later, in 1782, John Sones, who had been capitally convicted of horse theft at the Bury Assizes, was respited from execution by the trial judge on condition that he serve the King on the coast of Africa or in the East Indies.[83] In the same year, a man who had been tried at the same forum for burglary in Melford, "being found

81. See for example the case of Francis Wells in Cambridgeshire, CRO Q/So 6, p. 228.
82. SRO QS 347.96, *The Devereux Edgar Notebook*, transcribed by S. R. Schofield, 1956, vol.1, p. 130.
83. *Norfolk Chronicle*, 27 July 1782.

guilty of larceny only was permitted to enlist as a soldier."[84] (As this comment suggests, serious felonies were sometimes excluded from such a disposal). At about the same time, after James Castleton was sentenced to one year's imprisonment for stealing a coat, he was given the alternative of going for a soldier.[85] At the Bury Assizes in 1808, Henry Butcher was discharged for cutting out the tongue of a horse on condition that he entered the Marine Corps.[86]

Although penal enlistment was especially likely if it entailed service in a foreign theatre, many men would be released to locally encamped units. Thus, in 1780 a capitally convicted horse thief in Norwich received a pardon from the King on condition that he enlisted in the 4th Regiment of Foot, which was then quartered in the city.[87] Some such cases may have involved an element of bargaining in advance. In July 1799 Parson Woodforde noted that a servant who had stolen grain from a farmer had pleaded guilty at the Norfolk Assizes and "is to go for a soldier."[88]

Even the lower jury court sometimes imposed this penalty, in lieu of transportation, where they dealt with a clergyable felony (as they often did later in the century). For example, in 1781 John Pike was convicted of stealing a watch at the Norfolk Quarter Sessions and handed over to a press gang.[89] At the same forum, the following year, John Barnard received an identical disposal after he was convicted of grand larceny, as did John Waters, for stealing rabbits.[90]

Unsurprisingly, the process of recruiting offenders did not always run smoothly. Some of the men were of very bad character, occasioned problems while in the service, and discouraged honest volunteers from joining. In addition, it was often easy for men to desert while in Britain, despite the draconian punishments meted out for doing so by courts martial. These included execution by firing squad or, more commonly, a ferocious flogging.[91] For example, at Bury in 1760 John Heard of the

84. *Ipswich Journal*, 2 November 1782.
85. *Norfolk Chronicle*, 27 July 1782.
86. *Bury and Norwich Post*, 17 August 1808.
87. *Norfolk Chronicle*, 18 November 1780.
88. J. Beresford (ed.), *The Diary of a Country Parson, 1758–1802*, 1978, p. 38.
89. *Norfolk Chronicle*, 28 April 1781.
90. Ibid., 23 March 1782.
91. *Ipswich Journal*, 22 August 1741.

Western Battalion of the Norfolk Militia (not even a regular unit), then quartered in the town, received 200 lashes for desertion and was ceremonially drummed out with a halter round his neck.[92]

Many recruited offenders not only abandoned the colours but also quickly returned to a life of crime, often in their native counties.[93] For example, Jeremiah Theobald, who was eventually executed for the murder of Frances Phillips in 1782, had been tried for burglary at the Bury Assizes on an earlier occasion. After being convicted of the lesser offence of simple grand larceny, he had been permitted to "enlist for a soldier" in lieu of any other punishment. Evidently, he had quickly deserted to commit much more serious offences.[94]

Even those convicts who enlisted as sailors could re-offend quite quickly, despite being quartered on board ship. In 1783 Thomas Flowers was examined on suspicion of breaking open a grocer's warehouse in Norwich. Flowers had earlier been convicted at the Norfolk assizes of stealing a large quantity of cheese, but his sentence was respited on condition of serving on a Royal Navy ship, "from which he soon returned."[95] To reduce this risk, it was thought desirable that the convict be marched under guard directly to a warship. Even this was not always successful. In 1782 John Ewston, who had been convicted of various highway robberies and received the King's pardon on condition of serving as a soldier in the Indies, was sworn in and put on board an East Indiaman. Despite this, he was arrested shortly afterwards having been found at large in King's Lynn.[96]

---

92. *Ipswich Journal*, 16 August 1760.
93. P. King "War as a Judicial Resource. Press Gangs and Prosecution Rates 1740–1830," 2002, pp. 97–116.
94. *Norfolk Chronicle*, 2 November 1782.
95. Ibid., 22 November 1783.
96. Ibid., 16 March 1782.

Corporal Punishment

The Pillory and Stocks

The pillory was a wooden yoke erected on a post, with holes to secure the head and hands of the person undergoing punishment. During the eighteenth century it was used to punish, *inter alia*, those who committed lesser types of fraud, perjury, and attempted sodomy or rape ("assault with intent to rape").[97] Because it was used to deal with what were considered to be relatively minor crimes (misdemeanours) it was often imposed at quarter sessions. Frequently it was combined with short custodial or fiscal penalties, especially later in the century. For example, in 1752 John Grice was convicted of attempted sodomy at the Ipswich Quarter Sessions and sentenced to stand in the pillory for an hour at mid-day and to serve three months' imprisonment.[98] In 1783 William Smith, a swindler convicted of obtaining £12 worth of goods from a pair of linen drapers in Norwich, was sentenced to be pilloried on Castle Hill in the city, then to serve 12 months' imprisonment, before standing once more in the pillory with a paper fixed over his head denoting his crime.[99]

In practice it seems that the sentences of some of those being pilloried were abbreviated and occasionally even remitted altogether, if only on medical grounds. The number of people being pilloried also fell swiftly in the last quarter of the era, although use of the punishment continued into the following century; in 1815 Joseph Sharpe was sentenced to the pillory in Haverhill (Suffolk) for perjury.[100] After 1816 use of the pillory was restricted to this crime or subornation (persuading someone to commit perjury). It was not used at all after 1830, and the punishment was formally abolished in 1837.

The choice of timing for John Grice's period in the apparatus was deliberate. Exposure to public shame was an inherent part of the punishment, one that was encouraged by the authorities. As the social reformer Francis Place later noted, the hours immediately after mid-day saw more

97. H. Misson, *Memoirs and Observations in his Travels over England*, 1719, p. 218.
98. *Ipswich Journal*, 29 August 1752.
99. *Norfolk Chronicle*, 11 October 1783.
100. H. R. Barker, *History of, and Guide to, Bury St. Edmund's*, 2008, p. 88.

people in the streets. However, the popular role in proceedings went much further than mere observation. Crimes that were viewed harshly by the populace (or "mob") could produce an extremely aggressive response from spectators, with rubbish and even stones being thrown at those being pilloried. It was largely for this reason that Place was to remember it as a "barbarous punishment."[101] Typically, when Abraham Hearn and Ann Cran were exposed on the pillory at Chelmsford in Essex for sexual assault, both were pelted with rotten eggs as well as being subjected to a torrent of verbal abuse.[102] Similarly, when Peter Sparks was pilloried at Ipswich in 1769, he experienced "severe treatment by the populace." A soldier watching the events lost an eye after being accidentally struck by a misdirected potato.[103]

However, crowds were usually fairly discriminating about such abuse. Crimes that attracted less social opprobrium, or whose perpetrators manifest repentance, might attract more benign treatment from onlookers. A clear illustration of this phenomenon can be seen when Thomas Denny and Thomas Allen were pilloried at Norwich in July 1803. They had been convicted at the city quarter sessions a week earlier for falsely conspiring against another man from the city (probably some form of blackmail based on a spurious allegation of homosexuality).[104] An inscription was placed over their heads detailing their crime. Allen wept bitterly, but Denny enraged the crowd by smiling at them. They ignored Allen and threw rotten eggs and potatoes at Denny until he appeared to faint. On the advice of a medical observer, and the order of the attending sheriff, Denny was taken out of the pillory and conducted to the gaol, where, after being examined by several doctors, he was deemed to be in a fit state to be returned to the apparatus. However, all efforts to put him back in the pillory proved ineffectual; he lay over it until his hour was finished, amidst the execrations of the enraged multitude.[105] Interestingly, when Denny was initially taken out of the apparatus, the crowd

101. *Description of the Pillory, From the Diary of Social Reformer Francis Place*, 1829, BL Shelfmark add27826f172.
102. *Bury and Norwich Post*, 1 July 1807.
103. *Ipswich Journal*, 15 April 1769.
104. *The Bury and Norwich Post: Or, Suffolk, Norfolk, Essex, and Cambridge Advertiser*, 20 July 1803.
105. *The Bury and Norwich Post: Or, Suffolk, Norfolk, Essex, and Cambridge Advertiser*, 27 July 1803.

demanded that Allen, with whom they appeared to sympathise, should also be taken down. (At the end of the designated hour, both men were sent to the bridewell to undergo two years' imprisonment).[106]

Whatever the crime for which a man was pilloried, the quality of his experience in the apparatus would also depend on what steps the authorities were willing to take to protect him. Thus, in April 1756 a Mr Wye was pilloried in Ipswich. For the first 15 minutes, he was so well-guarded by the sheriff's officers that "few things were thrown at him." However, he was pelted "very smartly" with fruit and eggs for the remaining 45 minutes after these men were withdrawn.[107]

Time in the stocks, which held people by the ankles rather than the head and wrists, was usually imposed as a punishment for drunkenness or failing to pay a fine for a summary offence (such as profane swearing). It was often ordered by a magistrate sitting alone, and was a lesser and much less uncomfortable punishment than the pillory. It remained in use very much longer. As late as 1831 the Reverend Longe demanded that the stocks at Crowfield in Suffolk be replaced, and sent for a carpenter to make a new set.[108] The punishment was employed, albeit very infrequently in its final years, until 1872.

Flogging

Public flogging was the traditional punishment imposed for offences against morality, some other misdemeanours and, most commonly, petty theft. As with the stocks, it was also sometimes imposed in lieu of payment of a fine. The degree and vigorousness with which it was administered differed, often at the suggestion of the justices themselves. Frequently 20 lashes were inflicted. At other times, as many as 40 or as few as five or six strokes were ordered, especially, in the latter case, if the recipients were female or infirm. For example, at the Norfolk Quarter Sessions that opened at King's Lynn on 17 January 1758, five men from various nearby towns pleaded guilty to petty-theft indictments and were

106. C. Mackie, *Norfolk Annals*, 1901, p. 100.
107. *The Ipswich Journal*, 24 April 1756.
108. M. Stone (ed.), *The Diary of John Longe, Vicar of Coddenham, 1765–1834*, 2008, p. 130.

sentenced to 40 lashes each, these to be administered publicly the following day.[109] By contrast, when the frail Thomas Turner was convicted of the same crime at the Cambridgeshire Quarter Sessions in April 1763, the court stipulated just five lashes.[110] The beating was normally administered to the back of a convict who was stripped to the waist, and thrashed so that he (or she) was "bloody," as with William Ranson at Bury in 1784.[111]

The punishment might not be imposed, or would be reduced, if the convict became unwell after sentence. For example, in 1780 John Stangroom was convicted at the Norwich Borough sessions of stealing yarn from his employers, who were dyers in the town, and sentenced to a public whipping. Because a report from one of the city surgeons suggested that such a punishment "could not be inflicted upon him without endangering his life, the execution of his sentence was respited."[112]

Much might depend on the inclination and strength of the man inflicting the punishment. In 1777, as part of his traditional duties, the common hangman for Somerset whipped Robert Biggin through the streets of Cary for stealing potatoes. Because Biggin was an unpopular "old offender," local people raised a fund of 17s 6d to encourage the hangman to "do him justice" (flog him hard). Unfortunately for them, the hangman was elderly, and did not have the strength to administer much of a beating.[113]

Flogging was inflicted in three ways: in private, in a gaol or house of correction (this was fairly rare before the 1730s); in public, while the convict was tied to a post; or in public, but "on the move," while the convict was attached to the back of a cart being drawn through a certain area. Thus, in 1725, when Elizabeth Alden was convicted of petty larceny, she was flogged at the public whipping post on Castle Hill in Norwich.[114] By contrast, in March 1802 James Miller, convicted of stealing a sheet, was sentenced to be "whipped 100 yards in Bury Market Place."[115]

---

109. NRO C/S 1/12, mf 656 part 4.
110. CRO Q/SO 6, p. 251.
111. *Bury and Norwich Post*, 22 January 1784.
112. *Norfolk Chronicle*, 10 June 1780.
113. J. Beresford (ed.), *The Diary of a Country Parson, 1758–1802*, 1978, p. 95. Parish constables often flogged those convicted summarily.
114. *Evening Post*, 31 July – 3 August 1725.
115. H. R. Barker, *History of, and Guide to, Bury St. Edmund's*, 2008, p. 87.

As Alden's case shows, the courts were very willing to impose such sentences on women, even in public, during the first two-thirds of the era. Similarly, when Elizabeth Rivett was convicted of petty larceny at the Norfolk Assizes in Norwich in 1736, she was sentenced to a whipping in the city's marketplace, as was Ann Long in 1747.[116] However, judges and magistrates became increasingly reluctant to sentence females to corporal punishment after the 1760s, especially if it was to be imposed in public. It appeared unseemly, particularly as the woman's upper body was necessarily exposed. Fewer such sentences were passed and, where they were, more were conducted in private. Typically, in 1781, when Mary Newman was convicted of petty larceny in Norwich, she was whipped in a house of correction.[117] The following year, when two men and a woman (Letitia Stebbing) were convicted of petty theft at the Norfolk County Quarter Sessions, the men were sentenced to a public flogging, but Stebbing was privately whipped in Wymondham bridewell.[118] By the final years of the century, even this was in sharp decline, although it was not formally abolished until 1820.[119] Increasingly, females received short custodial sentences instead of corporal punishment. For example, in January 1783, at the City of Norwich Quarter Sessions, two women, found guilty of petty larceny, were sentenced to one month's hard labour in the house of correction rather than a flogging.[120] By the end of the century, this had become the usual punishment for females convicted of this offence, although sentences might extend to several months. When Mary Crack was found guilty of the same crime at the Bury Quarter Sessions in 1800, she was sentenced to three months' imprisonment in a local house of correction.[121]

The public whipping of males lasted significantly longer. Typically, in January 1785, after William Woods pleaded guilty to stealing a piece

116. *Country Journal Or The Craftsman*, September 4, 1736; *Whitehall Evening Post Or London Intelligencer*, 22–25 August 1747.
117. *Norfolk Chronicle*, 28 April 1781.
118. Ibid., 13 April 1782.
119. S. Devereaux, "The Abolition of the Burning of Women in England Reconsidered," 2005, pp. 83–84.
120. *Norfolk Chronicle*, 25 January 1783.
121. *The Ipswich Journal*, 25 January 1800. The use of imprisonment for this crime as well as for grand larceny (instead of transportation) helped to reduce the distinction between the two forms of theft by the end of the century.

of "Darbyshire" cheese at the Suffolk Quarter Sessions held at Woodbridge, he was discharged after being "publicly whipped at the rising of the court." However, by the final decades of the eighteenth century, a growing reluctance to flog men in public, if it could reasonably be avoided (for reasons of age, etc.), can be identified. Even in 1774 Daniel Catchpole was privately whipped after being convicted of petty larceny at the Bury Assizes.[122] After the Thetford Assizes in 1784, a chicken thief, Hammond Fox, was flogged in gaol.[123] This became more common in ensuing years.

By the 1790s, some men were receiving short custodial sentences for petty theft, rather than floggings, like many women. In 1794 Thomas Gisborne thought it a mark of a good JP that "[h]e will not consign to the lash the sturdy criminal, who, though he laughs at transient pain, might have been deterred at least from repeating his offence...by the irksomeness of solitude and labour."[124] Thus, at the Woodbridge Quarter Sessions in 1800, John Gillingham received six months in the bridewell for petty larceny.[125] Two years later, John King, convicted at Bury Quarter Sessions for stealing several boards, was sentenced to three months' imprisonment.[126] However, flogging lingered in England until the twentieth century, at least for young men and certain offences.

122. *Public Advertiser*, 9 August 1774.
123. TNA ASSI 33/6 and 33/7.
124. T. Gisborne, *An Enquiry Into the Duties of Men in the Higher and Middle Classes of Society in Great Britain*, 1794, p. 403.
125. *The Ipswich Journal*, 11 October 1800.
126. Ibid., 16 October 1802.

CHAPTER 14

Perspectives on Property Crime

Introduction

When eighteenth-century observers spoke about crime, they were normally referring to offences against property. These made up the great majority—usually at least 70 per cent—of felonies tried at assizes. For example, at the Court of Great Sessions in Chester (the equivalent forum for Cheshire), 84 per cent of all indictments in the years between 1760 and 1830 were for some form of property crime.[1] The proportion for the Great Sessions for Denbighshire in Wales between 1661 and 1730 was more modest, about half.[2] Lesser examples of these crimes, along with petty theft, were also a significant part of the quarter-sessions criminal caseload. Furthermore, very specific forms of low-value theft were among those statutory crimes that could be dealt with summarily by magistrates sitting alone or at petty sessions. This chapter will consider various aspects of property crime during the era.

Poverty and Crime

Most, but by no means all, of those who perpetrated crimes against property were poor. Many contemporary observers saw a close connection between want and offending. Roger North (1651–1734) thought that no amount of punishment could "prevent the effects of poverty, that is

1. J. Walliss, "Crime and Justice in Georgian Cheshire; The Chester Court of Great Sessions, 1760–1830," 2015, p. 45.
2. S. Howard, *Law and Disorder in Early Modern Wales*, 2008, p. 47.

stealing."[3] In 1783 an anonymous author suggested that most thieves were not of a naturally vicious disposition, but were driven by the most pressing need: "Their *vice* is hunger: and their crime is the gratifying that irresistible demand of nature, by the only possible means in their power, *stealing.*" He thought that if they were provided with sustenance crime would swiftly wither away.[4] He was not alone. By the late eighteenth century it was becoming a premise of much English debate that faulty public policy, rather than innate sin and human wickedness, lay behind a major part of the country's crime problems.[5] These views were frequently reiterated in a specifically East Anglian context. In 1781 a newspaper letter sent from Thetford claimed that the town and its environs had seen more property offences than for many years, "which is believed to be occasioned by such a number of people being out of employment."[6] Towards the end of the century, the Suffolk magistrate Thomas Ruggles deplored the life of "idleness, and theft, to which the children of the poor are prone."[7]

It was widely feared that former parish apprentices, who started life with huge disadvantages, were particularly prone to drifting into crime.[8] Among them were men like John Painter, from Downham Market, in Norfolk, who was orphaned when still an infant and put out to nurse by his parish before being "apprenticed" to a warrener. Subsequently, he joined a gang of smugglers and then progressed to more serious offences before being executed at the age of 35.[9] Unsurprisingly, many thieves and robbers were also uneducated. William Wright from Syleham, in Suffolk, executed in 1737 for a highway robbery committed in Norfolk, was

3. R. North, *A Discourse of the Poor. Shewing the Pernicious Tendency of the Laws Now in Force For Their Maintenance and Settlement,* 1753, p. 22.
4. Anon, *The Means of Effectually Preventing Theft and Robbery*, 1783, p. 86.
5. J. Innes, *Inferior Politics: Social Problems and Social Policies in Eighteenth-century Britain*, 2009, p. 218.
6. *Whitehall Evening Post (1770)*, April 19–21 1781.
7. T. Ruggles, *The History of the Poor; Their Rights, Duties, and the Laws Respecting Them,* 1794, p. 297.
8. T. Andrews, *An Enquiry into the Causes of the Encrease and Miseries of the Poor of England*, 1738, pp. 43–44.
9. *Daily Post*, 22 March 1737.

described as a "poor, stupid creature." Two men hanged with him were termed "stupid and indolent wretches."[10]

Nevertheless, despite these observations and illustrations, the direct relationship between poverty and crime was often quite tenuous. Although an apparent correlation between indictment levels and food prices has been identified for several counties during some parts of the eighteenth century, this is by no means universal.[11] For example, in south-west England there was frequently little or no connection between peaks in theft prosecutions and prices (as defined by the Schumpeter-Gilboy index) during the era.[12] Similarly, an examination of quarter-sessions theft cases in Oxfordshire between 1750 and 1800 suggests that there was only the most limited if any link between wage/price levels or inclement weather and peaks in indictment rates. The vast majority of those prosecuted at this forum for petty or minor theft were not destitute, in the sense that they were not unemployed or vagrants. Most also appear to have been neophytes to the criminal process.[13] Whatever may have been the situation in the county earlier in the period, even late-eighteenth-century Sussex does not appear to have seen much correlation between fluctuations in the number of larceny indictments tried at quarter sessions and grain prices, although there may have been some underlying link between prosecution levels and wider depressions in agriculture.[14]

A broadly similar picture presents itself in East Anglia. Theft defendants at quarter sessions and assizes were usually poor but not indigent people who were presented with a tempting opportunity to steal. Such temptation may have been exacerbated because they lived in a society with an unprecedented level of riches and a new abundance of alluring consumer goods. Sometimes such individuals may even have felt "mocked with the show of immense wealth and luxury amongst the rich."[15] Poverty clearly made people vulnerable to temptation and so to committing

10. *Daily Gazetteer,* 29 March 1737.
11. J. M. Beattie, *Crime and the Courts in England 1660–1800*, 1986, p. 235.
12. A. Williams, *The Criminality of Women in the 18th Century in The South West Of England*, 2000, p. 92.
13. A. Kilday, "'Criminally Poor?' Investigating the Link Between Crime and Poverty in Eighteenth Century England," 2014, pp. 520–521.
14. S. Wilson, "The Court of Quarter Sessions and Larceny in Sussex, 1775–1820," 1986, p. 82 and p. 92.
15. Anon, *The Means of Effectually Preventing Theft and Robbery*, 1783, p. 102.

theft. However, stealing was often just one facet of an otherwise (largely) legal "economy of makeshifts" employed by the poor to make ends meet which included paid work, the Poor Law, charity, credit, pawning, gleaning, and, for some urban women, prostitution.[16]

Some poor people eventually succumbed to temptation and stole, if only once or twice, but many did not. Variations in prosecution rates were as much affected by the changing reactions of victims and magistrates, which were themselves influenced by the media (especially newspapers) and events such as postwar disbandment, as by the "real" incidence of offending. Acute destitution, especially when manifest in the theft of food, was rare enough for it to be expressly recognised by assizes judges and juries as a specially mitigating factor. Conversely, when the perpetrator of a property crime was comfortably off, this was seen as greatly aggravating the offence, sometimes even justifying execution where clemency might otherwise have been expected.

Nevertheless, although many felons in East Anglia were neophytes to crime, there was also a significant minority of old offenders, distinct from its occasional opportunist thieves. Some people could not resign themselves to a life of very hard but badly remunerated labour or reliance on poor relief, and supplemented their incomes by fairly regular recourse to crime. For example, in late 1763, James Knights, a labourer from Tivetshall, in Norfolk, was thought to have been involved in a burglary in his parish, during which £60 in cash, £20 in banknotes, and ten gold rings had been stolen. The victim obtained a warrant to search Knights' house, which was located in a "lonesome" spot near the village. Parish constables then enforced the magistrate's warrant. Their search was highly revealing. A dead goose was found in Knights' bed, while a very large sum of money, the skins of numerous sheep with divers markings on them (suggesting a multiplicity of sources and thefts), and the heads and feathers of many other geese and turkeys were also found on the premises. Perhaps most strikingly of all, one of the constables conducting the search found a set of tools that he had himself lost earlier![17]

16. The phrase was first used by Olwen Hufton.
17. *London Chronicle*, 31 December 1763 – 3 January 1764.

It was not just men who fell into this category. Twenty years later, Elizabeth Pulley was charged with breaking into the shop of Elizabeth Minns at Hethersett, in Norfolk, on Christmas Eve. It was claimed that she had stolen two cheeses, four pieces of bacon, some half-pints of butter, several pounds of raisins and flour, and two rolls of worsted cloth. However, it was also noted that Pulley had already "been in the Castle [prison] four times, and convicted of a burglary at the assizes in 1781 in the same town, and sentenced to hard labour one year in the Aylsham Bridewell."[18] On this occasion, Minns was committed to Norwich prison by Thomas Beevor and later capitally convicted of burglary, but, again, reprieved from death at the ensuing assizes.[19] Clearly, she was something of a career criminal, if not a particularly good one.

Within this general group of habitual offenders there were small numbers of what might be termed professional criminals, who operated in a sophisticated manner seeking high-value returns, although their numbers were significantly lower than in the Metropolis. Prominent among them were the gangs that dealt in stolen horses and, of course, those engaged in smuggling (considered in *Chapters 16* and *23*). However, despite occasional chapbooks that suggested that career criminals mirrored the artisans of legitimate society by specialising in a specific form of offending, this was rarely the reality (smuggling, perhaps, sometimes apart). Many turned their hands to robbery, burglary, housebreaking, animal theft, and larceny as the opportunity presented itself.

For example, in 1736 four members of the Suffolk Gang were committed to Norwich Castle Gaol for a variety of offences. One of them was accused of highway robbery, another two of stealing corn from a barn at night, and one of receiving stolen goods.[20] Two years later, just before being executed for highway robbery, two married Suffolk men—35-year-old William Tink and 42-year-old Geoffrey Leaks—admitted to having "followed theft from their youth." After meeting at Bury, they had gone into partnership and "robbed in concert." Their crimes included stealing pigs in Essex and horses in East Anglia, before they "went on the

18. *Norfolk Chronicle*, 11 January 1783.
19. *Daily Advertiser*, 25 March 1783.
20. *Daily Gazetteer* (London Edition), 14 December 1736.

highway."[21] In 1766, after John Jeremy and George Woodbine were hanged for burgling a house in Wymondham and stealing cash and goods to the value of £10, it was observed that they were members of a gang that had been involved in "divers burglaries, felonies, stealing sheep, &c. which they have committed in different parts of this county."[22] Similarly, in April 1779, four men were hanged in Norwich for a midnight burglary during which cloth and clothing worth more than £12 had been stolen (a fifth was spared on condition of three years' hard labour on the Thames).[23] However, several other members of the same group were convicted of different robberies and burglaries at the same time, suggesting that they were an experienced gang that was fairly catholic in its crimes.[24]

It is difficult to portray many East Anglian thieves as "class warriors." As in most eras, much of the crime was *infra* not *inter* class and often committed against the most impoverished people. For example, in 1749 John Sullivan was executed for assaulting and robbing a sailor's wife of 20s in Great Yarmouth. She had just received her husband's monthly wages. Sullivan had carefully planned his attack and beaten her senseless in the process.[25] Similarly, one morning in 1781, a poor woman was robbed of a few shillings by a footpad near Watton (Norfolk). The money had been her parish allowance for having a husband away with the militia.[26] In the same year, several men broke into the house of Henry High, a day labourer at Blofield (Norfolk), in the middle of the night, and stole several articles.[27] In 1794 Thomas Osborne and two other men were committed to Bury prison for breaking into the house of George Mortlock, a labourer from Hundon, in Suffolk, and stealing six loaves, a pot of honey, a tablecloth and two shillings in cash.[28] None of the victims in these cases could remotely "afford" their losses.

21. Ibid., 19 April 1738.
22. *Public Advertiser*, 25 November 1766.
23. TNA ASSI 33/6.
24. *London Chronicle*, 22–24 July 1777.
25. *General Advertiser (1744)*, 29 August 1749; *Whitehall Evening Post Or London Intelligencer*, 21–24 October 1749.
26. *Norfolk Chronicle*, 15 December 1781.
27. Ibid., 25 August 1781.
28. Anon, *Last Dying Speech and Full Confession of Benjamin Brett*, 1794, p. 2.

The Role of Receiving

Second-hand goods of all descriptions were regularly bought and sold in eighteenth-century England. This made liquidating stolen items relatively easy by modern standards, and inevitably encouraged the commission of property crimes. Almost anything could find a buyer. The experiences of Robert Thompson are illustrative of this phenomenon. For most of the second half of the eighteenth century he lived an itinerant life of crime in the North of England and (sometimes) the South of Scotland, stealing everything that came his way, from handkerchiefs to horses. Provided that he put some distance between the places where he stole the items and those where he sold them, the length of which depended on the goods in question, they always found a ready market.[29]

Stolen items were usually sold on to ordinary people rather than specialist receivers, especially outside the Metropolis, which was very different from provincial England in this respect. It seems that many purchasers were not painstaking about ensuring the provenance of such goods. Provided that they could deny any awareness of the origins of items in a plausible manner, people were often willing to buy goods which must have excited some suspicions, if only because of the price. Of course, this was not always the case. In 1790 the employee of an ironmonger in Ipswich Buttermarket stole some stock from his master and took it to a Jewish shopkeeper in the town. Suspecting that the items were stolen, the shopkeeper asked the man to come back later in the day, saying that he could not purchase them immediately. He then told his daughter to summon some constables, who arrested the thief on his return. However, and significantly, this was considered noteworthy and somewhat unusual.[30]

Readily identifiable items were usually liquidated swiftly after they had been stolen, as any delay would allow victims to alert the public and pawnbrokers by printed and distributed handbills or newspaper advertisements. In late-eighteenth-century Bristol, it seems that most goods

29. R. Thompson, *Narrative of the Life and Transactions of Robert Thompson*, 1791, p. 16.
30. R. Halliday and B. Susser, "The Ipswich Jewish Community in the Eighteenth and Nineteenth Centuries," 2002, p. 153.

that were not taken for personal consumption were sold on within 24 hours of being stolen; a similar situation probably prevailed in Norwich and Ipswich.[31]

Many contemporary observers were convinced that effective action against receiving would greatly reduce the general level of offending, as the proceeds of most property crimes were sold on. Unfortunately, this was easier said than done. One possibility was increasing the penalties available. Historically, most cases of receiving had been treated as misdemeanours and punished accordingly. This was expressly reiterated by Parliament in 1702, and continued to be the case throughout the eighteenth century. For example, at the Suffolk Quarter Sessions held at Ipswich on 7 April 1758, Daniel Smith was sentenced to a public whipping after pleading guilty to receiving four ducks and turkeys from a female thief who pleaded guilty at the same sessions to petty larceny.[32]

However, in an effort to deter men and women (it was a common female crime) who were involved in receiving stolen goods on a regular basis, in 1691 the offence was made a felony carrying 14 years' transportation when committed in certain specific circumstances (an early use of the punishment). Normally, prosecutions under this heading were only possible after someone else had already been convicted of grand larceny for stealing the relevant items, and the convicted thief could not usually be a Crown witness in the ensuing prosecution. As a result, it was not indicted frequently. During the decade from 1751 to 1760, just one person was prosecuted for the statutory crime at an East Anglian Assizes. In 1753 at Bury, Barlee Banson faced two separate counts of receiving a total of ten geese, ducks and hens. He was acquitted on both charges. As this verdict suggests, throughout history, proving that a defendant knew or believed goods to have been stolen has proved exceptionally difficult in receiving cases, external signs, such as unusually low prices being asked, merely raising suspicion.[33] Nevertheless, at the Norwich City Assizes in August 1736, Ann Smith was convicted of the crime and sentenced to

31. See generally, M. Neale, "Making Crime Pay in Late Eighteenth-century Bristol: Stolen Goods, the Informal Economy and the Negotiation of Risk," 2011, pp. 439–459.
32. SRO g.125. B105/2/32.
33. Anon (Member of Parliament), *Further Observations On the Buyers or Receivers of Stolen Goods*, 1756, pp. 25–26.

14 years' transportation. She was acquitted of another, similar, count, as was her husband, suggesting a degree of professionalism.[34] Several other people received similar verdicts during the century.

Theft and Work Perquisites

Prior to the industrial revolution and the advent of factory-based manufacturing, many manual workers retained waste or surplus material from the production process, using it to supplement their relatively meagre earnings. This was often fairly easy, not least because traditional forms of manufacturing were frequently based on the "putting-out" system. For example, in the cloth industry, a considerable amount of piecework was done by out-workers, many of them female, who would be given wool to spin in their own homes, often with the assistance of their children and neighbours. In the early eighteenth century such work was sometimes sent as much as 50 miles from Norwich, going as far as Suffolk, using agents (frequently shopkeepers) to distribute the wool in spinning localities.

The exact status of "waste" retention varied widely over time and between English regions. Some manufacturers may have openly sanctioned the practice; others grudgingly tolerated it.[35] Nevertheless, its legality was frequently recognized prior to the eighteenth century. For example, in 1662, when a labourer named George Parke was tried for petty theft at the Norfolk Quarter Sessions held at Fakenham for "stealing" two wood blocks from his master, he was acquitted after he argued that it was normal for "woodsellers thereabout to carry home a faggot of rotten wood, & he taking the two blocks which were the great ends of wood then felled in lieu of such a faggot."[36] This does not mean that crime was customary. Such appropriations were viewed as legal entitlements, not cases of theft. However, and inevitably, matters were never that simple. Even in the seventeenth century, when the legitimacy of such perquisites was widely accepted, there were numerous grey areas

34. TNA ASSI 33/1.
35. R. J. Soderlund, "'Intended as a Terror to the Idle and Profligate': Embezzlement and the Origins of Policing in the Yorkshire Worsted Industry, c.1750–1777," 1998, p. 652.
36. J. Rosenheim (ed.), *The Notebook of Robert Doughty, 1662–1665*, 1991, p. 18.

relating to the quantity and quality of material that could be taken. Workers would often interpret these in their own favour, while, at the same time, not advertising what they were doing, well aware that their employers might feel that they had drifted into pilfering.

Whatever may have been the situation in earlier times, it seems that such defences were less readily accepted in the 1700s. Indeed, that there was a sustained attack on "traditional" work-related perquisites, during which they were redefined as theft, has been a major theme in studies of the period since the 1970s, and is borne out by some cases from the East Anglian region. For example, two porters, Hammond Webb and Joseph Kingsbury, were convicted at the Suffolk Assizes in 1787 for stealing some of the wool that they were employed to weigh for a factor in Sudbury. One of the reasons that clemency was suggested, after they had served two years in prison, was that they had held no felonious intent when taking the material; their crime had been based on an "Error from Precedent of Custom."[37]

Increasingly, attempts by outworkers to keep back wool, for personal use or sale, were frowned upon. However, prosecuting such embezzlement posed serious legal problems at the start of the era, necessitating parliamentary intervention. Because outworkers were voluntarily entrusted with the material that they transformed, purloining it for their own purposes could not, legally, amount to theft. (The principle of "possessorial immunity" on the part of a bailee was present in most European legal systems at this time.)[38] It might give rise to a civil action, but it was often impractical for a small weaving master to sue a poor cottage spinner who had kept back a few ounces of wool. At times a magistrate could deal with such cases informally, as they did with so many other matters, both civil and criminal. For example, in January 1708 Mordecai Simpson, a weaver from Stratford in Suffolk, complained that three years earlier he had delivered 28 pounds of combed wool, suitable for spinning, to "Widow Keeble" from Cheldmondiston in the same county. She had returned 14 pounds of it (presumably spun), and accounted for another eight pounds, but "never gave any account or satisfaction" for

37. TNA HO 47/10/8, ff 43–47.
38. G. P. Fletcher, "The Metamorphosis of Larceny," 1976, p. 475.

the remaining six pounds, which was worth 9s. Devereaux Edgar issued a warrant against the widow, who attended the magistrate and paid for it in his presence.[39] This was not entirely satisfactory, as it relied on the justice's personal authority being respected by all parties to the dispute.

During the 1700s the law on embezzlement was expanded to deal with this apparent lacuna in the penal repertoire, and to make unauthorized taking of such work materials a crime. For example, important statutes to punish the taking of wool, yarn, and cloth were passed in 1703, 1740, 1749, and 1774.[40] There were numerous others of lesser significance. Between 1726 and 1800 alone eleven embezzlement acts were passed in the woollen, worsted, and fustian trades.[41] It was hoped that these statutes would, *inter alia*, address "false" and "short" reeling in the cloth industry. The former entailed yarn being spun that was deficient in the requisite number of threads, although set on a standard-size reel. The latter involved yarn being reeled on a reel that was thinner than the standard circumference. By using these subterfuges, the spinner could appropriate some of the wool that had been delivered and also reduce her workload, albeit producing yarn of an inferior quantity and quality to that paid for.[42]

Most of the new crimes established by these statutes were summary offences, tried by magistrates sitting alone, rather than on indictment at assizes or quarter sessions. Thus, the 1703 act made false and short reeling, along with other forms of embezzlement by outworkers, a specific summary offence, liable to a fine that was linked to the amount taken, with 14 days' hard labour in the house of correction and a whipping in lieu of payment.[43] The sentences imposed for many new crimes of embezzlement were graduated, and depended on how many times an offender had been convicted on earlier occasions. For example, under one act (24 Geo III, c 44), spinners who committed a second offence could be fined 10s, while for a third offence it was £1 plus court costs. Only on a fourth

39. SRO QS 347.96, *The Devereux Edgar Notebook*, transcribed by S. R. Schofield, 1956, vol. 2, p. 161.
40. K. Wilson, *The Sense of the People: Politics, Culture and Imperialism in England, 1715–1785*, 1998, p. 309.
41. R. Porter, *English Society in the Eighteenth Century*, 2001, p. 150.
42. J. Styles, "Spinners and the Law: Regulating Yarn Standards in the English Worsted Industries, 1550–1800," 2013, pp. 147–150.
43. Ibid.

conviction did an offender face a mandatory spell of imprisonment and corporal punishment. Other statutes allowed for the imposition of a custodial sentence slightly earlier in a spinner's delinquent career.

The 1749 statute, the introduction of which had been strongly supported by Norwich worsted manufacturers, also targeted those who received such material, as they were thought to encourage appropriation by workers. Typically, the previous year, John Laws had been convicted in Norwich under an earlier act and fined £10 for knowingly receiving a quantity of embezzled yarn. (He paid up immediately, as the alternative was to be whipped in the marketplace).[44]

During the 1750s, growing numbers of Norfolk and Suffolk wool combers and yarn spinners prosecuted statutory reeling offences, something that was encouraged by an intense campaign against embezzlement conducted by Norwich manufacturers between 1751 and 1754. During this period, a Suffolk newspaper warned that the "enormous frauds" committed in earlier years would now be prosecuted if identified.[45] Martha Robinson of Great Blakenham learnt this to her cost when she was sentenced to a spell in Ipswich bridewell for false reeling.[46]

However, during the 1760s, a group of well-connected Yorkshire manufacturers embarked on an even more ambitious and organised campaign against false and short reeling. They established a private association, funded by subscription, which paid the cost of prosecutions and the salaries of at least two inspectors whose job it was to detect offenders. This scheme was highly influential in other parts of the country. In 1768, the master wool combers and yarn spinners of East Anglia adopted the Yorkshire model and established their own inspectorate. As in Yorkshire, this marked the beginning of another sustained campaign in the region against short reeling and a sharp increase in the number of prosecutions, one that would linger until the demise of hand spinning at the start of the nineteenth century. Thus 18 prosecutions were reported in

44. *General Advertiser (1744)*, 6 December 1748.
45. *Ipswich Journal*, 15 June 1754.
46. Ibid., 5 November 1763.

the *Norwich Mercury* in 1769 and another 27 in 1770, but just one in 1766 and none in 1767.[47]

So efficient was the inspectorate system that Norfolk and Suffolk MPs helped secure the passage of an act in 1774 reducing the punishment for a first reeling offence to a relatively modest 5s penalty. The preamble to the statute explained that this was necessary because the severity of existing penalties had discouraged prosecutions and deterred honest people from spinning. There was also a growing distaste for corporal punishment when inflicted on women. In a precursor to wider developments within the criminal justice system, severe but (in practice) selective deterrent punishments were replaced by a more systematic enforcement of milder penalties.[48]

Nevertheless, short-reeling survived to the end of the century, after which the industrialisation of cloth manufacture in the North began to make it irrelevant in both Norfolk and Suffolk. Thus, in 1780 Sarah Woodbine, from the Wicklewood (Norfolk) House of Industry, was committed to one month's hard labour in the Wymondham bridewell and publicly whipped for reeling false yarn "it being her third offence."[49] The following year, a large number of women from various central Norfolk villages were fined for reeling false or short yarn, and Susanna Joy of Great Melton was committed to bridewell for a month for the same offence.[50] In 1783 a general meeting of Suffolk yarn spinners was still able to lament that, because of short-reeling, clothmaking in the county had a worse reputation than that of counties with a better-regulated industry, as private tradesmen were unwilling to "expose themselves singly to the Odium of prosecuting Offenders."[51]

47. J. Styles, "Spinners and the Law: Regulating Yarn Standards in the English Worsted Industries, 1550–1800," 2013, p. 160.
48. Ibid., p. 161.
49. *Norfolk Chronicle*, 11 November 1780.
50. Ibid., 17 March 1781.
51. Ibid., 9 December 1783.

Gleaning and Theft

Gleaning uncut or fallen grain in reaped fields was widespread but not universal in eighteenth-century England; local customs and variations in provincial agriculture made it of limited significance in some counties, such as Yorkshire, and almost absent in a few others. However, in many arable regions, including Norfolk and Suffolk, it was a vital resource for poor labouring families, usually being carried out by women, children, and elderly men who were too frail for harder work. Gleaners might recover more than 4s worth of corn from just two acres of harvested crops.[52] In 1795 Lord Townsend noted that, during the two weeks after harvest, many of the poorest families in his part of North Norfolk picked up enough grain to last them for the best part of the winter.[53] Sometimes the proceeds of gleaning were even sold for cash rather than being used for personal consumption.[54] Occasionally it seems that gleaners were allowed access to fields where root vegetables had been harvested. For example, in 1777, after a plot of land that had produced 94 bushels of potatoes was ploughed in Bedfordshire, they recovered another two bushels from the ground.[55] Doubtless there were similar cases in Norfolk and Suffolk.

Whatever may have been the position with regard to vegetables, gleaning of grain had traditionally been viewed as a legal entitlement rather than a landowner's indulgence, not least because the practice (where carried out) was ancient and appeared to be supported by scripture.[56] In 1782 a newspaper correspondent complained that gleaners insisted that a farmer had no right to his own fields until they themselves had first had access to them, and would turn out any of his cattle that were put into the fields to feed before they had been gleaned.[57] Such attitudes could result in confrontations and violence.

In 1766, during the Norwich Riots, a local farmer was harassed specifically because he was felt to be an antisocial individual who had tried

52. *World (1787)*, 2 September 1790.
53. *Courier and Evening Gazette*, 17 April 1799.
54. A. Cirket (ed.), *Samuel Whitbread's Notebooks*, 1971, p. 89.
55. *St. James's Chronicle Or the British Evening Post*, 14–16 October 1777.
56. P. King, "Customary Rights and Women's Earnings: The Importance of Gleaning to the Rural Labouring Poor, 1750–1850," 1991, pp. 462–463.
57. *St. James's Chronicle Or the British Evening Post*, 12–14 September 1782.

to drive out gleaners from his fields. In 1772 an incident in Suffolk was even more serious. A farmer from Lawshall had acquired a bad reputation for being "severe" to the local poor. The most serious criticism was that he would not allow them to glean his fields but, instead, would let his own pigs and cattle into them to eat any spilled grain. One evening, up to eight heavily disguised men ambushed him in a dark lane when he was riding back from Sudbury market. They pulled him from his horse and beat him savagely, then dragged him through a river, before suspending him from a tree with a warning about "oppressing the poor any more."[58] More overtly, in 1788 about 100 people assembled in a "tumultuous manner" at Aldham, in Suffolk, and insisted on gleaning a farmer's wheat fields. When he tried to evict them, two women assaulted him.[59]

Despite periodic complaints and occasional conflicts, for most of the eighteenth century landowners appear to have accepted, if only grudgingly, that gleaning was a right. However, towards the end of the era, there was a change in attitude; agriculturalists became increasingly resistant to the practice per se, and demanded to know "how to prevent the gleaners from robbing the honest farmer."[60] In part this was because gleaning sometimes provided cover for the theft of already harvested wheat and barley, something that was, and always had been, indisputably a crime. For example, in August 1781, Elizabeth Bacon of Sprowston, in Norfolk, was charged with stealing a quantity of reaped barley from a local gentleman while in his fields.[61] It could also lead to the commission of other offences. Thus, in August 1708, Devereaux Edgar issued a warrant for the arrest of Elizabeth Green, a married woman, at the behest of Laurence Bacon, a yeoman farmer from Burstall, in Suffolk. It was alleged that Green had set an "ill example" to others by committing misdemeanours in the harvest field, throwing wheat sheaves about and pulling out corn from them.[62] Frequently the facts of such incidents were fiercely disputed and hard to establish. In 1782 one farmer allegedly thrashed an "insolent" female gleaner in his fields with a horsewhip after she took several

58. *General Evening Post*, 3–5 September 1772.
59. A. Randall, *Riotous Assemblies: Popular Protest in Hanoverian England*, 2006, pp. 319–320.
60. *St. James's Chronicle Or the British Evening Post*, 12–14 September 1782.
61. *Norfolk Chronicle*, 25 August 1781.
62. SRO QS 347.96, *The Devereux Edgar Notebook*, transcribed by S. R. Schofield, 1956, vol. 2, p. 199.

handfuls of his "unbound corn before his face." In reply she claimed that he had attacked her in an adjacent lane, while she was on her way to lawful gleaning, and prosecuted him at quarter sessions for the assault. The farmer was forced to settle the action by paying her 16s.[63]

In part the change in attitude towards gleaning occurred because farmers began to value fallen grain as potential animal feed, especially as the period saw a move from the use of the short-handled sickle to the heavier long-handled scythe as the standard harvesting tool. This made the process quicker (and so cheaper) and more responsive to the availability of good weather, but also produced considerably more wastage, spillage that could readily be recovered with a rake.[64] More generally, the whole notion of a "qualified ownership" of property, subject to customary restrictions, was in legal retreat during the era. As a result, some landowners sought to redefine gleaning as theft, unless they had first expressly authorised it, and started to use legal actions to resist gleaners' "rights."[65]

The substantive law on gleaning was something of a murky area until late in the century. In the early 1780s, one farmer concluded that it was so uncertain that "even the justices cannot determine how far they [aggressive gleaners] are punishable." He hoped that a legal decision would clarify the issue.[66] These duly came from Suffolk. In 1786 the case of *Worlledge v Manning* provided limited guidance on the issue. After the barley crop had been cut and cleared during the harvest of 1785, Benjamin Manning, a Timworth shoemaker, went on to the land of John Worlledge, a wealthy farmer in the adjoining parish of Ingham, to glean. Worlledge disputed his right to do so and brought an action for trespass in the Court of Common Pleas. The court decided in Worlledge's favour in May 1786 and awarded him damages on the basis that Manning was not resident in the parish in which he gleaned. A stranger had no right to do so.[67]

---

63. *St. James's Chronicle Or the British Evening Post*, 12–14 September 1782.
64. S. Hussey, "'The Last Survivor of an Ancient Race': The Changing Face of Essex Gleaning," 1997, p. 66.
65. P. King, "Gleaners, Farmers and the Failure of Legal Sanctions in England 1750–1850," 1989, pp. 115–116.
66. *St. James's Chronicle Or the British Evening Post*, 12–14 September 1782.
67. *Worlledge v Manning* (1786) East, 26 George III CB; 126 ER 34.

However, most gleaners worked in their own parishes, so that further guidance was needed on whether this was a legal right or an indulgence. This eventually occurred in 1788, in the case of *Steel v Houghton et Uxor* (the "Great Gleaning Case"), in which the Court of Common Pleas considered another case emanating from Timworth. (As the Manning case suggests, there was a history of tension over this issue in the village). On this occasion, it involved harvested barley fields being gleaned by locally settled poor people. Among them was Mary Houghton, who had gleaned without permission on the farm of James Steel, who then sued her for trespass. The background to these proceedings emphasised their role in the wider erosion of traditional rights, Mary Houghton's family lived in a cottage with customary rights on Lord Cornwallis's land, and had earlier tried to block local enclosures.[68]

After lengthy deliberations, the court's judges concluded by a majority of three to one that nobody had a right at common law to glean in the harvest field. It was an indulgence by the landowner, an act of charity, not a legal entitlement. Reflecting changing attitudes to "ownership," Lord Loughborough observed that the nature of property imparted "exclusive enjoyment," which meant that no one was obliged to permit gleaning. His colleague John Wilson noted that, although a farmer's conscience might "direct him to leave something for the poor, the law does not oblige him to leave anything." The Law of Moses was not directly applicable in England. The dissenting voice, the elderly Henry Gould, was more influenced by the value of scripture and previous judicial comments on the issue by distinguished jurists as sources of law.[69]

Although the 1788 case established an important precedent, it had little effect on gleaning in the short term, which continued almost unabated, even where it was not expressly permitted. In 1795 an Old Bailey judge freely accepted that, although it was not a legal right, reasonable jurors would not normally be willing to convict for theft in gleaning cases, even if permission from a landowner had not been forthcoming, provided that the gleaners had acted out of a sense of justified entitlement and taken

68. A. R. Buck, *The Making of Australian Property Law*, 2006, p. 27.
69. *Steel v Houghton et Uxor* (1788) 1 H Bl 51; 126 ER 32.

only fallen (rather than harvested) grain.[70] No gleaners were successfully prosecuted for theft in these circumstances during the eighteenth century. The 1788 case did not even fully register on popular consciousness. In 1811 a farmer asked the Bedfordshire JP Samuel Whitbread whether the poor had a right to glean on a farmer's land "without his leave." Whitbread made it clear that they did not have such a right.[71]

However, some farmers, aware that law was on their side, did try to force gleaners out of their fields. In their turn, gleaners continued to fight back by accusing the farmers involved of assault and bringing them before local magistrates where necessary.[72] Thus, in the early nineteenth century, Samuel Whitbread dealt with a gleaner, Elizabeth Kilby, who "complained of abuse in the field" whilst she was working, albeit that he quickly dismissed the case.[73] Although gleaning continued on a significant, albeit declining, scale in East Anglia until the end of the nineteenth century, and lingered on (as a source of chicken feed) until the advent of the combine harvester after the second world war, the practice was in slow retreat by the end of the 1700s.[74] It was gradually accepted as an indulgence, not an entitlement.

Servants and Property Crime

Domestic service was ubiquitous during the eighteenth century. Even small farmers and members of the middling orders had maids-of-all-work, albeit that they were sometimes recruited from the ranks of parish apprentices. Inevitably, servants were a major factor in property crime committed in a domestic environment, acting as both its perpetrators and as the protectors of stealable items.

Servants often stole from their masters, although, in these situations, modest appropriation of foodstuffs and beverages, which was often viewed as a perk of their position, should be distinguished from

70. *St. James's Chronicle Or the British Evening Post*, 19=22 September 1795.
71. A. Cirket (ed.), *Samuel Whitbread's Notebooks*, 1971, p. 36.
72. P. King, "Gleaners, Farmers and the Failure of Legal Sanctions in England 1750–1850," 1989, pp. 118–125.
73. A. Cirket (ed.), *Samuel Whitbread's Notebooks*, 1971, p. 44.
74. N. Verdon, *Rural Women Workers in Nineteenth-century England: Gender, Work and Wages*, 2002, p. 30 and p. 123.

the commission of "crimes," albeit that this distinction was inherently difficult, and there were fears that the former easily led to the latter.[75] Nevertheless, straightforward theft by domestic staff was not uncommon. As a trial judge observed at the Suffolk Assizes in 1802, there was "too much of this thing, stealing from employers."[76] Minor cases were usually dealt with by dismissal from position rather than by formal prosecution.

Servants were uniquely well-placed to steal because they usually had a detailed knowledge of, and ready access to, their employers' valuables. For example, in 1729 Edmund Smith, a servant from Nacton near Ipswich, stole £12 in money, a greatcoat, a shirt, a pair of breeches, and a brown mare from his master. A description of the offender and the missing horse was advertised in the *Ipswich Journal*, along with the offer of a reward.[77] Servants could also pose dangers away from home. In 1767 two boxes of silver and cash worth £200 were stolen from Michael Jacobs by his servant, described as a "Polish Jew" (his employer was also Jewish), while they were staying in a room at the *Plumbers Arms* at Wickhambrook, in Suffolk.[78]

The danger from domestic staff continued after they left their positions. In 1755 John Moyes was committed to Ipswich gaol for breaking into the house of John Gorbold of Covehithe, in Suffolk, where he had lately been a servant. He had stolen a significant sum of money while the family was out. Moyes was capitally convicted at the Bury Assizes but subsequently reprieved.[79] Although the breach of trust involved in such cases was always viewed as an aggravating feature, it declined with the passage of time between leaving employment and the commission of the offence. In 1789 Nash Grose, considering a petition on behalf of William Mayhew, who had been capitally convicted at the Bury Assizes of stealing plate worth £40 from his erstwhile master, expressly noted as one of the grounds for clemency that he had left his employment a

75. T. Broughton, *Serious Advice and Warning to Servants, More Especially Those of the Nobility and Gentry*, 1800, p. 8.
76. *Bury and Norwich Post*, 25 January 1802.
77. *Ipswich Journal*, 29 November 1729.
78. Ibid., 26 September 1767.
79. *Whitehall Evening Post Or London Intelligencer*, 5–8 April 1755.

considerable time before committing the crime, reducing the need for execution. He recommended that Mayhew be transported for life.[80]

The danger posed by servants explains the importance placed by employers on character references. In 1784 Parson Woodforde noted that a maid who had applied for a position in his household was unlikely to be acceptable. This was, in part, because her friends and associates lived in the North Norfolk village of Foxley, a place Woodforde "by no means approve[d] of." This distrust was based on the large number of felons in his part of the county who appeared to have originated from there. More ominously, the parson also noted that one of the maid's former masters had been the victim of a housebreaking during which all his plate had been stolen. The thief was never caught or identified. The suggestion was that the maid had been involved in some way.[81]

Servants posed special dangers to physically vulnerable employers. In 1711, towards the end of her life, the wealthy Norfolk gentlewoman Elizabeth Freke was, in her own words, a "diseased criple with a rhumatisme." She was largely confined to her chair.[82] Freke became convinced that her four domestic staff were stealing from her on a largescale and even plotting to murder her. Although she was a bitter and slightly paranoid woman, her fears do not appear to have been entirely unfounded. Her sister discovered that £100 worth of food and other items, along with a large consignment of linen and 84 bottles of wine and cordial, had gone missing, and Elizabeth belatedly realised that one of her employees was a convicted and clergied felon. She dismissed all her staff, but they returned in the night and (apparently) tried to force entry to her house. Alarmingly, her former maid, the "divell Sarah," knew where Elizabeth had hidden a large amount of cash on her premises. Freke later obtained arrest warrants against the group, but they fled the area before these could be enforced.[83]

However, the presence of servants also provided vital security, as they meant that houses were much less likely to be left unattended, something that greatly increased the prospects of victimisation. For example, in 1783,

80. TNA HO 47/8/36.
81. J. Beresford (ed.), *The Diary of a Country Parson, 1758–1802*, 1978, p. 160.
82. R. Anselment (ed.), *The Remembrances of Elizabeth Freke 1671–1714,* 2002, p. 158.
83. Ibid., pp. 270–272.

several men broke into the house of a Mrs Hambling, near Harleston, in Norfolk, while the family was away in Norwich. In their absence, the burglars were able to steal almost every moveable in the building. They even took the hangings from the bedsteads and the meat out of pickle casks. They also drank several bottles of wine that they found while stripping the house bare before removing their loot in a cart. (It was the hoofprints of the vehicle's horses that first alerted neighbours to the crime.)[84] More seriously, in 1782, after Frances Phillips was murdered and her house burgled, a newspaper noted that, given her wealthy status, it was "somewhat remarkable, that she had not a servant who lived in the house to defend her from [the] attacks of such lawless ruffians."[85]

By contrast, in 1741 three men invaded an isolated farmhouse in Melford (Suffolk) at about 9 pm one evening. At the time, a maid was alone in the building. She attempted to go to another, nearby, farmhouse for help, but was shot as she did so, although only slightly wounded. Nevertheless, being afraid that she had successfully summoned assistance, the three men fled.[86]

Servants were often fairly zealous about securing their employers' property from theft, if only for fear that they would themselves be blamed if anything went missing. Of course, the presence of domestic staff was not always enough. In 1781 a thief noticed that the servants in a Norwich banker's house were all upstairs, and used the opportunity to enter the premises and steal a case of knives and forks, along with six silver tablespoons, from a side board downstairs.[87] Nevertheless, the presence of servants deterred much crime.

Classification and Distribution of Property Crimes

Like other eighteenth-century offences, felonious property crimes can be divided into those that were clergyable and those that were not. Petty theft, the simple taking of goods or cash worth less than a shilling, was

84. *Norfolk Chronicle*, 8 February 1783.
85. Ibid., 26 October 1782.
86. *Ipswich Journal*, 28 March 1741.
87. *Norfolk Chronicle*, 6 January 1781. The case was thrown into a nearby stream by the escaping felon.

(uniquely) not capital in any circumstances, making clergy irrelevant, although the crime was technically a felony and always tried on indictment. By the late 1600s unclergyable offences included robbery, burglary, and housebreaking in most (but not all) circumstances. However, grand larceny—stealing goods or money worth 1s or more—was usually clergyable, with the exception of pickpocketing, theft of horses, theft from a church, and one or two other, rather arcane offences.

Nevertheless, in the century after 1688 a succession of statutes made further forms of grand larceny, committed in very specific circumstances, capital offences if prosecuted pursuant to an appropriately worded indictment. These can be viewed as a facet of the Bloody Code. Among them were: shoplifting goods worth 5s or more; theft of more than 40s from a dwelling-house; theft of sheep and cattle; and a host of other, more recondite, crimes, such as theft from a bleaching ground and from the mail. If, as was usually the case, a capital property crime such as burglary or theft from a dwelling-house necessarily encompassed theft, a finding of guilty to the latter crime could still be returned as a lesser verdict on the more serious count.

The felonious property crimes that were indicted at the regional assizes during the decade after 1751, other than those involving the theft of animals (dealt with in *Chapter 16*), one case of receiving (see above), and three counts of petty theft, can be considered in detail to give an indication of offence distribution at the higher jury court. There were 240 in total, counting each case as one prosecution, even if there were several defendants. A small number of fairly arcane offences were among them, including one case of stealing from a bleaching ground and two of "sacrilege" in the form of theft from a church (both unclergyable crimes). However, the vast majority were allegations of simple grand larceny, burglary, housebreaking, robbery, and theft from a dwelling-house of goods worth over 40s, in declining order of frequency. They will be considered in more detail in the following chapter.

CHAPTER 15

Grand Larceny and Capital Crimes Against Property

Grand Larceny

Clergyable grand larceny—theft of goods or cash worth 1s or more—was by far the most common property offence tried at the regional assizes, as it was elsewhere in England. It was also prosecuted fairly regularly at quarter sessions during the first two and last three decades of the eighteenth century. Furthermore, it was a frequently returned lesser verdict when a more serious felony, such as housebreaking, had initially been indicted at the higher forum. Juries were well aware that it was (effectively) not capital. As a result, they had far fewer qualms about convicting for the crime than they did for unclergyable property offences.

Being such a broad-ranging offence, grand larceny was committed in a huge variety of ways: at work, in taverns, in homes, on farms, in the street, and at public gatherings. Some cases were straightforward, others more complicated. In an extreme example of the latter from 1751, Stephen Warsse was transported for stealing a large amount of beer from Leonard Shelford, a major Thetford brewer. Over a period of several years Warsse had abstracted the beverage from casks that were about to be sent out, replacing what he took with water.[1]

In the decade from 1751 to 1760, the regional assizes tried 135 cases that were indicted as grand larceny, so that the offence made up more than half (about 56 per cent) of all property indictments heard in this

1. *Ipswich Journal*, 12 October 1751.

forum (animal theft being excluded). Of the 135 cases, 79 (about 56 per cent) produced at least one finding of guilt for the full offence charged. Another 25 (just over 18 per cent) did not produce convictions for grand larceny but resulted in at least one finding of petty theft being returned, the goods taken having been valued at less than 1s. A further 31 cases (about 23 per cent) produced outright acquittals for all accused. Of those convicted of the full offence, the vast majority were sentenced to seven years' transportation, although not all these sentences were necessarily carried out. A small number of grand-larceny convicts were merely clergied and discharged, or clergied and sentenced to a short spell in a house of correction under an act from 1706.

By contrast, nearly all those convicted of the lesser offence of petty theft were sentenced to a whipping, although after 1718 trial judges had a discretionary power to transport them. In East Anglia judges normally (though not invariably) accepted the jury's allocation of culpability in these situations. This meant that a small difference in ascribed value could be important. At the Suffolk Quarter Sessions held at Ipswich in January 1787, John Hammond was convicted of stealing a brass chattel valued at 2s, a minor case of grand larceny. He was sentenced to seven years' transportation. By contrast, at the same sessions John Double was found guilty of stealing a bucket of coals valued at ten pence, whipped, and discharged.[2]

Capital Forms of Larceny

During the early modern period, certain forms of grand larceny, committed in specific circumstances, were made capital offences by withdrawing them from clergy. Some of the earliest of these statutes were enacted in the sixteenth century, when pickpocketing and horse-theft were removed from the privilege. However, there had then been a period of almost a century when no *major* new forms of capital larceny were created. After 1689 the process resumed and accelerated quickly, so that many more

2. SRO QS B105/2/48.

forms of theft, committed in specific circumstances, attracted a death sentence.

Unlike most of the more arcane offences established under the Bloody Code, such as damaging certain named bridges, some (but not all) of these post-1689 forms of capital larceny were prosecuted fairly frequently, throughout the country. Among them were stealing goods worth more than 40s in a dwelling-house (withdrawn from clergy in 1713), the theft of sheep (withdrawn in 1741), and that of cattle (1742). Others, such as shoplifting (1699), were significant in the Metropolis, but prosecuted less frequently in many other parts of England and Wales. Clergy was also withdrawn from, *inter alia*, theft from warehouses, merchant vessels, the mail, and bleaching grounds, although these offences were not indicted often. Three of the most important eighteenth-century forms of capital theft other than those involving animals (dealt with in *Chapter 16*) are considered below.

Pickpocketing

Legally, picking pockets was a particular type of theft, one that involved "privately" (secretly) stealing goods or cash worth more than 1s from another's person. This was a long-standing capital crime, rather than a new Bloody Code offence, as it dated back to the Elizabethan era (8 El, c 4, v 6). It required a specially worded indictment. Picking pockets of goods below 1s in value remained petty theft and thus not capital under any circumstances. Additionally, openly "snatching" goods worth 12d or more from the person did not normally qualify, as it was not done secretly. As the century advanced the technical requirements for the offence, especially the meaning of "privately," came to be interpreted increasingly strictly, reducing its scope.[3] Nevertheless, in the Metropolis it was an important and regularly prosecuted form of property crime throughout the era. By contrast, in Norfolk and Suffolk pickpocketing was a relatively rarely indicted offence. There was also a smaller, albeit still significant, female involvement in the crime than was found in the

3. D. Palk, *Gender, Crime and Judicial Discretion*, 2006, pp. 69–70.

capital, where women made up half of all defendants. In this the East Anglian region broadly accords with gender patterns found on the Western Circuit in the early 1700s.

Taking the single years sampled for each decade until the end of the century, it seems that there were no prosecutions for the offence anywhere in East Anglia in 1735, 1747, or 1754. At the Norwich City Assizes held in August 1764, two men, John Kettle and Henry Norton, were tried for "stealing 4s secretly of Sam Bead." Both were acquitted. This appears to have been the only such case heard in the entire region that year.[4] There was just one prosecution in 1774. At the Thetford Assizes that year, a labourer named Matthew Yaxley was acquitted outright of picking the pocket of John Howard of more than £3. There were no prosecutions for the offence in 1784 and 1797, the remaining sample years. Thus there were two prosecutions, involving a total of three defendants, over the seven years sampled. To consider a longer but continuous period, there were no prosecutions for pickpocketing during the entire decade from 1751 to 1760.[5] As a result, it seems that, on average, fewer than three cases of pickpocketing were indicted in the region every decade. By contrast, ten people, all of them women, were prosecuted for the crime in the Metropolis during 1760 alone.

It also appears that nobody in East Anglia was hanged for the crime between 1735 and 1800. People had been executed in the region for the offence during the previous century. In 1629 a "purse-picker" had been "caught in the act" in court at the Thetford Assizes. The presiding judge had immediately had him examined by an attending JP, tried, and, after conviction, hanged (all in the space of four days).[6] In the six counties of the Western Circuit, nine people (including one female) were hanged for the crime between 1670 and 1729.[7] However, after the early eighteenth century, it was increasingly felt that imposing capital punishment for such an offence was, in William Blackstone's words, a "most severe

4. TNA ASSI 33/4.
5. TNA ASSI 33/2–3.
6. M. Green (ed.), *Diary of John Rous, Incumbent of Santon Downham, Suffolk, from 1625 to 1642*, 1856, pp. 48–49.
7. M. Eder, *"At the Instigation of the Devil": Capital Punishment and the Assize in the Early Modern England, 1670–1730*, 2014, pp. 71–75 and p. 113.

law." Even at the start of the era, Timothy Nourse had listed pickpockets amongst "lesser criminals" whose crimes did not deserve death.[8] Blackstone thought that the offence had only been made capital because of the ease with which it could be committed and the difficulty of preventing it.[9] Attitudes changed a little more slowly in the metropolitan area. It appears that 57 people were capitally convicted of the crime at the Old Bailey between the start of 1735 and the end of 1800. Of these, 14 were executed at Tyburn in the years up to 1754, after which hangings for the offence ceased, even in the capital.

Nevertheless, there were a small number of capital convictions for picking pockets or "secretly stealing from the person" at East Anglian assizes during the course of the century, albeit that they were all ultimately reprieved after 1735 (if not before). For example, in 1745 Elizabeth Macdonald was convicted at the Bury Assizes for picking the pocket of Daniel Richards of 13 guineas 1s.[10] Despite the large sum involved, she was swiftly granted clemency on condition of transportation.[11] Between 1768 and 1800, at least five people were found guilty of the full offence and reprieved. Among them was Thomas Thorpe, a Suffolk bricklayer, who was convicted in 1768 of stealing a silver watch and money from the person of a seaman who was asleep in bed at the Pickerell Inn in Ixworth.[12] In 1790 Henry Robinson was convicted at the Norfolk Assizes in Norwich for picking the pocket of a farmer at Downham Market the previous year, but immediately reprieved on condition of seven years' transportation.[13] Two years later, at the Suffolk Assizes, Robert Carman was capitally convicted for "privately stealing" a purse containing 9 guineas, a silver watch, and a silk handkerchief. Despite the high value, he, too, was administratively reprieved before the trial judge even left town.[14] More understandably, at the Lent Assizes for Norfolk in 1795, there was an immediate reprieve for stealing goods valued at 19s "privately from

8. T. Nourse, *Campania Folix. Or, a Discourse of the Benefits and Improvements of Husbandry*, 1706, p. 229.
9. W. Blackstone, *Commentaries on the Laws of England*, vol. 4, 1769, p. 241.
10. *Westminster Journal Or New Weekly Miscellany*, 17 August 1745.
11. *General Advertiser (1744)*, 13 August 1745.
12. *Public Advertiser*, 3 August 1768.
13. *Oracle Bell's New World*, 12 August 1789.
14. *General Evening Post*, 4–7 August 1792.

the person" (probably a low-value silver watch).[15] At the Summer Assizes for the same county, the following year, a pickpocket was reprieved after stealing goods and monies worth fully £25, again indicative of acute official reluctance in the region to hang those guilty of the crime.[16] In several other cases, defendants accused of pickpocketing were convicted of the lesser offences of grand or petty larceny.

There are some obvious reasons for the relative dearth of such cases in East Anglia. The crowds in which pickpockets could operate freely, and which were readily and regularly found in the capital, were much less common in the region, even in Norwich. Additionally, there were far fewer prostitutes in Norfolk and Suffolk than in the Metropolis, where a significant number were prosecuted under the statute for stealing from inebriated clients (partly explaining the high female involvement in the capital). However, it may also be that the authorities in East Anglia were reluctant to indict such women for picking pockets when they did steal, because they were less concerned about the crime. This seems to have been the situation in Bristol. Between 1780 and 1805 60 prostitutes went for trial in the western city after stealing from their clients, several of them twice or more, at both quarter sessions and assizes. In almost all cases their crimes were charged as simple larceny, their customers (the prosecutors) or the examining magistrates choosing not to try them for pickpocketing, which was indicted only once (for certain) in Bristol between 1741 and 1799.[17]

Of course, East Anglian pickpockets were still more likely to operate where large groups of people did congregate in the region, such as fairs and markets. Ironically, and as the case from 1623 suggests, this often included legal proceedings and public executions. It was a common observation of the time that there was "nowhere more filching, and picking of pockets, than at the execution of a felon."[18] At the Lent Assizes in Norwich in 1775, a young man was "detected in picking the

15. *St. James's Chronicle Or the British Evening Post*, 26–28 March 1795.
16. Anon, *Report from the Select Committee on Criminal Laws,* 1819, pp. 194–211. This list seems to miss off Robinson.
17. M. Pluskota, *Prostitution in Bristol and Nantes, 1750–1815: A Comparative Study*, 2011, pp. 72–73.
18. Anon, *A Dissertation on the Constitution and Effects of a Petty Jury,* 1737, p. 7.

pocket of one of the magistrates in the Nisi Prius court on the castle-hill." He was arrested and committed to prison to await the following assizes at Thetford.[19] Two years later Thomas Howlett was detained in London and produced at the Bow Street Public Office on suspicion of picking the pocket of John Baldwin at the Bury Assizes held in March 1776. Baldwin had lost bills and notes worth £90 when his pocketbook was taken. A cloth seller from Braintree (Essex) later became suspicious after making a sale to Howlett, who was eventually arrested and sent back to Suffolk for trial.[20]

Shoplifting

The Shoplifting Act of 1699 removed benefit of clergy from "privately stealing" goods worth 5s or more in retail premises, so creating a capital form of theft, provided (like pickpocketing) it was prosecuted under an appropriately worded indictment. If theft from a shop was valued at less than 5s but more than 11d, or not deemed to have been done "privately," even if for more than the former sum—for example, if the goods had been "snatched" in view of the shop owner—the crime would be simple grand larceny. If the stolen goods were valued at under 12d, the crime would be petty theft, even if the items had been taken secretly. The statute was introduced at the behest of London retailers.[21]

Shopkeepers were not obliged to indict for the capital rather than a lesser crime, and many did not, especially as the century advanced. Furthermore, if they did, juries could convict of lesser crimes, and this was also commonplace, particularly in the provinces.[22] Thus, in 1781, John Pike was tried at the Norfolk Quarter Sessions in Norwich for grand larceny after stealing several cheap handkerchiefs from a shopkeeper at Reepham (he was convicted of petty larceny and whipped in Aylsham market).[23] At the Suffolk Assizes in 1788, Thomas Hayward was sentenced

19. *Morning Post and Daily Advertiser*, 22 August 1775.
20. *Public Advertiser*, 5 June 1777.
21. T. Hitchcock and R. Shoemaker, *London Lives*, 2015, p. 61.
22. S. G. Tickell, *Shoplifting in Eighteenth-century England*, 2015, p. 182.
23. *Norfolk Chronicle*, 13 January 1781.

to seven years' transportation after being convicted of grand larceny for stealing goods from the shop of Samuel Leeds in Hemiston.[24]

There were two main ways in which a shoplifting charge could be reduced to ordinary theft: finding that one of the situational prerequisites for such a crime had not been proved or valuing the items taken below the strategic sum of 5s. An example of the latter occurred in 1735, when Robert Rochester, accused at the Bury Assizes of "privately stealing" in the shop of Samuel Bigg, merely appears to have been convicted to the value of 4s.[25] Similarly, at the Suffolk Assizes in March 1746, Thomas Smith was found guilty to the value of 4s 6d after being indicted for shoplifting goods worth 7s. More drastically, at the Norfolk Assizes in March 1748, Richard Wisking was prosecuted for shoplifting goods worth 15s but only found guilty to the value of 4s.[26] On an even more extreme scale, in August 1754, at the Norfolk Assizes, James Nelson was accused of stealing goods valued at 25 shillings from the shop of George Thomas, but merely convicted to the value of four shillings and ten pence.[27] In exceptional cases, the stolen goods were down-valued to below 1s so that the charge became one of petty theft. For example, at the Bury Assizes in 1735, John Jackson appears to have been found guilty of stealing goods from a shop to the value of 4d, although, in this case, the trial judge took the draconian and unusual (but legal) step of ordering his transportation for petty theft under the 1718 act; clearly, he felt that the jury's charity was excessive.[28]

Alternatively, a jury could convict of simple grand larceny after concluding that the technical requirements necessary for an offence to be made out under the 1699 act—most important, that the goods had been taken "privately"—had not been made out. This became more common after the early 1700s, as the 1699 statute was interpreted increasingly strictly.[29] Thus, Palgrave Cook, who was capitally tried for stealing goods from the shop of William Winters at the Norwich City Assizes in the

24. *The Times*, 28 March 1788, p. 3.
25. TNA ASSI 33/1.
26. Gray's Inn MS 45.
27. TNA ASSI 33/2.
28. TNA ASSI 33/1.
29. D. Palk, *Gender, Crime and Judicial Discretion: 1780–1830*, 2006, p. 70.

summer of 1734, was merely found guilty of grand larceny because the jury decided that he had not stolen the items in question "secretly." As a result, he was sentenced to seven years' transportation, and even this appears to have been commuted to being clergied, branded, and discharged.[30] Similarly, at the City of Norwich Assizes in March 1754, two men accused of shoplifting goods worth 7s from the retail premises of James Fuller were found to have stolen the items, but "not privately."[31] At the same forum in 1784, Mary Haslup was acquitted of shoplifting handkerchiefs and ribbons from the premises of Thomas Cole on the same basis, and merely found guilty of grand larceny to the value of 18s.[32] Any kind of break-in to secure items in a shop precluded an indictment under the 1699 act, and even the theft of cash (rather than goods) was eventually considered to be outside its scope.[33]

In East Anglia, as in most parts of the nation outside London, successful prosecutions under the 1699 statute appear to have been fairly rare, although the crime was indicted more frequently than pickpocketing, and executions were extremely unusual. The region was certainly not unique in this. Even during the first three decades of the century, of 83 people indicted for shoplifting on the whole of the Western Circuit, only seven (three of them female) were convicted, and of these, just two (both men) were hanged.[34] However, in Yorkshire, conviction rates for the full offence exceeded 25 per cent for some of the era, albeit that almost all those found guilty were reprieved from execution.[35]

In Norfolk and Suffolk (and as with pickpocketing) executions for the crime were almost unheard of after the early years of the eighteenth century. This is unsurprising. Representations from business interests operating in the quite different commercial conditions prevailing in the Metropolis had been the driving force behind the introduction of the 1699 statute. It regularly produced hangings in the capital until quite late in the century, and even a handful of executions during its last three

30. TNA ASSI 33/1.
31. TNA ASSI 33/2.
32. TNA ASSI 33/6 and ASSI 33/7.
33. S. G. Tickell, *Shoplifting in Eighteenth-century England*, 2015, pp. 175–179.
34. M. Eder, *"At the Instigation of the Devil": Capital Punishment and the Assize in the Early Modern England, 1670–1730*, 2014, p. 76.
35. R. Markless, *Gender, Crime and Discretion in Yorkshire, 1735–1775*, 2013, p. 255.

decades. Amongst the latter were the youthful George Reynolds, executed for stealing 12 hats in 1785, and William Brown, who died for lifting six watches from a shop in 1794.[36]

Things were different in East Anglia. Typically, when Iphemia Barnes was found guilty under the 1699 act at the Thetford Assizes in 1727, she was granted clemency.[37] Nevertheless, it seems that William Linger was capitally convicted of shoplifting at Norwich the following year and not, initially, reprieved.[38] It is not clear whether he was subsequently executed. According to one account, in 1737 John Bicker was convicted of shoplifting at the Bury Assizes and hanged.[39] However, other reports suggest, much more plausibly, that his crime was housebreaking.[40] In reality it seems that nobody was hanged in East Anglia for shoplifting in the years between 1735 and 1800. On the relatively few occasions when there were capital convictions, clemency followed.

Even so, prosecutions for the crime were not uncommon. Nine alleged shoplifters were tried (in seven prosecutions) in the region during the two-and-a-half years beginning in the summer of 1734 and ending at the close of 1736. Only one, Henry Coleman, tried at Bury in 1735, was convicted of the full offence, and he was subsequently reprieved, even though he had stolen a silver watch valued at 4 guineas from the shop of Mark Hawkins (presumably a jeweller). Four other men were convicted of a lesser offence (grand or petty larceny). The remaining four defendants were acquitted outright. (It was alleged that these men had operated in two pairs of shoplifters). In the decade after 1751, far fewer shoplifting cases came to court; just three defendants were indicted for the crime in two trials; all of the accused were convicted of simple grand larceny. By contrast, there were 101 prosecutions for shoplifting during the same ten-year period in the metropolitan area.

Prosecutions were being brought, and convictions secured, for the full offence to the very end of the period and beyond. Between 1768 and 1800,

36. *Public Advertiser*, 15 September 1785; *Public Advertiser*, 11 November 1785; *Public Advertiser or Political and Literary Diary*, 3 February 1794.
37. *Weekly Journal Or British Gazetteer*, 1 April 1727.
38. *Country Journal Or The Craftsman*, 24 August 1728.
39. *Daily Post*, 29 March 1737.
40. *London Evening Post*, 12–14 April 1737.

at least five people were found guilty of shoplifting at four trials. In 1803 and 1804 two more were convicted of the same crime.[41] Thus in March 1784 John Wilding was found guilty after shoplifting a gold timepiece worth £10 from the premises of Henry Browning, a Bury watchmaker. Although this was a fairly "grave" example of the crime, the trial judge immediately reprieved him on recommendation of seven years' transportation to America. (By then there was no prospect of such a sentence's being carried out).[42] In 1789 James Waterson was capitally convicted of stealing goods from a shop at Hibbard, in Suffolk.[43] He was later transported to Australia for life. The following year William Gant was found guilty of shoplifting two watches from retail premises at Downham Market, in Norfolk, but reprieved.[44] Less seriously, in 1796 John Ventris was convicted of shoplifting five pieces of muslin from a Bury linen draper, but (administratively) reprieved before the trial judge left town.[45]

Unsurprisingly, and as the examples set out above suggest, a disproportionate number of shoplifting cases came from Norwich, which had the largest and most developed retail industry in East Anglia, considerably greater than that found in Bury or Ipswich, and far larger than those in the small towns and villages. It was also more conscious of the "threat" posed by this sort of crime. Of the seven cases of shoplifting that went to trial between 1734 and 1736, four of them (including two with two defendants) came from the city. That one of the two pairs of men who were jointly indicted, John Mann and Timothy Ward, escaped being prosecuted for a second charge, on the basis that the matter had been "tried before" at an earlier sessions, would suggest a degree of criminal specialism, something that would accord with their stealing together. Working in pairs was a fairly common *modus operandi* in retail theft, with one person distracting the shopkeeper while the other stole, or, alternatively, carrying off goods that had initially been appropriated by a colleague and then passed on.

41. Anon, *Report From the Select Committee on Criminal Laws*, 1819, pp. 194–214.
42. TNA ASSI 33/6 and ASSI 33/7; *St. James's Chronicle Or the British Evening Post*, 3–6 April 1784; TNA HO 47/3/118.
43. *Oracle Bell's New World*, 12 August 1789.
44. *Whitehall Evening Post (1770)*, 20–23 March 1790.
45. *Sun*, 31 March 1796.

More surprisingly, only one of the seven cases involved a woman. This was markedly at variance to the position in the Metropolis and some other parts of the country, where females made up a majority, or at least a substantial component, of those indicted for shoplifting. For example, a random selection of cases from the Yorkshire Assizes between 1735 and 1775 produces a male/female ratio of 13 to 14.[46] In London about half of those prosecuted for the crime during the eighteenth century were female, while on the Northern Circuit almost two-thirds were women during the 100 years after 1726. Although the East Anglian sample is too small to allow many firm conclusions, there does, at least, appear to have been a higher male involvement in the crime than was found in some other areas. Nevertheless, as elsewhere, women still dominated certain types of shoplifting, such as that involving the theft of cloth. (About three-quarters of such cases in London and Northern England involved females).[47] Typically, in 1736 Elizabeth Dey was prosecuted under the 1699 act after she stole some cambric from a shop in Norwich, albeit that she was merely convicted of clergyable grand larceny, burnt in the hand, and discharged (a lenient disposal).[48] Almost 70 years later, in 1803, Elizabeth Eagle was capitally convicted of stealing a piece of printed cotton from a shop in Downham Market but immediately reprieved by the judge.[49]

Stealing from a Dwelling-house

Theft from domestic premises of goods worth more than 40s, where those premises had not first been broken into, was withdrawn from clergy in 1713 (12 Ann, c 7). It was often referred to as "stealing from a dwelling-house." The enabling act was partly introduced to deal with servants who were legally in their masters' houses but stole high-value

46. R. Markless, *Gender, Crime and Discretion in Yorkshire, 1735–1775*, 2013, p. 254.
47. S. G. Tickell, *Shoplifting in Eighteenth-century England*, 2015, p. 28 and p. 194.
48. *Daily Gazetteer*, 31 August 1736.
49. *The Bury and Norwich Post: Or, Suffolk, Norfolk, Essex, and Cambridge Advertiser*, 30 March 1803.

goods from them, or who deliberately allowed thieves into their employers' homes, so precluding charges of burglary and housebreaking from being brought.[50]

However, the offence was not confined to domestic staff or those connected with them; it covered anyone who stole from a dwelling-house without first "breaking and entering." Most of those accused of the crime were not servants. If, for example, a passerby noticed that a house door was open or unlocked, slipped inside, and took goods worth more than £2, they would be liable under the statute, as occurred with the heroine of Daniel Defoe's novel *Moll Flanders* of 1722. Flanders was indicted both for burglary and, under the 1713 Act, for stealing valuable lace, having "ventur'd into a house where I saw the doors open." She was acquitted of burglary, the jury accepting that she had walked (not broken) in, but capitally convicted for stealing goods worth more than 40 shillings in a dwelling-house.[51]

As Flanders' (fictional) experience suggests, a count under the 1713 Act was occasionally indicted as an alternative to one for housebreaking or burglary, in the event that a forced entry was not established on the evidence. In theory this was not always necessary. In *Comer's Case* in 1744 the "twelve judges" (actually nine, because of illness) agreed that it was possible to convict under the 1713 Act as a lesser (but still capital) crime on a burglary indictment providing the jury made it clear that they were acquitting of the more serious charge because breaking and entering had not been made out, and that all the other elements of the offence were set out in the indictment and established on the evidence. Otherwise, the correct lesser verdict would be one of clergyable grand larceny.[52] In practice it was normally easier to indict under the 1713 Act as an alternative count, as occurred with John Stubbins, who was accused of stealing £21 from a house at the Bury Assizes in 1760, albeit acquitted of both.[53] When Sarah Lloyd was prosecuted at the same forum in March 1800, she was less fortunate. She was acquitted of the burglary on the direction of

50. P. Humfrey, "Female Servants and Women's Criminality in Early Eighteenth-century London," 1998, p. 74.
51. D. Defoe, *The Fortunes and Misfortunes of the Famous Moll Flanders*, 1722, p. 3[illegible]5.
52. T. Leach, *Cases in Crown Law*, 1789, pp. 37–38.
53. TNA ASSI 33/3.

the judge. Being a servant who was already inside the residence, Lloyd "did not break into the house." However, she was convicted of theft from a dwelling-house, sentenced to death, and executed.[54]

Offences under the 1713 Act were prosecuted fairly frequently in East Anglia, far more so than either pickpocketing or shoplifting. Nevertheless, juries were often reluctant to convict for such crimes, and judges were usually loath to hang those found guilty when they did. This was not a regional phenomenon, being found throughout England. In the 17 years immediately after 1713, well under 30 per cent of cases tried on the Western Circuit produced convictions for the full offence.[55] In East Anglia conviction for simple grand larceny was a fairly common verdict when an offence was indicted under the 1713 Act and the trial jury thought that a crime had been committed. Such convictions were usually returned by down-valuing the stolen goods below the 40s limit, although finding that the alleged "dwelling-house" was another type of building might also have this effect, as occurred when James Douglas was tried at the Bury Assizes in 1754.[56]

Outright acquittals were usually genuine reflections of there being a doubt in the minds of the jury about the accused having had any involvement in a crime; partial verdicts were more commonly (though not invariably) cases of pious perjury. For example, three men were separately accused of "theft from a dwelling-house" at various East Anglian Assizes in 1751. All were convicted of simple theft, their stolen items having been valued at below the 40s limit.[57] Thus George Bellybone, accused of stealing goods worth just over £4 from the house of Thomas Dennis, was convicted to the value of 35s. More drastically, Thomas Mundy, accused of stealing goods worth more than £12 from the home of a widow named Ann Pratt, was convicted to the value of 39s, despite the large amount of money involved and a female victim. Finally, James Large was accused of stealing £13 16s 6d from a dwelling-house but convicted to the value of

54. TNA ASSI 33/3; Anon, *Trial of Joseph Clarke, the Younger, and Sarah Lloyd, at the Assizes, Held at Bury St. Edmund's*, 1800, p. 7.
55. M. Eder, *"At the Instigation of the Devil": Capital Punishment and the Assize in the Early Modern England, 1670–1730*, 2014, p. 116.
56. TNA ASSI 33/2.
57. TNA ASSI 33/2.

just 35 shillings.[58] Given these formulaic jury valuations, and the amounts alleged in the indictments, all appear to have been cases of pious perjury.

On a more statistical basis, and considering the sampled years after 1730, no one was prosecuted for the crime at any of the assizes held in the region during 1735 or 1747. In 1754 four cases were indicted as theft from a dwelling-house, but only one produced a capital conviction for the full offence. The others led to verdicts of simple theft.[59] The one capital conviction, that of James Hall at the Thetford Assizes, involved stealing the large sum of £34 13s in cash. He was subsequently reprieved. In 1764 two people were capitally convicted and reprieved before the regional assizes for separate cases of stealing in a dwelling-house. Both were tried at Thetford. Francis Crickmore had taken goods worth £5 from the residence of Samuel Buxton, while Mary Fisher stole goods worth £5 5 shillings from the home of Sir John Turner. (She was probably a servant.)[60] In 1774 there was one prosecution for the crime, at the City of Norwich Assizes. Martha Lester was capitally convicted of stealing goods worth more than £10 from the home of George Southern. She was sentenced to death but successfully "pleaded her belly," the jury of matrons finding that she was "quick with child" and so could not be hanged.[61] In 1784 there were four prosecutions for the crime, three of which produced full (but reprieved) convictions and one of them a lesser conviction for grand larceny after the goods taken were valued at 39s. In 1797 there were no prosecutions.

Thus, there were eleven prosecutions during the seven years sampled. Of these, seven (more than half) resulted in convictions for the full offence, none of which resulted in executions. However, another four cases produced guilty verdicts for simple theft. There were no outright acquittals. To take a shorter but continuous period of time, during the decade after 1751 there were 26 prosecutions for "theft from a dwelling house" at the regional assizes. Of these, just five (less than 20 per cent) produced at least one conviction for the full offence. Another 14 (more than half) resulted in at least one conviction for the lesser offence of

58. TNA ASSI 33/2.
59. TNA ASSI 33/4.
60. TNA ASSI 33/4.
61. TNA ASSI 33/6.

simple grand larceny. In seven cases (more than a quarter), all the defendants were acquitted outright. Although the verdicts returned differed considerably over time, it seems that, for much of the century, two people a year on average were indicted under the 1713 Act.

Very few people were hanged for the crime in East Anglia. According to the Select Committee on Criminal Laws of 1819, seven of the 46 people who were convicted of the offence in the region between 1768 and 1800 were "left for execution."[62] Even so, this does not tally with other reports, which suggest just two cases in this period. Convictions under the 1713 Act were easy to confuse with those for housebreaking, burglary, and robbery inside domestic premises, and this is what the 1819 committee, looking back over many years, seems to have done. For example, according to the Select Committee, one case of execution under the 1713 Act occurred at the Norfolk Assizes during Lent 1785. However, the only possible hanging, that of John Ferrett, involved the burglary of a Yarmouth widow's house.[63] In reality, stealing from a dwelling-house appears to have produced just three or (at the very most) four executions in the entire East Anglian area between 1735 and 1800. They were all particularly extreme cases, at least two involving gross breaches of trust.

At the City of Norwich Assizes in 1752, Daniel Wilson was capitally convicted of stealing goods worth £19 16s from Robert Horey's dwelling-house, which was also the Star Inn in the city's marketplace. His loot consisted of several silver tankards, mugs, and spoons. His execution was fixed for a week after the assizes finished, when he was duly hanged.[64] In 1768 Martha Green, a 20-year-old servant was hanged for stealing diamonds, garnets, and other jewellery of enormous value from her mistress's dwelling-house in Suffolk.[65] So serious was this crime that Sir John Fielding, the Bow Street Police Office magistrate, issued a public advertisement offering five guineas for her capture.[66] In 1799, at the Bury Assizes, Sarah Lloyd, a young maid working at Hadleigh, in Suffolk, was convicted of the same crime, committed in particularly

62. Anon, *Report from the Select Committee on Criminal Laws*, 1819, pp. 194–210.
63. *Public Advertiser*, 26 March 1785.
64. *General Advertiser (1744)*, 11 August 1752.
65. *St. James's Chronicle Or the British Evening Post*, 28–30 July 1768; *Public Advertiser*, 3 August 1768.
66. *Public Advertiser*, 28 June 1768.

aggravating circumstances, and executed (see below).[67] In 1743, William Goodward *may* have been hanged for the same crime after the Suffolk Assizes, although the details are uncertain.

Despite the paucity of executions, there was an average of considerably more than one reprieved capital conviction for this offence each year, even in the final three decades of the century. Some of them were quite grave manifestations of the crime. For example, at the Thetford Assizes in 1781, Robert Andrews was convicted of stealing 32 guineas from the house of Thomas Sutton in Shipdham but reprieved by the trial judge before he left the town.[68] Others had narrower escapes from execution. In March 1763 Edmund George and Jonathan Allen were sentenced to death at the Thetford Assizes for taking a box containing 19 guineas, along with an assortment of clothes, from a house. Influenced by the sum taken, the trial judge not only refused to reprieve them, but set their execution date for 2 April.[69] Nevertheless, this was ultimately put back, and, in August of that year, the two men were reprieved on condition of 14 years' transportation.[70] Presumably there had been a successful petition to the Crown asking for clemency in the meantime.

Given that juries were often reluctant to convict for offences under the 1713 Act, and judges loath to execute those found guilty, it might be wondered why so many lesser or middle-ranking examples of the crime were indicted, instead of being prosecuted as simple grand larceny *ab initio*. Sometimes it was probably done to give the defendants a scare. For example, in 1752, when John Francis and John Ashby were capitally indicted at the Thetford Assizes for stealing goods worth 43 shillings from the dwelling-house of a spinster, it was always extremely unlikely that the trial jury would fail to reduce the value of goods taken by four shillings to a non-capital 39s (as indeed occurred and for which both men were transported). In other circumstances—a single defendant and a male victim—this would probably have been charged as grand larceny from

67. *The Times*, 11 April 1800, p. 3; Anon, *Trial of Joseph Clark, the Younger, and Sarah Lloyd*, 1800, pp. 7–10.
68. *Whitehall Evening Post (1770)*, 22–24 March 1781.
69. *Lloyd's Evening Post and British Chronicle*, 25–28 March 1763.
70. *Lloyd's Evening Post*, 5–8 August 1763.

the start.[71] However, the willingness to indict for crimes under the 1713 Act also reflects a general reluctance by complainants and (even more so) examining magistrates to ignore the "black-letter" law emanating from Parliament on this issue. Instead, they preferred to leave it to the judge and jury to mitigate the consequences of such a prosecution.

Burglary and Housebreaking

More people were executed for burglary and housebreaking (taken together) than for any other crime in East Anglia. Both crimes usually involved the violation of a domestic residence for material gain. Between 1735 and the end of 1799, 45 people were hanged for the two offences in Norfolk, out of a total of 138 executed for the entire county (including the City of Norwich, King's Lynn, and Yarmouth). Thus, this type of crime contributed about a third of all executions. In Suffolk there were 51 cases out of 116 executions, making up somewhat less than half of the county's hangings. For the region as a whole, the combined figure of 96 out of 254 executions produces a result that was almost 40 per cent of the area's total. This was not unusual. As late as the 70 years after 1760, a quarter of those executed after being convicted at the Chester Great Sessions had been found guilty of burglary alone (the great majority prior to 1800).[72]

The high proportion of hangings for this form of crime reflects its ubiquity, the gravity with which it was viewed, and the number of offenders both caught and convicted. Its attractions were obvious. It did not normally require special skills or equipment to perpetrate, and it could be lucrative. In parts of Wales, the average proceeds of a prosecuted burglary in the 1730s were almost the same as a husbandman's wages for six months or that of a dairymaid for a year.[73]

71. TNA ASSI 33/2.
72. J. Walliss, "Crime and Justice in Georgian Cheshire; The Chester Court of Great Sessions, 1760–1830," 2015, p. 53.
73. N. Woodward, "Burglary in Wales, 1730–1830: Evidence From the Great Sessions," 2008, p. 73.

Burglary

Burglary was an unclergyable felony of long standing. Sir Nash Grose succinctly summed up its legal definition when presiding over a trial held at the Bury Assizes in 1800. It was "breaking and entering into a house in the night, when it is dark, by forcing the bolts, locks, or bars, so as to amount to a forcible entry."[74] Furthermore, as Sir Mathew Hale noted in the seventeenth century, the entry had to be with an "intent to commit a felony therein, whether the felony be actually committed or not." Thus it was necessarily nocturnal, taking place after sunset and before sunrise. It covered domestic residences but not such buildings as barns and outhouses, and required some form of "breaking" to gain entry. Obviously, this included smashing a window, as occurred when the dwelling-house of the Reverend Charles Topping was burgled in West Bradenham (Norfolk); three panes of glass were cut away from the kitchen window, allowing entry to the premises.[75] However, burglary also encompassed entry via picking a lock or using a skeleton or stolen key. It did not require that identifiable and permanent damage be inflicted on the building to gain access.[76] By contrast, walking through an open door to steal was not burglary. This meant that the distinction between the capital offence and a lesser crime might be dependent on whether the door by which offenders gained entry had been locked or bolted.[77] In theory, the offence was complete on entry with a felonious intent, even if no further crime actually occurred; this was usually to steal, much more rarely to rape or murder.

Burglary occasioned particularly acute public anxiety. As it was "perpetrated in the night, the surprise and terror it gives to the persons robbed, adds to the crime."[78] This was especially marked because of the lack of effective artificial light. Unsurprisingly, the winter months were the most problematic in this regard. During the long hours of darkness,

74. W. Notcutt, *Trial of Joseph Clarke, the Younger, and Sarah Lloyd, at the Assizes, Held at Bury St. Edmund's*, 1800, p. 7.
75. *Norfolk Chronicle*, 13 September 1783.
76. W. Blackstone, *Commentaries on the Laws of England*, vol. 4, 1769, p. 226.
77. Anon, *A Charitable Visit to the Prisons*, 1709, p. 28 and p. 30.
78. G. Jacob, *The Student's Companion: Or, The Reason of the Laws of England*, 1725, p. 14.

ill-disposed people were "more easily secreted, and of course the property and safety of individuals exposed to the greater danger."[79] This fear was particularly powerful in isolated rural areas. In 1701 one observer claimed that the popular dread of burglars in such parts was "greater than can well be express'd, or than the Inhabitants of Cities and Great Towns, who are well-guarded and secured by their numbers, can imagine."[80] This may explain the fear experienced by Parson Woodforde's niece and housekeeper in 1783, after the barn adjacent to their house in Weston Longville was broken into overnight. A bridle, a hatchet, and a pair of hedging gloves were stolen. Although this was not the most serious crime imaginable, she was so upset that Woodforde had to sit up with her the following night.[81]

In the decade after 1751, there were 49 prosecutions for burglary at the regional assizes, an average of almost five a year. Of these, 17 produced at least one conviction for the full offence. Another 17 resulted in convictions for the lesser crime of grand larceny, and 15 resulted in outright acquittals for all accused. Thus each category made up approximately a third of the total. The 17 cases that produced capital convictions during this decade led to only four executions, two in each county, the remainder resulting in conditional reprieves, so that less than 10 per cent of prosecutions and less than 25 per cent of convictions led to the gallows.[82] This is comparable with Essex at this time, but contrasts with an execution rate that may have been as high as two-thirds of all those convicted of burglary on the Western Circuit half a century earlier (1670 to 1729).[83]

Decisions on capital punishment turned on the facts of each case. A nocturnal "home invasion" of occupied premises in the early hours of the morning by a group of young men, in which owners and servants were tied up and threatened or physically abused, or a case in which high-value goods were stolen, was very different from a single, hungry man or (even more so) woman breaking into a house while it was empty, shortly

79. H. Jodrell, *A Charge Delivered to the Grand Jury of Norfolk, at the General Quarter Sessions Held on Wednesday, Jan. 16, 1793*, 1793, p. 11.
80. Anon, *Hanging, Not Punishment Enough*, 1701, p. 6.
81. J. Beresford (ed.), *The Diary of a Country Parson, 1758–1802*, 1978, p. 197.
82. TNA ASSI 33/2 and 33/3.
83. M. Eder, *"At the Instigation of the Devil": Capital Punishment and the Assize in the Early Modern England, 1670–1730*, 2014, p. 71.

after sunset, and helping themselves to the contents of a larder. Both types of crime occurred. For example, in December 1748, between five and ten (probably six) armed and disguised men broke into the house of Philippa Leman in Wenhaston, Suffolk, and carried off money, jewels, plate, and linen, valued at over £300.[84] During the incident, they tied up two domestic servants. They then went on to raid the house of a nearby farmer and took a further 80 guineas and various pieces of silver.[85] Indicative of the gravity with which these crimes were viewed, the King promised a pardon to any member of the gang who incriminated the others, while the victim offered a reward of £50 for their capture.[86] Many observers thought that this type of burglary was "so nearly related to murder that they seem to demand the same punishment."[87]

By contrast, at the Bury Assizes in March 1759, Mary Walker was convicted of burgling a quantity of pork and cheese at Hartest but immediately (administratively) reprieved by the trial judge.[88] In like manner, at the Norfolk Assizes in August 1774, Thomas Collins, a labourer, was found guilty of burgling the house of Lydia Boast but reprieved before the judge left the town, having been "recommended for pardon at instance of GJ [Grand Jury]." The reason for this is easy to identify. He had stolen bread and cheese worth just one shilling and six pence from Boast after entering her building, and was clearly motivated by pressing need.[89] In 1796 Thomas Risby and Thomas Sturgeon were convicted of burglary at the Bury Assizes but immediately reprieved by their trial judge for the same reason. They, too, had stolen bread and cheese.[90]

The threat or use of violence was always crucial to the decision to hang a convict. Sir Dudley Ryder expressly noted that he reprieved a burglar named Thomas Stebbing on the Home Circuit in 1754 because "nobody [was] put in fear."[91] Any kind of physical confrontation, even

84. *Ipswich Journal*, 10 December 1748.
85. *Whitehall Evening Post Or London Intelligencer*, 8–10 December 1748.
86. *London Gazette*, 3–7 January 1749.
87. J. Bransby, *The Ipswich Magazine, For the Year 1799*, 1799, p. 108.
88. *Ipswich Journal*, 31 March 1759.
89. TNA ASSI 33/5.
90. *Sun*, 31 March 1796.
91. Lincoln's Inn, Harrowby MSS 18–19, Document 19(f) *Legal Notebook of Sir Dudley Ryder*, 1754 and 1755, p. 5.

if no injury were occasioned to the victim, would greatly reduce the prospects of clemency (as it would for housebreaking). For example, at the Bury Assizes in April 1751, James Dunn was convicted of breaking into the house of Edmund West, of Botesdale, and threatening to murder him. He was hanged.[92] Similarly, in 1754 Samuel Agar and another man tricked their way into a house in Norwich and then threatened the owner with a pistol. He resisted and grappled with the men, who fled.[93] Agar was subsequently convicted and executed. The last hanging for burglary in Suffolk, as late as 1832, was a particularly extreme case in this regard. William Twitchett had entered the workhouse at Stradshill with another man and stolen a watch and other items belonging to the elderly governess there. Twitchett, unlike his colleague, had also beaten the woman in a "most savage manner on the head."[94]

Even without these aggravating features, groups of young men who committed burglary were often treated harshly, because such cases always had the potential to create violent confrontations if someone was inside the building. Thus, at the Thetford Assizes in 1736, three men were convicted of burgling the house of George Wellam and stealing money inside. Two of them, John Gilbert and Henry Barton, were hanged.[95] At the Bury Assizes the following year, two brothers, John and Burrell Kitchen, were executed for burglary in a combined house and shop in Needham Market.[96] At the same forum in 1741, John Knights, John Garnham, and James Garnham were all capitally convicted of breaking into the house of the Reverend Humfreys and executed.[97] It was not just high-status victims who received such protection from the courts. In 1787 three former soldiers, each about 20 years old, who had deserted several times during their military careers, were hanged at Rushmere for a burglary committed in the dwelling-house of Samuel Cowes, a gardener from Blundestone, in Suffolk.[98]

---

92. *Read's Weekly Journal Or British Gazetteer*, 6 April 1751.
93. *Whitehall Evening Post Or London Intelligencer*, 23–26 February 1754.
94. *The Morning Post*, 2 August 1832.
95. TNA ASSI 33/1.
96. *London Evening Post*, 26–29 March 1737.
97. *Ipswich Journal,* 28 March 1741; *Country Journal Or The Craftsman*, 4 April 1741.
98. *World and Fashionable Advertiser*, 21 August 1787.

Unsurprisingly, the value of items taken and the previous record of the convict were also important. Jonathan Sawyer was executed in 1780 for burgling the house of John Fisk, of Cretingham, in Suffolk, during which he merely stole a coat, a waistcoat, a few halfpence, and some tea. However, he was a habitual criminal. He had earlier been arrested near Attleborough for deserting from the army (he was a Suffolk man) but escaped by slipping out of his handcuffs "which he got rid of by having brought his hands under his legs, and forced the cuffs with the tine of a fork."[99] When John Manning was executed for burglary after the Lent Assizes for Norfolk in 1777, there were two aggravating factors: the nature of his victim and the amount taken. He had entered the house of a widow and stolen gold and silk worth more than £40.[100]

Nevertheless, even ostensibly serious burglaries could receive clemency in the right circumstances. In 1784 John Payne, a Barrow carpenter, broke into the house of a butcher from the same village at midnight, and stole more than £70 in money and some "writings."[101] Although capitally convicted at the ensuing Suffolk Assizes, he was reprieved before the trial judge even left Bury. Presumably there were special factors present, such as a business dispute that led him to believe he was entitled to the money.[102]

Housebreaking

Housebreaking was the diurnal equivalent of burglary and, like the nocturnal crime, also required forced entry. However, under an act of 1691, it was clergyable when no one was inside the premises during the commission of the crime and the defendant took goods or cash worth less than 5s.[103] For example, in December 1781 the house of Thomas Athow in Holt was broken into. A bureau was forced, but as it contained nothing the housebreakers "made off without any booty."[104] Assuming there

99. *Gazetteer and New Daily Advertiser*, 18 April 1780.
100. *London Evening Post*, 17–19 April 1777. TNA ASSI 33/6.
101. *Public Advertiser*, 20 March 1784.
102. *London Chronicle*, 3–6 April 1784.
103. M. Hale (updated by S. Emlyn), *Sir Matthew Hale's Historia Placitorum Coronae: The History of the Pleas of the Crown*, vol. 1, 1736, p. 547.
104. *Norfolk Chronicle*, 22 December 1781.

was no one at home at the relevant time, this would not have been a capital offence. For this reason, and fairly typically, at the Bury Assizes in August 1734, Christopher Wilson's indictment for the offence carefully noted that when he broke into John Hanniball's house there was "no person therein."[105] Otherwise, like burglary, the crime was not clergyable.

As a result, when Rebecca Wright was accused of housebreaking at the Norfolk Assizes in 1734, after entering the empty residence of Thomas Saul and stealing some of his goods, there were five possible scenarios open to the jury. They could have found her guilty of capital housebreaking for taking property worth more than 5s, though a reprieve would have been likely (the offence was not especially serious). Another possibility was that they could have found her guilty of taking goods worth less than 5s, or clergyable housebreaking. They might have found her guilty of taking the full sum charged, but concluded that there had been no "breaking in." This would then have become clergyable grand larceny. In yet another permutation, they could have found her guilty of stealing goods worth less than 1s without breaking in, or petty theft. Finally, they could have acquitted her outright. They followed the fourth course of action, and found Wright guilty to the value of just ten pence.[106]

Housebreaking was indicted less frequently than burglary. Daytime afforded fewer opportunities to enter properties. As a result, during the decade after 1751, there were only 16 prosecutions at the regional assizes for the crime, about a third of the total for burglary. Interestingly, the same relative proportions were found in Cheshire during the much longer period between 1760 and 1830.[107] Just four of the 16 cases produced convictions (a quarter of the total indicted) for the full offence. Ten more produced findings of guilt for the lesser offence of grand larceny, indicative of its occasioning a lower level of concern than burglary. The remaining two prosecutions resulted in outright acquittals (a much smaller proportion than for burglary).

However, unusually, all four cases that produced convictions in the decade from 1751 resulted in executions. Generally speaking, those who

105. TNA ASSI 33/1.
106. Ibid.
107. J. Walliss, "Crime and Justice in Georgian Cheshire; The Chester Court of Great Sessions, 1760–1830," 2015, p. 45.

were convicted of housebreaking were less likely to be hanged than burglars, as the crime was normally viewed less seriously than its nocturnal equivalent. Most housebreaking cases that resulted in a hanging had severely aggravating features; this proves to be the case with the four convictions referred to above. For example, in August 1751 four men (from two trials) were executed for the crime after the Bury Assizes. Three of them had been part of a group of at least four (and possibly six or seven) men who had broken into the house of the Reverend Ward at Blakenham some three years earlier and robbed him of his watch and other items. They were heavily armed with pistols and blunderbusses.[108] Essentially, this was a diurnal home invasion. One of the gang was allowed to turn King's evidence to secure the others' convictions and was discharged from prison at the end of the proceedings (itself an indication as to how determined the authorities were to secure guilty verdicts). In another case from the same sessions, Robert Clarke had broken into the house of Edmund Wale at Botesdale, in Suffolk, "with an intent to murder him."[109] The other two cases of housebreaking that resulted in execution during the decade involved large sums of money or, in the case of John Watling in 1753, repeat offences.[110]

Nationally, housebreaking normally had a significantly higher incidence of female involvement than burglary. For example, in eighteenth-century Wales women sometimes even outnumbered men accused of the crime.[111] Even so, in East Anglia they were very clearly in a minority of defendants.

Robbery

Robbery was a capital felony; it entailed theft with the use or threat of violence. If someone assaulted another person with an offensive weapon, with the ultimate intention of robbing them, yet without doing so, they committed a lesser statutory felony (7 Geo II, c 21) for which seven years' transportation could be imposed. At the Norfolk Assizes for Thetford

108. *General Evening Post*, 10–13 December 1748.
109. *General Advertiser (1744)*, 6 August 1751.
110. *London Daily Advertiser*, 24 April 1753.
111. N. Woodward, "Burglary in Wales, 1730–1830: Evidence from the Great Sessions," 2008, pp. 73–80.

that opened on 18 March 1749, Benjamin Bullock was convicted of assaulting Daniel Drake with a wooden stick "with intent to rob him of his goods" and received this disposal.[112] In 1783 two footpads were found guilty of this offence and their conviction and sentence was upheld by the 12 judges in London, although the pair were captured before getting round to making any demand for money.[113]

Highway Robbery

"Highway robbery" was by far the most common (prosecuted) form of the crime, and had been the first to be withdrawn from benefit of clergy in the seventeenth century, with all other manifestations of the offence following by 1691. If newspaper reports are accepted, it was not an uncommon crime. Even so, relatively few cases were prosecuted, and even fewer resulted in convictions. There were just three trials for highway robbery at the regional assizes in the 30 months from August 1734 and only one in the three years from 1777.[114] In part, this was because it was often difficult to detain robbers at the scene of their crimes or to prove cases against them if they were apprehended later. Jonathan Sawyer, who was eventually executed near Ipswich for burglary in 1780, gave an account of 15 unprosecuted robberies and other serious crimes that he and his gang had committed earlier.[115]

Even if suspects could be arrested, there were often considerable evidential difficulties when they came to trial, particularly on the crucial issue of identification, as the use of masks was commonplace, and many attacks took place at night. Typically, a highwayman captured at Great Yarmouth in 1733 was found in possession of a crepe hatband that had evidently been used to cover his face.[116] Arrests in such cases might be publicised, so that other potential victims could come forward and identify the suspect or his horse and accoutrements (often as important for

112. Gray's Inn MS 45.
113. R. Burn and G. Chetwynd, *The Justice of the Peace, and Parish Officer*, vol. 4, 1820, pp. 75–76. *R v Trusty and Howard* (1783) 1 East PC 418.
114. TNA ASSI 33/1 and 33/6.
115. *Gazetteer and New Daily Advertiser*, 18 April 1780.
116. *Weekly Miscellany (1732)*, 18 August 1733.

identification purposes as the highwayman). Thus, in 1739, after a man was committed to gaol on suspicion of robbing numerous people going home from Norwich market, a local newspaper reported: "Both man and horse may now be seen at Beccles."[117]

Of course, this procedure was not necessarily successful. In 1782 Michael Hardy, a highwayman who had been active in the area around Dereham, in Norfolk, was captured and committed to the county gaol in Norwich, accused of robbing two women at pistol point a few weeks earlier. Unfortunately, another case that he was suspected of perpetrating on the same day could not be resolved while the examining magistrate questioned him: "The person who was fired at by him the same evening attended the examinations, but could not swear privately to his person."[118]

Highway robbery was a permanent matter of concern, although it was in decline by the final years of the century. At the start of the era one observer claimed that its prevalence meant that all the pleasure of travelling had been destroyed. Even worse, the crime damaged trade and business, as a consequence of the robbing of coaches and the attendant "intercepting Letters of Correspondence and Advice; to say nothing of the insecurity of sending Exchequer and Bank-Bills by the Publick Conveyances."[119] Many East Anglian roads went through sparsely populated areas that had bushes and trees close to the highway, affording concealment and facilitating attacks from cover. Travellers were often carrying considerable amounts of cash and valuables, especially if they were farmers or traders returning from market or travelling to or from London or a provincial town, making them lucrative targets. When the crime eventually petered out, during the 1820s, it was partly due to improvements in the condition and security of roads, and to methods of banking, which had reduced the need to carry cash.

Highway robbery was an overwhelmingly male crime, although, unusually, at the Bury Assizes in August 1746, Mary Grimwood and two other women were jointly accused of robbing Thomas Southern on the road, taking more than £14. (All were acquitted).[120] The crime was in two

117. *Norwich Gazette,* 27 October 1739.
118. *Norfolk Chronicle,* 24 August 1782.
119. Anon, *Hanging, Not Punishment Enough,* 1701, p. 2.
120. Gray's Inn MS 45.

forms: that perpetrated by mounted highwaymen and that committed by horseless footpads. In 1759 a Suffolk tenant farmer encountered both in the space of a few minutes while on the robber-infested road from Beccles to Bungay. Initially, he was stopped by two footpads and robbed of 1 guinea 14 shillings. He was then allowed to ride on, but had gone only a mile before he was stopped again, by a man on horseback, who demanded his money. After he told the highwayman that he had just been robbed, he was allowed to proceed on his way.[121] Although legally these men had committed, or attempted to commit, the same offence, their crimes need separate consideration.

Mounted Highwaymen

In popular myth, mounted highwaymen were the aristocrats of crime. Sometimes, a gentlemanly gesture upheld this image, such as returning money to a poor victim. For example, William Tink and Jeffery Leaks gave back a halfpenny they found on a man they had robbed on Bury Heath.[122] Not infrequently highwaymen would go further, and leave even rich victims with their "charges." a small amount of money to allow them to complete their journeys. This was widely known. In the early 1740s, Jesse Walden and a companion robbed a gentleman in Norfolk, "but he hoping we would give him something to bear his Expences, we return'd him 5 s. of his Money again."[123] Additionally, most English highwaymen avoided lethal violence if they could, if only because it greatly reduced both the popular and the official reaction to their crimes.

However, if necessary, they could be brutal, as the threat of violence was integral to their trade, and not infrequently resorted to in practice. In 1783 two farmers who stumbled across the robbery of the Stowmarket diligence, as it was in progress, were warned to "ride on immediately or they [the highwaymen] would blow their brains out."[124] These were not empty threats, as travellers well knew. In 1722 it was "reported" that a passing female peddler who recognised three highwaymen who had

121. *Norwich Gazette*, 25 October 1759.
122. *Daily Gazetteer* (London Edition), 19 April 1738.
123. OBSP, Ordinary's Account, 7 April 1742: OA17420407.
124. *Ipswich Journal*, 8 February 1783.

intercepted the Bury coach between Epping and Stone Bridge, and foolishly revealed to them that she knew their identities, was given the option of being shot dead on the spot or having her tongue cut out. After many unavailing "tears and entreaties," she apparently submitted to having her tongue removed; it was then thrown into the road. Presumably, she was illiterate and could not write out the robbers' names.[125] More typically (and much more reliably), 40 years later, as John Harvey, a servant in Debenham, was returning from Woodbridge, he was attacked near Helmingham Park gate by three mounted men who demanded that he "stand and deliver." He did not comply, and one of the highwaymen fired a pistol at him. Harvey rode off and, being on a good horse, managed to escape after a pursuit of three miles.[126]

Highwaymen would intercept carriages, riders, and even pedestrians. Their mobility meant they could attack several targets over a relatively short period of time. In 1780 two men, one of them armed with a pistol, and both well-mounted, "infested" the turnpike road between Hockering and Easton, in Norfolk, for several nights in a row. On one evening alone, they stopped and robbed a number of people from various towns and villages who were returning home from Norwich market. Other travellers had a narrow escape. Among them was the Reverend Ives, from Bungay, who had been out collecting his tithes but was warned away by a local boy who overheard the two robbers talking while he (the boy) was setting rabbit traps. With echoes of the Wild West, the two young men had also visited several public houses near Hockering, while much in liquor, and behaved in a riotous manner—buying gunpowder, firing their pistol in the air, and abusing the landlord of one tavern while threatening other drinkers. Eventually, they were detected and chased by several local people, firing at one of their pursuers before escaping through the "goodness of their horses."[127]

As the above case suggests, owning a sound and strong animal was an essential prerequisite for successful highwaymen. The well-equipped ones would also have several firearms, usually pistols or pocket blunderbusses.

125. *Weekly Journal or British Gazetteer*, 28 April 1722.
126. *Ipswich Journal*, 2 January 1762.
127. Ibid., 18 November 1780.

Typically, in 1733 a highwayman captured in Great Yarmouth while in possession of two gold watches taken from an attack on a gentleman's carriage, had two pistols stuck into his breeches.[128] Others carried more, sometimes as many as half a dozen, as reloading the single-shot weapons of the period took time, and they were not entirely reliable. However, firearms were expensive, and carrying them too openly attracted suspicion, so that some men went on the road "undergunned." When a gentleman's gardener was robbed of three shillings and sixpence by two masked highwaymen near Heydon, in Norfolk, only one of his attackers carried a pistol; the other was armed with a knife.[129] A few robbers were reduced to using imitation weapons (see below).

The proceeds of crime could be substantial for competent highwaymen. In 1727 one robbed a gentleman near Attleborough and took £60.[130] The same year, John Huchen was committed to Norwich gaol for robbing a drover of more than £27 while on the road.[131] In an extreme case, Henry Salter, a wealthy maltster (malted grain was used to make beer), was robbed in April 1730, while returning to his home in Nacton, on the Suffolk coast, after doing business in Ipswich. The highwayman escaped with £195.[132] More typically, early one morning in December 1729, a pair of highwaymen stopped both the Norwich and Bury stagecoaches, which were en route to London. They stole £15 7s 6d from the former but just 30 shillings from the latter, as they were disturbed while robbing it. Even so, like all "professional" highwaymen, before they fled they had had the presence of mind to remove the bridles of the coach horses and then scatter the animals, both to prevent pursuit and to delay the authorities from being alerted. As was noted at the time, they "seemed to be fellows of great dexterity in their business."[133]

Such expertise was not universal. Those who were inexperienced, ill-equipped, or acting under impulse might have short careers. In 1780, after two highwaymen were pursued near Hockering, in Norfolk, one

128. *Weekly Miscellany (1732)*, 18 August 1733.
129. *Fog's Weekly Journal*, 29 August 1730.
130. *Daily Journal*, 12 May 1727.
131. Ibid., 4 May 1727.
132. *Weekly Journal or British Gazetteer*, 2 May 1730.
133. *British Journal (1729)*, 3 January 1730.

of them lost his hat and was forced to fire at the chasing villagers. The pair only narrowly escaped. It was later noted that, from their conduct, they appeared to be "young at their trade, and therefore, it is hoped, will soon be taken."[134]

Those being attacked would sometimes fight back. Carrying firearms was normal amongst prosperous travellers until late in the century. For example, in December 1773 John Roddle was killed after a powerful saddle-holstered pistol accidentally went off as he was mounting his horse in the yard of the King's Head, in Norwich.[135] An example of the hazards this posed to highwaymen, especially those who were not properly armed, can be seen in an attempted robbery that took place in Suffolk early one morning in 1776. A highwayman (the son of a local innkeeper) stopped the Norwich coach about one-and-a-half miles from Newmarket, but was immediately shot at and hit by a passenger firing from inside the carriage. He rode off a few yards before his wound caused him to fall from his horse. The highwayman was then taken to the *Red Lion Inn*, in Newmarket "but expired an hour after. He had no pistol but used an iron candlestick."[136]

Jesse Walden, awaiting execution in Newgate Prison, in London, provided some important details about the lives of highwaymen operating in the East Anglian region when relating his criminal biography to the Reverend James Guthrie, the prison ordinary. Although he was from Shoreditch, he had spent time "on the highway" in both Norfolk and Suffolk, itself an indication of the great geographical mobility of such men during the 1700s. They could easily move on before (or after) exciting suspicion.

On one occasion, while riding with a companion on a heath outside Bury, Walden stopped a gentleman who was apparently surprised to find that some highwaymen did not work alone. They took his silver watch, two guineas, horse, and saddle, and then rode ten miles to Thetford, where they spent the night. The next morning they robbed another gentleman of three guineas. After this the two men travelled to King's Lynn,

134. Anon, *Highwaymen*, p. 1. Printed reward notice published in Norwich 1780.
135. NRO NCR Case 6a/10/30.
136. *Ipswich Journal*, 13 January 1776.

where they remained until they had spent all their money, then went towards nearby Houghton, stopping on the way to rob one of the Earl of Orford's servants of the modest sum of six shillngs and six pence, but returning a "Silver Pocket Piece, worth about half a Crown ... upon his pleading Poverty." The pair then went on to Holt, where they diversified into other forms of crime, such as stealing geese. They next robbed a man near Cromer, but in another show of gallantry returned all his money, along with an extra shilling to drink their health, as he was a poor man, and had a large family. From there, they went to Eltham, in Norfolk, where they stole a local clergyman's horse but, finding it an unsatisfactory animal, turned it loose. The two men then relaxed in Norwich, enjoying the various entertainments, before heading back to London.[137]

Of course, as the case involving the innkeeper's son suggests, not all highwaymen were from "out of area." In 1715 it was noted that three individuals, captured the night before for robbing a gentleman near Hellesdonbridge had operated within a stone's throw of their homes, as "all appear to be Norwich-men."[138]

Footpads

Travellers were particularly afraid of footpads, because they were often forced to use serious violence when robbing. This might be employed to stop their victims on the road, to make sure that they were not physically in a position to flee, resist or pursue their attackers, or to ensure that they could not alert others after the criminals made their own, relatively slow, escapes. Unlike highwaymen, footpads were often armed with cudgels and knives rather than firearms. They usually lacked the graces that sometimes marked out their horsed brethren, although this was not invariably the case. For example, James Brown, a surgeon from Long Stratton, was on his way home from Norwich when two footpads stopped him on Dunston Hill. Unlike many of their colleagues, they had pistols, and held one to his breast while demanding his money with "dreadful imprecations." He handed over more than a guinea, but they

137. OBSP Ordinary's Account, 7 April 1742: OA17420407.
138. *Weekly Journal With Fresh Advices Foreign and Domestick*, 14 May 1715.

gave him back a "shilling to defray travelling expences [&], wish'd him a good night, and then made off."[139] John Cooper's experiences were more typical. A maltster from Long Melford, he was walking home from Sudbury market late one Saturday evening when he was knocked down by footpads and robbed of 13 guineas. The blows he received were "so violent as to deprive him of his senses for some time."[140]

Pedestrians on the roads between East Anglian towns and villages, unlike those in the Metropolis, were less likely to carry significant amounts of money. This meant that footpads sometimes had to attack mounted travellers, and so had to unhorse their victims. Occasionally this might be done by guile. For example, one evening in October 1770, a Mr Terry was returning to Hadleigh from Ipswich when he saw a man lying in the road. This individual begged his assistance and said that he had broken his leg. When Terry stopped to assist him, another man rushed out of an adjacent wood, caught hold of his coat, and "swore at him and bid him stop but Mr Terry clapped his horse with his spurs and rending his coat made his escape."[141]

More commonly, stopping mounted travellers necessitated a sudden attack from cover. In February 1766 Joshua Flack was knocked off his horse and robbed of £12 by two footpads between Stowmarket and Bury.[142] Similarly, at the start of 1809, a farmer from Cockfield, in Suffolk, was attacked by four footpads (possibly dressed in military grey), pulled off his horse, and robbed of more than £10.[143] Significant violence might be employed in such situations. One Saturday evening in March 1769, a Lawshall farmer was returning from Sudbury market when he was attacked in a field by two footpads, who pulled him from his animal and robbed him of £9. While doing so, they "beat him and cut his face in a terrible manner."[144] Footpads might also target slow-moving carts and carriages. Thus, in the small hours of a January morning in 1782, as James Altherton was driving his cart on a turnpike road near Hockering,

139. *Norfolk Chronicle,* 11 November 1780.
140. *Ipswich Journal,* 3 November 1781.
141. Ibid., 27 October 1770.
142. Ibid., 21 February 1766.
143. *Bury and Norwich Post,* 4 January 1809.
144. *Ipswich Journal,* 11 March 1769.

in Norfolk, he was stopped by two men carrying bludgeons. They beat him and robbed him of half a guinea and a silver watch.[145]

Even so, as Terry's case suggests, some mounted victims managed to escape. Similarly, one Sunday evening in 1766, a servant from Spexhall, in Suffolk, was returning from Halesworth when two footpads demanded his money and watch. When the man resisted, one of the pair tried to stab him in the chest with a knife. The blade penetrated the servant's clothes but, fortuitously, did not wound him. The traveller then beat back his assailant, put spurs to his horse, and rode off.[146] The following month footpads were also unsuccessful when they attacked a man named Barwick between Newmarket and Coolidge, in Suffolk. On this occasion, there was a "long scuffle" but Barwick escaped without being robbed by virtue of his powerful animal.[147]

As with highwaymen, where footpads were successful against mounted targets they would drive off their victim's horse. However, they might also steal it. For example, in 1767 a shoemaker's son from Melford was returning home from Sudbury market when three footpads accosted him. They took his watch, money, and horse, after which they rode off into a neighbouring county on the overburdened animal.[148] A similar crime occurred the following year. Two footpads attacked a farmer three miles outside Bury. They stole 3 guineas, some silver, and his horse. As with many such crimes, they also "beat him very much."[149]

Footpads would often target their victims in advance, identifying those who were likely to be carrying cash for commercial reasons, and sometimes even following them from a market or fair. In 1741 two men attacked a pedlar who had taken almost 14s selling cakes at a cockfight while he was on his way home to Clare in Suffolk. (He defended himself so stoutly that, although one of his arms was broken, he saved his money from the robbers).[150] In 1759 a tenant farmer going from Beccles to Bungay was stopped by two footpads and robbed of 1 guinea 14s. The

145. *Norfolk Chronicle*, 6 January 1782.
146. *Ipswich Journal*, 8 February 1766.
147. Ibid., 1 March 1766.
148. *Ipswich Journal*, 25 July 1767.
149. *St. James's Chronicle Or the British Evening Post*, 28–30 July 1768.
150. *Ipswich Journal*, 28 March 1741.

robbers had anticipated more as, earlier the same day, the farmer had paid a debt of £30, "which these fellows were informed he had about him."[151] Similarly, late one night in 1808, Richard Gosshawk, a Somerton jobber, was returning from Sudbury market on his pony when he was stopped by two footpads and violently robbed. They took £63 in notes and cash. It was thought that they had seen Gosshawk taking the money at the market, and deliberately targeted him.[152]

Footpads were usually less mobile geographically than highwaymen, and more likely to come from the region where they operated. Many were comparatively local men, some living within a day's walk or less of the scene of their crimes. In 1781 a Mr Potter, who kept the *Swan Inn* at Sharrington, was attacked near the village common by a single footpad, who robbed him of 13 shillings and sixpence in silver coins. The man was armed with a short gun and had a dog with him—not, perhaps, the most common companion for such a crime.[153] Footpads might pursue other, legitimate, trades at the same time as their nefarious activities, and there was often an improvised quality to their actions. Thus on one occasion it could be noted that a pair of footpads "appeared to be labourers."[154]

Execution for Robbery

Eighteen men were executed in Norfolk for highway robbery, including one case that involved robbery of the mail, between 1735 and 1799. One other man was hanged for robbery and rape, which can be disregarded for these purposes. To these can be added three men who were executed for highway robbery in Yarmouth and King's Lynn during these years after trial at their especially powerful borough courts. Eighteen men were executed at the Suffolk Assizes for highway robbery during the same period. (On several occasions, in both counties, pairs of men who had robbed together were hanged together). As a result, 39 men were hanged for robbery on the highway in the entire region between 1735

151. *Norwich Gazette*, 25 October 1759.
152. *Bury and Norwich Post*, 10 February 1808.
153. *Norfolk Chronicle*, 8 December 1781.
154. Ibid., 6 January 1781.

and 1799. This makes an average of just less than one execution for the crime every 18 months.

Throughout the period, it was widely thought that a conviction for highway robbery was likely to result in execution, indicating how seriously the crime was viewed. Certain forms of highway robbery were indeed unlikely to receive clemency. Foremost among them were attacks on mail coaches. For example, in 1790, after Thomas Jackson was capitally convicted at the Norfolk Assizes of robbing the mail between Stoke and Brandon, sentence of death was "almost immediately passed on him" and he was hanged.[155] Crimes in which high-value goods or large amounts of cash had been stolen were also likely to result in execution. Thus in 1733 22-year-old Samuel Partridge was hanged for a robbery committed near Ipswich, during which he had taken more than £31 in cash, a horse, and other items from the victim.[156] If serious violence had been employed, especially against a woman, a reprieve would also be unlikely. In 1787 John Crome was hanged after conviction for a highway robbery at the City of Norwich Assizes. During the crime, his victim had been assaulted.[157] As with other capital crimes, the commission of a series of offences discouraged clemency. Robert Fox was not helped when he admitted to two other robberies. He was hanged on Hardwicke Common near King's Lynn.[158] Even fairly "routine" highway robberies could lead to death if it was felt that a deterrent example was necessary at a particular time or place. In 1796 James Copsey and Daniel Burrows were both hanged after being convicted at the Bury Assizes for robbing a man of a (base) "metal" watch on a Suffolk road.[159] (By the 1740s, a secondhand watch made of brass could be had for as little as 5s and was within the means of some workingmen).[160]

Nevertheless, reprieves were regularly granted to those guilty of serious robberies that were not committed on the highway. For example, at the Norwich Assizes in 1750, John Townly was found guilty of robbing a

155. *World (1787)*, 18 March 1790.
156. *London Journal* (1720), 14 April 1733.
157. *Morning Chronicle and London Advertiser*, 8 August 1787; *Bath Chronicle*, 30 August 1787.
158. *London Chronicle*, 11–13 September 1783.
159. *Whitehall Evening Post (1770)*, 21–23 July 1796.
160. J. Styles, "Time Piece: Working Men and Watches," 2008, p. 45.

deaf-and-dumb boy of 6 shillings.[161] A year later, he was reprieved at the same forum, on condition of transportation for 14 years.[162] Much more pertinently, many cases of highway robbery also received clemency. For example, in 1727 three men were capitally convicted at the Bury Assizes of several robberies, but reprieved.[163]

Mercy was especially likely if several men had been convicted and an example could be made of one of them. For example, although Edward Plumb, one of three men found guilty of a highway robbery at the Norwich Assizes in August 1772, was hanged, his two co-defendants received clemency.[164] Similarly, in 1788 Richard and Abraham Young were convicted of robbing Henry Larner on the highway in Northwold (Norfolk) and stealing 1 guinea and some silver coins.[165] Richard was left for execution but Abraham was reprieved.[166] In like manner, at the Thetford Assizes in March 1799, two dragoons, William Mason and Thomas Dexter, were capitally convicted of a highway robbery committed at Gaywood the previous December. During the crime, they had "cruelly" treated an errand man from Lynn, and stolen cash and property worth more than £4.[167] At least one man had to be hanged as an example, and Dexter was duly executed. However, a petition was received asking for clemency on behalf of Mason. It appears that a pardon was prepared for him on condition of transportation for life. The grounds for mercy given by James Mingay, the trial judge, when consulted about the petition, were Mason's youth, he was a dutiful son, the crime was a first offence and he had apparently been led into it by his co-accused (the conveniently executed Dexter).[168]

Most of the cases of highway robbery that ended in a reprieve involved less serious examples of the crime, those characterised by small takings, amateurishness, an absence of brutality, or a combination of all of these factors. For example, Thomas Palmer was convicted at the Suffolk

161. *General Advertiser* (1744), 20 August 1750.
162. *Read's Weekly Journal Or British Gazetteer*, 10 August 1751.
163. *Daily Post*, 3 April 1727.
164. *Gazetteer and New Daily Advertiser*, 1 September 1772.
165. *The Times*, 21 March 1788, p. 3.
166. *Bath Chronicle*, 27 March 1788.
167. *London Chronicle*, 26–28 March 1799.
168. TNA HO 47/23/16, ff 107–121.

Assizes in March 1783 of robbing Joseph Crowder of just one shilling and escaped execution.[169] In 1790 "Royal" James King was convicted of highway robbery at Chisworth, near Norwich, but reprieved on condition of transportation for life.[170] His petition for clemency had stressed the relatively small amount taken and the fact that no one had been killed.[171]

Other mitigating factors could also be important. In 1740 James Curry was convicted of highway robbery at the Bury Assizes but subsequently reprieved (and possibly pardoned).[172] Curry was only 19-years-old, had made immediate admissions, and, perhaps most important, had also co-operated with the authorities in trying to secure his more experienced criminal associates and by providing information about their previous activities. Furthermore, his crime had occurred at 10 am rather than at night.[173]

Some highway robbers even benefitted from administrative reprieves, their sentences being commuted almost immediately after conviction by assizes judges. For example, at the Thetford Assizes in 1728, when John Hardy was convicted of highway robbery, Sir Bernard Hale immediately reprieved him on condition of transportation.[174] Hale later noted the presence of "favourable circumstances" in his post-sessions circuit letter.[175] At the Suffolk Assizes in 1783, Richard Smith was convicted of robbing Sarah Snell on the highway near Lavenham, during which crime he took a muslin apron and "other items of small value." Their trivial worth led the judge to reprieve him before he left Bury.[176] In March of the same year, Michael Handy (or Hardy) was convicted at the Norfolk Assizes for robbing a farmer's wife and another woman at pistol point on the highway near Frensham. Despite the ostensible gravity of the offence, during which a pan of silver clasps and a small amount of cash had been stolen from female victims, Handy was reprieved from his

169. *General Evening Post*, 22–25 March 1783.
170. *Whitehall Evening Post* (1770), 20–23 March 1790.
171. TNA HO 47/11/13, ff 61–70.
172. *General Evening Post*, 29 March – 1 April 1740.
173. *Weekly Miscellany (1732)*, 22 September 1739.
174. *Weekly Journal or British Gazetteer*, 6 April 1728.
175. TNA SP 36/7, ff 241–242.
176. *London Chronicle*, 23–26 August 1783.

death sentence before the trial judge left Thetford.[177] The judge's report on the case suggested that it was "as favorable a Case as a case of Robbery on the Highway can be." Handy was recommended to seven years' transportation (often replacing the traditional 14 years by the 1780s) as a condition of reprieve.[178] However, he continued to be held in Norwich Castle, as there was nowhere to send him, and eventually received a free pardon from the King in 1784.[179]

A decade later William Spark, a labourer from Rattlesden in Suffolk, was convicted of highway robbery at the Norwich Assizes, but, again, reprieved in favour of seven years' transportation before the judge left the city.[180] It was a strange case. Spark's victims, an adolescent brother and sister, Sarah and Richard Spalding, aged 15 and 16, respectively, had been robbed on the Scole-to-Billingford Road. Just seven pence in cash had been taken. Spark was of previous good character and had behaved well in prison. Most important, he appeared to be suffering from mental illness, "shewing the strongest Marks of a mind deranged, failure of Memory, mental Weakness, Childishness and the Incapacity to govern himself." William Henry Ashhurst, the trial judge, eventually recommended that his sentence of transportation (the initial reprieve condition) be replaced by one of six months' hard labour in the Wymondham bridewell.[181]

By the 1780s Martin Madan was deploring the number of highwaymen who benefitted from administrative reprieves, and claimed that an assizes judge had told him that he felt that such clemency should normally be extended where they "did not use much violence, or do any mischief to the persons they robbed."[182] Some cases from the time supported such an analysis. Edward Youngs received clemency after he was convicted for robbing Mary Copland on the highway near Colney (Norfolk) in 1781 and taking more than 2½ guineas. Despite the presence of a female victim, the judge reprieved Youngs before he left Norwich.[183]

177. *Whitehall Evening Post (1770)*, 20–22 March 1783; *London Chronicle*, 22–25 March 1783.
178. TNA HO 47/1/34.
179. *London Chronicle*, 15–18 May 1784.
180. *Lloyd's Evening Post*, 26–29 July 1793.
181. TNA HO 47/16/66, ff 275–279.
182. M. Madan, *Thoughts On Executive Justice*, 1785, p. 39.
183. *Gazetteer and New Daily Advertiser*, 15 August 1781.

On a more statistical basis, selected sessions for Suffolk, Norfolk, and the City and County of Norwich can be considered. At all three locations, between the middle of 1734 and the end of 1736, six men were indicted for highway robbery. Of these, just one was both convicted and executed. William Morris, a stove-maker by trade, was hanged at Norwich in August 1734 for a robbery in which he had taken several gold watches, cash, and other valuable items from a woman in a carriage that he attacked just outside the gates of Norwich. He was also rumoured to have been involved in several serious robberies in the Metropolis; i.e., there were multiple aggravating factors in his case. Morris was traced and captured when he wrote to his father in Norwich from temporary lodgings in Yarmouth, the letter apparently being intercepted.[184] By contrast, two other men, Robert Chesteney and John Broughton, were convicted at the same sessions for robbing another man but were reprieved and, the following March, pleaded their pardon at the Norfolk Assizes; presumably they were transported for 14 years as a condition of clemency. At the August Assizes for Suffolk in 1736, two more men were the subjects of bills of indictment. However, one of them was still at large, and the proceedings against the other, Philip Catton, failed when the grand jury threw out his bill as "ignoramus." Finally, at the Suffolk Assizes held at Bury in 1736, William Whitman was convicted of highway robbery but reprieved.[185] Thus only one convicted robber out of four was executed.

More typically, between the start of 1732 and the end of 1758, six men were executed for highway robbery in Suffolk, but three more were reprieved after conviction.[186] The 1819 Committee on Criminal Laws concluded that there had been 28 cases of highway robbery prosecuted to conviction at East Anglian Assizes during the 20 years from 1768 to 1787. These had resulted in just 18 executions. (A modern analysis suggests a figure of 16 executions). It seems that more than a third, perhaps almost 40 per cent, of convicted highwaymen in the region escaped death during this period. This broadly accords with some other, national estimates that suggest that the death sentences passed in 30 per cent of highway

184. *London Journal* (1720), 7 September 1734.
185. *Read's Weekly Journal Or British Gazetteer*, 11 September 1736.
186. P. Wright, *Death Recorded: Capital Punishment in Suffolk 1732–1900*, 2006, in unpaginated appendix.

robberies committed between 1749 and 1771 were commuted.[187] As in many other areas, East Anglia was fairly typical of the country as a whole.

Despite Madan's criticism, there was a rationale behind such mercy. Highwaymen rarely killed, even though they were committing a capital offence. Potential leniency if caught was one inducement for such behaviour. As Blackstone noted, slaughter on the roads was avoided because "highwaymen have a hope of transportation, which seldom is extended to murderers."[188]

187. A. R. Ekirch, *Bound for America: The Transportation of British Convicts to the Colonies, 1718–1775,* 1987, p. 35 at n. 14.
188. W. Blackstone, *Commentaries on the Laws of England,* vol. 4, 1769, p. 18.

CHAPTER 16

Animal Theft

Introduction

The theft of animals was a permanent issue in rural areas. Unsurprisingly for a heavily agricultural and pastoral region, it was a serious problem in East Anglia. In 1780, after the outhouse of a farmer at Carleton (just outside Norwich) had been broken into, and all his chickens taken, it was noted that his poultry had been "stolen every year for seven years last past, and two very good horses have been stolen from him in the [same] time."[1]

Historically, stealing animals valued at 1s or more from a field, yard, or barn was clergyable grand larceny, like any other theft at this value. If the animals were worth less than 1s, the crime would be defined as a case of petty theft. For obvious reasons, the latter possibility was most commonly the case when poultry was stolen. Most individual chickens and ducks would be worth under 12 pence. For example, at the Thetford Assizes in 1777, the appropriately named Henry Gosling was accused of stealing a hen and seven chickens, valued at 5s, an average of about 8d a bird.[2] According to William Goodwin, in January 1785 good quality, plump ducks and chickens were retailing at ten pence to 1s each in his part of Suffolk. Sometimes, even a couple of hens might be accurately valued at less than 1s. At the Yarmouth Borough Sessions in 1758, John Ellis was convicted of stealing two chickens initially valued by the prosecutor

1. *Norfolk Chronicle*, 23 December 1780.
2. TNA ASSI 33/6. He was merely convicted of petty theft.

at just ten pence.[3] However, two or more birds would usually be worth more than 12 pence if valued correctly. As a result, in 1801, after William Lockwood broke open a henhouse at Little Stonham, in Suffolk, and stole three chickens, he was convicted of grand larceny at the Bury Assizes.[4]

"Large" animals, such as pigs, goats, sheep, and horses would always be worth well over the petty theft limit. In 1777 a labourer named Jeremiah Harvey was convicted at the Bury Assizes of stealing four pigs, together valued at £3 3 shillings, or an average of just under 18 shillings each.[5] In 1784, at the Bury Assizes, a "fat hog" stolen from Susannah Bowen was valued, perhaps slightly optimistically, at £2.[6] Sheep were a little cheaper. Even a particularly plump animal, ready for market, the theft of which was tried at the Lent Assizes for Suffolk in 1747, was valued at only 10 shillings.[7] Many grazing sheep were worth far less, just five shillings or so. By contrast, if only because of their large size, a "good" cow, such as that stolen in Suffolk by Mathew Hindes in 1764, might be valued at as much as £5.[8]

Horses were usually the most valuable animals taken. For a typical example of cheaper animals, the standard bay mare that John Matthew was accused of stealing at the Lent Assizes in Bury in 1746 was set at £4 in value. An identical animal, the theft of which was tried at the Norfolk Assizes a few days later, was said to be worth £5.[9] Neither of these animals was remotely "special." A moderately "good" horse might fetch well over twice these sums. An excellent horse might cost far more than £30.

Nevertheless, as with other types of theft, complainants might artificially down-value several small animals or a large and expensive bird, such as a fat turkey, to below one shilling to make the consequences of conviction less serious and, perhaps, also ensure that it came within the province of their local quarter sessions. For example, at the Norfolk Quarter Sessions that opened at Walsingham on 28 April 1737, Andrew Chapman and Charles Gowing were indicted for petty theft, after stealing

3. NRO Yarmouth Borough Sessions Y/S/ 2/1–4 mf 1031.
4. *The Bury and Norwich Post: Or, Suffolk, Norfolk, Essex, and Cambridge Advertiser*, 1 April 1801.
5. TNA ASSI 33/6.
6. TNA ASSI 33/6–7.
7. Gray's Inn MS 45.
8. TNA ASSI 33/4.
9. Gray's Inn MS 45.

a goose, even though most birds of this type would have been worth more than 12 pence.[10]

Similarly, juries frequently down-valued grand larceny indictments in these situations. For example, at the Thetford Assizes in 1784, a labourer named Hammond Fox was convicted of petty larceny for stealing two chickens indicted as the more serious form of theft but valued by the jury at just ten pence.[11] At the Norfolk Quarter Sessions held at Norwich in October 1783, John Smith was also convicted of the lesser crime after stealing several chickens.[12] A more extreme instance of this occurred the following year, at the Suffolk Quarter Sessions held at Bury; William Ranson was accused of stealing eleven ducks but convicted of petty theft, even though the value of the birds must have been far in excess of the 11 pence limit.[13]

It was rare for prosecutors to down-value large animals to below a shilling; magistrates might frown on such behaviour, and even trial juries would be reluctant to do this. Nevertheless, in an extreme case of complainant down-valuing, John Cook pleaded guilty to stealing a pig valued at just ten pence by its owner at the Suffolk County Quarter Sessions held at Ipswich in January 1787. (He was sentenced to a public whipping in the town marketplace).[14] Similarly, in 1777 Benjamin Eves was convicted of stealing a pig at the Beccles Quarter Sessions and publicly whipped, suggesting that the animal was artificially valued at less than 1s, whether by its owner or the trial jury.[15] More typically of these cases, Thomas Browne received a sentence of seven years' transportation at the Bury Assizes in 1801 after being convicted of grand larceny for stealing a single "fat hog."[16] At the same forum in 1807, William Scotcher received the same disposal for stealing two pigs.[17]

Neither Browne nor Scotcher risked their necks because stealing hogs, whatever their value was always a clergyable crime. However, during the

---

10. NRO C/S 1/12 mf 656 part 4.
11. TNA ASSI 33/6 and 33/7.
12. *Norfolk Chronicle,* 11 October 1783; NRO C/S 1/12 mf 656 part 4.
13. *Bury and Norwich Post,* 22 January 1784.
14. SRO QS B105/2/48.
15. *Norwich Mercury,* 19 July 1777.
16. *The Bury and Norwich Post: Or, Suffolk, Norfolk, Essex, and Cambridge Advertiser*, 1 April 1801.
17. *Bury and Norwich Post,* 22 July 1807.

eighteenth century, the theft of horses, sheep, and cattle was or became capital *per se*, irrespective of their value, because clergy had been withdrawn from them by statute. Illustrative of the distinction, when Thomas Jacques was convicted of stealing horses at the Bury Assizes in 1786, he was sentenced to death, albeit reprieved from execution.[18] He remained in England, whether in gaol or on a hulk, and was subsequently released. In 1791 he was convicted again, this time for simple grand larceny after stealing a pig, and sentenced to seven years' transportation like other thieves.[19]

Capital Forms of Animal Theft

Stealing horses was popularly viewed as the most socially damaging and so heinous form of animal theft. For this reason, it had been withdrawn from clergy as early as 1545.[20] By contrast, the theft of sheep and cattle was viewed less seriously until well into the 1700s. Indeed, at the start of the period, Timothy Nourse expressly listed sheep thieves among "lesser criminals" whose crimes did not deserve death.[21] As a result, when William Burgess was convicted of stealing sheep at the Norfolk Assizes in 1729, he was clergied, branded, and discharged (a very benign sentence).[22] More typically, when Henry Wilson was convicted of stealing a cow at the Suffolk Assizes at Bury in August 1734, he was sentenced to transportation for seven years (the most common disposal after 1718 for grand larceny).[23] Similarly, at the Norfolk Assizes in Thetford the same year, Edmund Stone was transported for seven years for stealing sheep.[24] In a few parts of England, some cases of sheep theft were even heard at quarter sessions in the early 1700s.

18. *Whitehall Evening Post (1770)*, 30 March – 1 April 1786.
19. P. Wright, *Death Recorded: Capital Punishment in Suffolk 1732–1900*, 2006, Ipswich, in unpaginated appendix.
20. 37 Hen VIII, c 8, s 2.
21. T. Nourse, *Campania Folix. Or, a Discourse of the Benefits and Improvements of Husbandry*, 1706, p. 229.
22. *British Journal Or The Censor*, 9 August 1729.
23. TNA ASSI 33/1.
24. *London Journal (1720)*, 30 March 1734.

However, sheep stealing was hurriedly withdrawn from benefit of clergy in 1741, during a period of acute rural hardship, following complaints from farmers (especially those near London) and concern that the presence of the privilege might be encouraging such crimes. A parliamentary committee aimed at addressing the problem was convened and speedily reported on the problem, leading to legislation (14 Geo II, c 6). Cattle quickly followed suit, for similar reasons, in 1742 (15 Geo II, c 34).[25] Stealing pigs remained simple clergyable larceny throughout the period, however many animals were involved, and whatever their value. For example, at the Norfolk Assizes in 1734 John Wacham received seven years' transportation for stealing hogs, as did William Gates at the same forum in 1756, and Thomas Carter in 1768.[26] It was, of course, slightly illogical that pig theft was never capital. William Gates' seven hogs were valued at fully £10 (the equivalent of two "average" horses or more than a dozen sheep). Many observers, such as the elderly clergyman Dr Patrick Delaney, thought that the change in the law for the other two animals was "absurd" and even "monstrous."[27]

Background to the Crimes

The theft of large animals ranged from opportunistic crimes committed by poor individuals to those perpetrated by well-organised criminal networks, stealing on a commercial scale for resale. Theft by the former would usually involve taking a single animal, often a sheep, particularly in winter, and the removal of choice cuts of meat after swift butchery, with the rest of the animal (its fleece and entrails) normally being abandoned to prevent exposure. Frequently the theft would be for personal consumption. For example, at the Bury Assizes in March 1751, Digby Brownsmith was convicted of killing a wether sheep valued at 10s and stealing its two hindquarters. (He was immediately reprieved from execution by the trial judge).[28] Similarly, in 1780 three privates in the East Suffolk Militia were committed to Bury Gaol on suspicion of stealing a

25. J. M. Beattie, *Crime and the Courts in England 1660–1800*, 1986, pp. 144–145.
26. *London Journal (1720)*, 30 March 1734; TNA ASSI 33/2; *Public Advertiser*, 3 August 1768.
27. *The British Magazine, Or, Monthly Repository for Gentlemen & Ladies*, July 1766, p. 346.
28. TNA ASSI 33/2.

sheep at Benhall, in Suffolk.[29] It is likely that they had intended to roast and eat it. Nevertheless, even a single sheep, if successfully marketed, could be a real financial boon to a labouring man.

This form of animal theft was a fairly low-risk crime, at least when compared to stealing horses, cattle, or entire flocks. It could be hard to monitor pastured sheep on a regular basis as they might stray or die quite naturally (they were subject to relatively high mortality rates) without any human interference. As a result, small-scale losses were not always identified quickly, or immediately attributed to theft rather than other causes when they were.[30]

By contrast, professional animal theft normally involved the taking of horses for resale or, occasionally in East Anglia, flocks of sheep. Those involved often worked in gangs. These had a significant presence in both Norfolk and Suffolk. For example, in 1755 John Longden (he went by numerous aliases) was committed to Norwich Gaol for stealing two horses in Caister, on the Norfolk coast. When examined, he quickly admitted that he had been "wholly employed in horse stealing for about six years past." He claimed that he had operated throughout East Anglia with several other men.[31] Even so, he was reprieved from execution. By contrast, in the same year, John Hall was arrested, convicted, and executed for stealing a black mare at Wymondham. Although this was a relatively modest crime, Hall was thought to be one of the "most notorious horsestealers" that had been captured for more than a decade. It was said that he had carried out his nefarious trade for seven or eight years, was linked to almost all of the horse thieves arrested in the county over the previous 12 months, and had been involved in taking 50 animals in Norfolk alone.[32] Significantly, he had been acquitted of stealing another horse at the same assizes.[33] Similarly, Gibbon Houghton, who dealt in cattle on a commercial basis through an ostensibly legitimate business, was executed in 1767 for stealing eleven wether sheep from a marsh in the parish of Sudbourne, in Suffolk. He was strongly suspected of being a "very old

29. *Ipswich Journal*, 8 April 1780.
30. N. Woodward, "Seasonality and Sheep-stealing: Wales, 1730–1830," 2008, pp. 30–31.
31. *Read's Weekly Journal Or British Gazetteer*, 5 July 1755.
32. *Public Advertiser*, 6 November 1755.
33. TNA ASSI 33/2.

offender." On arrest, he was found in possession of 27 other sheep, with different identifying marks, which were thought to be the proceeds of similar thefts. When examined by a magistrate he also named others who had been involved with him in a sophisticated criminal trade in stolen animals.[34] Jonathan Norman, a convicted horse thief and another "old offender," also connected to a large gang from the region, was more fortunate: he was reprieved from execution in 1780.[35]

Unsurprisingly, butchers (who conducted their own slaughtering during the period) sometimes succumbed to the attraction of free meat, which was untraceable once an animal was cut up. For example, in 1782 William Town, a butcher from Polstead, in Suffolk, was committed to Ipswich Gaol for stealing three wether sheep from a farmer in Higham.[36] The following year, William Town and John Horn (Town's employee) were capitally convicted for the same crime at Bury Assizes.[37] They were both reprieved in favour of transportation. In his petition against the imposition of even this punishment, Horn claimed that his employer had bought the sheep, and they had then butchered them and sold on the meat.[38] The following year, John Kingsbury, a Sudbury butcher, was committed to Bury Gaol on suspicion of stealing six sheep.[39] In 1790 William Payne, a butcher from Great Waldingfield, in Suffolk, went to the same prison, accused of stealing a single ewe.[40] Animal theft by butchers was a nationwide phenomenon, being found in the Northeast of England as much as in East Anglia.[41] Of course, butchers could themselves be the victims of such crimes. One night in November 1701 a sheep belonging to George Bracolere, a butcher from Needham Market, in Suffolk, was stolen, killed and cut up on his premises, where it was being kept in an outbuilding prior to slaughtering. He suspected three local men, and obtained an arrest warrant against them.[42]

34. *Gazetteer and New Daily Advertiser*, 28 October 1767.
35. *Ipswich Journal*, 29 April 1780; *Whitehall Evening Post (1770)*, 15–17 August 1780.
36. *Norfolk Chronicle*, 3 August 1782.
37. *Parker's General Advertiser and Morning Intelligencer*, 26 March 1783.
38. TNA HO 47/1/47, ff 194–196.
39. *Ipswich Journal*, 8 February 1783.
40. *Bury and Norwich Post*, 3 February 1790.
41. G. Morgan and P. Rushton, *Rogues Thieves and the Rule of Law*, 1998, p. 85.
42. SRO QS 347.96, *The Devereux Edgar Notebook*, transcribed by S. R. Schofield, 1956, vol. 1, p. 15.

Some farmers, keen to augment their own flocks and herds at the expense of others, also perpetrated crimes of this type. Such cases could be very hard to prove at trial. In part, this was because the animals had to be positively identified to the court's satisfaction as belonging to the victim. This was especially difficult with sheep, which were less distinctive than horses and had less contact with their owners. In 1802 William Brand, a wealthy farmer charged with stealing four sheep, was acquitted at Bury Assizes for this very reason.[43] Nevertheless, identification was not impossible. Sheep were usually marked. Furthermore, to the trained eye they were distinguishable. At the Lincolnshire Assizes in 1797, a shepherd whose sheep had been stolen and recovered stated that he could identify them as his by their marks and "countenances." Defence counsel attacked this suggestion, and was "rather severe" when questioning the witness on such a possibility. Fortunately, the trial judge, Sir Francis Buller, was sympathetic, and informed the court that on another occasion he had heard a witness say that he "knew his sheep one from another by their faces."[44]

Another, even greater, problem when farmers were defendants was the difficulty of proving that the animals had been deliberately stolen, rather than straying into adjacent or nearby farms and joining their flocks and herds. In June 1701 the Suffolk magistrate Devereaux Edgar issued a warrant on behalf of George Cosens from Washbrook, in Suffolk, for the recovery of three "strayed or stolen" ewes that had gone missing from his grounds five months earlier, and been found in the custody of Samuel Woods of nearby Stutton. Recognising the impossibility of proving theft, Woods had initially been "civilly requested to restore" them by Cosens, and it was only when this request was ignored that he (Cosens) went to a magistrate.[45]

These factors may help explain why acquittal rates for sheep theft were higher than they were for stealing horses in some parts of England. However, this was not necessarily the case in East Anglia. In the decade after 1751, there were 42 separate trials for stealing horses at the regional assizes (counting those with multiple defendants as single prosecutions).

43. *Bury and Norwich Post*, 31 March 1802.
44. *Evening Mail*, 22–25 July 1796. This case is also interesting because the thief, a cottager, had already "sold" the sheep to a drover before he stole them.
45. SRO QS 347.96, *The Devereux Edgar Notebook*, transcribed by S. R. Schofield, 1956, vol. 1, p. 6.

Of these 29 resulted in at least one capital conviction, while 12 only produced acquittals. In the remaining case the defendant was so mentally disordered that he could not be tried. Ignoring this case, the conviction rate was just under 70 per cent for the decade. By contrast, during the same period, there were 26 prosecutions for sheep theft, of which 18 resulted in at least one conviction, producing a guilty rate of just over 71 per cent.[46] This similarity is not entirely surprising. Examining justices and grand juries provided a degree of evidential "quality control," excluding obviously weak cases.

The theft of large animals was an overwhelmingly male crime everywhere in the country throughout the century. For example, between 1670 and 1729, only 11 of the 773 people indicted for stealing horses on the Western Circuit were female, and most of these had worked with men.[47] No women at all were indicted for the crime in Cheshire between 1760 and 1830.[48] Similarly, only one woman, the notorious horse thief Margaret Catchpole, was capitally convicted for stealing such a beast in Suffolk between 1732 and 1800, and she was reprieved from execution.[49] Women who attempted to sell horses at fairs would normally arouse suspicion in what was a male-dominated trade. For the same reason, men who stole horses were often a little older than many other thieves, if only because it made it more plausible that they would legitimately own, and so be able to sell, such an animal. A majority worked alone when physically taking the horse, even if backed up by others. They tended to target less valuable animals that were out to pasture in fields, and so easier to steal, rather than the best horses, which were often secured in stables.

In contrast to stealing horses, the theft of fowl (most commonly chickens) was often opportunistic, frequently done for immediate consumption, and also had a significantly higher level of female participation. For example, and quite typically, at the Suffolk Quarter Sessions held at Ipswich on 7 April 1758, Susan Norman pleaded guilty to stealing two

46. TNA ASSI 33/2–3.
47. M. Eder, *"At the Instigation of the Devil": Capital Punishment and the Assize in the Early Modern England, 1670–1730*, 2014, p. 66.
48. J. Walliss, "Crime and Justice in Georgian Cheshire; The Chester Court of Great Sessions, 1760–1830," 2015, p. 45.
49. P. Wright, *Death Recorded: Capital Punishment in Suffolk 1732–1900*, 2006, pp. 52–53. *Observer*, 20 August 1797.

ducks and a pair of turkeys (down-valued as petty theft), and was privately whipped and discharged.[50]

Even so, not all such thefts were minor, especially when more valuable birds were involved or a large number were taken at the same time. At the Bury Assizes in March 1753, James Alexander was convicted and transported for stealing three cocks worth 18d, three hens worth the same amount, and 16 chickens valued at 4s, for a total value of 7s.[51] At the same forum in March 1797, Nathan Butcher was convicted of stealing geese valued at 10s and received the same disposal.[52] Sometimes birds were stolen on a commercial scale. In 1782, Parson Woodforde noted that late November was the time of year when "many idle fellows from Norwich go about the country stealing poultry to send them to London to make a penny of them." A neighbour of his had lost birds worth almost £4.[53] In 1774 Sir Charles Davers near Bury lost eleven fat turkeys, stolen by a gang that had already targeted most of the other farmers in the area.[54] Four years later, at the Thetford Assizes, Richard Tungate was acquitted of stealing 20 live turkeys valued at 40 shillings.[55] On an even greater scale, in October 1780, 58 geese were driven from the yard of a farmer in Barney (Norfolk) into a hollow, where 21 of them were killed and then carried away on horses by at least two people.[56]

Disposal of Stolen Animals

Ignoring those cases in which an animal was "borrowed" temporarily for a specific journey and then abandoned (the eighteenth-century equivalent of joyriding), disposing of stolen horses raised special problems. They were nearly always taken for live resale, not slaughter, unlike most other animals. Frequently they were publicly traded at fairs, where many people would have sight of them before they changed hands. The animals were often highly distinctive, and their identifying features were usually

50. SRO g.125. B105/2/32.
51. TNA ASSI 33/2.
52. TNA ASSI 33/6.
53. J. Beresford (ed.), *The Diary of a Country Parson, 1758–1802*, 1978, p. 132.
54. *Ipswich Journal,* 31 December 1774.
55. TNA ASSI 33/6.
56. *Norfolk Chronicle,* 14 October 1780.

carefully described in advertisements offering rewards for their return. As a result, successful horse theft often involved a considerable degree of professionalism, organization, skill, and even ruthlessness.

To reduce the risk of detection, many horse thieves tried to change the appearance of their stolen animals, cutting manes and tails, altering ear-marks, painting out or over blazes and stockings. In Norfolk, for example, in 1709, when Elizabeth Freke's stolen coach mare was recovered, it was found that the thief had "cut off his taile and his ears."[57] Gypsies were supposed to be particularly adept at effecting such transformations. Any saddles stolen with the animals would also be altered, with fresh buttons being added in different patterns.

Those who stole horses were usually careful to avoid disposing of the animals close to where they had been taken, especially just after the crime had been committed.[58] There was good reason for such caution. Victims might make considerable efforts to recover valuable horses, and trying to offload them at a local market could be dangerous, although distance did not necessarily guarantee safety. Famously, "Dick" Turpin was identified, convicted, and executed at York in 1739 after stealing a mare and foal many miles away at Heckington, in Lincolnshire.[59]

Even in the seventeenth century, when roads were extremely poor, almost half of all horses stolen on the Northern Circuit were sold or recovered more than 25 miles from where they had been taken, and only one in eight was found within six miles of the theft.[60] Successful thefts would have produced an even higher average, which would also have increased in the following century, as roads improved. In eighteenth-century Wales, most horse thieves lived close to the animals they stole; over half resided within five kilometres of the beasts. However, they disposed of them much further away. More than half the animals were sold more than 50 kilometres from where they were taken. A few were disposed of hundreds of kilometres away.[61]

57. R. Anselment (ed.), *The Remembrances of Elizabeth Freke, 1671–1714*, 2002, p. 261.
58. J. M. Beattie, *Crime and the Courts in England 1660–1800*, 1986, p. 169.
59. T. Kyll, *The Trial of the Notorious Highwayman Richard Turpin, at York Assizes on the 22nd Day of March, 1739*, 1739, pp. 1–3.
60. P. Edwards, *The Horse Trade of Tudor and Stuart England*, 1988, p. 112.
61. N. Woodward, "Horse-stealing in Wales, 1730–1830," 2009, p. 97.

When professional gangs were involved, they not only moved horses long distances before selling them, they sometimes even bought and sold animals among themselves, creating a chain of attendant documentation in the process, in case they were questioned about the provenance of their animals. Networks of unscrupulous dealers from around the country, willing to trade horses without asking too many questions, assisted their work.[62] They would also make sure that they knew where the stolen animals should not be sold on.[63]

In East Anglia, especially Suffolk, the London area provided an ideal place to dispose of animals. It was sufficiently distant without being far away, and also a fairly anonymous environment. Even so, some cases in which horses were sold on in the Metropolis resulted in prosecutions. Horse theft was unusual in that it was viewed as a "continuing crime," allowing cases to be indicted where the animal was found, if still in the thief's possession, as well as where it was taken. This meant that thieves did not necessarily have to be returned to the county where they had initially stolen the animal to be tried, unlike the perpetrators of most other crimes. Those who were resident in the capital and who had travelled out to the region to steal a horse before returning with the animal were often prosecuted at the Old Bailey.

A selection of cases is indicative of this phenomenon. In 1694 Henry Hooper, a 32-year-old man who had moved from Norfolk to London some years earlier, was capitally convicted at the Old Bailey after stealing a black gelding from Sir Edward Atkins at South Pickenham, in his native county. The crime was publicised in the *Gazette*, and both man and beast were found near Gray's Inn Lane.[64] In 1712 John Colebach from the City of London was indicted for stealing a mare from a field at Cotfield, in Suffolk. Its owner, John Jowers, advertised the theft, and Colebach was suspected after bringing the animal to the Castle and Faulcon tavern in Aldersgate Street. The "Prosecutor being sent to, came to Town

62. J. Poulter, *The Discoveries of John Poulter, Alias Baxter; Who Was Apprehended for Robbing Dr. Hancock, of Salisbury*, 1753, p. 39.
63. R. Thompson, *Narrative of the Life and Transactions of Robert Thompson*, 1791, p. 16.
64. OBSP, Trial of Henry Hooper, 21 February 1694: t16940221–31 and Ordinary's Account OA16940228.

and own'd [identified] her." Colebatch pretended that he had bought the horse from a Yorkshire butcher but was convicted.[65]

Similarly, in 1714 John Stokely from Whitechapel was seen riding a black mare worth £5 by a local watchman. This officer became suspicious and investigated. It transpired that the animal had been stolen while out to pasture in Suffolk. Again, its owner came to London to identify it and testify at the Old Bailey. Stokely was convicted, his implausible defence that he found the horse abandoned on the road "not being satisfactory."[66] Four years later, James Brown, from Shoreditch, was convicted of stealing a valuable brown gelding from a field at Denham, in Suffolk, while on excursion from the capital. He was caught when he tried to sell it.[67] In 1748 Thomas Chestney from Stepney, in Middlesex, travelled slightly further to steal a horse. He was convicted at the Old Bailey of stealing an animal from Henry Coxhead in Thetford. Coxhead's servant later identified the animal in Mile End and had Chestney arrested.[68]

However, some horse thieves, although arrested in the Metropolis, were sent back to the counties where they had committed their crimes. In 1796 William Spurgin was examined by a Bow Street magistrate on suspicion of stealing a mare from a publican near Bungay, in Suffolk, and selling it on at Smithfield Market, in London. The purchaser appeared at Bow Street with the horse, which was then formally identified by the victim, who had made the journey to the capital specifically for this purpose. Both men were bound over to prosecute the matter.[69] Spurgin was then returned to Suffolk and tried at the county assizes, where he was convicted and executed. Margaret Catchpole was more fortunate a year later. She stole a horse in Suffolk and then famously rode the 70 miles to London in less than ten hours, dressed as a man, to sell it with the assistance of a male lover. Although returned to Suffolk and capitally convicted at the Bury Assizes in 1797, she was reprieved.[70]

65. OBSP, Trial of John Colebach, 10 September 1712: t17120910–1.
66. OBSP, Trial of John Stokely, 30 June 1714: t17140630–43.
67. OBSP, Trial of James Brown, 10 September 1718: t17180910–7.
68. OBSP, Trial of Thomas Chestney, 7 September 1748: t17480907–1.
69. *London Packet or New Lloyd's Evening Post*, 19–21 October 1796.
70. *Observer*, 20 August 1797.

Conversely, some of those who stole horses in the metropolitan or other areas were prosecuted where they were arrested in East Anglia. In 1786 Robert Sutton and Henry Cross were capitally convicted of horse theft at the Norfolk Assizes in Norwich. They had stolen a gelding and a mare in Middlesex. Joseph Moore was convicted with them, after taking a mare in neighbouring Suffolk. All three men were subsequently executed.[71]

Concerns about putting distance between crime scene and sale also affected those who stole large numbers of sheep and (much less commonly) cattle. In 1764 John Lincoln stole a flock of 30 animals from William Bowle, a farmer at Wilby, in Norfolk. He then drove them through the night, a distance of some 20 miles, and sold them the following morning on Castle Hill, in Norwich, for £12. Even so, he was detected, and immediately confessed to the crime when examined by a magistrate in the city.[72] The sheep were valued in the gaol calendar at the sum he obtained for them, suggesting that this was roughly their market rate. Lincoln was convicted but reprieved from execution.[73]

Large animals were quite difficult to conceal, especially if alive, and magistrates might give orders to local constables to look for them. In February 1702 Devereaux Edgar received a complaint from Joseph Botwright that his sheep had been taken by "persons of ill repute" from around Akenham, in Suffolk. Edgar sent a warrant to the area's constables asking them to make a diligent search for the animals or their skins (in case they had already been slaughtered).[74]

Trial Forum

The theft of large animals (horses, sheep, and cattle) was nearly always prosecuted at assizes (or the Old Bailey in London), the odd sheep in the first two decades of the century apart. However, small animals

71. *Whitehall Evening Post (1770)*, 17–19 August 1786. Another man who had been capitally convicted with them for stealing a horse from a farmer in Necton (Norfolk) was reprieved.
72. *Public Advertiser*, 3 July 1764.
73. TNA ASSI 33/4. William Bowle received half the £10 statutory reward for prosecuting him to conviction.
74. SRO QS 347.96, *The Devereux Edgar Notebook*, transcribed by S. R. Schofield, 1956, vol. 1, pp. 2–3.

sometimes made an appearance at the higher court. Unsurprisingly, this was especially common if several had been taken at the same time, so that the allegation was grand larceny. For example, at the Bury Assizes in March 1797, a man was acquitted of stealing several ducks valued at three shillings.[75] Nevertheless, if the assizes were short of work or sitting at a convenient time, or if borough justices in the county were reluctant to try small larcenies, cases of petty theft involving a single fowl might be considered at the higher forum. The taking of one duck, valued at just ten pence, was listed for trial at the Bury Assizes in August 1794, rather than at local quarter sessions.[76]

Even so, the theft of poultry and domestic rabbits was usually the province of quarter sessions, being indicted as petty theft or even grand larceny (early in the century and during its last 30 years). For example, at the Suffolk Quarter Sessions held at Bury, in January 1772, two labourers from Wattisham were sentenced to seven years' transportation after they were convicted of stealing nine chickens from Thomas Game and selling them on to a common carrier at Bildeston.[77]

Trials for stealing pigs—creatures situated somewhere between "large" and "small" animals—alternated between the two forums and was partly contingent on the lower court's willingness to hear cases of simple grand larceny (which varied over time). In some regions, quarter sessions were reluctant to hear such cases. Of the 88 cases of animal theft heard at those for Oxfordshire in the second half of the eighteenth century, all but two involved poultry or other small creatures. One of the exceptions concerned the theft of a pig.[78] Rather more cases of hog theft went to East Anglian quarter sessions.

75. TNA ASSI 33/8.
76. Anon, *A Calendar of the Prisoners in the Custody of Margaret Baker, Keeper of His Majesty's Gaol of Bury St. Edmund's*, 1794, p. 1.
77. *Ipswich Journal*, 19 January 1771 and 25 January 1772.
78. A. Kilday, "'Criminally Poor?' Investigating the Link Between Crime and Poverty in Eighteenth-century England," 2014, pp. 507–526.

Execution and Animal Theft

Capital forms of animal theft were a major contributor to the list of executions in East Anglia. Between 1735 and 1799, 18 men were hanged in Norfolk for stealing horses, three for stealing sheep, and one for taking cattle. This produces 22 executions for all forms of animal theft from an overall total of 138 executions for the whole of Norfolk (including Yarmouth and King's Lynn) during this period. Thus, about a sixth of all executions in the entire county were for the theft of (large) animals. This places the crime well behind burglary and housebreaking (combined) but on a par with murder (22 cases including two of infanticide) and just ahead of highway robbery (20 executions). Suffolk saw eleven executions for the theft of animals during the same time, eight for stealing horses and three for taking sheep, out of a total of 116 executions for the county. As a result, to take the East Anglian region as a whole, there were 33 hangings for animal theft out of 254 executions, making up about 13 per cent of the total number. This relatively high figure is both indicative of the gravity with which the crime was viewed, its prevalence, and the possibility it afforded for securing convictions. As these figures also suggest, the vast majority of executions—almost 80 per cent—in both Norfolk and Suffolk were for stealing horses rather than sheep or cattle.

How does the East Anglian profile compare to that of other English counties? Staying on the Norfolk Circuit, at the Buckingham Assizes, between 1735 and 1799, nine people were executed on six occasions for horse theft. Four men were hanged for four separate cases of sheep-theft. Nobody was hanged for stealing cattle. At the Bedfordshire Assizes during the same period, four men were executed for horse theft on as many occasions, two men for sheep theft on two occasions, and (again) no one was executed for stealing cattle. On the Western Circuit, four men were hanged on two occasions at the Dorset Assizes for stealing sheep, and six men were hanged individually for horse theft. On the same circuit, after the Hampshire Assizes, 16 people were hanged on 14 occasions for horse theft, and four for stealing sheep (from as many cases). Nobody was hanged for cattle theft. At the Lancashire Assizes on the Northern Circuit, ten men were hanged on six occasions for horse theft, while none were executed for sheep or cattle theft. Thus it can be seen that, in its incidence of capital punishment for stealing animals, East Anglia stood out when compared to many, but certainly not all, English regions.

Reprieves from Execution

Despite the significant number of hangings, most capital convictions for the theft of large animals did not lead to execution, in East Anglia as elsewhere, especially in the latter decades of the era. The Reverend Martin Madan (1726–1790), a qualified barrister, thought that by the 1780s sheep and horse theft were ceasing to be capital offences in anything other than name. He claimed that fewer than one in 40 of those convicted of such offences were executed, so that perpetrators were "almost sure" of escape.[79] Madan's views were only slightly exaggerated. At the various assizes held for Norfolk and Suffolk during the 20 years between 1768 and 1787 (inclusive), 65 people were convicted of horse theft; five of them (less than 8 per cent) were eventually hanged (six if John Sherwood's combined arson and horse theft case is included). Over the same period and area, 31 people were capitally convicted for sheep theft, just four of whom were left for execution (other sources suggest only three men were actually hanged).[80] Similarly, ten people in the county were sentenced to death for stealing cows (including bullocks, steers, and heifers), but all of them were reprieved.[81]

Even in earlier years, only a minority of those convicted of such crimes were hanged. During the period running from the start of 1732 to the end of 1800 (18 months in the 1730s, six months in 1747, and all 12 months of 1793 are missing), a total of 75 years, there were 82 capital convictions for horse theft at the Suffolk Assizes (a few involved co-defendants being found guilty at the same time), of which ten resulted in executions, the other 72 people sentenced to death being reprieved. Thus, only a little over 12 per cent of those convicted for stealing horses in Suffolk were actually hanged. Significantly, half of these executions occurred in the

79. M. Madan, *Thoughts On Executive Justice*, 1785, p. 37.
80. www.capitalpunishment.org (Accessed 15 July 2015).
81. Anon, *Report From the Select Committee on Criminal Laws*, 1819, pp. 194–204.

first decade of the period under consideration. On the same assessment, between 1741 (when it became a capital offence) and the end of 1800, 36 people were convicted of stealing sheep in Suffolk, of whom just two were executed.[82] However, Henry Haylock was hanged for stealing 66 sheep in 1793 (a year is missing from the above source).[83] Even so, it is still less than 10 per cent of the total. To take the assizes from the entire region for the decade after 1751, 18 trials that produced convictions for sheep theft resulted in just one execution, that of James Palmer in Norfolk in 1751.[84]

Sheep

Prospects for execution if found guilty of sheep stealing were lower than they were for horse theft, but not enormously so, especially as the lack of the first decade for periods of mutual comparison exaggerates this phenomenon. The primary reason that there were far more executions for horse theft than sheep stealing in East Anglia was that many more men were convicted of the former crime. Nevertheless, it is true that the theft of small numbers (but not flocks) of sheep was much more likely to produce a reprieve than stealing similar numbers of horses after the former became a capital offence in the early 1740s. It was almost unheard of for a conviction for stealing one or two sheep to result in execution without severely aggravating factors being present. Typically, although William Elgin was sentenced to death at the Lent Assizes for Norfolk in 1747 after stealing two sheep worth (together) 10s, he received clemency.[85] The theft of small to medium numbers of sheep was also very likely to produce a reprieve.

Sometimes even cases involving much larger numbers of animals resulted in mercy, if other aggravating factors were absent and there was mitigation. After the assizes held at Bury in 1753, William Mann escaped death, despite stealing 34 sheep (they had been recovered swiftly). In 1758

82. P. Wright, *Death Recorded: Capital Punishment in Suffolk 1732–1900*, 2006, in unpaginated appendix.
83. *Star*, 25 July 1793.
84. TNA ASSI 33/2.
85. Gray's Inn MS 45.

Thomas Stibbard, a shepherd, was accused of "defrauding" 200 sheep and lambs, worth almost £100, from his master, a Mr Cook of Pinkney Hall, though the jury merely convicted him of stealing £4 worth of lambs. He was reprieved in favour of 14 years' transportation.[86] In 1785 Charles Plumb received an administrative (immediate) reprieve from his trial judge at the Norwich Assizes, although he had been convicted of stealing nine ewes, nine lambs, and three hoggets (young sheep) from a Swaffham farmer.[87] Two years later, at the Bury Assizes, John Wharby, who had stolen eleven sheep from a Lakenheath man, was also reprieved.[88]

As these cases suggest, throughout the century the great majority of capitally convicted English sheep thieves were transported.[89] Most of the East Anglian cases that produced a hanging involved the theft of a considerable number of animals—usually cases of rustling for resale—combined with a bad previous character on the part of the convict, involvement in a gang, evidence of a sophisticated or commercial *modus operandi*, a serious breach of trust, or a combination of these factors. For example, in 1749 John Gaiser was executed near Ipswich for stealing 20 sheep from a Mr Bennington at Capel, in Suffolk. This was the first such case in the county after the 1741 Act.[90] James Palmer, a shepherd who was executed for sheep theft after the Norwich Assizes in 1753, had stolen 32 of the animals in his charge in Barningham, in a gross abuse of his position.[91] Henry Haylock, capitally convicted and executed at the Bury Assizes in 1793, had gone even further than Palmer and taken a flock of 66 sheep.[92]

The general pattern in East Anglia for punishing sheep theft was duplicated elsewhere in England, such as the West Country.[93] It was even more marked in eighteenth-century Wales, where cases of sheep stealing that

86. *London Chronicle*, 27–30 May 1758; *Universal Chronicle Or Weekly Gazette*, 12–19 August 1758. A statutory reward was paid to four men involved in the prosecution.
87. *London Chronicle*, 23–26 August 1783.
88. *St. James's Chronicle Or the British Evening Post*, 10–12 April 1787.
89. J. Rule, "The Manifold Causes of Rural Crime: Sheep-Stealing in England, c.1740–1840," 1997, p. 240.
90. *Ipswich Journal*, 15 April 1749.
91. *London Daily Advertiser*, 1 May 1753; *Public Advertiser*, 28 August 1753.
92. *Lloyd's Evening Post*, 22–24 July 1793.
93. J. Rule, "The Manifold Causes of Rural Crime: Sheep-Stealing in England, c.1740–1840," 1997, p. 240.

resulted in execution usually involved offenders coming from a distance ("outsiders") who operated in a gang or group, and who faced several indictments at the same time.[94]

Nevertheless, in what appears to have been a short-term, centrally initiated policy of deterrent sentencing at a difficult time economically, especially in rural areas, there was an upsurge in executions for sheep stealing in the first several years of the nineteenth century. In 1801 Henry Warren was capitally convicted and executed in Suffolk for stealing just four ewes.[95] He was a married man of 46, with five (possibly eight) children, who claimed until his death that he bought the animals in good faith from a stranger.[96] At about the same time, in neighbouring Norfolk, James Chettleburgh was hanged at Thetford for stealing just six sheep in Saxlingham.[97] The following year William Rix, a married 25-year-old man, was executed for stealing ten sheep in his native parish of Denton, in Norfolk. (His youthful co-defendant, 19-year-old Christopher Smith, was reprieved).[98] This change in sentencing policy was paralleled elsewhere in England. For example, in the West Country there was a sharp increase in executions for sheep stealing in the first decade of the nineteenth century, with 1801 accounting for most of the 19 hangings for the crime on the Western Circuit during this time. This was a crisis year, and examples were clearly being made.[99]

Thereafter, the incidence of executions for sheep theft declined swiftly and steadily until repeal of the death penalty for the crime in 1832. Just two more men were executed in East Anglia after the early 1800s. Thomas Moy, a 32-year-old man with seven children, was hanged for sheep theft as late as August 1816. He appears to have farmed 100 acres of land at Binham, in Norfolk, his prosperous position making his criminal activity all the more reprehensible.[100] The final case, that of Robert Gibson,

---

94. D. Jones, "Life and Death in Eighteenth-century Wales," 1981, p. 543.
95. *The Ipswich Journal*, 28 March 1801; *The Hull Packet*, 7 April 1801.
96. *The Bury and Norwich Post: Or, Suffolk, Norfolk, Essex, and Cambridge Advertiser*, 15 April 1801.
97. Ibid., 8 April 1801.
98. Ibid., 1 September 1802.
99. J. Rule, "The Manifold Causes of Rural Crime: Sheep-Stealing in England, c.1740–1840," 1997, p. 249.
100. *The Bury and Norwich Post: Or, Suffolk, Norfolk, Essex, Cambridge, and Ely Advertiser*, 4 September 1816.

who was executed in April 1824 for stealing just two sheep, involved even more aggravating circumstances. These led the Lord Chief Justice, presiding over the Norfolk Assizes, to warn him that clemency would not be forthcoming. Gibson, a comfortably off man, had taken his son along on the criminal venture, so corrupting him, and had stolen the sheep for resale. There was also a local need to set a deterrent example.[101] Even so, he was extremely unlucky to hang for such a minor form of the crime at such a late date.

Cattle

Only one case of cattle theft produced an execution in East Anglia between 1742 (when the crime was made capital) and 1800. Cattle were less important than sheep to the agrarian economy of the region, and they were less likely to be stolen, if only because of their size and less tractable nature. For the same reason, they were not normally taken in large numbers (unlike sheep). The crime was prosecuted far less frequently than the theft of sheep or horses. In the decade after 1751 there were just two indictments for cattle theft at assizes in the region, albeit that both produced at least one conviction. Even so, nine men were convicted of the crime in Suffolk alone between 1742 and the end of the century.[102]

Despite the value of most cows, many of the men who were convicted of stealing cattle received an administrative reprieve, without even having to ask for mercy. For example, in 1780 Henry Geldon was found guilty at the Norwich Assizes of stealing a red-polled cow from an alehouse keeper, but reprieved by the trial judge before he left the city.[103] Four years later a labourer named John Murrills received the same disposal after he was convicted at the Bury Assizes for stealing two cows.[104] In like manner, at the same forum, in 1787, John Kingsbury was immediately granted clemency by the trial judge after being convicted of stealing a

101. *The Bury and Norwich Post: Or, Suffolk and Norfolk Telegraph, Essex, Cambridge, & Ely Intelligencer*, 31 March 1824.
102. P. Wright, *Death Recorded: Capital Punishment In Suffolk 1732–1900*, 2006, in unpaginated appendix.
103. *London Evening Post*, 12–15 August 1780.
104. TNA ASSI 33/6; *Whitehall Evening Post (1770)*, 5–7 August 1784.

"fat heifer."[105] On a larger scale, Richard Tilson received an administrative reprieve after being convicted of stealing three steers at the Thetford Assizes in 1793.[106]

Others had to petition for mercy. William Brentnall waited several months for clemency after being convicted of stealing three heifers, worth £15, at the Thetford Assizes in March 1760.[107] Although an "old offender," Mathew Hindes was also reprieved six months after being convicted of stealing a cow at the Bury Assizes in 1764.[108] Unsurprisingly, in 1792 29-year-old Daniel Henderson had to petition actively for a reprieve after being convicted of stealing ten steers from a field in Emneth (Norfolk), having been "left for execution" by the trial judge.[109] John Bradfield may have had an even closer escape. He was convicted at the Bury Assizes in 1795 for stealing five two-year-old heifers from a farmer in Norfolk.[110] He was not reprieved at the sessions and, on petition, his trial judge suggested that he receive mercy only on condition of transportation for life, a fairly draconian requirement. Doubtless the number of animals taken explains this reluctance.

In 1797, Robert Scott, a 58-year-old man, became the sole person to be executed in the region for cattle theft, after being sentenced to death at the Thetford Assizes for stealing six heifers and a steer.[111] It seems that this unusual punishment was partly imposed because of Scott's behaviour in trying to blame the crime on his own sons, who were acquitted at the same trial. This had "so incensed the minds of those, through whom mercy on these occasions so often and so properly flow, that he was deemed an improper object of his Majesty's clemency."[112] Nevertheless, he was not the last man to be hanged for the crime in the region. The final mini-surge in executions for animal theft early in the following

105. *The Times*, 6 April 1787, p. 3.
106. *The Times*, 2 April 1793, p. 3.
107. TNA ASSI 33/3.
108. *Public Advertiser*, 21 August 1764; TNA ASSI 33/4 1764. His prosecutor was awarded the £10 statutory reward.
109. *Evening Mail*, 3–6 August 1792.
110. *London Chronicle*, 31 March – 2 April 1795.
111. *London Evening Post*, 25–28 March 1797.
112. *Evening Mail*, 24–26 April 1797.

century helps explain why, in 1801, Richard Grafton was hanged for stealing a cow and three heifers after the Thetford Assizes.[113]

Horses

When it came to horse theft, stealing a single animal could, occasionally, be fatal, especially at the start of the period. For example, in 1741, at the Thetford Assizes, Peter Latten was convicted of stealing a mare, sentenced to death, and hanged.[114] This was particularly likely where an animal was especially valuable, or where the convict was thought to be an experienced criminal. In 1768 John Sherwood, a youth of between 16 and 18 years, was executed after stealing a colt from a farmer's stable in Carbroke in Norfolk. He had massively compounded this crime by setting fire to the building, presumably to cover his tracks. It had burnt down, the flames consuming another horse inside. Even worse, only the direction of the wind had prevented the fire from jumping to the main house.[115]

Nevertheless, execution was never the normal East Anglian disposal for stealing horses during the era, especially when only one or two animals had been taken, even early in the century. Thus, at the Thetford Assizes held in March 1726, a man who had been convicted of stealing a single horse was reprieved.[116] A few months later, four horse thieves—Burlingham Budd, Benjamin Lock, James Canham and Samuel Hagon—were capitally convicted at the Norwich Assizes but reprieved by the trial judge before he left the city.[117] At the Summer Assizes held at Bury in 1734, Robert Harold was found guilty of stealing a bay mare from William Woodbridge and received the same disposal.[118] At the same forum in 1749, two men, Jonathan Paul and Thomas Johnson, were also reprieved for (jointly) stealing a horse.[119]

113. *The Bury and Norwich Post: Or, Suffolk, Norfolk, Essex, and Cambridge Advertiser*, 8 April 1801.
114. *London Evening Post*, 21–24 March 1741.
115. *Public Advertiser*, 23 August 1768.
116. *Daily Post*, 28 March 1726.
117. *Country Journal Or The Craftsman*, 24 August 1728.
118. TNA ASSI 33/1.
119. *Ipswich Journal*, 12 August 1749.

Such clemency was particularly likely if the animal was of obviously limited value, such as the colt stolen by John Gosling in 1787, but it was by no means confined to such cases.[120] Sometimes even those who had stolen a number of horses escaped the gallows. Among them was George Hayes, convicted at the Thetford Assizes in 1728. Sir Bernard Hale immediately reprieved him on condition of transportation because of "favourable circumstances."[121] Similarly, at the Summer Assizes held at Bury in 1754, James Beckett and Robert Burnt were convicted of stealing several animals but reprieved.[122]

Much turned on a combination of the number and value of the horses taken, the sophistication of the defendant's *modus operandi*, and his character. For example, Peter Lattiman admitted he had several stolen horses in his possession, explaining his execution in 1741 after being found guilty of stealing just one animal.[123] By contrast, the report of Sir Nash Grose on a collective petition made on behalf of Edmund Roberts, who had been convicted of horse theft at the Bury Assizes, expressly noted that he was not thought to be part of a gang as a ground for commuting his death sentence to transportation for life.[124]

Other executed horse thieves had a record for different types of serious felony, something that was also indicative of the fluidity of most criminal careers. For example, John Painter, who was hanged for the crime in 1737, was thought to be one of a pair of men who had stolen from Watton Church (the grave offence of sacrilege).[125] Thomas Herring, executed for stealing a horse in 1756, admitted robbing a clergyman on the highway during his magistrate's examination and was suspected of other crimes that he eventually confessed to at the gallows.[126] Jeremiah Pratt, who was hanged after conviction on three indictments of horse theft, went by numerous nicknames and aliases (up to 20 of them), and

120. *St. James's Chronicle Or the British Evening Post*, 10–12 April 1787.
121. *Weekly Journal Or British Gazetteer*, 6 April 1728; TNA SP 36/7 ff 241–242.
122. *Ipswich Journal*, 17 August 1754.
123. *Daily Gazetteer*, 15 April 1741.
124. TNA HO 47/24/9, ff 75–80.
125. *London Evening Post*, 19–22 March 1737.
126. *Gazetteer and London Daily Advertiser*, 20 April 1756.

was an "old and great offender" who also confessed to several highway robberies while awaiting punishment.[127]

This willingness to extend clemency to horse thieves was a nationwide phenomenon, but to markedly different degrees depending on time and place. On the Western Circuit, between 1670 and 1729, somewhat more than half of those convicted for the crime were reprieved. Similarly, in Yorkshire, during the decade from 1735 to 1745, well over a third were executed.[128] By contrast, at times during the century as few as one in eight horse thieves were hanged in urban Surrey.[129] In notably lenient Wales, the figure was sometimes as little as 3 per cent of those convicted.[130]

In East Anglia there were 15 trials for horse theft at the regional assizes between August 1734 and August 1736 (five "cycles" in total) with eight mares and seven geldings being listed as the principal animals stolen. All of the cases involved individual defendants, except for a hearing at the Bury Assizes in 1736 in which three men stood trial for the theft of one animal. Thus a total of 17 men were tried for the crime. Nine were capitally convicted. Most of them were ultimately reprieved, usually on condition of 14 years' transportation, but three men (at the most), a third of the total, are recorded as having been hanged. Among them was George Chandler, executed after the Lent Assizes at Bury in 1736 for stealing a black gelding from Edmund Jenny.[131] His defiance at the gallows might suggest that it was not his first offence. Another was Robert Bird, who was also capitally convicted at the same time for housebreaking in Ipswich. Even so, he held "hopes of a transportation pardon" until his death warrant came down.[132] However, the decade after 1751 saw an increase in leniency; 45 men stood trial at assize for stealing horses, of whom 31 were convicted, and just two executed.[133]

127. *St. James's Evening Post*, 12–15 October 1745; *Westminster Journal or New Weekly Miscellany*, 19 April 1746.
128. R. Markless, *Gender, Crime and Discretion in Yorkshire, 1735–1775*, 2013, p. 271.
129. M. Eder, *"At the Instigation of the Devil": Capital Punishment and the Assize in the Early Modern England, 1670–1730*, 2014, p. 153.
130. N. Woodward, "Horse-stealing in Wales, 1730–1830," 2009, p. 83.
131. *Daily Gazetteer* (London Edition), 31 March 1736. *Daily Gazetteer* (London Edition), 13 April 1736.
132. *Daily Courant*, 22 April 1735.
133. TNA ASSI 33/2.

CHAPTER 17

Homicide Offences

Introduction

Homicide offences encompass the culpable taking of human life. By the eighteenth century, this class of crime was almost entirely made up of cases of murder (including infanticide), petty treason, and manslaughter. Neonatal infanticide, committed at or (much less commonly) within a few days of birth was *sui generis* as a crime, and is considered separately in *Chapter 20*. Petty treason was the murder of: a husband by his wife (its most common form); a master or mistress by his/her servant, apprentice, or maid; or a cleric by a subordinate, such as the killing of a rector by his curate. This offence was considered the most heinous form of homicide as it involved killing someone to whom a "special obedience" was owed.[1] As late as 1807 Martha Alden's cottage near Attleborough, in Norfolk, was pulled down by an enraged mob after she was convicted of killing her husband with a billhook.[2] Even so, and despite its special (if modest) extra evidential requirements and unusual punishment regime (see *Chapter 10*), it was essentially a specialist form of murder, which verdict, along with manslaughter, could be returned as a lesser offence on a petty treason indictment. Murder and petty treason were, unsurprisingly, capital crimes. Cases of the former were only rarely reprieved (infanticide apart), while the latter almost never received clemency.

---

1. E. Umfreville, *Lex Coronatoria*, 1761, p. 11.
2. *Hampshire Telegraph and Sussex Chronicle, etc.*, 17 August 1807.

By contrast, manslaughter, a lesser form of killing committed without "malice aforethought," the mental state (or *mens rea*) required for murder, was a clergyable crime that attracted relatively minor punishment throughout the period. It never resulted in execution, quite exceptionally rare convictions under the Statute of Stabbing of 1604 apart. This reflected perceived culpability; the era had a horror of killings committed in cold blood but was much more forgiving of those that occurred in other circumstances. In William Blackstone's words, "[M]anslaughter arises from the sudden heat of the passions, murder from the wickedness of the heart."[3]

For much of the period, a manslaughter verdict in East Anglia resulted in the clergied convict being branded on the left hand with an "M" and immediately discharged, as occurred at the Norfolk Assizes in Lent 1735, when William Watts was accused of murdering John Oldman but convicted of the lesser homicide.[4] Later that year, Christopher Hewett, described as a "lad," killed John Christmas by stabbing him in the heart with a penknife. At the Suffolk Assizes in March 1736 he was convicted of manslaughter rather than murder, then branded and released.[5] At the same forum in 1752, John Ford was also found guilty of the lesser form of homicide, clergied and discharged. He had beaten John Kingsbury of Melford who was subsequently "supposed to have died of bruises."[6]

However, by the latter part of the era, branding was often supplemented by a short custodial sentence. Although these were occasionally being added at assizes held on the Western Circuit in the early decades of the century, in many counties this change did not occur until the 1760s, and this seems to have been the situation in East Anglia.[7] For example, in August 1764 William Drury was branded and sentenced to three months' imprisonment after being convicted of manslaughter at the City of Norwich Assizes.[8] As this suggests, initially many such sentences

3. W. Blackstone, *Commentaries on the Laws of England,* 1769, vol. 4, p. 90.
4. TNA ASSI 33/1.
5. TNA ASSI 33/1.
6. *General Advertiser (1744)*, 4 August 1752.
7. M. Eder, *"At the Instigation of the Devil": Capital Punishment and the Assize in the Early Modern England, 1670–1730*, 2014, p. 41; J. M. Beattie, *Crime and the Courts in England 1660–1800*, 1986, p. 88.
8. TNA HO 33/4.

were for just a few months, but by the final decade of the era the almost standard penalty was a year's imprisonment. Typically, in 1802 William Cooper was tried at the Bury Assizes for murdering his wife. It appears that they had quarrelled, and a scuffle then broke out between them, during which he knocked her down, the fall causing fatal injury. Cooper was merely convicted of manslaughter, branded on the left hand, and sentenced to one year in prison.[9] Even so, the extreme difference in punishment meant that the distinction between murder and manslaughter remained absolutely crucial to English law in 1800.

Throughout the eighteenth century, it was unusual for manslaughter to be indicted by an assizes grand jury in its own right, even where such a verdict was the most serious one that could be expected on the evidence, and had earlier been produced by a coroner's inquest. Differentiating between homicides was felt to be something that should be left to a trial jury. The grand jury merely determined whether there was a case to answer for *any* type of killing. If so, it normally indicted for murder as a matter of course. This accorded with what Zachary Babington had recommended as "best practice" in 1677, when he concluded that a "grand jury ought to find it murther, where their evidence is that the party intended to be indicted had his hands in blood, and did kill the other person."[10] This was a nationwide phenomenon, and applied as much to Yorkshire as it did in East Anglia.[11]

For example, in 1736 a weaver named Francis Thurkil was tried for murdering his sweetheart, Sarah Turner, in a Norwich tavern. He had foolishly started playing with a loaded carbine belonging to a dragoon who was drinking there; it went off unexpectedly, hitting Turner in the head and killing her instantly. The same night, the coroner's inquest brought in a verdict of negligent manslaughter, and Thurkil was committed to prison, although he seemed quite distracted by grief.[12] It was obvious that manslaughter was the only form of homicide conviction that could possibly be anticipated.[13] The inquest itself described the death

9. *The Bury and Norwich Post: Or, Suffolk, Norfolk, Essex, and Cambridge Advertiser*, 11 August 1802.
10. In the full title of Z. Babington, *Advice to Grand Jurors in Cases of Blood*, 1677.
11. R. Markless, *Gender, Crime and Discretion in Yorkshire, 1735–1775*, 2013, p. 171.
12. *Read's Weekly Journal Or British Gazetteer*, 29 May 1736.
13. TNA ASSI 33/1; *Read's Weekly Journal Or British Gazetteer*, 29 May 1736.

as being occasioned by "misforturne."[14] Nevertheless, and typically, having decided there was a case to answer, the assizes grand jury brought in a murder indictment. The trial jury was left to make a decision on its merits, returning verdicts on both the grand-jury indictment for murder and the coroner's "inquisition" for manslaughter. (In these situations, if a murder conviction were secured on the former, no verdict would be returned on the latter). Thurkil was ultimately acquitted of any form of homicide offence. The same situation occurred at the trial of Robert Cay at the Suffolk Assizes in 1747.[15] Cay was accused of murdering Robert Love. The case was weak and, reflecting this, he stood trial on a murder indictment from the grand jury but on only a manslaughter inquisition from the coroner's hearing. Again the jury acquitted of any crime after concluding that Love "came to his death by misfortune and chance medley."[16]

This situation began to change early in the nineteenth century. Perhaps indicative of such a development in East Anglia, when Mary Mullenger was prosecuted (and convicted) at the Suffolk Assizes held at Bury in 1803 for the manslaughter of William Norman "in a scuffle," the offence was charged as the lesser form of homicide from the start by the assizes grand jury.[17]

Distribution of Homicide Verdicts

Most eighteenth-century murder indictments resulted in acquittals or convictions for the lesser offence of manslaughter. This lead some observers to complain that English jurors were prone to a "mistaken pity" for the accused in such cases, although, given the practice of indicting almost all killings as the most serious form of homicide, such results were not entirely unsurprising.[18] The distribution of the three main verdicts was fairly consistent around the country.

---

14. NRO NCR Case 6a/6/47.
15. Gray's Inn MS 45.
16. Gray's Inn MS 45.
17. *The Bury and Norwich Post: Or, Suffolk, Norfolk, Essex, and Cambridge Advertiser*, 3 August 1803.
18. Anon, *A Dissertation on the Constitution and Effects of a Petty Jury*, 1737, pp. 31–32.

In the Metropolis, a detailed sampling of homicide cases tried at the Old Bailey, taking one year for every decade from 1680 until 1834 suggests that just over half (51 per cent) of murder trials produced outright acquittals. About 29 per cent of the total resulted in a conviction for manslaughter, while 18 per cent produced convictions for the full offence of murder (the balance is made up of "unusual" verdicts, such as insanity).[19] The provinces were broadly similar. In Surrey just over half of all murder cases produced outright acquittals during the same period. A quarter resulted in verdicts of manslaughter, with the remainder returned as findings of murder.[20] A survey of homicide conviction rates (excluding those for infanticide) for Yorkshire between 1735 and 1775 suggests that 18.3 per cent of men (and more than 90 per cent of defendants accused of such crimes were male) were found guilty of the full offence, exactly the same proportion for manslaughter, and 58.1 per cent were acquitted outright.[21] Although much of the time frame is out of the era under consideration, in Cheshire between 1760 and 1830 murder was successfully prosecuted in less than a third of cases, with half of those indicted being found not guilty of any offence.[22]

Perhaps unsurprisingly, East Anglia produces a similar profile. The 20 "murder" cases tried during the seven sampled years from each decade between 1730 and 1800 can be considered. In nine murder trials (45 per cent), there were outright acquittals for all accused. In seven cases (about 30 per cent), the most serious conviction was for manslaughter for at least one defendant. Only four cases (20 per cent) resulted in at least one person's being convicted of murder. Of course, the sample numbers are small. Nevertheless, random perusal of other years supports the notion that only a relatively small minority of murder trials resulted in convictions for the full offence, and many produced complete acquittals.

For example, in 1736 (not a sampled year) there were four murder trials, resulting in one full conviction, one conviction for manslaughter, and two outright acquittals. Similarly, the 12 murder trials (ignoring infanticides)

19. G. Binder, "The Meaning of Killing," 2007, p. 93.
20. J. M. Beattie, *Crime and the Courts in England 1660–1800*, 1986, p. 97.
21. R. Markless, *Gender, Crime and Discretion in Yorkshire, 1735–1775*, 2013, p. 171.
22. J. Walliss, "Crime and Justice in Georgian Cheshire; The Chester Court of Great Sessions, 1760–1830," 2015, p. 49.

held at the three East Anglian assizes venues between the start of August 1746 and the end of August 1750 produce seven convictions—five of them for murder, two for manslaughter—and five outright acquittals. In the decade from 1751 to 1760 there were 16 homicide trials (infanticide again apart). In 15 cases the killing was indicted as murder, in one purely as manslaughter on a coroner's inquisition, the grand jury having decided there was no case to answer on any charge. Most involved a single accused, although three trials were of joint defendants, including one married couple. There were no homicide prosecutions at all in 1753 and 1759. Four of the 16 killings (a quarter) produced at least one conviction for murder. Seven cases (a little under half) produced at least one manslaughter conviction. Five (a little under a third) produced outright acquittals.

Moving on in time, the three years from 1777 to 1779 produced 13 homicide trials (again ignoring those for infanticide) at the regional assizes. All but one of these were indicted as murder, the exception being that of Benjamin Bowett, who was tried in 1779 purely on a manslaughter "indictment" from the summer of 1777 (whether a coroner's inquisition or a rare case of the lesser homicide being indicted by a grand jury) and found not guilty. Nine cases resulted in acquittals, including a case that was discharged for want of prosecution and another involving a press gang that initially produced a special verdict. Two produced at least one manslaughter conviction and two convictions for the full offence.[23]

As a result, it is safe to assume that each case (ignoring infanticide) that saw a murder conviction stood at the tip of about five homicide trials, so that the 57 murder convictions in the East Anglian region between 1735 and 1799 are the apex of at least 250 formal prosecutions for the same crime, or about four a year. Approximately 40 per cent of these produced outright acquittals, with the balance (still over a third) being made up of manslaughter or (very rarely) other verdicts, such as insanity.

23. TNA ASSI 33/6.

Offence Definitions

In the early seventeenth century, the distinguished jurist Lord Chief Justice Coke defined murder as occurring when a sane man unlawfully killed a person with "malice aforethought, either expressed by the party or implied by law, so as the party wounded, or hurt etc. die of the wound or hurt etc. within a year and a day of the same."[24] Examples of "implied" malice included, *inter alia*, killings committed by robbers and burglars while engaged in their crimes.

Self-Defence

By the eighteenth century, a successful claim to self-defence or defence of one's home or that of an employer normally precluded any type of homicide conviction at trial. However, at the start of the period, coroners' inquests might still leave such a matter to the assizes. For example, one night in January 1714, Robert Towell broke into the house of Nicholas Sharpington, in Norwich, while he and his wife were in bed and threatened to murder them. Nicholas then stabbed Towell with a sword.[25] This case produced a manslaughter verdict at the ensuing inquest, although there would, *prima facie*, appear to be a clear element of self-defence.

By contrast, in a case from Bury St Edmunds, at the start of 1798, Captain Huxley Sandon left his house in the care of a 17-year-old male servant. It had been the target of several attempted burglaries on earlier occasions. At 9 pm one evening, the young servant saw one of his master's dog's react to a noise in the yard. The youth picked up a loaded gun (left by his master for such an eventuality) and confronted a man there, immediately shooting him in the head. The dead man was a 60-year-old local wool comber of previous good character. Even so, he had climbed a seven-foot wall to get into the yard. The coroner's jury brought in a verdict of "Justifiable Homicide."[26]

24. It still forms the basis for the modern law of murder, albeit that some elements, such as the "year-and-a-day rule," have been abolished.
25. NRO NCR Case 6a/4/41.
26. *The Gentleman's Magazine*, Vol. 83, 1798, p. 71.

Manslaughter was a vital lesser verdict in murder cases and requires detailed consideration. Such verdicts were normally returned when the victim: had been killed by the defendant's gross (and so criminal) negligence; had died unpredictably as the result of a minor assault; or had provoked the killing in some legally "acceptable" manner. In practice, the last category was by far the most important.

Negligent Manslaughter

A tiny number of manslaughter verdicts were returned for causing death by severe negligence although, in what was a "robust" age, juries usually rejected such allegations if they came for trial. The case of Francis Thurkil has already been considered (see above). A similar case occurred almost 20 years later, in 1755. Eighteen-year-old John Wright was shot in the right side by a local hot-presser (Abraham Northern) who had been target shooting near the Bishop's Gate, in Norwich. The coroner's jury brought in a verdict of manslaughter.[27] However, Northern was acquitted at the City of Norwich Assizes in 1755. The gaol calendar described his offence as "slaying John Wright." Northern appears to have been tried purely on the coroner's inquisition, unlike Thurkil, the grand jury not finding a prima facie case for any homicide offence.[28]

Others in this situation were more fortunate, and did not even come to trial, especially later in the period. The more freakish the accident, the less likely it was that a manslaughter verdict would be returned by an inquest. Thus, in November 1754, after John Clarke was killed in a Norwich street by a piece of wadding that had been fired by members of a local club as part of a celebration, a verdict of accidental death rather than manslaughter was returned, although the society was also fined 5s by the inquest jury.[29] No prosecution was brought. In February 1804 a similar inquest verdict was returned after 12-year-old Robert Andrews accidentally shot 16-year-old Mary Wilson of Dilham in the forehead.

27. *Read's Weekly Journal Or British Gazetteer*, 19 July 1755; NRO NCR Case 6a/8/56.
28. TNA ASSI 33/2.
29. NRO NCR Case 6a/8/44.

Wilson "lingered" for some time afterwards, but eventually died in the Norfolk and Norwich Hospital.[30]

Manslaughter by "Non-Lethal" Blows

In 1762 Sir Michael Foster noted that if a man were to give another a "box on the ear, or strike with a stick, or other weapon not likely to kill, and unluckily and against his intention kills, it is manslaughter." This was reiterated periodically throughout the era.[31] For example, in September 1755 a husbandman named John Howlett was committed to gaol accused of killing Sarah Clarke after striking her on the head with a whip.[32] Howlett was subsequently convicted of manslaughter at the Suffolk Assizes, branded, and discharged.[33] In a more extreme case, in early August 1778, Henry Keymer, a land surveyor, died in Dereham of wounds shortly after he was "cruelly treated and beat by a riotous mob at Felthorpe, in Norfolk."[34] Four men were identified and arrested for murder the following morning and committed to Norwich Castle by the coroner.[35] They were tried at the county assizes the same month. One man, Robert Bell, who had struck Keymer with a stick, was indicted as principal, and the other three as accessories for aiding and abetting him. All were acquitted of murder but convicted of manslaughter, for which they were branded and sentenced to between six months and a year in gaol.[36]

Manslaughter following Provocation

The two essential prerequisites for provocation to be advanced successfully as a (partial) defence to murder had crystallised during the seventeenth century. First, the killing had to be committed while the perpetrator was acting in the "heat of blood." Calculated revenge could

30. NRO NCR Case 6a/14/54.
31. R. Beville, *A Treatise on the Law of Homicide, and of Larceny at Common Law*, 1799, p. 75.
32. *London Evening Post*, 13 September 1755.
33. TNA ASSI 33/2.
34. *Lloyd's Evening Post*, 14–17 August, 1778.
35. *General Evening Post*, 15–18 August, 1778.
36. TNA ASSI 33/6.

not be manslaughter. In this context, timing, and any delay between provocation and reaction were vital. Second, the perpetrator's mental state (or "passion") must have been occasioned by an adequate and legally recognised form of provocation. Both factors were present when John Framingham, an apothecary from Swaffham, in Norfolk, was tried at the Thetford Assizes in 1733 for murdering a young attorney from the same town. He was merely convicted of manslaughter, as the killing appeared to have been committed in the "height of passion, without prepense malice, and after the greatest provocations given by the deceased that he was capable of."[37]

Four categories of provocative conduct were ultimately recognised as sufficient at law: a grossly insulting assault; witnessing an attack upon a friend or relative; seeing an Englishman unlawfully deprived of his liberty; and witnessing one's wife in the act of adultery. The last category was usually enough to reduce any charge for an attendant killing to manslaughter, however it was inflicted, even if it involved an inherently deadly weapon, such as a sword, and an unarmed victim. Thus, at the Norfolk Assizes in 1729 it was noted "John Capes for killing a man that kept company with his wife, [was clergied for manslaughter and] branded."[38]

Nevertheless, the first category, a grossly insulting assault, was statistically by far the most important category of manslaughter.[39] If a man was provoked by more than words, and then retaliated in hot blood, even using inherently lethal weapons such as a knife, club, or firearm, and a death resulted, any conviction was likely to be for manslaughter, even in circumstances where the defendant could not claim self-defence. As the killer's actions were an overreaction, but not grossly so, the lesser verdict was appropriate.

There usually had to be some physical battery to constitute legally adequate provocation. A purely verbal insult was not normally enough. For example, in 1736 Robert Brett "fell into a passion" and beat his foul-mouthed but non-violent wife Ann. It appears that he snapped after being constantly nagged, an account that was supported by his

37. *London Journal (1720)*, 24 March 1733.
38. *British Journal or The Censor*, 9 August 1729.
39. M. N. Berman and I. P. Farrell, "Provocation Manslaughter as Partial Justification and Partial Excuse," 2012, p. 1036; *R v Mawgridge* (1706) Kel 119.

neighbours, who thought highly of him. Ann died from her injuries a few days later. Even so, Brett was executed at Melton, in Suffolk, after being convicted of murder.[40]

Of course, returning manslaughter verdicts in any case where "Blow had been returned for Blow" would be unjust. As counsel for the Crown pointed out in 1705, when arguing a special verdict before the Westminster judges at Serjeants' Inn, this would mean that a killer could never be convicted of murder unless his victim was "so base a coward as to suffer another to cut his throat before his face, without resisting his assaulter."[41] The use of force in self-defence would not be provocation.

Nevertheless, it did not take much to be seen to be voluntarily "participating" in a brawl, which action would then preclude a murder verdict. For example, in April 1757 Charles Parr, Jeffry Warns, and Robert Sillys were drinking in a public house at Thursford, in Norfolk, and playing a game called Hustling in the Hat. A quarrel arose, and Parr punched Warns several times with his fist and then picked up a poker and struck him on the head, killing him "on the spot." Sillys allegedly held Warns while Parr struck the fatal blow. Parr made his escape, but Sillys was held at the scene and committed to the county gaol in Norwich.[42] Parr joined him there a few days later, after being arrested at King's Lynn.[43] At trial he was merely convicted of manslaughter, and Sillys was acquitted altogether.[44]

In an even more extreme case, from 1796, two men stood trial at the Suffolk Assizes for the murder of James Mayes during an altercation in October the previous year. The victim had been a private in the Northumberland Militia. The defendants, William Martin and Edmund Taylor, had seen him with a young woman in the small hours of the morning and "attempted to take her away." A scuffle ensued in which Mayes was killed. It was alleged that he had been kicked while on the ground.[45] Both defendants were subsequently acquitted outright. The (perhaps

40. P. Wright, *Death Recorded: Capital Punishment in Suffolk 1732–1900*, 2006, p. 19.
41. Anon, *A Full and True Account of the Tryal, Examination, and Proceedings Against Mr. John Maugridge a Kettle-Drummer*, 1705, p. 1.
42. *Public Advertiser*, 19 April 1757.
43. *London Evening Post*, 23–26 April 1757.
44. *Public Advertiser*, 13 September 1757.
45. *The Times*, 13 October 1796, p. 3.

surprising) failure of the Crown even to secure a manslaughter verdict in this case may have been indicative of hostility towards the local garrison.

Obviously, if one of the parties in an interpersonal conflict had been entirely passive before a dispute came to lethal violence, a murder verdict was almost certain to follow. This was unusual. Only one such "quarrel," that which occurred between Thomas Clarke (a butcher's "slave") and John Bonney at Norwich in 1750, produced a conviction and execution between 1735 and 1799, and in this case the victim had not raised a hand to his killer or threatened to do so.[46]

Both men had gone to a tavern in the city as part of a small group. After they had consumed some beer, a dispute arose between them, Clarke accusing Bonney of drinking too much, and unsuccessfully trying to wrest his mug away. He then slapped Bonney, who did not react, but warned Clarke that he would get a warrant against him for assault from a Justice of the Peace the next day. The men continued drinking, but half an hour later, Clarke picked up an iron poker from the pub's fire, and gave Bonney two "severe strokes" for threatening him with a warrant, fracturing his skull in the process. The Norwich City coroner's inquest quickly brought in a finding of wilful murder.[47] Several of the witnesses called at the trial at the City of Norwich Assizes held in August 1750 suggested that Clarke had a "barbarous and unhumane disposition" and had shown no remorse when told the following morning that Bonney was dying. (According to one account, a dozen witnesses were called at trial to establish the defendant's malign disposition.)[48] The complete lack of physical reaction or voluntary participation in any conflict by Bonney meant that it was not a "fight" but an assault, one that had been carried out with a potentially lethal weapon. This, combined with the defendant's bad reputation, explains why the case produced a full murder rather than manslaughter verdict.[49] Clarke was duly hanged.

---

46. *Read's Weekly Journal Or British Gazetteer*, 25 August 1750.
47. NRO NCR Case 6a/8/1.
48. *Whitehall Evening Post Or London Intelligencer*, 18–21 August 1750.
49. *Read's Weekly Journal Or British Gazetteer*, 25 August 1750.

Manifest Criminality

The distinctions between lawful self-defence, manslaughter, and murder were often fine. To a considerable extent, eighteenth-century courts extrapolated "malice" (a deliberate intention to kill) from the external physical circumstances of the case put before them, what might be termed its "manifest criminality," rather than attempting to delve too deeply into the individual's mind at the time of the crime. Once certain circumstances were present, the onus was (effectively) on the defendant to persuade the court that he had not possessed malice aforethought.[50] Indeed, Sir Michael Foster suggested that in murder cases, once a killing had been established, "all the circumstances of accident, necessity, or infirmity are to be satisfactorily proved by the prisoner."[51]

This approach meant that the use of a weapon or poison was often a *sine qua non* for securing a murder (rather than manslaughter) conviction when a death occurred during a violent confrontation. In the metropolitan area during the eighteenth century, of 43 sampled cases where a murder verdict had been returned, 39 (about 90 per cent) involved the use of weapons, albeit not all of them purposely manufactured. In 22 murders a knife or sword was employed; in one, an axe; nine cases involved the use of firearms of various types; in two, staffs were used to batter the victims; in the remaining five, domestic implements, such as a poker, were employed as improvised weapons. The four "weaponless" murders are also highly revealing. One involved the use of poison, which can be viewed as a form of weapon for these purposes. In another two, the victims died of strangulation, an act that offered little opportunity for ambiguity. The final case involved the savage thrashing, without a weapon, of a child, an inherently frail victim. This was the only case in which a weaponless beating produced a murder conviction.

A broadly similar situation was found in the East Anglian region. The 19 killings that produced murder convictions and executions at the various sessions of the Norfolk Assizes held between 1735 and 1799 can be considered in this regard (ignoring the one case of newborn infanticide

50. G. Binder, "The Meaning of Killing," 2007, pp. 95–97.
51. M. Foster, *Crown Law,* 1762, p. 255.

that produced a hanging). The *modus operandi* for these murders can be firmly identified in eleven cases. In several of the others it can be guessed at. For example, when James Cliffen, a footpad, beat and robbed two elderly brothers, killing one of them in the process, it is likely that he used some kind of blunt instrument. However, this is not certain and so is not included in the total. Of the eleven murders two involved stabbing with a knife, and one with a pitchfork; there were four cases of poisoning (including one done to procure an abortion which killed the pregnant woman); four involved the use of a blunt instrument (a wooden staff, an iron poker, a wooden lever, and a large stick), and there was one case of a fatal shooting with a firearm (a pistol).

If no weapons were employed, the prospects of a murder conviction fell greatly. In East Anglia, as elsewhere, it was not easy to be found guilty of murdering an adult with fists. For example, in 1751 John Ginn was convicted of manslaughter at the Bury Assizes, after he struck James Mumford on the side of his head, occasioning a single bruise from which the victim subsequently died.[52] The slightly freakish element to the case, a single punch causing death, makes the verdict unsurprising.

A more extreme example occurred in 1779, after Thomas Meadows, a corporal in the Royal Marines, who were recruiting in East Anglia, enlisted Robert Alderson in Sudbury. Meadows struck him a vicious punch in the stomach for a minor transgression. This prevented Alderson from marching as fast as the other recruits. When their group reached the *Duke's Head* near Long Stratton, in Norfolk, Alderson lay down to rest, but was dragged from his bed by Meadows, who then beat him so violently that he expired at the inn shortly afterwards. Richard Eaton, a Norfolk coroner, committed Meadows to Norwich Castle gaol for murder.[53] Even so, when tried at the Norfolk Assizes in July that year for murder by "beating with his hands," he was acquitted outright, not even a manslaughter conviction being returned.[54] Similarly, in October 1784 a quarrel arose between a butcher unfortunately named Death, from Hargrave, in Suffolk, and Samuel Savage, his former journeyman. Savage

52. *General Advertiser (1744)*, 6 August 1751; TNA ASSI 33/2.
53. *General Advertiser and Morning Intelligencer*, 2 June 1779.
54. TNA ASSI 33/6.

knocked Death down with a blow to the head that killed him almost immediately. Savage was committed to Bury gaol after the coroner's jury investigating the death brought in a verdict of "willful murder."[55] Nevertheless, he, too, was not convicted of this crime at the ensuing assizes.

Acquittal for murder in the absence of weapons was not a rule of law. In extreme cases, beatings inflicted without a weapon *could* produce murder convictions, even with an adult victim. Thus, in 1790 Bartholomew Quaim was tried at the Ely Assizes for murdering his wife during a ferocious quarrel as they were going home from a public house. He beat and kicked her "cruelly," and she died from a burst spleen.[56] Significantly, the jury could not decide whether this constituted murder or manslaughter and returned a special verdict. At the request of the prisoner, the court provided him with counsel to argue the legal point in front of the Court of King's Bench, which decided that he was guilty of murder.[57] Quaim was duly hanged on Kennington Common, in Surrey, on 7 February 1791. However, it was rare for spousal killings that had not involved the use of a weapon to produce murder convictions until the middle of the nineteenth century.

As in the Metropolis, the deaths of small children, killed without a weapon, were also an exception to the general situation. Benjamin Brett killed his four-year-old stepson at Ketton (Suffolk) in 1794 by violently throwing the infant to the ground and was executed for murder.[58] As in the capital, strangulation of adults was also an exception. Richard Ringe was convicted of murder at the Bury Assizes in 1763 after throttling his master while he slept.

Lethal Brawls

Because of the role of physical provocation in reducing murder indictments to the lesser form of homicide, the great majority of manslaughter verdicts, whether in East Anglia, London, or Surrey, were returned in cases where killings occurred as a result of sudden violent altercations

55. *Felix Farley's Bristol Journal*, 16 October 1784.
56. *Ipswich Journal*, 9 February 1791.
57. *Whitehall Evening Post (1770)*, 22–25 January 1791.
58. Anon, *Last Dying Speech and Full Confession of Benjamin Brett*, 1794, pp. 1–2.

between two or more men.[59] Despite its generally falling homicide rate, eighteenth-century England was still a quick-tempered society, possessed of what might almost be termed a "brawling culture." This meant that social encounters could turn sour quickly, and conflicts over essentially trivial matters swiftly escalate to lethal violence. A selection of cases from the region, not all of which ended in death, is indicative of this phenomenon.

In May 1777, after two men "had some words" at a shoemaker's shop in Hundon, Suffolk, one of them picked up one of the cobbler's knives and gave the victim a "wound in the body to the depth of three inches of which he lies with little hope of recovery."[60] In May 1780 John Cunningham, an Ipswich butcher stabbed Thomas Gusterson, a local labourer, in an outburst of pure tetchiness. Gusterson, who was personally acquainted with Cunningham, had gone into the latter's shop, where the owner was eating turnip tops, and helped himself to some of the vegetables, without permission, dropping the plate in the process. This infuriated Cunningham, who said, "[D]—n your blood, I'll run my spado into you, and instantly stabbed him with great violence in the breast, with a knife." Purely by chance, this did not produce a fatal wound.[61]

Others were not so lucky. In December 1716 23-year-old John Catton had an argument over a book with John Rolling in the latter's house in Norwich. While they were scuffling, Rolling struck Catton a mortal blow on the head. The coroner's inquest returned a manslaughter verdict.[62] In the same city in 1724, another inquest reached the same decision after two men had an argument and started fighting while walking together in a churchyard. During the altercation, Daniel Firman kicked Thomas Money in the "privy parts," inflicting injuries from which he eventually died.[63]

The presence of alcohol greatly increased the possibility of such disputes having fatal outcomes. In eighteenth-century Cheshire many inquest findings of manslaughter involved men who had fallen out after

59. J. M. Beattie, *Crime and the Courts in England 1660–1800*, 1986, p. 97.
60. *Ipswich Journal*, 10 May 1777.
61. *Norfolk Chronicle*, 13 May 1780.
62. NRO NCR Case 6a/4/64/1. Latin copy for the Assizes at 64/2.
63. NRO NCR Case 6a/5/4.

drinking together in a tavern, alehouse, or public space.[64] A case from Essex provides a specific example of such an altercation. In August 1776 some inebriated husbandmen, celebrating the end of the harvest, agreed to wrestle. This quickly turned into vicious fighting, during which one man received a paralysing blow to the head. It was noted that all too often in such situations, harvesters, instead of merrily socialising over the "liquor they are partaking of, often go quarrelling and abuse each other and commit such acts as they have cause to repent afterward."[65]

East Anglia was much the same. In November 1733 James Croskill met his brother Peter in a Norwich alehouse and, having drunk an immoderate quantity of ale, the pair quarrelled and fought. As a result, James fell and severely bruised his head, from which injuries he later died.[66] The matter was set down for trial at the City of Norwich Assizes in August the following year. However, no offence was listed or verdict recorded in the gaol calendar for that sessions.[67] Similarly, in October 1780 the landlord of a public house at Winburgh near Dereham, in Norfolk, "having some words with a man drinking at his house, they went to blows, when the landlord beat him in so terrible a manner that he died that night." The coroner's jury brought in a verdict of manslaughter, and the publican was bailed to appear at the next assizes.[68] Again, he does not appear to have come for trial at the ensuing Lent sessions at Thetford, and was certainly not convicted.[69]

The conjunction of alcohol and a readily available weapon was particularly dangerous. In November 1711 John Hammond stabbed James Hunt in the *Rampant Horse* public house in Norwich. The coroner's inquest returned a verdict of manslaughter, suggesting a sudden quarrel. (A Latin copy of the indictment was prepared to facilitate a prosecution at assizes).[70] In 1715 Edward Browne, a "gentleman," stabbed 40-year-old Robert Houghton with a sword in the *Fleece Tavern*. Gentlemen still wore

64. J. Sharpe and J. Dickinson, "Coroners' Inquests in an English County, 1600–1800: A Preliminary Survey," 2011, p. 263.
65. *Ipswich Journal*, 31 August 1776.
66. NRO NCR Case 6a/6/28.
67. *London Evening Post*, 10–13 August 1734; TNA ASSI 33/1.
68. *Gazetteer and New Daily Advertiser*, 11 October 1780.
69. *Whitehall Evening Post (1770)*, 22–24 March 1781.
70. NRO NCR Case 6a/4/10/1.

swords as part of their normal dress at this time, although, by the middle of the century, it was no longer "done" to wear blades in many provincial towns and cities, such as the spas at Bath or Tunbridge Wells.[71] The fact that the coroner's inquest returned a finding of manslaughter would, again, suggest some active participation by the victim in the incident.[72]

Soldiers posed particular problems in this regard. Even at mid-century, it was still normal for NCOs and other ranks to wear swords and bayonets with their regimentals, both on and off duty. This, combined with heavy recreational drinking, facilitated potentially lethal quarrels: "Nothing being more common than for a soldier, hot with spirit of gin, and high in blood, to draw his Toledo [sword] and hack away."[73] For example, at the two assizes held in August 1760 for Norfolk and the City and County of Norwich, three men were tried for murder in as many hearings. Two of the cases involved soldiers as defendants.[74] Corporal Matthew Bowers had been a member of the 67th Regiment of Foot engaged with his sergeant in recruiting at the *White Lion* in Swaffham. They had asked a local tailor, Robert Lane, who was drinking in the tavern, if he was interested in enlisting. Their enquiry was rebutted firmly and "words arose." Lane stripped to the waist to fight and struck the sergeant, who then defended himself with his halberd. At this, Lane ran into the street after Corporal Bowers, who stabbed him in the heart with his sword.[75] At trial Bowers was indicted for murder and capital manslaughter under the Statute of Stabbing 1604 but merely convicted of common-law manslaughter.[76] At about the same time, Sergeant Thomas Smith from the "Old Buffs" was tried at the City of Norwich Assizes. According to the coroner's inquest, he had stabbed 26-year-old Paul Smith (probably unrelated) with a sword in the kitchen of the *White Swan* alehouse in the parish of St Peter Mancroft the previous November.[77] Like Bowers,

71. C. Jones, *Some Methods Proposed Towards Putting a Stop to the Flagrant Crimes of Murder, Robbery, and Perjury*, 1752, p. 5.
72. NRO NCR Case 6a/4/51/1.
73. C. Jones, *Some Methods Proposed Towards Putting a Stop to the Flagrant Crimes of Murder, Robbery, and Perjury*, 1752, p. 7.
74. *London Chronicle*, 12–15 April 1760; *Whitehall Evening Post Or London Intelligencer*, 2–5 August 1760.
75. *Public Ledger Or The Daily Register of Commerce and Intelligence*, 8 July 1760.
76. *Lloyd's Evening Post and British Chronicle*, 4–7 July 1760.
77. NRO NCR Case 6a/8/133; *London Chronicle*, 2–5 August 1760.

he was prosecuted for murder, and under the 1604 Act (see below), but merely found guilty of manslaughter, for which (like Bowers) he was branded in the left hand and discharged.[78]

The Statute of Stabbing

The 1604 Statute of Stabbing (1 Jac 1, c 8) had been introduced to counter a perceived tendency amongst jurors in the early seventeenth century to reduce murder to manslaughter when there had been serious verbal but not physical provocation. It limited the circumstances in which a killer who used a blade without first being struck or physically threatened could avoid the gallows by dint of an apparent lack of "malice aforethought."[79] Essentially, it created a form of capital manslaughter. The lethal wound had to occasion death within six months (unlike the year and a day for murder) and affected only the individual who had struck the blow, rather than any secondary parties to the crime.[80] However, although the crime was formally repealed only in 1828, by the eighteenth century it was rarely prosecuted. On those few occasions when it was indicted, it was usually an alternative count to murder and often failed to produce a conviction if there was an acquittal on the more serious charge. This can be seen at John Browne's trial in August 1747. Anticipating problems on a murder count, the prosecution had also indicted Browne for "stabbing Robert Blyth with a knife against the [1604] statute." By the 1700s, many observers thought that contemporary juries would normally view killings committed after purely verbal provocation as murder, so that the 1604 act was merely declaratory of the common law. Browne was only convicted of ordinary manslaughter, branded, and discharged.[81]

78. TNA ASSI 33/3.
79. B. J. Brown, "The Demise of Chance Medley and the Recognition of Provocation as a Defence to Murder in English Law," 1963, p. 314.
80. T. S., *A Dissertation Concerning the Evil Nature and Fatal Consequence of Immoderate Anger and Revenge*, 1725, pp. 57–58.
81. M. Eder, *"At the Instigation of the Devil": Capital Punishment and the Assize in the Early Modern England, 1670–1730*, 2014, p. 50.

Duels and Other Arranged Fights

Duelling was less common in England and Wales than in some continental countries, such as France and Spain. Even so, it occasioned at least 200 deaths in the period between 1785 and 1845, although it was in continuous decline from the end of the eighteenth century.[82] However, duelling was less popular in the provinces than it was in London. Only a tiny number of high-status individuals died in this fashion in East Anglia. Among them, just before the start of the period, was Sir Henry Hobart, who was killed in a sword duel with Oliver Le Neve, a lawyer from Great Witchingham, which took place at Cawston Heath, in North Norfolk, in August 1698. Le Neve was found guilty of manslaughter, some 18 months later, having fled and returned in the meantime.[83] In the same year, a quartermaster killed an ensign from his own regiment in a duel held in Norwich.[84] Military officers provided a disproportionate number of duellists.

Of course, in East Anglia as elsewhere, many duels did not result in deaths or even injuries, especially as, in England, they were much more likely to be conducted with pistols rather than swords after the early 1760s, and some duellists were reconciled after a harmless exchange of shots. For example, in 1785 a duel was fought between a naval officer and a former officer from the same service at Chapel Field, in Norwich. The occasion of the conflict was an argument the previous night over a tankard of porter (beer). Fortunately, when they exchanged shots early the following morning, they both missed.[85]

Although few in number, duels lingered in the region into the nineteenth century. Thus, in 1802 one was fought on Mousehold Heath, near Norwich, between Robert Alderson, a barrister who was resident at Bungay (and future recorder of Ipswich) and a Mr Grigby. The latter felt that he had been unfairly treated during cross-examination by Alderson while giving evidence at the Suffolk Assizes, and, refusing to

82. See generally, S. Banks, "'Very Little Law in the Case': Contests of Honour and the Subversion of the English Criminal Courts, 1780–1845," 2008, pp. 575–594.
83. *Post Boy (1695)*, 21=23 March 1700.
84. *Flying Post Or The Post Master*, 22–24 September 1698.
85. *Public Advertiser*, 13 August 1785.

accept the lawyer's explanation, sent him a challenge. Each man fired twice, without success, although Grigby's first ball went through the tails of Alderson's coat. A "cordial reconciliation" was subsequently effected between the two men.[86] Ignoring the *casus belli* (itself a sign of the more robust lawyer-conducted cross-examination that became common after about 1780), and the fact that a barrister and future judge felt obliged to participate in the process, the conduct and eventual result of the duel was not unusual.

Not much more than a fifth of the 200 fatal duels in England and Wales between 1785 and 1845 resulted in a matter's going for trial. By far the most common verdict when they did was not guilty, followed in frequency by a finding of manslaughter, provided that the duel was deemed to be "fair." Only a handful of cases produced murder convictions, and, in these, the death penalty was usually reprieved in favour of a sentence of imprisonment.[87] The legal basis for such a benign approach was fairly dubious, and the subject of considerable contemporary criticism from those who thought it encouraged the "disgraceful practice."[88]

Social elites were careful that formal duels, with their de facto semi-legal status, did not extend to commoners. As a result, there was no lower-class equivalent combat, conducted with (for example) knives. However, there was a "popular duel" in eighteenth-century England, albeit not one that was carried out using lethal weapons. This was the formally organized bare-knuckle fight between two men with a grudge against each other. Such fights were usually subject to a system of rules: participants shaking hands before the bout, hitting a man on the ground not being tolerated, etc. Deaths that occurred as a result of such staged but often vicious fights (not an infrequent occurrence) almost never produced a verdict more serious than manslaughter, if they were prosecuted at all, provided the requisite formalities had been followed and, occasionally, even if they had not.

---

86. C. Mackie, *Norfolk Annals*, vol. 1, 1901, p. 14.
87. S. Banks, *A Polite Exchange of Bullets: The Duel and the English Gentleman, 1750–1850,* 2010, p. 137.
88. G. Sharp, *A Tract on Duelling: Wherein the Opinions of Some of the Most Celebrated Writers on Crown Law are Examined and Corrected*, 1790, p. 2.

For example, in 1786 several farm labourers quarrelled while playing cricket at Haverhill, in Suffolk. Two of them decided to fight in an organized manner. Another two of the players agreed to be "sidesmen" (seconds). Unfortunately, the sidesmen also quarrelled, and, after a few blows, one of them, Robert Webb, pulled out a knife and stabbed his opponent in the belly, the knife striking his backbone. He also attempted to stab his victim's brother. The wounded man lingered for a few hours and then died. The coroner's jury that sat on the body brought in a verdict of wilful murder, and Webb was committed to gaol.[89] Even so, he was not subsequently convicted of murder, despite his apparent departure from the "rules of the game." He had warned the dead man not to strike any further blows before stabbing him, which may explain his escape.[90]

The treatment of such "grudge matches," was similar to that meted out for prearranged prizefights for an agreed purse that produced fatalities. Many of these were not prosecuted, resulted in acquittals or, at the worst, findings of manslaughter. For example, in 1781 Matthew Alefoot was tried for murder at the Norfolk Assizes for killing a man named Hardy in a boxing match but convicted of the lesser homicide.[91]

Insanity

There were a few verdicts other than a conviction, acquittal, or finding of manslaughter that could be returned at murder trials. A finding of insanity, the only exculpatory mental state recognised at common law, was one of the most important.[92] Insanity was a general defence to all crime, but does not appear to have been used in misdemeanour cases tried at quarter sessions, perhaps because justices could commit "furiously mad and dangerous" people to custody under the Vagrancy Act 1714.[93] It is also likely that many felonies less serious than murder, and in which there was a question about the defendant's mental state, did not proceed

89. *Norfolk Chronicle*, 16 August 1786; *Whitehall Evening Post (1770)*, 10–12 August 1786.
90. *The Times*, 18 August 1786, p. 3.
91. *Norfolk Chronicle*, 11 August 1781.
92. See generally, J. Brydall, *Non Compos Mentis: or, The Law Relating to Natural Fools, Mad-folks, and Lunatick Persons*, 1700.
93. T. Ward, "Magistrates, Insanity and the Common Law," 1997, p. 796.

to trial, hence not appearing very often in the records. However, this could not easily be done with killings. Insanity was normally a matter for a jury to decide, unless the defendant's condition was quite blatant. An example of the latter occurred in February 1751. Henry Case, a "lunatic" and inmate in the Bethel Hospital for the Insane, in Norwich, appears to have escaped prosecution after he killed Richard Perrin by striking him on the head several times with a deal board.[94] By definition, his condition had already been established. The hospital had been founded by bequest in 1713, specifically for the reception of lunatics rather than the mentally defective ("such as are fools or idiots from their birth"). It was a smaller copy of its more famous (and much older) London counterpart. At times the hospital attracted inmates from other parts of East Anglia. It tried to produce a relatively secure regime in which blades were kept well away from patients.[95]

Although the legal definition of insanity was slightly vague, an ability to distinguish between right and wrong was considered fundamental. Eighteenth-century assizes judges and juries did not lightly accept such claims, as they often led to the immediate discharge of the accused, even in the most serious cases. For example, in 1794, after the child-killer Ann Gosling was found at the Suffolk Assizes to be mad, the court merely ordered her parish officers to "keep and treat her as an insane person."[96] Unsurprisingly, the onus of proof was on the defendant to establish that they were not *compos mentis* (as it still is).[97] Judges actively discouraged acquittals on this basis when they thought guilty verdicts appropriate.[98]

The courts usually required some provable history of eccentric behaviour, prior to the killing that brought a suspect to court, before they would accept such a defence. The support of the gaoler who had supervised the defendant's custody prior to trial was also very helpful. Ann Gosling was fortunate in that she was known to have been "struggling

94. NRO NCR Case 6a/7/148.
95. M. Winston, "The Bethel at Norwich: An Eighteenth-century Hospital for Lunatics," 1994, p. 31 and p. 42.
96. Anon, *The Trials of Samuel Hammond, For the Murder of Ann Avey; and Ann Gosling, For the Murder of John Sage*, 1794, pp. 12–16.
97. *Arnold's Case* (1724) 16 St Tr 694.
98. Lincoln's Inn, Harrowby MSS 18–19, Document 19(f) *Legal Notebook of Sir Dudley Ryder*, 1754 and 1755, p. 4.

with fits" before she killed her illegitimate two-year-old grandson and, in addition, her gaoler had come to the conclusion that she was "out of her mind." Gosling had cut the infant's throat, fearing that he would otherwise be committed to the local workhouse, which, she felt, was a worse fate than going to heaven.[99] Various other tests and criteria were formulated by contemporary specialists, such as Dr William Rowley, including whether the defendants' minds had been affected by grief, love, or "religious enthusiasm."[100]

Nevertheless, Gosling was not alone in experiencing success when advancing insanity as a defence. At the Thetford Assizes in 1725, a woman "who cut her daughter's head off, was found lunatick."[101] Two years later, Samuel Pulham was tried for murder at Bury but "appearing to be lunatick was acquitted."[102] During the Lent Assizes of 1741, Sir William Chapple kept a diary of proceedings on the Norfolk Circuit. In his notes Chapple explained why Mary Stubbing, a married woman who had been accused at the Suffolk Assizes of murdering her nine-month-old male infant by throwing him into the River Lark, had been acquitted: she "looks like a weak woman & has been out of her head at times a great many yeares."[103]

99. Anon, *The Trials of Samuel Hammond, For the Murder of Ann Avey; and Ann Gosling, For the Murder of John Sage,* 1794, pp. 12–16.
100. W. Rowley, *Truth Vindicated Or, The Specific Differences of Mental Diseases Ascertained*, 1790, p. 40.
101. *Weekly Journal Or Saturday's Post*, 27 March 1725.
102. *Daily Post*, 3 April 1727.
103. M. Caswell, *Married Women, Crime, and Questions of Liability in England, 1640–1760*, 2012, p. 89.

CHAPTER 18

Murder

Introduction

Although the eighteenth century saw a high mortality rate from disease and accident this did not make people blasé about premeditated killing. Considerable efforts were made to find and prosecute those who committed such crimes. Indicative of this, at the Bury Assizes in 1812, Edmund (or Edward) Thrower was indicted for murdering Elizabeth Carter and her father at Cratfield, in Suffolk, some 19 years earlier. The pair, who lived together, had been hacked and beaten to death with a hatchet one night in October 1793.[1] Thrower had admitted the murder to another man shortly after it was committed, but the man had dismissed his claim as untrue. However, over the years other information had emerged, and by a "chapter of accidents" and a random conversation among magistrates about a group of notorious murders that took place in London in 1811, a case was built up and Thrower arrested. A witness from the time of the murder was called at the trial and, there being "strong circumstantial evidence" to support his informal admissions, Thrower was convicted, sentenced to death, and duly executed.[2]

Of course, the number of murder convictions is much smaller than the total for all homicides, because the latter includes the numerous convictions for manslaughter. It is vastly smaller than the actual number of unlawful killings because it does not include those that resulted in unjustified acquittals, did not produce suspects, or went entirely undetected.

1. *Morning Chronicle*, 1 November 1793.
2. *The Times*, 24 March 1812, p. 2 and 2 April 1812, p. 2.

Nevertheless, it is indicative of the forms of killing that were deemed to be most reprehensible by eighteenth-century society, and justifies close examination for that reason.

Between the start of 1735 and the end of 1799, 57 people were executed for murder in the five East Anglian jurisdictions that had the power to impose capital punishment. Of these, 24 were in Suffolk, 27 in Norfolk and Norwich combined, four in Yarmouth, and two in King's Lynn. Three involved the murder of newborn illegitimate babies by their mothers and can be ignored for these purposes. Murder convictions and executions are *almost* the same, as murder was an offence that only rarely attracted a reprieve, while hangings usually took place swiftly enough after conviction (especially from 1752) for very few murderers to die in prison in the meantime.

Even so, at least two men during this period convicted of the full offence of murder in the region (other than for infanticide) were reprieved; they were Thomas Harper and the child William York. Such clemency was found elsewhere in the country as well. On one assessment, 11 per cent of murder convictions on the Western Circuit between 1670 and 1730 ended in reprieves.[3] Furthermore, one or two murder convicts died prior to execution. In March 1769 Thomas Clevelong was capitally convicted at the Thetford Assizes for abetting the murder of a Mr Haslip, a surveyor and customs officer, in February of the previous year. However, judgment was temporarily respited on legal grounds.[4] Clevelong was carried to London to receive his sentence, where he died in Newgate prison the following January.[5] More problematic is that, although the majority of those executed for murder had been convicted alone for killing a single person, there were a number of double convictions and executions, in which two people hanged for the same murder, and one or two cases in which there had been more than one victim.

More reliably, between 1735 and 1799, 19 killings in Suffolk were prosecuted to at least one conviction and attendant execution for murder (ignoring a single case of infanticide). Similarly, 23 Norfolk homicide

3. M. Eder, *"At the Instigation of the Devil": Capital Punishment and the Assize in the Early Modern England, 1670–1730*, 2014, p. 40.
4. *St. James's Chronicle Or the British Evening Post*, 23–25 March 1769.
5. *Ipswich Journal*, 6 January 1770.

prosecutions produced at least one conviction and execution for murder over the same period (ignoring two infanticides). This leaves 23 murder cases that resulted in at least one execution for the full offence. These 42 cases will be the subject of analysis.

Classification of Murders

Extrapolating patterns from murder convictions requires that they be classified. This is impossible to do in an entirely satisfactory manner, not least because several potential categories overlap. For example, Charles Drew killed his much-disliked father to secure an inheritance. Should this be seen as a domestic murder or as one related to acquisition, such as the killings perpetrated by some footpads?

While presiding over the trial of John and Nathan Nichols at the Bury Assizes in 1794, Sir William Ashurst noted that there were three primary motives for murder: "the first is, a lawless thirst for plunder; the second, a gratification of carnal or impure desires; the third, spleen, malice, rancour, or hatred."[6] This list is not entirely satisfactory. The first, very important, category encompasses what might be termed "instrumental murders" committed in the course of property crimes. However, killings committed in the course of a sexual offence (the second category) were exceptionally rare. The final category identified by Ashurst is too broad.

Instead, a four-fold division has been employed in this study, and where there has been an overlap, the best "fit" for any individual killing has been chosen, usually by examining the dominant purpose behind the crime. The first category is that of "domestic murders." This is very broadly construed to include the killing of live-in servants by family members and vice versa. Frequently, servants and apprentices were integral members of their employers' families during the eighteenth-century, and the violence they described as being meted out to them, and occasionally took to petty sessions, had many similarities to that sustained by battered wives. The murder of servants and apprentices through the abuse of domestic power, manifest in, for example, sustained beatings and

6. Anon, *The Trial of John and Nathan Nichols*, 1794, p. 7.

deprivation of food over time, will also be dealt with in this category.[7] Conversely, it will also include vengeful servants and apprentices who perpetrated such killings against their masters or their employers' families.

The second category is that of "instrumental" murders, killings carried out in the course of property crimes, such as robbery, housebreaking, and burglary. The murder of law-enforcement officers, while engaged in their duties makes up the third category, albeit that they are widely construed so as to include private security guards such as gamekeepers or soldiers aiding the civil power. The fourth, "miscellaneous" category, covers all other murders, including, *inter alia*, those stemming from non-domestic but spontaneous quarrels that did not produce a manslaughter conviction (exceptionally rare), killings that were not domestic but occasioned by calculated and planned revenge, and the one murder in the context of a sexual offence. These four categories will be dealt with *seriatim*.

Domestic Murders

Although the proportion of murders arising out of a domestic context was slightly smaller than in the modern era (assuming that infanticide is ignored), it was still substantial, and the largest of the four categories considered.[8] Of the 19 Suffolk cases, 12 can, very broadly, be described as "domestic." A majority of these were instances of spousal murder. However, they included an illegitimate child who was killed to save expense; a stepson killed in a fit of temper; a daughter, beaten and starved to death; another daughter, deliberately killed by her father and brother; and a parricide. Of the 23 Norfolk murders, nine can be described as domestic. These include four cases of uxoricide. However, the group also included (at a pinch) a man who murdered his former homosexual lover's fiancée and (even less satisfactorily for purposes of classification) a man who poisoned his pregnant lover while attempting to procure an abortion. Thus, for the region as a whole, 21 of the 42 cases that produced murder convictions, exactly half, had a domestic background.

7. S. D'Cruze, *A Pleasing Prospect: Social Change and Urban Culture in Eighteenth-century Colchester*, 2009, p. 172.
8. J. Sharpe, "Domestic Homicide in Early Modern England," 1981, p. 34.

Modus Operandi of Domestic Murder

A significant number of domestic murders in East Anglia were planned well in advance. Perhaps surprisingly, many involved poison as their *modus operandi.* By contrast, its use in Denbighshire (Wales) between 1660 and 1730 has been described as "exceptional," although the power and ubiquity of poisons increased as the 1700s advanced.[9] It is also noteworthy that, although poison has sometimes been thought of as a female weapon, men often employed it to kill within the region.

Poison, especially arsenic, had many attractions. It was widely available, and freely sold to deal with infestations of rats and mice. Its prevalence could have tragic results, even in the absence of any malice. For example, in November 1712 Margaret Latten died after taking what she thought was "physick" from another woman to cure herself of the "itch." Neither of them realised it was yellow arsenic.[10] In 1783 a man from Bury whose house was infested by rats, spread a slice of bread with arsenic, and left it out to poison them. Unfortunately, his young son got up early, noticed the bread, and ate it, dying in agony a day or so later.[11]

Poisoning posed serious problems for the criminal justice system. The symptoms of arsenic and several other toxins could easily be confused with those of other illnesses, and there were no sure techniques to detect their presence after death until well into the nineteenth century. However, by the eighteenth century physicians had developed a number of (unreliable) tests to identify the ingestion of poison. For example, Lord Chief Justice Gibbs, presiding over the trial of Elizabeth Woolterton for "murder by poison" at the Bury Assizes in 1815, correctly assumed that one well-known test for arsenic had been employed: "I suppose you tried it by fire?"[12] In reality, this test (the poison gave a distinct coloured flame when burnt) was of the most limited value. Nevertheless, doctors continued to rely on it. In March 1767 an autopsy was carried out on

9. S. Howard, *Crime, Communities and Authority in Early Modern Wales: Denbighshire, 1660–1730*, 2003, p. 201.
10. NRO NCR Case 6a/4/19.
11. *Bury and Norwich Post*, 24 April 1783.
12. Anon, *The Trial at Large of Eliz. Woolterton for the Wilful Murder of Robert Sparkes, A Child Six Years Old*, 1815, p. 15.

the body of the pregnant but single Anne Adkins, from St Swithin's parish, in Norwich, due to fears that she had been murdered. The inquest examining her death firmly concluded that there were "[n]o signs of poison or other means of destroying her."[13]

When poisoning cases did come to trial, it was often difficult to secure convictions in the absence of direct evidence. At the City of Norwich Assizes in July 1735, John Davis was accused of the murder by poison of Ann Rowe, a Norwich widow who was "called his wife." He appears to have pleaded guilty to bigamy, and was clergied for this offence, but acquitted outright of murder.[14] (He was also suspected of bigamously marrying and murdering another woman in Sussex.)[15]

Despite these problems, several cases of male-perpetrated poisoning in a domestic context were "proved." Thus, John Norton was convicted of murdering his wife in this fashion at the Bury Assizes in 1734.[16] More than half a century later, Aaron Fakenham murdered his spouse by putting arsenic in a kettle of water with which she made her breakfast tea. He subsequently admitted that he had planned to sell all his possessions after her death and then move away from the area, cruelly abandoning their four-year-old son to the mercy of his Norwich parish.[17] It was a well-planned crime; he had purchased the arsenic almost three months earlier "under the pretence of poisoning rats." His lengthy admissions to a coroner's inquest were held to corroborate: his wife's "dying declaration" (an exception to the hearsay rule), an autopsy that found disfigurement in her stomach, and the fact that white powder had been discovered in a teapot (albeit that this utensil was inadvertently thrown away before "testing").[18] Fakenham (like Norton) was executed.[19]

More unusually, in 1742 Robert Carlton was hanged on Diss Common for committing sodomy with his young lodger and apprentice, John Lincoln, and for fatally poisoning Lincoln's fiancée. The younger man had been "entirely kept" by Carlton until he tired of the relationship and

13. NRO NCR Case 6a/9/80.
14. *General Evening Post*, 2–5 August 1735; TNA ASSI 33/1.
15. *Weekly Miscellany (1732)*, 17 May 1735.
16. *Penny London Post*, 29 March 1734.
17. *Whitehall Evening Post (1770)*, 1–3 October 1789.
18. *The Times*, September 30 1789, p. 3, and August 3 1790, p. 3.
19. *Morning Post and Daily Advertiser*, 30 September 1789.

their covert way of life, and switched his affections to a woman, Mary Frost. Carlton was infuriated by this, and warned that if Lincoln "ever brought his whores near to him he would do them some mischief." A few weeks later the couple announced their intention of marrying. The tailor attempted to dissuade Lincoln from this course of action, and apparently threatened to poison his fiancée. When this failed, he pretended to be reconciled to the turn of events, and invited them to a supper of boiled mutton. At the meal, he poisoned Frost's food (apparently by means of the salt he gave her) before urging her to "eat heartily."[20] That night she became violently sick and "swelled very much." She convulsed for a while and then died, despite attempts to purge her. An autopsy was performed, and when the doctors involved "open'd her they found all her entrails quite affected by the poison." Lincoln gave evidence for the prosecution at his erstwhile partner's hearing.[21] Thomas Bacon, an apothecary from Diss, also testified that he had earlier sold "sublimate of mercury" to Carlton, ostensibly to kill vermin (it was a popular alternative to arsenic). It seems that up to a quarter of an ounce was used to murder Mary.[22] Carlton was convicted; before his execution he admitted sodomy, but attempted to blame others for the poisoning.[23]

More typically of such cases, in 1788 Henry Sell, a disgruntled and vengeful servant of 17, was convicted at the Lent Assizes at Thetford and executed for murdering his master's wife, Elizabeth Clark, at Walsoken, in Norfolk. He had put arsenic in the tea he prepared for the couple. After copious vomiting they sent for a surgeon, who prescribed camomile tea and something to induce further purging. Clark recovered, but, unfortunately, this was not enough to save his wife.[24]

In 1792 William Anthony gave his lover arsenic, from which she died. It seems to have been intended to procure an abortion rather than kill Sarah Cusher, the prospective mother, who was six months' pregnant by Anthony, but it killed both mother and foetus.[25] Sadly, this was a fairly

20. *London Evening Post*, 23–25 March 1742.
21. *Norwich Gazette*, 13–20 March 1742.
22. *Universal Spectator and Weekly Journal*, 27 March 1742.
23. *Norwich Gazette*, 13–20 March 1742; *Norwich Gazette*, 3–10 April 1742.
24. Anon, *The Trial of Henry Sell, For the Wilful Murder of Mrs. Elizabeth Clark*, 1788, p. 4.
25. *Lloyd's Evening Post*, 23–26 March 1792.

regular consequence of induced abortions at this time. Although the killing of the mother was accidental, that of the foetus was deliberate, and the attendant "malice" was legally transferred to the mother, allowing Anthony to be convicted of murder and hanged.

Some other well-planned domestic killings were carried out away from the home using extreme physical violence. William Suffolk, a man of almost 50, was executed on Castle Hill, in Norwich, for killing Mary Beck, a "young" woman (other accounts suggest she was 41), who had rejected his proposal of marriage. Suffolk met her on a common near North Walsham, knocked her down with a large stick, and continued hitting her until he thought she was dead. However, she survived for long enough to give information about her attacker to the authorities. Perhaps unwisely, Suffolk made full admissions when questioned.[26]

Similarly, in a largely unexplained crime from 1794, the father and brother of Sarah Nichols, from Fakenham, in Suffolk, waylaid her in the countryside, beat her with a hedge-stake, and then strangled her.[27] Both were convicted of murder and executed. However, in the same year Samuel Hammond, a young postilion in service to a gentleman from Walsham (Norfolk), was more fortunate when accused of murdering his sweetheart, Ann Avey, in a similar fashion. She had tried to pressure him into publicising the banns of their marriage, as she was six months' pregnant by him. Hammond arranged to meet her. Avey's bruised body was subsequently found in a field with her throat and face cut in a "most shocking manner."[28] After (allegedly) killing her, Hammond had returned to work and played cards with his fellow servants in their kitchen as if "nothing had happened to hurt his mind."[29] In this case, the lack of direct evidence and the absence of a confession proved fatal to the prosecution and the trial jury acquitted.

In another gruesome and well-planned domestic killing, carried out in 1769, Jonathan Vincent, a married man from Laxfield, in Suffolk, murdered his 30-week-old illegitimate daughter, Mary Canham, to "save

26. *Observer*, 26 March 1797.
27. *London Packet Or New Lloyd's Evening Post*, 26=28 March 1794.
28. *Morning Post*, 27 January 1794.
29. *Sun*, 18 February 1794.

expense."[30] The child was the fruit of his relationship with a neighbour's maid. After the servant was dismissed from her position for pregnancy, Vincent allowed her 1s a week as child support. However, after a while, he started to complain about the expense, and asked to take the child from her 18-year-old mother. When she refused, he took both of them into his household, ostensibly to assist with looking after his ill wife and three legitimate children. One day, while Mary's mother was out, he struck the child a fatal blow on the head. The care that Vincent later took to negotiate the price of his own coffin prior to execution would suggest that, although comfortably off, he was something of a miser, explaining his reluctance to be put to unnecessary expense. He was capitally convicted and executed at the Bury Assizes.[31]

It was not only men who killed for such brutally practical reasons. In an equally macabre case, albeit just outside the period, Ann Arnold was convicted at the Bury Assizes in 1813 for the murder of her illegitimate son, a child of less than five years old. She removed his clothes and threw him into a remote pond in a field at Spexhall, in Suffolk, where he drowned, despite repeated appeals for help. Ann had given birth to another illegitimate child, nine months earlier, and the genitor was willing to marry her, provided the older child was put into the custody of its father (who paid her 1s 6d a week maintenance for the boy). However, the father was not willing to take him, leading his mother to her drastic action.[32]

Festering familial grievances could also result in well-planned (rather than impulsive) domestic killings. In 1787 Timothy Hardy slashed his brother-in-law John Aggus's stomach open with a knife in the *Lamb Inn* of Norwich (where John lived) while pretending to shake his hand. He appears to have held a longstanding grudge against Aggus, and had been regularly criticised by the latter's wife (his sister) for being dissolute. Hardy unavailingly attempted to kill himself afterwards, but sustained only a minor wound. Aggus died a few hours later, despite the best efforts

30. *St. James's Chronicle Or the British Evening Post*, 3–6 June 1769.
31. *Ipswich Journal*, 22 July 1769; *Middlesex Journal or Chronicle of Liberty*, 22–25 July 1769.
32. *The Bury and Norwich Post: Or, Suffolk, Norfolk, Essex, Cambridge, and Ely Advertiser*, 31 March 1813.

of three surgeons. Hardy later suggested that there were other relatives that he would have killed, had he been given the opportunity to do so.[33]

Other domestic murders were more sudden and spontaneous, albeit not qualifying as cases of manslaughter. One of the most notorious instances occurred in 1705. William Gilbert from Toddington, in Norfolk, married a well-to-do woman who brought him a dowry of £500 and a flock of sheep worth another £300. Unfortunately, the marriage turned sour very quickly, as Gilbert squandered this new wealth and discovered the pleasures of drink, loose women, and dissolute companions, something that also affected his previously benign character, so that he quickly became very cruel towards his spouse, "using her more like a slave than a wife." There was only one child of the union, a well-behaved daughter, though at the time of her death his wife was more than seven months' pregnant with another. One August evening, William came home very drunk and started blaspheming. When his wife asked him to desist, he cut her throat and then stamped on her body. When his young daughter tried to intervene, he threw the child against a wall and then beat out her brains with a hammer. Gilbert expressed contrition as soon as he sobered up. Unusually for the era, he pleaded guilty to murdering his family and was hanged four days after conviction at his own request, although greater delays in execution were normal until 1752.[34]

Seven men were hanged for killing their wives in Norfolk and Suffolk between 1735 and 1799. As some of the cases already cited suggest, and as today, uxoricide often followed a history of physical abuse. Stephen Watson's murder of his wife was, apparently, quite shocking. She had given birth only a week earlier. The "cruelties" that Watson inflicted on her apparently excited general horror at the Thetford Assizes in 1795.[35] However, one or two cases came out of the blue. At the Bury Assizes in 1775, George Smith admitted poisoning his wife. There was no apparent reason for the killing, as they had previously lived in seeming amity. Smith, a "most stupid, illiterate fellow" successfully asked for a one-week respite before execution, after which he was hanged.[36]

33. *General Evening Post*, 17–20 November 1787.
34. Anon, *The Wicked Husband, and Unnatural Father*, 1705, pp. 1–8.
35. *General Evening Post*, 31 March – 2 April 1795.
36. *Craftsman or Say's Weekly Journal*, 26 August 1775.

Only one woman was executed for murdering her husband (technically, petty treason) in the East Anglian region over the same period. Although only 21, Margaret Beddingfield had been married to a prosperous Suffolk farmer (John) for four years. She began an affair with her husband's young farmhand, Richard Ringe, and resolved to murder her spouse with her new lover's assistance. She promised Ringe marriage as soon as he "destroyed her husband." After they failed to persuade a maid to poison John's food, Richard strangled him while he slept in his bed. The couple initially escaped detection, only being caught when the maid broke her silence. The pair were convicted at the Lent Assizes in 1763 and executed at Ipswich.[37]

As the Ringe case suggests, and as in all eras, adultery and romantic triangles could spawn homicidal violence. In 1795 Henry Bennington killed his master with a pitchfork whilst working in a stable, and buried him in an adjacent yard. He made full admissions to the crime when examined by a JP. Bennington acknowledged that he had had "criminal connections" with his master's wife but (unlike the Ringe case) denied that she had had any involvement in the killing.[38]

Murder by Abuse of Power

The use of "correctional" violence, and the physical mistreatment of young servants, apprentices, and children, was widespread during the eighteenth century. Typically, one of the eleven preserved coroners' inquests that produced homicide verdicts in Norwich in the first two decades of the century involved murder by "hard usage" of an infant by his parents.[39]

Correctional violence was considered quite proper, provided it was kept within recognised bounds. If it went beyond "acceptable" levels, and significant injury resulted, assault charges could be laid. If it was inflicted improperly, but not in such a way that a fatality was likely, and a death did ensue, it would normally be deemed a case of manslaughter at most.

37. Anon (An eminent short-hand writer), *The Genuine Trial of Margery Beddingfield and Richard Ringe*, 1763, pp. 3–43.
38. *General Evening Post*, 31 March – 2 April 1795.
39. NRO NCR Case 6a/4/68/1 and 68/2.

Indicative of this, in 1801 William Steward, an Essex farmer, was committed to Chelmsford Gaol accused of striking a servant boy, William Bayliss, on the head with the iron end of a plough staff. The youth had died a fortnight later. Remarkably, it was noted that another servant boy had died in a workhouse a few months before through the same man's "cruelty," albeit that Steward was merely charged with assault on this occasion.[40] Despite this history, he was not convicted of Bayliss's murder.

However, throughout the period, the deliberate use of potentially lethal force that resulted in death could produce a murder conviction, especially if a weapon was employed.[41] Furthermore, English courts appear to have gradually lowered the bar at which such conduct was viewed as "unacceptable."[42] Nevertheless, the dividing line between acquittals, convictions for manslaughter, and findings of murder could be very fine, producing different verdicts in broadly similar situations. A cluster of cases from the region drawn (by chance) from a single year is indicative.

In 1784 Mary Ramplin of Felsham, in Suffolk, was accused of murdering her younger namesake and daughter-in-law "by beating." (There was also an allegation of neglect and withholding food). She was acquitted outright at the Bury Assizes.[43] In the same year, at the Norfolk Assizes, a butcher named Higgs was accused of murdering a shepherd boy he had employed to secure some sheep prior to slaughter. The lad had negligently allowed the sheep to escape and, in his irritation, the butcher hit the boy with a stake that came readily to hand, fracturing his skull. Mr Justice Nares, summing up to the jury, noted, "Every master has a right moderately to chastise his servant, but the chastisement must be on just grounds, and with an instrument properly adapted to the purposes of correction." The jury produced a manslaughter verdict, apparently not viewing the stake as a grossly improper instrument, given that it was picked up on impulse, in the heat of passion, and concluding that the defendant did not intend to kill the boy.[44] (By contrast, in 1761 Edward Johnson, a chimney sweep, who had killed his apprentice,

40. *Bury and Norwich Post,* 22 April 1801; *Ipswich Journal,* 18 April 1801.
41. R. Beville, *A Treatise on the Law of Homicide, And of Larceny at Common Law,* 1799, p. 62.
42. J. M. Beattie, "Violence and Society in Early-Modern England," 1985, pp. 50–51.
43. *Ipswich Journal,* 8 May 1784; *Morning Herald and Daily Advertiser,* 9 August 1784.
44. Discussed in *The King v Sarah Hazel* (1785) 1 Leach 368.

Edward Stanley, was convicted of murder at the Bury Assizes, executed at Sudbury, and then hanged in chains in the town).[45]

Another case from 1784, that of Sarah Hazel, raised even more difficult legal issues in this regard. Sarah, a day labourer's (second) wife, and a pregnant woman of just 22 years of age, was accused of murdering her stepdaughter Mary "by beating." She had thrown a heavy stool at the ten-year-old child (some accounts give her age as 13) in Buxton, Norfolk, after she became annoyed at Mary's defective spinning. The stool struck the child on the temple, as a result of which she "lingered" for a short while, in a stupefied condition, then died.[46] Two days later her body was pulled from the River Bure at Lamass. The coroner's inquest was initially unable to decide how she had met her death. However, shortly afterwards, Sarah and her husband, John, were committed to the Castle Gaol, in Norwich, after a local magistrate heard sworn evidence from a Buxton clergyman and then extracted a confession from Sarah.[47]

The case raised the crucial issue (*inter alia*) of whether Sarah was guilty of murder or manslaughter.[48] The trial jury at the Norfolk Assizes concluded that she had not intended to kill the child and returned a special verdict, the facts of which were initially reserved for the 12 Westminster judges and eventually debated in the Court of King's Bench. Ultimately, this body did not produce a decision, and Sarah was kept in the King's Bench prison for a year. In his report on the case, Lord Loughborough suggested that, given the exceptional circumstances, even were Sarah to be convicted of murder she might be reprieved, and, if she were guilty only of manslaughter, the term of imprisonment she had already served was equal to the normal (late eighteenth-century) punishment for the crime. He recommended a free pardon, and claimed that this had the backing of all the judges.[49] Sarah eventually received such a pardon and was released. (For purposes of analysis, this case is treated as one of manslaughter.)

45. *London Chronicle*, 21–24 March 1761.
46. *The King v Sarah Hazel* (1785) 1 Leach 368, 168 E.R. 287.
47. *Morning Chronicle and London Advertiser*, 7 June 1784.
48. *Public Advertiser*, 3 May 1785.
49. NA HO 47/4/2, ff 2–3.

In reality, it seems that the jury's reluctance to return a manslaughter verdict *ab initio* was prompted by Sarah's concerted attempt to conceal the death. She announced that her stepdaughter had disappeared and conducted mock searches, although she (Sarah) had actually weighted Mary's corpse down and thrown it into the river. Although Sarah's husband had also been accused of the crime, the allegation against him was thrown out by the assizes grand jury.[50] Nevertheless, John was acutely unpopular. On his release from prison he was surrounded by a mob, treated in a "cruel manner," and ducked in the local river, albeit while tied to a rope. He was rescued by local peace officers but then pursued through the city streets.[51]

"Parish apprentices" were particularly vulnerable to mistreatment. These were bastards, orphans, or (sometimes) children whose parents were alive but permanently dependent on parish relief. They were "put out" to service when they were deemed old enough. Legally, they had to be over seven years of age, but many were just eight or nine, and few more than ten, when entrusted to the care of people who would, in theory, teach them a trade or domestic skills. This spared parishes the expense and inconvenience of raising the children themselves. In practice, parish apprentices were often used for any work that needed doing, indoor or outdoor, by employers who had been attracted by the parish-paid financial premium (£3 or £4) for taking them, and the prospect of cheap labour.

Such children were frequently apprenticed some distance from their parish of origin, if only because it was widely thought that if the apprentice had not been returned within 40 days they would have gained settlement and so become the responsibility of their new community. Unfortunately, it also meant that there was often no one to protect them, even though the overseer of the poor in their home parish was supposed to monitor their progress. Furthermore, their new masters were sometimes drawn from the "very dregs of the poor." The parish officers who arranged such "mock apprenticeships" were not overly concerned as to whether such guardians might be savagely cruel and "beat, abuse,

50. *Morning Herald and Daily Advertiser*, 5 June 1784; *London Chronicle*, 12–14 August 1784.
51. *Felix Farley's Bristol Journal*, 21 August 1784.

strip-naked, starve" the new employee. Although a few JPs were careful about giving their approval to such arrangements, and tried to establish the good character of prospective employers before they did so, such men were rare, and parish officers could usually avoid them. Most magistrates were much less diligent, and their clerks could be bribed to encourage their agreement.[52]

Parish apprentices were not entirely devoid of legal protection. If their masters had recourse to "unacceptable" violence they might face charges of assault. For example, at the Beccles Quarter Sessions in 1785, Thomas Hotblack was found guilty of assaulting and ill-treating a girl who had been bound to his service from the House of Industry at Shipmeadow, in Suffolk. He was fined £5 and imprisoned to a maximum of two months until it was paid. At the same time, Thomas Fox, a butcher from Shottisham, in Suffolk, was fined £1 and imprisoned for a month for "assaulting and ill treating his apprentice bound from the house of industry at Melton."[53] In practice, however, most such cases never came to official notice, if only because young apprentices were heavily dependent on their employers.

Unfortunately, such assaults could have fatal consequences. In September 1767 Mary Larter, a parish apprentice working on a farm in Suffolk, died after extreme mistreatment by her employers. Larter was brought to the nearby Framlingham Workhouse and tended by Mary Fisk before succumbing to her illness and injuries. She told Fisk that a day or so earlier she had been churning butter while sick. When she told her mistress that she was too ill to continue, she was ignored. When Larter fainted the following day, while milking, she was whipped by her master with a riding crop and hit on the back with a stick by her mistress, who also shoved her against a pump, making her nose bleed. Larter eventually collapsed in a field, where a local man found her and took her to a JP, where she made a complaint before dying. The coroner's inquest concluded that this was a case of murder.[54] It seems that

52. T. Andrews, *An Enquiry Into the Causes of the Encrease and Miseries of the Poor of England*, 1738, pp. 43–44.
53. *Ipswich Journal*, 2 April 1785.
54. D. Smith and L. Smith, *Sudden Deaths in Suffolk 1767–1858: A Survey of Coroners' Records in the Liberty of St Etheldreda*, 1995, p. 111.

the farmer and his wife absconded after an arrest warrant was issued for causing the death of their maid by ill treatment.[55] No conviction for the crime ultimately ensued.

Such cases always raised difficult questions of degree. The courts were fairly robust about the "rough and tumble" of domestic life. For example, Mary Beart, a married woman, was tried at the Lent Assizes at Thetford in 1736 for the murder of Elizabeth Newman, a parish apprentice, by beating the girl and not allowing her sufficient food or drink. Her husband was not charged. (It was normally a woman's responsibility to discipline female domestics.)[56] Beart was acquitted of any offence.[57] Similarly in 1784, Thomas and Elizabeth Howlett were indicted at the Norfolk Assizes for killing eight-year-old Mary Sparkes by "neglect" and refusing to give her sufficient food "with intent to murder." Unusually, and perhaps anticipating how difficult it would be to secure a homicide conviction, the Howletts were also prosecuted on an alternative count of assaulting the young girl. They were acquitted of the murder but convicted of the assault, for which Elizabeth received six months in a House of Correction and Thomas three months in gaol.[58]

Children who were not servants might also receive such abuse, even from their parents. In April 1717 Thomas Tompson from Norwich, aged just seven years, died after being assaulted by his worsted weaver father and mother, Thomas and Susanna, and being placed in a coal hole in the kitchen of their house. He had been refused food for a week, and died a few days after the ordeal. The city coroner brought in a verdict of murder, and prepared a Latin copy of their inquest for the assizes.[59] Fifty years later Robert Bee and his wife, Mary, from Beccles, in Suffolk, were charged with the murder of their son, who, it was said, had been starved to death.[60] They were not subsequently convicted. However, in 1785 John and Elizabeth Wilkinson from Felixstowe were found guilty at the Bury Assizes, and then hanged, for murdering their daughter,

55. *Ipswich Journal*, 5 September 1767.
56. W. Gough, *Domesticall Duties*, 1634, p. 671.
57. TNA ASSI 33/1.
58. TNA ASSI 33/6–7.
59. NRO NCR Case 6a/4/68/1 and 68/2.
60. *St. James's Chronicle Or the British Evening Post*, 16–19 January 1768.

Martha, by "cruelly beating and starving her to death."[61] Elizabeth, who was viewed as particularly vicious, drew comparison with the infamous Mrs Brownrigg (a metropolitan child-killer).[62]

There was some truth to the popular notion of the wicked stepmother. Martha was John's offspring from an earlier marriage. Similarly, at the City of Norwich Assizes in 1790, David and Elizabeth Dickerson were tried together for starving to death David's daughter from an earlier relationship. Although nine when she died, she was terribly malnourished. However, the surgeon who had examined her was unable to rule out an organic cause for her condition and death. Despite the three-hour trial revealing many "unfeeling and aggravating circumstances" in the couple's treatment of the child, the jury, after an hour's deliberation, "finding they could not punish them short of death, brought in a verdict of Not Guilty."[63] By contrast, this did not prevent a conviction in 1812, after eight-year-old Mary Ann Smith died having been subjected to a regime of beating, exposure, and starvation, which included spending three December nights in a freezing shed. She was the eldest of three children from her father's previous marriage. Although her stepmother had been the prime mover in what occurred, there was wilful neglect by her father. Both were convicted and executed at Ipswich.[64]

Men could also be cruel to stepchildren. Benjamin Brett's third wife brought with her from her earlier marriage a son who was a little under four years old. He would sometimes accompany Brett to work. One day the child would not stop crying, and, in an explosion of temper, Brett threw him to the ground, where he struck his head. He expired some hours later. Brett was convicted at the following assizes although he maintained that he had not intended to inflict serious harm on the child. He was executed in August 1794.[65]

61. *Public Advertiser*, 2 April 1785; *Ipswich Journal*, 2 April 1785.
62. *Public Advertiser*, 2 April 1785.
63. Anon, *Hanging, Not Punishment Enough*, 1701, p. 1.
64. *The Lancaster Gazette and General Advertiser, for Lancashire, Westmorland, &c.*, 4 April 1812; *The Times*, 2 April 1812, p. 3.
65. Anon, *Last Dying Speech and Full Confession of Benjamin Brett*, 1794, pp. 1–2.

Instrumental Murders

"Instrumental" killings—those carried out in the course of a robbery, burglary, housebreaking, or theft—were the second-most-common type of murder in eighteenth-century East Anglia. Between 1735 and 1799 nine of the 23 cases that led to murder convictions in Norfolk (ignoring those for infanticide) appear to have occurred as an adjunct to the commission of property crimes. In Suffolk the figure was four out of 19 cases. This makes a total of 13 out of 42 cases for the region (or 31 per cent). On one assessment, this situation differs from that found in Wiltshire, where, between 1752 and 1796, such killings have been described as "very rare," allegedly making up just 3.1 per cent of all homicides (albeit that this includes findings of manslaughter).[66]

Several of the East Anglian cases involved robbery on the highway. For example, in 1748 William Salter, a bricklayer, was convicted on two counts for the highway robbery and murder of Christopher King on Holt Heath, in Norfolk. During the attack he gave his victim "several mortal wounds & bruises on the back part of his head with a wooden staff."[67] Salter was executed after the Lent Assizes held at Thetford the following year.[68] In 1785 James Cliffen, a footpad, was also hanged for combining murder with highway robbery. He had attacked two elderly brothers on a footpath near the Yaxham Road. Before taking their valuables, Cliffen "knocked them both down." One of the men died from his injuries shortly afterwards.[69] Although the doctrine of "felony murder" was not fully developed until the nineteenth century, its presence during the era encouraged convictions for the most serious form of homicide.

In a slightly more complicated scenario, in March 1743, John Codlin (or Quadling) was convicted and executed for murdering the elderly Bunwell carrier Simon Pottill (or Pottle) the previous November.[70] It appears that the carrier was returning from Norwich with Codlin, a young man

66. C. Emsley, *Crime and Society in England: 1750–1900*, 2010, pp. 42–43.
67. Gray's Inn MS 45; *General London Evening Mercury*, 29–31 July 1746.
68. *London Evening Post*, 19–22 March 1748; *Old England*, 26 March 1748.
69. J. Beresford (ed.), *The Diary of a Country Parson, 1758–1802*, 1978, p. 167; *Public Advertiser*, 26 March 1785.
70. *London Evening Post*, 19–22 March 1743.

who had asked for a ride home. They stopped at several public houses on the way, and Pottill was probably intoxicated when he died. As his wagon crossed Caldwell Common, near Pottill's home, Codlin attacked him and slit his throat. He then stole Pottill's purse, which contained 33s, cut the carrier's horse free and rode it back to Norwich, where he abandoned the animal. After Pottill's body was found the following morning, enquiries were made in the public houses that the two men had visited. These swiftly led to Codlin's arrest the following afternoon, with a bloody knife still in his possession. He was imprisoned in the County Gaol at Norwich Castle, tried at Thetford Assizes, hanged on Caldwell Common in April 1743, and buried without a church service.[71]

A not dissimilar case occurred 34 years later, when John Rye murdered Joseph Snelling. The dead man was a carrier from Lincolnshire who had been in Norfolk delivering a load of wool. On his way home, Snelling was stopped by Rye, who offered to help drive his team in exchange for food and drink. While Snelling was sleeping in the back of the (now empty) wagon, as it went through Little Frensham, Rye hit him on the back of the head with a wooden cleaver and killed him.[72] Rye was clearly motivated by the prospect of material gain; at his trial he faced five other indictments for theft and stealing horses. (These were not proceeded with in light of the murder verdict).[73]

Other murders involved robberies that had been committed away from the highway. In 1736, a group of "lewd" women from a tavern in the same town were accused of murdering an inebriated Dutch sailor. Their victim was found strangled, floating in the town harbour, with the tips of his ears, in which he had worn gold earrings, cut off. Only one of the women, Elizabeth Thompson, was convicted and executed for the crime, after trial at the town's powerful borough sessions.[74] In another case, Robert Bullen, the eighteen-year-old son of a Norfolk farmer, visited Yarmouth in the summer of 1750, where he was allowed to go for a brief pleasure trip with a group of sailors. Afterwards he was shown round the town by one of them, John Barchard. As thanks, Bullen treated

71. *Westminster Journal or New Weekly Miscellany*, 26 March 1743.
72. *London Packet or New Lloyd's Evening Post*, 19–21 March 1777.
73. TNA ASSI 33/6.
74. *Weekly Miscellany (1732)*, 27 September 1735.

Barchard to drink, but in doing so revealed that he had several gold and silver coins on his person. Barchard decided to take this money, and, when they came to a secluded spot, unsuccessfully attempted to push the inebriated youth into the sea. When Bullen resisted, Barchard hit him with a rock and stabbed him 20 times in the head. He then robbed his body and left it concealed in the sand. Barchard was quickly arrested, convicted, and executed. As with many killings of the period, a conjunction of alcohol, making the victim vulnerable and having a disinhibiting effect on the perpetrator, and the presence of a weapon, the customary sailor's knife, had fatal consequences.[75]

Alcohol was also present in 1790, when John Beckett murdered Edward Allen after they had been drinking at the King's Head in Wroxham, near Norwich. It was known that Allen lived an extremely thrifty life and had amassed a considerable amount of cash as a result, which was hidden in his home. Beckett left the pub early and some time later unavailingly attempted to break into Allen's empty house with a spade. As he left the scene, Beckett ran into Allen as he came home from the tavern. Beckett knocked him down and cut his throat with a penknife, so that Allen's "head was almost separated from his body." Beckett then robbed the dead man's corpse of three-and-a-half guineas. He was immediately suspected of the crime, and a bloody knife and cash were found in his pocket.[76] Beckett was convicted and executed.

Other cases of instrumental murder were more carefully planned. In October 1782 a wealthy gentlewoman named Frances Phillips who lived alone in an isolated farmhouse was robbed and murdered near Mildenhall, in Suffolk.[77] Despite being a wealthy landowner she was noted for her rather "parsimonious disposition," so that it was widely thought that she had a great deal of cash hidden in her home. One night several men called and told her they had seen a dog worrying her sheep. Phillips dressed and went with them to investigate. Her body was later found a quarter of a mile from her house, hidden under a sack, with injuries to

75. NRO Yarmouth Borough Sessions Y/S 2/1–3, mf 1031; *London Evening Post*, 11 August and 15 September 1750.

76. *General Evening Post*, 16–18 February 1790.

77. T. Notcutt, *The Trial at Large of Jeremiah Theobald, Otherwise Hasell, and James May, Otherwise Folkes*, 1783, p. 19. Phillips employed only non-residential help.

the head and throat. The killers had then returned to her home and taken £150 worth in cash and valuables before making good their escape. Two suspects were swiftly identified. After a long examination, at an inquest held by one of the county's coroners, they were committed to Bury Gaol, subsequently being convicted and executed.

Physically confronting thieves always posed serious risks. In 1787 William Hawke, a miller from Beccles, and Thomas Mayhew, a waterman from Bungay, murdered another waterman named Henry Scarle. Scarle had suspected that the two men were planning to steal from a wherry for which he was responsible. He lay in wait for the pair the same night. Unfortunately, they beat him savagely and then threw his body into the river. The pair fled but they were immediately suspected and a reward offered for their capture.[78] They were arrested at Botesdale, in Suffolk, while trying to get to London. Both men were convicted at the Thetford Assizes and executed.[79]

Murder of Law-Enforcement Officers

Four murder convictions, from slightly less than 10 per cent of the cases that returned such verdicts between 1735 and 1800, were secured where "law-enforcement officers," loosely construed to include those working in a private capacity, had been killed in the execution of their duties. There were two such murders in Suffolk. In 1735 William Cam, a dragoon engaged in escorting seized contraband, was shot dead by a group of men including John Bigg and John Wilson, both of whom were later executed for the crime. More than a decade later, Stephen Pettit, a carpenter and smuggler, was convicted of the murder of Joseph Keys, an Ipswich "serjeant" (a salaried law-enforcement official for the town), who had been carrying Pettit to prison.[80] Before his death Pettit admitted the killing but claimed that he had only intended to "disable" Keys in order to escape.[81]

78. *Whitehall Evening Post (1770)*, 17–20 February 1787.
79. *The Times*, 31 March 1787, p. 3.
80. *General Evening Post*, 3–5 March 1748; *Jacobite's Journal*, 26 March 1748; *Westminster Journal or New Weekly Miscellany*, 9 April 1748.
81. *Westminster Journal or New Weekly Miscellany*, 16 April 1748.

There were also two cases in Norfolk. In 1744 Robert Capps shot and mortally wounded a bailiff named Joseph Laughter who tried to enforce a writ on him at Capps' house in Hockering. Laughter had been the lead man of three bailiffs, and had been told by Capps "you are a dead man" just before the latter discharged a pistol into him. The coroner's inquest immediately brought in a verdict of wilful murder.[82] Capps was subsequently convicted and executed.[83] In November 1785 Joseph Wakefield was one of a group of men who bludgeoned Thomas Thwaites, Lord Townshend's gamekeeper, when he confronted them on one of their nocturnal forays. Thwaites died from his injuries shortly afterwards.[84] Wakefield was convicted of murder at the Thetford Assizes in March 1788 and hanged.[85]

Not all such cases ended in convictions. In September 1784 a dragoon and a customs officer were shot dead by smugglers at Hunstanton, in Norfolk. The soldier was hit by four balls and died almost immediately; the customs officer lingered for 36 hours before succumbing to his wounds.[86] The ensuing murder prosecutions resulted in acquittals (see *Chapter 23*).

Miscellaneous Murders

The remaining seven cases (a sixth of the total) cover a range of less important categories that do not fit readily into the other three groups. Amongst them was a "quarrel" in a tavern in which the victim had not "participated" in any sense, so that a murder, rather than manslaughter, verdict was returned. They also include a highly unusual case in which James Thacker, a Royal Navy midshipman, was executed in Yarmouth for murdering John Augur, a local keelman (sailor in a cargo lighter), in the town. Augur had been pressed into the navy and was trying to escape when Thacker "shot him thro' the head."[87] This group also contains the

82. *Daily Gazetteer* (London Edition), 8 May 1744.
83. *London Evening Post*, 11–14 August 1744 – 14 August 1744.
84. *Bath Chronicle*, 30 August 1787.
85. *General Evening Post*, 20 March 1788.
86. *Whitehall Evening Post* (1770), 30 September – 2 October 1784.
87. *London Evening Post*, 3–6 April 1742; *Country Journal or The Craftsman*, 22 May 1742.

sole case of murder in the course of rape (that of Toby Gill) and a rare instance of planned revenge in a non-domestic context. In 1791 Thomas Briggs owned a cow that had been pastured on Roger Benstead's farm. When Briggs arrived to take his animal away, an altercation ensued between the two men, during which Benstead was shot in the back. He fled, though mortally wounded, and made his way home, where he died a short while later. Before expiring he identified his attacker, and Roger Benstead and his son were soon apprehended. The trial of both Bensteads and a youth named Thomas Harper took place in March 1792. The elder Benstead was convicted and hanged.[88] The motive for one more case in the "miscellaneous" category, the murder of a bricklayer by John Rudderham in King's Lynn, is not clear.[89]

88. Anon, *The Trial of Roger Benstead the Elder, and Roger Benstead the Younger*, 1792, p. 14.
89. *Gazetteer and New Daily Advertiser*, 28 January 28.

CHAPTER 19

The Incidence of Homicide

Introduction

English homicide rates had been in uneven decline for several centuries by the late 1600s. In 1819 the Parliamentary Committee on Criminal Laws concluded that this fall had continued during the "long" eighteenth century, so that the per capita murder rate in most parts of the country was significantly lower than it had been in 1688.[1] Much modern scholarship supports their analysis. One calculation suggests an average of 2.3 homicides per 100,000 people nationally during the first half of the eighteenth century, but only 1.4 in its second.[2] More locally, it has been estimated that in the first decade of the century Kent saw a homicide rate of 3.1 cases per 100,000 people, but only 1.6 in its final ten years, with the 1720s seeing a particularly large fall, the 1740s a short-term reversal in the trend, and the last forty years of the era a degree of stability.[3]

Of course, care must be taken when extrapolating general trends from studies conducted in the Home Counties (let alone the Metropolis). Nevertheless, it is apparent that the decline was not an even one. Coroners' inquests from Cheshire support the widely accepted notion of a rapid fall in homicide rates around the middle of the seventeenth century, followed by a slower but still significant per capita fall until about the middle of the eighteenth century but, and a little unusually, with a small upturn

1. *The Times*, 7 July 1819, p. 2.
2. M. Eisner, "Modernization, Self-control and Lethal violence," 2001, p. 629.
3. J. S. Cockburn, "Patterns of Violence in English Society: Homicide in Kent 1560–1985," 1991, p. 78.

occurring during the final 50 years of the period.[4] The "general pattern" in provincial England might be tentatively described as one of significant decline in the first half of the eighteenth century, with some variation on timings depending on region, this being followed by a mild decline (or even stability) until the end of the century, so that there was a national rate of 1.2 or 1.3 cases per 100,000 people during the decade after 1810.[5]

It should be noted that the phenomenon of a general decline in killings at this time was not special to England, although the country had been in the vanguard of falling homicide rates at the end of the medieval period. Perhaps unsurprisingly, in Denbighshire there also appears to have been an overall downward trend between 1661 and 1730, albeit (as in England) complicated by short-term fluctuations.[6] However, it was also found over much of North Western Europe, including Flanders, Holland, and Germany. Sweden and Finland saw a particularly steep fall between 1650 and 1750.[7]

Homicide in East Anglia

Did eighteenth-century East Anglia reflect the broader national trend? In the most heinous forms of homicide, those classified by the courts as murder, the improvement is slightly less obvious and more nuanced, not least because of an unusual final decade, even after factoring in regional population growth of about 50 per cent during the course of the century.

In Norfolk, there were three executions for murder in the decade from 1735 to 1744, and two in the following decade. The 20 years from 1755 to 1774 witnessed no executions. The years 1775 to 1784 saw one hanging, while the following decade had a spurt in executions, with 13 people being hanged for the murder of 12 people. In Suffolk four people (accused of three murders), four people, three people (for two murders), four people, and four people (for three murders), were executed in each

4. J. Sharpe and J. Dickinson, "Coroners' Inquests in an English County, 1600–1800: A Preliminary Survey," 2011, p. 257.
5. P. King, "The Impact of Urbanization on Murder Rates and on the Geography of Homicide in England and Wales, 1780–1850," p. 684.
6. S. Howard, *Law and Disorder in Early Modern Wales*, 2008, p. 53.
7. J. Kivivuori and M. Lehti, "Homicide in Finland and Sweden," 2011, p. 150.

of the five decades after 1735. However, in the years from 1785 to 1794, seven people were hanged for five murders.

The cluster of murder convictions in Norfolk and Suffolk in the middle of the 1790s appeared surprising, even at the time. After Samuel Hammond was charged with murdering his pregnant lover in 1794, a local newspaper noted, "This makes the fourth person committed in Suffolk for murder, and who will take their trials at the next Assizes."[8] It is possible that the 1790s were something of a statistical quirk, although it was an economically difficult time, with widespread political tensions occasioned by the Revolutionary and Napoleonic wars. The region was not alone in seeing an enhanced number of deliberate killings. In Scotland the 1790s have been described as a "murderous decade."[9] Allowing for population increase, the years prior to 1785 might suggest a slow decline in the incidence of homicide in East Anglia from the 1740s.

Much more important, murder convictions do not reflect the numerous homicides that were defined as manslaughter, produced undeserved acquittals, thrown out by grand juries, or not even prosecuted. For example, in Great Yarmouth on 14 July 1746, four people—Thomas Gray, Robert Smith, John Cully, and Elizabeth Cully (John's wife)—were remanded in custody for the murder of an unmarried woman. A year later they came for trial at the special borough sessions with power of gaol delivery that commenced on 13 July 1747. However, on this occasion the four were acquitted by proclamation and discharged, no one appearing to prosecute the case. Bizarrely, at the same sessions, a man named Wood who was the defendant in another murder case involving the shooting of a seaman who had died in Yarmouth was also released by proclamation for the same reason.[10]

As a result, when seeking homicide patterns it is best to consider all prosecutions for any type of killing, whatever the outcome. This can be done using the sample years from each decade from the 1730s to the 1790s. The focus will be on the number of homicide trials, rather than on the number of defendants, which can be distorted by incidents involving

8. *Morning Post*, 27 January 1794.
9. W. W. J. Knox and L. Thomas, "Homicide in Eighteenth-century Scotland: Numbers and Theories," 2015, p. 57.
10. NRO Yarmouth Borough Sessions Y/S 2/1–4 mf 1031.

large groups and gangs. For example, on one occasion, all 17 members of a press gang were tried for one murder.[11]

Homicide During Sample Years

A total of five deaths came to court in the region as homicides during 1735, resulting in as many separate prosecutions for murder. All the cases involved individual killings, and in all but one there were single defendants. These resulted in: three outright acquittals or (in one case) discharge by the grand jury without a matter going for trial; one conviction for the lesser offence of manslaughter; and one case that produced two convictions for the murder of one man (the multi-defendant trial).

In 1747 six people in the region faced five murder indictments in as many trials (one with two co-defendants). One case (that with co-defendants) produced outright acquittals. Two more produced convictions for the lesser offence of manslaughter, while two produced convictions for the full offence of murder. In 1754 three men stood trial for murdering two men in as many hearings. The case with co-defendants produced outright acquittals. A few months later, Thomas Theobald was prosecuted for the murder of William Rampley. He was convicted of the lesser offence of manslaughter.[12]

In 1764 three people were prosecuted for as many murders at the regional assizes courts. Two cases produced acquittals, and one a conviction for the lesser offence of manslaughter. Nobody was accused of any type of homicide offence in the region in 1774. In all of 1784, just three cases of homicide came before the regional assizes. Unusually, two of them involved women as sole defendants. One was (effectively) convicted of manslaughter, and one acquitted outright. The third case involved husband-and-wife co-defendants. Both were acquitted.

In 1797 the killing of two individuals (in separate incidents) resulted in as many murder trials at the regional assizes. (This figure does not include two women who were prosecuted for infanticides). In one case, two men stood trial at the Suffolk Assizes as co-defendants. Both were

11. TNA ASSI 33/6.
12. TNA ASSI 33/2.

acquitted. Another, essentially domestic, killing produced a conviction and execution for murder. The gaol calendar for that year also notes that, at the Suffolk Assizes in 1797, Joseph Hull (or Hall) was convicted of an "assault that occasioned death," fined 1s, and discharged. A contemporary newspaper report described his offence as "manslaughter."[13] Even so, the punishment imposed strongly suggests that the matter was indicted only as an ordinary misdemeanour assault, perhaps because of problems in establishing causation. Conversely, the gaol calendar also records that a labourer named Luke Rice was tried and acquitted of the murder of an unknown man.[14] However, contemporary reports suggest that he was, in reality, tried for taking part in a riot in Norwich, during which the *Shakespeare Tavern* was almost pulled down (albeit that a death may have occurred at some point in the process).[15]

Summary of Sample Years

Taking the yearly sample for each decade from the 1730s to the 1790s produces, successively, five, five, two, three, zero, three, and two trials involving an allegation of homicide. Thus there is a fairly constant total after about 1750, prior to which a sharp fall *may* have occurred. However, there was some population increase during this time, suggesting a slightly more marked per capita decrease during the latter half of the era than revealed by the figures, and supporting the general picture of a significant, but uneven, decline in homicide rates during the first half of the century followed by a relatively modest (and uneven) fall after the middle of the era.

Evidence from Inquests

Of course, even the figures for homicide cases that came to court do not come close to the incidence of killing, as some cases did not produce suspects, and a few were not even identified as such, the deaths being

13. *Bell's Weekly Messenger*, 20 August 1797.
14. TNA ASSI 33/8.
15. *St. James's Chronicle Or the British Evening Post*, 24–26 August 1797; *London Evening Post*, 10–12 August 1797.

attributed to accidents or misfortune. Nevertheless, the ancient English system of coroners, which considered killings that were formally identified or suspected as homicides, probably ensured that the number of overlooked killings was not substantial (see *Chapter 6*), infanticide perhaps apart.

Inquest records also (tentatively) suggest that homicide became less common after the early years of the century, which would accord with indictment patterns and most paradigms for the era. For example, for the period from July 1700 to February 1720 some 119 inquests have been preserved for the City of Norwich. Viewing these as exhaustive would be dangerous, as the first eleven years produced only 25 inquests. The city grew in ensuing years, but not at such a rate that the difference could be explained without assuming that there were either much more interventionist coroners or that many inquest documents are missing for the early years of the century. However, the consistency in the range of preserved documents suggests that, if this happened, it occurred across the board. The *proportionate* distribution of case type is significant. Of the 119 cases, eleven, about 9 per cent of the total, involved homicides, whether cases of murder, manslaughter, or (in four cases) infanticide.

By contrast, coroners' inquests for the Liberty of St Etheldreda, in Suffolk, produced just five identifiable and "culpable" killings over the last 33 years of the eighteenth century, of which four took place in a domestic context, three of them involving children or adolescents, and two of these occurring via abusive treatment. In the final third of the eighteenth century, it is clear that this large part of Suffolk was not particularly "homicidal."[16]

Conclusion

East Anglia shared fully in the general (uneven) decline in homicide seen in the wider nation at this time. As a result, by the first half of the nineteenth century, Suffolk was one of four predominantly rural and agricultural English counties (along with Sussex, Cornwall, and Berkshire)

16. D. Smith and L. Smith, *Sudden Deaths in Suffolk 1767–1858: A Survey of Coroners' Records in the Liberty of St Etheldreda*, 1995, pp. 23–60.

that had extremely low rates of homicide indictment by national standards (under one case per 100,000 in 1840), while Norfolk was in the next tranche of low homicides (between one and one-and-a half per 100,000 people). They were in stark contrast to "industrialised" counties such as Lancashire, Cheshire, and Staffordshire, which returned relatively high homicide rates at this time (above 2.5 per 100,000) and may not have seen any decline in their incidence of killing during the late eighteenth century.[17] Much of the East Anglian fall had occurred during the first half of the eighteenth century, with a much gentler decline thereafter. Some of the explanations for this change are explored in *Chapter 22*.

17. P. King, "The Impact of Urbanization on Murder Rates and on the Geography of Homicide in England and Wales, 1780–1850," 2010, p. 683 and p. 685.

CHAPTER 20

Infanticide

Introduction

The murder of newborn babies was a fairly regular phenomenon during the eighteenth century. Infanticide made up a substantial majority of female-perpetrated killings in East Anglia, as it did throughout the country, and a significant proportion of all homicides, even if not prosecuted.[1] For example, in the 1690s and early 1700s, cases of infanticide may have equalled all other types of homicide considered by coroners in the Palatinate of Chester, although this was a fairly extreme case.[2] Similarly, albeit of more limited statistical value, of the eleven preserved inquests that produced findings of homicide (of all types) for the City of Norwich, between 1700 and 1720, four were for infanticide, such as that of the newborn female baby discovered in a "cockey" (dyke) in Norwich in May 1710.[3]

Even among killings that went to formal trial a substantial component involved the murder of neonates. On the Western Circuit, between 1670 and 1729 (a few records are missing), 406 cases of infanticide were tried, compared to 752 indictments for other types of murder.[4] More modestly, at the assizes held for Northumberland and Newcastle between 1657 and 1720, there were 12 infanticide cases and 50 for other types of homicide

1. A. Williams, *The Criminality of Women in the 18th Century in the South West of England*, 2000, p. 200.
2. P. Spierenburg, *History of Murder*, 2008, p. 148.
3. NRO NCR Case 6a/3/11.
4. M. Eder, *"At the Instigation of the Devil": Capital Punishment and the Assize in the Early Modern England, 1670–1730*, 2014, pp. 38–40.

(again, there are gaps in the records), the latter making up just under a fifth of the combined total.[5] In Wiltshire, during the second half of the era, they made up about a quarter of all prosecuted killings tried at assizes.[6]

In eighteenth-century East Anglia, the proportions varied, but were broadly similar to those found in the North and Wiltshire, with infanticide making up about a fifth of all homicides tried at the regional assizes. For example, two of the 12 homicide cases (about 17 per cent) heard in the 30 months from the summer of 1734 involved infanticide.[7] There was a somewhat higher number at the regional assizes held between the start of August 1746 and the end of August 1750 (four-and-a-half years' worth of hearings)—five of 16 homicide trials involving 17 defendants (about 30 per cent)—concerned women accused of murdering neonates.[8] The decade from 1751 to 1760 saw a rather more modest number; three of the 20 homicide trials in the region (about 15 per cent) were for infanticide, with a fourth involving an older infant, (unusually) killed by her father.[9] At a similar level, during the three years from 1777, two of 14 homicide trials (about 14 per cent) involved infanticide cases.[10] Considering prosecuted cases of infanticide in the sampled years for each decade during the last two thirds of the century, there were none in 1735, none in 1746, one in 1754, none in 1764, none in 1774, none in 1784, and two cases in 1797. Collating these data, it seems that an average of less than one case a year came for trial in the region between 1735 and the end of the century.

It should not be thought that infanticide was a "normal" facet of everyday life. On one estimate, its incidence in England and Wales was relatively modest, between 0.20 and 0.30 cases per 100,000 people in the second half of the period, although such a calculation is enormously difficult to make, and so of limited reliability. Furthermore, the rate of neonaticide may have declined during the era.[11] It has been suggested that such a fall, if it occurred, can be explained by a link between infanticide

5. J. Bath, *Violence and Violent Crime in the North East, c.1650–1720*, 2001, p. 12.
6. C. Emsley, *Crime and Society in England: 1750–1900*, 2010, pp. 42–43.
7. TNA ASSI 33/1.
8. Gray's Inn MS 45.
9. TNA ASSI 33/2 and 33/3.
10. TNA ASSI 33/6.
11. N. Woodward, "Infanticide in Wales, 1730–1830," 2007, p. 101 and pp. 106–107.

and the strength of the country's economy. According to this analysis, real wages rose in the late-seventeenth and early-eighteenth centuries, so reducing the temptation to kill newborn babies.[12] Whatever the merits of this theory, coroners' inquests for the substantial Liberty of St Etheldreda in Suffolk identified no cases of newborn infanticide during the last third of the eighteenth century (for which records are complete), although, in 1790, an unnamed baby had been found "stillborn" in Foxhall.[13]

A decline in infanticide would be especially significant because the era witnessed an apparent growth in bastardy, which provided the backdrop to most prosecuted cases. This phenomenon may have occurred because the century saw an increased emphasis on full coitus, which slowly replaced lesser alternatives, such as simple fondling, as the primary form of extra-marital sexual activity, even though methods of contraception remained basic.[14] Other social developments, such as increased population mobility and changes in the marriage laws, may also have influenced the apparent increase in illegitimacy.

Profiles of Infanticide Cases

Small bodies were periodically found dumped in privies, ditches, dunghills, haystacks, and ponds, or buried in fields and hedges. Undoubtedly, numerous others were never found at all, diminutive corpses swiftly decomposing in the soil or water. A selection of cases from Norwich reveals fairly typical examples. The city coroners considered at least three infanticides over a four-year period from 1712. In March of that year, William Riches found the body of a female neonate buried amongst the muck in a storage bin, as he was engaged in emptying it. A verdict of "Murdered by person unknown" was returned at the inquest.[15] The same conclusion was reached at an inquest held in May 1715 into the death of a newborn female baby found drowned in a well on the estate of a

12. R. Roth, "Homicide in Early Modern England 1549–1800: The Need for a Quantitative Synthesis," 2001, pp. 33–67; R. Roth, "Biology and the Deep History of Homicide," 2011, pp. 535–555.
13. D. Smith and L. Smith, *Sudden Deaths in Suffolk 1767–1858: A Survey of Coroners' Records in the Liberty of St Etheldreda*, 1995, pp. 23–60.
14. T. Hitchcock, "Sex and Gender: Redefining Sex in Eighteenth-century England," 1996, p. 79.
15. NRO NCR Case 6a/4/12.

Mr Pockett.[16] Less than a year later, in April 1716, the body of another female baby was found in a "house of office" (privy), again producing a verdict of murder by an unknown person.[17] Despite this local gender distribution, sex does not normally appear to have been a major factor in the decision to kill an illegitimate baby in England, although it may have been slightly more significant in Wales, at least during the final decades of the era.[18]

Similar cases from other parts of East Anglia can be considered on a more random basis. In 1742 it was noted that a newborn child had been found in a privy in Brook Street, Ipswich, "where the surgeons think it was born alive and murdered."[19] The following year, at Lavenham, in Suffolk, the corpse of a male baby was found abandoned in a pond next to a public footpath, close to some houses.[20] In 1767 several labourers found the body of a female baby in a ditch in Suffolk. It had been covered in cloth and was thought to have been dead for about six weeks. Unusually in such cases, a surgeon who examined the corpse thought that the infant had lived for several days before being killed.[21]

The great majority of prosecuted infanticides were committed immediately after the delivery of a baby by an unmarried woman, often a young servant, who had usually concealed her pregnancy as best she could beneath the cloaks and wide hoop skirts of the era, and then given birth alone. This was a general pattern throughout Britain; in eighteenth-century Scotland, nearly all infanticides were committed at birth or shortly afterwards.[22] Of course, the profile for prosecuted and actual (including undetected) cases is likely to be very different. Young "live-in" servant maids had minimal privacy, greatly increasing the risk of exposure. Furthermore, there were a few exceptions to this general pattern in East Anglia. Not quite all cases involved neonates. In 1777

16. NRO NCR Case 6a/4/43.
17. NRO NCR Case 6a/4/12 and Case 6a/4/56.
18. J. Dickinson and J. Sharpe, "Infanticide in Early Modern England: The Court of Great Sessions at Chester, 1650–1800," 2002, p. 49; N. Woodward, "Infanticide in Wales, 1730–1830," 2007, p. 116.
19. *Ipswich Journal*, 6 February 1742.
20. Ibid., 5 March 1743.
21. Ibid., 16 May 1767.
22. W. W. J. Knox and L. Thomas, "Homicide in Eighteenth-century Scotland: Numbers and Theories," 2015, p. 54.

Margaret Clarke from Mildenhall was committed to Bury Gaol accused of murdering her five-week-old illegitimate child (also named Margaret Clarke).[23] Slightly more commonly, some of the mothers accused of the crime in the region were married (see below).

Method of Killing

Most infanticides in eighteenth-century East Anglia involved suffocation, drowning, exposure, or strangulation. This was the normal pattern for England and Wales. In the Principality, 80 per cent of infanticides were carried out using these four methods, and the English total may have been even higher.[24] Typically, in July 1751 Mary Flower was accused (and acquitted) of throttling her newborn male baby at the Bury Assizes.[25] Frequently the same act resulted in both the death and disposal of the infant. Thus, in December 1754 Martha Plumb, the servant to an Ipswich gentleman, gave birth alone to a female bastard.[26] The inquest presided over by the town's two coroners and 12 jurors concluded that she then threw her baby into the vault of a "necessary house" (privy), where it suffocated "amongst the filth and muck."[27] (Plumb was taken into custody but acquitted at the ensuing assizes).[28] In 1777 it was claimed that Sarah Balls murdered her newborn female baby by wrapping her in a mantle and hiding her under the boards in a nearby privy, so that she "perished in inclement weather." Balls, too, was acquitted at the Bury Assizes.[29]

However, a few cases of neonaticide were more obviously violent. In March 1752 the body of a male baby was found inside a periwig box, dumped in a passage in the parish of St Michael-at-Plea, in Norwich. According to a Dr Maltby, who gave medical testimony at the ensuing Inquest, he had been born alive and then received a violent blow to the right side of his head.[30] In October 1759 the same verdict was returned

23. *London Evening Post*, 15–17 May 1777.
24. N. Woodward, "Infanticide in Wales, 1730–1830," 2007, p. 116.
25. *London Daily Advertiser and Literary Gazette*, 6 August 1751.
26. *Read's Weekly Journal Or British Gazetteer*, 21 December 1754.
27. SRO Sessions Roll 42, 2nd July 1755, c/2/9/1/1/1/77–21.
28. *Read's Weekly Journal Or British Gazetteer*, 21 December 1754.
29. TNA ASSI 33/6.
30. NRO NCR Case 6a/8/10.

after a baby girl was found on a muckheap in St Clement's parish in the same city, with a "cord put through her cheeks."[31] Sometimes both overt violence and asphyxiation were present. In May 1758 an inquest concluded that a male baby found by Fye Bridge staithe, in Norwich, had been" [m]urdered by being marked with bruising in several parts of the body, then thrown in the river by an unknown hand."[32]

Identifying Perpetrators

Records from eighteenth-century coroners' hearings in the region suggest that many, perhaps the majority, of identified neonatal infanticides did not produce suspects, let alone prosecutions. Most tellingly, all four of the preserved infanticide cases considered by the two Norwich city coroners (see above) in the 20 years after 1700, an era when the authorities were still keen to prosecute for the offence, involved this scenario. The only case investigated in which a named single woman gave birth to a (male) baby, who died shortly afterwards, was attributed to natural causes rather than murder.[33] This suggests that trials for the crime were the tip of a significantly larger infanticide "iceberg," especially as many cases must have gone entirely undetected.

Nevertheless, serious attempts were made to find the genitors of victims of infanticide; it was not a crime that was tacitly accepted, even in the early part of the eighteenth century. There was no popular justification for such killings, and many people (especially women) were keen to expose suspected perpetrators. Similarly, the authorities made serious attempts to identify baby-killers. For example, in 1748, when the corpse of a five-day-old female infant was found in a basket, fastened to a gate in the Norfolk parish of Rushford, William Steggles, the local overseer of the poor, offered two guineas (provided by the parish) for the identification of its mother.[34] In 1783 an inquest held at Hardwick, in Norfolk, considered the body of a female infant that had been found in a local field. Vermin had gnawed the baby's corpse, and pecked out her

31. NCR NCR Case 6a/8/132.
32. NRO NCR Case 6a/8/97.
33. Although some are probably missing because they were referred to the assizes.
34. *Ipswich Journal*, 12 March 1748.

eyes. However, her legs had been wrapped up in a piece of linen marked BBE3. The jury brought in the standard verdict (for these situations) of murder by a person or persons unknown. Even so, this was not the end of the matter. It was hoped that the "marks on the piece of linen will lead to a discovery of the perpetrators of this horrid deed."[35] It is likely that the cloth was publicly displayed to this end. However, such efforts were often fruitless. Even if a likely suspect was found, it was not always possible to prove that she was the mother. Soon after the discovery in Brook Street, Ipswich (see above), a young woman was arrested and questioned but subsequently released without charge.[36]

Gender and Marital Status

That nearly all East Anglian infanticide defendants were women is unsurprising. Few men were tried for the crime during the eighteenth century, and this phenomenon was almost universal within England and Wales. For example, in Yorkshire, between 1735 and 1775, it seems that just over 6 per cent of infanticide defendants were men, all of whom were acquitted.[37] In Wales the figure may have been slightly higher, at 9 per cent, although this figure also encompasses the early decades of the following century.[38] Nevertheless, this does not mean that there was no male involvement in the crime in the region, even if some men escaped prosecution, as the following cases show.

In 1751 Jonathan Bloom was committed for trial for murdering his "bastard child," William, by drowning; he was acquitted at the Norfolk Assizes.[39] (That the infant had a name suggests that he was not newborn). More pertinently, in 1769 a wealthy farmer and his housekeeper from Aldeburgh, in Suffolk, absconded after a warrant was issued for their arrest. Their maid had accused them of murdering an illegitimate child. The farmer had, allegedly, buried it in his garden a few hours after it was

---

35. *Norfolk Chronicle*, 8 February 1783.
36. *Ipswich Journal*, 6 February 1742.
37. R. Markless, *Gender, Crime and Discretion in Yorkshire, 1735–1775*, 2013, p. 189.
38. N. Woodward, "Infanticide in Wales, 1730–1830," 2007, p. 114.
39. *General Advertiser (1744)*, 23 July 1751; *General Advertiser (1744)*, 6 August 1751.

born.[40] At the Suffolk Assizes held in August 1770, a rich farmer named Barry and his housekeeper—presumably the same couple—were acquitted of the murder of their bastard after a hearing lasting four hours.[41] (Interestingly, neither appears to have been held in custody prior to the trial).[42] In 1777 it was claimed that a Suffolk farmer named Richard Petchy (presumably the genitor) had aided one Margaret Clarke in killing her illegitimate baby. He was committed to prison with Clarke as an accessory to the crime.[43] At the ensuing assizes it was alleged that the killing had been occasioned by the couple "squeezing and bruising" the infant to death. Even so, both defendants were acquitted.[44] It is likely that considerably more men were involved in such killings, without their crimes coming to light or court, if only because their assistance prevented exposure.

That nearly all East Anglian women convicted of infanticide were single also accords with the national situation. However, this does not mean that married women did not commit the crime or, more interestingly, were never prosecuted for murdering their newborn babies, even though it is generally thought that infanticide played little role in regulating the size of English families at this time. For example, at least two married women were acquitted of killing neonates (as can be assumed because the babies are not named) during the period from 1746 to 1749. Among them was Margaret Jones, found not guilty of suffocating her baby by putting it in a box, at the Norfolk Assizes in July 1748.[45] These cases were certainly not unique. In 1734, at the Suffolk Assizes, Jane Wells, another married woman, was prosecuted and acquitted of the crime. Again, this phenomenon was not confined to the East Anglian region. In Wales between 1730 and 1830, nine of 182 female infanticide defendants were married, although several of these women probably did not kill their own babies, but assisted single daughters to do so, etc.[46] Even so, in some areas at least, infanticide may have been slightly more common among

40. *Ipswich Journal*, 29 July 1769.
41. *General Evening Post*, 1618 August 1770.
42. Anon, *A Kalendar of the Prisoners Now Confined in Ipswich Gaol*, 1770, p. 1.
43. *London Evening Post*, 15–17 May 1777.
44. TNA ASSI 33/6.
45. Gray's Inn MS 45.
46. K. Watson, "Women, Violent Crime and Criminal Justice in Georgian Wales," 2013, p. 259.

married women, and the authorities a little more willing to indict them for the crime, than has sometimes been thought.

However, cases in which married women were accused of infanticide almost always resulted in acquittals, if only because it was hard to prove that the baby had been born alive and then deliberately killed without having recourse to a statute from 1624 (21 Jac I, c 27) that facilitated the prosecution of single women (see below). In an era of high infant mortality it was extremely difficult to exclude a natural explanation for newborn deaths, such as the baby being "overlain" in a shared bed. This was a regular occurrence throughout the century. For example, in 1800 the eleven-month-old son of a journeyman shoemaker from Bury was overlain and suffocated by a young woman whose breasts needed drawing and who had fallen asleep.[47] Beyond these practical issues, there was an apparent reluctance to find married women guilty of the crime.

Verdicts

Even single East Anglian women accused of killing their newborn bastards were normally acquitted during the 1700s. Indeed, on one assessment, most women in the region were being found not guilty of the crime by the end of the seventeenth century.[48] This became especially marked after the 1720s, and by the second half of the century an acquittal was the "standard" verdict in the region, quite exceptional cases apart. Again, this closely accords with the national pattern.

A selection of figures is indicative. All three cases of infanticide that were tried in the region between 1734 and 1737 resulted in acquittals.[49] Similarly, although three women (one of them married) were prosecuted for infanticide in a "spike" of cases tried at the Summer Assizes for Suffolk held at Bury in 1746, all were found not guilty.[50] In like manner, all three cases of female perpetrated infanticide that came before the regional assizes in the decade after 1751 (in 1751, 1754, and 1756) resulted in acquittals. During the three years between 1777 and 1779, there were

47. *Bury and Norwich Post*, 2 January 1800.
48. J. Thorn (ed.), *Writing British Infanticide: Child-murder, Gender, and Print, 1722–1859*, 2003, p. 36.
49. J. Sharpe, *Crime in Early Modern England 1550–1750*, 1998, p. 94.
50. Gray's Inn MS 45.

just two prosecutions for infanticide at the regional assizes (in 1777), both of which resulted in not-guilty verdicts. Some prosecutions did not even reach a full trial. At the Norfolk Assizes held in August 1781, the grand jury found "no true bill" against Eleanor Eckleston, who was charged with having wilfully murdered two illegitimate children.[51] By then only the strongest cases produced convictions.

In the middle of the seventeenth century, the conviction rate for infanticide had been much higher. This was partly a result of the relatively strict application of a statute dating from 1624 (21 James 1, c 27) that created a legal presumption that the concealed birth, death, and disposal of an illegitimate baby signified murder unless the mother could prove it had been stillborn by calling a plausible witness (often impossible). "Malice aforethought," the mental state necessary for murder, was assumed in these situations.[52] As a result, it was not necessary to prove that the baby had been born alive and then deliberately killed, as would normally have been the case with a standard murder allegation.

However, after the Restoration the conviction rate for infanticide fell fairly rapidly, as the 1624 Act was increasingly disregarded, although it remained in force until 1803.[53] During the period between 1670 and 1729, almost 70 per cent of infanticide cases on the Western Circuit were thrown out by an assizes grand jury or resulted in acquittals.[54] The proportions for Denbighshire, in Wales, where there were 14 prosecutions for infanticide between 1660–1730, but only four convictions, were almost identical.[55]

The proportion of defendants found guilty continued to decline during the early eighteenth century. It has been suggested that, by about 1715—at the Old Bailey, at least—the 1624 statute was being ignored, and the same sort of proof was needed to convict an unmarried mother of murdering her baby as was required to convict on any charge of murder.

51. *Norfolk Chronicle*, 11 August 1781.
52. Z. Babington, *Advice to Grand Jurors in Cases of Blood*, 1680, p. 172.
53. M. Francus, "Monstrous Mothers, Monstrous Societies: Infanticide and the Rule of Law in Restoration and Eighteenth-century England," 1997, pp. 133–156.
54. M. Eder, *"At the Instigation of the Devil": Capital Punishment and the Assize in the Early Modern England, 1670–1730*, 2014, p. 44.
55. S. Howard, *Crime, Communities and Authority in Early Modern Wales: Denbighshire, 1660–1730*, 2003, p. 63.

From the 1740s this was joined by a positive desire on the part of judges, jurors and doctors, to acquit such women, if at all possible, even if some evidence for murder was available.[56]

This time profile is a little precise for what was often a gradual process, even in London. In the provinces, at least, it differed to some extent from judge to judge and circuit to circuit. Some traditionalist members of the judiciary continued to stress the 1624 Act long after 1715. In East Anglia, convictions for the offence, although a small minority of the total number of cases brought, were still being secured during the third decade of the era. For example, at the Bury Assizes in 1723, Susan Sturgion was "condemn'd for the murder of her bastard child."[57]

Nevertheless, the notion of a two-stage process in the decline of infanticide convictions is valuable. During the early years of the eighteenth century the legally "special" nature of the crime was gradually abandoned, albeit on a de facto rather than a de jure basis. The 1624 Act was being tacitly ignored in East Anglia by the end of the 1720s, as it was elsewhere in the country. By then courts in the region were usually very reluctant to convict of neonaticide simply because there had been obvious concealment and no witness to swear to the contrary. They required proof that the mother had deliberately killed her living baby, just as they would with the murder of an adult. This had been the case for decades by 1785, when an experienced Suffolk JP, urging the formal repeal of the 1624 statute, noted that "judges and juries had reduced it in general practice nearly to a shadow."[58] This process was bolstered by the acceptance of a range of judicially established extra-legal defences, such as the pre-birth preparation of baby clothes.

Around the middle of the eighteenth century, this development was joined by a positive reluctance to see women convicted of the crime if an innocent explanation for a baby's death that was not patently ludicrous could be advanced. By then convictions were usually being secured in East Anglia only when there was an admissible and reliable confession

56. M. Clayton, "Changes in Old Bailey Trials for the Murder of Newborn Babies, 1674–1803," 2009, p. 353.
57. *Evening Post* (1709), 8–10 August 1723.
58. J. Jebb, *Thoughts on the Construction and Polity of Prisons: With Hints for Their Improvement*, 1785, p. 34.

by the suspect, the baby's injuries were quite obviously of human origin (such as its throat having been cut with a blade, etc.), or, ideally, both were present.

It has been suggested that women who adopted obviously violent methods of killing their offspring were viewed as "monstrous" in a way that ordinary mothers, who merely smothered their babies or dropped them in privies, were not, explaining why convictions were still secured in such cases. According to this analysis, the latter killed to preserve their reputation and working-class status rather than flouting convention, so encouraging sympathy.[59] However, in reality, much more seems to have turned on simple evidential considerations. Even if juries wanted to be "kind," they required facts in order to be merciful. There had to be "plausible deniability" on the part of the defendant.

Even apparently strong infanticide cases often failed to produce a conviction after the mid-century. For example, in 1765 Mary Wyatt, a 19-year-old woman from Sudbury, in Suffolk, was committed to Bury Gaol on "violent suspicion of murdering her bastard child."[60] Despite the prima facie case, no conviction ensued. The following year, Mary Stacy, a maid working for a Norwich brazier, was committed to gaol on suspicion of murdering her newborn female infant, whom she had delivered herself, by cutting the baby's throat from "ear to ear."[61] An inquest held on the infant by the Norwich coroner, Christopher Newman, swiftly brought in a verdict of "wilful murder" against Stacy.[62] Nevertheless, she too was acquitted at trial a few weeks later, despite the nature of the baby's wound.[63]

These developments can be identified throughout England, albeit with slightly different timings. A survey of cases for Yorkshire between 1735 and 1775 indicates that over 82 per cent of females accused of infanticide were certainly acquitted at trial (as were all of the few men accused of the crime), a figure that rises to almost 87 per cent if those who were

59. M. Francus, *Monstrous Motherhood: Eighteenth-century Culture and the Ideology of Domesticity*, 2012, p. 100.
60. *Public Advertiser*, 9 July 1765.
61. *Public Ledger*, 22 July 1766.
62. *St. James's Chronicle Or the British Evening Post*, 19–22 July 1766.
63. *Gazetteer and New Daily Advertiser*, 6 August 1766.

discharged for want of prosecution are added to the total. Verdicts in about nine per cent of cases are not known. Only 4.4 per cent of women were definitely convicted in this northern county.[64] In East Anglia, less than ten per cent of infanticide cases produced convictions after 1735.

This change in attitudes eventually extended to East Anglia inquest juries, albeit to a more modest extent than at assizes, if only because much less turned on their decisions. Inquests became more reluctant to find that abandoned newborn babies had been murdered. Even in the first half of the period they had been reasonably discriminating about such cases, appreciating that some babies were stillborn and then subject to irregular disposal, as an inquest concluded was the case with a female child found in the river near the malthouse staithe in Norwich in September 1740, or a male baby "not born alive" discovered in a wooden box placed in St Stephen's churchyard in the same city a year later.[65]

This conclusion became more common at inquests after the middle of the century, especially when the mother was identified. For example, in July 1761 Mary Parker, a single woman, "privately delivered" in Norwich a baby boy who was later found dead.[66] This was, in theory, within the ambit of the 1624 statute and should have produced a presumption of murder. Even so, after examination and testimony from two "men midwives," the inquest returned a verdict of "still born." The same verdict was returned in April 1767, after Elizabeth Hart, a single woman, "privately delivered" a baby boy, who was also later found dead in the city. In January the following year, Mary Fisher, another single woman who had also "privately" given birth, received the same verdict, after evidence was, again, given by two male midwives. (One of them had testified at the other two inquests.)[67]

Even more blatantly, in early 1779, some men going to work at Lakenheath, in Suffolk, noticed a man and woman burying something in a field. They suspected that the couple were hiding smuggled goods (indicative of its prevalence in the county) and excavated the hole after the couple had left. Instead, they discovered the body of a newborn baby.

64. R. Markless, *Gender, Crime and Discretion in Yorkshire, 1735–1775*, 2013, p. 189, table 4.6.
65. NRO NCR Case 6a/710.
66. NRO NCR Case 6a/9/9.
67. NRO NCR Case 6a/10/10.

A local surgeon was called to the scene and concluded that it had been murdered. The parents were recognised as travelling people who were well-known in the district, and a search ensued. The man escaped, but the woman was held. Even so, an inquest held a day or so later concluded that the baby had been stillborn.[68]

Reprieves

Unlike most other murderers, a significant number of women who were capitally convicted of killing their illegitimate babies were reprieved from execution. This was a nationwide phenomenon. According to one assessment, as early as the period from 1670 to 1729, a third of those convicted of infanticide on the Western Circuit received clemency, albeit often on condition of transportation (42 of 123 identifiable cases).[69] In East Anglia Susan Tyler received mercy after conviction at the Norwich Assizes in 1732.[70] A little more obliquely, in 1728 Anne Hall was, it seems, convicted and "condemned" in Norwich for murdering her bastard child, but reprieved after it was concluded that she was "lunatick." This might have been a ground for acquittal at trial. However, it was also felt that those who became insane after trial should not be hanged until they recovered their senses. Remarkably, Hall had committed a similar crime on an earlier occasion. As a result, it was ordered that she "now be confin'd to prevent such unhappy accidents."[71] Presumably this would have been in a local house of correction. In Suffolk just two women were capitally convicted of infanticide between 1732 and 1800 (four years are missing from the records). One of them, Sarah Lock, was found guilty of murdering her illegitimate baby in 1745.[72] However, at the following sessions her sentence was commuted to transportation for 14 years.[73]

As a result of these dispensations, only three women (about half of those convicted) were executed in the entire East Anglian region for

68. *Ipswich Journal*, 9 and 16 January 1779.
69. M. Eder, *"At the Instigation of the Devil": Capital Punishment and the Assize in the Early Modern England, 1670–1730*, 2014, p. 147.
70. *Daily Post*, 28 March 1732.
71. *Country Journal Or The Craftsman*, 24 August 1728.
72. *Westminster Journal Or New Weekly Miscellany*, 6 April 1745.
73. *Penny London Post Or The Morning Advertiser*, 9–12 August 1745.

infanticide during the 65 years after 1735, and the last of these was not a "typical" case. Rebecca Howard was hanged in 1797 for murdering her five-week-old illegitimate infant by drowning him in a river.[74] She had convicted herself, as, "stung with remorse, she confessed the fact."[75] (She did challenge a prosecution witness at trial.)[76] At the gallows she warned other young women to be on their guard against deceitful men.[77] One of the remaining two executions for infanticide after the mid-century involved Elizabeth Martin, a domestic servant living in Yarmouth, who was convicted of murdering her illegitimate male baby at the town borough sessions in 1769; she was the last woman to be hanged there during the century.[78] One disadvantage of such an unusual forum was that local knowledge and hostility was likely to be present amongst trial jurors, perhaps increasing the prospects of a capital conviction in this type of case. The execution of Susan Dunwich (or Dulwich) in 1771, after the Suffolk Assizes, had fewer obviously distinguishing features.[79]

Despite these developments, cases of infanticide were still prosecuted quite regularly until the end of the era, if not as frequently as they had been at the start of the century, even in situations in which an acquittal was highly predictable. It seems that the authorities saw some benefit in the process of indictment or, at least, did not feel that they could disregard or tacitly ignore such cases. Of course, the women involved would spend time in prison awaiting trial, which was a punishment in itself. For example, in 1736 Mary Foreman from Wotton spent six weeks in custody after being committed to Norwich Castle gaol by a Norfolk coroner, before she was acquitted of murdering her newborn illegitimate baby at the Norfolk Summer Assizes.[80] They would also be publicly shamed, an acquittal rarely restoring their reputation.

74. *Morning Post and Fashionable World*, 12 September 1796.
75. *True Briton (1793)*, 12 September 1796.
76. TNA ASSI 33/8.
77. *London Chronicle*, 17–19 August 1797.
78. *London Chronicle*, 23–26 September 1769.
79. *Public Advertiser*, 13 August 1771.
80. *London Daily Post and General Advertiser*, 31 August 1736.

The 1803 Act

Rather belatedly, given its long abandonment in practice, and after several unsuccessful attempts to repeal it in earlier decades, the 1624 Act was abolished in 1803, Parliament noting that its "true sense and meaning" was uncertain, and that it had been difficult to apply in practice. The 1803 Act (43 Geo III, c 58) included a provision allowing juries that acquitted defendants of murdering their newborn offspring to return a verdict of "guilty" to the lesser offence of concealing a birth, a new crime that carried a maximum sentence of two years' imprisonment. This became the "normal" verdict in infanticide cases when jurors did not acquit outright. In reality, many such cases were probably homicides. Typically, Elizabeth Pells, charged at the Suffolk Assizes in 1805 with murdering her illegitimate baby, was "acquitted of the murder, but sentenced to 6 months' imprisonment for secreting its birth."[81] Similarly, at the Thetford Assizes in 1808, Elizabeth Sparrow was accused of murdering her bastard and, in the alternative, secreting its birth. She was acquitted of the former but found guilty of the latter charge, for which she received a year's imprisonment.[82] In previous years these women would probably have been acquitted outright and discharged. After 1803 cases in which convictions for murdering illegitimate children were secured usually involved slightly older infants rather than newborn babies.

Conclusion

Murder is sometimes identified as a "crime apart." If so, newborn infanticide was a "crime apart within a crime apart" during the 1700s. It was never commonplace, always deprecated where it occurred, and the authorities refused to turn a blind eye to such killings when they did happen. Nevertheless, in East Anglia as elsewhere in eighteenth-century England, infanticide occurred with some regularity and did not normally elicit the horror caused by other forms of deliberate killing. Increasingly the invidious choices that single mothers faced elicited sympathy, or at

81. *The Bury and Norwich Post: Or, Suffolk, Norfolk, Essex, and Cambridge Advertiser*, 7 August 1805.
82. Ibid., 30 March 1808.

least acceptance, rather than hostility, from (male) jurors and judges, perhaps because many of them had indulged in extra-marital coitus themselves. To a growing extent, this was reflected in their verdicts, provided these could be returned without being seen to openly condone the murder of the newborn.

CHAPTER 21

Sexual Offences

Introduction

The 1700s witnessed a slightly more liberal attitude towards consensual heterosexual conduct than had been seen in the previous century. Nevertheless, when it came to sexual crimes, change was modest. The law on these offences did not alter much during the era, although there were differences of emphasis and intensity in its enforcement. Throughout the period, the most serious sexual offences were unclergyable felonies that did not lightly produce convictions but which usually resulted in executions on the few occasions when they did. Most important among them were rape and sodomy, the latter being committed with either humans or animals (bestiality). Other sexual crimes were normally classified as misdemeanours and viewed much less seriously, at least officially, as a result.

Rape

English courts applied slightly different definitions to rape during the course of the eighteenth century. There was no dispute that it involved having carnal knowledge of a woman "by force against her will," but there was considerable debate, and varied legal opinion, as to whether this required both penetration and ejaculation or merely the former.[1] In 1723 John Sturgion was tried for rape at the Bury Assizes but acquitted on

1. W. Hawkins, *A Treatise of the Pleas of the Crown*, Book 1, 1724, p. 108.

the basis that the complainant could not swear to the "emissio seminis" inside her.[2] At other times, penetration alone appears to have been sufficient, or at least to have brought about a presumption of ejaculation.[3]

Despite its theoretical gravity, rape was not a commonly prosecuted offence anywhere in eighteenth-century England. It was indicted much less frequently than murder. For example, there were 39 prosecutions for the crime (including those thrown out by the grand jury) at the Great Sessions in Cheshire between 1760 and 1830, just over one every two years.[4] In Yorkshire, during two eleven-year periods between 1735 and 1775—that is, a total of 22 years—just 18 cases of rape, or less than one a year, were presented to a grand jury at assizes, despite the large size of the county.[5] If anything, it was indicted even less frequently in Norfolk and Suffolk. The sampled years for each decade during the last two thirds of the era can be considered. There were no cases in 1735. There was just one case in 1747. There was one case in 1754. There were no cases of rape prosecuted in the area's Assizes in 1764, 1774, 1784, or 1797.

Considering slightly longer continuous periods, there was one prosecuted case in the two-and-a-half years from August 1733. Similarly, Francis Cooper was the only rape defendant indicted in the four-and-a-half years from August 1746. Taking the entire decade after 1751, there was just one prosecution for the crime. John English was convicted of raping a spinster named Mary Woolard in her father's house at Barking in Suffolk.[6] In the three years from 1777 to 1779 there were no indictments for the crime. Thus the regional assizes, taken together, probably averaged little more than two prosecuted rapes each decade, or about one per county.

This low indictment rate almost certainly reflected the reluctance of victims and institutions to complain about and process cases (respectively) rather than the real incidence of rape. Victims were nervous about coming forward, and magistrates were often hesitant about committing

2. *Weekly Journal Or British Gazetteer*, 17 August 1723.
3. E. Hyde, *A Treatise of the Pleas of the Crown*, vol. 1, 1803, p. 436.
4. J. Walliss, "Crime and Justice in Georgian Cheshire: The Chester Court of Great Sessions, 1760–1830," 2015, p. 48.
5. R. Markless, *Gender, Crime and Discretion in Yorkshire, 1735–1775*, 2013, p. 226.
6. TNA ASSI 33/2.

men accused of the crime for trial. Even if they did, grand juries might refuse to indict them. Thus, in Surrey the assizes grand jury threw out almost half of all such cases between 1660 and 1800.[7] More specifically, and by way of illustration, in Gloucestershire in 1770, an allegation of rape by a married woman against an acquaintance did not get to trial, although supported by some independent evidence, the assizes grand jury dismissing the bill of indictment after "apprehending the woman to have been drunk." She, like her assailant, had been drinking gin and milk before the incident took place.[8] More locally, in 1802, after Phillis Eggleton was convicted of stealing various items of clothing from the poorhouse at Necton, in Norfolk, where she was an inmate, it was noted that she had earlier prosecuted two men for rape. However, the assizes judge had asked the governor of the poorhouse if he thought that she was to be "credited on her oath." He had replied in the negative; the grand jury then "of course found no true bill against them."[9] (This case also illustrates the unrecorded, even legally dubious, manoeuvrings that might go on behind the scenes in such forums.)

Even if proceedings resulted in a hearing, securing a conviction for the full offence was difficult, because of its strict evidential and legal requirements and what might be termed a general climate of scepticism towards such claims. This was especially marked if the complainant did not have an unsullied reputation. When two Norfolk farmers, Thomas Morley and Thomas Walker, were accused of raping Eliza Everett, a farm worker, on the highway, they appear to have been acquitted because she admitted to an examining magistrate that she had been "criminally connected with young men since she was 14." Everett still possessed a piece of fabric she claimed to have torn from one of her assailants' coats, but this was not enough.[10]

Numerous rape allegations ran into the sand for a variety of other reasons. For example, Timothy Gray was accused of raping a Suffolk spinster named Martha Porter in 1734, but did not come for trial because

7. J. H. Langbein, *The Origins of Adversary Trial*, 2005, p. 45.
8. M. McGarvie (ed.), *The King's Peace, The Justice's Notebooks of Thomas Horner of Mells, 1770–1777*, 1997, p. 29.
9. *The Bury and Norwich Post: Or, Suffolk, Norfolk, Essex, and Cambridge Advertiser*, 24 March 1802.
10. A. Clark, *Women's Silence, Men's Violence: Sexual Assault in England 1770–1845*, 1987, p. 73.

he failed to answer to bail, which had been granted despite the gravity of the allegation. He appears to have been executed for highway robbery after the Summer Assizes in Surrey in 1735.[11] Interestingly, he had been acquitted of another robbery at the Old Bailey a short while before he died, when he mentioned the rape allegation made against him in East Anglia, claiming that it had been a malicious prosecution for political reasons, his foes having "got a woman in Suffolk to swear a rape against me."[12]

In August 1770 Samuel Buck was accused of raping Elizabeth Estaugh at the Suffolk Assizes, where he was acquitted.[13] In April 1782 two drovers, John Swan and John Allison, were committed to Norwich Castle gaol, accused of stopping Elizabeth Broughton on the road between Swaffham and Shouldham, robbing her of a coloured linen handkerchief, and "ravishing" her.[14] The following month Thomas Warf, an "old offender," was committed to the same prison, charged on the oath of Amy Jarwood, a married woman, with breaking into her house one Sunday night a few days earlier and "violently assaulting and ravishing her."[15] Neither of these cases appears to have resulted in a conviction.

There was nothing unusual in the modest East Anglian success rate for rape prosecutions, which was in line with those for most other English regions. For example, on the Western Circuit between 1670 and 1729, of the 54 men indicted for the crime, 46 (85 per cent) were tried and acquitted or their cases were thrown out by the grand jury. (A few instances are probably missing from the above total).[16] Indeed, the East Anglian conviction rate was positively high compared to that in Wales at this time, where about half of those charged with rape were not even tried at the great sessions, and of those cases that did reach a petty jury almost none resulted in conviction.[17] Against this, and apparently something of

11. TNA ASSI 33/1.
12. OBSP, Trial of Thomas Gray, 11 September 1735: t17350702–22.
13. Anon, *A Kalendar of the Prisoners Now Confined in Ipswich Gaol*, 1770, p. 1; *General Evening Post*, 16 August 1770–18 August 1770.
14. *Norfolk Chronicle*, 13 April 1782.
15. Ibid., 11 May 1782.
16. M. Eder, *"At the Instigation of the Devil": Capital Punishment and the Assize in the Early Modern England, 1670–1730*, 2014, p. 57.
17. K. Watson, "Women, Violent Crime and Criminal Justice in Georgian Wales," 2013, p. 252.

an exception, in Cheshire, over 40 per cent of rape cases that went for trial during the 70 years after 1760 produced convictions.[18]

Despite the attendant difficulties, five men were executed for four rapes that were unaccompanied by a more serious charge (i.e. murder) in Norfolk between 1735 and 1799. All were fairly heinous examples of the crime. Thus, in 1747 Francis Cooper, an 18-year-old youth, was executed for raping a girl who was under ten.[19] Similarly, in 1772, William Pilling, a man of almost 60, was convicted at the special General Sessions of the Peace for King's Lynn for raping a ten-year-old girl and duly hanged.[20] Samuel Creasy, who raped Mary Gage of East Walton near the footpath in the parish of Wormegay in 1781, compounded his crime by robbing her of 8s in silver. He, too, was executed.[21] In 1799 James Fleming and Samuel Windham, a pair of soldiers from the 30th Regiment of Foot, along with a third private (allowed to turn Crown evidence to ensure the conviction of the others), gang-raped eleven-year-old Rebecca Brighton and inflicted injuries which contributed to her later death, though they were not charged with murder.[22] Gang rapes, especially those in which the victim sustained serious injuries, were viewed as the most heinous form of the crime and, if proved, nearly always led to execution. As the case suggests, the authorities were also willing to go to considerable lengths to secure convictions in such circumstances. Both men were hanged.

No one was executed for rape in Suffolk between 1735 and 1800, other than Toby Gill in 1750, a black army drummer in a dragoon regiment who was also convicted of the murder of Ann Blackmore in what seems to have been a drunken sexual attack. He raped and strangled her with her own handkerchief after she refused to comply with a "lewd proposal," although some aspects of the case remain unclear.[23] Nevertheless, William Holmes, a severely disabled (due to military wounds) pauper from the House of Industry in Melton was hanged in 1805 for "ravishing" two girls in the same establishment, one under eleven, and the other under

18. J. Walliss, "Crime and Justice in Georgian Cheshire; The Chester Court of Great Sessions, 1760–1830," 2015, p. 50.
19. *Old England*, 29 August 1747.
20. *Morning Chronicle and London Advertiser*, 20 October 1772.
21. *Norfolk Chronicle*, 11 August 1781.
22. *London Chronicle*, 26–28 March 1799.
23. *Country Journal Or The Craftsman*, 15 September 1750.

12, years of age.[24] In 1812 John Took was capitally convicted of raping his eldest daughter, a child of 13, at the Bury Assizes.[25] He was executed a month later. Took was described as manifesting "extreme ignorance and insensibility." This may have extended to his family. His wife and two children were in the crowd that assembled to view his execution, engaged in collecting money, although the sheriff (one of whose tasks it was to supervise executions) ordered two constables to take them out of sight before Took was "turned off."[26]

Although rape was, ostensibly, one of the most serious offences in the criminal canon it did not automatically lead to execution for those convicted of the crime, though the majority did hang.[27] Rapes without "aggravating" features (child victims, great brutality, attendant robbery, etc.) did not always end in death. Thus, on the Western Circuit between 1670 and 1729, three of the eight men (over 37 per cent) who were convicted of rape escaped the gallows.[28] In Cheshire, about a century later, between 1760 and 1830, over half (eight of 14) of the men sentenced to death for rape were reprieved.[29] A small number of men found guilty of rape in eighteenth-century East Anglia also received clemency. For example, John English was reprieved on condition of 14 years' transportation.[30]

Characteristics of Rape Cases

Many eighteenth-century rape victims were children or adolescents, in East Anglia as elsewhere in the country.[31] A statute of 1576 had made it a felony, without benefit of clergy, to have intercourse with any female child under the age of ten.[32] As a result, consent in cases involving such

24. *The Lancaster Gazette and General Advertiser, for Lancashire, Westmorland, &c.*, 20 April 1805.
25. *The Bury and Norwich Post: Or, Suffolk, Norfolk, Essex, Cambridge, and Ely Advertiser*, 25 March 1812.
26. *The Ipswich Journal*, 18 April 1812.
27. G. Walker, "Rereading Rape and Sexual Violence in Early Modern England," 1998, p. 1.
28. M. Eder, *"At the Instigation of the Devil": Capital Punishment and the Assize in the Early modern England, 1670–1730*, 2014, pp. 147–149.
29. J. Walliss, "Crime and Justice in Georgian Cheshire; The Chester Court of Great Sessions, 1760–1830," 2015, p. 52.
30. *London Evening Post*, 15–18 December 1753; *Whitehall Evening Post Or London Intelligencer*, 6–9 April 1754.
31. Anon, *The Tryal and Condemnation of Mervin, Lord Audley Earl of Castlehaven*, 1699, p. 6.
32. M. Levine, "A More Than Ordinary Case of 'Rape', 13 and 14 Elizabeth 1," 1963, p. 163.

children became irrelevant.[33] It was merely necessary to prove that intercourse had occurred for the crime to be established.[34]

The victimisation of children reflected their vulnerability in an era when the demarcation between childhood and adulthood was less emphatic than it is today, and when there was a greater adult willingness to exploit it. For example, in February 1777 a schoolmaster from Bury was committed to prison for attempting to rape one of his nine-year-old female pupils.[35] In March the following year, William Wiseman was acquitted at the Thetford Assizes of raping three-year-old Mary Mann and (an alternative count) of attempting to do so. A three-year-old would not have been able to give evidence, making effective prosecution difficult.[36] Similarly, William Snelling was convicted of attempting to rape a child of just over seven years of age at the Bury Assizes in 1812. He was sentenced to serve two years' imprisonment and to stand in the pillory at Bury marketplace.[37]

Perhaps more typically of such cases, in April 1749 Mary Woods, a girl of eleven (possibly 12) from Grundisburgh, in Suffolk, was brought before John Sparrow by parish officers and swore on oath in front of the JP that John Mayhew, a local husbandman, had had sexual intercourse with her on several occasions three years earlier, and again the previous year "every time by force and violence." On the first occasion, Mayhew had just recovered from smallpox and was taking the air when he met her in a field and "lay with her." Despite her youth, Mary was apparently in an advanced stage of pregnancy when she reported the matter to the justice (the two events were probably connected), something that was confirmed by local surgeons. An arrest warrant was issued against Mayhew.[38]

Female servants were particularly vulnerable to rape. Sometimes their masters were the perpetrators. In an alleged example from 1799, Robert

33. W. Blackstone, *Commentaries on the Laws of England*, vol. IV, 1769, p. 212.
34. E. Hyde, *A Treatise of the Pleas of the Crown*, vol. 1, 1803, p. 436.
35. *Ipswich Journal*, 17 February 1777.
36. TNA ASSI 33/6.
37. *The Bury and Norwich Post: Or, Suffolk, Norfolk, Essex, Cambridge, and Ely Advertiser*, 25 March 1812.
38. *Penny London Post Or The Morning Advertiser*, 7–10 April 1749; *Whitehall Evening Post Or London Intelligencer*, 6–8 April 1749.

Adcock and John Green were acquitted at the Norfolk Assizes of raping Phoebe Rackey after it "appeared that a tender connection had previously subsisted between the prosecutrix and the prisoner Green, with whom she lived as servant." Green's counsel asked for a copy of the indictment (a necessary precedent to an action for malicious prosecution). However, the court refused his application, suggesting that they did not feel that the prosecution was obviously unfounded.[39] Indicative of the stress of giving evidence in such cases, then as now, the trial had been adjourned at an earlier hearing after the complainant fainted twice while testifying.[40]

Even more frequently, employees raped their co-workers. For example, in January 1708 Elizabeth Watner, a spinster and servant in Falkenham (Suffolk) was looking after a small child, on her own, in her employer's house. Robert Brown, a day labourer for the same master, asked her for two blankets to seal a barn while he dressed corn. He allegedly followed her upstairs when she went to get them from a bedroom, and threw her onto a bed, with Elizabeth "cryeing out & shrieking loud at the same time for helpe." There was no one to come to her assistance and he raped her. Her two-week hesitation in reporting the matter to anyone was almost certainly fatal to any attempt at prosecution.[41] Rape victims were expected to make an immediate outcry, and it was a "strong presumption against a woman, that she made no complaint in a reasonable time."[42] Similarly, at the Thetford Assizes in 1758, Joseph Bloomfield was acquitted of ravishing Ann Reynolds, a spinster. Both prosecutor and defendant were the servants of a Mrs Pigg in Downham Market.[43]

Attempted Rape

Assault with intent to rape (i.e., attempted rape) was an indictable misdemeanour. As such, it could be prosecuted at either the assizes or at quarter sessions. Practice differed in English regions on trial distribution for the offence between these two courts. For example, two-thirds

39. *London Chronicle*, 26–28 March 1799.
40. *London Packet or New Lloyd's Evening Post*, 22–25 March 22.
41. SRO QS 347.96, *The Devereux Edgar Notebook*, transcribed by S. R. Schofield, 1956, vol. 2, p. 162.
42. G. Jacob, *The Student's Companion: Or, The Reason of the laws of England*, 1725, p. 166.
43. *London Evening Post*, 1–4 October 1757; TNA ASSI 33/3.

of such charges in Yorkshire, during a selection of years taken from the period between 1735 and 1775, were prosecuted at assizes.[44] By contrast, in Middlesex, it seems that most offences went to the lower forum. In Norfolk and Suffolk both courts were used.

Because it was a misdemeanour and not a felony, a jury faced by a rape indictment could not return a lesser verdict of guilty to the inchoate offence. However, for the same reason, an acquittal for rape due to a technical defect (such as lack of penetration) could be re-prosecuted as an "assault with attempt to rape" without infringing the rule of *autrefois acquit*. Thus, at the Bury Assizes in 1723, after John Sturgion was acquitted of the more serious crime due to a lack of ejaculation, a new bill was prepared, and he was immediately re-prosecuted for "assault with intent to ravish," convicted, and sentenced to be pilloried and two months' hard labour.[45] This was not unusual, as expert medical witnesses were often reluctant to commit themselves specifically on the issue of penetration.[46] Of course, this problem could be avoided by trying the defendant on alternative counts for both offences at the same time, although the presence of the inchoate crime on the indictment tended to undermine the prospects of a conviction for the more serious offence.

In May 1756 John Stone, a chimney sweep, was accused of having sexual relations with an eight or nine year-old girl in a turnip patch in Great Snoring. When examined by a local JP he apparently confessed to the crime.[47] As the child was below the age of ten, consent was irrelevant, and Stone was tried for rape at the following Norfolk Assizes. He was acquitted on this count. However, anticipating legal problems, he had also been indicted for an alternative count of assaulting the girl with intent to ravish her, for which he was duly convicted and sentenced to a year in gaol and a fine of one shilling, and also ordered to find sureties for his good behaviour for two more years.[48] Similarly, at the Norfolk Assizes in August 1760, Edward Lawrence faced alternative indictments of assault with intent to ravish one Susannah Curtis and for the full offence

44. R. Markless, *Gender, Crime and Discretion in Yorkshire, 1735–1775*, 2013, p. 222.
45. *Weekly Journal or British Gazetteer*, 17 August 1723.
46. D. Harley, "The Scope of Legal Medicine in Lancashire and Cheshire, 1660–1760," 1994, p. 53.
47. *Public Advertiser*, 18 May 1756.
48. TNA ASSI 33/2.

of rape with the same victim. Again, he was merely found guilty of the lesser crime, and ordered to stand in the pillory, fined 6s 8d, sentenced to two months' imprisonment, and required to find sureties for his good behaviour for three years.[49] (The fine constituted half a "mark.")

Legally, the misdemeanour differed from the capital crime only in not requiring penetration. However, as some of the examples already alluded to suggest, it was viewed much less seriously than the completed offence, and sentenced accordingly. To consider an extreme case, in 1723 William Heath came before the Suffolk Quarter Sessions sitting at Ipswich, accused of attempting to rape a woman, but was merely ordered "to be sent as a vagrant to the place of his habitation."[50] The official punishment for attempted rape normally involved any combination of the pillory, a fine, and a short sentence of imprisonment. Very leniently, at the City of Norwich Assizes in 1753, Edward Edrington pleaded guilty to assaulting a spinster named Mary Miles with intent to ravish her and was fined just six shillings and eight pence.[51]

However, like attempted sodomy (see below), the crime attracted popular hostility. As late as 1807, Abraham Hearn and Ann Cran (his female accomplice) were severely pelted with rotten eggs while in the apparatus in Chelmsford (Essex) and "assailed with indignant shouts and execrations."[52] A few years earlier, at the Dover Borough Sessions in Kent, after a linen draper was convicted of committing the same crime against a six-year-old girl, he estimated that up to 4,000 people came to watch him in the pillory. He was savagely pelted with stones and excrement from close range, the attending constables apparently making little effort to protect him.[53] As with many other misdemeanours, members of the upper orders could sometimes avoid such punishment by paying a suitably heavy fine. For example, in 1772 a "gentleman" who was convicted of attempting to rape a child who was under eleven years of age was merely fined £400.[54]

---

49. *Public Ledger Or The Daily Register of Commerce and Intelligence*, 5 August 1760.
50. SRO QS B/105/2014, p. 191.
51. TNA ASSI 33/2.
52. *Bury and Norwich Post*, 1 July 1807.
53. Anon, *The Trial of Mr. Savill, Linen-Draper, Margate*, 1800, pp. 22–23.
54. *Ipswich Journal*, 22 August 1772.

The relatively mild official punishment imposed for the lesser offence appears to have encouraged juries to convict. Many prosecutions were probably brought for attempt when, in reality, the full (and capital) crime had been committed. As a misdemeanour, attempted rape could also be compounded quite legally, with complainants being "paid off." This occurred fairly frequently. In Cambridge (also on the Norfolk Circuit), in 1751, a bill of indictment was brought at the Assizes against four university students for assault with intent to ravish one Elizabeth Norman. The grand jury found a "true bill" against three of them. However, the trial was put over to the following assizes. Perhaps mindful of their social backgrounds, the three young men were "warmly exhorted by his Lordship to make ample satisfaction to the girl in the meantime."[55] This was a nationwide phenomenon. Welsh women regularly accepted payment to drop such prosecutions (and those for the full offence) at the great sessions of the principality. For example, in 1763 the Welsh diarist William Thomas noted that a man from Burthin, near Cowbridge, "ravished his servant maid, about 18 years of age. She served him with a warrant, he feared to be punished, determined the matter and paid her £10 for abuseing her."[56]

Of course, the possibility of a pay-off also meant that spurious allegations could be made maliciously for financial gain. This was a risk to which the courts were acutely sensitive. In August 1706 Ann Ewen, a married woman from Ramsholt, in Suffolk, complained to a JP that a sailor named Roger Clarke kept entering her house and demanding "carnal use of her body." He allegedly offered her money for such a service and threatened that she would "not be at quiet" until she agreed. The Ewens lived in an isolated house a quarter of a mile from other residences, and Ann claimed that she was afraid Clarke would rape her. He was summonsed by the magistrate and entered into a personal recognisance of £20 to appear at the next county quarter sessions to answer Ewen's allegation of assault (a misdemeanour). A friend of Clarke's, Robert Batty, also entered into a further recognisance of £10 to ensure his appearance. At the same time, Ann Ewen was bound over to prosecute him in the

55. *Ipswich Journal*, 27 July 1751.
56. K. Watson, "Women, Violent Crime and Criminal Justice in Georgian Wales," 2013, p. 252.

sum of £20. The use of recognisances to prosecute misdemeanours was relatively unusual. However, the magistrate was aware of rumours that the allegation might be unfounded and just a "contrivance between husband and wife to gett a piece of money of Clark." Both of them were, apparently, of "ill fame" while Clarke had a good reputation. The magistrate also considered the possibility that the couple might be indicted for conspiracy at the following sessions.[57] In a more concrete example, in March 1715 Devereaux Edgar received depositions from several witnesses that an apparently "idle" servant named Rebecca Lee had threatened to accuse her master, Richard Garwood, of raping her in his cowhouse, so as to be "revenged on the old rogue." Lee was discharged from Garwood's service and sent to a house of correction.[58]

Even the misdemeanour was not a generic crime, covering a wide range of sexual assaults; its *mens rea*, an intent to rape, had to be made out. During the eighteenth century, sexual assaults committed without intent to rape, such as groping, would usually be prosecuted as simple assaults (if indicted at all), albeit often punished a little more severely than ordinary examples of the crime. For example, at the Suffolk Quarter Sessions held at Beccles in 1797, a blind man was sentenced to a month's imprisonment for "making love somewhat rudely" to a female shopkeeper in Lowestoft.[59] A more serious charge was heard in 1806 at the Ipswich Quarter Sessions, where a 60-year-old man was sentenced to two years' imprisonment for "indecently offering violence" to a six-year-old child.[60]

A jury could also return a lesser verdict of common assault on a count for assault with intent to rape. For example, in Wales, seven cases of the latter crime that were tried at the Court of Great Sessions between 1730 and 1830 produced verdicts of common assault (15 produced convictions for the full offence).[61] Normally this would attract a more modest penalty, although, on some occasions, a trial judge might not agree with the jury's decision and sentence accordingly.

57. SRO QS 347.96, *The Devereux Edgar Notebook*, transcribed by S. R. Schofield, 1956, vol. 2, pp. 183–184.
58. Ibid., p. 403.
59. *Oracle and Public Advertiser*, 9 October 1797.
60. *The Times*, 21 July 1806, p. 3.
61. K. Watson, "Women, Violent Crime and Criminal Justice in Georgian Wales," 2013, p. 252.

Sodomy

Sodomy was a capital offence, having been made an unclergyable felony by a statute of 1533 (25 Hen 8, c.6). This was repealed in 1553, but re-enacted a decade later, remaining on the statute book without alteration until 1828. It could be committed by "Man with Man, (which is the most common Crime) or Man with Woman; or by Man or Woman with a Brute Beast."[62] Sodomy involving animals is considered under the next section, as "bestiality." Consensual male-female sodomy, or that between husband and wife (even if not consensual), rarely came to court, although it was still, technically, a felony. In 1785 Martha Cordy from Worlingworth, in Suffolk, occasioned confusion when she complained to local JPs that her husband had buggered her or, as she put it, treated her in a "very indecent and unnatural manner." As the case appeared to be altogether unprecedented in their experience, the justices involved thought that they ought to have advice from other magistrates. As a result, a meeting was held in Ipswich at which the assembled JPs heard Martha's evidence. A warrant was then issued against her husband, who was arrested and held in Ipswich gaol until the following morning, when he came before a distinguished three-man bench of justices for examination and was remanded for trial at the following Spring Assizes.[63] (Initially, he was refused bail, though on his second application to the Court of King's Bench, almost two months after his arrest, it was granted in the sum of £200).[64] However, as Giles Jacob's quotation suggests, the crime's most common manifestation involved men having sexual relations with other men. (Lesbianism was never illegal.)

Homosexuality was widely deplored in eighteenth-century England as a heinous sin against God, nature, and the law. Such antipathy was marked even by some contemporary European standards. In the latter part of the period, a German visitor commented on the non-tactile nature of Englishmen's relationships with each other (they shook hands rather

62. G. Jacob, *The Students Companion: Or, Reason of the Law*, 1743, p. 239.
63. *Ipswich Journal*, 3 September 1785.
64. *William Goodwin of Street Farm, Earl Soham, Diaries Dated from 1785–1810*, Vol. 3, HD 365/3, transcribed by Mrs. J. Rothery of Earl Soham, August 2001. www.earlsoham.org (Last accessed 15 December 2015).

than embracing) and noted, "They speak in no part of the world with so much horror of this infamous passion [homosexuality], as in England."[65] In 1726 one observer seriously suggested that anyone convicted of such an offence should be tied up by the common executioner, in open court, and a "Skilful Surgeon be provided immediately to take out his Testicles, and that then the Hangman sear up his Scrotum with an hot Iron."[66]

Nevertheless, the everyday treatment of homosexuals did not necessarily reflect this type of rhetoric. Normative statements did not always mirror reality. Indicative of this, it seems that unwanted homosexual advances that were not forced on the recipient were often dealt with informally. For example, in 1773 in Somerset, a man named Smith was the target of a workmate's "detestable" approaches as they walked home from the pub. Smith subsequently informed his colleagues at the cloth-manufacturing establishment where he was employed. They appear to have dealt with the case by arranging an impromptu "stang riding," in which eleven fellow clothworkers assaulted the homosexual by "hoisting him on a pole" and then carried him through the streets of Frome while blowing a horn. Interestingly, their victim was confident enough to complain about his treatment to a local JP, who summoned the eleven men. When they appeared before him, he reprimanded them "sharply" and warned them against any repetition of what had occurred. Nevertheless, in view of the "heinousness" of the complainant's behaviour, he discharged them without any further action.[67]

Much more violently, in 1737 a Bristol man who had attempted sodomy on a drunken victim was mobbed and severely pelted through the city streets: "The Butchers too got him into their common Beast-Penn, and dragg'd him thro' the Filth till the Wretch was almost suffocated."[68] Other cases were simply ignored. In 1737 the Reverend John Swinton, a don at Wadham College, Oxford, appears to have used his powerful

65. M. D'Archenholz, *A Picture of England*, 1791, p. 197.
66. Letter to the Editor of *The Weekly Journal: Or, The British Gazetteer*, 14 May 1726.
67. M. McGarvie (ed.), *The King's Peace, The Justice's Notebooks of Thomas Horner of Mells, 1770–1777*, 1997, pp. 94–95.
68. *Newcastle Courant*, 5 February 1737.

position to avoid any repercussions from a string of aggressive sexual advances towards undergraduates, college servants, and a local barber.[69]

It is difficult to establish how common sodomy was in eighteenth-century England, especially outside the metropolitan area, which clearly had what might (very loosely) be termed a "homosexual subculture" by the early 1700s, with "molly houses" where gay men would meet to "Practise and Propagate the detestable Sin of Sodomy."[70] According to some assessments, there were 20 such houses in the capital during the 1720s, along with recognised "cruising" grounds.[71] This phenomenon was not confined to London. In the first half of the era Bristol, which was smaller than Norwich for the initial 30 years of the century, acquired a national reputation for such activity, something that eventually forced a local clergyman to publish a defence of his city in 1756.[72]

It would be surprising if the county town of Norfolk, and even Bury and Ipswich, had been entirely devoid of such a subculture, and its presence is occasionally hinted at in reported cases. For example, John Griggs, an elderly Ipswich man, was a repeat offender. In 1747 he was convicted of attempted sodomy and "severely pelted" in the pillory.[73] Five years later he was accused of the same crime and committed to prison to await trial.[74] In 1790, when two men were executed for the crime at Ipswich, one of them addressed the spectators at the gallows, "exhorting them to take warning by his untimely end."[75] This suggests that they knew they were not alone in their secret vice.

In purely rural parts, instances of homosexuality probably took place on a more sporadic basis, sometimes perhaps serving as a sexual displacement activity for otherwise heterosexual men. Nevertheless, for most of the period it may have occurred fairly regularly in slightly larger communities. For example, according to Francis Blomefield, Robert Carlton,

69. See generally, Anon, *A Faithful Narrative of the Proceedings in a Late Affair between The Rev. Mr. John Swinton, and Mr. George Baker*, 1739.
70. Letter to the Editor of *The Weekly Journal: Or, The British Gazetteer*, 14 May 1726.
71. R. Norton, "Recovering Gay History from the Old Bailey," 2005, pp. 40–42.
72. S. Poole, "Bringing Great Shame Upon This City: Sodomy, the Courts and the Civic Idiom in Eighteenth-century Bristol," 2007, p. 114.
73. *Westminster Journal Or New Weekly Miscellany*, 31 October 1747.
74. *General Advertiser*, 25 August 1752.
75. *Bath Chronicle and Weekly Gazette*, 15 April 1790.

who was eventually executed at Diss (Norfolk) for sodomy and murder in 1742, had been a trainee tailor there when young, but at the end of his apprenticeship was "led astray by a company of sodomites." He became a practising homosexual and for over 20 years was "notoriously guilty of that abominable sin." Even so, no formal complaints were made against him in the small town, and he was able to conduct a successful business and private life without any difficulty.[76] Clearly, Carlton and his lover were not the only active homosexuals living in Diss at this time. Writing a few days after his execution and gibbeting, Francis Blomefield observed that his publicly displayed body was a just example to "all such villains, & especially to those of this place, who were concerned with him in his detestable practices."

Public and official responses towards homosexuality also became a little more muted and nuanced in the years after the intense campaign against vice conducted by the Reformation of Manners Societies petered out in the 1730s. (Norwich had had its own society by 1700.)[77] It has even been argued that the eighteenth century saw a small and gradual de facto extension of sexual freedom with regard to homosexual acts.[78] While sodomy remained punishable by death, many people were prepared to turn a blind eye to it as long as it was covert, consensual, and restricted to adults, albeit that this tolerance was punctuated by periodic outbursts of activism and draconian punishment.

Trial for Sodomy

It was extremely difficult to prosecute the substantive offence of sodomy successfully, as contemporary observers well knew.[79] There were complicated prerequisites for proving the felony. Most important, as with rape, there normally had to be direct evidence from a witness of penetration and even, it was sometimes thought, ejaculation.[80] In 1738, after a

76. Manuscript account written by Francis Blomefield, preserved in the Bodleian Library under MS. Gough Norfolk 43.
77. For more on these societies see G. Durston, *Whores and Highwaymen*, 2012, pp. 109–114.
78. F. Dabhoiwala, *The Origins of Sex: A History of the First Sexual Revolution*, 2012, p. 128.
79. M. D'Archenholz, *A Picture of England*, 1791, p. 197.
80. G. Jacob, *The Students Companion: Or, Reason of the Law*, 1743, p. 239.

soldier was accused of committing sodomy with a Bristol youth, it was noted, "The Boy has sworn to the Emission, which makes the Crime of a Capital Nature." This was later confirmed by an examination of bed sheets.[81] For this reason the Crown allowed Robert Carleton's erstwhile partner and lodger to give evidence for the prosecution, even though he was not a child and so was himself guilty of the crime.[82] (If buggery was committed consensually with a man of the age of discretion, both the "agent and patient" were felons, "But if with a man under the age of discretion, *viz.* 14 years old, then the buggerer only is the felon.")[83] Without his testimony on this issue, securing a conviction would have been difficult. This also helps explain why well-to-do men, with greater opportunities for privacy, were only rarely prosecuted successfully for the crime.

Because of these evidential problems, even apparently strong cases might fail to secure convictions. For example, at the quarter sessions held at Lowestoft in 1755, Robert Heaken was committed to gaol pending trial at Bury Assizes, charged on the oaths of "several Persons, as well as his own Confession, with committing the Act of Sodomy with T. W."[84] This was Thomas Wye, a Royal Navy officer. Nevertheless, at the Bury Assizes held in March 1756, Heaken and another man, named Thompson, also accused of sodomy with Wye, were discharged for want of prosecution.[85] Wye was merely convicted of assault with intent to bugger Heaken, and sentenced to six months' imprisonment, a fine of six shillings and eight pence, and three (separate) hours in the Ipswich pillory.[86]

This result was typical of the rest of England. A selection of jurisdictions from the South West between 1730 and 1800 are indicative. In the most "successful" forum, Bristol, 58 people were prosecuted for sodomy offences, although three were for bestiality (see below) and many others were tried (and 16 convicted) for the inchoate crime. However, 36 men were acquitted outright. Only six were capitally convicted. Nobody was

81. *Newcastle Courant,* 10 June 1738.
82. *Norwich Gazette,* 20–27 March 1742.
83. M. Hale, *Historia Placitorum Coronae. The History of the Pleas of the Crown,* vol. 1, 1736, p. 670.
84. *London Evening Post,* 11 October 1755.
85. *Oxford Journal,* 10 April 1756.
86. TNA ASSI 33/2.

found guilty of the full offence in Somerset, Gloucestershire, or Wiltshire during the same period.[87]

Execution for Sodomy

Unsurprisingly, given this state of affairs, there were only three executions in the entire East Anglian region for sodomy, apart from that of Robert Carleton (who was also convicted of murder) between 1735 and 1800. Interestingly, these occurred late in the era, in Suffolk. In March 1790 John Southwell and John Smith were convicted of committing the "detestable crime" with each other at the Bury Assizes, sentenced to death, and then sent back to Ipswich to be hanged.[88] In August 1797 the 70-year-old William Powell was convicted of the "unnatural crime" at the same forum and executed in Bury.[89] Powell had been a pauper in Melford workhouse when he committed his offence, perhaps explaining why it came so provably to light.[90] Nevertheless, as late as 1830, Samuel Wright was executed for sodomy in Suffolk (the last man in the region to experience this fate), albeit that it was a particularly heinous case. He had buggered a nine-year-old boy at Claydon, probably repeatedly, having first "corrupted his mind."[91] The last Englishmen to be hanged for the crime were executed in London in 1835, although sodomy was only formally made non-capital in 1861 (the death penalty had survived a change in legislation in 1828).

As with rape, a small number of men who were capitally convicted for the offence were reprieved, but the majority went to the gallows. Among the former was a soldier in Bristol in 1738, and another military man, Captain Robert Jones, in 1772, who was reprieved on condition of (self-administered) transportation for life.[92] More locally, in 1763 a labourer named John Culling was sentenced to death at the Bury Assizes

87. S. Poole, "Bringing Great Shame Upon This City: Sodomy, the Courts and the Civic Idiom in Eighteenth-century Bristol," 2007, p. 119.
88. *Whitehall Evening Post (1770)*, 25 March 1790; *The Times*, 27 and 31 March 1790, p. 4.
89. *Observer*, 3 September 1797.
90. *Bury and Norwich Post*, 19 July 1797.
91. *Suffolk Chronicle*, 3 April 1830.
92. *Derby Mercury*, 28 September 1738; *Daily Advertiser*, 3 November 1772.

for committing sodomy with eleven-year-old John Chattin.[93] Culling subsequently received a free pardon from the King, perhaps reflecting doubts about the safety of the conviction, or concern that his co-accused, Samuel Ray, who was on bail and had not appeared for trial, was the prime mover in the matter.[94]

Attempted Sodomy

Very commonly, and as with rape, those accused of homosexual offences were merely prosecuted for, or ultimately convicted of, the inchoate crime. There were three prosecutions for assault with intent to commit sodomy at the regional assizes in the decade after 1751, but just one for the full (consensual) offence. There were two such prosecutions at assizes in the three years from 1777, but none for the full crime. As with attempted rape, many other prosecutions for this crime took place at the lower jury forum. For example, in 1752 John Griggs was convicted of attempted sodomy at the borough sessions for Ipswich and sentenced to be pilloried and to serve three months' imprisonment.[95]

Attempted sodomy did not require proof of penetration, was legally defined as a misdemeanour, and did not attract very serious official punishment as a result. This encouraged juries to convict. The crucial distinction was widely appreciated at the time. To take an example from Surrey in 1716, JPs examined a carpenter named David Dartnell about an incident with another man after they had shared a bed at the Greyhound Inn in Southwark (a common arrangement for travellers at the time). Thomas Reeves apparently made homosexual advances to Dartnell, which do not appear to have been resisted. A night of sexual activity seems to have followed but, as Dartnell stressed, without penetration occurring: "Mr Reeves never threatened or offered to turn him."[96] In

93. *St. James's Chronicle*, 26–29 March 1763.
94. *Lloyd's Evening Post and British Chronicle*, 25 March 1763–28 March 1763; *Ipswich Journal*, 6 August 1763.
95. *London Daily Advertiser*, 1 September 1752.
96. Transcript of examination of David Dartnall in 1716, Surrey Record Office QS2/6/1717/Eas/87.

reality, a high proportion of these "inchoate" offences probably involved full homosexual relationships.

Many such crimes were consensual. For example, at the Suffolk Assizes in 1756, John Holly was tried for permitting Edward Hoves to commit buggery with him. He was acquitted but immediately re-prosecuted and convicted for allowing Hoves to "lay hands on him" with intent to commit sodomy. (He was sentenced to two months in the county gaol).[97] Similarly, at the Bury Assizes in 1779, John Carter was accused of "permitting William Bell to commit sodomy on him." Bell was also accused of assault with intent to commit sodomy, although the act was obviously consensual. The two men were convicted of the inchoate offence and received identical disposals: the pillory, a fine and a year's imprisonment.[98] In 1768 Peter Sparkes and William Kerry, two carpenters from Bury, were committed to the town gaol on "strong suspicion of having committed sodomitical practice." Clearly this, too, was consensual.[99]

However, some men were indicted for attacks with intent to commit sodomy on an unwilling victim who would, of course, not be prosecuted. For example, in 1777, James Bulbrook, a 60-year-old wool comber from Chevington in Suffolk, was committed to Bury Gaol accused of forcibly attempting to sodomise John Kemp, a Suffolk labourer, and further charged with wounding Kemp in the face with a knife after he resisted the "un-natural practice."[100] Bulbrook was convicted at the Bury Assizes in July of the same year, and, reflecting the gravity of his crime, sentenced to three years' imprisonment. In this case verdicts were not returned on alternative, lesser counts of non-sexual assault with a knife and common assault that had been brought in the event the more serious offence was not made out.[101] This appears to have been fairly common practice in such cases. At the Bury Assizes in August 1783 the Reverend William Aldington was indicted for an assault with intent to commit a "detestable crime," but merely convicted of common assault. Nevertheless, the trial judge did not think the verdict correct, and, aware of the

97. TNA ASSI 33/2.
98. TNA ASSI 33/6.
99. *Ipswich Journal*, 13 August 1768.
100. *Public Advertiser*, 8 July 1777.
101. TNA ASSI 33/6.

defendant's resources and "fully convinced of his abominable practices, sentenced him to pay a fine of one hundred pounds."[102]

Part of the "normal" punishment on conviction for attempted sodomy, even if consensual, was to stand in the pillory, this often being supplemented by a short prison term or fine. These penalties tended to be slightly more severe when passed at assizes. For example, at the Bury Assizes in 1741 Mathew Colman and William Utting were convicted of "sodomical practices" and ordered to stand in the pillory at Lowestoft. Colman was also sentenced to two years' imprisonment, while Utting was required to provide sureties for his future good behaviour for seven years.[103] Similarly, in 1769 at the Bury Assizes, Peter Sparks was found guilty of "sodomical practices" and ordered to stand in the pillory for two hours and to remain in Ipswich gaol for 12 months.[104] The following year, at the same forum, Francis Limmer, who had repeatedly attempted to sodomise three young labourers from Lowestoft between April and August 1770, was sentenced to two sessions in the pillory and imprisoned for six months.[105] Less seriously, in 1761 Thomas Herd was convicted of the same crime at the Bury Assizes, sentenced to stand in the pillory at Ipswich between 11 am and 1 pm, and also fined 13s 6d (one mark).[106]

Punishments were similar at the lower jury court, if sometimes slightly more lenient. Thus, at the Suffolk County Quarter Sessions held at Ipswich in 1752, John Grice was found guilty of attempted sodomy, and sentenced to stand in the pillory and to three months' imprisonment.[107] At the same forum in 1761, William Atkinson and Thomas Wright were convicted of sodomitical practices, and received an identical disposal, albeit pilloried in Stowmarket, one after the other.[108] This seems to have been almost the standard sentence in the lower jury court. More than 50 years later, in October 1814, Charles Pegg, a 67-year-old man, was found guilty at the Norwich Borough Sessions of an "unnatural assault"

---

102. *Norfolk Chronicle*, 23 August 1783.
103. *Ipswich Journal*, 25 July 1741.
104. *Ipswich Journal*, 18 March 1769.
105. *Middlesex Journal Or Chronicle of Liberty*, 18–21 August 1770; Anon, *A Kalendar of the Prisoners Now Confined in Ipswich Gaol*, 1770, p. 1; *General Evening Post*, 16–18 August 1770.
106. *Ipswich Journal*, 25 July 1761.
107. Ibid., 29 August 1752.
108. Ibid., 24 January 1761.

on William Harbord, and also sentenced to three months' imprisonment and one hour in the pillory, which he duly served.[109]

Throughout the era, pilloried homosexuals attracted acute popular hostility. They could expect the roughest reception of anyone placed in the apparatus. As a German visitor noted, the "fury of the populace is unbounded, and even the better sort of people have no compassion for the culprit."[110] Elsewhere in England some homosexual men died as a result of the injuries they sustained in the pillory, as occurred at Bristol in September 1737 and at Stratford (Essex) in April 1763.[111] When Thomas Herd was pilloried in Ipswich for attempted sodomy, in the same year, he was more fortunate. He escaped with his life but was "severely pelted by the populace."[112] Similarly, when John Griggs, a man in his fifties, was convicted of attempted sodomy with a 16-year-old youth at the quarter sessions held at Ipswich in October 1747, he was "well pelted by the spectators."[113]

Perhaps not surprisingly, given these circumstances, after William Snell and John Carter were convicted of attempted sodomy at the Bury Assizes in 1779, and sentenced to a spell in the pillory in the town marketplace (along with a 5s fine and a year in prison), they feared a violent reception.[114] As a result, Snell tried to kill himself by ingesting arsenic. Unfortunately, it initially had no effect on him, so that he was fully conscious when put in the pillory and "pelted." As he was being carried back to prison, the poison took effect and he died that evening. The coroner's inquest later returned a verdict of suicide, which by then was usually limited to clear-cut cases or those involving nefarious defendants (both criteria applied to Snell). He was buried at a crossroads with a stake driven through his body, the traditional but increasingly rare disposal for suicides during the eighteenth and early nineteenth centuries.[115]

109. *The Bury and Norwich Post: Or, Suffolk, Norfolk, Essex, Cambridge, and Ely Advertiser*, 26 October 1814.
110. M. D'Archenholz, *A Picture of England*, 1791, p. 197.
111. *Stamford Mercury*, 22 September 1737; *Lloyd's Evening Post*, 4–6 April 1763.
112. *Ipswich Journal*, 1 August 1761.
113. Ibid., 10 and 24 October 1747.
114. TNA ASSI 33/6.
115. *Ipswich Journal*, 31 July 1779.

The degree of popular opprobrium that these offences attracted helps to explain why, throughout the country, such an allegation, even if entirely fabricated, was often used for blackmail. In Norwich, in the summer of 1790, two men "accosted a gentleman's servant in the passage leading from the Ditches, threatening to charge him with an unnatural crime, if he did not give them some money." On this occasion, they had mistaken the character of their mark. The servant, conscious of his innocence, beat one of the men quite severely, while the other made off. Other victims were not so strong-willed in the face of potential disgrace; apparently, it was not the pair's first blackmail attempt.[116]

Bestiality

Cases of bestiality (sodomy with animals) appear to have been a regular, though not common, feature of rural life at this time, despite the existence of harsh punishments for the crime established by the 1533 statute (25 Hen. 8 c. 6), under which buggery committed with beasts was as much a capital felony as that with man. Even in the eighteenth century, there was often little distinction in terminology between homosexual acts and bestiality. In both cases, one party penetrated another in what was considered a deviant manner. However, with animals, buggery could be committed by intercourse *per anum* or *per vaginam*, by either a man or (with some difficulty) a woman.[117]

As one might expect, an examination of English legal records, such as those for Somerset between 1740 and 1850, suggests that prosecuted bestiality was disproportionately committed by young men in rural areas during summer months, with mares and cows or, much less frequently, ewes and sows. (In the early nineteenth century, the 12 judges concluded that it could not be committed with a chicken, as it was not a "beast.") In an era when men normally married around their mid-twenties, the practice provided males in places with little or no access to prostitutes or other willing women with a penetrative sexual outlet, albeit not one that many men had recourse to. There are only occasional suggestions that

116. *Norfolk Chronicle*, 10 July 1790.
117. *R v Jacobs* (1817) Russ & Ry 331.

those accused of the crime had a specific fetish for animals (zoophilia). Prosecuted cases often involved the violation of a creature owned by someone other than the defendant, explaining why these crimes came to notice and also why they were indicted. Females could be guilty of the crime: "Women are within this statute, and if they commit this crime with a beast, incur the same punishment."[118] However, conviction required that they be penetrated by an animal, almost always a dog, and was exceptionally unusual.[119]

Committing such a crime with larger animals was necessarily fairly difficult. In a case from Yorkshire in May 1670, a couple out for a walk witnessed a mare being approached by a man who was "jumping at her with his body, in unseemly and beastly manner." Sometimes, the mare or cow would be put into a ditch, to make congress easier. A cover might also be put over the animal's head to make it more tractable.[120]

Throughout the era, prosecutions for bestiality were uncommon in England, as they had been since the advent of the 1533 act, although there was a small cluster of cases in the South West early in the nineteenth century.[121] Convictions were extremely rare, as they were in most of Western Europe apart from Sweden (where up to 700 people were executed for the crime between 1630 and 1778).[122] The "victims" could not speak, and the activity was usually carried out in the privacy of barns or in isolated fields. Most important, and as with rape and sodomy with men, the need to prove penetration made it extremely difficult to secure guilty verdicts. Eyewitnesses who were willing to swear to this as a certainty were necessarily few and far between, and the courts were often reluctant to accept anything less than direct evidence of penile entry. A mare's bushy tail could provide crucial concealment.

Nobody was executed for the crime in East Anglia between 1735 and 1799, and, as elsewhere, even prosecutions were rare. For example, no

118. H. Dagge, *Considerations on Criminal Law*, 1772, p. 374.
119. T. Courtney, "'Not Having God Before his Eyes': Bestiality in Early Modern England," 2011, p. 149.
120. E. Fudge, "Monstrous Acts," 2000, pp. 20–25.
121. C. J. Griffin, "Animal Maiming, Intimacy and the Politics of Shared Life: The Bestial and the Beastly in Eighteenth and Early-nineteenth-century England," 2012, p. 310.
122. T. Courtney, "'Not Having God Before His Eyes': Bestiality in Early Modern England," 2011, p. 149.

one is recorded as having been indicted for bestiality in the entire region in the two-and-a-half years encompassing the second half of 1734 and the whole of 1735 and 1736.[123] In the decade after 1751, only one man was tried for the crime at the entire region's assizes. In 1759 William Asker was acquitted of buggery with a mare at the Thetford Assizes. Despite this verdict, a witness was allowed a guinea by the court as costs for giving evidence, suggesting that the trial judge thought the prosecution was properly founded.[124] In the three years from 1777 to 1779, there were no indictments for the crime.

Nevertheless, Asker was not alone. In 1767 Samuel Elden, a septuagenarian farmer from Trunch, in Norfolk, was committed to Norwich gaol, accused of the "most abominable act of bestiality" on the sworn evidence of a man and woman.[125] He had apparently had intercourse with a mare in a pasture close to his home.[126] Even so, he does not seem to have been convicted. In 1770 Samuel Scales was committed for trial at the Bury Assizes for committing bestiality, also with a mare.[127] He was held in Ipswich gaol pending his hearing and appeared for trial with another man (who seems to have been on bail), but both were acquitted.[128] In 1785 John Taylor was charged with bestiality at Hintlesham, in Suffolk, and committed to Ipswich gaol, but not ultimately convicted.[129] Most significantly, albeit shortly after the end of the eighteenth century, in 1814 George Maulkin was hanged after conviction for bestiality at the Suffolk Assizes.[130] The last execution for the crime in England occurred as late as 1826 in neighbouring (to Suffolk) Essex, where Isaac Smith was hanged for bestiality with a donkey.[131] Even so, prosecutions for the full offence do not seem to have averaged much more than one case a decade in the entire East Anglian region.

---

123. TNA ASSI 33/1.
124. TNA ASSI 33/3.
125. *St. James's Chronicle Or the British Evening Post*, 25–28 July 1767.
126. *Public Advertiser*, 28 July 1767.
127. Anon, *A Kalendar of the Prisoners Now Confined in Ipswich Gaol*, 1770, p. 1.
128. *Middlesex Journal Or Chronicle of Liberty*, 18–21 August 1770.
129. *Ipswich Journal*, 21 May 1785.
130. *The Bury and Norwich Post: Or, Suffolk, Norfolk, Essex, Cambridge, and Ely Advertiser*, 10 August 1814.
131. Ibid, 26 July 1826.

Unlike rape and sodomy with men, the inchoate offence was only rarely indicted in bestiality cases. However, although John Waiste was acquitted of sodomy with both man *and* beast at the Suffolk Assizes in 1797, he *was* convicted on a separate count of attempted buggery with a mare. He was sentenced to two years' "solitary imprisonment."[132]

Minor Sexual Offences

An array of lesser sexual offences, which did not involve overt violence or penetration, also found their way in front of the lower jury court. For example, although a ten-year-old could give sufficient agreement to preclude a rape charge, the age of female consent in eighteenth-century England was 12. It was a common-law misdemeanour, albeit rarely prosecuted, to have consensual intercourse with a girl between ten and 12 years of age.[133] More general provisions against "disorderly behaviour" could also be pressed into service to deal with minor sexual offences. Thus, at the Ipswich Quarter Sessions in 1803, James Wright received a second conviction for "publicly and indecently exposing himself." He was sentenced to serve a year's imprisonment and to stand in the pillory.[134]

Conclusion

Successful prosecution for all felonious sexual offences, whether rape, bestiality or sodomy with men, was very difficult, so that only a handful of people (a total of eight) were executed for such crimes in the entire region between 1735 and 1800. Nevertheless, the existence of capital punishment, and its occasional but very public implementation, helped to uphold the strict code of sexual morality ostensibly expected of a Christian society. The legal problems entailed in prosecuting these crimes to conviction meant that the realities of the world could readily be accommodated and the day-to-day control of sexual misconduct left to lesser offences and milder punishments. Even these were not a common occurrence.

132. *Bell's Weekly Messenger*, 20 August 1797.
133. E. Hyde, *A Treatise of the Pleas of the Crown*, vol. 1, 1803, p. 436.
134. *The Times*, 14 March 1803, p. 3.

It seems that policing sexual boundaries was often left to communities, and these frequently turned a blind eye to transgressive behaviour if it was discreet, consensual, and not excessively disruptive.

CHAPTER 22

Non-Lethal Violence

Introduction

At the start of the eighteenth century, violence was a common facet of many personal relationships and pastimes. Frequently it was little noticed or remarked upon because it was so prevalent, and, for the same reason, did not generate much public concern. In families, schools, institutions, workplaces, and neighbourhoods, in both public and private, violence within certain (very important) limits was an acceptable means of expressing authority, maintaining discipline, preserving status, and even pursuing leisure activities. Age-old custom bestowed a degree of popular legitimacy on physical force when used by certain people. Among them were husbands dealing with their wives, parents with their children, employers with their (youthful) employees, and communities with their local deviants. This was part of a much wider "culture of violence."

Eighteenth-century England was not a squeamish society by modern standards, or even some of those found elsewhere in Europe at the time.[1] Brutal sports and hobbies were still widespread. When the normally Anglophile François de la Rochefoucauld visited Suffolk, he was appalled by the national penchant for cockfighting, something that, he felt, was a "game of cruelty, a relic of barbarity."[2] Huge sums might be wagered on these contests. One series held at Thetford in 1729 that was

1. See, for example, C. P. Moritz, *Travels in England in 1782,* 2nd edn., 1797, p. 242.
2. N. Scarfe, *A Frenchman's Year in Suffolk,* 2011, p. 82.

sponsored by two gentlemen from Norfolk and Suffolk was scheduled to last over three days, and involved at least 31 fights.[3]

Even worse, for most of the period, bull-baiting still took place in or near the major towns of the region. For instance, one was held at the Ipswich racetrack in 1784, and promised large rewards to the best dogs.[4] As late as 1792, a 12-year-old girl was tossed by an exasperated bull at such an event in Bury and so badly injured that it was feared she would die. Other people were nearly killed or gored by the same animal after it got loose and ran through the principal streets of the town before his "numerous idle pursuers" caught up with him.[5]

East Anglia was also a stronghold of eighteenth-century football; its enthusiasm for the game was (remotely) matched only in Lancashire and London. It was not the regulated association game that emerged during the nineteenth century, and could be very violent, with reports of people being killed during contests. (The sport was also sometimes used as a cover for disturbances over enclosures).[6] A notice for a Whitsun football match to be played at Battisford Tye near Stowmarket, in Suffolk, urged "no man [playing] to strike a man when he is down."[7]

Even more bloody, bare-knuckle prizefighting was a popular spectator sport. Crowds would often relish the attendant brutality. Thus, in 1777 two young men from Charsfield, in Suffolk, fought a bare-knuckle contest for a prize of just five shillings. It lasted 20 minutes, during which one of the contestants was so badly hurt that he died of his injuries a few hours later, even though the conduct of the bystanders in "suffering the fight to continue after the deceased was scarce able to stand is much condemned by every man of humanity."[8]

This "culture of violence" was shared by elements of all classes in 1700. For example, at the start of the eighteenth century, many "respectable" men, such as Sir William Chayton and Sir Walter Calverley, were aficionados of cockfighting. However, such attitudes were no longer equally

3. *Ipswich Journal*, 18 October 1729.
4. Ibid., 30 October 1784.
5. *Bury and Norwich Post*, 7 November 1792.
6. A. Harvey, *Football*, 2005, p. 53.
7. *Ipswich Journal*, 25 April 1745.
8. Ibid., 8 November 1777.

distributed throughout society.[9] Members of the middling and some (not all) elements of the upper orders, in particular, were beginning to evince concern at some of its manifestations. This would become increasingly widespread as the century advanced. By the early decades of the 1800s, there had been a fundamental change, especially among educated people. As a result, there were growing efforts to narrow the "legitimate" manifestations of violence. It was increasingly identified as a social pathology and a matter of concern.[10] The explanation for this change has attracted a number of "meta-narratives."

The Civilising Process

One of the most important and influential of these explanations is that of a "civilising process," formulated by the German sociologist Norbert Elias during the 1930s. This involved an interaction between social structure, culture, and individual personality in the move from medieval to modern European societies. According to Elias, factors as diverse as the growing state monopoly of violence, the extension of interdependent market economies, and the promulgation of a culture that promoted self-restraint all worked to reduce the incidence of serious violence.[11]

Research over the last quarter of a century has produced a considerable amount of academic support for his analysis.[12] However, although it has greatly influenced most modern explanations for the apparent decline in violence in the centuries after 1660, Elias's theory has been refined. Some academics have emphasised different factors in the process. For example, several have stressed a cultural shift towards "empathy." A small role in this process has even been attributed to the late-eighteenth-century expansion in literacy and the attendant emergence of novels, on the basis that they encouraged their readers to identify with people who were different to themselves.[13]

---

9. J. C. Wood, "Criminal Violence in Modern Britain," 2006, pp. 77–90.
10. J. C. Wood, *Violence and Crime in Nineteenth Century England: The Shadow of Our Refinement*, 2004, p. 29.
11. H. Thorne, "Explaining Long Term Trends in Violent Crime," 2001, pp. 69–86.
12. P. Spierenburg, "Violence and the Civilizing Process: Does It Work?," 2001, pp. 87–105.
13. S. Pinker, *The Better Angels of Our Nature: A History of Violence and Humanity*, 2012, pp. 211–214.

It should also be noted that several modern scholars remain sceptical about aspects of the Elias thesis.[14] Instead, some have stressed the importance of social stability and feelings of political legitimacy in relation to the incidence of homicide and serious violence in England and elsewhere, detecting an increase when these became attenuated, as in the years immediately after the end of the Napoleonic Wars in 1815, and a decline when they were reinforced, as occurred in the years following the Glorious Revolution of 1688.[15] North of the border, it has been suggested that eighteenth-century fluctuations in Scottish homicide rates were more affected by political tensions and socio-economic dislocation than by any cultural change in manners, with high homicide rates early in the century coinciding with tensions occasioned by the Act of Union in 1707 and the Jacobite Rising in 1715.[16] According to this analysis, states that are viewed as repressive lose any moral right in the eyes of their subjects to the exclusive use of physical violence.[17] The general improvement in the economy, a rise in national solidarity, and the relaxation of demographic pressure during the early years of the eighteenth century may also have played a role. It is even possible that religious toleration and the expansion of poor relief played some part in the process.[18]

In England, at least, the apparently irregular decline in homicide rates, with falls being followed by plateaus, does not sit entirely comfortably with notions based purely on a gradual cultural change. Of course, the two theories are not mutually incompatible; both could have been operative at the same time, with an underlying downward trend in lethal violence based on cultural change being checked periodically by the effects of political crisis.

Whatever the explanation, English society became more sensitised towards violence during the eighteenth century. This appears to have

14. G. Schwerhoff, "Early Modern Violence and the Honour Code: From Social Integration to Social Distinction?," 2013, pp. 27–46.
15. R. Roth, "Yes We Can: Working Together Toward a History of Homicide that is Empirically, Mathematically, and Theoretically Sound," 2011, p. 133.
16. W. W. J. Knox and L. Thomas, "Homicide in Eighteenth-century Scotland: Numbers and Theories," 2015, p. 57.
17. M. Eisner and A. Nivette, "Does Low Legitimacy Cause Crime? A Review of the Evidence," 2013, p. 37.
18. R. Roth, "Homicide in Early Modern England 1549–1800: The Need For a Quantitative Synthesis," 2001, p. 38.

manifest itself in the generally declining homicide rate considered in *Chapter 19* and the increased concern about penal execution discussed in *Chapter 10*, but was also reflected in a new attitude towards non-lethal violence, especially after the middle of the era. Previously acceptable behaviour was increasingly condemned as detrimental to public order and even immoral. People became a little less ready to resort to physical force and more willing to have recourse to alternative means of settling disputes and asserting power and authority. There was increased concern about "cruelty," although this process still had a long way to run in 1800.[19]

Illustrative of this change, bull-baiting became one of the first blood sports to be targeted by magistrates, in the latter decades of the eighteenth century, not least because of the social disruption and danger that it occasioned to bystanders, although the Justices did not find it easy to end the "inhuman" practice.[20] For example, in 1795 the aldermen of Bury called a meeting of its inhabitants specifically to discuss "suppressing the barbarous custom of Bull baiting."[21] Moving region, in 1777, John Brand noted with relief that the custom of throwing stones at cocks on Shrove Tuesday had finally died out amongst his fellow North Country men.[22] Another manifestation of this phenomenon was a gradual change in judicial and popular attitudes towards assault.

Assault

Assault was (and is) a broadly defined offence of non-lethal violence. It includes both physical attacks and threats that put the victim in immediate fear of such an attack. (The former was sometimes termed "battery" and also constituted a civil wrong). For much of the eighteenth century, most assaults were not viewed seriously, and a "robust" approach was taken towards all but the gravest manifestations of the crime. In January 1707, after John Garnham thrashed William Cooper with a whip on the highway near Rushmere, in Suffolk, his victim merely asked a magistrate for "suertys of the peace against the said Garnham as goeing in danger

19. J. C. Wood, "Criminal Violence in Modern Britain," 2006, vol.4, no. 1, pp. 77–90.
20. *Bury and Norwich Post,* 7 November 1792.
21. J. Fiske, *The Oakes Diaries*, 1991, p. 286.
22. J. Bath, *Violence and Violent Crime in the North East, c.1650–1720*, 2001, p. 97.

of his life."[23] Similarly, in November 1711 Samuel Brett, a wool comber from Woodbridge, in Suffolk complained that he had been assaulted in the street by John Piggot, a local joiner. During the attack, he had been threatened, beaten, and stabbed in his arm (to the bone) with a chisel. He claimed that, as a result, he had been in "danger of bleeding to death." However, his initial demand was (again) merely to "prayeth suerties of the peace" against Piggot.[24]

Illegal violence that fell short of murder was normally defined as a misdemeanour, rather than a felony, even if very serious, and was often tried at quarter sessions as a result. Whether tried at that forum or assizes such crimes were normally punished "by fines according to the heinousness of the offence, and perhaps imprisonment."[25] Fiscal penalties could range from small sums to quite substantial amounts of money, depending on the gravity of the crime and the defendant's means. Thus, at the Suffolk County Sessions sitting at Beccles in April 1716, Moses Williams was fined £5 for an assault.[26] A decade later, after Edward Haws was convicted at the Norfolk Assizes for assaulting and "dangerously wounding" John Elding with a knife, he was fined £50, "but by reason of his poverty [this] was mitigated to 10l [£10]."[27] In August 1747 Richard Pendor was fined just 20s at the Suffolk Assizes for assaulting a married woman.[28] Most fines were even smaller, especially when the court was made aware of a private settlement between the parties (see below). Similarly, until late in the century, on the rare occasions when a custodial sentence was imposed for the crime, it tended to be short. For example, when Simon Lewis was convicted at the Thetford Assizes in March 1754 of assaulting John Pettingell he was fined 13s 4d (a mark) and sentenced to three months' imprisonment.[29]

Even attempted murder was often treated (legally) as a grave form of assault, and so a misdemeanour, although there were a few specific

23. SRO QS 347.96, *The Devereux Edgar Notebook*, transcribed by S. R. Schofield, 1956, vol. 2, p. 160.
24. Ibid., p. 244.
25. T. Barlow, *The Justice of Peace: A Treatise Containing the Power and Duty of That Magistrate*, 1745, p. 48.
26. SRO QS B/105/2014, p. 116.
27. *London Journal (1720)*, 20 August 1726.
28. Gray's Inn MS 45.
29. TNA ASSI 33/2.

exceptions to this general situation (see below). In Blackstone's words, the "bare intent to murder is no felony." For example, at the Bury Assizes in 1768, Thomas Alexander was fined 13s 4d, imprisoned for a year, and required to find sureties for his good behaviour for three years for assaulting a constable in the execution of his duty.[30] One report suggests that he had attacked the constable and another man, intending to kill them.[31]

Felonious Assaults

A handful of the gravest, but also the most specific, non-lethal assaults were legally classified as felonies during the eighteenth century and (in practice) necessarily prosecuted at assizes. Among the most important was that created by Lord Coventry's Act of 1670 (22 & 23 Car II), whereby an unclergyable felony was committed if anyone lay in wait for their victim and then with "malice aforethought" cut out their tongue, put out one of their eyes, slit or cut off their nose, or otherwise inflicted severe injury with intent to maim or disfigure. The legal prerequisites for this crime were highly technical, and strictly applied, so that it was rarely indicted and produced even fewer convictions.[32] For example, only one case was prosecuted on the entire Western Circuit between 1670 and 1729, and that produced an acquittal.[33]

Interestingly, one of the few cases that produced both a conviction and an execution during the eighteenth century occurred in Suffolk. In 1721 a local barrister named Arundel Coke became envious of his childless brother-in-law Edward Crispe's wealth, money that would pass to him if the latter died. He sought a man to kill Crispe, and eventually settled on a labourer named John Woodburne. After numerous abortive attempts, Coke invited Crispe to his house for dinner and then lured him into the grounds of a nearby churchyard, where he was attacked with a billhook. The crime was bungled; Crispe survived, and was able to identify his two assailants after recovering the power of speech. He had

30. *St. James's Chronicle Or the British Evening Post*, 28–30 July 1768.
31. *Public Advertiser*, 3 August 1768.
32. W. Blackstone, *Commentaries on the Laws of England*, 1769, vol. iv, p. 207.
33. M. Eder, *"At the Instigation of the Devil": Capital Punishment and the Assize in the Early Modern England, 1670–1730*, 2014, p. 61.

sustained dreadful injuries, including, fortuitously for the prosecution, a slit nose. The legally qualified Coke strenuously argued that, as he had intended to kill—not maim or mutilate—his victim, he was outside the remit of the 1670 act. However, the judge at assizes refused to accept this (a slightly controversial decision). Coke was convicted and executed at Bury in March 1722.[34] The case was particularly shocking because of the defendant's high social status, his profession (Blackstone thought he was a "disgrace" for this reason), and ancient local family. It cast a pall over the town; a few years later Defoe noted that the barbarous crime had "made the place less pleasant for some time, than it us'd to be."[35]

There were a few other specialist provisions whereby non-lethal violence could be capital. For example, the Black Act of 1723 made it a capital felony for poachers to shoot at people in certain circumstances, even if no one was hit.[36] Thus, in 1779 Thomas Bell was executed for firing at Lord Walpole's gamekeeper, albeit without killing him.[37] John Chapman was convicted under the same statute and hanged in 1808, after shooting at William Bussey (Lord Ellenborough's gamekeeper).[38] There were one or two even more arcane and rarely prosecuted felonious assaults. One was introduced in 1711, after Anthony de Guiscard unsuccessfully tried to stab Lord Robert Harley to death with a penknife while being questioned by the Privy Council. It was then made a capital offence to attempt to kill or to assault a Privy Councillor in the execution of his duty (9 Anne, c. 16).[39] (This statute is also indicative of the hurried and ad hoc manner in which many Bloody Code Acts were passed into law.)

A major process of *legal* change in this respect would only begin with Lord Ellenborough's Act of 1803 (43 Geo III, c 58), which effectively created several new, potentially capital crimes of violence, including attempts to kill, disable, or commit grievous bodily harm with firearms

34. *Daily Journal*, 6 April 1722; W. Blackstone, *Commentaries on the Laws of England*, vol. 4, 1769, p. 207.
35. D. Defoe, *A Tour Through the Whole Island of Great Britain*, 1978, p. 75.
36. 9 Geo I, c 22.
37. *Public Advertiser*, 23 March 1779.
38. *The Bury and Norwich Post: Or, Suffolk, Norfolk, Essex, and Cambridge Advertiser*, 30 March 1808.
39. J. F. Stephen, *A History of the Criminal Law of England*, 1883, p. 113; P. Jones, "Antoine De Guiscard, 'Abbé de la Bourlie,' 'Marquis de Guiscard'," 1982, p. 110.

or other lethal instruments, such as knives.[40] For example, Ann Clark was capitally convicted at the powerful King's Lynn Borough Sessions held in January 1814 for stabbing her husband, William Clark, master of the trading vessel *Flora*, in July 1813. She was sentenced to death.[41] However, in this case, a petition to the Crown signed by 302 people from the town, asking for clemency, was referred to Robert Bevill, the recorder of Lynn, for consideration. There was a lot of mitigation. William had been able to return to sea within three hours of the attack, which was prompted by a dispute about financial support. A reprieve in favour of transportation was recommended.[42]

Assault as a Quasi-Civil Action

For much of the period, it seems that the primary aim of many complainants when making a criminal allegation of assault was to secure financial compensation or (less commonly) some other form of redress for their injury, rather than the punishment of their assailant. As previously discussed (in *Chapter 2*), the majority of these allegations were settled informally, by JPs, usually sitting alone. Indeed, prosecutions for assault were often only brought after attempts at securing an informal settlement had failed. For example, in 1774 a man named George appeared before the Somerset JP Thomas Horner accused of assaulting one William Pobjoy. Horner "recommended an agreement; but Pobjoy insisting on high terms, George found sureties and entered into recognisance to appear at next sessions, to answer etc."[43]

Even when formal prosecutions on indictment were brought for assault, they were often viewed as a useful way of pressuring the defendant into making a private arrangement with his alleged victim. As a result, there were considerable affinities between civil and criminal proceedings in this regard. As late as 1780, Sir John Hawkins, chairman of the Middlesex Bench, advised the county quarter-sessions grand jury that

40. P. Handler, "The Law of Felonious Assault in England, 1803–61," 2007, p. 188.
41. *The Morning Chronicle*, 7 February 1814.
42. TNA HO 47/53/3, ff 10–20.
43. M. McGarvie (ed.), *The King's Peace, The Justice's Notebooks of Thomas Horner of Mells, 1770–1777*, 1997, p. 125.

assaults, although "nominally offences against the King, and therefore fineable at the Discretion of his Justices, are, nevertheless, nearly similar in the nature to the civil action of trespass."[44] Prosecuting assaults by indictment was less expensive than bringing a civil claim for battery, and, if such cases did come for trial, allowed the prosecutor to present evidence that would be inadmissible at a civil hearing, not least his own sworn testimony.

If the parties to an indicted assault agreed terms in private, the court would be made aware of the settlement. For much of the century, the defendant would then plead guilty and (normally) receive a nominal fine of 1s or a similar sum, as magistrates and judges co-operated in the process.[45] A slightly macabre example of this "traditional" approach to assault can be seen in a case from 1784. Thomas Hurrel, a farmer from Hundon, in Suffolk, his wife, Rose, and one John Daye were all convicted at the Bury Quarter Sessions of assaulting Mary Colver by forcing her to get up in the night, whilst she was in labour, and then driving her in a tumbrel to Cavendish, during which time she was delivered of a baby. However, the defendants "having made ample satisfaction to the aggrieved party were discharged with the payment of a small fine."[46]

This situation also prevailed when assaults were prosecuted at East Anglian assizes, where, for most of the century, fines of twelve pence were the most common penalty imposed after a guilty plea. Guilty was also the most frequent plea at arraignment for the crime. A cluster of cases at the Bury Assizes in 1751 is indicative. At these sessions, a man and woman admitted assaulting the Reverend Thomas Cook; although this involved an attack on a "man of the cloth," both were fined just 1s. At about the same time, Edmond Mace also pleaded guilty to assault and was fined the same amount. Even more pertinently, Stephen Blomfield retracted a not-guilty plea that he had entered the previous year to assaulting a married woman and admitted the crime at these sessions. Again, he was fined 1s. It is likely that an accommodation had been reached in the meantime, of which the court was made aware. As this

44. J. Hawkins, *A Charge to the Grand Jury of the County of Middlesex,* 1780, pp. 26–27.
45. N. Landau, "Indictment for Fun and Profit: A Prosecutor's Reward at Eighteenth-century Quarter Sessions," 1999, p. 533.
46. *Ipswich Journal,* 24 January 1784.

suggests, changes of plea from not guilty to guilty were fairly common in assault cases, the trial of a matter having been put over from the sessions in which arraignment originally took place, allowing time for negotiations. Mary Betts did the same thing at the Bury Assizes in August 1749, and was also fined 1s.[47]

This approach continued late into the century. At the City of Norwich Assizes held in August 1764, two men were accused of assaulting and falsely imprisoning William Burgess. They both pleaded guilty and were fined just 1s each before being discharged.[48] In like manner, at the Lent Assizes held at Thetford in 1774, John Sagrot and John Newberry, who were described as "yeomen," and who had been jointly indicted for assaulting John Peverett the previous summer, "confessed" the indictment and were, again, fined just 12 pence each, which they immediately paid in court.[49]

Of course, a guilty plea sometimes reflected overwhelming evidence against the accused, rather than a private accommodation. Furthermore, not *all* admissions were met by nominal penalties. At the Suffolk Quarter Sessions sitting at Beccles in 1723, a man pleaded guilty to two separate assaults and was fined 20 shillings for one and ten shillings for the other.[50] However, such cases were in the minority.

Sentences would usually be more severe if a defendant in an assault case were convicted following a not guilty plea. After Richard Ponder was found guilty at the Bury Assizes in August 1747 of assaulting Elizabeth Hawkins, he was fined 20s.[51] At the City of Norwich Assizes in 1751, Isaac Lillington, who had pleaded not guilty to assault and then been convicted was fined six shillings and eight pence (half a mark). Much more severely, at the Norfolk Quarter Sessions held in Norwich on 11 July 1751, after Richard Prior was tried and convicted for assault, he was fined £10 and committed to Norwich Castle gaol until it was paid. At the same sessions, William Girling, described as "Esquire" and so clearly

47. TNA ASSI 33/4; Gray's Inn MS 45.
48. TNA ASSI 33/4.
49. TNA ASSI 33/5.
50. SRO QS B/105/2014, p. 196.
51. Gray's Inn MS 45.

a man of some status, was fined £100 on each of two assaults (reflecting his means and position).[52]

In 1755, eight people appeared before the regional assizes, in six cases of simple assault. Two men, accused of separate offences, pleaded not guilty, and were tried and acquitted. Five men, accused of three assaults, pleaded guilty and were each fined 1s. (Unusually, two of them had been cross-summonsed, each admitting to assaulting the other.) Four of them were discharged at court after paying their fines, but the fifth, Francis Thompson, was held in custody until he could produce the 12 pence required. By contrast, Thomas Baker was convicted after a trial of assaulting Martha Merrals, a spinster, and sentenced to three months' imprisonment in the county gaol, the only man so punished.[53]

Changing Attitudes to Assault

A change in judicial and magisterial as well as social attitudes towards low-and-medium level non-lethal violence started to occur in the final decades of the eighteenth century. Even by the 1760s William Blackstone was becoming concerned about judicial support for what were, essentially, compounding agreements in assault cases. He felt that they undermined the rule of law. By the end of the era, although nominal fines were still frequently imposed after guilty pleas, this was no longer necessarily "standard" practice. A growing number of cases resulted in contested public trials in which those convicted were subject to substantial fines and even significant sentences of imprisonment. For example, at the Beccles Quarter Sessions in 1801, John Taylor received 12 months in the house of correction for assault. At about the same time, at the Ipswich Quarter Sessions, Charles Wink was fined £5 and imprisoned for two months for assaulting a woman.[54] When John Hicks was convicted of assault at the Suffolk Assizes in 1805, he received a year in gaol.[55] Assault was ceasing to be a quasi-civil matter, even in its less serious

52. NRO C/S 1/1 mf 653. At the same sessions Thomas Clamp pleaded not guilty to assault and was acquitted.
53. TNA ASSI 33/3.
54. *The Ipswich Journal*, 10 October 1801.
55. *The Bury and Norwich Post: Or, Suffolk, Norfolk, Essex, and Cambridge Advertiser*, 7 August 1805.

manifestations, although there were no formal changes in the law until the early nineteenth century.[56]

The process whereby a great majority of those convicted of simple assault at the lower jury court were no longer fined a shilling (or less) occurred at slightly different times around the country. In relatively remote Cornwall, as late as the 1790s, 88 per cent of those convicted merely paid a small fine, but only 58 per cent did so in the decade after 1800.[57] In other parts of the country, the change started earlier. In East Anglia, it appears to have been under way before the end of the eighteenth century. For example, in 1781, a trio of men convicted of separate assaults at the Norfolk Quarter Sessions received custodial sentences. Two were imprisoned for six months, while James Pegg received nine months.[58]

The two approaches to assault overlapped for some years. Perhaps indicative of this, at the Suffolk Quarter Sessions held at Ipswich on the 18 July 1783, Thomas Godbold and his wife, Sarah, were indicted for assaulting a woman and pleaded guilty. They were fined 1s each and discharged. However, at the same sessions, Thomas Gosling pleaded guilty to assaulting John Barnes but was sentenced to six months' imprisonment.[59]

Conclusion

At the start of the eighteenth century, East Anglian society, like that in the rest of the country, was not greatly concerned about non-lethal violence, exceptional cases apart. It was a facet of "normal" life. During the 1700s, a change in manners and attitudes seems to have altered the way in which such behaviour was viewed. By the close of the century, this change also influenced the way in which the law was applied. English society had embarked on a slow journey, at the end of which (well after 1800) non-lethal violations of physical integrity would be viewed more seriously than low-level property crime, the converse of the situation that had prevailed in the early 1700s.

56. P. King, "Punishing Assault: The Transformation of Attitudes in the English Courts," 1996, p. 72.
57. P. King, *Crime and Law in England, 1750–1840: Remaking Justice from the Margins*, 2006, p. 259.
58. *Norfolk Chronicle*, 28 April 1781.
59. SRO B105/2/47, pp. 52–53.

CHAPTER 23

Smuggling and Poaching

Introduction

There was no form of crime that was unique to East Anglia. However, there were several that were disproportionately associated with Norfolk and Suffolk. Most important, the two coastal counties had a large amount of often highly organised smuggling. Additionally, poaching was a prevalent activity in what was a largely rural and extremely game-rich region.

Although different in character, poaching and smuggling had several things in common. They provided almost classic examples of "social crime"—behaviour that was sanctioned by the criminal law but which possessed a considerable degree of popular legitimacy and support. It was often difficult to persuade ordinary people that they were truly "criminal" or in any way morally wrong. As the Newgate Prison ordinary observed, "The common People of England in general, fancy there is nothing in the Crime of Smuggling, but cheating the King of a small Part of his Revenue; and that there is no Harm done to the Community in general, or to the Properties of particular Persons."[1] Two years later the Duke of Richmond reiterated this analysis, complaining that the "common people of this country have no notion that smuggling is a crime."[2] Similarly, many poor people felt that taking wild animals was a legitimate enjoyment of nature's providence. As a witness to a parliamentary select committee observed in 1826, "The general opinion is that game is

1. Ordinary's Account, 16 November 1747: OA17471116.
2. J. Briggs et al, *Crime and Punishment in England: An Introductory History,* 1996, pp. 75–76.

not private property. They say God has made the game of the land free and left it free."[3] Hens in coops were "possessions"; pheasants, hares, and partridges ("game") living in the wild were not.

Despite their considerable popular legitimacy, it was feared that both poaching and smuggling were major entry points into mainstream crime. This was important, as the era was intellectually committed to a notion of progressively deteriorating criminal careers, whereby minor offences inexorably led on, by stages, to "enormous crimes."[4] In 1740 prosecuting counsel at Charles Drew's trial and the defendant himself placed the latter's descent into murder on his early association with Suffolk smugglers and poachers.[5] Forty years later, an East Anglian commentator suggested that smuggling was the "great nursery of highwaymen, housebreakers, and every desperate offender against the laws."[6] Three years further on again, another observer from the region argued that experience showed that the two offences were the "beginning and foundation of almost every other capital crime."[7] Even towards the end of the century, William Godschall was still convinced that both poaching and smuggling "lead directly to horse-stealing, and the gallows."[8]

Although slightly surprising to modern eyes, this regularly reiterated analysis was supported by the careers of several prominent East Anglian felons. Among them was 41-year-old John Blade, executed at Norwich for horse-theft in 1737. Keen to travel, he had joined a gang of smugglers before becoming involved in highway robbery in Norfolk.[9] Similarly, in 1752 the smuggler Thomas Fidgett, a member of a gang that had killed a customs officer, confessed at the gallows to having stolen from Shelfanger Church (sacrilege) as well as burgling the houses of numerous substantial people in various Norfolk villages.[10] In 1780 accounts supplied

3. J. Rule and R. Wells, *Crime, Protest and Popular Politics in Southern England, 1740–1850*, 1997, p. 158.
4. Anon, *A Charitable Visit to the Prisons*, 1709, p. 37.
5. Anon, *The Suffolk Parricide; Being, the Trial Life, Transactions, and Last Dying Words of Charles Drew*, 1740, p. 5.
6. *Norfolk Chronicle*, 18 November 1780.
7. *Norfolk Chronicle*, 27 September 1783.
8. W. M. Godschall, *A General Plan of Parochial and Provincial Police*, 1787, p. 6.
9. *Daily Gazetteer*, 29 March 1737. He also attended fairs in the same county, gulling people into rigged and unlawful games, such as "pricking at the girdle" and "thimble and balls."
10. *Ipswich Journal*, 11 April 1752.

to the Dereham justices in Norfolk also suggested that the prominent highwayman John Ewston had started life as a smuggler.[11]

Smuggling and poaching could bring about the commission of other crimes in a more direct manner. They might lead to serious violence, and they sometimes precipitated conventional property offences. For example, in 1780 William Broughton of Barton Bendish, in Norfolk, was committed to Norwich Castle Gaol for stealing a brown mare specifically to transport smuggled goods from the coast.[12] Three years later, the crew of a smuggling cutter from Hunstanton, keen to replenish their vessel for a journey to Flushing, went ashore at Trimingham, in Norfolk, and plundered food and bedding from houses in the village, threatening to murder the occupants if they resisted.[13] In April of the same year, Robert Eagle, the secretary of a prosecution association, claimed that those who took rabbits from warrens frequently carried them away using horses stolen from neighbouring pastures.[14]

Smuggling

Smuggling was endemic on the Norfolk and Suffolk coasts for much of the eighteenth century. It had been present long before this period, and could be found long afterwards, but during the 1700s it reached an almost industrial scale. The government, under pressure to finance a succession of costly wars, but reluctant to place too many extra financial burdens on wealthy and landed individuals, sought revenue from high duties on what had become almost everyday commodities by the early 1700s. Some of these were sold at three times their wholesale price across much of the Continent. This provided a strong incentive to bring in contraband, and huge amounts were landed in often largescale operations.

For example, in 1745 a parliamentary committee reported that a gang of 50 men had run a cargo of tea and brandy into Benacre, in Suffolk. Two weeks later, a group of 60 smugglers repeated the feat, as did one of 70 men a few days after that. Sometimes dozens of horses were involved,

11. *Norfolk Chronicle*, 18 November 1780.
12. Ibid., 22 January 1780.
13. K. Hipper, *Smugglers All: Centuries of Norfolk Smuggling*, 2001, pp. 78–79.
14. *Norfolk Chronicle*, 12 April 1783.

and carts pulled by teams of four animals were often used to carry contraband away. It was estimated that in the last six months of 1745 alone, 1,835 horseloads of tea were landed on the Suffolk coast, usually from cutters of 30 to 40 tons.[15] Little had changed 35 years later, when a Norfolk newspaper claimed that gangs of 40 or 50 men could be seen riding during the day in the "most audacious and triumphant manner" from the coast to London, with heavily laden carts and horses, openly carrying firearms.[16] Men and women from coastal communities might assist these gangs on an ad hoc basis when contraband was being landed, further swelling the numbers involved.

The East Anglian counties were favoured for such ventures because fewer soldiers were garrisoned on their extensive and often lonely coasts during wartime than in Kent, Sussex, and Hampshire, the other main counties for smuggling from the continent. Furthermore, fewer Royal Navy warships patrolled offshore in the North Sea than in the English Channel, although they tended not to be overly concerned about smuggling during periods of conflict. Boulogne, Calais, and Dunkirk became major centres for the trade, with some East Anglian smugglers having their own houses in these ports.

Four commodities dominated smuggling in the region: tea, spirits (usually Dutch gin or French brandy), coffee, and tobacco. Typically, in 1764 the cargo of a smuggling cutter driven ashore near Aldeburgh included 25 "halves" (half "ankers/anchors" of just under 20 litres a unit) of brandy and gin, five hundredweight of tea, and between two and three hundredweight of coffee.[17] Similarly, in 1792 a lugger that had been stopped off Yarmouth and escorted into port was found to be carrying 611 half ankers of gin and brandy and 50 bags of tea, along with 12 boxes and six bags of tobacco.[18]

Of the four, tea was probably the most important commodity between about 1718 and 1784. The country consumed vast quantities of the beverage. In the 1780s François de la Rochefoucauld noted that in Suffolk

15. E. K. Chatterton, *King's Cutters and Smugglers 1700–1855*, 1912, p. 182.
16. *Norfolk Chronicle*, 18 November 1780.
17. *Ipswich Journal*, 22 September 1764.
18. *The Times*, 19 January 1790, p. 3.

"even the humblest peasant will take his tea twice a day."[19] According to some calculations, the duty payable until the advent of the Commutation Act of 1784 ranged from 65 per cent to 110 per cent of the net cost, so the price advantage of smuggled tea was enormous. Tea was also light and extremely valuable, making shipping and distribution on shore relatively easy and profits correspondingly high. In Norfolk, during the 1740s, it was customary to smuggle it in oiled (and so waterproof) bags, each weighing 25lb.

Of course, using contraband goods was not entirely devoid of risk for purchasers. Inevitably there was a greater chance of inferior or adulterated products being traded. An Act of 1730 (4 Geo II, c14) noted that *terra japonica* was sometimes used to dye tea that had been diluted by the addition of other types of leaf. This could be dangerous if not used properly. In 1783 a prosperous woman from Shotley, in Suffolk, died, and her husband and four servants fell ill, after drinking smuggled tea. Poisonous substances had been used to give their tea a finer colour.[20] Nevertheless, the trade was so well-organized that this does not appear to have been a particularly acute risk.

It is difficult to estimate how much contraband tea was drunk in England. Witnesses giving evidence to the 1745 parliamentary committee on smuggling estimated that at least three million pounds of tea had been smuggled annually over immediately preceding years. Estimates for the period just before 1784 were more detailed. The deputy accountant general of the East India Company thought that during the decade from 1773 to 1782 about 7 million pounds of tea and between two million and three million pounds of "fictitious tea" were smuggled into Britain and its dependencies each year. (The latter was an inferior mixture of tea dust with foreign matter.) Thus illicit imports constituted over half of an estimated total of 18 million pounds of tea being consumed in Britain and Ireland.

After duty was slashed in 1784 to 12.5 per cent *ad valorem*, consumption of legally imported tea quickly tripled. The importing of smuggled

19. N. Scarfe, *A Frenchman's Year in Suffolk*, 2011, p. 19.
20. *Ipswich Journal*, 1 November 1783.

tea swiftly fell to a relative trickle, as the fall in duty made it unprofitable.[21] A year after the reduction, the Suffolk surgeon William Goodwin noted in his diary that it appeared almost at an end, prior to which the "Contraband Trade sold two parts out of three of ye Teas consum'd in the Kingdom."

Many high-status and "respectable" people consumed smuggled goods. In 1783 one East Anglian observer lamented that the encouragement given to smugglers by "different ranks of people is astonishing and truly alarming!"[22] In 1785 William Goodwin noted that in earlier years almost everyone "from the highest to the lowest were either directly or indirectly concern'd and of course abettors of the practice."[23] They included the Norfolk resident Sir Robert Walpole, at least in his early years. More typically, in 1777 Parson Woodford recorded that "Andrews the smuggler" had brought him six pounds of tea, which he purchased for ten shillings and six pence a pound. The cleric and his housekeeper had been startled when Andrews discreetly alerted them to his presence by whistling under their parlour window as they were going to bed.[24]

Inevitably, in these circumstances, sympathy for those who perpetrated the crime extended to many of the men who sat on assizes juries, explaining why so many major smuggling prosecutions from the area were brought at the Old Bailey in London when possible (smuggling was a crime against the state). In 1783 a not guilty verdict returned on a notorious smuggler at the Thetford Assizes led to general "rejoicings."[25] An even more extraordinary case was tried at the Norfolk Assizes in March 1785. Two notorious smugglers, William Gunton and John Kemble, were accused of murdering a dragoon and a customs officer engaged in anti-smuggling operations. Unusually, as they stemmed from the same incident, the killings were prosecuted separately. The jury in the first trial returned an acquittal "contrary to the general expectation of the

21. Cheung, H. and Mui, L. H., "'Trends in Eighteenth-century Smuggling' Reconsidered," 1975, p. 29.
22. *Norfolk Chronicle*, 27 September 1783.
23. *William Goodwin of Street Farm, Earl Soham, Diaries Dated from 1785–1810*, Vol. 3, HD 365/3, transcribed by Mrs. J. Rothery of Earl Soham, August 2001. www.earlsoham.org (Last accessed 15 December 2015).
24. J. Beresford (ed.), *The Diary of a Country Parson, 1758–1802*, 1978, p. 131.
25. *Norfolk Chronicle*, 27 September 1783.

court." Counsel for the prosecution then appears to have successfully moved for what was popularly thought to be a retrial but was, in fact, a prosecution for the second killing (and so not a violation of *autrefois acquit*) while observing that "if a Norfolk jury were determined not to convict persons guilty of the most atrocious crimes, who were smugglers, there was an end of all justice." At the same time, he ordered a fresh indictment to be prepared, and successfully asked that none of the jury involved in the first hearing should be permitted to sit on the second trial. The two men were tried again, "when the same evidence was delivered against them, and the jury after being out of court near three hours brought them in a second time, *Not Guilty*."[26] Local jurors were simply not prepared to convict these men.

Interestingly, and anticipating the possibility of such an outcome, the prosecuting solicitor in the case had investigated the jury list, and identified prospective jurors who appeared to have links with smugglers. As a result of this information, four men were "stood by" at the trial by prosecuting counsel, albeit that this still did not produce the desired verdict.[27] The Crown had also made contingency plans for indicting the two defendants in London for simple smuggling if they were acquitted of the murders.

Although smugglers had a considerable degree of genuine community support in Norfolk and Suffolk, they also had the power to intimidate if it was not forthcoming. One East Anglian gang, several of whose members were captured by dragoons in 1751, was described as being made up of "desperate fellows; who always went about with fire-arms, and kept people in awe."[28] Such men were capable of ruthless action against anyone who crossed them. For example, in 1745 30 smugglers broke open a house in Beccles in the middle of winter and pulled a poor man from his bed. He was then whipped with a cat o' nine tails, dragged out in just a nightshirt, although there was snow on the ground, and abducted.[29] In 1780 a gang of almost 20 smugglers attempted to murder a man named

26. *Public Advertiser*, 26 March 1785.
27. N. Holmes, *The Lawless Coast: Smuggling, Anarchy and Murder in North Norfolk in the 1780s*, 2008, p. 69.
28. *Whitehall Evening Post Or London Intelligencer*, 22–24 October 1751.
29. *Ipswich Journal*, 9 March 1745.

Diggens who kept an inn at Rainham, in Norfolk "whom they supposed to have informed against them for some smuggled goods which were lately seized." They broke into his house at night, when he was away, held his wife and servants, and threatened to kill him unless they were reimbursed the £60 value of the seized goods. Fortunately, Diggens was warned of the danger before returning. He raised the alarm with Lord Townshend, whose servants drove off the smugglers. Even so, Diggens and his family had to move out of their home.[30]

Most smugglers were working men. To those on low incomes, the crime offered easy money. Typically, Thomas Puryour, a Sussex smuggler, labourer, and husbandman, was drawn to the nefarious trade because he "got more Money, and earned it at an easier Rate, than in the Calling in which he was bred up."[31] However, smuggling gangs usually included a few tradesmen or tenant farmers and, occasionally, more elevated members of society. For example, in 1751, when dragoons captured eleven members of a particularly "cruel" Norfolk gang, seven of them were described as labourers, but one, John Harvey, was termed a "yeoman" while another was a blacksmith and one a butcher.[32] In the same year, it was noted that James Holt, a notorious smuggler, had been the parish clerk of Benacre, in Suffolk.[33]

It was not just coastal communities that became involved in smuggling. The trade extended deep into the interior of the region. The inland town of Hadleigh, in Suffolk, was a major centre for smuggling throughout the period, although many miles from the sea. It produced a long-lived and large gang, reputed to be up to 100 men strong, which regularly landed huge quantities of contraband on the coast near Sizewell. Members of the Hadleigh gang resisted all official attempts to suppress their organization. For example, in April 1735 a customs collector received information that 400 pounds of tea had been hidden in a house near the town. He seized it with the support of another excise officer and four dragoons. The officials then secured it overnight in the *George Inn*. However, the following day, as they escorted the tea to Ipswich, they

30. *Norfolk Chronicle*, 18 November 1780.
31. *Ordinary's Account*, 16 November 1747: OA17471116.
32. *Whitehall Evening Post Or London Intelligencer*, 22–24 October 1751.
33. *Ipswich Journal*, 29 June 1751.

were intercepted by up to 20 mounted men, armed with blunderbusses, pistols, and fowling pieces. During the engagement that followed, this gang recovered the tea and shot the four dragoons; one of them later died from his wounds. The receiver general of customs offered a reward of £100 for the capture of the ringleaders, and £50 for lesser members. Witnesses duly came forward and identified some of them as coming from Hadleigh and nearby villages.[34] Two were ultimately convicted and executed for the murder. Nevertheless, the gang continued to operate. Twelve years later, its leader, John Harvey, was convicted at the Old Bailey for carrying firearms in a group of three or more people while engaged in smuggling (a clergyable statutory felony introduced a few years earlier). He was transported for seven years.[35]

Groups of smugglers could range over considerable distances. In 1751, at the Old Bailey trial of Edward Dixon, Samuel Salmon, a Crown witness, stated that he had been at Benacre in 1746 with the "Suffolk Company," a smuggling gang of 20 men. However, the cutter they were expecting did not arrive, so they went on to Walsham, on the Norfolk coast, to wait for it there, before returning to Suffolk. Salmon was acquainted with Dixon, who belonged to the "Norfolk Company," which also had about 20 men at its core. This band could arm themselves with a selection of blunderbusses, carbines, pistols, and hangers (short swords) when necessary. They had access to up to 60 horses. Every member of the gang had a private mark to identify his share of the contraband brought in.[36] In October 1780 a gang of Kentish men, operating far from their native county on the Suffolk coast, seized the brother of an excise officer from a tavern in Yaxley and held him aboard their ship until it had been unloaded. (He was treated in a "humane fashion" before being released with a guinea for his trouble.)[37]

Although a high proportion of smuggled goods were destined for the London market, a network of small-scale dealers helped to distribute contraband throughout East Anglia. Typically, in 1731, a woman from Yarmouth was held in Norwich and found to have several pounds of tea

34. *London Gazette*, 13–17 May, 1735.
35. OBSP, Trial of John Harvey, 14 October 1747: t17471014-6.
36. OBSP, Trial of Edward Dixon, 3 July 1751: t17510703-33.
37. *Lloyd's Evening Post*, 30 October – 1 November 1780.

quilted into her petticoat, presumably for sale there.[38] Over 20 years later, in the same city, 25 pounds of tea was seized at the house of a woman who kept a small shop in St Martin's parish. She was the widow of Samuel Eager, a smuggler who had died some time earlier in Newgate.[39]

Policing the Trade

The presence of smuggling gangs meant that, although East Anglia was a largely rural area, law-enforcement agencies were regularly faced by large bands of aggressive and well-armed men. It was obviously unreasonable to expect part-time village constables to confront such groups, even if they had been so minded. As a result, dealing with them was primarily the responsibility of the Customs Service. During the 1680s, revenue officers had been provided with cutters to allow them to patrol coastal waters, so that they operated on both land and sea. Some smuggling vessels were intercepted before they made landfall. In 1765 armed cutters seized smuggling prizes worth £170,000 off the British coast.[40] In one local example, a case from 1780, the cutter *Bee* brought a 250-ton brig, the *Isabella,* into Harwich, after officers searching the vessel discovered 230 gallons of gin and 110 pounds of tea hidden in her hold. (This meant that the entire vessel could be detained as a prize.)[41] Customs officers also had a significant presence on land, with mounted "riding officers" intercepting smuggled goods as they were landed and distributed, even deep in the interior of the country.

It could be a dangerous occupation. A parliamentary enquiry held in 1736 concluded that, over the previous 12 years, 250 customs officers had been injured and six killed in the line of duty, although, as the figures suggest, even smugglers would usually try to avoid inflicting lethal injuries if possible.[42] A selection of cases is indicative of the risks. In July 1708 John Sawyer, a boatman with the customs, found two half ankers of contraband brandy in the possession of William Cook near Shotley,

38. *Daily Journal,* 13 January 1731.
39. *General Advertiser,* 31 October 1752.
40. *Gazetteer and New Daily Advertiser,* 28 January 1766.
41. *Norfolk Chronicle,* 29 July 1780.
42. S. Jarvis, *Smuggling in East Anglia 1700–1840,* 1987, pp. 20–21.

in Suffolk. He seized and marked them with a "broad Arrow" to show that they had been taken for the Crown. However, when the spirits were put on a horse, Cook leapt on the animal and rode away; Sawyer pursued him. After being cornered, he stabbed Sawyer in the hand and escaped with the brandy.[43]

In March 1745, shortly after a small-scale seizure of tea and brandy, a low-ranking customs officer was stopped at Clopton tollgate by two men, who forced him into a wood, then stripped him and whipped him severely, before leaving him with his hands bound. It took him well over an hour to get free.[44] The following year, smugglers seized Abraham Bailey, a former excise officer who kept a coffee shop in Yarmouth, while on a visit to the small and isolated Norfolk coastal parish of Horsey. They appear to have thought that he was a government spy. He was whipped mercilessly in the hamlet's churchyard, tortured to reveal information, hung over the arm of a tree, and then left almost for dead. (In response, Bailey gave evidence against several of them at the Old Bailey in a series of trials over ensuing years).[45]

Even more seriously, in March 1769 Thomas Clevelong was capitally convicted at the Thetford Assizes for his involvement in the murder of a customs officer named Haslip in February the previous year.[46] Haslip had been one of several officers who had been so badly beaten after they had seized a smuggler's boat that "some of their brains gushed out." He died from his injuries, as did one of his boatmen. Clevelong, the only man arrested for these murders, died of natural causes in Newgate Prison in December 1769.[47]

Unsurprisingly, Revenue officers were well-armed, and operated in groups where possible. Sometimes, this was sufficient. For example, in 1784 a dozen excise officers seized a large quantity of smuggled spirits but were attacked near Woodbridge by a gang of 30 men, aiming to recover the confiscated liquor. A violent confrontation ensued, lasting almost an

43. SRO QS 347.96, *The Devereux Edgar Notebook*, transcribed by S. R. Schofield, 1956, vol. 2, p. 182.
44. *Ipswich Journal*, 9 March 1745.
45. OBSP, Trial of Robert Cunningham, 7 September 1748: t17480907–38.
46. *St. James's Chronicle Or the British Evening Post*, 23 March 1769–25 March 1769.
47. K. Hipper, *Smugglers All: Centuries of Norfolk Smuggling*, 2001, p. 50.

hour, until the excise men put the smugglers to flight. Nearly all members of the gang were wounded in the battle. The officers were armed with carbines, pistols, and broadswords, explaining their triumph.[48]

On numerous other occasions, the civil authorities were simply not strong enough to deal with smuggling gangs and their supporters, a situation that was exacerbated because some customs officers were elderly or corrupt; it was a poorly remunerated profession, and they lived in the communities they policed, making bribery to turn a blind eye a constant danger.

For example, in April 1777 two excise officers from Bungay, in Suffolk, received information that smuggled goods were being stored in Metfield. They found a large body of men there loading contraband. The smugglers immediately attacked the two officers with pitchforks and clubs, disarmed them of their pistols, and confined them in a nearby house until they had escaped with three wagons and five carts filled with spirits and tea.[49] In one of the most extreme cases, up to 200 people assembled at Thornham, in Norfolk, one Sunday morning in 1783 and spent five hours unloading a large smuggling cutter. They safely carried the goods away totally unmolested, the watching customs officers "not having assistance enough to oppose them."[50] In the same year a customs cutter commanded by a Captain Haggis returned from a cruise with a smuggling boat that had been seized offshore while full of contraband. However, before its contents could be secured, 20 mounted smugglers fell upon Haggis and his small crew and beat them with sticks in an "unmerciful manner."[51]

This weakness in the face of large groups of smugglers necessitated using the army to aid the civil power on a relatively frequent basis. The distances that had to be covered in large counties, such as Norfolk and Suffolk, and the need for speed, meant that these were often drawn from dragoon regiments. Thus, in 1751 the departure of the Third Dragoon Guards from Norwich was "much regretted" as they had broken a major and well-armed gang of smugglers that had "been a terror in those parts,

48. *Ipswich Journal*, 22 May 1784.
49. Ibid., 26 April 1777.
50. *Norfolk Chronicle*, 27 September 1783.
51. Ibid., 13 May 1780.

where they had committed the most unheard-of cruelties."[52] Similarly, in 1764 it was noted that two troops of General Howard's Dragoons were being stationed at Stowmarket, Woodbridge, Saxmundham, and Walton to "check the proceedings of the Smugglers."[53] In August 1783 a skirmish occurred near Theberton, in Suffolk, between a party of smugglers and five dragoons in which one of the former was killed and two horses were wounded.[54]

Infantry troops were also sometimes employed in this role. For example, late in 1747 a party of the Welch Fusiliers confronted a 30-man group of armed smugglers near Sizewell, in Suffolk. When they refused to surrender, the soldiers opened fire, killing two smugglers, capturing two more, and putting the rest to flight. (The prisoners were sent to London by sea to prevent rescue attempts.)[55] The same regiment was in action again the following year, when William Rowland, a smuggler and former Ipswich butcher "was taken in bed by a party of Welch Fusiliers commanded by Lieut Marly and on Tuesday was sent by sea to London." (The farmer who sheltered him was committed to the county gaol.)[56]

Even locally raised militia regiments could become involved, although this was not ideal, because their loyalties might be suspect. (One observer thought that three-quarters of such soldiers were likely to secretly aid and abet smugglers).[57] Thus, in December 1751 William Jackson, an excise officer, accompanied by a party of the "Huntingdonshire Rangers," seized three carts carrying 50 half-ankers of gin near Tottington. They safely conducted the spirits to the excise office in Swaffham.[58] Similarly, one night in May 1780, an excise officer accompanied by a party of soldiers from the West Suffolk Militia seized a large quantity of gin on Lowestoft beach. They also recovered a chest containing several cutlasses, 12 pistols, and ammunition, perhaps explaining why it had been thought necessary to bring soldiers.[59]

52. *Whitehall Evening Post Or London Intelligencer*, 22–24 October 1751.
53. *Ipswich Journal*, 14 January 1764.
54. *General Evening Post*, 30 August – 2 September 1783.
55. *Ipswich Journal*, 12 December 1747.
56. Ibid., 16 January 1748.
57. *Gentleman's Magazine*, vol. 8, 1738, p. 453.
58. *Norfolk Chronicle*, 15 December 1781.
59. *Norfolk Chronicle*, 20 May 1780.

Troops also provided escorts for captured smugglers, preventing their escape or rescue by colleagues, although this was not always successful. For example, John Pixley, who had been convicted at the Thetford Assizes for leading a group of smugglers and sentenced to transportation, escaped from George Gynne, the keeper of the Norfolk Gaol, and an escorting troop of dragoons. He was eventually arrested in London.[60]

Poaching

Although historically a longstanding phenomenon, poaching became a major rural issue during the eighteenth century, especially in East Anglia. This reflected changes in both the nature of field sports and the law governing the taking and sale of game. During the 1600s, hawking and netting had been popular forms of hunting. After 1700 the advent of increasingly reliable and effective flintlock guns meant that shooting became the dominant form of blood sport. From the middle of the century it also became increasingly organized, with estates and gamekeepers working to optimise the number of pheasants, partridges, and hares that were preserved within their bounds, and the size of shooting parties and their "bags" getting correspondingly larger. At about the same time, in 1755, Parliament effectively imposed a complete ban (in theory) on the commercial trade in game, even though there was a large market for such meats amongst poulterers, innkeepers, and victuallers in London and provincial towns and cities such as Norwich and Ipswich. Sir James Macintosh later suggested that these laws, although aimed at the protection of game, had instead created a "clandestine traffic, highly injurious to the morals of the labouring classes."[61] Improved roads also allowed faster and easier access to urban areas for poached game from the country.

The historiography of poaching has often emphasised a strong link between the crime and the increasing degradation of the landless (as a result of enclosure) agrarian labour force in the country's cereal heartlands, and particularly counties such as Norfolk and Suffolk. Nevertheless,

60. OBSP, supplementary material for John Pixley, 3 September 1740: s17400903–1; *Daily Gazetteer*, 25 April 1739.
61. House of Commons Debate on 2 March 1819, *Hansard*, vol. 39, cols. 777–845.

several academics have questioned this analysis, and stressed the organized and even semi-commercial nature of some eighteenth-century poaching, suggesting that its motivation went far beyond mere survival and personal consumption. Both forms of the crime were well-evidenced in East Anglia.

Certainly, there was largescale organized poaching, carried out by potentially violent gangs and aimed at producing substantial amounts of game for commercial sale. For example, in 1741 the city marshal in London seized 60 partridges from a coach arriving from Suffolk, birds that had been "sent up by the poachers in that county for sale to this City."[62] During the second half of the century, large gangs of commercial poachers, often over a dozen strong, operating a highly profitable black market for game, frequently raided the pheasant and partridge preserves found on the estates in the region. As an East Anglian gentleman noted in 1780, poachers were quite flagrant about their activities on the Norfolk coast, "for game they say they must and will have, for Norwich must be supplied."[63] The following year it was noted that five well-known poachers who had been apprehended near Walsingham came from the county capital.[64] Clearly they were not local men putting food on their tables. They had gone far out into the countryside to take game, presumably with a view to reselling it in Norwich or London.

Nevertheless, between 80 per cent and 90 per cent of poaching prosecutions, even in the early decades of the nineteenth century, were for the relatively minor offence of "trespass in pursuit of game during the day-time" (diurnal poaching) and could be dealt with summarily. This suggests that poaching was usually not a serious, premeditated crime but one resorted to casually or out of need, a view supported by the considerable degree of genuine popular support given to many poachers throughout the country.[65] For example, in 1753 the effigy of a man in Marlborough (Wiltshire) was hung from a tree and burnt "for informing

62. *London Evening Post*, 1–3 September 1741.
63. P. B. Munsche, *Gentlemen and Poachers—The English Game Laws 1671–1831*, 1981, *A Kalendar of the Prisoners Now Confined in Ipswich Gaol* pp. 22–23.
64. *Norfolk Chronicle*, 8 December 1781.
65. H. Osborne and M. Winstanley, "Rural and Urban Poaching in Victorian England," 2006, pp. 187–188.

against several poachers of game."[66] Hostility towards such men was just as great in East Anglia.

Poaching and the Law

The 1671 Game Act provided the cornerstone for the game laws until 1831, although it was amended and supplemented by numerous further statutes in the intervening period. This produced a legal regime that was notorious for its complexity and obscurity. In 1764 Richard Burn thought that many of its provisions were ungrammatical and even nonsensical. He unavailingly urged that the game laws be revised and reduced into "some order."[67] The legislation did not cover animals such as pigeon, rabbits, or deer (which were not "game"), although taking these creatures on other people's land was usually criminal, and sometimes contrary to a specialist statutory provision, such as the 1723 "Black Act."

Traditionally, the 1671 statute has been viewed as a quintessential piece of class legislation. Whether this analysis is entirely justified is a matter of considerable debate; however, it is understandable. In theory, the act prevented unqualified individuals from hunting game, even on their own land, so limiting long-established property rights. This helps explain why some small farmers in East Anglia destroyed pheasant nests when they found them on their property, leading to a serious doubt as to "whether the game laws tend to destroy rather than preserve game."[68]

To be "qualified" to hunt game an individual had to own land, whether freehold or leasehold, worth £100. A number of other people were included or gradually added to those so qualified if they could not meet this requirement, such as the eldest sons of men who were eligible. If an unqualified man killed game, or attempted to do so, he committed an offence. Thus, in 1781 Lancelot Howlet from Norwich was tried before Justice Roger Kerrison for taking a gun and dogs to kill game on the land of Sir John Berney at Kirby "and being a person not qualified so to do, paid the penalty."[69] Inevitably, the authorities sometimes made

66. *London Evening Post*, 13–15 November 1753.
67. R. Burn, *The History of the Poor Laws: with Observations*, 1764, p. 274.
68. *Ipswich Journal*, 23 September 1789.
69. *Norfolk Chronicle*, 22 December 1781.

mistaken assumptions about the wealth of ostensibly humble individuals. For example, in 1793 a miller from Tuddenham, in Suffolk, was accused of shooting a hare when not qualified. Summoned before a magistrate to answer the complaint, he "cooley threw down" documentary details of his estate, showing that he had property worth more than the requisite £100 per annum; the summons was dismissed.[70]

In practice, a blind eye was often turned towards a technical lack of qualification, provided that the person shooting game either owned the land or had the permission of the landowner to do so. In 1769 the lord lieutenant of Suffolk responded to claims that he had been officious in enforcing the laws on poaching against neighbours who had coursed hares on his land by pointing out that he "not only permits gentlemen, duly qualified, but does not even hinder the yeomanry or farmers from coursing or hunting on his manors."[71] The inference was that the latter were technically not always qualified to do so but that this was being ignored. This accords with many contemporary reports. Most of those prosecuted for poaching had done so nefariously, on strangers' land, for gain rather than sport.

During the eighteenth century minor cases of poaching, such as non-violent diurnal poaching for personal consumption, would normally be determined summarily, by a single magistrate, as a result of the 1671 act.[72] More serious cases, such as poaching committed at night or by gangs, might be heard at quarter sessions, although, by the 1700s such cases were comparatively rare. Thomas Blythe was one of only a few poachers to go before the Suffolk Quarter Sessions when he appeared at Beccles in 1724.[73] Similarly, at the Norfolk Quarter Sessions held at Norwich in 1771, two men were convicted of poaching on a gentleman's estate and then assaulting his servants when they were pursued. One man was fined £50 and the other £25; they were committed to Norwich Castle prison until the money had been paid.[74] Of course, if a grave crime such as murder were committed during the course of a poaching expedition, it

70. *True Briton (1793)*, 16 October 1798.
71. *Public Advertiser*, 28 November 1769.
72. P. B. Munsche, *Gentlemen and Poachers—The English Game Laws 1671–1831*, 1981, p. 212.
73. SRO QS B/105/14, p. 201.
74. *Public Advertiser*, 17 April 1771.

would be heard at the assizes, as would any of the variety of rather arcane poaching related felonies established by the Black Act of 1723 and other statutes, such as shooting at a gamekeeper.

As some of these cases suggest, and contrary to popular belief, the punishments imposed for lesser forms of the crime were not normally draconian. In 1782 a group of five "noted poachers" who had already been in custody several times for poaching were brought to Norwich Castle under a strong guard, having been apprehended on Lord Townshend's estate at Rainham. Despite their previous record, they were merely committed to prison for three months and fined 20 shillings each.[75] In 1784 a gamekeeper caught John Blois of Aldham using a net to catch partridges near Hintlesham, in Suffolk, "but the net being delivered up the fine was mitigated to 10s."[76]

As with other crimes, victims of major poaching operations might offer rewards for the arrest and conviction of those responsible. In January 1764 William Beal Brand offered ten guineas to anyone revealing the identity of a group of "idle and disorderly persons" who had snared and netted a large number of hares in his wood at Polsted, in Suffolk.[77] However, many landowners would attempt to prevent poaching before it occurred rather than seek its perpetrators afterwards. As a result, in the last decades of the century there were often violent confrontations between groups of poachers and gamekeepers.

Poaching Battles

A selection of cases from the 1780s illustrates how vicious such conflicts could be. At the start of December 1781, two poachers near Methwold, in Norfolk, beat a gamekeeper so savagely that his life was "despaired of."[78] A few weeks later, 18 armed poachers entered a plantation at Blickling belonging to the Earl of Buckingham. Their shots alerted the gamekeepers, who went out to confront them. A desperate affray ensued, in which the keepers were violently beaten with gun butts and large clubs set with

75. *Norfolk Chronicle*, 5 January 1782.
76. *Ipswich Journal*, 25 September 1784.
77. *Norfolk Chronicle*, 4 February 1764; *Ipswich Journal*, 4 February 1764.
78. *Norfolk Chronicle*, 8 December 1781.

iron spikes. One man, Jacob Blyth, subsequently died of his wounds, and another, James Gibbons, was gravely injured, with several more receiving lesser wounds. A reward of £100 was offered for information that led to the poachers' convictions. It is clear that the keepers had fought back, as it was noted that some of the poachers might themselves have "marks of blows upon them." Interestingly, this notice was specifically brought to the attention of those who lived in any "Neighbourhood where suspected Poachers usually dwell."[79] Four years later a group of 12 poachers attacked an elderly Suffolk gamekeeper and "thrashed him like clover." He subsequently died of his wounds.[80]

Mantraps and Spring Guns

The use of mantraps and spring guns during the last quarter of the eighteenth century was a response to the poaching problem in areas of East Anglia, where such machines first appeared in the late 1770s, after Lord Walpole installed them in his own woods. Other regional landowners, such as Lord Walsingham and Lord Townshend, quickly followed. They subsequently spread to most parts of rural England.

Mantraps were usually trip-spring-operated steel jaws with sharp spikes as teeth that closed on a man's leg when activated and held him fast, inflicting significant injury (the spikes could be well over an inch in length). Spring guns were pulley-operated, wire-initiated, unattended firearms that would fire buckshot or swan shot over fixed lines or, after turning on a plate, discharge in the direction of the person who had touched the wire. Such devices had obvious attractions. They were permanently on duty, fearless, and incorruptible. They were also cheap, at least compared to the cost of having a sufficient number of retainers patrolling at night. Even more important, they avoided the need to directly confront potentially violent gangs of armed men.[81]

Landowners who set such traps were supposed to give notice of the fact (by means of signs, advertisements, and, sometimes, a public crier) or

79. Ibid., 29 December 1781.
80. Anon, *The Trial of Joseph Wakefield and Henry Smith*, 1788, pp. 1–5.
81. P. B. Munsche, *Gentlemen and Poachers—The English Game Laws 1671–1831*, 1981, p. 72.

risk being sued for any injuries or deaths they caused, even if the victim was a trespasser. Thus, in 1780 an advertisement in the *Norfolk Chronicle* noted that, because much game had been destroyed on the estates belonging to Lord Walpole around Wolterton, Wickmere, Mannington, and Saxthorpe: "This is therefore to give Notice, that from and after the 24th of this Inst., Mantraps and Spring Guns will be placed in the several Gardens, Plantations, Woods, and Coppices abovementioned."[82] Two years later, an advertisement in the same newspaper declared, "Notice is hereby given, that Man-traps and Spring-guns will this Day be set in the Woods, Plantations, and Gardens, belonging and adjoining to Barningham Hall, near Holt, in Norfolk."[83] Similarly, in September 1793 a warning was published after poachers killed a considerable amount of game near Langham Hall, in Suffolk. As a result, it was noted that steel traps were being set every night in adjacent woods and plantations.[84] Many thought that such advertisements were inadequate, and that there should be no difference in law between "an affixed notice and no notice at all; the idea of setting such frightful traps is bloody and inhuman."[85]

Nevertheless, mantraps could be brutally effective. For example, one night in 1785 four poachers in a Suffolk wood blundered into them. When they were found the following morning, three were still alive but "had their thighs broke by the crackers and traps." The fourth was dead from the injuries he had sustained.[86] Unfortunately, mantraps were also entirely indiscriminate in their operation. In 1781 a gentleman who was legally shooting in a covert near Holt, in Norfolk, set up a bird that ran into the wire of a spring gun. The gun went off, hitting his dog, and missing its master by only a few feet.[87] Nationally several people who were not poachers were killed or injured by these engines. For example, in 1790, spring guns killed two of Lord Berkely's servants.[88] This made them unpopular with ordinary people. In 1791 it was claimed that some of the

82. *Norfolk Chronicle*, 9 November 1780.
83. Ibid., 16 November 1782.
84. *Bury and Norwich Post*, 25 September 1793.
85. *Morning Chronicle and London Advertiser*, 22 August 1774.
86. P. B. Munsche, *Gentlemen and Poachers—The English Game Laws 1671–1831*, 1981, p. 73.
87. *Norfolk Chronicle*, 8 December 1781.
88. *English Chronicle Or Universal Evening Post*, 6–9 February 1790.

rural poor were so angry at the general use of mantraps (and game-law prosecutions) that they were destroying partridge eggs in retaliation.[89]

Furthermore, experienced poachers often became adept at spotting and avoiding such contraptions, sometimes even reversing them. In 1795 the gamekeeper to a Norfolk nobleman set a mantrap for a suspected poacher without realising that, as he did so, his quarry was observing him. When he left, the poacher moved the trap so that it covered a path frequently taken by the keeper. Just before daylight the next morning, the keeper was heard calling out for help and was "found personating his intended visitor in the trap."[90]

Even so, spring guns and mantraps had their supporters until well into the early nineteenth century among men who thought that they were the "only means of opposing the attacks of those freebooters who take their midnight perambulations in quest of pheasants."[91] It was also argued that local men, poaching alone, and taking animals for their family pot, usually knew where they were situated.[92] They were primarily a deterrent to gangs of commercial poachers, often operating at night, and coming from "out of area." Ultimately an act of 1827 made it illegal to set mantraps, spring guns, and other engines calculated to destroy human life or inflict grievous bodily harm outside a dwelling-house.

89. *Morning Post and Daily Advertiser*, 10 September 1791.
90. *Norfolk Chronicle*, 31 August 1795.
91. *Norfolk Chronicle*, 8 December 1781.
92. P. B. Munsche, *Gentlemen and Poachers—The English Game Laws 1671–1831*, 1981, p. 75.

CHAPTER 24

Protest Crime

Introduction

As in most parts of eighteenth-century England, a significant stratum of East Anglian society, at least the bottom third of the population, lived a highly marginal, often hand-to-mouth existence of acute poverty. This group was extremely vulnerable to economic pressure, whether manifest in rises in grain prices, increased levels of unemployment, or a depression in wage levels. Even in good times they depended on long hours of hard work to secure a basic level of subsistence. In bad times their lives could easily be viewed as intolerable. Their attitude towards their "betters" varied. Nevertheless, an undercurrent of sullen resentment appears to have been an almost steady state amongst both rural and urban poor in East Anglia, albeit usually qualified by a resigned acceptance of the status quo and manifest in little more than grumbling.

Most poor people in Norfolk and Suffolk, as in the rest of England, were entirely disenfranchised, despite their large numbers. They had almost no political means of registering their grievances, and very few that were legal, although peaceful demonstrations might (sometimes) fall into the latter category. For example, during the harsh year of 1766 it was noted that a group of labouring people had assembled at Melford, in Suffolk, and then gone to villages and farms in the neighbourhood complaining about the "dearness of provisions and declared they would not work unless the price of necessaries of life were lessened or the wages heightened to 16 pence a day instead of one shilling." They subsequently dispersed without trouble.[1]

Nevertheless, such resentment did not always express itself in a peaceful or lawful manner. The poor sometimes had recourse to various extra-legal forms of protest when times were particularly bad or issues especially vexing. There were regular, if isolated, attacks on the property of those members of the "establishment" who had offended individuals or local groups, whether as employers, justices of the peace, clergymen (the last two sometimes overlapping in the latter part of the century), or in some other capacity.

This chapter will deal with various forms of localised criminal damage that were not done for gain but motivated by grievances, whether political or personal. Most commonly they were manifest in cases of incendiarism, animal maiming, and malicious damage to trees, crops, fences or other property. It will also consider the poison-pen letters that often threatened these attacks. Unpopular farmers or other establishment figures might see their ricks or barns burnt, cows and horses hamstrung or killed (but not stolen), plantations cut down, and wheat trampled; they might receive anonymous threatening correspondence from people whose ire they had excited. The perpetrators of these crimes tended to be disproportionately drawn from males in their late teens and early twenties, if only because they had less to lose, although some older men and not a few women became involved. Such individuals normally carried out their crimes at night, for obvious reasons.[2]

Arson

Incendiarism was an important form of protest crime. It usually brought no material benefits to its perpetrators, although it gave them personal satisfaction. Most cases of arson were motivated by grievances, whether personal, political, or both. However, there were a few exceptions to this general rule. For example, in 1735 Richard Prince was capitally convicted

1. *Norfolk Chronicle*, 4 October 1766.
2. C. J. Griffin, "'Cut Down by Some Cowardly Miscreants': Plant Maiming, Or the Malicious Cutting of Plants as an Act of Protest in Eighteenth and Nineteenth-century Rural England," 2008, pp. 29–54.

at the Lent Assizes for Norfolk of burning down the dwelling-house of Thomas Post; he was subsequently reprieved.[3] Prince had worked for Post, stolen from his house, and then fired the building to cover the crime.[4] Sarah Lloyd did the same thing in 1800. In 1779 William Spalding set light to his own home in Hartest, Suffolk, as part of an attempted insurance fraud (the building was covered for £100).[5]

Where revenge *was* a motive for arson, it was sometimes based on very personal factors. Thus, in early 1791 Mary Adams set fire to outbuildings belonging to a farmer named Burgess from Bawburgh, in Norfolk. She was a former servant there, and had herself gone by the "alias Burgess," suggesting some kind of publicly acknowledged relationship with her erstwhile employer.[6] Adams had been discharged by the farmer in acrimonious circumstances some three weeks earlier, and had subsequently been overheard threatening reprisals. She lit multiple fires on his premises with a flint and striker, so that hayricks, a pigsty, stables, and several barns all burned to the ground. Six valuable horses, along with assorted pigs, cows, and poultry, perished in the blaze.[7] (Adams was executed, her apparent status as a bigamist not helping her cause).[8] Similar factors may have lain behind Debora Harris's crime in 1728. She was capitally convicted in Norwich of setting fire to a man's dwelling-house.[9]

Nevertheless, incendiarism was often prompted by wider grievances. In the first third of the nineteenth century it was to become particularly prominent as a form of protest in rural East Anglia. There were major outbreaks in 1815–1817, 1822, 1825, 1829–1833, and 1835–1837. However, it was not a new phenomenon, even then. It had its roots far back in the previous century, although it was less common than it became in the 1800s, especially after 1830, when the advent of lucifer matches made

3. TNA ASSI 33/1.
4. *Country Journal or The Craftsman*, 29 March 1735.
5. *Ipswich Journal*, 25 March 1780.
6. *Whitehall Evening Post (1770)*, 26–29 March 1791.
7. *Morning Chronicle*, 3 January 1791; *Evening Mail*, 13–15 April 1791.
8. *Evening Mail*, 13–15 April 1791.
9. *Country Journal Or The Craftsman*, 24 August 1728.

it much easier to start fires than had previously been the case using a tinderbox.[10]

For example, in 1781 James Grice was left for execution after being capitally convicted of burning down a barn in Norfolk that contained a "great quantity of corn."[11] Late one Saturday evening the following year, a major fire destroyed another large barn at Worlington, in Suffolk. Had it not been for the intervention of passersby, it would probably have spread to the adjacent dwelling-house, with possible loss of life. There was little doubt that it had been deliberately started.[12] In 1785 Mary Collins was committed to Bury Gaol accused of setting fire to a barley stack at Brundish, in Suffolk.[13] In 1790 a magistrate committed Sarah Allen and Ann Flower to the bridewell for setting fire to the workhouse at Lawshall, in Suffolk, in what was clearly a political 'statement'.[14]

The loss occasioned by arson could be enormous. The blaze at Worlington caused damage estimated at £600, with many cows being killed in the fire.[15] When Thomas Sutton was capitally convicted at the Thetford Assizes in 1808 for burning a barn full of barley and a rick belonging to Major General Money of Trowse Newton the value lost was placed at £700.[16]

It is apparent that, although the actual perpetrators of such crimes might be few in number, they sometimes attracted much more widespread support, and were not lightly given up to the authorities. In 1800 a huge fire broke out at Boy's Hall in Halstead, in Essex, just over the Suffolk border. It began in a large barn filled with crops and spread to haystacks, causing hundreds of pounds' worth of damage. There was apparently every reason to believe that arson was committed, using gunpowder as an accelerant. Two troops of cavalry were sent to assist, as the "poorer inhabitants were very remiss in affording help where the

10. D. Jones, "Thomas Campbell Foster and the Rural Labourer: Incendiarism in East Anglia in the 1840s," 1976, pp. 5–43.
11. *Norfolk Chronicle*, 28 April 1781.
12. *Norfolk Chronicle*, 3 August 1782.
13. *Ipswich Journal*, 1 August 1785.
14. *Bury and Norwich Post*, 2 June 1790.
15. *Norfolk Chronicle*, 3 August 1782.
16. *The Bury and Norwich Post: Or, Suffolk, Norfolk, Essex, and Cambridge Advertiser*, 30 March 1808.

exigency of the circumstances demanded."[17] Not only was the owner of the farm hated enough by someone to have been the victim of arson, but the local poor appear to have approved of his treatment and been blatant about their views. Very likely the perpetrator(s) came from within their community.

Securing convictions in arson cases was difficult. It was often hard to be sure whether a fire had started by accident or been caused deliberately, making identifying suspects almost impossible. Even if they could be found, it might be difficult to prove a case against them. For example, one winter afternoon in 1784 a fire broke out in the warehouse of a yarn manufacturer at Glemsford, in Suffolk. It was thought to have been arson, and a person was arrested on suspicion of the crime. Even so, he was subsequently discharged.[18] In Suffolk just five people were capitally convicted for as many cases of arson between the start of 1732 and the end of 1800 (four years are missing from this period), and two of these had combined their incendiarism with conventional crimes such as stealing from a dwelling-house.[19]

It might be expected that the few individuals who were convicted would face draconian punishment, reflecting both the gravity of the crime and the difficulty of proving it in court. This was certainly the case in some parts of the country. Between 1670 and 1729 69 per cent of men (eleven out of 16 cases) convicted of incendiarism on the Western Circuit were hanged (women there fared a little better).[20] In Cheshire between 1760 and 1830 both convictions for arson resulted in executions.[21]

However, in East Anglia there appears to have been a slightly greater chance of mercy. Of the five people capitally convicted of arson in Suffolk during the last 68 years of the era, two escaped the gallows, although one of them, a 13-year-old girl who was convicted at the Bury Assizes in 1735, had extreme youth on her side. She had set fire to a barn, and the

17. *Bury and Norwich*, 22 October 1800.
18. *Ipswich Journal*, 4 December 1784.
19. P. Wright, *Death Recorded: Capital Punishment In Suffolk 1732–1900*, 2006, in appendix.
20. M. Eder, *"At the Instigation of the Devil": Capital Punishment and the Assize in the Early Modern England, 1670–1730*, 2014, p. 63.
21. J. Walliss, "Crime and Justice in Georgian Cheshire; The Chester Court of Great Sessions, 1760–1830," 2015, p. 54.

flames spread to an adjacent mansion, which burned down.[22] Interestingly, two of the three people who were hanged for the crime in Suffolk were female. Amongst them was Ann Catchpole, who was executed at Ipswich in 1771 for setting fire to her master's straw stack.[23] In Norfolk two people were executed for arson during the same period. John Sherwood, a youth of about 17, who was hanged in 1768, had also been convicted of horse theft. After taking a colt from a farmer in Carbrook, he had set fire to the stables, killing another horse and endangering the main house.[24] Mary Adams (previously discussed) was executed in 1791. Shortly after the period, Thomas Sutton (see above) was hanged following the Thetford Assizes in 1808. Correctly anticipating death for such a heinous case of arson, he behaved in a "most audacious manner" towards the judge.[25]

Animal Maiming

Animal maiming or killing was another periodic feature of the time, especially in rural areas. If conducted with malice against the owner of the creature (rather than the animal itself) it was, in theory, a capital felony under the 1723 Black Act.[26] However, like arson, by no means all such cases were carried out on an inter-class basis. Although some were a form of political or social protest, others were motivated by personal factors.

It was fairly difficult to steal large animals successfully, especially horses and cattle, but comparatively easy to wound them, something that caused both inconvenience and considerable expense to their owners. Although hamstringing was popularly associated with this form of crime, many animals were simply stabbed (not necessarily fatally) or, in the case of sheep, had their throats cut. Less seriously, in August 1746 16 people were fined three shillings and fourpence each at Bury, after they admitted riotously assembling while armed and "beating and illusing the cattle of Richard Newton."[27] A few cases appear to manifest a macabre and

22. *Read's Weekly Journal Or British Gazetteer*, 16 August 1735.
23. *Bingley's Journal Or Universal Gazette (1771)*, 30 March – 6 April 1771.
24. *Public Advertiser*, 26 April 1768; *Gazetteer and New Daily Advertiser*, 3 August 1768.
25. *The Bury and Norwich Post: Or, Suffolk, Norfolk, Essex, and Cambridge Advertiser*, 30 March 1808.
26. L. Radzinowicz, "The Waltham Black Act: A Study of the Legislative Attitude Towards Crime in the Eighteenth Century," 1945, p. 66.
27. Gray's Inn MS 45.

cruel sense of humour. In 1784, it was noted that a group of "villains" who had frequently stolen poultry and cheese from a farmer at Stutton in Suffolk, had the "barbarity to fasten his cows tails together in such a manner that some of their tails were torn off by struggling to separate."[28]

A selection of cases from the region is indicative of more typical forms of the crime. Poison featured quite regularly, as did the use of a bladed weapon. In 1762 26 hounds belonging to William Moseley of Fornham All Saints in Suffolk died suddenly, so that there was "great reason to believe all were poisoned by some wicked person or persons." (Moseley offered a reward of 20 guineas for their identification).[29] At the Bury Assizes in March 1779, Isaac Stapleton was acquitted of maliciously wounding four horses valued at £27 belonging to Solomon Boggis. (Generous prosecution costs of over £5 were allowed to Boggis).[30] In October 1800 some "evil disposed person or persons" poisoned several pointers and spaniels at a parsonage in Hartest.[31] In March the following year, William Pooley was committed to Ipswich gaol, "charged with stabbing and maiming a mare."[32] One night in June 1808 a Suffolk man "cruelly cut out the tongue of a fine horse the property of James Filewood of Sible Hedingham."[33] The same thing happened to a horse in Melford (in Suffolk) two months later.[34]

How frequently animal maiming occurred is difficult to assess. Many cases almost certainly went unreported, and the prosecution rate was correspondingly low. Information is sparse for the 1700s. However, in the following century just 89 cases were recorded in Norfolk and 68 in Suffolk (some involved several animals) between 1830 and 1870. Nevertheless, in 1834 it became such a problem in the Fakenham area of Norfolk that a meeting was called to form an association to insure members against the killing or maiming of their horses and cattle.[35]

---

28. *Ipswich Journal*, 13 November 1784.
29. *Ipswich Journal*, 1 January 1763.
30. TNA ASSI 33/6.
31. *Bury and Norwich Post*, 10 October 1800.
32. *The Bury and Norwich Post: Or, Suffolk, Norfolk, Essex, and Cambridge Advertiser*. 1 April 1801.
33. *Bury and Norwich Post*, 15 June 1808.
34. *Bury and Norwich Post*, 17 August 1808.
35. J. E. Archer, *"A Fiendish Outrage"? A Study of Animal Maiming in East Anglia: 1830-1870*, 1985, pp. 148–149.

Criminal Damage

Criminal damage to inanimate objects was another regularly employed form of protest, although hedge, plant, and tree cutting and destruction have often been neglected as fields of study, unlike incendiarism and animal maiming. In certain circumstances they were capital offences, albeit almost (but not quite) always reprieved. In some respects, they could be more damaging than arson, as it was usually harder to insure against such losses. They could also be difficult to detect while being committed. Unlike cases of incendiarism, the attention of the victim and his neighbours was not necessarily drawn to the scene of a crime shortly after it occurred, while injured flora, unlike fauna, could not squeal in pain, alerting local people. Targeted trees were often located in outlying areas, well away from houses and farmyards.[36]

Some such attacks were small scale. At the Bury Assizes in July 1751, four men were tried and acquitted of destroying Edward Browne's hedges and fences. One of them, Edmund Nunn, was also acquitted of assaulting John Browne, a charge presumably connected to the incident.[37] Other cases involved larger groups. At the Suffolk Quarter Sessions in 1788, eight men were tried for rioting near Hadleigh. They were part of a group led by John Naven that had cut down fences and trees belonging to the Reverend Talbot. Naven was convicted, fined 20 guineas, and sentenced to three months in prison.[38]

Threatening Letters

Those of the poor who were literate, or who had access to people who could read and write, might send anonymous but highly threatening letters to men they resented. Again, this was probably a much under-reported crime. In 1762 Isaac Boggis, from Colchester in neighbouring (to Suffolk) Essex, found a letter pushed under his door warning of the

36. C. J. Griffin, 2008, "'Cut Down by Some Cowardly Miscreants': Plant Maiming, Or the Malicious Cutting of Plants as an Act of Protest in Eighteenth and Nineteenth-century rural England," pp. 36–37.
37. TNA ASSI 33/2.
38. *Bury and Norwich Post*, 9 April 1788.

consequences of introducing machinery that would threaten employment, and warning him that the writer would "blow your brains out if ever you consent to have a rowing mill, I have a great family and before I see them want I will be dammed if I don't blow you and your house and your family to hell for no more than the truth."[39] Similarly, at the Bury Assizes in March 1797, a Suffolk labourer named Charles Peak was accused of sending letters threatening to kill John Amyas but acquitted at trial.[40] Such letters were common enough for the Harleston Association for Prosecuting Felons to list them in 1799 as one of the crimes for which they would fund a prosecution.[41]

Protest crimes rarely involved more than small groups of perpetrators. However, during periods of acute stress, popular resentment could manifest itself in major outbreaks of riot and disorder, the subject of the next chapter.

39. *Ipswich Journal*, 10 April 1762.
40. TNA ASSI 33/8.
41. Anon, *Rules and Regulations, Entered Into by the Members of the Harleston Association For Prosecuting Felons*, 1799, pp. 1–14.

CHAPTER 25

Riots and Disturbances

Introduction

The eighteenth century witnessed hundreds, if not thousands, of popular disturbances. Arguably, "collective bargaining by riot" served as an extra-legal channel by which poor people could make their grievances known to local or national government. Sometimes almost choreographed warnings were given to those who were perceived to be violating community norms before more drastic mob action was taken, as occurred at Great Tey, in Essex, in 1727, when a landholder in the village decided to plough and plant (rather than graze) a field that had always previously been used for communal activities.[1] At other times, they were more spontaneous.

Riots were ascribed a degree of legitimacy by the authorities, if only tacitly. Their perpetrators would often have their complaints listened to, and acted on, at least to some degree. Local officials would be forced to engage in a difficult balancing act, trying to uphold the law while yielding on some issues, aware that simple coercion was not a realistic option. This sometimes required a considerable degree of sangfroid. In 1756 John Hewitt, an alderman and justice for Coventry, was faced by a crowd of angry colliers complaining about the price of bread. Determined not to let them think he was frightened, he invited them into his front parlour, and assured them that he would publish the laws against manipulating grain prices, but at the same time was careful to avoid making promises

1. J. Pearson, "Threshing Out the Common in Community: The Great Tey Riot of 1727," 1998, p. 50.

that could not be kept.[2] Another aspect of this balancing act was that the consequences for most of those involved in serious disturbances were relatively modest, even where considerable damage had been caused. Unfortunately, this was often qualified by a draconian deterrent example being made of a few selected individuals.

The Riot Act

The Riot Act of 1715 (1 Geo I, St 2, c 5), which came into force in August of that year, having passed swiftly through Parliament in just three weeks, was an important weapon in the eighteenth-century arsenal of riot-control measures, and bears examination, as it was regularly used in East Anglia. It had been introduced after a series of major disturbances, including the Sacheverell Riots of 1710 and the Coronation Riots of 1714. It authorised certain local officials, such as JPs, mayors, and sheriffs, to declare any group of 12 or more people to be unlawfully assembled and to order them to disperse immediately. Anyone who failed to do so within an hour of its delivery was, in theory, guilty of an unclergyable felony. The warning had to be read out to the crowd, and had to follow the precise wording contained in the statute. Reading the requisite words could be very difficult during a fluid disturbance.

The Riot Act did not prejudice the power of the authorities to use force to stop a violent riot before the hour was over; it created a new (if rarely prosecuted) offence of failing to disperse. There was considerable debate as to the amount of force that could properly be used on those who failed to do so after the requisite hour. However, the act stated that if rioters were killed, maimed, or hurt while being dispersed, those who had wounded them would be exempt from suit, perhaps encouraging a robust interpretation.

Reading the Riot Act could be quite effective when dealing with low-to medium-level disturbances. For example, in November 1733 two parliamentary candidates for Norfolk entered Yarmouth accompanied by 50 carriages and 400 horsemen. As members of the "court party" they were

2. J. Hewitt, *A Journal of the Proceedings of J. Hewitt*, 1790, p. 3.

associated with the acutely unpopular new excise regime. Local people mobbed them in an "outrageous" manner for several hours, shouting abuse, throwing dirt, and breaking the windows of several carriages. Eventually the town clerk, accompanied by a local JP, read the proclamation, upon which the crowd "immediately dispers'd."[3] In other situations, reading the act was entirely ineffectual. It seems that one of its most important functions was to act as a general alert to those engaged in protests that matters were deemed to be "serious" by the authorities and at risk of going "too far."

Causes

People rioted for many reasons during the era. The introduction of turnpikes, enclosure, excise duties, taxes, wage levels, and press gangs were among their grievances. Some of them were quite arcane. For example, in 1760 an attempt to raise the duty on beer, from five to eight shillings per barrel, which drove up the retail price of the beverage, sparked "tumults" in Norwich.[4]

Religion prompted the worst single outbreak of English disorder during the century, the metropolitan Gordon Riots of June 1780, which were initially motivated by the Relief Act of 1778 and its repeal of some anti-Catholic legislation. Religious disturbances were not entirely absent in East Anglia, although they occurred on a much smaller scale than in the capital. Some of the worst were linked to the presence of James Wheatley, an itinerant preacher, who launched a "crusade" in late 1751 to reform Norwich. (John Wesley had earlier expelled Wheatley from the Methodist movement.) Thousands apparently attended his lectures, and supporters claimed a "spirit of seriousness" was detectable in the city as a result, with greatly reduced levels of public cursing.

However, Wheatley's activities also prompted acute antagonism among local people, including members of the city's Hell Fire Club of wealthy libertines. These men gathered mobs armed with marrowbones and cleavers, provided their members with drink, and urged them to attack

3. *Grub Street Journal*, 6 December 1733.
4. A. Randall, *Riotous Assemblies: Popular Protest in Hanoverian England*, 2006, p. 53.

Wheatley's religious gatherings. A popular rallying cry was "Church and King, down with the meetings." The mobs would also shout and throw fireworks, dirt, and stones at those who attended them. Several people were injured, including Wheatley himself. The wooden meetinghouse that he built was destroyed. Wheatley's group appears to have felt that the city authorities were rather backward in taking action to suppress the trouble, although the Riot Act was sometimes read to those causing the disturbances.[5] Far from protecting his group, magistrates even entertained a charge that had been laid against Wheatley for preaching without being duly qualified.[6] The firebrand cleric's career eventually ended in a sexual scandal, and he moved away from the city, bringing the unrest to an end. There were much more modest disturbances occasioned by antagonism towards mainstream dissenters and non-conformism. For example, in August 1783, just after divine service was finished at a Methodist meeting house at Holt, in Norfolk, "a mob broke into it, pulled down the pulpit, and did considerable mischief there."[7]

Local politics could also be a source of popular unrest. A major riot that took place at Sudbury, in Suffolk, in November 1771 started as an electoral dispute. The conduct of the Sudbury Corporation had enraged local people who besieged its members in the town Moot Hall, holding them captive, without light or sustenance, until late in the evening, and threatening their lives until they agreed with the mob's demands.[8] Ultimately, a party of dragoons marched into the borough to assist the civil magistrates preserve order.

The introduction of workhouses, in place of out relief for the rural poor, became a cause of major disturbances in Suffolk during the 1760s. Such establishments were not a new phenomenon, especially in urban areas, dating back to the previous century. However, the Workhouses Act ("Knatchbull's Act") of 1723 (9 George I, c 7) gave them a new impetus. It authorised churchwardens, overseers of the poor, and vestries to construct workhouses and to offer accommodation in them as a mandatory

---

5. Anon, *A True and Particular Narrative of the Disturbances and Outrages That Have Been Committed in the City of Norwich,* 1752, p. 24.
6. *General Advertiser*, 3 December 1751.
7. *London Chronicle*, 23–26 August 1783.
8. *London Evening Post*, 2–5 November 1771.

alternative to out relief. It also allowed parishes e to combine as unions to set up workhouses. Nevertheless, in predominantly rural areas small-scale combinations were often not felt to be viable, and some parts of provincial England had little recourse to them during the century. East Anglia was something of an exception. In 1756 Admiral Edward Vernon and several other Suffolk gentlemen drew up an ambitious plan, centred on the union of the Carlford and Colneis hundreds, to establish a large workhouse at Nacton. It opened in March 1758.

According to one view, conditions in the new establishment were not particularly harsh. The food was plain but usually adequate, the working hours long but the tasks assigned to inmates not especially heavy. One local observer even thought that good order and "plenty without profusion" characterised the new institution. There were punishments for the idle and disorderly, but there were also rewards for the sober and industrious. Inmates enjoyed "as much liberty as that station ought to enjoy."[9]

However, liberty was the crucial issue. To the rural poor, the entire regime had a quasi-penal quality. As one (national) observer noted in 1738, whatever workhouses might be termed, they were, in effect, prisons, and their inmates were being punished for being poor.[10] In Suffolk this impression was not helped by (possibly exaggerated) reports that inmates could not go outside them in their leisure hours, whether to visit the local village or, if children, to play in adjoining fields. (One supporter likened the reality to the restricted freedom found in gentlemen's boarding schools.)[11]

Other observers also took a much harsher view of the conditions found in these establishments, and suggested that they often degenerated into places of "misery to the aged, and nurseries of vice to the young." Some were very large, drawing inmates from an extensive catchment area, requiring many poor people to go some distance from their homes to "pine among strangers."[12] When Parson Woodhouse visited the workhouse

9. *London Chronicle*, 23–25 February 1764.
10. T. Andrews, *An Enquiry Into the Causes of the Encrease and Miseries of the Poor of England*, 1738, pp. 7–9.
11. *Lloyd's Evening Post*, 20–23 September 1765.
12. T. Gisborne, *An Enquiry Into the Duties of Men in the Higher and Middle Classes of Society in Great Britain*, 1794, pp. 291–292.

near West Dereham in 1781, he observed that it had 380 poor inmates housed in a very large building who did not "look either healthy or cheerful." He also noted that 27 had died since the previous Christmas.[13] This state of affairs did not just trouble residents. Because many Englishmen were poor, and life was often precarious, large numbers of people were potentially vulnerable to a turn of fortune that might force them to seek relief, and oblige them to enter a workhouse.

Although only the Nacton House of Industry was fully complete in 1765, it had already been decided to extend the model to other hundreds in Suffolk, and work had started on further institutions. This occasioned great public concern, and threatening letters were sent to those involved in the scheme. A large mob eventually assembled to pull down the Nacton establishment. A passing gentleman encountered groups of 15 or 20 people on their way to the building. Most of them were poor, but they included several small farmers. Some had travelled a considerable distance to take part. They were armed with clubs and pitchforks, and freely declared that they intended to pull down the House of Industry, so that "the poor might be maintained in their several parishes as usual." The crowd eventually amounted to between 150 and 200 people. Local justices attempted to dissuade them and failed, after which the Riot Act was formally read and a small group of soldiers readied. During the very brief engagement that followed, an officer was knocked to the ground, and one of the rioters was stabbed (not fatally) in the side with a bayonet. The crowd then dispersed, with seven or eight being captured as they fled. Newspaper correspondents were struck by the involvement of several women in the disturbance.[14]

At the same time as the trouble at Nacton, a much larger mob of about 500 people attacked the partially completed House of The Poor at Bulcamp, which was intended for the indigent from the Blything hundred. Being unopposed, they razed the building to the ground.[15] The damage cost up to £2,000 to repair. Two labourers from Theberton, Daniel Manning and Benjamin Preston, along with James Strewger, a carter from

13. R. Porter, *English Society in the Eighteenth Century*, 1981, p. 148.
14. *Lloyd's Evening Post*, 20–23 September 1765.
15. Ibid.

Wenhaston, were subsequently detained for the attack at Bulcamp and taken to Ipswich gaol by a small group of cavalrymen.[16]

Although some Suffolk magistrates asked for a special commission to try the workhouse rioters immediately (as occurred after the disturbances at Norwich the following year), the government did not find this necessary, and they went for trial at the scheduled assizes in March 1766. Several people were convicted, but the punishments they received were notably light—very short custodial sentences and relatively small fines—albeit that they had been held in custody for six months prior to their trials.[17] Although these protests did not halt the schemes in progress, plans to adopt such a system in some other parts of East Anglia were abandoned for up to a decade.[18]

Threats to employment were another frequent cause of popular disorder during the era. In 1719 there were major disturbances in the streets of Norwich by weavers who were angered by the lack of trade, and alarmed at the growing fashion for wearing foreign calico, a cheap and cool substitute for wool. Anybody who was seen walking in public while wearing the cloth was mobbed.[19] These riots and attacks had originated in London, where there were disturbances in Spitalfields amid demands by the Weavers' Company for Parliament to pass an act forbidding the use of foreign plain calicos. (The import of printed calicos had been banned in 1700.)[20] It was claimed that the Norwich weavers had then acted after being "spirited by designing people" to follow the example set in the capital. There were reports of a body of weavers marching to London to support the disturbances there.[21] Initially, Norwich magistrates found it difficult to deal with the disturbances, but these were eventually suppressed by soldiers from the locally based artillery company, "several of the rioters receiving wounds in the Fray, and a great many sent prisoners to the castle, so that now they are perfectly quiet."[22]

16. *St. James's Chronicle Or the British Evening Post*, 17–20 August 1765.
17. *Public Advertiser*, 27 March 1766.
18. C. J. Griffin, *Protest, Politics and Work in Rural England, 1700–1850*, 2013, p. 27.
19. *Weekly Journal Or Saturday's Post*, 18 July 1719.
20. F. McLynn, *Crime and Punishment in Eighteenth-century England*, 1989, p. 220.
21. *Weekly Journal Or Saturday's Post*, 20 June 1719.
22. *Weekly Packet*, 4–11 July 1719.

East Anglia did not witness the major riots over balloting for the militia seen by Bedfordshire, Yorkshire, Gloucestershire, Surrey, and Lincolnshire, after the force was reformed in 1757. Nevertheless, each parish had to provide at least one fit man for the Suffolk or Norfolk militia. Volunteers were often not forthcoming, so villagers had to draw lots (certain men were exempt). Those who could afford to pay £20 or £30 to a substitute, or to subscribe to an insurance scheme in case they were chosen, were not too troubled if they drew the short straw. Of course, many could not do this, and several men absconded when selected. Among them was 22-year-old Robert Gibson, from Holt, in Norfolk, whose capture warranted a half-guinea reward in 1780.[23] Two years later, one guinea was offered for the arrest of 18-year-old Thomas Bullard, who disappeared after being chosen to serve in the Suffolk Militia for the parish of Frostenden.[24]

Concern about the issue prompted a minor popular disturbance at Fakenham in September 1757. A small mob seized the militia lists from the area's constables and marched to a tavern, where the local high constables had been waiting to receive them. However, local JPs, conveniently meeting at quarter sessions nearby, addressed the crowd, assuring them that they could not be forced to serve overseas if selected (a perennial concern). On being advised of this, most dispersed, the remainder leaving after the Riot Act was read to them. The militia lists were returned.[25]

Popular entertainments also regularly produced low-level disturbances. In 1753 it was noted that an unlawful fair that had been held in the parish of Somersham, Suffolk, for several years, had been the occasion for "great riots and disorders." The authorities banned it, and warned that anyone who tried to hold such a fair there in future would be prosecuted.[26] Even the official response to minor pilfering could occasion trouble. In December 1720 there was a major "uproar" in Norwich, after a group of constables went to a street outside the city gates to arrest some people for stealing wood and turnips from Sir Lambert Blackwell's land. At

23. *Norfolk Chronicle,* 15 April 1780.
24. *Ipswich Journal,* 2 November 1782.
25. P. Muskett, *Riotous Assemblies: Popular Disturbances in East Anglia, 1740–1822,* 1984, p. 12.
26. *Ipswich Journal,* 8 May 1753.

this, the "mob rose and abus'd the constables, and would not suffer 'em to seize the offenders." They began to commit various acts of disorder.

The disturbance prompted the city sheriffs to use their power to raise a "posse" to suppress it. This was the normal abbreviation after the mid-seventeenth century for the *posse comitatus* ("power of the county"), a group of citizens officially assembled to deal with an emergency. When these men arrived at the scene they were met with a shower of stones. A woman armed with a penknife even stabbed one of the sheriff's men. The "proclamation," i.e., the Riot Act (see above) was then read, but to no effect. The disturbance was quelled only by the arrival of artillery-men from the nearby garrison. Three or four rioters were then arrested.[27]

Food Riots

Food, bread, flour, or grain riots—the terminology depended on circumstances—made up the great majority of serious popular disturbances during the eighteenth century, especially in the eastern counties. As such, they are deserving of special consideration.[28] Nevertheless, as with many of the riots already discussed, it is necessary to be careful when ascribing a single cause to such disturbances. They were often multifaceted events, and cannot readily be explained by simple models. Many fed on long-standing grievances and popular resentment caused by numerous issues, such as low wages and the scarcity of employment, not just the price of flour and bread, even though this was usually the catalyst. As one observer noted, normally "every rioter had a motive of his own, relative to himself."[29] Ultimately, general poverty and a sense of political powerlessness lay behind many, if not most, popular disturbances.

The purchase of food consumed at least half an average family budget during the eighteenth century. At the very bottom of the social scale the proportion was often much higher. As in most previous ages, bread was the staple food for ordinary people. The poorer the individual was, the greater his dependence on a cereal-based diet. It has been estimated

27. *Weekly Journal Or British Gazetteer*, 24 December 1720.
28. A. Randall, *Riotous Assemblies: Popular Protest in Hanoverian England*, 2006, p. 2.
29. A. Ramsay, *Observations Upon the Riot Act, With an Attempt Towards the Amendment of It. By a Dilettante in Law and Politics*, 1781, p. 2.

that, in late eighteenth-century Berkshire, an agricultural labourer with five children sometimes spent two thirds of his income on flour alone.[30] (Potatoes were grown but they were much less important than in Ireland.) This was especially true in the eastern and southern counties of England. Although small amounts of fish, cheese, eggs, green vegetables, and meat (particularly bacon) supplemented their diet, the price of bread was always crucial to the survival of those on low incomes. Indicative of this, in the exceptionally difficult year of 1795, the poor from 17 parishes in the vicinity of Hadleigh, in Suffolk, complained to the directors of the local House of Industry about their "miserable situation." A bushel of wheat cost 4s, more than most men earned in a week, and a labourer: "probably has five or six children to maintain."[31]

In East Anglia bread was usually made from wheat rather than barley flour, especially in the second half of the century, although the latter (and cheaper) cereal was still sometimes used, even in the 1790s. In January 1796 it was one of the grievances of labourers around Stowmarket, in Suffolk, that they were forced to eat brown barley bread rather than wheaten loaves. They paraded the streets of the town carrying pieces of the offending bread on sticks, declaring that they would not eat it while there was better available.[32]

Although a vital commodity, the price of bread was not stable. It was, of course, dependent on the cost of grain, which could fluctuate enormously during the 1700s. Frequently it more than doubled, and sometimes even trebled, between periods of dearth and glut. For example, the price of wheat sold at Windsor was at its lowest for the century in 1743, when it dropped to 2 shillings and eleven pence a bushel. In both 1706 and 1732 it was only slightly higher, just three shillings and three pence. It peaked at the end of the century, when it reached the quite enormous sum of 16 shillings in 1800. However, it had been eleven shillings and sixpence in 1709 and the same price in 1795 (its second-highest price during the era).[33] Despite these fluctuations, there was a general upward trend in the average price of grain during the latter decades of

30. R. Wells, *Wretched Faces: Famine in Wartime England 1793–1801*, 2011, p. 17.
31. *Courier and Evening Gazette*, 17 October 1795.
32. P. Muskett, *Riotous Assemblies: Popular Disturbances in East Anglia, 1740–1822,* 1984, p. 37.
33. J. Stevenson, *Popular Disturbances in England, 1700–1870*, 1979, p. 92.

the century, something that was partly linked to England moving from net exporter to net importer of the commodity. Thus the average price for wheat was 34 shillings and eleven pence per quarter-hundredweight between 1713 and 1764 but 55 shillings for the same amount in the final third of the century.

Short-term variation in the price of grain occurred for a variety of reasons, most of which were related to the abundance of previous harvests, which in turn were usually linked to the effects of weather. In 1780 it was noted that a recent rise in the price of wheat could readily be explained. A reduced quantity of corn had been planted, as low prices at the start of 1779 had encouraged farmers to diversify into other crops. There had also been continuous heavy rains when crops were being sown, alternate bouts of severe frost and rain after sowing, and one of the driest summers on record.[34] By contrast, "plenty" quickly reduced grain prices. In some (not all) parts of Norfolk, in the otherwise very difficult year of 1795 "all the crops proved highly successful so that a considerable reduction of the price of corn is expected."[35]

A willingness to allow imports of the staple from abroad during times of hardship, and the ability to source such grain, could also make an important difference to domestic prices. In May 1801 wheat fell by up to 20s a quarter on the London market, as a result of a "great influx of foreign corn."[36] Importation might be very difficult during wartime, but was not impossible, even then. For example, despite the conflict with France, in October 1782, notice was sent to grain merchants in Ostend that the port of London had been "opened for the importation of foreign wheat, etc., in order that they might make it known to the captains of neutral vessels."[37]

Even more important, a willingness to ban English corn exports to foreign countries could help keep domestic prices down. In normal times some East Anglian grain was sent to Europe, especially the Netherlands, where there was a major international market for the foodstuff. Even in the 1720s Daniel Defoe, visiting the cereal-producing country around

34. *Norfolk Chronicle*, 11 November 1780.
35. Ibid., 31 August 1795.
36. *Bury and Norwich Post*, 13 May 1801.
37. *Norfolk Chronicle*, 28 December 1782.

Ipswich, had observed "sometimes they load corn here for Holland, especially if the market abroad is encouraging."[38] In 1755 it was noted that "prodigious quantities" of corn had been carried from all over eastern and central England to King's Lynn and shipped to the Netherlands.[39] The consequences of internationalisation can be seen in a petition to the Privy Council sent by John Patteson, the mayor of Norwich, which was considered on 24 September 1766. Patteson asked for an end to the export of large amounts of grain to Europe, much of it through East Anglian ports. He noted that foreign demand was being driven up by harvest failure on the Continent, especially in Italy, Catalonia and the Greek-inhabited parts of Turkey.

Typically, Parliament introduced a ban in December 1739, in the light of poor harvests, but prematurely lifted it in 1740, possibly as a result of pressure from corn merchants. The ban was reintroduced later the same year, after serious disturbances.[40] Such embargos were implemented quite strictly. At the start of December 1740, it was noted that although three small vessels had recently sailed from Ipswich to Holland carrying grain (beating the reintroduced ban), a fourth, which was ready to sail, had been stopped by the reimposed embargo late one Friday night.[41] In the same year a coastal vessel bound from Wisbech to Calais was seized while at sea and found to contain 1,400 quarterns of barley, apparently being exported in violation of the embargo. It was escorted to the Port of London, "sufficient proof having been made that said barley was design'd for sale in foreign parts."[42]

However, the biggest drain on local grain supplies in East Anglia was not Holland but the Metropolis. As Defoe noted of the corn produced around Ipswich in the 1720s, a "very great quantity is continually shipped off for London." The ease of access to the ever-growing capital provided by improved roads greatly facilitated this. According to Arthur Young, writing in 1769, "all sensible people attributed the dearness of

38. D. Defoe, *A Tour Through the Whole Island of Great Britain*, 1978, p. 71.
39. *Read's Weekly Journal Or British Gazetteer*, 23 August 1755.
40. R. Markless, *Gender, Crime and Discretion in Yorkshire, 1735–1775*, 2013, p. 287.
41. *Ipswich Journal*, 6 December 1740.
42. *Common Sense Or The Englishman's Journal*, 2 August 1740.

their country to the turnpike roads."[43] The government's recognition that bread riots in the Metropolis would be politically disastrous further exacerbated the problem.

A number of long-standing statutory and common-law offences existed to combat speculation and profiteering in basic commodities, especially grain. The most important of these was forestalling—buying up commodities before they came to market, usually by intercepting sellers and purchasing their stock, then taking it on to market and selling at a higher price. This was an ancient common-law crime, heavily reinforced by statute in 1552. However, there were other forms of speculation that were also subject to criminal sanctions, such as regrating and engrossing. The former entailed the buying of corn in a market and selling it again within four miles. As successive sellers had to make a profit, this necessarily drove up prices. The latter offence entailed acquiring large quantities of corn with the intention of selling it again. This allowed small groups to artificially raise the price of provisions. Such crimes were usually dealt with by fiscal penalties for a first offence, but those convicted for a third time could sometimes be pilloried and imprisoned.[44]

Because East Anglia was not an especially wealthy region, local stocks of grain were quickly affected by the higher prices that could readily be obtained in the capital during shortages. In 1800 even Lord Chief Justice Kenyon acknowledged that it had been claimed that if practices such as regrating were deemed to be criminal, the "metropolis would be starved, as it could not be supplied by any other means." Unfortunately, wage levels remained relatively stable in times of dearth and expensive bread, despite occasional attempts to link the two. For example, JPs at the Bury Quarter Sessions in 1795 unavailingly asked their county MPs to bring in a parliamentary bill to regulate the price of labour, so that it fluctuated with that of corn.[45] As a result, whenever prices rose sharply, subsistence became difficult for the poor of the region.

---

43. S. Renton, "The Moral Economy of the English Middling Sort in the Eighteenth-century: The Case of Norwich in 1766 and 1767," 1996, p. 120.
44. J. Gonson, *The Charge of Sir John Gonson Knt. to the Grand Jury of the Royalty of the Tower of London, and Liberties and Precincts Thereof*, 1728, p. 10 and p. 123.
45. *Courier and Evening Gazette*, 17 October 1795.

The history of bread riots in East Anglia went back centuries. During the years from 1527 to 1529 three consecutive poor harvests led the mayor of Norwich to note that there was "so great scarceness of corne that aboute Christmas the comons of the cyttye were ready to rise upon the ryche men." There had also been major grain riots in 1629. Nevertheless, the eighteenth century saw some of the most serious disturbances. Such riots lingered into the nineteenth century, only fully petering out in the 1840s after the repeal of the Corn Laws.

Although it has sometimes been claimed that the notion of a "feminine food riot" is largely a myth, and that women normally joined rather than initiated such disturbances, it is apparent that they featured prominently in many East Anglian disturbances, especially those local to their homes. Sometimes their presence may have served as a shield, encouraging restraint on the part of both the authorities and the crowd itself.[46] For example, in 1800 it was reported that a farmer at Ipswich market, who had refused the apparently reasonable price of £3 10 shillings for each coomb (four bushels) of his wheat, was subjected to popular haranguing, much of it female. A group of women lined the side of a street through which he had to pass and "assailed him with a volley of abuse, happily no other weapons were used and the tumult subsided."[47]

It is now well-appreciated that such riots were not simple outbreaks of mob disorder, although they inevitably attracted some straightforward hooliganism. Theft was often frowned upon by those involved, and even actively prevented, especially before the 1800s. Indicative of this, it was reported that some of the Bury rioters of 1772 threatened, "to hang any of their own party who should steal anything."[48] Similarly, the targets of their destruction were often carefully selected. In 1767 Lord Chief Justice Wilmot recognised this in the context of a Norfolk disturbance, noting that crowds rarely burnt down houses because "[c]onflagration affects friends and enemies alike; and therefore pulling down houses, when mobs go beyond breaking of windows, is the common mode of

46. N. Rogers, *Crowds, Culture and Politics in Georgian Britain,* 1998, pp. 230–231.
47. *Bury and Norwich Post*, 10 September 1800.
48. *London Evening Post*, 16–18 April 1772.

expressing their resentment."[49] However, it is also clear that some riots were more disciplined than others, this being, perhaps, a reflection of the quality of local leadership.

Rioters were normally possessed of a sense of justified grievance, and appealed to what they viewed as the "traditional" order of society. Their aim was usually to see food prices returned to what they had been in "normal" years. Frequently vendors would be forced to sell at this price during disturbances, rather than having their grain seized outright, in instances of *taxation populaire*. Disturbances were legitimised by a popular belief in what has been termed a paternalist "moral economy." This has often been contrasted to the emerging market economy. The former was characterised by traditional values, while the latter reflected the unfettered political economy associated with Adam Smith type liberalism.[50] In more concrete terms, those involved in food riots usually manifested antipathy towards men who they believed were using their power over the market during times of shortage to maximise their profits at the expense of consumers. They sought unadulterated food, sold in honest measures, at a reasonable price.

Belief in such a moral economy was certainly not confined to the poor. Most members of the middling and upper social orders accepted, however grudgingly, the legitimacy of popular demands. In 1765 a newspaper correspondent observed that the abandoned lives and "irreligious conduct of the poor, require but little to be said in their favour but if they cannot have bread for about one penny per pound, and mild beer for three halfpence a full pint, they have great reason to complain."[51] In the first half of the eighteenth century, and to a declining extent during the ensuing 50 years, it was widely accepted that society and its economic activity should be arranged so that the most basic needs of the poor were met (the notion did not extend to any luxuries), as the "honest, laborious

49. *John Drinkwater, Esq. v The Royal Exchange Assurance Company* 1 January 1767 (1767) Wilmot 282, 97 E.R. 109.
50. See generally, E. P. Thompson, "The Moral Economy of the English Crowd in the Eighteenth Century," 1971, pp. 76–136.
51. *St. James's Chronicle Or the British Evening Post*, 5–7 September 1765.

and industrious, man is entitled to the necessaries and enjoyments of life, proportioned to the relative situation in which he is placed."[52]

Until the mid-eighteenth century there was little dispute as to why it was necessary to enforce the moral economy. It was not purely a matter of Christian decency, although this came into the equation. It was recognised that exorbitant grain prices created "uneasiness, discontent, and murmuring, especially among the lower sort of people." In the difficult year of 1740, Edward Chandler, the Lord Bishop and *custos rotulorum* of the County Palatine of Durham, addressed the 18-man quarter-sessions grand jury for that city about the need to refrain from engrossing corn and grain. He stressed both practical and moral considerations. At times of public scarcity and distress such activity not only offended God but also encouraged the people to "commit mad and violent actions in return." As a result, it was wrong to value the private gain of a few traders above the lives of thousands of labourers and their families. Chandler urged that the 1552 Act setting out the regulatory regime for grain be strictly enforced.[53]

The need for honest measures explains why bakers who sold underweight loaves were regularly prosecuted, either summarily or at quarter sessions. It was vital for social harmony that such practices were dealt with firmly. For example, at the King's Lynn Sessions held on 15 April 1738, Elizabeth Gulstrop was fined 40 shillings for "selling bread contrary to the Assize." (Most of the fine was later remitted.)[54] In this context, the "Assize" referred to the "Assizes of bread" that set standard weights and measurements for loaves. Similarly, 70 years later, three Essex bakers were summarily convicted of the same crime, and ordered to pay two shillings and sixpence for each ounce by which one of their loaves had been deficient. This amounted to a significant sum of money. One of them had sold 29 loaves that were, together, 91 ounces underweight.[55]

52. H. Jodrell, *A Charge Delivered to the Grand Jury of Norfolk, at the General Quarter Sessions Held on Wednesday, Jan. 16, 1793*, 1793, p. 10.
53. E. Chandler, "A Charge Delivered to the Grand-Jury, at the Quarter-sessions Held at Durham, on Wednesday, the 16th of July, 1740," 1740, pp. 1–10.
54. NRO, King's Lynn Sessions Book, KL/C 20/1.
55. *Bury and Norwich Post*, 7 December 1808.

Preserving reasonable prices for foodstuffs was much more difficult. The existence of crimes such as forestalling was premised on a belief that farmers and dealers sometimes combined to rig grain markets to keep prices unnaturally high. By the 1750s the opponents of marketing offences were claiming that such allegations, although frequently made by the public, were largely unfounded. It did not require a conspiracy or market manipulation to raise prices when supplies were low and grain could move to more lucrative markets; the law of supply and demand was enough. Poor harvests led to a "shortness of crops and the smallness of the quantity at market."[56] As the demand for grain was constant—indeed, increasing with the growing population—prices inevitably rose. Some went further and argued that prosecutions for forestalling actually damaged the market mechanism.

Despite such opinions, there were regular prosecutions for marketing offences during the first half of the century. Thus, on 9 October 1738, the King's Lynn sessions grand jury found a "true bill" against Thomas Munk for "forestalling the market" in the town.[57] In June 1740 the Westminster judges ordered that the laws against market manipulation be "strictly observed and effectually carried into execution."[58] However, their enforcement gradually petered out in the latter decades of the era: 1766 was the last time there was any significant encouragement from the centre for the prosecution of forestallers and engrossers. Much of the legislation on this issue was repealed in 1772 (12 Geo III, c 71).

The process of abolition was not universally supported, even as it occurred. Despite the strong "hint" from Parliament that prosecutions for regrating and similar practices should no longer be countenanced, it was widely thought that there were residual common-law powers to punish such behaviour. William Blackstone supported this analysis. Furthermore, a few lesser regulatory statutes had not been repealed in 1772. There were sporadic attempts to enact more, rather than fewer, controls on the price of foodstuffs, and to enforce those that still existed, during the last two decades of the century, especially in 1795 and 1796, when

56. *London Chronicle*, 12–14 January 1758.
57. NRO, King's Lynn Sessions Book 1726–1752, KL/C 20/1.
58. *Daily Gazetteer*, 30 June 1740.

grain prices were particularly high. As late as 1800 (a year of quite extreme dearth), the mayor and Corporation of Colchester, in Essex, agreed to prosecute, at the town's expense, forestallers within the borough, and offered a "liberal reward" for the detection of such offenders.[59]

Lord Kenyon, who became Chief Justice in 1788, and who was sympathetic to the notion of surviving common-law controls on those profiteering in foodstuffs, even set limited precedents for such actions at the very end of the eighteenth century. For example, in 1800 a hop dealer was prosecuted for having spread rumours suggesting that existing stocks of the flowers were almost exhausted, to encourage other dealers to wait to bring their hops to market, so driving up the price of his own stock. Looking at the broader issues in the case, Kenyon was adamant that if a number of rich people bought up a considerable part of the grain and food supply in order to take an exorbitant advantage, to the public detriment, it would be a "most heinous offence against religion and morality, and against the established law of the country."[60] However, Kenyon's death in 1802 brought a close to this strain of judicial thought, and prosecutions for such matters largely came to an end.[61] Even so, another repealing statute was required in 1844 to fully effect their abolition (7 & 8 Vic, c 24).

Major Grain Riots in the Region

For most of the first 40 years of the eighteenth century, harvests were good and grain prices fairly low in East Anglia, as in the rest of England. Nevertheless, there were short periods of acute hardship that sometimes produced localised disturbances. For example, there was a major food crisis in 1709 and longer-lasting and severe problems in the late 1720s. At the County Assizes for Norfolk in 1726, ten people were indicted for a "notorious riot" at Cley, during which they cut open and spoilt many sacks of corn.[62]

59. *The Ipswich Journal*, 11 October 1800.
60. *The King v Waddington* (1800) 1 East 143, 102 E.R. 56.
61. D. Hay and N. Rogers, *Eighteenth-century English Society*, 1997, p. 111.
62. *London Journal (1720)*, 20 August 1726.

This relatively benign situation began to change towards the end of the 1730s. In 1737, anticipating future problems occasioned by the movement of foodstuffs, Parliament found it necessary to introduce legislation making it a capital felony to steal or destroy corn in a granary or on a merchant vessel.[63] Poor harvests in 1739 and 1740, which were caused by very harsh weather, meant extremely high prices. This was to occasion problems throughout East Anglia, and even worse ones in some other parts of the country. Nevertheless, as a major cereal-producing coastal area, the eastern counties were exposed to the particularly dismaying sight of grain being shipped away from their region.

In June 1740 a group of men from Norfolk, were involved in a major riot across the county border in Wisbech (Cambridgeshire). During the disturbances, the mob almost pulled down one house and broke the windows of several more, forced open three or four granaries and made the owners of others give them their keys. In total, they carried off 20 "lasts" (one last was 80 bushels) of wheat and forced several local gentlemen and tradesmen to give them small sums of money. They then sold the wheat publicly at 1d a bushel or carried it to their homes. The cost of the damage was put at between £500 and £600.[64] At the Cambridgeshire Assizes in August 1740, Robert Pogsen, their "Captain," and three other men from Upwell, in Norfolk, were capitally convicted of riot and carrying away corn. (Significantly, their sentences appear to have been commuted.) Five others from the same town were sentenced to seven years' transportation for larceny, as were an equal number from Wisbech and other surrounding towns and villages. Several other men were whipped after being convicted of lesser offences, and a great number more were discharged without their prosecutions going ahead.[65] There were other regional disturbances that year. For example, in November 1740 it was reported from Sudbury in Suffolk that the "poor people have been disorderly lately in stopping several wagons loaded with grain, some of which they plundered."[66]

63. R. Markless, *Gender, Crime and Discretion in Yorkshire, 1735–1775*, 2013, p. 290.
64. *Ipswich Journal*, 5 July 1740.
65. *London and Country Journal*, 26 August 1740.
66. *Ipswich Journal*, 29 November 1740.

However, by far the worst incident in the area, and perhaps the whole country, occurred in Norwich during the summer of 1740. The high price of flour, combined with the dearness of other provisions, at the same time as local clothworkers' wage levels were under considerable pressure, produced a major riot: "Many thousands of the mob are about the town committing disorders on account of the price of corn and [because] the weavers are lowering the journeymen's wages."[67] Given its population, even this figure suggests that a significant tranche of the city's adult inhabitants, and those resident nearby, were caught up in what occurred.

On 5 July 1740, John Nuttall, the mayor, supported by the city's recorder, steward, and magistrates, wrote to Sir William Yonge, the Secretary of War, asking for a party of dragoons commanded by Cornet Gabriel Bilson to remain in Norwich to suppress further riots rather than moving to Wisbech, as they had been ordered (to prevent any recurrence of the disturbances there). He felt that there was "great reason to apprehend there may be a Rising of the Common People of this City under a pretence to prevent Corn being sent from here to Yarmouth to be exported."[68] He was right. During the ensuing outbreak crowds forced bakers to sell their corn at a set price, broke open several granaries, and forcibly carried away great quantities of corn. Very unusually, up to nine members of the "mob" were also killed by the authorities, although most estimates place it at five or six individuals.[69]

A local resident later gave a detailed account of the development of the riot in a letter to a national newspaper. The "common people" of the city had initially assembled on a Sunday morning, and produced a "sort of riot" after fishermen had suddenly increased the price of mackerel from one and a half pence to two pence apiece. This quieted down quite quickly, not least because fish was not a hugely important part of the local diet. Unfortunately, the following morning, the "meanest of the people" reassembled, visited every baker in Norwich, and pinned a notice on their doors, purporting to offer wheat at 16 shillings a coomb, which was well below the prevailing market price. Panicking, the mayor

67. *Ipswich Journal*, 5 July 1740.
68. TNA SP 36/51, f 254.
69. *London Evening Post*, 12–15 July 1740.

and court met at the town hall, in the marketplace, and decided to call in the military. Nevertheless, and reflecting the traditional process of accommodation, they also published a notice announcing that they would put into effect a recent proclamation forbidding the export of grain, hoping that this would calm the situation. It failed to have the desired effect, and that evening the mayor committed four people to prison for participating in the disturbances. This infuriated the crowd, which broke into the gaol and released them, while smashing windows in the prison. At this point, an "unthinking gentleman" made the fatal mistake of seizing a musket from a nearby dragoon and shooting a rioter through the head. This immediately enraged the populace and prompted further and severe conflict. By the evening, three men, two women, and a boy had been shot dead, and many others wounded.[70]

In a letter to the Duke of Newcastle, John Nuttall was clearly aware that the shooting was not something to be taken lightly. He claimed that after the mob broke open the prison they had assaulted the magistrates and soldiers with stones so that they were "obliged to repel Force with Force, by which means 5 persons were killed."[71] The mob then dispersed, but reassembled the following morning, when it attacked the houses of the mayor and aldermen (most of whom hid or fled). The authorities and leaders of the mob then negotiated a temporary truce.

Nevertheless, the next (Wednesday) morning, the crowd gathered again and looted a small ship carrying wheat and rye that was in the River Wensum (which ran through the city). They then went round Norwich demanding cash from its wealthy inhabitants, and threatening to pull down their houses if it was not forthcoming. On the Thursday morning they regrouped, after being summoned by horns, and divided themselves into bands, which marched in different directions from the city, following banners, and demanding that the farmers and wealthy residents of nearby villages give them money and strong ale. If they failed to pay, their crops were trampled, animals injured, and houses damaged. Some members of these groups sheltered under rural hedges that night, to sleep off the effects of the alcohol they had consumed. Friday was calmer, if

70. *London Evening Post*, 17–19 July 1740.
71. TNA SP 36/51, f 286.

only because a large force of dragoons had garrisoned the town hall.[72] Relative tranquillity then gradually returned to Norwich.

The legal repercussions of the riot were very modest, as was normal in these situations, and something that occasioned annoyance to several observers. In August 1740 just two men, Andrew Lister and Robert Bezett, were convicted and executed together on gallows specially erected for the purpose on Castle Hill in Norwich, the minimum number that was consistent with enforcing subordination.[73] This was typical of the rest of the country. In Yorkshire relatively few rioters were arrested for any offence arising out of their participation in the food riots of 1740. Even those who were subsequently convicted escaped the severest punishments.[74]

The years after 1740 saw a number of flashpoints when major disturbances over the price of grain were narrowly avoided. The most significant of these occurred in late 1756 and early 1757, after war had broken out with France. Heavy rain in the summer of 1756 affected the harvest, and resulted in the speculative buying of grain, further driving up prices. There were riots in Leicester, Coventry, Northampton, Derby, and the West Country. East Anglia, where harvests had not been as bad as some other parts, remained relatively quiet. Even so, an infantry regiment was sent to Norwich in November as a precautionary measure. On this occasion, effective action appears to have been taken by both the authorities and wealthy inhabitants in most parts of the two East Anglian counties to subsidise bread prices. For example, in May 1757 1,200 poor people in Norwich were supplied with "good white wheat household bread at half price."[75]

Nevertheless, 17 men and three women came for trial at the Norfolk Assizes, accused of stealing parcels of flour valued at £40 from Joseph Cole of Dilham, in what was clearly a major disturbance. Eleven were acquitted, but nine were convicted of grand larceny and initially sentenced to seven years' transportation. However, they were kept in custody for a month while a decision was reached on their future. It was swiftly

72. *London Evening Post*, 17–19 July 1740.
73. *Universal Spectator and Weekly Journal*, 6 September 1740; H. T. Dickinson (ed.), *A Companion to Eighteenth-century Britain*, 2002, p. 102.
74. R. Markless, *Gender, Crime and Discretion in Yorkshire, 1735–1775*, 2013, p. 316.
75. P. Muskett, *Riotous Assemblies: Popular Disturbances in East Anglia, 1740–1822,* 1984, p. 10.

reported, "[i]nterest is making for a mitigation of their punishment."[76] Stealing flour in the course of a riot was not the same as "normal" theft. It is very unlikely that they were sent to America. The standard pattern of extreme selectivity, combined with general leniency, appears to have prevailed. Interestingly, this incident had occasioned fairly minimal reporting in the newspapers, the *Public Advertiser* merely noting, "We hear the excessive price of corn, has occasioned a riot in the county of Norfolk."[77]

In an echo of 1740, a major grain riot took place in Norwich in September 1766. Nationally, grain prices had reached very high levels that month, even by the standards of a difficult decade, reflecting an extremely bad harvest the previous summer caused by a late spring frost and heavy rain in July.[78] Domestic harvests had been poor since 1763, while that for 1765 had been bad over much of the Continent, something that had drawn already depleted stocks across the Channel.[79] This prompted major disturbances in many English towns and cities. In September 1766 the *Annual Register* (a yearly compendium of memorable events) noted that there had been at least 30 significant riots around England, as a result of the "rising of the poor; who have been driven to desperation and madness, by the exorbitant prices of all manner of provisions."[80] Oxford, Worcester, and Gloucester were all badly affected.

At the end of that month, Norwich saw one of the most serious, but also the most geographically isolated, of these disturbances. A crowd of poor people gathered in the market place on Saturday, 27 September and began to overturn stalls. They drove the mayor and local justices away when they tried to intervene. The situation quickly escalated. A huge crowd attacked and partly destroyed the mills in West Wymer. They then spent the evening attacking the city bakers' shops and houses, and breaking their windows and furniture, despite having the Riot Act read to them on several occasions. At midnight, they partly demolished

76. *Public Advertiser*, 13 September 1757.
77. *Public Advertiser*, 2 May 1757.
78. W. J. Shelton, *English Hunger and Industrial Disorders: A Study of Social Conflict during the First Decade of George III's Reign*, 1973, p. 31.
79. A. Randall, *Riotous Assemblies: Popular Protest in Hanoverian England*, 2006, p. 91.
80. D. Cox, "The 'Bread and Butter Riots' of 1766": Civil Unrest in the Black Country 1750–1837," 2002.

the *White Horse Tavern*.[81] The following day, having been reassembled by horn blowing and flag-waving (as in 1740), they recommenced their activities, even leaving the city to destroy two nearby malthouses. On their return they resumed their attacks on the bakers and other commercial premises, although they showed some discrimination between targets, depending on the proprietors' local reputation.

At this point the mayor of Norwich, John Patteson, called out the city constables and "staffmen." The latter were effectively self-appointed special constables drawn from the "respectable" inhabitants and enlisted for the emergency. Together they successfully intervened to stop the rioting.[82] This was done quite aggressively; they "attacked [and dispersed] the rioters, whilst they were demolishing a house on Tombland."[83] All the main streets in Norwich were illuminated after dark, and upwards of 500 well-to-do residents armed with staves patrolled all night, with the strong encouragement of the authorities. A party of dragoons summoned from Colchester eventually arrived as well but ("thank God") the rioters had gone home beforehand, avoiding the risk of a hugely sanguinary confrontation, like that of 1740. (By contrast, eight rioters were reportedly shot dead in Worcestershire during the same wave of disturbances). Almost 30 of the riot's alleged ringleaders were arrested and committed to the city gaol to await trial, where they were guarded by elements of the local militia.[84]

Despite the destruction they had wrought, the imprisoned rioters received considerable popular sympathy and understanding, even from respectable people, and were given donations of food and money, for which they advertised their thanks in a local newspaper.[85] Equally significantly, the authorities, both national and local, took immediate steps to deal with some of their grievances. A royal proclamation, made just

81. NRO NCR Case 6h/6/12.
82. A. Randall et al (eds), *Markets, Market Culture and Popular Protest in Eighteenth-century Britain*, 1996, pp. 122–123.
83. Anon, *The History of the City and County of Norwich: From the Earliest Accounts to the Present Time*, 1768, p. 347.
84. *Public Advertiser*, 6 October 1766. Up to 96 were brought to trial for similar offences at Gloucester.
85. A. Randall et al (eds), *Markets, Market Culture and Popular Protest in Eighteenth-century Britain*, 1996, p. 124.

before the disturbances began, forbidding the export of wheat, was put into force, and, shortly afterwards, the government issued licences allowing its importation.[86]

Nationally, bread riots were often followed by a wave of well-publicised "benevolence" towards the poor.[87] This was certainly the case in East Anglia. Less than a week after the 1766 riots, magistrates in Norwich were "taking every method to reduce the price of provisions, and this day butter was sold for two-pence a pint less than last week, and all things in proportion."[88] The following month, still alarmed about the continuing cost and scarcity of grain, they urged Norwich MPs to raise the issue in Parliament and to take concrete measures to bring down the cost of bread and essentials.[89] Steps were also taken in some other parts of East Anglia to reduce prices. There was also a stricter enforcement of the legislation against forestalling and regrating. Other, innovative approaches to limiting the price of staples were sometimes adopted. In November 1766, for example, the principal inhabitants of Debenham, in Suffolk, meeting to find ways of dealing with the "dearness of all sorts of provisions" in their area, resolved to emulate the plan produced by justices in the Carlford and Babergh hundreds of the county. Under this scheme, the difference between four shillings and sixpence and the prevailing market rate for a bushel of wheat would be put on the poor rates when grain was sold to local members of the "necessitous and orderly poor."[90]

Private philanthropists, especially those with a public position, might also make a contribution. For example, in November 1766, Thomas Fonnereau, noting the very high cost of food and impressed by the apparently peaceable behaviour of the industrious poor of Sudbury (unlike that of the inhabitants of Norwich) ordered a large quantity of wheat to be sold at four shillings a bushel. Several hundred local people were supplied with grain at this price.[91] Similarly, at the start of 1767 the *Ipswich Journal* carefully informed its readership that Sir Charles Bunbury, a Suffolk MP,

86. G. Rude, *The Crowd in History: A Study of Popular Disturbances in France and England, 1730–1848*, 2005, p. 43.
87. A. Randall et al (eds), *Riotous Assemblies: Popular Protest in Hanoverian England*, 2006, p. 119.
88. *Public Advertiser*, 6 October 1766.
89. *Gazetteer and New Daily Advertiser*, 4 November 1766.
90. *Public Advertiser*, 25 November 1766; *Gazetteer and New Daily Advertiser*, 26 November 1766.
91. *Ipswich Journal*, 15 November 1766.

had supplied the "most distressed and deserving poor" of Great Barton with subsidised wheat at four shillings and sixpence a bushel and rye at three shillings a bushel, along with a weekly donation of four stones of free beef for making broth.[92]

At the same time, the flagrant defiance of the law that had occurred at Norwich in 1766 could not pass unnoticed. The mayor and other city magistrates took evidence against those involved throughout the second week of October; 13 people eventually stood trial on capital charges (a tiny proportion of those involved). A special commission of gaol delivery and oyer and terminer was held in December the same year, presided over by Sir Henry Gould (a King's Bench judge), to deal with the large number of suspects being held in gaol. (Two other Westminster judges were sent to hold similar ad hoc assizes in Berkshire, Gloucestershire, and Wiltshire to deal with the disturbances there.)[93] These special assizes would allow the gaols to be cleared and a swift deterrent example set.

The petty jury panel consisted of manufacturers and tradesmen from the city.[94] These were the same type of men who had been on the receiving end of the destruction. Even so, they appear to have been very discriminating with their verdicts, as were the authorities with their punishments. In Norwich eight men were capitally convicted. Six were eventually reprieved, four of them (Robert Royce, John Crawforth, James Fleming, James Codner) on condition of transportation for life, one on condition of transportation for 14 years, while the other died in prison some time later. Another man, Henry Nobbs, who had thrown butter at the city swordbearer and been sentenced to death for other offences, was pardoned in the summer of 1767.[95]

However, as in 1740, two men were not so fortunate. John Hall and David Long had been found guilty of demolishing a malthouse (vital for the numerous breweries in the city) and were executed. It was hoped that their punishments would "make a lasting impression on the minds of everyone."[96] Though heavily involved in the riots, they were probably

92. *Public Advertiser*, 27 January 1767.
93. *London Evening Post*, 18–20 November 1766.
94. *Public Advertiser*, 9 December 1766.
95. *Gazetteer and New Daily Advertiser*, 28 July 1767.
96. *Public Advertiser*, 9 December 1766.

no more active than many other men. As Edmund Burke later noted, after a major incident of this type, the fate of convicts often depended more upon the "accidental circumstance of their being brought earlier or later to trial than to any steady principle of equity applied to their several cases."[97] Several more people were acquitted at trial or had their cases referred to quarter sessions for lesser acts of disorder. Among them was Elizabeth Parr, the only woman tried, who was sentenced to three months' imprisonment at the January Quarter Sessions. Susannah Soons, who had been prosecuted for inciting others to attack bakers' houses, was merely bound over to keep the peace.[98]

Although the Norwich riot of 1766 was very serious, other parts of East Anglia were not greatly affected that year, though there were disturbances at Burnham Market, and popular "regulators" forcibly reduced prices at Ipswich and Woodbridge markets. By contrast, in 1772, the very high price of corn and other provisions led to numerous food riots throughout the region, especially in Suffolk.[99] In early April that year there were major disturbances in Ipswich and Bury St Edmunds. Anticipating problems in what were difficult times, the Bury justices had already opened a public fund for the support of local poor people, and many well-to-do people subscribed to it, so that wheat flour could be sold to the needy at a subsidised price. A hundred soldiers also arrived in the town, albeit without powder and ball, with a view to deterring trouble.

Nevertheless, these precautions failed to prevent large numbers of rioters assembling in Bury one night. They visited local millers, "fixing" the price of flour, before moving on to farmers and setting the price of wheat at four shillings a bushel. A similar commitment was obtained from local maltsters. All of these agreements were put in writing and signed by the relevant parties. The rioters also raided the house of a carpenter named Baddock who was thought to be hoarding grain, and made him promise to sell it at their set price. The contents of every wagon loaded with grain that entered the town were sold for four shillings a bushel,

97. E. Burke, "Some Thoughts On The Approaching Executions, Humbly Offered to Consideration," 1839, pp. 197–200.
98. A. Randall et al (eds), *Markets, Market Culture and Popular Protest in Eighteenth-century Britain*, 1996, p. 128.
99. P. King, *Crime, Justice and Discretion in England 1740–1820*, 2003, p. 165.

and numerous millers were threatened with having their premises pulled down if prices were not lowered. Subsequently, the mob forced those who dealt in cheese and butter to fix their prices at five pence and four and a half pence a pound, respectively. A day or so later they visited tradesmen and grocers in Bury, forcing them to sell at the same prices. Such behaviour even extended to more expensive foodstuffs. Two carts on their way to London from Ipswich carrying slaughtered calves were stopped, and the veal sold for two and a half pence to three pence a pound. The rioters also went out to nearby villages. They visited a miller at Ixworth and inflicted £10 of damage to his premises, then put him on a table and "auctioned" him before driving him through the streets while beating him with sacks.[100]

However, the following day, when the mob reassembled, they were "attacked" by more than 1,000 "respectable" townsmen, apparently raised by the civil authorities. By then, the rioters' numbers had been reduced to about 100 by the effects of three days of disturbances and some heavy drinking, and they quickly fled. Seven or eight were captured and committed to prison. The town became quiet again. Military units near Ipswich and Sudbury had been alerted to assist the magistrates but were not needed. In a show of force similar to that seen in Norwich, 500 mounted farmers eventually paraded around the town in ranks of three before being inspected by local gentlemen. During the disturbances, they had been reluctant to bring food into Bury, and its butchers had avoided slaughtering animals, forcing the inhabitants to fast.[101]

No one was hanged as a result of these disturbances. At the August 1772 Assizes in Bury, the prisoners were "mostly rioters, whose sentences were whipping, fines and imprisonment."[102] William Hempsted, a wool comber from Horningsheath, in Suffolk, even escaped prosecution by publishing an advertisement in which he admitted that, without appreciating its consequences, he had accompanied a mob that assembled outside the house of Christopher Metcalfe. He begged "pardon for my offence and promise never to be guilty of any such misdemeanour in future."[103]

100. *London Evening Post*, 11–14 April 1772; *London Evening Post*, 25–28 April 1772.
101. Ibid., 16–18 April.
102. *Bingley's Journal*, 15–22 August 1772.
103. *Ipswich Journal*, 2 May 1772.

As in 1766, local elements of the "political nation" subsequently sought to subsidise grain prices. In neighbouring Essex, where there had also been disturbances, there was no pretence as to the motivation for such largesse. When the gentlemen and principal inhabitants of Colchester offered to subsidise bread they warned that the offer would be withdrawn if disturbances continued.[104]

Although the price of grain remained high over the ensuing 20 years, it did not reach the levels seen in 1772, and though there were some minor disturbances during this period, there do not appear to have been any largescale riots. However, in the autumn of 1792 the situation became very difficult again. In February 1793 Charles Stisted, a magistrate for both Suffolk and Ipswich, wrote to London to seek approval for dropping the prosecution of six merchant sailors who had been involved in a riot at Ipswich in November the previous year, on condition that they enlist in the Royal Navy.[105]

More seriously, in October 1792 there was a major riot at Great Yarmouth in Norfolk. It appears to have been prompted by a combination of low wage levels among local sailors and high bread and provision prices. During the initial disturbance, some of the town's shipowners were "roughly treated." The situation was temporarily pacified when seamen were offered a pay increase. However, rumours quickly spread that there was to be another riot at the forthcoming Saturday market. The chief magistrate in the borough also received an anonymous letter, threatening his life and property—"your head will come from your shoulders and your house to the ground"—if prices did not come down as a result of his issuing "publick orders" to all the bakers in the town.[106] As predicted, a few days later, mobs began to seize or destroy foodstuffs at the market. Anticipating this, the authorities made three arrests during numerous "skirmishes."[107] However, that evening a crowd of up to 300 people forced their release after an attack on the local gaol and sessions house.

---

104. *Middlesex Journal or Chronicle of Liberty*, 18–21 April 1772.
105. TNA HO 42/24/225, ff 555–556.
106. Letter dated October 21st 1792, at TNA HO 42/22/222.
107. Anon, *The Trials of the Offenders Apprehended for the Riots in the Borough of Great Yarmouth, Norfolk, October 27th, 1792*, 1792, pp. iii-iv.

As at Norwich 26 years earlier, order was restored by the local civic authorities and magistrates' assembling the borough constables, reading the Riot Act to the mob, and, most important, calling out the "principal inhabitants of the town." The latter, armed with staves, seized several of the ringleaders, took them to prison, guarded the gaol from rescue attempts, and quelled the riot before a small force of 18 dragoons arrived. They then patrolled the streets with the troops.[108] It was a matter of considerable satisfaction that the Yarmouth riots of 1792 were suppressed "without the intervention of military force." Nevertheless, they were serious enough for Henry Jodrell, the recorder of Great Yarmouth, to write to the Home Secretary, seeking a meeting.[109]

As in 1766, special sessions were held within weeks of the disturbances to try the suspects. Because of the town's unusually powerful borough sessions, these were heard before local magistrates and the recorder at a special hearing in November 1792 rather than at an improvised assizes.[110] As in many such cases, considerable leniency was shown towards those prosecuted. This moderation was aided by the apparent lack of political motivation among those involved, something that was always a concern for the authorities after the French Revolution, and which had, apparently, been manifest in a recent disturbance in Birmingham. The rioters cry at Yarmouth was simply "The dearness of provisions."[111] As a result, no one was capitally convicted and executed.

However, three men—Thomas Smith, a labourer, and two sailors, Thomas Bully and John Houghton—were tried for conspiring and riotously assembling to release those who had been put in the Great Yarmouth gaol. Houghton had been seen with a large stick, leading a band of up to 20 men and demanding the keys to the prison. Smith was acquitted outright. Bully and Houghton were acquitted of the conspiracy but sentenced to two years' imprisonment for rioting.

Ann Robinson, a married woman, was indicted for a robbery committed during the disturbances but sentenced to seven years' transportation

108. TNA HO 42/22/106, f 278. Charles Townshend of Honingham later noted that they had attacked the mob and subdued them. TNA HO 42/22/80, ff 204–205.
109. TNA HO 42/22/115, ff 298–299.
110. *The Times*, 13 November 1792, p. 3.
111. *The Monthly Review; or, Literary Journal*, vol. x, 1793, p. 90.

after being convicted of simple grand larceny.[112] She had taken a large leg of pork, worth six shillings, from William Collins, a local farmer, butcher, and market trader. Collins had been pressured to sell his meat at a lower price than he wished by the crowd and had tried to walk away from the market. He was followed by the mob, knocked down, and kicked. Anne Robinson allegedly "pulled his hair and beat him." She then took some of the meat from underneath him, so founding the robbery count. However, at the start of 1795 there was a collective petition from prominent inhabitants of Great Yarmouth, including the magistrates and mayor, for a free pardon. (Robinson had already served more than two years in Yarmouth Gaol while awaiting transportation.)[113]

The 1790s were to be an extremely difficult time. Wheat yields were very low due to unseasonably bad weather over several years during the middle of the decade, while the war against revolutionary France disrupted European markets for grain, making it very difficult to import extra supplies, even where it was allowed. Prices rose very steeply as a result. At times during the late 1790s and early 1800s there were near-famine conditions. Again, local elements of the political nation appreciated that something had to be done. During the winter of 1795 to 1796 many towns and villages in Norfolk and Suffolk raised subscriptions to help their own poor, usually by subsidising the price of wheat. Even so, there were disturbances on a regular basis between April 1795 and January 1796.

For example, in May 1795 a riot occurred in Sudbury after a wagon loaded with flour passed through the town on its way to London. It was stopped by a crowd, including several women, who insisted on its contents being sold at one shilling and sixpence a pound. The owner of the wagon immediately sought aid from the town mayor, who tried to quell the disturbance by swearing in two "creditable persons" as special constables and reading the Riot Act. The West Norfolk Militia also paraded. The wagon was eventually escorted out of Sudbury and continued its journey to the capital. Indicative of a tradition of accommodation, the mayor promised to call a meeting of the principal inhabitants to address

112. TNA HO 42/22/203, ff 506–507.
113. TNA HO 47/19/46, f 140.

the issues facing the local poor.[114] A few days later some of the latter visited him and complained that it was impossible, given the high price of provisions, and the "inadequate price for labour" for them to support themselves and their families. Their grievances were listened to and a petition sent to Parliament with 1,000 signatures, calling attention to their plight.[115] The situation quietened down, although there were less serious problems at Ipswich in June.

Unfortunately, the Privy Council asked the Home Secretary to send letters to the county authorities encouraging them to enforce the free movement of grain within England. They noted that the export of corn to other countries had been strictly prohibited for several months and claimed that, bolstered by alternatives, there was sufficient to last until the next harvest.[116] In August 1795 Robert Stearn and a mob assembled in the village of Bures (Suffolk) and during a "riot" took wheat from the premises of John Barnard and Lawrence Bull that they illegally sold to the crowd at "prices beneath the value."[117] The following month there was another disturbance at Sudbury prompted by the high price of corn. A wagon belonging to a man named Hayward was stopped on the road to Colchester at the crack of dawn by a largely female crowd of about 100 people, who took 20 sacks of fine flour. After disposing of it, they returned the empty sacks to Hayward and offered him £40 in payment, which he refused to accept "as he means to bring action against the town." His load would have fetched £70 in London.[118]

In December 1795 a group of men and women "riotously assembled" and stole wheat from two boats in the Mildenhall River and a barn at Great Bealings, in Suffolk. At the following assizes held at Bury, five of them were sentenced to just three months' imprisonment each.[119] In the same month the Marquis of Townshend, whose seat was at Raynham Hall, in Norfolk, wrote to the Home Secretary, the Duke of Portland, describing a disturbance that had taken place in the small port of Wells

114. *Bury and Norwich Post*, 13 May 1795.
115. *Lloyd's Evening Post*, 13–15 May 1795.
116. TNA HO 42/35/106, ff 245–251.
117. *Sun*, 31 March 1796. At the Bury Assizes in March 1796, Stearn was sentenced to one year in prison and ordered to find securities for his future good behaviour.
118. *Norfolk Chronicle*, 23 September 1795.
119. *Sun*, 31 March 1796.

over the shipping of flour to London. A large number of riotous women, supported by some men, had prevented a consignment of flour from sailing. As the local magistrate was away, Townshend and the Reverend Dixon Hoste, the rector of nearby Tittleshill, felt that it was their duty to go to Wells and deal with the matter. They also ordered a company of the Pembrokeshire Militia stationed in Holt to go to Warham to await further orders. Hoste warned the women that their conduct was illegal and advised them of its possible consequences. He also reminded them that they had previously been supplied with flour shipped in from Yarmouth and that, once peace was restored, the magistrates would be willing to attend to their needs. Having twice read the Riot Act, Townshend ordered the militia to march in. The soldiers drove the mob away with bayonets and secured the safety of the ship and its flour. Townshend thought that their action had prevented similar disturbances occurring in other parts of Norfolk.[120] The following year, in April 1796, a group of people in Norwich, exasperated by a sudden and unexpected rise in the price of flour, "assembled riotously" in the marketplace but were dispersed by the magistrates, with several of their number being committed to prison.[121]

These problems continued on an intermittent basis to the very end of the era. The summer of 1800 was to see the highest grain prices ever recorded. This produced disturbances in various parts of East Anglia, some small, others on a very largescale. Some were disciplined, others descended into serious disorder. Thus, in early September 1800, a "tumultuous" crowd that was, again, largely made up of women "attacked the person" of a miller in King's Lynn, Norfolk. They then went to his house, where they broke all the windows with stones and mud. Ultimately it was necessary for local magistrates to read the Riot Act to make them disperse. However, the next day the crowd reassembled in the marketplace and marched back to the miller's house, where they "repeated their former outrages, and were not dispersed but with the utmost persuasions."[122]

---

120. TNA HO 42/37/173, ff 306–307.
121. *Bell's Weekly Messenger*, 8 May 1796.
122. *Albion and Evening Advertiser*, 12 September 1800.

By contrast, a remarkably disciplined and effective case of crowd action occurred at Harwich, in Suffolk, a few days later. A large crowd of people, again, many of them female, assembled in the town market, where traders were about to sell various foodstuffs, including butter, onions, eggs, and potatoes. The crowd conferred among themselves and decided that the prices were far too high. They agreed a new price list, and presented it to the traders, who were told to accept between half and two-thirds of what they had been asking. When they resisted, the mob took and distributed the traders' food at the rates they had proposed, in the presence of the mayor. They then marched on his house and demanded that the price of bread and meat (not on sale that day) be lowered, threatening to repeat their behaviour when these came to market. The mayor promised to do everything in his power to achieve a reduction in prices. That afternoon he summoned some of the town's inhabitants and asked them to "regulate the prices of provisions." Some traders coming by boat to Harwich from other parts of the county learnt about what was happening ashore before landing, and attempted to turn back. However, a group of young men from the town set off after them in a rowing boat, and forced them to land and distribute their goods at the new prices. Unlike near-contemporary events at Ipswich, there was no disorder in Harwich: "No hurt was done by the mob, neither was there any property plundered: they confined themselves to insisting that the prices should be lowered."[123]

At the very end of the period, technological change began to occasion popular concern. Amongst the most hated innovations were threshing machines powered by horses or water. However, it was not until the following century that these produced major disturbances. At the Norfolk Quarter Sessions in 1815, four labourers were imprisoned for rioting at Hockham and destroying a threshing machine.[124] In the same year farm labourers rioted at Downham Market, in Norfolk, over low wages. The yeomanry were called out, and the Riot Act read, after which the crowd gradually dispersed. Another disturbance followed shortly afterwards, during which two women and numerous men were arrested. They were

123. *Oracle and Daily Advertiser*, 18 September 1800.
124. C. Mackie, *Norfolk Annals*, vol.1, 1901, p. 138.

tried at the Norfolk Assizes in August 1815. Sixteen were capitally convicted but only two of them, Daniel Harwood and Thomas Thody, were hanged.[125] There were major riots in Brandon and Downham Market the following year. Unusually by most eighteenth-century standards, these were accompanied by widespread and overt looting.[126]

Political Concerns After 1789

For much of the century, the authorities were fairly sanguine about popular disorder. It was widely appreciated that disturbances and protests over specific grievances were intended to prompt a remedial response, rather than being a challenge to authority per se.[127] This attitude was manifest in litigation between the owner of one of the malthouses that had been burnt down in the Norwich riot of 1766 and his insurer. The latter argued that a clause in their contract excluded liability where the damage had been caused by a "usurped power," and that the mob of 300 people involved met this definition. A majority of the judges in the Court of Common Pleas found for the plaintiff. Lord Chief Justice Wilmot was unconcerned about any political motivation behind the riot.[128]

However, after 1789 a growing awareness of the political ideas emanating from revolutionary France enhanced the anxiety occasioned by popular disturbances, even when they were motivated by grain prices. There was slightly more cause for such concern in East Anglia than in some other parts of England, even if the connection was often exaggerated. During the final years of the eighteenth century, Norwich (along with Sheffield) was considered to be one of the two most radical centres in England. William Pitt even dubbed it the "Jacobin city."[129]

In December 1792 an "incendiary letter" was put up in Earl Soham, in Suffolk, threatening to pull down Melton House and Soham Lodge and expressing a wish for "no King no Clergy." A similar letter had earlier

125. C. Mackie, *Norfolk Annals*, vol.1, 1901, p. 137. *The Morning Chronicle*, 12 September 1816.
126. P. Muskett, *Riotous Assemblies: Popular Disturbances in East Anglia, 1740–1822*, 1984, pp. 49–50.
127. J. Brewer and J. Styles (eds) *An Ungovernable People. The English and Their Law in the Seventeenth and Eighteenth-centuries*, 1980, pp. 12–16.
128. *John Drinkwater, Esq. v The Royal Exchange Assurance Company* (1767) Wilmot 282, 97 E.R. 109.
129. I. Smith, "Reactions to Radicalism in Norwich 1789–1801," 2015, p. 6.

been found in Helmingham Park threatening Lord Dysart's person and house.[130] A printed-paper circulated in Norwich in October 1795, signed by "A friend to reform," complained about the poverty and hardship caused by the war with France and called for reform. Its author also deplored the House of Commons as being made up of "land-monopolists, commissaries, contractors and pensioners."[131] In the same year, the Norfolk magistrate Robert Fellowes noted in a letter to the Home Office that a public meeting had been held at the village of Saxlingham during which a man wearing a hat with a cockade had made a speech and given away leaflets demanding radical political reform. Several similar meetings had, apparently, been conducted, as the high price of bread provided an excuse for ill-disposed people to radicalise the poor.[132] In July 1796 the seventh anniversary of the destruction of the Bastille was celebrated at the *Rose Tavern* in Norwich. At about the same time, the radical John Thelwall gave a speech to 400 people praising human liberty, the rights of man, the jury system, freedom of the press, and the American republic, and calling for the abolition of slavery.[133]

Thelwall was himself to become the cause of a riot the following year. In 1797 he was set to give a lecture in Norwich when a group of soldiers from an Irish cavalry regiment, carrying bludgeons, rushed into the room, shouting, "Down with the Jacobins!" They hit out at the people waiting for the talk to begin and "demolished" the lecture hall, smashing up furniture in the process. As their numbers increased (other soldiers and some civilians joining them), they moved on to several alehouses, which they also gutted or severely damaged. In the early hours of the following morning, by which time their numbers had swollen to several hundred, they searched the *Dove*, unavailingly looking for Thelwall and various "seditious papers" which they had been told were hidden

130. *William Goodwin of Street Farm, Earl Soham, Diaries Dated from 1785–1810*, vol. 2, HD 365/2, transcribed by Mrs. J. Rothery of Earl Soham, August 2001. www.earlsoham.org (Last accessed 15th December 2015).
131. TNA HO 42/36/85, ff 189–192.
132. TNA HO 42/36/85, ff 189–192.
133. *Morning Post and Fashionable World*, 22 July 1796.

there.[134] Subsequently the owners of the taverns made substantial claims for damages against the city.[135]

"Ordinary" members of the social elite, such as Parson Woodforde, shared some of the official concern about the politics behind popular disturbances during the final decade of the century. In 1792 the mayor and other prominent inhabitants of King's Lynn met at the town hall and passed a resolution expressing their support for the King, and determination to prevent any seditious meetings (none were actually planned in the area). At the same time, they were delighted to receive a deputation from the "Labouring Class" who presented a letter signed by many local people stating that they were equally ready to defend the King and constitution, and promising to "maintain good order amongst themselves."[136]

Conclusion

The great majority of serious riots and many lesser disturbances in eighteenth-century East Anglia were motivated by poverty and powerlessness, whether directly or indirectly. Unsurprisingly, the most serious conflicts took place in urban areas, though they often attracted people from adjacent rural parts. Towns had the requisite numbers of people who could rise quickly. There were purely rural riots, but these were less common, and also less prone to getting out of control. In an era of limited communications, popular protest was harder to initiate and then sustain in country areas. Labourers in these parts were also usually subject to greater social control and more fearful of upsetting the farmers who employed them.[137]

Dealing with major disturbances posed considerable problems for the authorities, whether justices, aldermen, sheriffs, mayors, or the well-to-do residents of the towns involved. They were reluctant to employ the military, even if soldiers were available, if this could possibly be avoided. The terrible events at Norwich in 1740, and the damage to community

134. *London Evening Post*, 1 June 1797–3 June 1797.
135. NRO 6h/11/16–21.
136. *Diary or Woodfall's Register*, 11 December 1792.
137. A. Randall et al (eds), *Markets, Market Culture and Popular Protest in Eighteenth-century Britain*, 1996, p. 153.

relations that followed, along with cases in England and Wales in which borough officials who had employed troops that killed rioters had themselves faced trial (even if they were ultimately acquitted) served as a warning about its dangers. As a result, the army directly confronted mobs in only about one in six riots nationally, although their presence sometimes provided a deterrent to further disorder after a disturbance had been suppressed.[138] Towards the end of the century, the Reverend Thomas Gisborne was restating widely held opinion when he urged magistrates to put an end to disturbances solely by the use of those means "which are commonly employed by the civil power. Let him be tender of calling in the soldiery; and still more tender of commissioning them to shed blood." (He accepted that, if all else failed, a "cautious application of military force" might be necessary.)[139]

Normally the most important role in suppressing serious urban riots in East Anglia, especially after the mid-century, was not the military but moderately prosperous residents, many (but not all) of whom might even have been described as members of the "middling orders." Such people were much more numerous in urban areas than they were in rural parts, as towns had many more skilled artisans, craftsmen, merchants, and shopkeepers. They could be assembled in substantial numbers, and even formally sworn in as special constables or members of the *posse commitatus*. The willingness of these people to unite against rioters, with the encouragement of the authorities, was crucial. Not only were they familiar with their towns, they were much less likely to be carrying lethal weapons (rather than staves), and were reluctant to have unnecessary recourse to lethal force, if only because they would live with those they policed in the future.

It was such men, numbered in the hundreds, who helped bring the major disturbances in 1766, 1772, and 1792 to an end. Some insight into their origins, and how they were recruited, is provided by an account from Coventry. After major grain riots in the city in August 1756, Joseph Hewitt noted that the "civilized part of the town" had a meeting with

138. J. Bohstedt, *Riots and Community Politics in England and Wales, 1790–1810*, 1983, pp. 156–158.
139. T. Gisborne, *An Enquiry Into the Duties of Men in the Higher and Middle Classes of Society in Great Britain*, 1794, p. 294.

the mayor and nineteen borough justices at St Mary's Hall. Local constables were summoned, and each of them was told to bring with them the names of two "able assistants." Furthermore, every principal inhabitant in the city was asked to have three or four good men in his house, ready to assist the civil magistrates if necessary.[140] However, large numbers of such men were not raised lightly. It seems that the general mayhem often had to have reached what were widely thought to be "intolerable" levels before this option was viable. It is a mistake to imagine that those recruited were devoid of sympathy for their poor neighbours.

Most riots in the East Anglian region, as in other parts of England, were "dialogues of disorder;" frequently they had an almost choreographed quality. They were carried out with an eye firmly on local justices. "Statements by conduct" from the crowd were met by responses from those charged with their "care."[141] For example, assembling in front of the house or work premises of someone who was deemed to have violated community values, and then threatening to pull their building down, was a widespread form of communal action throughout the era. It could be used against millers, farmers, constables, and even local JPs. Moreover, the prudent response from their targets when confronted by such mobs was well-known, and usually followed. They might attempt to calm the situation by offering beer, cheese, and even small sums of cash to compensate members of the crowd for the "trouble" of making their views heard.[142] They would often be mollified by such behaviour and move on to their next target. Occasionally, such steps were not enough, and damage would occur. Even this was usually limited. The individuals inside such houses were rarely badly hurt and were frequently left physically unmolested.

This form of protest, and the official response to it by local elites, was part of a wider culture, duplicated across much of England. In exchange for the mob's observing informal rules, the authorities knew that they had to be highly selective about prosecuting and punishing rioters when order was restored. Most escaped unscathed. Only a select few would

140. J. Hewitt, *A Journal of the Proceedings of J. Hewitt*, 1790, pp 4–5.
141. A. Randall, *Riotous Assemblies: Popular Protest in Hanoverian England*, 2006, p. 312.
142. E. Stockdale, *Law and Order in Georgian Bedfordshire*, 1982, pp. 8–9.

be prosecuted, from whom a tiny number were capitally convicted and then executed. This tradition of accommodation continued into the following century. Although East Anglia was heavily involved in the Swing Riots of 1830, these disturbances were noted for a general absence of serious violence.

CHAPTER 26

General Conclusion

As has been seen in the course of this book, in many respects an examination of both crime and the justice system in eighteenth-century Norfolk and Suffolk replicates the picture found in most other English regions that were not in the immediate orbit of the Metropolis or situated at the extremities of the country. Even visitors from Surrey or Cumberland would have found comparatively little in East Anglia that differed radically from their own areas, although they might have seen a slightly different set of priorities and significant differences in some (not all) patterns of crime and punishment. Many of the apparent idiosyncrasies of the region were closely matched elsewhere. Similarly, it shared in most of the legal developments that emanated from the centre. Whatever had happened in earlier centuries, by the 1700s these did not usually disappear into a morass of provincial inaction but were, instead, modified using a variety of local mechanisms such as jury nullification. Furthermore, the broader cultural changes that affected English society during the era, such as the increased level of general squeamishness, were as evidenced in the East Anglian region as they were elsewhere in the country.

Although the effectiveness of the English criminal justice system was a matter of considerable discussion amongst literate people throughout the era, the debate largely reflected experience in and around the huge and constantly growing Metropolis, with its rapidly segregating society and, towards the end of the era, the problems occasioned by the swiftly industrialising and urbanising North. As Hewling Luson noted in 1787 (albeit with some exaggeration), most country dwellers retained their virtue: "To them, many of the crimes and miseries incident to the lower order of the people in large manufacturing and corporate towns, and which abound in the Metropolis, are scarcely known, even by report."[1]

In many respects, an examination of East Anglia serves only to highlight how utterly extraordinary London was, and how dangerous it is to extrapolate generalisations for the wider country from what occurred in the capital. The Metropolis may have been a phenomenon, but it still held a *relatively* small proportion of the national population. Whatever might have been the situation in the capital, serious crime was not a *huge* social problem in Norfolk and Suffolk. It loomed large for those who owned valuable but portable property, lived in isolated dwellings in remote areas, or who had to travel the region's roads on a regular basis, especially if they needed to carry large sums of money when they did so. It was a perennial nuisance for the rest of the population, something that had to be carefully guarded against, but was just one of the many insecurities of eighteenth-century life, and quite modest when compared to the risk of losing employment, falling gravely ill or of dying prematurely from disease or accident.

Grave crimes, especially if they involved extreme violence, were comparatively rare and frequently in decline. Where they did occur, they were often bucolic in nature, manifest in the theft of domestic animals and commercial poaching. Minor crime was another matter altogether; it was much more widespread. However, society had a high ability to absorb such deviance, and most of it could be dealt with informally, particularly when committed by local people. The lack of convenient access to the criminal justice system in large parts of the two East Anglian counties encouraged recourse to such settlements, although the increased level and speed of population mobility was beginning to challenge the effectiveness of extra-legal controls.

The majority of people in eighteenth-century Norfolk and Suffolk did not feel that they were living through a law-and-order "crisis" for most of the period, although there were occasional panics, especially during economically difficult times and after mass demobilisations, these sometimes being fanned by alarmist reports in the burgeoning number of

1. H. Luson, *Inferior Politics, Or, Considerations on the Wretchedness and Profligacy of the Poor, Especially in London and Its Vicinity*, 2nd edn., 1787, p. 22.

newspapers available. The generally low level of serious crime, combined with recourse to informal disposals, also helps to explain why the use of draconian state-administered sanctions in the region, whether death, transportation, or significant periods of imprisonment, was fairly modest, even sparing, for what was a comparatively populous area. There was certainly no reign of judicial terror in the region.

In the capital the traditional criminal justice system *may* have been transformed in the century after 1690, but it would be a slight exaggeration to say the same of East Anglia.[2] Unlike London, the system found in Norfolk and Suffolk that was inherited from the previous century remained largely viable for most of the era. Although its defects were widely acknowledged, so were its strengths. Indeed, for much of the period, there was a widespread feeling that it would be entirely satisfactory if it could only be made to function a little more efficiently, whether by private or government initiatives.

It was the prevalence of such attitudes, combined with a fear of central government involvement and the increased expense that came with it that explains the largely incremental and often modest nature of change during the 1700s. Frequently, and in time-honoured English fashion, this was effected by institutions gradually "mutating" over the years. Thus, as problems developed in recruiting JPs from "traditional" elite backgrounds, minor gentlemen and then clerics were added to the commissions of the peace. Difficulties in finding constables were resolved by the provision of modest rewards and increased volunteerism.

Where there was radical reform, whether it was manifest in shoplifting becoming a capital crime in 1699, the introduction of short-term imprisonment for clergyable felony in 1706, or the advent of transportation for the same crimes in 1718, it often originated in London, and was frequently the result of active petitioning by bodies in or near the capital, even if it necessarily affected the provinces. Conversely, justified change in the Metropolis was sometimes delayed for fear of the precedent it would set in the rest of the country, which contained the great majority of the national population, and where it might still not necessary.

2. T. Hitchcock and R. Shoemaker, *London Lives*, 2015, p. 9.

Furthermore, such radical change as did occur had often been the subject of considerable debate among informed observers for many years; it did not come out of nowhere. Just as there were few dramatic beginnings, there were few sudden endings. Punishments and disposals fell out of fashion, but lingered on, and were used on an occasional basis, for many years after they had largely been replaced by newer alternatives.

Something that also becomes clear when considering the ancillary records, in so far as they survive or are alluded to in the relevant archives and reports, is just how much was going on "behind the scenes." The foreman of a grand jury might inform the trial judge on the Crown side at assizes that he felt a conviction was suitable for an administrative reprieve. The grand jury itself could be informed of doubts as to the credibility of a prosecution witness when deciding whether to return a "true bill." Local magistrates might support petitions against execution, transportation, or even imprisonment. Some of these representations were purely oral, and have left no formal record. Many others, even if written, have been lost. They are the (often irrecoverable) "meat" on the bare bones of the criminal justice system of the era, one that was less arbitrary and much more considered and thorough than is sometimes suggested in the modern literature.

It is often said that the eighteenth century was a "golden age" for discretionary justice. Certainly England acquired a sanguinary penal code during the era, just as society became increasingly reluctant to impose the death penalty. As a result, the country's black-letter law departed from its practice to an unprecedented degree. This was largely done by exercising discretion, the use of which, according to the eminent judge and politician Sir William Grant (1752–1832), eventually amounted to a "general confederacy of prosecutors, witnesses, counsel, juries, judges, and the advisers of the Crown, to prevent the execution of the criminal law."[3]

Nevertheless, such an analysis, though true, can also be misleading. Once a serious matter was within the criminal justice system, discretion was neither exercised in a vacuum nor in a wildly arbitrary manner. Decisions were not plucked from the air. The same factors were considered on

3. House of Commons Debate 2 March 1819, *Hansard*, vol. 39, cols. 777–845.

a repeated basis, and were widely known, although, at the margins, the temperament of individual actors, whether complainants, judges, jurors, or magistrates, could be vital.[4] Even so, an informed observer, apprised of the details of a case and its defendant, could usually have made a fairly reliable prediction as to the likely verdict and sentence. The ubiquity of such factors, and the manner in which they were normally viewed, also helps explain why cases could be processed so quickly through the system. They were being pushed into well-worn templates, rather than made the subject of highly personalised consideration.

In practice, the various parts of the East Anglian justice system worked reasonably well for most of the time. The region did not normally witness random or extra-legal decisions, at least when it came to serious matters, and most people had some level of access to, and protection from, the criminal law. However, and vitally, East Anglia, like all other parts of provincial England, lacked an effective system of "quality control" for its criminal justice system. Consequently, there were periodic exceptions to the general situation, some of them quite glaring, due to the failure of one or more of its component parts, whether coroners, constables, jurors, JPs, or judges. Apparently bizarre, draconian, or even excessively lenient decisions sometimes slipped through the net.[5] These were not typical of the wider system (although more common in summary matters) but occurred with some regularity and provided the foundations for many of the less flattering contemporary portraits of criminal justice at this time as well as some modern critiques of its administration.

Until the late seventeenth century, society had been fairly sanguine about these aberrations and failings. In part, this was because they were not well-publicised. The lack of general concern also reflected an awareness that "respectable" people were unlikely to be on the receiving end of the injustices they occasioned. As a result, at the start of the period, many observers still took a holistic approach towards the occasional glaring failures of the system, and its more frequent "below par" performances, whether manifest in mistaken convictions or sentences, legally unserved areas, corrupt and drunken constables, or tyrannical, absent,

4. W. Blackstone, *Commentaries on the Laws of England*, 1769, vol. 4, p. 15.
5. Ibid.

or incompetent justices, and viewed them as the unfortunate but necessary price to be paid for enforcing the criminal law, one that had to be set against the system's numerous successes.

This rather robust and impersonal attitude gradually changed during the course of the eighteenth century. The expansion of printed media meant that people were increasingly aware of such lapses, which also cast doubts on the wider system, even if it was often undeserved. As the barrister and coroner Edward Umfreville noted in this context in 1761, "one scabbed sheep may infect the whole flock, which may reasonably become suspected by the appearance of a spotted companion."[6] There was growing anxiety about the significant minority of cases that were severely mishandled. There was also increasing concern that some of the factors that influenced the exercise of judicial and executive discretion, such as a defendant's previous character and associations, were based on informational sources that were unreliable—something that was made worse by increased social mobility—or inherently unfair. This reflected a major change in attitudes towards what might broadly be termed "due process." It provided some of the background to legal change during the era.

That the criminal justice system worked reasonably well for much of the time helps to explain why it enjoyed a significant degree of legitimacy among a majority of the population for most of the eighteenth century. This was vital, as a sense of legitimacy is closely linked to popular willingness to comply with and obey the rules of a state, whether they protect property or physical integrity.[7] Such legitimacy is particularly remarkable, as it has frequently been suggested that there was clearly one law for the rich and another for the poor in eighteenth-century England.[8] As a matter of strict black-letter law, this was not true, apart from the modest legal privileges enjoyed by England's tiny number of aristocrats. Nevertheless, eighteenth-century England was a highly unequal society and, inevitably, this hugely affected exposure to its criminal justice system.

---

6. E. Umfreville, *Lex Coronatoria*, 1761, p. vii.
7. M. Eisner and A. Nivette, "Does Low Legitimacy Cause Crime? A Review of the Evidence," 2013, p. 3.
8. J. M. Beattie, *Crime and the Courts in England 1660–1800*, 1986, p. 10; R. Porter, *English Society in the Eighteenth Century*, 1990, p. 150.

Even at the time, many observers, such as Adam Smith, appreciated that the criminal law largely served to protect the interests of those who had a stake in society against those of the poor, and that it was often natural for the latter to seek to appropriate the possessions of the former.[9]

However, it was not merely its effectiveness that explains the absence of widespread alienation towards the English criminal justice system of the era. Just as important is that it was essential for the system to have a considerable measure of popular support to function at all. There was not a hermetic seal between governors and governed. Both the rich and the "middling sort" of people were heavily involved in its administration. Assizes judges and JPs drawn from the former worked in relative harmony with trial jurors made up of the latter. Given the dearth of guilty pleas in felony cases, all serious criminal sanctions (effectively) required the approval of a jury of fairly ordinary men before they could be imposed. Just as important, and moving down the social scale, elements of the "common people" played a major role in policing their own society, whether as constables, as part of the "hue and cry," or by sitting on coroners' juries.

Nevertheless, it is also apparent that, although a sense of legitimacy reached far down into English society, it was not universal. For the lowest stratum of society, at least a third of the population, the situation was much more nuanced. In 1753, when a gentleman referred to "our tyranny over the poor," it was this group he had in mind.[10] Its members ascribed legitimacy to aspects of the criminal justice system, but this was often fairly grudging, frequently highly qualified, and sometimes totally absent. Such poor people might agree that murder and sodomy were deserving of condign punishment. However, there were large parts of the criminal code where, whatever the black-letter law, offences were not viewed as properly "criminal" in any meaningful sense. Obviously, these included, *inter alia*, smuggling, poaching, gleaning without permission after 1788, pilfering from employers, and the seizure of grain during food riots. Perhaps more significantly, some "conventional" crimes, committed in certain circumstances, were not viewed as terribly reprehensible.

9. A. Smith, *Wealth of Nations*, 1999, pp. 297–310.
10. R. Porter, *English Society in the Eighteenth Century*, 1990, p. 150.

These included, inter alia, non-violent thefts, especially (but not solely) of foodstuffs, from those who were perceived as being able to "afford" their loss.

Even so, violent conflict was still usually avoided, even with this large and impoverished provincial proletariat of landless labourers and permanently pressured cloth workers, although it has been argued that, by the early nineteenth century, agrarian capitalism had a harsher face in Norfolk than in many other English counties, and produced more desperate protest amongst its rural labourers.[11] The relative absence of both the means of blatant coercion and a political philosophy that would justify recourse to such an option encouraged or required a degree of sensitivity on the part of the governors, a determination not to push matters "too far" in any given situation. This is not to suggest that East Anglian society existed as a cohesive whole, working in social harmony. It was not governed by the sociological equivalent of the Gaia hypothesis, in which the various actors in a complex environment interact to produce a smoothly self-regulating system. However, East Anglia, like most of provincial England, normally managed to operate without its governors having largescale recourse to force. They knew when to yield, or at least to soft-pedal, and were prepared to listen, if only grudgingly. As has been seen, this was reflected in a considerable tolerance for grievance-motivated public disorder and hardship-driven crime. Doubtless, in the final decade of the century, many gentlemen in Norfolk and Suffolk, as elsewhere in England, could not help noting that the ostensibly powerful and much lauded apparatus of the French state had rapidly collapsed under pressure in 1789.

11. D. Hay, "Patronage, Paternalism, and Welfare," 1998, p. 44.

Frequently Used Abbreviations

ASSI	Assizes Papers
BL	British Library
HO	Home Office
MF	Microfiche
NRO	Norfolk Record Office
SRO	Suffolk Record Office
SP	State Papers
TNA	The National Archives
NCR	City of Norwich Coroner's Inquests
OBSP	Old Bailey Sessions Proceedings
CRO	Cambridgeshire Record Office
OA	Ordinary's Account
QS	Quarter Sessions

Bibliography

Contemporary Journals and Newspapers Cited

Albion and Evening Advertiser
Annual Register
Applebee's Original Weekly Journal
Bath Chronicle
Bath Chronicle and Weekly Gazette
Bedfordshire Mercury and Huntingdon Express
Bell's Weekly Messenger
Bingley's Journal
British Journal Or The Censor
Bury and Norwich Post
Caledonian Mercury
Chester Chronicle and General Advertiser
Common Sense Or The Englishman's Journal
Country Journal Or The Craftsman
Courier and Evening Gazette
Coventry Mercury
Craftsman Or Say's Weekly Journal
Daily Advertiser
Daily Courant
Daily Gazetteer
Daily Post
Diary Or Woodfall's Register
English Post
Exeter Flying Post
Felix Farley's Bristol Journal
Freeholder's Journal

Gazetteer and London Daily Advertiser
Gazetteer and New Daily Advertiser
General Advertiser
General Evening Post
Gloucester Journal
Grub-street Journal
Guardian
Hampshire Telegraph and Sussex Chronicle
Harrop's Manchester Mercury
Ipswich Journal
Jacobite's Journal
Lloyd's Evening Post and British Chronicle
Lloyd's Evening Post
London Chronicle
London and Country Journal
London Daily Advertiser
London Daily Post and General Advertiser
London Evening Post
London Journal
London Packet Or New Lloyd's Evening Post
London Post
London Spy Revived
Mist's Weekly Journal
Middlesex Journal Or Chronicle of Liberty
Morning Chronicle and London Advertiser
Morning Herald and Daily Advertiser
Morning Post and Daily Advertiser
Morning Post and Fashionable World
Norfolk Chronicle
Norwich Mercury
Norwich Gazette
Old England
Old Whig Or The Consistent Protestant
Oracle and Daily Advertiser
Oxford Journal

Parker's General Advertiser and Morning Intelligencer
Penny London Post Or The Morning Advertiser
Public Advertiser
Public Advertiser Or Political and Literary Diary
Public Ledger
Read's Weekly Journal Or British Gazetteer
Remembrancer
Royal Cornwall Gazette, Falmouth Packet & Plymouth Journal,
St. James's Chronicle Or the British Evening Post
St. James's Evening Post
Sun
Telegraph
The British Journal
The British Magazine, Or, Monthly Repository for Gentlemen & Ladies
The Bury and Norwich Post: Or, Suffolk, Norfolk, Essex, and Cambridge Advertiser
The Daily Journal
The Derby Mercury
The Flying Post
The Gentleman's Magazine
The Hull Packet and Humber Mercury
The Ipswich Journal
The Leicester Chronicle: Or, Commercial and Agricultural Advertiser
The Leicester Journal
The Leicestershire Journal
The London Chronicle Or Universal Evening Post
The London Journal
The Middlesex Journal
The Mirror of the Times
The Monthly Review; Or, Literary Journal
The Morning Post and Gazetteer
The Morning Post
The Post-Boy
The Spectator
The Tatler
The Times

True Briton (1793)
Universal Chronicle Or Weekly Gazette
Universal Spectator and Weekly Journal
Weekly Journal, Or The British Gazetteer
Westminster Journal Or New Weekly Miscellany
Whitehall Evening Post (1770)
Whitehall Evening Post Or London Intelligencer
World and Fashionable Advertiser

Articles and Books

Allen, D. (1997), "Daniel Browninge of Crowfield: A Little-Known High Sheriff of Suffolk and the Stowmarket Assizes of 1695," *Proceedings of the Suffolk Institute of Archaeology and History,* vol. XXXIX, part 1, pp. 28–47.

Allen, D. et al (2000), *Ipswich Borough Archives 1255–1835: A Catalogue,* Ipswich: Suffolk Records Society.

Allen, F. (1739), *The Reasonableness and Necessity of Human Laws and Penalties. A Sermon Preached at the Assizes Held at Reading… Tuesday, March the 6th, 1738–9,* London.

Andrews, A. (1856), *The Eighteenth Century Or Illustrations of the Manners and Customs of Our Grandfathers,* London.

Andrews, T. (1738), *An Enquiry into the Causes of the Encrease and Miseries of the Poor of England,* London.

Anon (1681), *Seasonable Cautions for Juries, Solicitors and Witnesses, to Deterre from Man-catching,* London.

Anon (1701), *Hanging, Not Punishment Enough, For Murtherers, Highway Men, and House-Breakers,* London.

Anon (1705), *A Full and True Account of the Tryal, Examination, and Proceedings against Mr. John Maugridge a Kettle-Drummer,* London.

Anon (1705), *The Wicked Husband, and Unnatural Father: Being a Sad and Deplorable Relation of one William Gilbert, a farmer of Toddington Near Lynn in Norfolk,* London.

Anon (1709), *A Charitable Visit to the Prisons. Containing Suitable and Proper Advice or Counsel to those Who are Confined There,* London.

Anon (1709), *An Impartial Account of the Malicious Prosecution of John Comyn, and Chadwick Chambers. By Robert Deans of Maidstone, and His Accomplices, on Pretence of Their Robbing the said Deans on the Highway*, London.

Anon (1711), *A Bill for Erecting a Work-house in the City and County of the City of Norwich, For the Better Employing and Maintaining the Poor There*, London.

Anon (1722), *The Tryal and Condemnation of Arundel Coke Alias Cooke Esq; and of John Woodburne Labourer, for Felony, In Slitting the Nose of Edward Crispe Gent*, London.

Anon (1724), *A Narrative of the Proceedings in France, For Discovering and Detecting the Murderers of the English Gentlemen, Sept. 21, 1723, near Calais*, London.

Anon (1727), *A Method Whereby Criminals Liable to Transportation May be Render'd Not Only Useful But Honest Members of the Publick*, London.

Anon (1733), *Abstract of Several Acts*, London.

Anon (1737), *A Dissertation on the Constitution and Effects of Petty Jury*, Dublin.

Anon (1738), *An Enquiry into the Causes of the Increase and Miseries of the Poor in England*, London.

Anon (1740), *The Suffolk Parricide; Being, The Trial Life, Transactions, and Last Dying Words of Charles Drew, of Long-Melford, in the County of Suffolk*, London.

Anon (By a gentleman of Bury) (1740), *The Genuine Trial of Charles Drew, For the Murder of His Own Father, at the Assizes Held at Bury St. Edmund's: on Thursday, March 27, 1740* (2nd edn.), London.

Anon (By an attorney at law) (1742), *The Law of Arrests in Both Civil and Criminal Cases*, London.

Anon (1750), *The Life of Benjamin Barker, A Notorious Highwayman, From His Youth to His Death*, London.

Anon (1752), *A True and Particular Narrative of the Disturbances and Outrages That Have Been Committed in the City of Norwich, Since November to the Present Time*, London.

Anon (1752), *The Complete Juryman: Or, A Compendium of the Laws Relating to Jurors*, London.

Anon (1753), *A Compassionate Address to the High and Mighty in Behalf of the Poor Distressed Prisoners*, London.

Anon (Member of Parliament) (1756), *Further Observations On the Buyers or Receivers of Stolen Goods, Particularly, of Lead, Iron, Copper, Brass, Bell-metal, and Solder*, London.

Anon (1756), *The Coroner's Guide: Or, the Office and Duty of a Coroner* (2nd edn), London.

Anon (1758), *An Essay on the Office of Constable* (2nd edn.), London.

Anon (1759), *The Genuine Account of the Life and Trial of Eugene Aram, For the Murder of Daniel Clark, Late of Knaresborough in the County of York,* London.

Anon (An eminent short-hand writer) (1763), *The Genuine Trial of Margery Beddingfield and Richard Ringe*, London.

Anon (1765), *A Proposal For the Relief and More Comfortable Maintenance of the Poor of the County of Norfolk*, London.

Anon (1768), *The History of the City and County of Norwich: From the Earliest Accounts to the Present Time,* Norwich.

Anon (1770), *A Kalendar of the Prisoners Now Confined in Ipswich Gaol… Who Are to be Tried at the Next General Assizes of Oyer and Terminer, … 9th August 1770*, Bury St. Edmunds.

Anon (1771), *A Dialogue Between a Lawyer and a Country Gentlemen, Upon the Subject of the Game Laws,* London.

Anon (1772), *The Norfolk Tour: Or, Traveller's Pocket Companion. Being a Concise Description and Present State of all the Noblemens and Gentlemens Seats, As Well as of the Principal Towns, and Other Remarkable Places, in the County of Norfolk*, London and Norwich.

Anon (1779), *The Trial at Large of Thomas Clarke, Thomas Carty, and John Deane, Who Were Tried, Convicted, and Received Sentence of Death, For Robbing Thomas Marsh on the King's Highway, at Yoxford, etc.*, Bury St Edmunds.

Anon (1783), *The Means of Effectually Preventing Theft and Robbery; Together With Our Present Cruel Punishments of Those and Other Crimes*, London.

Anon (1783), *The Trial at Large of Jeremiah Theobald,* Ipswich.

Anon (1785), *Internal Police of the Kingdom Very Much Neglected,* London.

Anon (1786), *The Trial of John Shilling, For the Wilful Murder of Mr. John Raven, of Burnham Westgate, Carrier, at the Lent assizes, 1786, Holden at Thetford, before Sir George Nares, Knt.*, Bury St. Edmunds.

Anon (By a magistrate) (1787), *Some Hints towards a Revival of the Penal Laws, The Better Regulating the Police, and the Necessity of Enforcing the Execution of Justice,* London.

Anon (1788), *The Trial of Thomas Harper, For Shooting Thomas Briggs, of Lakenheath in the County of Suffolk* (2nd edn.), King's Lynn.

Anon (1788), *The Trial of Joseph Wakefield and Henry Smith, (the Former of Whom Only Was Convicted) For the Murder of Mr. Thomas Twaites … In the Month of November, 1785*, Bury St Edmunds.

Anon (1788), *The Trial of Henry Sell, For the Wilful Murder of Mrs. Elizabeth Clark, Wife of Mr. Wm. Clark, Farrier, at Walsoken, in Norfolk. At the Lent Assizes 1788, Holden at Thetford*, Bury St Edmunds.

Anon (1790), *Statement and Propositions From the Society for Giving Effect to His Majesty's Proclamation Against Vice and Immorality*, London.

Anon (1791), *General Regulations for the Government of the New Goal* [sic], *At Ipswich, for the County of Suffolk; As Drawn Out at the General Quarter Sessions of the Peace, Held by Adjournment, on Tuesday, the Second of February, 1791*, Ipswich.

Anon (1792), *The Trials of the Offenders Apprehended for the Riots in the Borough of Great Yarmouth, Norfolk, October 27th, 1792, At a Special Session, Held 21st Nov. Following, at Yarmouth*, London.

Anon (1792), *The Trial of Roger Benstead the Elder, and Roger Benstead the Younger, For the Wilful Murder of Thomas Briggs, of Lakenheath, in Suffolk*, Bury St. Edmunds.

Anon (1793), *An Address to the Public, From the Friends of Freedom. Assembled at Their Club, at the Goose and Gridiron, St. Giles's; on Saturday, Feb. 1, 1793: Containing a Protest Against the Late Associations for the Prosecution of Felons*, London.

Anon (1794), *Last Dying Speech and Full Confession of Benjamin Brett*, Bury St Edmunds.

Anon (1794), *The Trial of John and Nathan Nichols: (Father and Son) For the Wilful Murder of Sarah Nichols, Daughter of the Former, and Sister of the Latter*, Bury St Edmunds.

Anon (1794), *A Calendar of the Prisoners in the custody of Margaret Baker, Keeper of His Majesty's Gaol of Bury St. Edmund's, For Trial at the Summer Assizes*, Bury St Edmunds.

Anon (1795), *The Poll for Electing A Coroner for Norfolk, Occasioned by the Resignation of Mr. Francis Munhall*, Norwich.

Anon (1795), *At A Meeting of the Grand Juries for the County of Suffolk … For Taking into Consideration the Present Very Heavy Expence that Attends Executing the Office of Sheriff*, Bury St. Edmunds.

Anon (By a friend to the constitution) (1796), *Observations On the Duty and Power of Juries, As established by the Laws of England* (2nd edn.), London.

Anon (1799), *Rules and Regulations, Entered Into By the Members of the Harleston Association for Prosecuting Felons*, Bury St. Edmunds.

Anon (1800), *Trial of Joseph Clark, the Younger, and Sarah Lloyd*, Ipswich.

Anon (1800), *The Trial of Mr. Savill, Linen-Draper, Margate, Who was Falsely and Maliciously Charged with Assaulting Mary Bayly, With Intent her Carnally to Know and to Abuse,* London.

Anon (1811), *The Crown Circuit Companion* (8th edn.), London.

Anon (1815), *The Trial at Large of Eliz. Woolterton for the Wilful Murder of Robert Sparkes, A Child Six Years Old*, Bury St Edmunds.

Anon (By a juryman) (1819), *Notes and Observations On Criminal Trials*, London.

Anon (1819), *Report from the Select Committee on Criminal Laws, &c.; Ordered by the House of Commons to be Printed, 8th July 1819*, London.

Anon (1836), *Penny Cyclopaedia of the Society For the Diffusion of Useful Knowledge*, vol. 5, London: Charles Knight.

Anon (Historical Manuscripts Commission) (1895), "The Corporation of Bury St. Edmunds: Minute-books (1652–1835)," at pp. 144–155 in *The Manuscripts of Lincoln, Bury St. Edmunds etc.: Fourteenth report, Appendix; part VIII*, London.

Anon (2000), "The Parish Constable in Georgian Times," *Barwicker*, No. 59, p. 50

Anselment, R. (ed.) (2002), *The Remembrances of Elizabeth Freke, 1671–1714*, Cambridge: Cambridge University Press.

Archenholz, J. W. von (1791), *A Picture of England, Containing a Description of the Laws, Customs and Manners of England*, Dublin.

Archer, J. E. (1985), "'A Fiendish Outrage'? A Study of Animal Maiming in East Anglia: 1830–1870," *The Agricultural History Review*, vol. 33, No. 2, pp. 147–157.

D'Archenholz, M. (1789), *A Picture of England, Containing a Description of the Laws, Customs, and Manners of England*, London.

Armstrong, M. (1781), *History and Antiquities of the County of Norfolk*, vol. 1, Norwich.

Ashby, R. (1724), *A Relation of a Visit to Three Malefactors, Condemn'd at the Assizes at Thetford in Norfolk, Anno 1721–2*, London.

Ayres, J. (ed.) (1984), *Paupers and Pig Killers: The Diary of William Holland, a Somerset Parson, 1799–1818*, Stroud: Sutton Publishing.

Baldwin, R. (1776), *Considerations on Some Laws Relating to the Office of Coroner,* Newcastle.

Banks, S. (2008), "'Very Little Law in the Case': Contests of Honour and the Subversion of the English Criminal Courts, 1780–1845," *King's Law Journal*, vol. 19, pp. 575–594.

Banks, S. (2010), *A Polite Exchange of Bullets: The Duel and the English Gentleman, 1750–1850*, Woodbridge: Boydell Press.

Barker, H. R. (2008), *History of, and Guide to, Bury St. Edmund's*, Bury: Andesite Press.

Barlow, T. (1745), *The Justice of Peace: A Treatise Containing the Power and Duty of that Magistrate*, London.

Bath, J. (2001), *Violence and Violent Crime in the North East, c.1650–1720*, Newcastle University (PhD thesis).

Beattie, J. M. (1986), *Crime and the Courts in England 1660–1800*, Oxford: Oxford University Press.

(2007), "Sir John Fielding and Public Justice: The Bow Street Magistrates' Court, 1754–1780," *Law and History Review*, vol. 25, no. 1, pp. 61–100.

Bentley, D. (1998), *English Criminal Justice in the Nineteenth Century*, Hambledon: Hambledon Press.

Campbell, B. and Overton, M. (1993), "A New Perspective on Medieval and Early Modern Agriculture: Six Centuries of Norfolk Farming c.1250–c.1850," *Past & Present*, no. 141, pp. 38–105.

Beresford, J. (ed.) (1978), *The Diary of a Country Parson, 1758–1802*, Oxford: Oxford University Press.

Berman, M. N. and Farrell, I. P. (2012), "Provocation Manslaughter as Partial Justification and Partial Excuse," *William and Mary Law Review*, vol. 52, no. 4, pp. 1027–1107.

Berry, C. (1810), *A Concise History and Directory of the City of Norwich; For 1811*, Norwich.

Beville, R. (1799), *A Treatise on the Law of Homicide, and of Larceny at Common Law*, London.

Binder, G. (2007), "The Meaning of Killing," pp. 88–114 in Dubber, M. and Farmer, L. (eds), *Modern Histories of Crime and Punishment*, Redwood City: Stanford University Press.

Bird, J. (1799), *The Laws Respecting Parish Matters* (2nd edn.), London.

Bird, M. (ed.) (2013), *The Diary of Mary Hardy 1773–1809*, vol. 1, Kingston-upon-Thames: Burnham Press

Black, J. (1986), "Newspapers and Politics in the 18th century," *History Today*, vol. 36, issue 10, pp. 36–42.

Blackerby, S. (1715), *The Justice of Peace His Companion* (3rd edn.), London.

(1717), *Cases in Law: Wherein Justices of Peace Have a Jurisdiction, As Well By Their Commission, As by Act of Parliament... Being the Second Part of The Justice of Peace's Companion,* London.

Blackstone, W. (1765–9), *Commentaries on the Laws of England,* vols. 1–4, Oxford: Clarendon Press.

Blomefield, F. (1739), *The History of the Ancient City and Burgh of Thetford in the Counties, of Norfolk and Suffolk Shewing It's Rise, Increase, Decrease, and Present State,* Fersfield.

(1806), *An Essay Towards a Topographical History of the County Of Norfolk,* vol. iii, London.

Bogart, D. (2005), "Did Turnpike Trusts Increase Transportation Investment in Eighteenth-century England?," *The Journal of Economic History,* vol. 65, no. 2, pp. 439–468.

Bohstedt, J. (1983), *Riots and Community Politics in England and Wales, 1790–1810.* Boston: Harvard University Press.

Bohun, E. (1693), *The Justice of Peace His Calling and Qualifications,* London.

Braddic, M. J. (2010), *State Formation in Early Modern England, c.1550–1700.* Cambridge: Cambridge University Press.

Bransby, J. (1799), *The Ipswich Magazine, For the Year 1799,* Ipswich.

Brereton, C. D. (1827), *The Subordinate Magistracy and Parish System Considered: In Their Connection with the Causes and Remedies of Modern Pauperism,* Norwich.

Brewer, J. and Styles, J. (eds.) (1980), *An Ungovernable People. The English and their law in the Seventeenth and Eighteenth Centuries,* London: Hutchinson.

Briggs, J. et al (1996), *Crime And Punishment in England: An Introductory History,* London: Routledge.

Broome, W. (1737), *A Sermon Preach'd at the Assizes in Norwich, August 8th, 1737,* Norwich.

Broughton, T. (1800), *Serious Advice and Warning to Servants, More Especially Those of the Nobility and Gentry,* London.

Brown, A. (1996), *Prosperity and Poverty: Rural Essex 1700–1815,* Chelmsford: Essex Record Office.

Brown, B. J. (1963), "The Demise of Chance Medley and the Recognition of Provocation as a Defence to Murder in English Law," *American Journal of Legal History,* vol. 7, no. 4, pp. 310–318.

Brydall, J. (1700), *Non Compos Mentis: Or, The Law Relating to Natural Fools, Mad-folks, and Lunatick Persons*, London.

Buck, A. R. (2006), *The Making of Australian Property Law*, Sydney: The Federation Press.

Burke, E. (1839), "Some Thoughts on the Approaching Executions, Humbly Offered to Consideration," pp. 197–200, in *The Works of Edmund Burke*, vol. v, Boston: Little, Brown.

Burn, R. (1764), *The History of the Poor Laws: With Observations*, London.

Bushaway, R. (1981), "'Groveley, Groveley and All Groveley': Crime and Conflict in the English Woodland," *History Today*, vol. 31, issue 5, pp. 37–45.

Campbell, B. and Overton, M. (1993), "A New Perspective on Medieval and Early Modern Agriculture: Six Centuries of Norfolk Farming c.1250–c.1850," *Past & Present*, no. 141, pp. 38–105.

Care, H. (1703), *English Liberties: Or, the Free-Born Subject's Inheritance*, London.

Carew, B. M. (1749), *An Apology for the Life of Bampfylde Moore Carew*, London.

Caswell, M. (2012), *Married Women, Crime, and Questions of Liability in England, 1640–1760*, Queen's University (Canada) (PhD thesis).

Chandler, E. (1740), *A Charge Delivered to the Grand-Jury, At the Quarter-sessions Held at Durham, on Wednesday, the 16th of July, 1740. Concerning Engrossing of Corn and Grain, and the Riots that Have Been Occasion'd Thereby*, Durham.

Chatterton, E. K. (1912), *King's Cutters and Smugglers 1700–1855*, London: George Allen.

Cheung, H. and Mui, L. H. (1975), "'Trends in Eighteenth-century Smuggling' Reconsidered," *The Economic History Review*, New Series, vol. 28, no. 1, pp. 28–43.

Cirket, A. (ed.) (1971), *Samuel Whitbread's Notebooks*, Ampthill: Bedfordshire Historical Record Society.

Clark, A. (1987), *Women's Silence, Men's Violence: Sexual Assault in England 1770–1845*, New York: Pandora Press

Clark, G. (2001), "Farm Wages and Living Standards in the Industrial Revolution: England, 1670–1869," *Economic History Review*, vol. 54, no. 3, pp. 477–505.

Clayton, M. (2009), "Changes in Old Bailey Trials for the Murder of Newborn Babies, 1674–1803," *Continuity and Change*, vol. 24, pp. 337–359.

Clemis, J. D. (1999), *Government in an English Provincial Town: The Corporation of Ipswich, 1720–95*, University of Leicester (PhD thesis).

Cockburn, J. S. (1969), "Seventeenth-century Clerks of Assize—Some Anonymous Members of the Legal Profession," *The American Journal of Legal History*, vol. 13, pp. 315–332.

(1972), *A History of English Assizes, 1558–1714*, Cambridge: Cambridge University Press.

(ed.) (1977), *Crime in England 1550–1800*, London: Methuen.

(1991), "Patterns of Violence in English Society: Homicide in Kent 1560–1985," *Past & Present*, no. 130, pp. 70–106.

Cockburn, J. S. and Green, T. A. (eds) (1988), *Twelve Good Men and True: The Criminal Trial Jury in England 1200–1800*, Princeton: Princeton University Press.

Cohen, S. (1972), *Folk Devils and Moral Panics: The Creation of the Mods and Rockers*. London: MacGibbon & Kee Ltd.

Coldham, P. W. (1988), *The Complete Book of Emigrants in Bondage, 1614–1775*. Baltimore: Genealogical Publishing Company.

(2011), *Emigrants in Chains. A Social History of Forced Emigration to the Americas of Felons, Destitute Children, Political and Religious Non-Conformists, Vagabonds, Beggars and Other Undesirables, 1607–1776*, Baltimore: Genealogical Publishing Company.

Colquhoun, P. (1800), *A Treatise on the Police of the Metropolis*, London.

(1803), *A Treatise on the Functions and Duties of a Constable*, London.

Cooper, T. (1620), *The Cry and Revenge of Blood*, London.

Corfield, P. (1987), "From Rank to Class: Innovation in Georgian England," *History Today*, vol. 37, issue 2, pp. 36–42.

Costello, K. (2012), "The Writ of Certiorari and Review of Summary Criminal Convictions, 1660–1848," *Law Quarterly Review*, vol. 128(3), pp. 443–465.

Cox, D. (2002), "The 'Bread And Butter Riots' of 1766," *Civil Unrest in the Black Country 1750–1837*, part 1, Black Country Society, www.blackcountrysociety.co.uk (Retrieved 15 March 2015).

(2005), *Cinderellas and Packhorses: A History of the Shropshire Magistracy*, Logaston: Logaston Press.

(2015), *Crime in England 1688–1815*, London: Routledge.

Dabhoiwala, F. (2012), *The Origins of Sex: A History of the First Sexual Revolution*, London: Allen Lane.

Dagge, H. (1772), *Considerations on Criminal Law*, Dublin.

Daunton, M. J. (1995), *Progress and Poverty: An Economic and Social History of Britain 1700–1850*, Oxford: Oxford University Press.

Davey, B. J. (1994), *Rural Crime in the Eighteenth Century: North Lincolnshire 1740–80*, Hull: The University of Hull Press.

Davies, O. (1999), "Witchcraft: The Spell that Didn't Break," *History Today*, vol. 49, no. 8, pp. 7–13.

D'Cruze, S. (2009), *A Pleasing Prospect: Social Change and Urban Culture in Eighteenth-century Colchester*, Hatfield: University of Hertfordshire Press.

Defoe, D. (1722), *The Fortunes and Misfortunes of the Famous Moll Flanders*, London.

(1978) (originally published 1724–26), *A Tour Through the Whole Island of Great Britain*, Harmondsworth: Penguin.

Devereaux, S. (1999) "The Making of the Penitentiary Act, 1775–1779," *The Historical Journal*, vol. 42, issue 2, pp. 405–433.

(2005), "The Abolition of the Burning of Women in England Reconsidered," *Crime, Histoire & Sociétés/Crime, History & Societies*, vol. 9, no. 2, pp. 73–98.

(2005), "The Promulgation of the Statutes in Late Hanoverian Britain," pp. 80–101 in Lemmings, D. (ed.), *The British and Their Laws in the Eighteenth Century*, Woodbridge: Boydell & Brewer.

(1998), "The Criminal Branch of the Home Office 1782–1830," pp. 270–308 in Devereaux, S. et al (eds.), *Criminal Justice in the Old World and the New.* Toronto: University of Toronto.

Dickinson, H. T. (2002), "Popular Politics and Radical Ideas," at pp. 97–111, in H. T. Dickinson (ed.), *A Companion to Eighteenth-century Britain*, Oxford: Blackwell.

Dinwiddy, J. R. (1982), "The Early Nineteenth-century Campaign Against Flogging in the Army," *English Historical Review*, vol. XCVII, pp. 308–331.

Disney, J. (1786), *An Address to Grand-Juries, Constables and Church Wardens*, London.

Dodsworth, F. M. (2008), "The Idea of Police in Eighteenth-century England: Discipline, Reformation, Superintendence, c.1780–1800," *Journal of the History of Ideas*, vol. 64, issue 4, pp. 583–605.

Dolins, D. (1726), *The Third Charge of Sir Daniel Dolins, Kt to the Grand-Jury, and other Juries of the County of Middlesex*, London.

Durston, G. (2005), "Magwitch's Forbears: Returning from Transportation in Eighteenth-century London," *Australian Journal of Legal History*, vol. 9, no. 2, pp. 137–158.

(2012), *Whores and Highwaymen: Crime and Justice in the Eighteenth-century Metropolis*. Hook: Waterside Press.

Eastwood, D. (1997), *Government and Community in the English Provinces, 1700–1870*. Basingstoke: Macmillan.

(2002), "Local Government and Local Society," at pp. 40–54, in H. T. Dickinson (ed.), *A Companion to Eighteenth-century Britain*. Oxford: Blackwell.

Eccles, A. (2012), *Vagrancy in Law and Practice under the Old Poor Law*. Farnham: Ashgate

Eden, F. M. (1797), *The State of the Poor; Or, An History of the Labouring Classes in England, From the Conquest to the Present Period*, vol. 1, London.

Eden, W. (1781), *Principles of Penal law*, London.

Eder, M. (2014), *"At the Instigation of the Devil": Capital Punishment and the Assize in the Early Modern England, 1670–1730* (2nd edn.), Hilgertshausen-Tandern.

Edwards, D. (1774), *Sermons For the Use of Condemned Malefactors ... To Which is Added, An Original Dialogue Between the Minister and Two Convicts Ordered for Execution*, London,

Edwards, P. (1988), *The Horse Trade of Tudor and Stuart England*, Cambridge: Cambridge University Press.

Eisner, M. (2001), "Modernization, Self-control and Lethal violence," *British Journal of Criminology*, vol. 41, pp. 618–638.

(2003), "Long-Term Historical Trends in Violent Crime," *Crime and Justice: A Review of Research*, vol. 30, pp. 83–142.

Eisner, M. and Nivette, A. (2013), "Does Low Legitimacy Cause Crime? A Review of the Evidence," Cambridge: Violence Research Centre Working Paper.

Ekirch, A. R. (1987), *Bound for America: The Transportation of British Convicts to the Colonies, 1718–1775*, Oxford: Clarendon Press.

Emmerichs, M. (2001), "Getting Away with Murder?: Homicide and the Coroners in Nineteenth-century London," *Social Science History*, vol. 25, no. 1, pp. 93–100.

Emsley, C. (2010), *Crime and Society in England: 1750–1900* (4th edn.), London: Routledge.

Evans, E. J. (1975), "Some Reasons for the Growth of English Rural Anti-Clericalism c.1750–c.1830," *Past & Present*, no. 66, pp. 84–109.

Fielding, J. (1762), *Extracts From Such of the Penal Laws, As Particularly Relate to the Peace and Good Order of this Metropolis*, London.

Fisher, G. (1995), "The Birth of the Prison Retold," *Yale Law Journal*, vol. 104, pp. 1236–1252.

Fisher, G. (1997), "The Jury's Rise as Lie Detector," *Yale Law Review*, vol. 107, no. 3, pp. 575–713.

Fisher, P. J. (2007), "Getting Away with Murder? The Suppression of Coroners' Inquests in Early Victorian England and Wales," *Local Population Studies*, vol. 78, pp. 47–62.

(2013), *The Politics of Sudden Death: The Office and Role of the Coroner In England and Wales, 1726–1888,* University of Leicester (PhD thesis).

(2011), "Edmund Whitcombe and the Detection of Homicide in Georgian Shropshire," *Family & Community History*, vol. 14, issue 1, pp. 3–23.

Fiske, J. (Ed) (1991), *The Oakes Diaries: Business, Politics and the Family in Bury St. Edmunds 1778–1827.* Woodbridge: Suffolk Records Society/Boydell & Brewer Inc.

Fitzsimmonds, J. (1751), *Free and Candid Disquisitions on the Nature and Execution of the Laws of England, Both in Civil and Criminal Affairs,* London.

Fletcher, G. P. (1976), "The Metamorphosis of Larceny," *Harvard Law Review*, vol. 89, no. 3, pp. 469–530.

Fletcher, R. (1910), *The Pension Book of Gray's Inn (Records of the Honourable Society) 1669–1800*, vol. II, London: Chiswick Press.

Flynn, S. and Stevens, M. (1995), "Petty Criminals, Publicans and Sinners: Petty Sessions Records in the Berkshire Record Office," *Journal of the Society of Archivists*, vol. 16, no. 1, pp. 41–53.

Foster, M. (1762), *A Report of Some Proceedings on the Commission of Oyer and Terminer and Gaol Delivery for the Trial of the Rebels in the Year 1746 in the County of Surry and of other Crown Cases. To which are added Discourses Upon a Few Branches of the Crown Law,* Oxford: Clarendon Press.

Francus, M. (1997), "Monstrous Mothers, Monstrous Societies: Infanticide and the Rule of Law in Restoration and Eighteenth-century England," *Eighteenth-century Life*, vol. 21, no. 2, pp. 133–156.

(2012), *Monstrous Motherhood: Eighteenth-century Culture and the Ideology of Domesticity*, Baltimore: Johns Hopkins University Press.

Friedman, D. (1995), "Making Sense of English Law Enforcement in the Eighteenth Century," *University of Chicago Law School Roundtable*, vol. 2, issue 2, pp. 475–505.

Fudge, E. (2000), "Monstrous Acts," *History Today*, 2000, vol. 50, no. 8, pp. 20–25.

Gardiner, R. (1655), *England's Grievance Discovered, In Relation to the Coal-trade With the Map of the River of Tine, And Situation of the Town and Corporation of Newcastle,* London.

(1710), *The Compleat Constable* (4th edn.), London.

Gardner, T. (1754), *Southwold, An Historical account of Dunwich, Antienty a City, Now a Borough; Blithburgh, Formerly a Town of Note, Now a Village; Southwold, Once a Village, Now a Town-Corporate*, London.

Gatrell, V.A.C. (1996), *The Hanging Tree: Execution and the English People 1770–1868*, Oxford: Oxford University Press.

Gay, N. (1947), *Glorious Dunwich: Its Story Through the Ages*, Ipswich: Suffolk Press

Gent, J. D. (1720), *An Humble Proposal to Prevent the Beginnings of Theft*, London.

George, R. (1708), *Honour and Conscience Call'd upon: Or, the Duty of Faithfulness and Satisfying Trust Urg'd, in a Sermon Preach'd at the Assizes at Bury St Edmonds In Suffolk, March 23. 1707/8*, Norwich.

Gilboy, R. (1934), *Wages in Eighteenth-century England,* Cambridge: Harvard University Press.

Gillespy, E. (1793), *A Disquisition Upon the Criminal Laws; Shewing the Necessity of Altering and Amending Them,* Northampton.

Gisborne, T. (1794), *An Enquiry Into the Duties of Men in the Higher and Middle Classes of Society in Great Britain,* London.

Glassey, L. (1979), *Politics and Justices of the Peace, 1675–1720,* Oxford: Clarendon Press.

Godschall, W. M. (1787), *A General Plan of Parochial and Provincial Police*, London.

Gonson, J. (1728), *The Charge of Sir John Gonson Knt. to the Grand Jury of the Royalty of the Tower of London, And Liberties and Precincts Thereof*, London.

Gough, G. (1981), *The History of Myddle*, Harmondsworth: Penguin.

Gray, D. (2013), "Making Law in Mid-eighteenth-century England: Legal Statutes and Their Application in the Justicing Notebook of Phillip Ward of Stoke Doyle," *Journal of Legal History*, vol. 34, no. 2, pp. 211–233.

Gray, D. and King, P. J. R. (2013), "The Killing of Constable Linnell: The Impact of Xenophobia and of Elite Connections on Eighteenth-century Justice," *Family & Community History*, vol. 16, no. 1, pp. 3–31.

Green, M. (Ed) (1856), *Diary of John Rous, incumbent of Santon Downham, Suffolk, from 1625 to 1642*, London: Camden Society.

Green, T. A. (1985), *Verdict According to Conscience,* Chicago: Chicago University Press.

Griffin, C. J. (2008), "'Cut Down by Some Cowardly Miscreants': Plant Maiming, or the Malicious Cutting of Plants as an Act of Protest in Eighteenth and Nineteenth-century Rural England," *Rural History*, vol. 19, issue 1, pp. 29–54.

Griffin, C. J. (2012), "Animal Maiming, Intimacy and the Politics of Shared Life: The Bestial and the Beastly in Eighteenth and Early Nineteenth-century England," *Transactions of the Institute of British Geographers*, vol. 37, pp. 301–316.

(2013), *Protest, Politics and Work in Rural England, 1700–1850*, London: Palgrave Macmillan.

Grosley, M. (1772), *A Tour to London: Or, New Observations On England, and Its Inhabitants*, vol. 3, Dublin.

Haigh, C. (2004), "Clergy JPs In England And Wales, 1590–1640," *The Historical Journal*, vol. 47, issue 2, pp. 233–259.

Hale, M. (1713), *The History of the Common Law of England*, London.

(Updated by Emlyn, S.) (1736), *Historia Placitorum Coronae. The History of the Pleas of the Crown*, London.

(Updated by Wilson, G. and Emlyn, S.) (1800), *The History of the Pleas of the Crown*, vol. 1, London.

Halifax, C. (1791), *The Constable's Sure Guide; Or Every Constable His Own Lawyer*, London.

Halliday, R. and Susser, B. (2002), "The Ipswich Jewish Community in the Eighteenth and Nineteenth Centuries," vol. 40, part 2, *Proceedings of the Suffolk Institute of Archaeology and History*, pp. 151–163.

Hanawalt, B. A. (1975), "Fur-Collar Crime: The Pattern of Crime Amongst the Fourteenth-century English Nobility," *Journal of Social History*, vol. 8, pp. 1–17.

Handler, P. (2007), "The Law of Felonious Assault in England, 1803–61," *Journal of Legal History*, vol. 28, issue 2, pp. 183–206.

(2007), "The Law of Felonious Assault in England, 1803–61," *The Journal of Legal History*, vol. 28, issue 2, pp. 183–206.

Hanway, J. (1785), *The Defects of Police*, London

Hardman, P. (2007), *The Origins of Late Eighteenth-century Prison Reform in England*, University of Sheffield (PhD thesis).

(2013), "Fear of Fever and the Limits of the Enlightenment: Selling Prison Reform in Late Eighteenth-century Gloucestershire," *Cultural & Social History*, 2013, vol. 10, issue 4, pp. 511–531.

Harley, D. (1994), "The Scope of Legal Medicine in Lancashire and Cheshire, 1660–1760," pp. 45–63 in Clark, M. and Crawford, C. (eds.), *Legal Medicine in History*, Cambridge: Cambridge University Press.

Harvey, A. (2005), *Football: The First Hundred Years*, London: Routledge.

Hasted, E. (1797), *The History and Topographical Survey of the County of Kent,* vol. 1, Canterbury.

Hawkins, J. (1780), *A Charge to the Grand Jury of the County of Middlesex, Delivered at the General Session of the Peace, Holden at Hicks-Hall, in the said County, on Monday the Eleventh Day of September, 1780,* London.

Hawkins, W. (1724), *A Treatise of the Pleas of the Crown,* Book 1 (2nd edn.), London.

Hawles, J. (1680), *The Englishman's Right: A Dialogue Between a Barrister at Law and a Juryman,* London.

Hay, D. (1976), "Property, Authority and the Criminal Law," pp. 17–64, in P. Linebaugh et al (eds), *Albion's Fatal Tree: Crime and Society in Eighteenth-century England,* London: Random House.

(1982), "War, Dearth and Theft in the Eighteenth Century: The Record of the English Courts," *Past and Present,* vol. 95, pp. 117–160.

(1998), "Patronage, Paternalism, and Welfare," *International Labor and Working-Class History,* vol. 53, pp. 27–47.

(2000), "Master and Servant in England: Using the Law in the Eighteenth and Nineteenth Centuries," at pp. 227–264 in Steinmetz, W. (ed.), *Private Law and Social Inequality in the Industrial Age,* Oxford: Oxford University Press.

(2002), "Dread of the Crown Office: The English Magistracy and King's Bench 1740–1800," at pp. 19–45 in Landau, N. (ed.), *Law, Crime and English Society 1660–1830,* Cambridge: Cambridge University Press.

Hay, D. and Craven, P. (eds.) (2004), *Masters, Servants, and Magistrates in Britain and the Empire,* Chapel Hill: The University of North Carolina Press.

Hay, D. and Rogers, N. (1997), *Eighteenth-century English Society: Shuttles and Swords.* Oxford: Oxford University Press.

Hewitt, J. (1790), *A Journal of the Proceedings of J. Hewitt, Senior Alderman, Of the City of Coventry* (2nd edn.), Coventry.

Higgs, J. (1742), *A Guide to Justices or Modern English Precedents for the Direction of Justices of the Peace and Their Clerks* (2nd edn.), London.

Highmore, A. (1783), *A Digest of the Doctrine of Bail in Civil and Criminal Cases,* London.

Hillen, H. J. (1907), *History of the Borough of King's Lynn,* vols. 1 and 2, Norwich: East of England Newspaper Co.

Hindle, S. (1998), "Power, Poor Relief, and Social Relations in Holland Fen, c.1600–1800," *Historical Journal,* vol. 41, no. 1, pp. 67–96.

Hitchcock, T. (1996), "Sex and Gender: Redefining Sex in Eighteenth-century England," *History Workshop Journal*, vol. 41, pp. 72–90.

Hitchcock, T. and Shoemaker, R. (2015), *London Lives: Poverty, Crime and the Making of a Modern City, 1690–1800*. Cambridge: Cambridge University Press.

Hodshon, R. (1736), *The Honest Man's Companion: Or, The Family's Safeguard*, Newcastle upon Tyne.

Holmes, N. (2008), *The Lawless Coast: Murder, Smuggling and Anarchy in the 1780s on the North Norfolk Coast*, Dereham: The Larks Press.

Houston, R. A. (2010), *Punishing the Dead?: Suicide, Lordship, and Community in Britain, 1500–1830*, Oxford: Oxford University Press.

Howard, J. (1789), *An Account of the Present State of the Prisons and Houses of Correction in the Norfolk Circuit*, London.

Howard, S. (2003), *Crime, Communities and Authority in Early Modern Wales: Denbighshire, 1660–1730*, University of Wales (Aberystwyth) (PhD thesis).

Howard, S. (2008), *Law and Disorder in Early Modern Wales: Crime and Authority in the Denbighshire Courts, c.1660–1730*, Cardiff: University of Wales Press.

Howe, J. (1793), *A Charge Delivered to the Grand Jury at the General Quarter Sessions of the Peace for the County of Suffolk: Holden by Adjournment at Ipswich on Friday, January 18, 1793*, Ipswich.

Humfrey, P. (1998), "Female Servants and Women's Criminality in Early Eighteenth-century London," pp. 58–84, in Smith, G. T. et al (eds.), *Criminal Justice in the Old World and the New: Essays in Honour of J M Beattie*, Toronto.

Humphries, T. (1776), *A Preservative From Criminal Offences*, Shrewsbury.

Hussey, S. (1997), "'The Last Survivor of an Ancient Race': The Changing Face of Essex Gleaning," *The Agricultural History Review*, vol. 45, no. 1, pp. 61–72.

Hyde, E. (1803), *A Treatise of the Pleas of the Crown*, vol. 1, London.

Impey, J. (1782), *The New Instructor Clericalis, Stating the Authority, Jurisdiction, and Modern Practice of the Court of King's Bench*, London.

Impey, J. (1800), *The Office and Duty of Coroners*, London.

Innes, J. (2009), *Inferior Politics: Social Problems and Social Policies in Eighteenth-century Britain*, Oxford: Oxford University Press.

Irvine, S. (2011), *Surgeons and Apothecaries in Suffolk: 1750–1830, City Slickers and Country Bumpkins—Exploring Medical Myths*, University of East Anglia (PhD thesis).

Jackson, M. (1994), "Suspicious Infant Deaths: The statute of 1624 and Medical Evidence at Coroners' Inquests," pp. 64–86, in Clark, M. and Crawford, C. (eds.), *Legal Medicine in History*, Cambridge: Cambridge University Press.

(1997), *New Born Child Murder*, Manchester: Manchester University Press.

Jacob, G. (1725), *The Student's Companion: Or, The Reason of the Laws of England*, London.

(1739), *Every Man His Own Lawyer: Or, A Summary of the Laws of England in a New and Instructive Method*, London.

(1743), *The Students Companion: Or, Reason of the Law* (3rd edn.), London.

Jacob, W. M. (2007), *The Clerical Profession in the Long Eighteenth Century, 1680–1840*, Oxford: Oxford University Press.

Jarvis, S. (1987), *Smuggling in East Anglia 1700–1840*, Newbury: Countryside Books.

Jebb, J. (1785), *Thoughts on the Construction and Polity of Prisons: With Hints for Their Improvement*, Bury St. Edmunds.

Jenkins, P. (1986), "From Gallows to Prison? The Execution Rate in Early Modern England," *Criminal Justice History*, vol. 7, pp. 52–60.

(2002), *The Making of a Ruling Class: The Glamorgan Gentry, 1640–1790*, Cambridge: Cambridge University Press.

Jennings, P. (2012), "Policing Drunkenness in England and Wales from the Late Eighteenth-century to the First World War," *Social History of Alcohol and Drugs*, vol. 26, pp. 69–92.

Jodrell, H. (1793), *A Charge Delivered to the Grand Jury of Norfolk, At the General Quarter Sessions Held on Wednesday, Jan. 16, 1793, At the Shire-House on the Castle-Hill, Norwich* (2nd edn.), Norwich.

Jones, C. (1752), *Some Methods Proposed Towards Putting a Stop to the Flagrant Crimes of Murder, Robbery, and Perjury*, London.

Jones, D. (1976), "Thomas Campbell Foster and the Rural Labourer; Incendiarism in East Anglia in the 1840s," *Social History*, vol. 1, no. 1, pp. 5–43.

(1980), "Life and Death in Eighteenth-century Wales: A Note," *Welsh History Review*, vol. 10, no. 4, pp. 536–548

Jones, P. (1982), "Antoine De Guiscard, 'Abbé de la Bourlie,' 'Marquis de Guiscard,'" *British Library Journal*, pp. 94–113.

Kay, R. (2014) *The Glorious Revolution and the Continuity of Law*, Washington: Catholic University of America Press.

Keith-Lucas, B. (1980), *The Unreformed Local Government System*, London: Croom Helm.

Kent, J. R. (1995), "The Centre and the Localities State Formation and Parish Government in England, Circa 1640–1740," *The Historical Journal*, vol. 38, no. 2, pp. 363–404.

Kilday, A. (2014), "'Criminally Poor?' Investigating the Link Between Crime and Poverty in Eighteenth Century England," *Cultural and Social History*, vol. 11, no. 4, pp. 507–526.

King, P. (1987), "Newspaper Reporting, Prosecution Practice and Perceptions of Urban Crime: the Colchester Crime Wave of 1765," *Continuity and Change*, vol. 2, issue 3, pp. 423–454.

(1988), "Illiterate Plebeians, Easily Misled: Jury Composition, Experience and Behaviour in Essex 1735–1815," pp. 254–304, in J. S. Cockburn and T. Green (eds.) *Twelve Good Men and True. The Criminal Trial Jury 1216–1800*, Princeton: Princeton University Press.

(1989), "Gleaners, Farmers and the Failure of Legal Sanctions in England 1750–1850," *Past and Present*, vol. 125, no. 1, pp. 116–150.

(1991), "Customary Rights and Women's Earnings: The Importance of Gleaning to the Rural Labouring Poor, 1750–1850," *The Economic History Review*, vol. 44, no. 3, pp. 461-476.

(1992), "Legal Change, Customary Right, and Social Conflict in Late Eighteenth-century England: The Origins of the Great Gleaning Case of 1788," *Law and History Review*, vol. 10, issue 1, pp. 1–31.

(1996), "Punishing Assault: The Transformation of Attitudes in the English Courts," *Journal of Interdisciplinary History*, vol. 27, pp. 43–74.

(2002), "War as a Judicial Resource. Press Gangs and Prosecution Rates 1740–1830," at pp. 97–116 in N. Landau (ed.), *Law, Crime and English Society 1660–1840*, Cambridge: Cambridge University Press.

(2003), *Crime, Justice, and Discretion in England 1740–1820*, Oxford: Oxford University Press.

(2004), "The Summary Courts and Social Relations in Eighteenth-century England," *Past & Present*, no. 183, pp. 125–172.

(2006), *Crime and Law in England, 1750–1840: Remaking Justice from the Margins*, Cambridge: Cambridge University Press.

(2010), "The Impact of Urbanization on Murder Rates and on the Geography of Homicide in England and Wales, 1780–1850," *The Historical Journal*, vol. 53, issue 3, pp. 671–698.

King, P. and Ward, R. (2015), "Rethinking the Bloody Code in Eighteenth-century Britain: Capital Punishment at the Centre and on the Periphery," *Past and Present*, vol. 228, no. 1, pp. 159–205.

King, P. and Carter Wood, J. (2015), "Black People and the Criminal Justice System: Prejudice and Practice in Later Eighteenth and Early-nineteenth-century London," *Historical Research*, vol. 88, issue 239, pp. 100–124.

Kinnear, M. (1990), "The Correction Court in the Diocese of Carlisle, 1704–1756," *Church History*, vol. 59, pp. 191–206.

Kivivuori, J. & Lehti, M. (2011), "Homicide in Finland and Sweden," *Crime and Justice*, vol. 40, no.1, pp. 109–198.

Koyama, M. (2012), "Prosecution Associations in Industrial Revolution England: Private Providers of Public Goods?," *The Journal of Legal Studies*, vol. 41, issue 1, pp. 95–130.

Knox, W. W. J. and Thomas, L. (2015), "Homicide in Eighteenth-century Scotland: Numbers and Theories," *The Scottish Historical Review*, vol. 94, no. 238, pp. 48–73.

Kyll, T. (1739), *The Trial of the Notorious Highwayman Richard Turpin, At York Assizes on the 22nd day of March, 1739*, York.

Landau, N. (1984), *The Justices of the Peace 1679–1760*, Berkeley: University of California Press.

(1998), "Appearance at the Quarter Sessions of Eighteenth-century Middlesex," *London Journal*, vol. 23, no. 2, pp. 30–51.

(1999), "Indictment for Fun and Profit: A Prosecutor's Reward at Eighteenth-century Quarter Sessions," *Law and History Review*, vol. 17, no. 3, pp. 507–536.

(2002), *Law, Crime and English Society 1660–1830*, Cambridge: Cambridge University Press.

(2005), "Summary Conviction and the Development of the Penal Law," *Law and History Review*, vol. 23, no. 1, pp. 173–189.

Landsman, S. (1990), "The Rise of the Contentious Spirit: Adversary Procedure in Eighteenth-century England," *Cornell Law Review*, vol. 75, pp. 498–609.

Langbein, J. H. (1983), "Shaping the Eighteenth-century Criminal Trial: A View from the Ryder Sources," *The University of Chicago Law Review*, vol. 50, no. 1, pp. 1–136.

(1983), "Albion's Fatal Flaws," *Past & Present*, no. 98, pp. 96–120.

(1987), "The English Criminal Trial Jury on the Eve of the French Revolution," pp. 13–39, in Schioppa, A. P. (ed.), *The Trial Jury in England, France, Germany 1700–1900*, Berlin: Duncker & Humblot.

(1999), "The Prosecutorial Origins of Defense Counsel in the Eighteenth-century: The Appearance of Solicitors," *Cambridge Law Journal*, vol. 58, pp. 314–365.

(2003), *The Origins of Adversary Criminal Trial*, Oxford: Oxford University Press.

(2012), "The Disappearance of Civil Trial in the United States," *Yale Law Journal*, vol. 122, pp. 522–573.

Langeluddecke, H. (1998), "'Patchy and Spasmodic'? The Response of Justices of the Peace to Charles I's Book of Orders," *English Historical Review*, vol. 113, no. 454, pp. 1231–1248.

Langford, P. (1991), *Public Life and the Propertied Englishman: 1689–1798*, Oxford: Clarendon Press.

(2005), *Eighteenth-century Britain: A Very Short Introduction*, Oxford: Oxford University Press.

Layard, D. (1772), *Directions to Prevent the Contagion of the Jail-distemper: Commonly Called the Jail-fever*, London.

Leach, T. (1789), *Cases in Crown Law*, London.

Lee, R. J. (2003), *Encountering and Managing the Poor: Rural Society and the Anglican Clergy in Norfolk 1815–1914*, University of Leicester (PhD thesis).

Lemmings, D. and Walker, C. (2009), *Moral Panics, the Media and the Law in Early Modern England*, Basingstoke: Palgrave Macmillan.

(2005), "Criminal Trial Procedure in Eighteenth-century England: the Impact of Lawyers," *The Journal of Legal History*, vol. 26, pp. 73–82.

(2011), *Law and Government in England During the Long Eighteenth Century: From Consent to Command*, New York: Palgrave Macmillan.

Levine, M. (1963), "A More than Ordinary Case of 'Rape', 13 and 14 Elizabeth 1," *American Journal of Legal History*, 1963, vol. 7, pp. 159–163.

Loar, C. (2010), "Medical Knowledge and the Early Modern English Coroner's Inquest," *Social History of Medicine*, vol. 23, no. 3, pp. 475–491.

Luson, H. (1787), *Inferior Politics; Or, Considerations on the Wretchedness and Profligacy of… London*, London.

Ma, Y. (2008), "Exploring the Origins of Public Prosecution," *International Criminal Justice Review*, vol. 18, pp. 190–211.

Mackerell, B. (1738), *The History and Antiquities of the Flourishing Corporation of King's-Lynn in the County of Norfolk*, London.

Mackie, C. (1901), *Norfolk Annals*, vol. 1, Norwich.

Madan, M. (1785), *Thoughts On Executive Justice: With Respect to Our Criminal Laws, Particularly On the Circuits* (2nd edn.), London.

Maddison, M. E. W. (1986), *The Justices of the Peace and the Administration of Local Government in the East and West Ridings of Yorkshire Between 1680 and 1750*, Leeds University (PhD thesis).

Markless, R. (2013), *Gender, Crime and Discretion in Yorkshire, 1735–1775*, Roehampton University (PhD Thesis).

Marriot, W. (1795), *The Country-Gentleman's Lawyer; And the Farmer's Complete Library, Containing All the Laws Now in Force Which Particularly Relate to Country Gentlemen,* London.

McCafferty, J. (2009), *Capital Punishment*, Chicago: Aldine Transaction.

McGarvie, M. (ed.) (1997), *The King's Peace, The Justice's Notebooks of Thomas Horner of Mells, 1770–1777*, Frome: Frome Society for Local Study.

McGowen, R. (1999), "From Pillory to Gallows: The Punishment of Forgery in the Age of the Financial Revolution," *Past and Present,* vol. 165 (1), pp. 107–140.

McLynn, F. (1989), *Crime and Punishment in Eighteenth-century England*, London: Routledge.

McMullan, J. (1787), "Crime, Law and Order in Early Modern England," *British Journal of Criminology*, vol. 27, no. 3, pp. 252–274.

Meeres, F. (2010), *A History of Bury St Edmunds*, Chichester: Phillimore & Co Ltd.

Melling, E. (Ed.) (1969), *Kentish Sources. VI Crime and Punishment,* Maidstone: Kent County Council.

Meyer, W. (2011), *Beyond the Seas: Eighteenth-century Convict Transportation and the Widening Net of Penal Sanctions*, University of California (Berkeley) (PhD thesis).

Middleditch, T. (1815), *The Trial at Large of Eliz. Woolterton, for the Wilful Murder of Robert Sparkes, A Child Six Years Old*, Bury St. Edmunds.

Misson, M. and Ozell, J. (Trans.) (1719), *Memoirs and Observations in his Travels Over England*, London.

Moir, E. (1969), *Local Government in Gloucestershire 1775–1800*. Bristol: Bristol and Gloucestershire Archaeological Society.

Morgan, G. and Rushton, P. (1998), *Rogues Thieves and the Rule of Law*, London: UCL Press.

Morgan, G. and Rushton, P. (2004), *Eighteenth-century Criminal Transportation*, Basingstoke: Palgrave Macmillan.

Morgan, J. (1787), *The Attorney's Vade Mecum, and Client's Instructor, Treating of Actions: Such as Are Now Most In Use; Of Prosecuting and Defending Them,* vol. 2, London.

Morgan, K. (1989), "Petitions Against Convict Transportation, 1725–1735," *The English Historical Review,* vol. 104, no. 410, pp. 110–113.

Moritz, K. (1886), *Travels in England in 1782,* London: Cassell and Company.

Munsche, P.B. (1981), *Gentlemen and Poachers — The English Game Laws 1671–1831*, Cambridge: Cambridge University Press.

Murray, D. J. (2013), *Crown and Community: The Coroner in Early Modern England, 1580–1630,* University of Calgary (MA thesis).

Muskett, P. (1984), *Riotous Assemblies: Popular Disturbances in East Anglia, 1740–1822,* Ely: EARO.

Muyden, M. V. (ed.) (1902), *A Foreign View of England in the Reigns of George I and George II; The Letters of Monsieur César de Saussure, to His Family.* London: John Murray.

Neale, M. (2011), "Making Crime Pay in Late Eighteenth-century Bristol: Stolen Goods, the Informal Economy and the Negotiation of Risk," *Continuity and Change*, vol. 26, issue 3, pp. 439–459.

Neeson, J. M. (1984), "The Opponents of Enclosure in Eighteenth-century Northamptonshire," *Past & Present*, no. 105, pp. 114–139.

Nelson, R. (1715), *An Address to Persons of Quality and Estate… To Which is Added, An Appendix of Some Original and Valuable Papers,* London.

North, R. (1753), *A Discourse of the Poor. Shewing the Pernicious Tendency of the Laws now in force for Their Maintenance and Settlement,* London

Norton, R. (2005), "Recovering Gay History from the Old Bailey," *London Journal*, vol. 30 (1), pp. 39–54.

Notcutt, T. (1783), *The Trial at Large of Jeremiah Theobald, Otherwise Hasell, and James May, Otherwise Folkes, For the Wilful Murder of Mrs. Frances Phillips of Eriswell, in the County of Suffolk*, Ipswich.

Notcutt, W. (1800), *Trial of Joseph Clarke, the Younger, and Sarah Lloyd, at the Assizes, Held at Bury St. Edmund's, March 20, 1800*, Bury St. Edmunds

Nourse, T. (1700), *Campania Folix. Or, a Discourse of the Benefits and Improvements of Husbandry,* London.

Nourse, T. (1706), *Campania Folix. Or, a Discourse of the Benefits and Improvements of Husbandry* (2nd edn.), London.

Oldham, J. (2011), "Informal Law-Making in England by the Twelve Judges in the Late 18th and Early 19th Centuries," *Law and History Review*, vol. 29, no. 1, pp. 181–200.

Ollyffe, G. (1731), *An Essay Humbly Offer'd, For An Act of Parliament to Prevent Capital Crimes*, London.

Osborne, H. and Winstanley, M. (2006), "Rural and Urban Poaching in Victorian England," *Rural History*, vol. 17, no. 2, pp. 187–212.

Paley, R. (1991), *Justice in 18th-century Hackney: The Justicing Notebook of Henry Norris and the Hackney Petty Sessions Book*, London: London Record Society.

Paley, W. (1814), *The Law and Practice of Summary Convictions on Penal Statutes by Justices of the Peace*, London.

Palk, D. (2006), *Gender, Crime and Judicial Discretion: 1780–1830*. Woodbridge: Royal Historical Society/Boydell Press.

Parker, J. (1749), *Conductor Generalis, Or, The Office, Duty and Authority of Justices of the Peace, High-sheriffs, Under-sheriffs, Coroners, Constables, Gaolers, Jury-men, and Overseers of the Poor* (2nd edn.), New York.

Parkin, C. (1776), *The History and Antiquities of Yarmouth, In the County of Norfolk. Collected from Antient Records, And Other Authentic Materials*, King's Lynn.

Patten, J. (1975), "Population Distribution in Norfolk and Suffolk during the Sixteenth and Seventeenth Centuries," *Transactions of the Institute of British Geographers*, no. 65, pp. 45–65.

Pattenden, R. (1999), "The Exclusion of the Clergy from Criminal Trial Juries: An Historical Perspective," *Ecclesiastical Law Journal*, vol. 5, issue 24, pp. 151–163.

Paul, G. O. (1783), *A Second Address on the Subject of a Reform of Prisons*, Gloucester.

(1789), *Address to his Majesty's Justices of the Peace for the County of Gloucester*, Gloucester.

Pearce, T. (1756), *The Compleat Justice of the Peace, and Parish Officer*, London.

Pearson, J. (1998), "Threshing Out the Common in Community: The Great Tey Riot of 1727," *Rural History*, vol. 9, issue 1, pp. 43–56.

Philalethes (1748), *English Liberty in Some Cases Worse Than French Slavery: Exemplified by Animadversions Upon the Tyrannical and Anti-constitutional Power of the Justices of the Peace*, London.

Philonomos (1751), *The Right Method of Maintaining Security in Person & Property to All the Subjects of Great-Britain*, London.

Pinker, S. (2012), *The Better Angels of Our Nature: A History of Violence and Humanity*, Harmondsworth: Penguin.

Plint, T. (1851), *Crime in England: Its Relation, Character, and Extent, as Developed from 1801 to 1848*, London.

Plumb, J. H. (1969), *England in the Eighteenth Century*, Harmondsworth: Penguin.

Pluskota, M. (2011), *Prostitution in Bristol and Nantes, 1750–1815: A Comparative Study*, University of Leicester (PhD thesis).

Poole, S. (2007), "Bringing Great Shame Upon this City: Sodomy, the Courts and the Civic Idiom in Eighteenth-century Bristol," *Urban History*, vol. 34, no. 1, pp. 114–126.

(2008), "'A Lasting and Salutary Warning': Incendiarism, Rural Order and England's Last Scene of Crime Execution," *Rural History*, vol. 19, no. 2, pp. 163–177.

(2015), "'For the Benefit of Example': Crime Scene Executions in England, 1720–1830," at pp. 71–101 in R. Ward (ed.) *A Global History of Execution and the Criminal Corpse*, Basingstoke: Palgrave Macmillan.

Porter, R. (1990), *English Society in the Eighteenth Century*, Harmondsworth: Penguin.

Poulter, J. (1753), *The Discoveries of John Poulter, Alias Baxter; Who Was Apprehended for Robbing Dr. Hancock, of Salisbury* (7th. edn.), Sherborne.

Prest, W. (1986), *The Rise of the Barristers: A Social History of the English Bar 1590–1640*, Oxford: Clarendon Press.

Pue, W. (1983), "The Criminal Twilight Zone: Pre-trial Procedures in the 1840s," *Alberta Law Review*, vol. 21, pp. 335–364.

Pyle, T. (1716), *The Wisdom of a Government in Distributing Punishment or Mercy to State-Criminals. A Sermon Preached at the Lent-Assizes Holden at Thetford*, London.

Radzinowicz, L. (1945), "The Waltham Black Act: A Study of the Legislative Attitude Towards Crime in the Eighteenth Century," *The Cambridge Law Journal*, vol. 9, pp. 56–81.

(1948–56), *A History of English Criminal Law and its Administration from 1750*, vols. 1–3, London: Stevens & Sons.

Raithby, J. (1811), *The Statutes at Large, of England and of Great-Britain*, vol. 10, London.

Ramsay, A. (1781), *Observations Upon the Riot Act, with An Attempt Towards the Amendment of It. By a Dilettante in Law and Politics*, London.

Randall, A. et al (eds.) (1996), *Markets, Market Culture and Popular Protest in Eighteenth-century Britain*, Liverpool: Liverpool University Press.

Randall, A. (2006), *Riotous Assemblies: Popular Protest in Hanoverian England*, Oxford: Oxford University Press.

Rastall, W. D. (1815), *A Practical Guide, to the Quarter and other, Sessions of the Peace*, London.

Rawcliffe, C. and Wilson, R. (2004), *Norwich Since 1550*, London: Hambledon.

Renton, S. (1996), "The Moral Economy of the English Middling Sort in the Eighteenth-century: The Case of Norwich in 1766 and 1767," at pp. 115–136 in Randall, A. and Charlesworth, A. (eds) *Markets, Market Culture and Popular Protest in Eighteenth-century Britain and Ireland*, Liverpool: Liverpool University Press.

Reresby, J. (1734), *The Memoirs of Sir John Reresby*, London.

Ritson, J. (1791), *The Office of Constable: Being an Entirely New Compendium of the Law Concerning That Ancient Minister for the Conservation of the Peace, etc.*, London: Whieldon and Butterworth.

Rokeby, T. (1887), *The Diary of Mr Justice Rokeby*, London: Wyman and Sons.

Ruggles, T. (1794), *The History of the Poor; Their Rights, Duties, and the Laws Respecting Them. In a Series of Letters*, London.

Rule, J. and Wells, R. (1997), *Crime, Protest and Popular Politics in Southern England, 1740–1850*, London: Continuum.

Rule, J. (2004), "The Labouring Poor," pp. 183–195 in Dickinson, H. T. (ed.) *A Companion to Eighteenth-century Britain*, Oxford: Blackwell.

Rushton, P. and Morgan, G. (2004), *Eighteenth-century Criminal Transportation: The Formation of the Criminal Atlantic*, New York: Palgrave Macmillan.

Riche, N. (1967), *The Agricultural Revolution in Norfolk*, London: Frank Cass.

Ritson, J. (1809), *The Jurisdiction of the Court Leet* (2nd edn.), London.

Rogers, N. (1998), *Crowds, Culture and Politics in Georgian Britain*, Oxford: Clarendon Press

Rowley, W. (1790), *Truth Vindicated Or, The Specific Differences of Mental Diseases Ascertained*, London.

Rosenheim, J. (1989), "County Governance and Elite Withdrawal in Norfolk, 1660–1720," at pp. 95–125 in Beier, A. L. et al (eds.) *The First Modern Society: Essays in English History in Honour of Lawrence Stone*, Cambridge: Cambridge University Press.

(ed.) (1991), *The Notebook of Robert Doughty, 1662–1665*, Norwich: Norfolk Record Society.

(1993), "Documenting Authority: Texts and Magistracy in Restoration Society," *Albion: A Quarterly Journal Concerned with British Studies,* vol. 25, no. 4, pp. 591–604.

Roth, R. (2001), "Homicide in Early Modern England 1549–1800: The Need for a Quantitative Synthesis," *Crime History & Societies*, vol. 5, no. 2, pp. 33–67.

(2011), "Biology and the Deep History of Homicide," *British Journal of Criminology*, vol. 51, no. 3, pp. 535–555.

(2011), "Yes We Can: Working Together Toward a History Of Homicide That is Empirically, Mathematically, and Theoretically Sound," *Crime, History & Societies,* vol. 15, no. 2, pp. 131–145.

Rude, G. (2005), *The Crowd in History: A Study of Popular Disturbances in France and England, 1730–1848,* London: Serif.

Rule, J. (1992), *Albion's People, English Society, 1714–1815*, London: Longman.

(1997), "The Manifold Causes of Rural Crime: Sheep-Stealing in England, c.1740–1840," pp. 127–145 in Rule, J. and Wells, R. (eds) *Crime, Protest and Popular Politic in Southern England 1740–1850,* Winchester: The Hambledon Press.

Rushton, P. and Morgan, G. (2003), "The Magistrate, the Community and the Maintenance of an Orderly Society in Eighteenth-century England," *Historical Research*, vol. 76, no. 191, pp. 54–77.

S., T. (1725), *A Dissertation Concerning the Evil Nature and Fatal Consequence of Immoderate Anger and Revenge*, London.

Scarfe, N. (Trans. and ed.) (2011), *A Frenchman's Year in Suffolk: French Impressions of Suffolk Life in 1784*, Martlesham: Boydell & Brewer.

Schwerhoff, G. (2013), "Early Modern Violence and the Honour Code: From Social Integration to Social Distinction?," *Crime, History & Societies*, vol. 17, no. 2, pp. 27–46.

Scott, J. (1773), *Observations On the Present State of the Parochial and Vagrant poor,* London.

Seller, J. (1671), *A Booke of the Punishments of the Common Laws of England*, London.

Shakesheff, T. (2003), *Rural Conflict, Crime and Protest: Herefordshire 1800–1860*, Woodbridge: Boydell Press.

Sharp, G. (1790), *A Tract on Duelling: Wherein the Opinions of Some of the Most Celebrated Writers on Crown Law are Examined and Corrected… In Order to Ascertain the Due Distinction Between Manslaughter and Murder*, London.

Sharpe, J. (1981), "Domestic Homicide in Early Modern England," *Historical Journal*, vol. 24, issue 1, 1981, pp. 29–48.

(2001), "Crime, Order and Historical Change," pp. 109–138, in Muncie, J. and McLaughlin, E. (eds) *The Problem of Crime* (2nd edn.), London: Sage Publications.

Sharpe, J. and Dickinson, J. R. (2011), "Coroners' Inquests in an English County, 1600–1800: A Preliminary Survey," *Northern History*, vol. 48, no. 2, pp. 253–269.

Sharpe, J. (2012), "Reporting Crime in the North of England Eighteenth-century Newspaper: A Preliminary Investigation," *Crime, History & Societies*, vol. 16, no. 1, pp. 25–45.

Shaw, J. (1733), *Parish Law: Or, A Guide to Justices of the Peace, Ministers, Churchwardens, Overseers of the Poor, Constables, Surveyors of the Highways, Vestry-Clerks, and All Others Concerned in Parish Business*, London.

(1756), *The Practical Justice of Peace, And Parish and Ward-Officer: Or, A Treatise Shewing the Present Power and Authority of These Officers*, vol. 1, London.

Shelton, M. (1726), *A Charge Given to the Grand-Jury, at the General Quarter-Sessions of the Peace, Holden at St. Edmunds-Bury For the Liberty Thereof; In the County of Suffolk: On the 11th of October, An. Dom. 1725*, London.

Shoemaker, R. (1991), *Prosecution and Punishment: Petty Crime and the Law in London and Rural Middlesex, c.1660–1725*, Cambridge: Cambridge University Press.

Shorrocks, D. M. M. (1954), "Eighteenth Century Petty Sessions Records in Kent," *Bulletin of the Society of Local Archivists*, no. 14, pp. 10–13.

Silverman, L. (2001), *Tortured Subjects: Pain, Truth, and the Body in Early Modern France*, Chicago: University of Chicago Press.

Sinclair, J. (2007), "Why Has Imprisonment Emerged as the Predominant Form of Punishment for Serious Crimes in England?," *UCL Jurisprudence Review*, vol. 13, pp. 37–52.

Slack, P. (1795), *The English Poor Law, 1531–1782*, Cambridge: Cambridge University Press.

Smith, A. (1999), *Wealth of Nations: IV-V* (4th edn.), Harmondsworth: Penguin.

Smith, B. P. (2005), "The Presumption of Innocence and the English Law of Theft: 1750–1850," *Law and History Review*, vol. 23, no. 1, pp. 133–173.

(2006), "The Emergence of Public Prosecution in London, 1790–1850," *Yale Journal of Law & the Humanities*, vol. 18, issue 1, pp. 29–62.

(2007), "English Criminal Justice Administration, 1650–1850," *Law and History Review*, vol. 25, no. 3, pp. 593–634.

Smith, D. and Smith, L. (1995), *Sudden Deaths in Suffolk 1767–1858: A Survey of Coroners' Records in the Liberty of St Etheldreda*, Ipswich: Suffolk Family History Society.

Smith, G. T. (ed.) (2013), *Summary Justice in the City. A Selection of Cases Heard at the Guildhall Justice Room, 1752–1781*, London: London Record Society.

Smith, R. (1695), *Mistaken Justice: Or, Innocence Condemn'd, In the Person of Francis Newland*, London.

Snell, E. (2005), "Representations of Criminality and Victimisation in Provincial Newspapers: The Kentish Post 1717 to 1768," *Southern History*, vol. 27, pp. 48–75.

(2007), "Changing Discourses of Crime: Representations of Criminality in the Eighteenth-century Newspaper Press," *Continuity and Change*, vol. 22, issue 1, pp. 13–47.

Soderlund, R. J. (1998), "'Intended as a Terror to the Idle and Profligate': Embezzlement and the Origins of Policing in the Yorkshire Worsted Industry, c.1750–1777," *Journal of Social History*, vol. 31, no. 3, pp. 647–669.

Spierenburg, P. (2008), *A History of Murder: Personal Violence in Europe from the Middle Ages to the Present,* Cambridge: Polity.

(2001), "Violence and The Civilizing Process: Does It Work?," 2001, *Crime, History & Societies*, vol. 5, no. 2, pp. 87–105.

Stephen, J. F (1883), *A History of the Criminal Law of England*, London: Macmillan.

Stevenson, J. (1979), *Popular Disturbances in England, 1700–1870*, Harlow: Longman.

Stone, M. (ed.) (2008), *The Diary of John Longe, Vicar of Coddenham, 1765–1834*, Woodbridge: Boydell Press.

Styles, J. (1982), "An Eighteenth-century Magistrate as Detective: Samuel Lister of Little Horton," *The Bradford Antiquary*, vol. 10, part 47, pp. 98–117.

(2008), "Time Piece: Working Men and Watches," *History Today*, vol. 58, no.1, pp. 44–50.

(2013), "Spinners and the Law: Regulating Yarn Standards in the English Worsted Industries, 1550–1800," *Textile History*, vol. 44, no. 2, pp. 145–170.

Steedman, C. (2012), "At Every Bloody Level: A Magistrate, A Framework-Knitter, and the Law," *Law and History Review*, vol. 30, pp. 387–422.

Tancred, C. (1727), *Essay for a General Regulation of the Law,* London.

Tarlow, S. and Dyndor, Z. (2015), "The Landscape of the Gibbet," *Landscape History*, vol. 36, issue 1, pp. 71–88.

Thomas, C. (2011), "'Not Having God Before His Eyes': Bestiality in Early Modern England," *Seventeenth Century*, vol. 26, issue 1, pp. 149–173.

Thomas, M. and Sign, N. (2012), *The Loyal Suffolk Hussars. The History of the Suffolk Yeomanry 1794–1967*, Solihull: Helion & Company.

Thompson, E. P. (1971), "The Moral Economy of the English Crowd in the Eighteenth Century," *Past and Present*, vol. 50, no. 1, pp. 76–136.

Thompson, R. (1791), *Narrative of the Life and Transactions of Robert Thompson*, Newcastle.

Thorn, J. (Ed) (2003), *Writing British Infanticide: Child-murder, Gender, and Print, 1722–1859*, Newark: University of Delaware Press.

Thorne, H. (2001), "Explaining Long Term Trends In Violent Crime," *Crime, History & Societies*, vol. 5, no. 2, pp. 69–86.

Tickell, S. G. (2015), *Shoplifting in Eighteenth-century England*, University of Hertfordshire (PhD thesis).

Umfreville, E. (1761), *Lex Coronatoria*, London.

Vaisey, D. (ed.) (1994), *The Diary of Thomas Turner, 1754–1765*, Oxford: CTR Publishing.

Verdon, N. (2002), *Rural Women Workers in Nineteenth-century England: Gender, Work and Wages*, Woodbridge: Boydell Press.

Verey, D. (ed.) (2003), *The Diary of a Cotswold Parson*, Stroud: Sutton Press.

Waddell, B. (2012), *God, Duty and Community in English Economic Life, 1660–1720*, Woodbridge: Boydell Press.

Wake, R. (2013), *Southwold and its Vicinity, Ancient and Modern*, Charleston: Nabu Press.

Walker, G. (1998), "Rereading Rape and Sexual Violence in Early Modern England," *Gender & History*, vol. 10, pp. 1–25.

Walliss, J. (2013), "Representations of Justice Executed at Norwich Castle A Comparative Analysis of Execution Reports in the Norfolk Chronicle and Bury and Norwich Post, 1805–1867," *Law, Crime and History*, vol. 2, pp. 30–51.

(2015), "Crime and Justice in Georgian Cheshire; The Chester Court of Great Sessions, 1760–1830," *Journal on European History of Law*, vol. 6, no 1, pp. 38–55.

Ward, R. (Ed) (2015), *A Global History of Execution and the Criminal Corpse*, London: Palgrave Macmillan.

Ward, T. (1997), "Magistrates, Insanity and the Common Law," *Criminal Law Review*, p. 796.

Watson, K. (2006), "Medical and Chemical Expertise in English Trials for Criminal Poisoning, 1750–1914," *Medical History*, vol. 50, no. 3, pp. 373–390.

(2013), "Women, Violent Crime and Criminal Justice in Georgian Wales," *Continuity and Change*, vol. 28, issue 2, pp. 245 272.

Welch, S. (1754), *Observations On the Office of Constable,* London.

Well, R. (2011), *Wretched Faces: Famine in Wartime England 1793–1801*, London: Breviary Stuff Publications.

Whatley, R. (1729), *A Friendly Admonition to Gentlemen in the Commission of the Peace* (2nd edn.), London.

White, W. (1845), *History, Gazetteer, and Directory of Norfolk,* Sheffield.

Williams, A. (2000), *The Criminality of Women in the 18th Century in the South West of England,* University of Plymouth (PhD thesis).

Willis, J. (2005), "Transportation Versus Imprisonment in Eighteenth and Nineteenth-century Britain: Penal Power, Liberty, and the State," *Law & Society Review*, vol. 39, pp. 171–210.

(2008), "Punishment and the Cultural Limits to State Power in Late 18th-century Britain," *Punishment & Society*, vol. 10, no. 5, pp. 401–428.

Wilson, K. (1998), *The Sense of the People: Politics, Culture and Imperialism in England, 1715–1785*, Cambridge: Cambridge University Press.

Wilson, S. (1986), "The Court of Quarter Sessions and Larceny in Sussex, 1775–1820," *Criminal Justice History*, vol. 7, pp. 73–94.

Winston, M. (1994), "The Bethel at Norwich: an Eighteenth-century Hospital for Lunatics," *Medical History*, vol. 38, no. 1, pp. 27–51.

Wise, E. (1751), *The Remarkable Tryal of Thomas Chandler, Late of Clifford's Inn, London, Gent. Who was Tried and Convicted at the Lent Assizes at Reading, 1750,* Reading.

Wood, J. C. (2004), *Violence and Crime in Nineteenth-century England: The Shadow of our Refinement,* London: Routledge.

(2006), "Criminal violence in modern Britain," *History Compass*, vol. 4, no. 1, pp. 77–90.

Woodford, T. (1749), *A Discourse Concerning Some of the Most Important Branches and Parts, of the Office of the Justices of the Peace*, London.

Woodward, N. (2007) "Infanticide in Wales, 1730–1830," *The Welsh History Review*, vol. 23, Number 3, 2007, pp. 94–125.

(2008) "Burglary in Wales, 1730–1830: Evidence from the Great Sessions," *The Welsh History Review*, vol. 24, no. 2, pp. 60–91.

(2008), "Seasonality and Sheep-stealing: Wales, 1730–1830," *Agricultural History Review*, vol. 56, no. 1, pp. 25–47.

(2009), "Horse-stealing in Wales, 1730–1830," *Agricultural History Review*, vol. 57, no. 1, pp. 70–108.

Wright, P. (2006), *Death Recorded: Capital Punishment In Suffolk 1732–1900*, Ipswich: Pawprint Publishing.

Wrigley, E. A. (2007), "English County Populations in the Later Eighteenth-century," *Economic History Review*, vol. 60, pp. 35–69.

Wyatt, I. (2008), *Calendar of Summary Convictions at Petty Sessions 1781–1837*, Bristol: Bristol and Gloucestershire Archaeological Society.

Yates, N. (2007), *Eighteenth Century Britain: Religion and Politics 1714–1815*, London: Routledge.

Zouch, H. (1786), *Hints Respecting the Public Police*, London.

Index

Lightning Source UK Ltd.
Milton Keynes UK
UKOW05f1650111216
289693UK00002B/21/P

9 781909 976115